IDEAS
ARE WEAPONS

The

History and Uses of Ideas

BY

MAX LERNER

†

New York

THE VIKING PRESS

1939

*For permission to reprint articles and reviews the author
wishes to thank the editors and publishers as indicated in the
list of acknowledgments appearing on pages 541–4.*

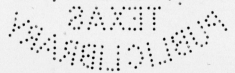

FOR ANITA

Foreword

Generally when a writer wants to make a book out of his essays and reviews, he attributes it to the importuning of his friends. They want copies of his articles, perhaps, and he has run out of his supply. I suppose that writers are much like politicians. The one pants for his job, the other for his book—yet neither must seem to pant. Each hides his basic human eagerness behind an elaborate screenwork of protestation. For myself, I must confess that no one importuned me into making this book. I did it because I want to see the various studies between covers, because they are thus more available than when scattered over twenty or thirty publications, and because I wrote them knowing pretty well all the time that I intended in the end somehow to put them together.

I feel they belong together. If a writer is to grow and survive as a writer, and not just as a fellow going through the motions of putting words together, something in him must be organic—shifting its forms but with a core of unity. There are all the subjects in the world to pick from; and you nibble a little at this and a little at that. There are all the books and ideas in the world, past and present, to write about; and you have to make a heart-breakingly limited selection. But all the time it is not you who are making the selection. There is something in you of which you are only dimly aware, reaching out, feeding upon your reading and experience, taking ever clearer shape and sharper contours.

That something in me has for some time been an interest in ideas as things to be studied—their shape and structure, their origins, their history, their changes and chances, their migrations, their uses. But you cannot have just an amorphous interest in ideas. And eventually I discovered that what interested me mainly was not their symmetry or logical structure or even their validity. What interested me was their history, the way in which they emerged out of the biographies of their creators and out of the class movements and tensions of their time, and the way in which they have finally taken the shape of the uses to which they have been put. I saw, in short, that my approach to ideas is an instrumental one: that I have increasingly sought to view them as weapons in the personal struggles that every individual has for the resolution of his tensions, and in the struggles for power and order that every age has and every culture.

When I saw that clearly, several years ago, the book began to take definite shape in my mind. I might have written it afresh, using what I had done only as raw material. Or I might have taken my essays and reviews over the whole period, and revised them and linked them together into a continuous book. I refrained from either course, partly because I think that the record of a development, however uneven, has an interest of its own; but mainly because I have a considerable regard for the essay form. Each of these pieces was originally written as an essay—even those that were externally book reviews or encyclopedia articles—and it is as essays that I want them to be read.

They are essays in ideas. That is why so many of them use as their point of departure some book and nearly all of them some craftsman in ideas. It has become a truism to say that our bustling and impersonal age has killed the familiar essay as a form; but it is equally true that our age of quick and transitory books and even quicker and more transitory book-reviews has almost killed the essay in ideas, as distinguished from the discussion of public affairs. A book today is rarely the occasion for the sort of extended inquiry into ideas that it was in Macaulay's day and in Matthew Arnold's and Sainte-Beuve's. It has become instead the occasion for quick summaries, oblique judgments, *ex cathedra* utterances. "Your business as thinkers," Justice Holmes once said, "is to see the relation between your fact and the framework of the universe." That is still our business.

It is our business especially in what Alfred North Whitehead has called "adventures in ideas." The studies that follow roam over many fields—law, literature, politics, economics, history, education, sociology, social psychology—and cover none with any comprehensiveness. I have done what I could to repair the gaps. Both essays in Part I are new in the sense that they have been written especially for this book, and not a few of the pieces in the rest of the book have been similarly written during the past year to fit into the general pattern. But if there is an organic principle in these explorations, it must be sought not in what I have covered or failed to cover, but in the inner unity of a cohesive point of view.

Most of the people whom I discuss are the men who have strongly influenced our contemporary thinking, and shaped what we call the modern mind. Some of them have been scholars, some journalists, some administrators, some politicians. Several have been revolutionists, some hard-bitten conservers of the established order, but most of them have been progressives in the sense that they have recognized the need for continual change in ideas and institutions. This is especially true of the Americans, most of whom fall into the period of social consciousness since the turn of the century. Had Vernon Parrington lived to complete the third volume of his *Main Currents in American Thought*, the writing of many of these studies would have been easier and the results better.

This book was completed, as several chapters will indicate (especially the title chapter in Part I and the chapter on Hitler), after the Soviet-Nazi non-aggression pact and Hitler's attack on Poland. Both these events are likely to have far-reaching consequences for the working thinker. In a sense we have come to the end of an epoch marked on one side by the first world war and on the other by the outbreak of the second. That epoch has been one of the most turbulent in world history, yet the one on which we are entering seems destined to be even more so. For the craftsman in social theory this forms a remarkable laboratory for testing his hypotheses but a difficult one in which to express them. For if it is true that ideas have been weapons thus far, it is likely to prove doubly true in the future; and in a sense far more military and manipulative than I had intended in my title.

MAX LERNER

October 1939

Contents

Part I: The Uses of Ideas

Part II: A Gallery of Americans

Part III: Some European Thinkers

Part IV: Ideas and Society

The Uses of Ideas

1

Ideas Are Weapons

Among the intellectual exiles from Germany after Hitler's capture of power in 1933 was a keen political and legal theorist, Professor Hermann Kantorowicz. I sat in a seminar with him for a short time at the University in Exile, one of the many brilliant achievements in Alvin Johnson's crowded life. "You would not understand this perhaps," he said to us, "because you have not experienced it as we have in Germany. There is an important distinction between thoughts and ideas. Men possess thoughts but ideas possess men."

I shall not easily forget the impact of his remark and the illumination it carried. It was not that the distinction between the words "thoughts" and "ideas" meant much to me in itself. Let us rephrase the statement. Let us say we are dealing with the whole realm of what, for lack of a better term, we shall call ideas—the whole intellectual realm. One phase of it is the rational: and here men are in possession of the ideas, using them to clarify their world and subject it to order. The other phase is the irrational: and here the ideas—big sweeping ideas like racism, individualism, Nazism, communism, democracy—are in possession of men. They possess us as evil spirits were once said to have entered into witches and possessed them and made them do their bidding. Under the spell of these ideas a madness seems to sweep over a people, like an engulfing sea that sweeps away the dikes that rationality has painfully and prayerfully built against it over the centuries.

It is the recognition and exploitation of this possessive power of ideas that makes the genius of our age. The great intellectual revolution of the seventeenth century was the discovery of scientific method and its possibilities. That of the eighteenth century was the charting of the map of reason and the subjecting of social institutions to the test of rationality. That of the nineteenth century was the discovery of the world as process rather than as structure, with ascertainable laws of development both in the biological realm (Darwinism) and in the historical and social realm (Marxism). The intellectual revolution of the twentieth century is likely to prove the charting of the *terra incognita* of the irrational and the extraction of its implications for every area of human thought.

If ever the story of this exploration of the irrational is written, it will be one of the exciting adventures in the history of ideas. Such forerunners as Stendhal, Dostoyevsky, and Nietzsche, who searched out the hidden fastnesses of the mind as only men of a tortured imagination can do, belong in the story. Freud is its dominating figure: as our century grows older the serious discussion of his work will be separated from the faddist wranglings over it, and we shall see more clearly his massive influence in exploring the "psychology of the depths" and setting our intellectual task for decades to come. The unfortunate things are that Freud is still regarded primarily as a creative figure in individual psychology, and that to the social sciences he is a pariah. Politics as an art has begun to build upon some of his insights, but politics as a science scorns to. We shall have to place Bergson in the story as well: his *élan vital* is a Gallic version of Nietzsche's *der dunkle Drang*—a life force that sweeps away logical constructions and is the matrix for revolutionary impulse. Sorel will be part of it, with his theory of the social myth and his emphasis of the desire of men to be part of the winning movements of history. Pareto will be part of it—the Pareto who wanders learnedly over the centuries, showing by brilliant illustration how men have built intellectual systems to rationalize their basic drives toward conformity or change. And Hitler will be part of it: for Hitler, whatever his ignorance of the academic lore of psychology, has shown that he has the intuitions of a genius in propaganda—and by intuitions I mean here simply the capacity to translate remembered experience into new and effective action.

This is not the place for an extended discussion either of the new age of propaganda or of the discovery of the irrational. For the present purpose, both must be taken as givens. What I want to emphasize here is how radically this has affected our intellectual orientation. It involves nothing short of a Copernican revolution in ideas. Many of us do not yet know it, because there is always a lag between intellectual change and our awareness of it; but it is nevertheless a fact that the rational right-thinking man has as surely ceased to be regarded the center of our intellectual system as the earth has ceased to be regarded the center of our planetary system.

This is bound to play havoc with intellectual history as it has been traditionally written. There have been two principal traditions in intellectual history. One has been the history of ideas, viewed narrowly in a genteel Matthew Arnold sense as the best that has been thought and said by accredited spokesmen in the proper quarters, and written, after the manner of Deuteronomy, as a genealogical succession of schools of thought. The second has been the history of states of social consciousness, or what Whitehead and after him Carl Becker have called "climates of opinion."

To these must be added now a third approach—that of seeing the history of ideas as the expression of broad social and class forces. Here we may place Taine in France in his studies of English literary history; Franz Mehring in his studies of German literature and especially in his *Lessing-Legende;* Harold Laski in England in his studies of the history of European political thought; and, in America, Charles Beard and Vernon Parrington in their approach to American intellectual history. Some of these are Marxian in their emphasis, the others only loosely related to the class interpretation. They have in common what Karl Mannheim, in his *Ideology and Utopia,* has called the "unmasking" of ideologies. They view the history of thought as a succession of defensive and aggressive movements directed toward class and group interests and power relations. Their assumption is that both the intellectual apologies for a social order and the intellectual attacks upon it need to be recognized as such before we can lay bare the social impulsions behind the work of individual thinkers.

The great merit of this approach is that it goes beyond the rhetoric of ideas. It is not content to consider them at their face-value, or to deal with them as in a pecuniary culture we deal with coins —so many counters of standardized value that have become ends in themselves. It deals with ideas as symbol-formations, half revealing and half concealing the real purposes beneath. It sees that the idea has meaning only in a dynamic context of a struggle over power and values.

But even after one has spelled out these merits, the approach

still suffers from overrationalism. It concentrates on the thinker
and the idea, and on the conscious or unconscious but none the less
rational interests behind both. We shall have to shift our emphasis
so as to include not only the conditions of the creation of ideas but
also the conditions of their reception, not only the impulsions behind the ideas but also the uses to which they are put, not only the
thinkers but also the popularizers, the propagandists, the opinion
skill-groups, the final audience that believes or disbelieves and acts
accordingly. This is, in a sense, a naturalistic approach. It follows
through to the actual shapes the idea assumes in its various uses and
transformations. And this takes us out of the realm of the rational
and of validity into the realm of the irrational and of belief.

For whatever may have been the personal intent or the biographical dilemmas of a thinker (an Adam Smith, an Emerson, a
Nietzsche, a Lenin, a Spengler), we do not see his idea as a whole
until we see the things that time and men have done to it. Ideas have
not only origins and internal consistency; they have also direction
and consequence. That Adam Smith would be used to impede economic progress by breaking the government restraints on the concentration of economic power, that Emerson would end up in the
homilies of Elbert Hubbard and in editorials against labor legislation, that Nietzsche would be used to exalt a nationalism he despised, that Lenin would become an excuse for an equally mechanical extreme leftism and extreme opportunism, that Spengler would
serve to bolster the crudest sort of racism—these may seem only
deliciously ironic commentaries on the human comedy, or atoms
in the senseless whirl of history. Neither explanation seems valid
to me. Nor would I agree that these are merely instances of the
distortion of ideas, and therefore irrelevant. For in the history of
ideas even their distortions are part of their meaning—the unfolding of a line of direction inherent in the ideas themselves.

The Copernican revolution in intellectual history will not have
borne fruit until we adopt a completely naturalistic approach to
them. The meaning of an idea must be seen as the focus of four
principal converging strains: the man and his biography; the intellectual tradition; the social context, or the age and its biography;
the historical consequences of the idea, or the successive audiences
that receive it. When we have grasped this we shall have grasped also
the force of the irrational in the history of ideas, the role of propa-

ganda as well as of individual creativeness, the role of insecurity and fear as well as of class and national interest, the role of instinctual drives as well as of logical formulations. We shall, in short, be viewing the idea not wishfully but with our eye on what happens to it.

But does this mean a surrender on our part to the force of the irrational? By no means. There is an enormous difference between the recognition of the role of the irrational and the glorification of it. It is our failure to make this distinction that has largely prevented us from making use of the new insights into the irrational. Liberals and democrats alike have striven hard to keep their skirts clean of any contamination from the irrational—lest by recognizing it they strengthen it and thus play into the fascists' hands. The result is that the term "ideologies," in the sense of systems of belief that serve to energize a culture and make it cohesive and give it a fighting strength, has come to have a meaning restricted to the fascist and communist countries.

If we had more clearly recognized the distinction I speak of, we might have made greater strides than we have made thus far to the problem of reconciling Freud and Marx. The work of Freud himself is from this point of view revealing. Unlike Nietzsche, Sorel, and D. H. Lawrence, who not only recognize the force of the irrational but glory in it, and who seek to get at it through intuition and rhapsody—i.e., by the use of the irrational—Freud approaches it by rigidly scientific and rational procedures of study. Another example is Thomas Mann, whose novels, such as *The Magic Mountain* and the *Joseph* series, are profound explorations of depth-psychology, yet organize these perceptions of the daemonic in the human psyche into a framework of values that looks to the life of reason. We have here the foreshadowing of the task of political science in our time—in fact, of the principal task of our age: that of finding a resolution between the necessary role of the irrational and the demands of social rationality.

It is in some such terms that we shall have to approach the problem and fact of race. The fascists have used it so fantastically and unscrupulously that the rest of us feel as if we ought not to come even within hailing distance of the concept. Yet this is to adopt almost as untenable a position as that of some of the scholars who have been so frightened at the Marxist implications of the class-concept that they refuse to admit the existence of classes. Racial strains and racial differences do exist: for us to deny it is to play into the hands of the fascists by seeking to throw a veil of silence over a patent fact. But we must approach the race-concept scientifically. And thus far what science—both in biology and in anthropology—tells us is that racial strains are not clearly defined even physically and that their psychological and cultural by-products (if any exist) have not proved amenable to scientific study. But to say this is not to deny the role of something approximating a racial factor in history, nor to give up the task of studying its secondary products.

I have little doubt that, more than anything else, what will ultimately defeat fascism is its anti-scientific bias. The shape that ideas take is relative to the culture and era in which they develop and are used; yet there are internal standards of validity in ideas themselves. The sum of those internal standards is what, for lack of a better term, we call "science," although the philosophers may prefer to call it "truth." The notions we have about science and the methods we use for it will also vary, but the existence of scientific standards cannot be brushed aside either by skepticism or by state fiat. And a culture that sets itself against science by expelling its physicists and biologists and chemists, its doctors and its engineers, is not a culture that will survive. Not only will its armaments be defective, and its synthetic products ultimately unusable; more important, that regard for fact and its validity upon which survival depends will inevitably wither away.

For some time we have believed that there was a sharp difference between nations with "ideologies" enforced by state power and those in which the state was ostensibly neutral and allowed a competition of ideas. Several things have happened to bridge this sense of difference. One is that we have come more and more to view democracy as an ideology. Another, and recently more important, was the shock of the diplomatic rapprochement between Nazi Germany and the Soviet Union through a non-aggression pact, with the consequences that followed.

For we have come to see that just as, for the purposes of power-politics, we have had to manufacture an ideology of whose existence we had hitherto been only dimly aware, so it has also been possible for the totalitarian states to ignore their ideologies when power-politics demanded a decent ideological ignorance. The discovery shocked most of us, not because we had underrated the force of power-politics but because we had overrated the compulsion of ideologies. We had assumed that the Soviet Union would cleave to its doctrine or perish; and it has preferred to suspend its doctrine. We thought that Hitler's acts were governed by a fine ideological frenzy; and he turned out to be only a man governed by a desire for power so great that, as Hermann Rauschning has pointed out in *The Revolution of Nihilism,* it admits of no other fixed principles. In the one case the survival of socialism in Russia seems to have been the imperative; in the other the principle of dynamism—of the restless conquest of power, with whatever allies, until Germany shall have established its hegemony over the world. The two imperatives are, of course, in the end irreconcilable; but before the end comes there may be several way-stations where they can still consort.

What we are dealing with is the cynicism of *Realpolitik* that still cuts across ideological considerations as it has always done, not because they are irrelevant, but because it uses and discards ideas as one might use and discard weapons. We ought not to feel too smug in our superiority, however. The cynicism that the German-Russian pact displayed is not limited to the Nazi and Soviet ruling groups. It is a cynicism which today characterizes every ruling élite, even in the democracies.

It is instructive to recall the attitude of the élite toward the religion of emperor-worship in the Roman Empire as Gibbon describes it. The élite were sophisticated enough to be completely skeptical of it, yet they went through the forms because the demands of cohesion required that the underlying population should still believe. There is a similar dichotomy developing today between the ruling groups and the masses in every culture. By this dichotomy the ruling groups deal with power-politics and the masses are fed the proper ideas and the minimum security. Nor is this true only of the totalitarian states. In the democracies as well, statesmen are willing to betray ideologies: as witness Chamberlain's fealty to Hitler at Berchtesgaden—the Canossa of our era; and his cynical act at Munich of scrapping democratic Czechoslovakia in order to turn Hitler in the direction of the Soviet Union. And in the democracies too the ruling economic groups are skeptical of majority rule, making only the most necessary concessions to the masses in the form of economic security, and using the opinion industries to manipulate the minds of the people.

This is, of course, in the hard-bitten tradition of Machiavelli. If it is a new Machiavellianism, what is new is only the greater complexity of the task, and the need for operating simultaneously on three fronts—the economic, the political, the ideological. The basic difference here between the capitalist totalitarianisms and the capitalist democracies is that in the former the military, economic, and propaganda skill-groups are openly part of the government and can afford to be summary in their commands; while in the latter great subtlety is still required in order to conform with the rhetoric of democracy.

Is there then no real difference between the totalitarianisms and the democracies in their attitude toward the use of ideas? Thus far the difference has not been clear. But it can be made clear and it does exist.

It does not lie, as many would have us believe, in the assumption that a totalitarian state uses ideas for its purposes whereas a democracy does not. Ideas do not exist in the void, separated from the purposes and survival of the culture. In every culture they are weapons. They were used in the making of the Russian Revolution and they have been used in the consolidation of the Soviet power. They played their role in the Nazi revolution, and they have been conscripted for its entrenchment and extension. If we are to be successful in retaining democratic institutions and expanding their meaning, we must be clear about the meaning of democratic ideas, we must make those ideas persuasive, and we must above everything make them an integral part of our daily lives.

The important difference is the difference between the *instrumental* approach to ideas and the *manipulative* approach. The instrumental approach recognizes that ideas are used in behalf of a way of life and in the struggles for its achievement. But it is also humanist. It understands that, if democracy is to mean anything, it must have respect for the common man and not use him cynically as a pawn in the political game. The manipulative approach sees the common people only as so much material to be used. It has no more respect for that material than it would have for counters in any game. If you view ideas instrumentally, your primary regard is for their validity and for the creative action they will evoke through that validity, and for the social cohesion that will result. If you view them manipulatively, your only regard is for the use you can make of them. They become instruments not for creativeness but for contrivance.

The discoveries we have made in the realm of the irrational are important in the struggle for democracy because they pose the task and condition its achievement. Democratic ideas will have validity not because of any moral perfection in themselves but because they fulfill men's needs for security, for stature, for participation in a cultural experience. This means economic change, and of a drastic nature. It means a change in educational procedures which will place the full force of our educational agencies—the school, the press, the radio, the movies—behind the achievement of a socialized democracy. It means the enrollment of new skill-groups, especially those of economic, legal, engineering, and labor technicians, in the government of industry. It means an affirmativeness in our pursuit of cultural goals which will convert our old democratic stereotypes into ideas winged with fire, to touch the imaginations of the young.

The assumption of the fascist thinkers is that only the underlying masses are irrational, and that the ruling élite is a caste endowed with a divine rationality. They are men like gods, equipped to understand and exploit the weaknesses of the common herd but themselves untouched by the same weaknesses. This has unfortunately been the assumption of our liberal élites as well, insofar as they have recognized the problem of the irrational. But the assumption of a democratic culture must be at once more modest and more realistic. Granted individual differences, we are all—élite and mass—of the same basic human material. There can be no ruling caste that is not subject to the same irrationalisms as the people ruled. And there can be no noble and enduring democratic culture unless those who are leaders, while showing the way, do so with an understanding both of their own limitations and the creativeness of the mass.

I suspect that fascism will die in the end not only because of military adventurism and economic collapse, but also because it will have overreached itself in the realm of ideas. To pursue *Macht-politik* as Hitler has been pursuing it means to be cynical of idea-systems and contemptuous of the minds you are manipulating. This cynicism and contempt may seem for a time to go unpunished. But all the time they are destroying the only principle of cohesiveness a culture can have—belief on the part of the common people in a way of life. When that crumbles the culture crumbles. War and economic collapse will simply remove the outward props, and reveal the inner principle of disintegration.

Hermann Rauschning has spoken of the lack of principle on the part of the Nazi élite as nihilism. He is right. But the ironic thing about his book is the note of hurt and disillusion in it, as if his original trust in the Nazi ideology had been betrayed. What he does not see is that the fear of the masses which first led him to join the Nazi movement is exactly the essence of the nihilism that developed out of the movement. What is cynical about Hitler, as about every adventurist leader, is not his lack of fixed principle. It is his basic contempt for people. And that means ultimately his hatred of life.

Ideas are necessarily weapons. But they will be effective as weapons only if the uses to which they are put are life-affirming. If the craftsmen in ideas have a belief in the possibilities of human society and a sense of the dignity of ordinary people, that will be the best safeguard of those ultimate standards of validity that we call science and truth.

1939

2

Freedom in the Opinion Industries

LIKE other Americans I get letters from Europe that have always the same note: Europe is doomed; can a free society survive in America? It is now fashionable to answer Yes. The new note in speeches, books, and editorials is either "the coming victory of democracy" note or the "America is different" note. A native democratic *élan* is excellent, but, aside from the fact that every exhorter uses democracy in a different sense, it has thus far been left largely in the realm of exhortation. The New Deal program has bogged down not only because of its own lack of plan and cohesion, not only because of the bitter opposition of its enemies, but also because of the sabotage of those who should have been its friends—the very liberals who have been whipping themselves to new heights of fervor in defense of the democratic principle.

If we are honest with ourselves we will not blink the fact that we are entering one of the blackest crisis periods in our history. Whoever is elected in 1940, the outlook is bearish from any humanist angle. Already budgets are being cut, taxes eased for big enterprise, labor-protective legislation repealed, new labor-smashing laws introduced, strikes met with repression, educational expenditures whittled away, alien-baiting and Red-baiting measures passed—and all while we engage in top-flight oratory about making democracy work. I have been reading a recent history of criminal-syndicalism legislation after the World War, and the story is a grim one. But nothing in the palmiest days of Palmer, Lusk, and the Centralia hysteria can equal the new tidal wave of reaction that is descending upon us. From Boston to San Francisco, from the Mexican border to Madison, there are ungentle preparations being made by corporate capitalism to take over just as soon as the New Deal has relaxed its grip.

I do not say this to register myself on the Jeremiah rolls. I say it because the fact that the once advancing democratic armies in America are now in full retreat is a fact that needs explaining. The current explanations run in terms either of "the swing of the pendulum" or of "the tyranny of words." But pendular theories are only a polite way of saying: "I don't know, but I won't admit it." And before words can have the power to become tyrants, the minds of people must be prepared for the tyranny through demoralization. My own belief is that the turning-point in that demoralization came with the 1937 "recession." The reactionary press campaign, which had reached a fierce intensity during the 1936 elections without showing any marked effect on them, was now resumed with a much greater probability of success. The masses had voted for Mr. Roosevelt, not for any sophisticated reasons but because he had reached them by the propaganda of the deed—the actual accomplishments of the New Deal. They had caught the contagion of his assurance and felt that, whatever happened, he would be master of the occasion. But such a sense of confidence could not survive a new and drastic depression. The Roosevelt image had lost much of its magic. And when that had happened it became easy for the Coughlins and the Gerald Winrods and the Fritz Kuhns and their fellow-travelers to marshal their forces effectively on the battleground of opinion.

We are in the midst of a sharp struggle over opinion, and there is a sharper one still to come. Everyone feels a swing of the country's mood to the right—a swing well engineered and maneuvered. The pattern itself is clear: anti-Semitic (Coughlin, Kuhn, and eight hundred-odd fascist organizations), anti-labor and vigilantist (Ford, Girdler, Associated Farmers), Red-baiting (Dies, the Catholic hierarchy), anti-alien (the xenophobes in Congress and out), anti-democratic (all of them). What is not so clear is how far the swing will go before it is checked, and what is likely to check it. One answer is that a direct grappling with the problems of unemployment and shrinking capital investment will check it. And it is a good answer—if it can be translated into reality.

Yet it is well to remember that we are witnessing something that is to no small extent a synthetic achievement in the realm of opinion itself. The fascists have demonstrated in one country after another that it is possible to create a Red scare where there are few Reds and even those are ineffectual, a Jew-hate orgy where the Jews represent no real "problem," an anti-labor drive where labor is moving peacefully toward its own proper place in an economic democracy, an anti-alien drive where the aliens have added richly to our culture, and a contempt for democratic methods where democracy is striving courageously to carry the burden of a collapsing capitalism. The fascists have gone in for the synthetic creation of opinion in much the way that an autarchic regime goes in for the creation of artificial sugar or rubber.

In short, we are in what may be ironically called a new Golden Age of propaganda. The last Golden Age came with the discovery and spread of advertising technique, the revelations in the army intelligence tests of the low level of popular thinking, and the underscoring the World War gave to the irrational character of all political thinking. The new Golden Age, using all that, has added to it the control (either by a state monopoly or by a class monopoly) of the channels and sources of opinion, and their systematic exploitation for state or class ends. As Harold Lasswell says, "A new skill group has come into existence in modern civilization . . . skill in propaganda has become one of the most effective roads to power in modern states." And that propaganda skill is at the service of those who are ruthless enough to use it and can pay for it. I differ from Lasswell here only in emphasizing not the propaganda skill group itself but the class and state interests in whose service it is enlisted.

As there is a new Golden Age of propaganda, so also there is a new Unholy Alliance in the winning and maintaining of power. There was once a phrase that passed current among historians— "the barons of the bags and the barons of the crags." There are groups in every culture today corresponding to these—and the unholy alliance is between them. The barons of the bags are the holders of economic power, acting through their government and dependent upon it. The barons of the crags are the newspaper publishers and editors, the masters of the radio, the propagandists, the back-stage manipulators of opinion—those who occupy the strategic passes to the castles of the mind and who exact their heavy toll from all comers. We have often asked ourselves how it happens that reactionary governments in England and France have remained in power despite the patent fact that they do not express

the majority will. One answer is that two deeply entrenched minorities in each country are holding onto governmental power through
sheer tenacity, and will not relinquish it except at the cost of revolution. They know that in politics as in the law of real property the
possessors are blessed before all others—and they use every method
to avoid giving up possession.

The vast new fact that is emerging out of the struggle for majority rule is that our fates are currently being determined by two
sorts of minority strategy. A few men within the political governing
group make decisions that condition the destiny of peoples. Nothing is clearer than that Chamberlain's whole appeasement policy
was dictated by the fear that the defeat of Hitler and the collapse of fascist prestige would mean a genuine democratic victory
throughout Europe. And the important thing is that he was able
so to play on the fear of war of the English people that they accepted his appeasement policy; and then, when Hitler's territorial
ambitions turned to the West rather than the East, he was able
to play upon the English instinct for survival and modify his appeasement policy even to the extent of bidding for a Soviet alliance and introducing conscription. Moreover, nothing could be
clearer than that Czechoslovakia would have chosen to fight rather
than be absorbed, if a few men in the governing group had not preferred German domination to the acceptance of Soviet aid. One
of them expressed it: "I would rather be invaded by Hitler than
helped by Stalin"; and the important thing is that he was able to
make his own personal preference override the exactly opposite
preference of millions.

What happened yesterday in Spain and Czechoslovakia, what
is happening today in England and France, may happen tomorrow
in America. The Roosevelt government has weakened the hold
of the Big Money group and has even succeeded in undermining
the blind faith we once had in the barons of opinion, but it has not
succeeded in controlling or displacing either group. They are still
in control in the two strategic centers of American life. Their great
weakness used to lie in their pathetic reliance upon money in the
old sense—money to be used in buying power; and Chamberlain's
government in England, with its cowardly betrayal of Spain to
Franco and its bewildered hope that it could then buy Franco off
by loans, is the classic illustration of this. But that is an old-fash-

ioned and vestigial capitalist view. The newer groups are today learning the subtler uses of money. They understand not only that money must be used very delicately and indirectly—behind the rhetoric of majority rule and the screen of a free press—to buy power, but also that power must be captured and retained in order to protect money. I should be greatly surprised if the economic groups behind the Chamberlain government ever allow their kind of Cabinet—whether under Chamberlain or Hoare or Simon or some essentially reactionary coalition—to be replaced by a genuinely democratic government, short of civil war. I should be equally surprised if that happened soon in France. Nor do I think the matter is likely to come to civil war. In a time of confusion, when the big battalions of the majority are distracted and demoralized, the compact and ruthless storm troopers of opinion march in and take possession.

That is beginning to happen today in America. If the liberals do not know it yet they are blind. If they fail to act they are committing suicide.

How have they acted thus far to insure the survival of a free society? Whatever the contribution of the politicians and administrators, the contributions of the intellectuals seems to have been the fetishism of the principle. Many of them recognize the extent of fascist propaganda and the preparation of fascist terrorism in America today. Some of them even recognize the extent to which the formation of opinion in America today is a class monopoly, and the hopelessness of taking active measures for greater economic effectiveness and social well-being while that is true. Nevertheless, they persist in asserting that though the heavens may fall and the democratic state be destroyed, they will not qualify in the slightest the principle of *laissez-faire* in the opinion industries.

Of course, they do not see it quite that way. To them the realm of opinion-formation is not an industry but the sacred and untouchable province of the individual. They do not see that since Jefferson's day two things have happened that have wholly changed the conditions of freedom—first, the unremitting thrust of economic empire until it has subdued the political and the social unit to the corporate sway; second, the replacement of the free small newspaper by the mastodons of the press and radio, and the perfection of propaganda techniques to swell the power of those who control opinion.

The newspaper industry is one of the outstanding examples of the crowding out of the relatively free small enterprise by big capital. One reason why William Allen White is so tragic as well as so exciting a figure in modern journalism is that, as the editor and publisher of the Emporia (Kansas) *Gazette,* he stands for a world that was but that is no longer—stands for it with complete integrity but with a final ineffectiveness. The huge independent newspaper, such as the New York *Times,* which could not be replaced nor effectively met in competition except by an enormous capital investment; the newspaper chain, such as that of Hearst, Scripps-Howard, Gannett, Paul Block; the powerful press associations, such as the Associated Press or the United Press; the special-features syndicates, the new and powerful pictorial weeklies, the advertising agencies—these have left the William Allen Whites in splendid isolation, attractive but none the less museum-pieces. The temper of this group may be judged by the fact that for seven years now it has been consistently anti-New Deal while a majority of the people have been consistently pro-New Deal. It can be judged even better by reading the speeches and resolutions at the last convention of the American Newspaper Publishers Association—one that had every index of a convention of the right-wing Republicans after the dissenters among them had been expelled and only a rump was left. The fact is that these gentlemen express the interests and the sentiments of Big Enterprise not only because of advertisers' pressures, but basically because they are themselves Big Enterprise. We cheer when a J. David Stern attempts to break this solid phalanx as he did for a time with the New York *Post;* but the reason Stern failed was that no single individual can alone break the phalanx, so long as the rest remain solid. And while a Stern was trying to do that in New York, there were hundreds of cities and towns with only a single newspaper or with several owned by the same company—and with no competition of ideas in either case.

Given these conditions, it is idle to talk any longer of "freedom" of press and opinion as though it were synonymous with the absence of governmental intervention of any sort. The fact is that here, as in other industries dominated by big corporate enterprise, *laissez-faire* has come to mean not freedom for all but the tyranny of a few.

Liberalism fights for its dogmas inch by inch before it yields them. The doctrine of the final triumph of the idea—that the truth, even though unaided, must prevail—died a hard death, if indeed it may be said to have died at all. But even more tenacious is the linked notion that there exists anything like a competitive system for ideas. To say that because I can get up and spout on a soap-box in Union Square or write in the *Nation* or start a newspaper in competition with Mr. Hearst or Mr. Howard I have a freedom of opinion comparable to theirs is fantastic. I speak with the voice of one, Mr. Howard with the voice of millions. It is not because he is a better man than I, or because his ideas are truer or sounder, or because they represent more authentically the humanist tradition. It is because he has a major control in an opinion industry and I do not. My freedom to start a newspaper in competition with him is as real as my freedom to enter the field against the United States Steel Corporation. The fact in each instance is that it is hollow to talk of "freedom," whether economic freedom or freedom of opinion, except where there is equality or at least a framework of governmental control to reduce inequality.

Justice Holmes himself came close to recognizing this. "The best test of truth," he said in *Abrams v. U.S.*, "is the power of the thought to get itself accepted in the competition of the market." I am willing to take my stand on that statement of freedom of the press—but it involves a genuine competitive situation for ideas. There is another dictum of Holmes that is equally important, from *Coppage v. Kansas,* to the effect that there can be no freedom of contract between worker and employer except where there is already equality of bargaining power. It remains for our generation to fulfill the implications of Holmes's thought by projecting his position in *Coppage v. Kansas*—a position that has today become the new basis of labor law—into the realm not only of the workers' wages but of the formation of their thought.

Freedom is not *laissez-faire*. We have come by this time to recognize that in the area of our economic life, but in the area of opinion we still cling to the belief that it is. It has taken us decades of social blundering to understand that economic freedom in the sense of

the unregulated decisions of an irresponsible capitalism is no longer
possible. We had better face the fact that the opinion industries are
as much "affected with a public interest" as any others. A nation
that has decided on a program of democratic control of the rest of
its industrial area endangers the entire structure of control by allowing the corporate interests to shape public opinion at will. It is very
well for liberals to speak of making a weapon of liberalism; but the
fetishism of the principle is far different from the wielding of the
weapon. It seems to be the essence of passive liberalism to make a
fetish of freedom. It is perhaps natural for an organism which sup-
presses all impulses toward action that it should deflect the energy
thus stored up into the channels of the adoration of its own tolerance.

But all ideas have their uses. There has been much discussion
among liberals of the problem of means and ends. We tend to forget that here, as elsewhere, absolutes are arid, and that ends and
means are interrelated. Freedom is an end with respect to economic
security: a culture that does not give scope to diversity of opinion
is an unfree culture no matter how economically secure it may be,
and the whole economic life of that culture is crippled. But freedom is also a means with respect to economic security, majority
rule, cultural creativeness. To have an abstract freedom of opinion
in a culture that is so organized that freedom (or, better, *laissez-
faire*) of opinion plays into the hands of economic scarcity and
economic tyranny is but sand in our mouths—not nourishing but
a matter for gritting of teeth. And that is actually the case with us.
Freedom of opinion is precious in itself, yet it is also self-defeating
if it is not used to ensure the free building up of majority opinion,
the orderly replacement of one majority by another, the refashioning of economic institutions to achieve the maximum security for
all. Freedom has little meaning except in the context of equality,
just as economic equality has only a stunted meaning except in a
free society.

We must organize our freedom of opinion in such a way as to
make it usable and not academic. But how do it? It is not an easy
task, and it has its risks. The first step is to face the problem and
face it in a tough-minded way. The question of means can then
be tackled. My own preference is to extend the principles of the

TVA "yardstick" and the SEC "truth in securities" into the opinion industries.

We must avoid a government-operated radio as in Great Britain, and we must avoid a government-monopolized press as in Germany, Italy, Russia. I propose the TVA principle in our radio system: in addition to, and side by side with, the great private broadcasting chains, let us have two major airways reserved for the government and run for it not by its bureaucrats but by the guild of radio artists. That it can be done has been demonstrated with brilliant success by the Federal Theater, which has changed the contours of American dramatic art and prodded the creative forces of the theater from their slumber. Why should not a similar Federal Radio chain, run non-commercially and without advertising, serve to set a standard for the other chains to live up to, and serve to broadcast the merciless truth about our social conditions when the other chains fear to? The radio is inherently a better mechanism to use in the competition of ideas than is the press. To begin with, the air already belongs to the nation and there can be no question raised legitimately of confiscation. The radio chains have their present position on sufferance. It would be only a step forward to use two of these strategic airways directly for public purposes and turn them over to the technicians, just as the actual teaching in our school and university system is in the hands of technicians.

With respect to the movies, the TVA principle would have to be different: it would have to be a private TVA. But why should not socially conscious money enter the movie industry, and set up great producing units that will put out the sort of films toward which Hollywood is only now beginning to make some feeble gestures? And why should not an RFC that finances all sorts of schemes be used to finance culturally productive enterprise of this sort? This would involve tackling the problem of distribution outlets as well; and there is much to be said for a framework of governmental controls over these outlets. It would involve also using the new film consumer organizations to give utterance to protests against the cowardly and the shoddy and to shape the supply in relation to the demand.

As for the press, the only solution is the long and hard road of creating competition by the deliberate and large-scale process of creating new competitors. There is no inherent economic law toward gigantism among newspapers. We could do with a good many more newspapers, even though it meant that none of them could be leviathans. Here too, wherever there is a locality where there is no competition of ideas in the press, socially conscious money must enter to create competition—and it would be a legitimate function of the government to subsidize individuals and cooperatives that want to start such newspapers, much as we subsidize new housing. In the end, in the hands of good working newspapermen and -women, they would pay for themselves financially and more than pay for themselves in cultural enrichment. Alexander Meiklejohn has suggested that our press be socialized like our universities. We could do much worse and we are doing much worse. But there is another possibility: to use the government power and the whole liberal tradition to bring about competition of ideas in a press that remains free from government control; which is, in the best sense, to socialize the press.

Given the reorganized opinion industries, one can turn to the problem of the control of outright propaganda with some hope of success. The problems of the internal organization of the opinion industries involve problems of power; the propaganda problem is one of truth. The first involves the adequate representation of diverse points of view, equality of bargaining power in opinion, the accessibility of adequate information for the common man; the second involves a ban on flagrantly distorted information, intended deliberately as a poison for the public mind. The first involves the break-up of the opinion monopolies and the creation of a positive framework for competition in ideas; the second involves the regulation of cut-throat competition and fraudulent practices in opinion. Of these the first is most important as a long-run matter if we are ever to have a genuine market for ideas; but the second is more urgent in the short run as a matter of sheer democratic survival.

In meeting the propaganda danger, something like the SEC pattern would be the most effective procedure. We have a Truth in Securities Act, to make sure that there is no rigging of the stock market, that there are no false prospectuses, no unethical practices in the marketing of stocks and bonds. Yet we allow rigging of the opinion market, unethical practices in the marketing of ideas. Are our securities more precious to us than our security, our stocks more delicate plants than our ideas, our investors more in need of protection than our common people? We have a Wheeler-Lea Act against false advertising of drugs and cosmetics; are we to have nothing to protect us against the infinitely more dangerous advertising of anti-labor, anti-democratic, anti-Semitic lies?

I know that liberals will immediately say: Why could not a Truth in Opinion Act be used against the left as well as the right? The answer is that it is already in use against the left. Anti-alien and anti-radical measures are already being passed in Congress and in virtually every state legislature. Have any of the corporate heads or any of their legal aids protested against them? The Dies Committee is already smearing the left with its so-called investigations; has it done anything substantial to investigate corporate fascism and regional fascism in America? We know perfectly well that before the legislation was enacted to control business, labor was already hemmed in by a *de facto* regulation. There was always a danger that the regulatory structure imposed upon business would be turned against labor as well; and, indeed, the Federal Courts tried their best to do so. Yet the total effect has been on the whole to carry through the original legislative intentions. The liberals and the left need not fear the creation of precedents that may be used against them. When a time of crisis comes, it will not be past precedents that count; new precedents, as Hitler has shown in Germany, can easily be created in the interests of ruthless power. What must be feared is not precedents but the sort of social breakdown that will make all precedents, good and bad, equally irrelevant.

To avoid this social breakdown we must move at the same time in the direction of a clear economic program, calling for democratic control of industry; and also in the direction of regulation of anti-social propaganda. Individuals of the highest caliber would be required to man a board such as I have suggested. There come to my mind men like Lloyd Garrison, Alexander Meiklejohn, Alvin Johnson, William Allen White—men wise in the way of words, tolerant of their latitude, but so tenacious of the ethics of the thinking craft that they could recognize the spurious and dishonest. The task of such a board would be to require complete information about the provenance and financing of political statements, bring the underground pamphlet literature above ground, see that all inflammatory radio statements are backed up by a bill of particulars, allow for the answering of controversial material—and, if necessary, ban the material that is poisonous and spurious. The decisions of this board would be, of course, reviewable by the courts under the rule of law. With any sort of good direction the task of the board would become that of monitor rather than censor; and as one of the consequences the press and radio would in the long run set up their own code of ethics. Such a law would be hard to write, as are all laws to begin with. Yet surely it would be no more difficult than the drafting of the SEC.

All of this would not proceed on the principle that there need be no tolerance for the intolerant. I think that is an unnecessarily dangerous principle. To pick the intolerant would be a subjective matter; to hound them, an all too easy absolutism. What we want to create for all is a set of rules of the game within which tolerance and intolerance shall operate.

What chance has such a program of becoming a reality? In the immediate future, very little. The confusion between *laissez-faire* and genuine freedom in the opinion industries is unlikely to be dissipated easily, and as long as it remains in the popular mind any attempt, however prayerful and innocuous, to restore competition in ideas will lead to anguished howls from the monopolists—and the howls will be echoed through the entire country. Nevertheless, we must continue our attempts to clarify our thinking in this area. One of the crucial reasons for the failure of progressive movements in the past has been their unwillingness or inability to operate in this area, with the result that the mass mind has been turned against them and they have been doomed to a melancholy soliloquy. There can be little doubt that soliloquy is a beautiful art form, but it has no place in politics.

American history is the story of the attempts of the minority will to suppress the democratic consciousness. It is the story, therefore, of successive upsurges of democratic strength, each of which has threatened to break the minority power. The year 1932 represented such an upsurge. There will be another. When it comes, the progressives must understand that unless they can restore freedom in the opinion industries, they are again doomed to a brief flurry of excitement and reformism and then to a frustrate soliloquy.

1939

PART TWO

———————◆———————

A Gallery of Americans

1

John Marshall's Long Shadow [1]

THIS year (1935) marks the centenary of John Marshall's death. Thus far our only commemoration has been the Schechter decision, in which the Supreme Court paid its greatest member the dubious honor of turning its back on his tradition of judicial nationalism. In 1901, when the centenary of his first term of court was celebrated, there was much greater éclat. John Marshall dinners were held in all the large cities and the corporation lawyers and political bigwigs made John Marshall speeches. Those were the days of a triumphant nationalism, just home from Cuba and the Philippines. Those were the days when the Populists were storming the state legislatures, and when the bigwigs were finding an effective incantation against them in lauding the man who had fashioned judicial review. Today a Marshall commemoration would be a double-edged sword. The Republicans fear it because Marshall exalted the national power and used the commerce clause (as Mr. Roosevelt and the New Dealers have sought to use it) as a lever by which he might move the economic universe. The Democrats fear it because Marshall exalted the judicial power, made the judges men like gods, and gave an enormous impetus to the fetishism of the Constitution.

Thus does a sense of politics temper our historical devotions with discretion. But what inner contradictions were there in Marshall's thought that will explain these cross-currents of his influence today?

The shambling but iron-willed Richmond lawyer who was to preside over the Supreme Court from 1801 to 1835 did not seem

---

[1] I have since published a revised and greatly expanded version of this essay, as "John Marshall and the Campaign of History"—(March 1939) 39 *Columbia Law Review* 396–431—which will eventually form a chapter of a book on the Supreme

earmarked by fate to play his great role. He was a frontier boy, but of good proprietary stock. He had been brought up in a high-minded and conventional home, his formal schooling was fragmentary, his legal training casual. Pope, Blackstone, and Burke formed his mind; Hamilton's *Federalist* was his American Bible; George Washington was his archetypal hero. In such an education the Revolutionary War was a curious interlude, a sort of shadow-play in which Marshall went gallantly through all the motions of a minor young hero, experienced Valley Forge and came home to Virginia to be idolized by the girls. But that did not keep him, later in life, from repudiating "the wild and enthusiastic notions" of his youth. In the turbulent years of the Confederation he was dismayed at the agrarian unrest; as a member of the Virginia legislature he fought for ratification; he served a term in Congress; went to France on the famous XYZ mission; was Secretary of State in the closing years of John Adams's administration. For a time it looked as if Marshall were only a second-string Federalist politician, caught like the other Federalists in a blind alley of history.

His class roots were theirs. His disarming democratic ways, casting a spell over his biographers, have tended to conceal this fact. An entire mythology has grown up around all the little tender and mildly heterodox ways in which the great Chief Justice half outraged and half titillated his friends by forgetting the dignity of his position. But while Marshall was no New England Brahmin or New York fashionable, he was actually a man of substance, with a deep personal and psychological stake in property. His business and political connections were with the men of funds and funded income, the lawyers and *rentiers,* the landowners and speculators, the shipbuilders, the merchants and manufacturers. He was himself a large landowner, up to the neck in suits over land titles. You have here only the lag that you will find in any man between his boyhood conditionings and his manhood maturities. The boyhood patterns linger on, outliving their utility or even their congruity, like the college-boy folkways in the chairman of a finance board, or a debutante whimsey in a dowager of fifty.

Much has been made also of Marshall's nationalist feeling, espe-

Court. The essay in its present form was written during the New Deal constitutional crisis, immediately after the Schechter decision, and may have some value in that context.

cially by his biographer Senator Beveridge, who uses it to pattern Marshall's entire career. But it must be remembered that Marshall was to show himself, on the bench, as the best of the Federalist political strategists. And nationalism, however fatefully it may have been rooted in Marshall's personality, was also good strategy. After the XYZ affair Marshall came home to find himself a national hero, toasted everywhere. He saw that the common man, who would not respond to Federalist aristocratic theory, would respond to the same property interests when they were clothed in the rhetoric of the national interest. It was a crucial discovery and Marshall was to make the most of it on the judicial front, where he was to fight the battles of business enterprise.

For his mind was not that of the great lawyers, with their heavy erudition, their tortuousness, their narrow legalism, but the mind of a captain of industry with its powerful concentration on a single purpose. Like the elder Pierpont Morgan, he had mastered the art of finality; like him, he possessed a footloose opportunism in the service of a singular tenacity; like him, he was to be a magnificent dictator, dwarfing and intimidating his colleagues, polarizing around himself as a dominant personality the forces that were later to be institutionalized in the Court.

This was Marshall—a man who was not really to find himself until he reached the Court, and who seems miraculously to have turned up in American history at just the point where a rising capitalism most needed him. So near a miracle does this seem that I am ready to pardon Senator Beveridge his four volumes of ecstasy and hosannas. Yet Justice Holmes seems nearer the truth. "A great man," he writes of Marshall, "represents a great ganglion in the nerves of society, or, to vary the figure, a strategic point in the campaign of history, and part of his greatness consists of his being *there*." Marshall's role was to effect a nexus between the property interests under an expanding industrialism and the judicial power under a federal system of government. He was to be the strategic link between capitalism and constitutionalism. And for occupying that position in the campaign of history his experience and the nature of his mind fitted him superbly. Rarely in American history has the exterior tension of events been matched so completely by an interior tension of preparation and purpose on the part of the exactly right man.

Marbury v. Madison (1803) showed Marshall's daring and his mastery. He was seizing the first occasion to affirm the power of judicial review. Nor was his urgency either accidental or whimsical. It was the last-ditch necessity of the Federalist property groups when confronted by Jefferson's victory at the polls. The question of judicial review had been allowed only a few volcanic rumbles at the Constitutional Convention and after. Fearing the common man, the Federalists had not forced the issue. But when they were swept out of the presidency and Congress by the "revolutionary" wave of 1800, there was nothing to do but seek refuge in the judiciary, affirm its supremacy, and claim for the Court the final right to pass on the constitutionality of legislation and the distribution of powers.

Marbury, one of the "midnight appointments" as justice of the peace, had not had his commission delivered. He now sought from the Court a writ of mandamus commanding the Secretary of State to give it up. Marshall was faced by a dilemma. If he denied Marbury's claim it would be an admission of judicial powerlessness. If he upheld it, Jefferson would undoubtedly say what Jackson is reputed to have said thirty years later: "John Marshall has made his decision, now let him enforce it." But Marshall, by a maneuver, managed to administer a public spanking to the new administration, assert judicial supremacy, yet leave Jefferson helpless to strike back. Marbury's commission, he said, was a valid one and Marbury had a vested right in it which it was the function of "a government of laws and not of men" to protect; having a right he had also a remedy, which was mandamus. *But* the Supreme Court, by its reading of the Constitution, could not have jurisdiction over such cases; and the section of the Judiciary Act that sought to confer such jurisdiction was therefore unconstitutional.

It mattered little to Marshall that if his conclusion was valid and the Court had no jurisdiction, then his whole opinion up to that point was superfluous as law—an *obiter dictum* that was sheer political maneuver. Nor did it matter that to declare the section of the Judiciary Act unconstitutional he had to wrench it beyond all principles of statutory interpretation. He was setting the classic example for "judicial statesmanship." It was the formative period of American political life, when every important move was decisive for later power configurations. Legalisms did not count; what counted was the daring, decisive coup. From a legalistic point of view alone, *Marbury v. Madison* has a nightmarish fascination. If ever the history of the Court is written with the proper cosmic irony here will be the cream of the jest. Upon this case, as precedent, rests the power of judicial review. Yet every part of its reasoning has been repudiated by commentators and decisions of later courts which none the less continue to exercise the power it established. "Nothing remains of *Marbury v. Madison*," writes Professor Grant, "except its influence." And its influence continues to grin at us from the Cimmerian darkness like the disembodied smile of the Cheshire cat.

What is the nature of Marshall's contribution to judicial review? He did not originate it, nor did he single-handed establish it beyond all dislodgment. He added nothing substantial to the argument of the Federalists in the "great judiciary debate" in the Senate in 1802. Ultimately, the whole of the theory is in No. 78 of the Federalist Papers; in fact, much of Marshall's career may be viewed as a process of reading Hamilton's state papers into the Constitution. And yet his having translated these ideas into judicial action is Marshall's decisive achievement.

As to the permanence of his work, I find much in Louis B. Boudin's forceful contention that judicial review as we know it is primarily a post-Civil War creation, and that *Marbury v. Madison* actually decided only the Court's power to determine its own jurisdiction. And yet the prestige of the case went far beyond its strict legal effect; everything the Court drew upon after the Civil War in completing judicial review is already to be found in Marshall's opinion. And while the Court did not use judicial review against Congress again until the Dred Scott case a half-century later, it was because in all economic matters the property interests wanted to expand the national power. Where judicial review *was* used effectively during this period was with reference to state power. Marshall's role in this entire process was to give judicial review a foothold, use it for the immediate interests of the capitalism of his day, tie it up with the powerful appeal of nationalism, and entrench it where a later stage of capitalism could take it up and carry it further for its own purposes.

The state legislatures in Marshall's day had an unseemly habit of being responsive to the economic plight of the common man. What was needed was a way of using judicial review to keep them in check. Marshall's "contract clause" opinions were the answer. They stretched contract far beyond its contemporary meaning and gave it a sanctity overriding every consideration of public policy or economic control. Next to judicial review this doctrine of vested rights, as Professor Corwin has called it, was probably the most important invention in the history of the Court. It dominated the constitutional scene up to the Civil War, and it served as a model after which later doctrines, such as due process of law and liberty of contract, could be fashioned.

The first of these "contract cases," *Fletcher v. Peck* (1810), has been described as "a cornerstone of legal structure laid in mud." Behind it is one of the most malodorous episodes in American history, the Yazoo land frauds. Georgia had sold a strip of Indian lands half the size of New England to a land-speculation company for a cent and a half an acre. And every legislator save one had received a large bribe of land stock which could be disposed of for cash. The scandal broke, the people of Georgia, in a fury, elected a new legislature and rescinded the corrupt act. But meanwhile the speculators had sold their stock to Northerners, who now brought a trumped-up suit before the Court. Marshall's decision is breath-taking. He held that the Court could not concern itself with the alleged corruption of the Georgia legislature, and that the original grant was a contract that could not be impaired.

In the context of the land speculation of the day, the decision takes on meaning. Gambling in land values represented the principal financial activity in expansionist America at the turn of the nineteenth century, before industrialism came to overshadow everything else. Some of the most prominent men of the day had been involved in the Yazoo land transactions. Marshall himself knew land and loved land; land speculation was the breath of life in the circles that he moved in. The Fletcher case served as model during the next quarter-century for a series of important decisions in which Marshall and Story led the Court in holding the flimsiest of land titles legal. While hoping to encourage stability through the enforcement of contract, Marshall was actually encouraging the reckless development of economic resources and flagrant corruption in politics. The decisions were decidedly in harmony with the progress of an exploitative capitalism.

The contract ·cases made Marshall the best-hated man in the country. State bankruptcy laws, squatter laws, tax laws fell under the interdict of "vested rights." Marshall made clearest the philosophy underlying all these decisions in *Ogden v. Saunders* (1827), in which a revolt of his colleagues had for once forced him into a solitary dissent. In an opinion breathing a weird Rousseauist natural-rights mysticism he insisted that "the obligations created by contract . . . exist anterior to and independent of society." But the case that comes closest home to us is the famous Dartmouth College case (1819), in which the issue was whether New Hampshire could make any changes in the charter it had granted the college. Every schoolboy knows Webster's eloquent plea ("It is, sir, as I have said, a small college. Yet there are those who love it") and how Marshall, whom the Yazoo land scandals had left cold, wept over it. But few schoolboys know that the case had ultimately less to do with colleges than with the charters of business corporations; that sanctity of contract was invoked to give them immunity against legislative control; and that business enterprise in America has never had more useful mercenaries than the tears Daniel Webster and John Marshall shed so copiously that day. Later developments have stripped the decision of some of its starkness, yet the overmastering fact is that it set up an inviolability of corporate charters that has had slowly to be qualified, instead of starting at the opposite pole with a rule of legislative discretion and control.

It is, however, not with the states but on the national judicial-economic front that Marshall's greatest meaning for today lies. I can say this without succumbing uncritically to the elements of sheer rhetoric in Marshall's nationalism. That rhetoric, like the rhetoric of sanctity of contract, is best cleaved by the sundering blade of the logic of business interests. Its hollowness is most shockingly revealed by Marshall's serious negotiations with the New England secession movement on the eve of (and even during) the War of 1812. In the face of a war that was being fought for the agricultural rather than for the industrial and mercantile groups, his principles of nationalism were dangerously shaken. Marshall had little of the deeper national consciousness of the common man, based on national expansion and adventure and on the promise of American life. His was a theoretical, a strictly judicial nationalism.

Its guiding logic was the relation of the national power to the scope of industrial development. This is brought out clearly in his two famous nationalist decisions, *McCulloch v. Maryland* (1819) and *Gibbons v. Ogden* (1824). The first involved the constitutionality of the Second United States Bank. Marshall made it the occasion of his most resounding opinion, building a doctrine of implied national powers on the "necessary and proper" clause, and waving away Maryland's attempt to tax the bank with "the power to tax involves the power to destroy." Thus Marshall showed himself master of the two-way stretch, interpreting national powers broadly and state powers narrowly. In *Gibbons v. Ogden*, the steamboat case (Marshall's only popular decision), he construed the power of Congress to regulate commerce among the states so broadly that it became one of the most effective elastic clauses of the Constitution. These decisions were part of the upswing of a rising capitalism. Through them Marshall sought to strengthen congressional jurisdiction over the two main lines of business expansion of the day—a national banking system and a national transportation system. In the early stages of industrial capitalism, the function of a central government was to ensure favorable conditions for the development of business enterprise.

Marshall here had the advantage of working with the course of history. He had vision enough to see that political power had to be coterminous with the scale of economic activity. He saw it only dimly, and it was obscured in his mind by a hatred of states' rights and of the common man, and by a protective obsession about the rights of property. But his historical meaning for us lies none the less in this dim insight of his. The position of his opponents, such as Jefferson and John Taylor, embodied an archaic economic vision, whatever the merits of their political views. They dreamed the Physiocratic dream of a society that was even then beyond recall—a republic of small farmers. They failed to see that technology was settling that question for them, and that the issue was now not between states' rights and national power, but between some form of control and no control at all. If, instead of following a policy of states'-rights obstructionism, they had come out frankly for national legislative control of the developing industrial system, Marshall's much vaunted nationalism would quickly have changed to a different tune. What it amounted to was aid and tolerance for business enterprise, both of them on a national scale.

As American capitalism developed, it was inevitable that the mere absence of restraint over private property should no longer be adequate to resolve the deepening contradictions of economic life. In the search for new methods of economic control through the federal government, Marshall's judicial nationalism proved a memorable instrument. The Marshall technique of interpretation became a tradition that created new uses not only for the commerce power, but for the taxing and spending power of Congress as well. It is this technique which, since the eighteen-seventies, has formed one facet of judicial liberalism. And it was upon the continuation of this technique that the administration laid its hope for the New Deal legislation. Indeed, a very good case could have been made out, on the basis of continuous precedents since the Swift case in 1905, when the nature of our market economy had already become clear to some of the Justices, that all important business enterprise today is interstate commerce, that the whole industrial process is an unbroken chain flung out over a national market, and that every important link in that chain is therefore a link in interstate commerce.

But the important question, as we have since learned, is not whether the Court *could if it would* interpret the commerce clause broadly enough to validate legislative control of industry, but whether it *would if it could*. And to explain its unwillingness we have to go back to Marshall as surely as we do when we wish to explain its competence. Marshall's class interest took two forms in his own thinking: the doctrine of the vested rights of property and the doctrine of judicial nationalism. Each of these has given rise to a tradition that has been followed in the later history of the Court, the first principally by the conservatives, the second principally by the liberals. And it need scarcely be added that the dominant one has been not the broad interpretation of the Constitution in the interests of federal jurisdiction over industry, but the setting up of the Supreme Court as the guardian of the vested interests. In Marshall's thought, in the period of a rising capitalism, these two streams could flow together smoothly and feed each other. But the movement of economic events has caused a deepening cleavage between them.

Today, in a period of capitalist crisis, to follow Marshall's vested-rights tradition means to entrench further the hegemony of Big Ownership; to follow his tradition of judicial nationalism means for a time to salvage capitalism, but to salvage it by stripping it of some of its powers; and, more important, it means to maintain tolerable standards of wages and working conditions. Today, even more than in Marshall's time, the issue is one between national control of business enterprise and no control at all. What the Court thus far has done has been to turn its back on everything in the Marshall tradition that was worth following, everything that was an abiding part of the campaign of history. And it has chosen to cling to that part of his tradition which was narrow, immediate, and actuated chiefly by a jealous and exclusive class interest.

For the liberals on the Court this was no easy choice. Nor did they make it as a deliberate preference for the interests of business enterprise. And here, for explanation, we must turn to a third element in Marshall's thought—that of constitutionalism, the supremacy and sanctity of the Constitution and of the Supreme Court as its exclusive interpreter and guardian. A potential liberal minority on the Court, far removed from a defense of reactionary capitalism, is none the less fearful of what may lie ahead in the unexplored vistas of hitherto unparalleled federal control of industry. And they find nothing to fall back upon except an austere constitutionalism and Marshall's doctrine of judicial supremacy. Like *Marbury v. Madison,* the Hot Oil and Schechter decisions express (for some of the Justices) a jealousy of the executive power, and the insistence of the judiciary that it alone can apportion powers among government departments. That is the meaning of the contentions about the delegation of congressional powers to the Executive.

Unfortunately the Court liberals do not see that the constitutionalism which they regard as the safeguard of the polity is, in the hands of the Court majority, not the expression of a tortured and sensitive conscience, but a stubborn defense of the *status quo.* And on the part of many people outside the Court this heritage from Marshall becomes a militant vigilantism that is violently opposed to any form of social change, is fed by Hearstian poisons, and is one of our peculiarly American forms of supernationalism. It defeats the very purposes that Marshall's real judicial nationalism stood for. And it promises to form a considerable part of whatever fascist future the unkind gods may have in store for us.

Thus there are three Marshalls alive today—a hundred years after his death: the Marshall of expanded national power, the Marshall of the protection of the vested interests, and the Marshall of a sacred constitutional fetishism. And it is the great irony of his place in the campaign of history that the last two have combined to kill their brother.

1935

2

Taney Redivivus[1]

THERE has for some time been a feeling that history, acting through her agents the historians, has done something less than justice to Roger B. Taney. There have in the past few years been thunderings and reverberations of an approaching revaluation, of which Carl Swisher's book [2] is a part. Louis Boudin, in his *Government by Judiciary* (1932), took a bold step in revaluing Taney's importance, although his analysis is far different from Mr. Swisher's. Felix Frankfurter's *The Commerce Clause under Marshall, Taney, and Waite* devotes a sharply etched study to Taney, placing him second only to Marshall in the Supreme Court's history. C. W. Smith's recent *Roger B. Taney: Jacksonian Jurist* gives him a high rank in our political thought. The theme of all these books is *Taney redivivus*.

Mr. Swisher's must be counted the definitive work on Taney. It is clear, painstaking, and comprehensive and will rank as one of the solid achievements of American biography. The book has every mark of having been built up from the ground, with material quarried from all the printed and manuscript sources, the latter in several instances hitherto unknown. Fact and opinion have been scrupulously winnowed, the chaff of hypothesis separated from the wheat of actuality. Most important, the result is by no means dry-as-dust scholarship, but a living historical portrait. I shall in several instances have to quarrel with the Taney that emerges from these pages, having some chaffy hypotheses of my own as to the authentic stamp of the man's ideas. But the essential

---

[1] Readers interested in following the Supreme Court theme through this book may wish to go from these essays on Chief Justices Marshall and Taney to the essays on Justices Holmes, Brandeis, and Black below, in Part II, and then to the essays in Part IV on "The Supreme Court and American Capitalism," "Minority Rule and the Constitutional Tradition," and "Vested Rights and Vested Interests."

[2] *Roger B. Taney*, New York, Macmillan, 1935.

fact is that there *is* a Taney that emerges—not an insubstantial fiction but the result of an honest and able attempt to give the shape of a historical figure and his thought.

Until very recently Chief Justice Taney had been regarded as a second-rate figure, narrow and localist in his outlook, notable only because he strove to undo the work of the Marshall court. He had been damned by conservatives for his "partisan" fight in Jackson's Cabinet against the United States Bank and by liberals for his Dred Scott decision in support of the slavocracy. He has thus suffered the fate reserved for those whose acts, whatever unity they may have had in their own day, have had that unity shattered by the unfolding of history. It is only recently that the pendulum of opinion has begun to swing back again, partly because we have moved farther away from the tensions of the Civil War and Reconstruction periods but more largely because the expansion of the Court's power has made us more concerned about American democracy. And so we go back to Taney, with his Jacksonian rages against financial concentration and corporate power, with his restricted view of the judicial power, as to a road not taken that we might with advantage have traveled.

Mr. Swisher is conscious of performing a work of historical reshaping. He complains, with a bitterness that eats through his scholarly urbanity, of the raw deal that Taney was given by Burgess, Rhodes, and William Graham Sumner. His concern is to vindicate Taney against his detractors and thus to give him the retributive justice that has thus far been denied him. It is clear that in telling Taney's story he has had his eye not only upon the deeds of history but upon the misdeeds of the historians as well.

Yet the need of revaluation should not blind us to the fact that the revaluation may itself have a bias. In each period the estimate of Taney has been responsive to the dominant winds of doctrine. Swisher points out quite clearly that Burgess and Rhodes, when they wrote about the Civil War and the events leading up to it, were writing from the viewpoint of Northerners after the victory, and that the conservative American historians, Channing, McMaster, Bassett, and Sumner, when they wrote about the war between Jackson and the Bank of the United States, were writing from the viewpoint of latter-day Whigs. Swisher himself would be more or less than human if he did not have a political orientation of his own, and I wish—as Max Weber always advocated—that he had set down the boundaries of his own bias for us to discount. Actually he writes of Taney with the bias of the liberal who distrusts finance capital, believes in democracy, is skeptical of the solutions that industrialism has imposed, and stresses human rights as against property rights. It is no accident that the book was written in the presidency of Franklin D. Roosevelt. In no other climate of opinion could the viewpoint it represents have flourished so. I happen personally to like this bias pretty well, but I think every bias should be recognized and set forth.

It is to Mr. Swisher's credit that, although his primary interest in Taney is in Chief Justice Taney, he has given ample space— perhaps more than ample—to his participation in the Bank War. This was in a sense necessary because, to correct past distortions, a careful scholar had to go back in every case to the original manuscripts and reconstruct the detailed story from them. American financial historians will welcome this emphasis; American constitutional historians will regret it. But a more important question than the apportionment of space is the explanation of a man's mind and career. And I suspect that one reason Swisher dwells on the Bank War period is to underline Taney's essential anti-corporate radicalism.

Taney started as a Whig and became a Jacksonian, hated by the businessmen and bankers of the country and feared by such orthodox Marshallian constitutionalists as Justice Story and Chancellor Kent. Swisher explains this shift by saying that Taney was influenced by the anti-mercantilist bias of the tobacco planters among whom he grew up in the Maryland tidewater region— planters who felt "a deep distrust and dislike for the mercantile and creditor class" and for "the predatory financial interests." While Swisher is on the whole not given overmuch to precipitous generalization, he seems to have a weakness for the environmental approach. The tidewater tobacco economy plays in this book somewhat the same role that the California frontier played in molding Mr. Justice Field's mind in Swisher's first book.

I do not by any means want to quarrel with the environmental-class approach. But Swisher's use of it strikes me as being rather too static. Of all instruments of interpretation, that of class and environment should be a moving, complex, dynamic thing. One has to explain not only how the Whig became a fervid Jacksonian, but how the Jacksonian radical—once he came to the Supreme Court—turned out to be a mildish liberal, weighing precedents along with the best of them. Then one must go on to explain how the radical (or liberal) who cared so much about human rights as against property rights became finally the champion of slave property rights in his anti-humanist decisions in the Dred Scott and other cases; and how a man who had talked about limiting the judicial power came finally to take one of the revolutionary steps in its expansion.

Previous liberal defenders of Taney have sought to present the Dred Scott case as a mistake and an aberration. Swisher, fortunately, does not make any such attempt. For even mistakes have their roots in a man's thinking and need to be integrated with the rest of his actions. The fact is that the Dred Scott case is by no means an isolated incident in Taney's development; many of the elements in the Dred Scott opinion are to be found in the rest of his work. In his desire not to see Dred Scott as an isolated incident, Swisher seeks to make a consistent figure out of Taney, and in the process he swallows Dred Scott and much of the social philosophy of Southern planterism. I believe that the better view is not to seek consistency in Taney so much as continuity—the continuity of a liberal whose anti-corporate bias still leaves him room for a strong property bias, responding with honesty but with a tragic shift of social outlook to the complex tensions of the most bewildering period of American history. Taney had a stubborn personal strength, but he was not one of the makers of history. He was caught in one of the swirling eddies of history, and the result was the gyrations of doctrine that puzzle us.

All of which should make my own bias abundantly clear.

1938

3

The Heritage of Emerson

RALPH WALDO EMERSON has been most widely read as an edifying essayist and has latterly come to be valued for his incisive and pattern-breaking poetry. Yet his chief importance is as a thinker. He was not a systematic philosopher; and there is little in his metaphysics that cannot be found in Plato and Kant. His gnomic wisdoms do, however, sum up to a philosophy and his atomistic utterances cohere somehow into a well-defined point of view.

While he was transcendentalist enough to believe in the existence of innate ideas that do not result from but transcend experience, he avoided entangling alliances with the transcendentalist movement as such. And he adopted much the same policy toward Unitarianism, Fourierism, perfectionism, abolitionism, and all the millennial and humanitarian programs that shot up luxuriantly in the suppressed and crotchety atmosphere of New England society. He wanted freer air to breathe than he could find in any sect, creed, cult, or movement. For all his pride in being rooted in his provincial soil, he was more truly a citizen of the world than of Massachusetts. His intellectual coming of age dates from his first trip to Europe, where he was exposed to the thought of Goethe, Carlyle, Coleridge, Wordsworth, and Landor. This completed the fusion in his mind of the strands of influence deriving from sources so diverse as Platonism, Protestantism, romanticism, Swedenborgian mysticism, the sacred books of the East, and homely Yankee observation. The resulting configuration became, on his return to Concord, a sharp cuneiform instrument for valuations which he impressed on the clay of contemporary American life.

With a godlike aplomb Emerson set himself to rethink his world afresh; with an almost flagellant anxiety he lay in ambush for his materials, surprising every stray perception and intuition, setting them down in his journals and hammering out of them finally his completed lectures and essays. He became the center of an intellectual renaissance in New England. With a characteristic sanity he sought the sources of new energy within the same confines of American life where he found exhausted traditions and sinister growths. It is that which accounts for the dual aspect of his thought as a criticism of his times and an exploration of the new America. He denounced the spiritual barrenness of American life, its growing materialism and acquisitiveness, the narrowness of sect and party, the deadening effect of institutions, the clinging to European traditions, and the obedience to the voice of authority. While he lacked Carlyle's capacity for moral indignation (he substituted for it a somewhat irritating oracular tone of his own), Emerson must be ranked with him as a great ethical critic of society.

But the whole tendency of Emerson's being lay not toward criticism but toward affirmation. The most insistent note of affirmation that he sounded was an intellectual and ethical individualism—what William James summed up as "the sovereignty of the living individual." Whether he was aware of it or not, Emerson was fulfilling in his thought the deepest meaning of the Protestant Reformation—designating the individual as the unit of judgment and interpretation. From this central preoccupation lines may be drawn touching every important doctrine at the periphery of Emerson's social thought. The individual must choose his own calling, guide his own conduct, form his own opinions, construct his own religion, even fashion his own history. Nothing is important except as it is relevant to his purposes; nothing is sacred except his own mind; he can learn nothing except as he himself relives it. Standing at the conflux of time he has at his disposal the social heritage of the past and before him a future bounded in its possibility only by his own creative imagination.

Doctrine such as this shot like lightning through the dour Calvinist atmosphere of New England; it fitted the mood of a pioneer society in the West; its easy harmonies were welcome in a country threatened by sectional struggle; there were even aspects of it that could be found to meet the needs of an emerging industrial society. In fact, it was the tragedy of Emerson's teaching that it could be turned about to serve purposes he never dreamed of and causes he would have abhorred.

How have we used our heritage from Emerson? The conception of society as dynamic and experimental, which is the most permanent and valuable element in his social thought—that at any moment our social thinking must start afresh with a clear field and no shackling traditions—has been lost sight of. What we have chiefly heeded has been his buoyant and almost unctuous optimism. His opposition to state coercion, amounting in his own thought almost to philosophical anarchism, has gone to support *laissez-faire*. His emphasis on the sovereignty of the individual has strengthened a formal ballot democracy. His ethical individualism has furnished a basis for economic individualism. His doctrines of self-reliance and opportunity are excellent homilies on the prevailing virtues of a capitalist economy. The denial of the existence of evil and the principle of compensation can be used to bridge inequalities of income and social status. While Emerson was still engaged in building his doctrine, the industrial revolution came to America and turned all the social consequences of his precepts topsy-turvy.

Beyond this his chief weakness as a social thinker lay in his overestimate of the role of the individual in the social process and his underestimate of the place of the institution. This vitiates, for example, whatever theory of history may be found implicit in his *Representative Men*. His *English Traits*, however, is a brilliant study in the dangerous realm of national psychology and makes a much juster estimate of the force of tradition. But throughout his thinking one feels that his world was not a society but a collection of individuals. He did not offer, nor did he envisage the need of, any mechanisms whereby individual judgments would add up to a social judgment or individual creativeness would be translated into social action.

1931

Thoreau: No Hermit

WHEN just out of Harvard, Thoreau came under the powerful sway of Emerson's mind and did his formative thinking as a member of the Concord group of transcendental-
ists. He eventually liberated himself, however, from Emerson's
influence, and at no time was he taken in by the transcendentalist
excesses of the Concord group or by the millennial dreams that
grew thick as huckleberries on the Concord bushes. The sources
of strength in his thinking came rather from other strains—an
absorption with the Greek classics, a prolonged study of the Orien-
tal teachings, the Graeco-British tradition of individualism, the
nature-worship of the French and German philosophers and the
English romantic poets, and finally a conscious modeling upon the
way of life of the American Indians.

But Thoreau was not one to be too deeply influenced. He was
impervious to anything that did not fit into that continual quest
for a practical solution of the problems of his own individual life
which he called his philosophy. But implicit in his highly personal
essays and nature soliloquies and journal entries is a devastating
attack upon every dominant aspect of American life in its first
flush of industrial advance—the factory system, the corporations,
business enterprise, acquisitiveness, the vandalism of natural resources, the vested commercial and intellectual interests, the cry
for expansion, the clannishness and theocratic smugness of New
England society, the herd-mindedness of the people, the unthinking civic allegiance they paid to an opportunist and imperialist
government.

He despised everything derivative and secondary. His criticism
of American society sprang from the rebellion of the pioneer spirit.
For he was seeking on an intellectual and moral frontier the zest
and immediacy of the original pioneer effort and protesting pas-

sionately against the cultural crudity and the materialism of the pioneer in an industrial age. He rejected the factory system because it meant the exploitation of others; he rejected the cult of success and the Puritan creed of persistent work because it meant the exploitation of oneself. His economics anticipated Ruskin's by defining the cost of a thing as the amount of life that has to be exchanged for it; his aesthetics anticipated William Morris's by declaring that no beauty can exist in commodities that does not flow from a creativeness in the lives of those who fashion them. He recounts in *Walden* (1854) a two-year experiment in living in a hut in the woods, stripping the husk of civilization to the core, and setting up his own economy of wants and satisfactions. He found that the economic system was making unreasonable demands on him, and so he proceeded to sabotage it, entering upon a conscientious withdrawal of efficiency which was none the less earnest because it was restricted to his own life. Similarly he sabotaged the government by refusing to pay taxes, and he spent a night in the village jail as an exultant political prisoner. His essay *Civil Disobedience* (1849) is a sharp statement of the duty of resistance to governmental authority when it is unjustly exercised; read by Gandhi in 1907, it became the foundation of the Indian civil disobedience movement. Thoreau's three speeches on John Brown (1859–60; republished in vol. X of the *Collected Works*) extol his insurrectionary attempt at Harpers Ferry and denounce the shortsighted coercion of the government that martyred him.

As a social critic Thoreau was uncompromising: his thought was tighter than Emerson's, less optimistic, less given to the resolution of opposites. It was a taut, astringent rejection of everything, that could not pass the most exacting tests of the individual life. In that sense there was something of the nihilist about Thoreau, and his thought effected an almost Nietzschean transvaluation of values.

But his hermit-like individualism may easily be overemphasized, just as his absorption with nature has been overemphasized. Both must be seen as part of a rebellion against the oversocialized New England town, in which the individual was being submerged, and against the factory system which saw nature only as so much raw material and sought to subdue it to the uses of profit. He was not so limited as to believe that the individual could by his own action stem the heedless onrush of American life, or succeed wholly in rechanneling it; yet, being a transcendentalist, he believed that a sharp moral protest such as that of John Brown, once clearly made, is ultimately irresistible. While he regarded individual development as the only aim of society, and the individual's moral sense as the only test and ultimately the only safeguard of institutions, he did not envisage the individual as the necessary cadre of society. "To act collectively is according to the spirit of our institutions," he wrote in *Walden,* and he follows this with a plea to extend the social services of the community and to make every New England village the basis of a venture in adult education. Nor did he wholly turn his back on the machine as an instrument of production: his emphasis was rather on its cultural consequences in his own day.

It was one of his characteristic paradoxes that the man who could solemnly call his fellow-townsmen together to read them a protest against the imprisonment of John Brown or the return of a fugitive slave could also profess an unconcern with most of the burning political issues of the day, and insist that his business was not to change the world but to solve the problem of living in it. He could say: "God does not sympathize with the popular causes," and at the same time have so deep a sense of the relation between a great culture and the common concerns of life that he has come down as perhaps the leading American nativist; commenting on the fact that no literature had yet grown up around "the Man of the Age, come to be called workingman," he remarks that "none yet speaks to his condition, for the speaker is not yet in his condition." It was his tragedy to be forced by the crudities of an expanding capitalism into a revulsion against society and its institutions that has until recently obscured the real force of his social thought. But there is about that thought a spare and canny strength and a quality of being unfooled that will survive even such a tragedy.

1934

5

The Lincoln Image

ARE people moved by Lincoln today? And if so, what is the image that moves them? I have sought some light on such questions in this year's (1939) birthday crop of books on Lincoln. Each of the three gives us a different facet of his evocative power. One [1] is Lincoln seen through the swift, devouring eyes of a smart young contemporary, John Hay, who had acid for everyone but devotion for his chief. The second [2] is Lincoln seen through the understanding eyes of one of the best of today's middle generation of dramatists. The third [3] is Lincoln seen through the myriad loving and magnifying eyes of the common folk. And the striking fact is that, although each is caught from a different angle, there is considerable congruity between these Lincolns of history, drama, and legend. I do not know whether separately or together they make the "real" Lincoln. I leave such matters to those with greater certitude about impaling historic actuality. I find it more exciting to ask what pattern of Lincoln's personality is emerging from the past and what its directive force is for the future.

Sherwood has done a brave play, striving to fuse the private with the public Lincoln. I suspect, of course, that most of those who have seen it have gone away feeling that what made Abe Lincoln President was that he lost Ann Rutledge and was wooed and driven by Mary Todd. That is less Sherwood's weakness than our own: we have a desire to bring the historic great down to our everyday level, and we would rather remember that Abe was de-

---

[1] *Lincoln and the Civil War in the Diaries and Letters of John Hay.* Selected and with an introduction by Tyler Dennett. New York, Dodd, Mead, 1939.

[2] *Abe Lincoln in Illinois: a Play in Twelve Scenes,* by Robert Emmett Sherwood. With a foreword by Carl Sandburg. New York, Scribner, 1939.

[3] *Lincoln Talks: a Biography in Anecdote.* Collected, collated, and edited by Emanuel Hertz. New York, Viking, 1939.

lightfully clumsy in love-making, or unconsolable over Ann, or caught in Mary's more powerful will, than what his views were on slavery and labor.

Yet the fact remains that Sherwood has not been wholly successful. He has two themes. One is of slow, painful growth—the making of a man for whom the resolution of his personal conflicts is not complete until he has reached some degree of political maturity. The second is democracy as a living credo. The two are never fused. Perhaps it is because the theme of growth is a dynamic one, and he has handled it thus through the twelve lean and muscular scenes; while the temptation in developing the democratic theme is to do it through such symbolism as that of the westward-moving settlers in the seventh scene. What best unites the two themes, although scarcely mentioned, is the Civil War symbol. For Lincoln, no less than the nation, was a house divided against himself, threatening always to secede from himself. And the belief that finally moved him to summon up a new sense of wholeness was his belief in ordinary people like himself and his neighbors, and of a nation built upon them. "The prayer which Lincoln gives for a sick boy," Sherwood tells us in a brilliant essay on the play's genesis and intent, "is in effect a prayer for the survival of the United States of America."

At the end of Sherwood's play, Lincoln is leaving for his inauguration, heavily guarded. Tyler Dennett's collection, which puts all the relevant John Hay letters and diaries together for the Civil War and Reconstruction periods, takes him up at that point, and the note of danger and stress is never absent. Hay's Lincoln is the crisis leader, and the theorists of leadership in a democracy would do well to study this volume. Here are the fruits of that period of growth and democratic deepening that we saw in *Abe Lincoln in Illinois*. The smoldering young Billy Herndon, Lincoln's law clerk in the Sherwood play, has been replaced by the acidulous young John Hay, Lincoln's secretary. It is good to see Lincoln through the eyes of the young men about him. In Herndon's impatient eyes Lincoln was weak and hesitant, moving too slowly toward a sense of the slavery crisis. To Hay, Lincoln is too indulgent to the treacherous and incompetent around him; with a mixture of the admiring and protective, he talks of him as the "Tycoon" and the "Ancient." Hay is no radical, and not much of a democrat: he turned out later to be considerable of an imperialist. What draws him to Lincoln? It is a sense of the difficulties that beset the President in war-beleaguered Washington—the bullying ways of Cabinet members, the incompetence of the generals, the importunities of favor-seekers, the milk-and-wateriness of preacher folk, the hot-headedness of the Abolitionists, the sabotaging of the Copperheads. Here is a crisis democracy if there ever was one.

And the Lincoln who emerges from it is none the less heroic because he is not a mystic or a fanatic. He is the brooding man of thought whom events have spurred to action. He has an infinite capacity for patience. When he has a message or state paper to prepare he goes about for days, turning it over in his mind. We catch glimpses of him talking to an Indian delegation, arguing about Daniel Webster and his importance in American history, speaking at Gettysburg ("The President, in a fine, free way, with more grace than is his wont, said his half-dozen words of consecration, and the music wailed, and we went home through crowded and cheering streets"), waiting in McClellan's house for the general to come back from a wedding party, only to have McClellan snub him on his return and go straight to bed. ("This unparalleled insolence of epaulets," Hay remarks bitterly, and the President answers that "it was better at this time not to be making points of etiquette and personal dignity.") But we see him also with a will steeled to his task, unrattled even when Washington seemed in extreme danger, taking what measures were necessary to suppress treason, sending an unending stream of messages to his generals about strategy, having by an immense personal effort to supply them with the sheer will to win the war. This is an embattled Lincoln in the midst of cowardice, disloyalty, defeatism. If we want a parallel in our time, let us think of Negrín, whose efforts, however, were not crowned by victory because he was betrayed from without.

Hertz's new book is a miscellany of trivia. But when you add them up they come close to amounting to Abraham Lincoln. The weakness of the book is that it is neither biography nor portrait: it is too inclusive to be either, for each involves selection. The editor has simply gathered all the stories about Lincoln and dumped them between the covers of a book. It is curious to see the editor of the tough-minded *Hidden Lincoln* of last year doing this, since many of the stories here give us a mushy and idealized Lincoln. Yet there is a logic in what he has done. I take it that what Mr. Hertz objects to primarily is not the Lincoln legend as such, but the curtains that have been put up to screen Lincoln's lusty honesty, the literary and official attempts at prettifying. He objects to the selective because the selective is always secondary and artificial—and the artifice has generally come from the hands of reaction. Just as *The Hidden Lincoln* was the material Herndon had gathered from people who knew Lincoln directly, so *Lincoln Talks* represents the immediate impact of Lincoln upon thousands whose lives crossed his. A good deal of nonsense has been written about the folk mind. Yet it is true that the legendry that clusters about a great man often gives a more complete picture of him than may be found in the scholars and prettifiers.

There is much in *Lincoln Talks* that our own generation has forgotten. "Financial success," Ben Tillman quotes Lincoln as saying, "is purely metallic. The man who gains it has four metallic attributes—gold in his palm, silver on his tongue, brass in his face, and iron in his heart." There are other remarks to the same purpose. Yet when a colleague of mine made a speech to a Rotary Club pointing out that Lincoln was in his day considered something of a radical, he was met by a shocked silence. The banker pays a fat sum to go to a Lincoln's Day dinner; he wipes out Lincoln's belief in the masses, his sense of the brotherhood of workers in every land—and what remains for him is the Lincoln who helped forge what has become the party of an irresponsible capitalism. But it is not only the Rotarian and the banker who see a truncated Lincoln. Just as to Mary Antin, as an immigrant child, George Washington was the boy who could not tell a lie and became the Father of his Country, so to the common man today Lincoln is the rail-splitter, the ragged boy who rose to be President, the Great Emancipator who in the end suffered martyrdom. Was he radical or conservative, weak or decisive, democrat or oligarch, pro-labor or anti-labor? The question scarcely occurs to us.

The fact is that between the generations that told the Lincoln stories and our own generation there have intervened the decades of finance capitalism. They have wiped the Lincoln image from our minds because Lincoln as democrat, as labor sympathizer, as "Father Abraham" with his compassion for the suffering of the people, was an inconvenient Lincoln. What has remained is the barest attenuation of a man—just enough to give sanctity to the birth of the Republican Party—and the self-made man who has added fuel to the myth of individual success. There is a historical seemliness in this, of course, given Charles Beard's interpretation of the Civil War as the decisive triumph of capitalist enterprise. Yet Lincoln did not foresee those consequences. There is considerable evidence that he saw the Civil War as a struggle between two concepts of labor—free and slave—and became most alarmed at the extreme Southern doctrine that slavery was the natural condition of the working class.

Is there a new and revived Lincoln image in the making? I think so. These books, along with Hertz's *Hidden Lincoln* and Carl Sandburg's magnificent volumes on the "Prairie Years," are among its first signs. The fact that Sherwood's *Lincoln* has been playing to packed houses has some meaning. So also has the Abraham Lincoln Brigade. Even the old John Hay portrait of Lincoln the War President and Commander-in-Chief of faltering armies has a new meaning today.

For the Lincoln image that is faithful to history and the recollections of his contemporaries is one almost providentially made for our present national crisis. It is of a Lincoln who was first of all a deeply human being, with the rich earth flavor and the gusto out of which a culture is made; who had a long tolerance for all modes of belief while he had an unshakable faith in majority rule; who was willing to grant every reasonable concession to the tenacious and blind slave-owning class in order to preserve national unity, yet when the fight was forced on him insisted on fighting hard and fighting for victory; who did not let his will be paralyzed in a crisis, but knew that when the time came for action it had to be decisive action; who was unwilling to fetishize civil liberty and make an absolute of it, seeing that if the Union were not saved civil liberty would not mean much, yet who fought against the wholesale suppressions demanded by the Radical Republicans; a Lincoln who died while planning a reconstruction without bitterness or vengeance.

If such an image does not have power to steel our will and give it a quiet strength, and thus shape our history, it will be because the capitalism that Lincoln accepted has already overpowered the democracy of which he dreamed and for which he died.

1939

6

Mr. Justice Holmes

Justice Holmes: Flowering and Defeat [1]

THIS is a sad essay, for much of my reading recently (1935–36) has been in the opinions of the Supreme Court, and their narrow unyielding quality has sent my mind back to the towering figure by the side of whom Chief Justice Hughes seems merely a politician and Justice Sutherland a schoolmarm. The triumph of the present reactionary Supreme Court majority is in a real sense a triumph over Justice Holmes and the memory of Justice Holmes. In the same sense it is a triumph of legalism and business enterprise over literature and the philosophic mind. As I have watched the Supreme Court majority during the past fifteen months riding roughshod over every principle of humanism and tolerance that Holmes ever stood for, my mind has turned back with increasing frequency to Holmes himself—to his decisions and his speeches and his letters, all fit to stand with the great writing of America and its noblest thinking. I have turned back in quest of the roots of his flowering and defeat.

What emerges most clearly as one reads Holmes and reads about him is that here was a whole man. His genius—and it *was* genius— did not proceed from eccentricity, nor did it rise up from revolt. It was not the schizoid genius of a Poe, or the tight austerity turned into flame of an Emerson, or the truncated genius of a Melville. There was a wholeness about Holmes which could come only from

---

1 This essay was written in 1936, before President Roosevelt's reorganization proposal and his Court appointments brought a new liberalism into the Supreme Court. I have nevertheless allowed it to stand as written, since the trends it refers to were not transitory and we shall have to reckon with them again. For a more extended analysis of these trends, see the essay on "Corwin and the Judicial Power" below, and in Part IV "The Supreme Court and American Capitalism."

the flowering of the greatest aristocracy America has so far had—
the New England intellectual aristocracy.

The picture that we have of Holmes as he grew into maturity
is the picture of a young New England intellectual aristocrat, with
literary and philosophical tastes, sweeping to success in his chosen
profession of the law. He had chosen the law deliberately as a
pathway to expression and not because some inner need or some
cruel urge and pressure of the time dictated that career and that
alone. He had a hunger for greatness or distinction of some sort
and a hunger for adventure. He got his chance at the second during the Civil War, in which he was wounded three times and distinguished himself for bravery. When he came back from war he
was ready to plunge just as intensely into the battles of peace, if
only he could get an adversary formidable enough. That may be,
indeed, why he chose law: simply because to fashion something
great and enduring out of such barren and unyielding material
one would need to have a firm sculptor's hand, and ample heat
of the brain with which to govern the chisel. "In our youths," he
afterwards said, "our hearts were touched with fire. It was given
to us to learn at the outset that life is a profound and passionate
thing."

It was this conviction that enabled him to master the technicali-
ties of legal study, read his fill of the English Yearbooks, get out his
edition of Kent's *Commentaries* and his book on *The Common
Law*. But even as a young lawyer he was still absorbingly interested
in philosophy. In an office on Beacon Street, with the shades drawn,
the gas-light flaring, whisky bottle on the table, and Holmes's tall
frame leaning against the fireplace mantel, he and William James
would spend the evening in talk, "twisting the tail of the cosmos."

He seemed to have all the gifts the gods could offer: family, wit,
elegance, grace, a profound belief in life, a quiet self-assurance, a
deep sense of security. He was of the leisure class, he lived and
talked in the grand manner, with just enough hint of the casual,
the profane, and the shocking to make it clear that the grand manner was something he adopted deliberately while he viewed it
objectively. His success was like an irresistible force. He taught
at Harvard College; got the first professorship of law for which
there was an opening; and, barely launched on legal teaching, was
elevated to the Supreme Court of Massachusetts. No wonder that

later he was able to touch the hearts of all young men with fire. For what he did for them was to take a profession that was rapidly becoming too commercialized and sordid even for the strong stomachs of American youth and invest it with nobility, grandeur, daring.

Holmes came to the bench already equipped with a philosophy which he had compounded somehow out of Plato, Emerson, and William James and out of his own already fabulous experience. It was not a self-contained philosophic system in which the ends always met. More often than not he brought to the writing of one of his opinions merely a series of sharp insights and sharper phrases, which he would proceed to lick into shape and give an organic structure mainly by his unflagging vitality. His thought flowed from an insistence that any fact had to validate itself before it could disturb his desire to let past experience stand. "All that I mean by truth is what I can't help thinking. . . . But I have learned to surmise that my *can't helps* are not necessarily cosmic."

But he had not rid himself of the influence of Plato, or of Plato in Emerson. Try as he would to wash his thought in the cynical acid of pragmatism, he still lived considerably in the realm of essences. There was always a straining for the universal, a restlessness until he had shown "the relation of his fact to the framework of the universe." Although he was called a sociological jurist, the values and experience he cared most about were of invariance rather than change. He had his eye peeled always for the curious uniformity with which the human animal behaves, whatever the century: he sought identities, whereas his colleague Brandeis always sought mutations. His equipment in the lore of human uniformity was profound; his equipment in the sciences of social change was less impressive. He gave lip-service to economics, and said that the man of the future in law was not the black-letter man but the economist; yet his own economics was fragmentary and almost archaic.

But beyond philosophy or economics, Holmes was ridden by two myths: that of the soldier and that of the gambler. Life was a campaign, requiring heroic and disciplined individual qualities. Life was a throw of the dice, but the stakes were worth the risks. Both myths, it will be seen, are of the leisure class. His memory of the war made his approach to life that of the good soldier; his philosophy was an aleatory philosophy—the gods playing at dice with human destinies; his theory of law was that it was merely "the rules of the game." With this framework it was amazing how successful Holmes was in handling the problems of a complicated industrial world. On the Massachusetts bench his tough and skeptical conservatism allowed the existing legal rule—embodying all the changes and chances of the past—to stand unless the new doctrine forced its way in. On the United States Supreme Court he turned his skepticism toward the process of judicial interpretation itself, and would allow the action of the legislature—embodying men's experience and the risks they were willing to take in learning how to govern themselves—to stand unless it seemed entirely unreasonable. What had seemed conservatism at first now seemed radicalism.

But Holmes was no radical. He was against any "tinkering with the institution of property." "The notion that with socialized property we should have women free and a piano for everybody seems to me an empty humbug." After rendering an opinion favorable to some strikers he went on very sedulously to disclaim having any illusions that strikes were economically valid. He saw them merely as "a lawful instrument in the universal struggle for life." In fact, his whole conception seems at times an aristocratic refinement on Darwinism. He believed in the law of the economic jungle, but he wanted to see the beasts behave like gentlemen and observe the rules of the game. He was able to come out in protection of trade unionism on the ground that it gave the employees "equality of bargaining power"—that is, a good gambling chance. But to apply an individualistic approach or a philosophy of risk and gamble to American business was a thankless task. Business was more adept at that than was anything dreamed of in Holmes's philosophy: it had Holmes licked even before the word "Go." Given monopoly conditions, law could not be regarded with Olympian calm. To view thus the position of the worker as against the large corporation, or the small businessman as against the holding company, was at best a bitter sort of irony.

Like Henry Adams, Holmes was the flowering of an aristocracy that felt itself bewildered under the impact of the new industrialism. But while Adams analyzed with a poignant awareness the sources of his defeat, Holmes gallantly and robustly proclaimed that one could still live in a world like this. Even aristocrats could. The function of the aristocrat was to maintain the great traditions while the forces loose in an industrial world battled it out to a conclusion.

But Holmes is dead, and his influence lingers only with a few dissenters, protesting in a diminuendo. The prevailing tone of style and thought in the Supreme Court decisions is now set by Justice McReynolds and Justice Sutherland. But while Holmes's defeat shows that the pre-industrial aristocratic tradition cannot grapple with the problems of finance capitalism, he will always be proof that the tradition could generate a superb personality, a gallant philosophy, and a great style.

1936

The Scar Holmes Leaves

MR. SHRIVER has given us a volume of Holmes miscellanies [2] —the early reviews and comments written between 1870 and 1873 by the young editor of the *American Law Review*, plus some fugitive bits of the famous Holmes fleece that had not yet been gathered from the famous Holmes hedges, plus a bundle of letters written to his Chinese friend John C. H. Wu. The letters are easily the heart and prize of the collection—of them, more later. For the rest, it is good to have some of the early notes and comments, with their strong shop-talk flavor and the insight they give us into the mind of a hard-working young lawyer —good to have them if only to assure ourselves that there was a period in his life when even Holmes could be a bit prosy and matter-of-fact, and when not all the arrows that he shot were tipped with flame. It is good also to have the few uncollected papers of his later years, as further examples (if any were needed) of that exact proportioning of the statement to the occasion which makes Holmes's occasional utterances among the outstanding ones in the

---

2 *Justice Oliver Wendell Holmes: His Book Notices and Uncollected Letters and Papers*. Edited by Harry C. Shriver, with an introduction by Harlan Fiske Stone. New York, Central Book Co., 1936.

language, comparable to Lincoln's, and possessing a shade more grace than his if a shade less vigor.

This book, by the very fact that it *is* a somewhat dressed-up scrapbook, may now be added to the 1913 volume of *Speeches* and the 1920 volume of *Collected Legal Papers* to complete the round-up of Holmes's scattered writings within book covers. Add to these three volumes the treatise on *The Common Law* (which should be required reading in every first-year law course in the country as a supplement to the case books), the 1873 edition of Kent's *Commentaries,* and a very few still uncollected signed articles, and you have the total harvest of Holmes's writings outside of his judicial opinions and the main body of his letters. When Holmes's literary executors have given us what letters and personal documents they have been able to wrench loose from his tenacious sense of privacy, we shall finally have the material on which to base an estimate of a man who, by every standard, was one of the completest persons to have emerged out of our culture.

The editing of the volume leaves something to be desired. We have now reached the stage of Holmes-worship where we treasure every fragment of his, not only for its essential quality, but also for its place in the complete whole. This is the spirit in which Mr. Shriver has approached his task. He has reprinted a whole set of unsigned book reviews and comments, originally discovered by Felix Frankfurter. It is no iconoclasm to say that while it may be a good thing to gather up every scrap that a great man writes, there is very little that is unusual or distinguished about these comments. There are to be sure, as Justice Stone points out in his Introduction, some startling intimations in some of the early papers—in an 1879 article an understanding of the legislative character of the judicial process, the extent to which notions of public policy enter into the decision of cases, some shrewd adumbrations (as early as 1871–72) of the value and also the limitations of the case method in the study of law, some early statements of Holmes's "prediction theory" of the law, a very striking paragraph on class legislation in connection with the 1872 strike of the London gas-stokers. It may be that I am overcritical, but it seems to me that this does not justify the ritual sacrifice of two-thirds of the 240 pages of text to the gods of completeness. Such material would be interesting—in fact, indispensable—to anyone preparing a Holmes biography or a critical estimate of the development of his thought. The ordinary student and reader, however, will find these ideas best developed in his later speeches and opinions.

The letters to John C. H. Wu are especially revealing. They are the heart of the book, and they are alone worth its price. They are the letters of an old New England aristocrat, laden with years and honors, to a young Chinese student of law and philosophy. Wu seems to have sent Holmes an article of his on Chinese law. He was twenty-two; Holmes was eighty. Holmes answered gracefully but in a noncommittal fashion. Gradually his interest was stirred, and the letters ripened into a steady exchange of correspondence over eleven years, including a period when Wu was in China as professor and judge and a period when he came to Cambridge on a fellowship. The last letter was written when Holmes was ninety-one. Together they offer the greatest amount of light that has thus far been shed from any single source on Holmes's personality.[3]

We see an old man, concerned about his age, expecting to die any year, but gallant, generous, graceful—taking the time to dip into his rich experience and nourish an eager and hungry youth; we see a general in the campaign of life painstakingly teaching a soldier the rules of warfare; we see a man who has found success and a deep core of peace within himself gently nurturing the troubled spirit of a young man just starting out; we see a teacher writing to a student with infinite frankness and infinite tact. Holmes is at his best in these letters. He chats about his reading, striking off amazingly keen critical comments in passing. Thus about Whitman: "I don't care very much for his posing as a message-bearer and his Messiah Jesus attitude, but I think that he is the most important poet America has produced." About Hegel: "He could not persuade me that a syllogism could wag its tail . . . he could not persuade me that his King of Prussia was God." About Spengler's *Decline of the West:* "A stimulating humbug of a book." About John Morley: "I used to think that in his world Harriet Martineau was the Virgin and John Stuart Mill the prophet." About Bertrand Russell: "He argues in detail what

<hr>

[3] The most important series of Holmes letters—the correspondence with Harold J. Laski—has not yet been published. Professor Mark Howe is also editing the very interesting correspondence between Holmes and Frederick Pollock.

I had taken as not needing further argument and in his general view of the universe seems to me . . . to wobble between sentiment and reason." About John Dewey's *Experience and Nature:* "As badly written as possible. I could not have given an account of any page or chapter and yet he seemed to me to have more of our cosmos in his head than I ever found in a book before." His test of a great book is a simple one: that it should "leave a scar on my mind." And it is by that test that his own thought must be judged.

He writes of law, defining it as "a statement of the circumstances in which the public force will be brought to bear upon men through the courts." Of justice: "I hate justice, which means that I know if a man begins to talk about that, for one reason or another he is shirking talking in legal terms." This note of tough-mindedness recurs throughout the book, forming a sort of counterpoint to the note of fiery idealism. The tough-minded note is sounded especially when he is talking of political realities. He has scant respect for talk about equality. "I hardly think of man as so sacred an object as Laski seems to think him. I believe that Malthus was right in his fundamental notion . . . every society is founded on the death of men. In one way or another some are always and inevitably pushed down the dead line." He hated also talk of neighborly love, and wrote it down as humbug. He had "an imaginary society of jobbists, who were free to be egotists or altruists on the usual Saturday half-holiday provided they were neither while on their job."

Nor did he think much of "the human ultimate that man is always an end in himself. . . . We march up a conscript with bayonets behind to die for a cause he doesn't believe in. And I feel no scruples about it. Our morality seems to me only a check on the ultimate domination of force, just as our politeness is a check on the impulse of every pig to put his feet in the trough. . . . When it comes to the development of a *corpus juris* the ultimate question is what do the dominant forces of the community want and do they want it hard enough to disregard whatever inhibitions may stand in the way." This was the ripe fruit of an idea he had expressed more than fifty years before, in 1873, in his comment on the gas-stokers' strike. "This [Herbert Spencer's] tacit assumption of the solidarity of the interests of society is very common, but seems to us false. . . . In the last resort a man rightly prefers his own interest to that of his neighbor. . . . All that can be expected from modern improvements is that legislation should easily and quickly, yet not too quickly, modify itself in accordance with the will of the *de facto* supreme power in the community, and that the spread of an educated sympathy should reduce the sacrifice of minorities to a minimum. . . . The more powerful interests must be more or less reflected in legislation, which, like every other device of man or beast, must tend in the long run to aid the survival of the fittest. . . . It is no sufficient condemnation of legislation that it favors one class at the expense of another, for much or all legislation does that." Thus his view of politics and law is seen as a curious compound of social Darwinism, the Marxian class-concept, and a hard pragmatic semi-Austinian recognition of the realities of a social system, all tempered by a tolerance of other people's views and a humorous unwillingness to erect his own notions into absolutes.

But Holmes never tired of saying that he saw law and politics only as parts of the cosmos. It is the cosmos with which his letters are most concerned. His attitude toward it was always that of a gallant humility, and a shrug of the shoulder that did not preclude the most arduous effort. "A man must accept limits," he writes. And again: "We begin with an act of faith, with deciding that we are not God, for if we were dreaming the universe we should be God so far as we knew." But within these limits that the cosmos imposes he believed in human heroism. "If . . . you bear the fire in your belly, it will survive and transfigure the hard facts." He had learned the "hard facts" on the battlefield in the Civil War. "The reality was to pass a night on the ground in the rain with your bowels out of order and then after no particular breakfast to wade a stream and attack the enemy. That is life." And it was this sense that he had of life which led him to despise logic-chopping and theorizing, and to speak generally in an anti-intellectualist vein. He called speculation *in vacuo* "churning the void to make cheese." Thus also his feeling about absorption with the forms of thought. "The only use of the forms is to present their contents, just as the only use of a pint pot is to present the beer . . . and infinite meditation upon the pot never will give you the beer." When he pushed his thought back as far as it would go, he found finally "the mystery of the universe," admiration for the insight of the artist into that mystery, an emphasis on will ("the capacity to want something fiercely and want it all the time, and sticking to the rugged course"), and, in the end, "faith in effort." "If I were dying my last words would be: 'Have faith, and pursue the unknown end.' "

This is Holmes in the last glorious decade of his life. He was no philosopher in any technical, close-knit sense. He was a literary psychologist, a moralist who did not impose his moral code upon others, a liberal who makes us redefine the term because there was nothing merely humanitarian in him, an aphorist in the great tradition, a magician with words, a man who for one could turn the stuff of his experience into wisdom, a legal craftsman who always knew his tools were subordinate to his products, a human being almost inhumanly capable of remaining unfooled by the shams of life and undefeated by its perplexities. He had his limitations, but this is no place to discuss them at any length. I have written elsewhere [4] that he was ridden by two myths—that of the soldier and that of the gambler. Life was a campaign, and one had to be a good soldier. Life was a throw of the dice, and one had to take one's chances without grumbling, and abide by the rules of the game. Out of such myths it was possible for a man who was the very perfection and flowering of the New England aristocracy to fashion the rules for a great and good life. But as one reads the letters and occasional papers of his last decade, one is more than ever convinced that the greatness of Holmes lies in his insight into the problem of the individual life, whatever the society, and not into the problems of social construction or reconstruction. For all his pragmatism he has his eye on the universals and the identities of life, not on its mutations and on the fierce conditionings it offers the majority in any particular culture. It is fundamentally a gentleman's universe in which Holmes lives, a universe of the elite. While we may question how usable his system of thought will be for us in the turmoil on which we are entering, we can only be grateful that American culture in its brief span was able to fashion such a product.

1937

---

[4] See above, "Justice Holmes: Flowering and Defeat."

Holmes, Frankfurter, and the Austerity Theory

NO BOOK this year (1938) will be more intensively read between the lines than Professor Frankfurter's.[5] In fact many people are likely to scan the interstices who have no mind for the lines themselves. We owe this fact to the accident (or is it an accident?) that the foremost scholar on recent Supreme Court history is also the most assiduously discussed prospect for filling the current Supreme Court vacancy.[6] We owe it also to the paradox that one of the most controversial figures in American life has always, despite the persuasive stream of his talk in private conversation, been reticent about the public expression of his views. This man whose mind has touched and influenced so many others in law, government, business, education, has a way of making every word count. The more the magazines and newspapers write about him, the less he seems to write for them, by a sort of Gresham's Law which dictates that bad writing drives out good.

Those who come to the book for the light that it sheds on Frankfurter as well as on Holmes will not be disappointed. For no man can write about another without writing at the same time about himself, and every man who has written about Holmes has managed to write something of himself into Holmes. But Mr. Frankfurter has done more. He has written a good deal of himself into his discussion of the Supreme Court and the judicial process, and he has done it courageously. Never in our history has anyone so prominently mentioned for appointment to the Court written in so critical a vein of its conservative tendencies.

There is no indictment, no finger-pointing. Mr. Frankfurter's method is one of deadly objectivity. In each of his three lectures he considers a phase of Holmes's work on the Supreme Court—his views on "property and society," on "civil liberties and the individual," and on "federalism." He begins each lecture with a brief introduction giving the factual social setting for the Court's work in each field, and then proceeds to Holmes's views. The effect is to show that one can be human and reasonable although a Supreme

---

[5] *Mr. Justice Holmes and the Supreme Court.* Cambridge, Harvard University Press, 1938.

[6] This essay was written before Professor Frankfurter's appointment as Associate Justice of the United States Supreme Court.

Court judge, and to reveal the chasm that separated Holmes and some of his liberal colleagues from the Court majority during his years of tenure. It is as if there were, in the sense in which Disraeli spoke of the "two nations" in England, two Supreme Courts instead of one. Without this factual context, Holmes's opinions are great utterance; with it they take on, in addition, the accents of inevitable statesmanship.

Mr. Frankfurter's eye is always on Holmes and his opinions. Yet the book is also a study of the judicial process, in the sense in which a profound book on Keats would have to contain at the same time a theory of the creative process in poetry. Mr. Frankfurter loves the judicial process, whatever he may think of some of its practitioners. And he is plain-spoken about its frustrations because he believes so deeply in its possibilities. It is partly because of this *odi et amo* at the base of Mr. Frankfurter's attitude toward the Supreme Court and partly because the book is about Holmes that it contains his best writing thus far. The sentences crackle and glow, the argument moves swiftly, and there is a sustained brilliance of phrase that gives an edge even to his poised and balanced judgments.

There can be no quarrel with the estimate of the greatness of Holmes's opinions. But since the book is also an inquiry into the nature of the judicial process, I am inclined to linger over the analysis of how Holmes arrived at his judgments.[7] Mr. Frankfurter underscores Holmes's capacity to "transcend personal predilections and private notions of social policy"—what I should call the "austerity theory" of the judicial process. But if Holmes was so completely above the battle, it would seem harder to apply Mr. Frankfurter's social-context method of approach to him than to any judge in the Court's history. It fits the early Brandeis or the present Black; one can even use it for the inverted sociology of Field or Sutherland. But it is surely one of the prime paradoxes about Holmes that one who averted his eyes from social needs should have written opinions that coincided with, let us say, those of Justice Brandeis, which were frankly sociological.

---

[7] For a more extended discussion of the theory of the judicial process, the reader may wish to refer to the essay in Part IV below, "The Supreme Court and American Capitalism," section 5.

There are several hypotheses for resolving this paradox. One is that Holmes was a social neutral Olympian whose credo about the Court's power happened by the merest accident to jibe with our deepest social needs. I say "by the merest accident," for if Holmes was a completely disinterested mind who always gave the legislatures *carte blanche,* there can be no strictly logical relation between his decisions and the needs of America; for all we know, the legislators might have wholly misgauged the social needs, and judicial tolerance have been no blessing.

Mr. Frankfurter seems inclined to a second and more forceful view of the austerity theory. He points out that Holmes's tenure on the Court coincided with an upsurge of regulatory legislation in the interest of "bringing to the masses economic freedom commensurate with their political freedom." Thus Holmes's policy of a *laissez-faire* attitude toward the legislatures would be likely to have the same social consequences as a more affirmative method of deciding cases in terms of their social context. Holmes's opinions took on, as it were, the color of the legislature's sense of social need. Logically such a sociology is still strongly tinged with the accidental, but it is accident geared to historic trend.

My own leaning would be away from either of these explanations and toward a third. It may be true, as Mr. Frankfurter observes of Holmes, that "he had an artist's craving for perfection and sought it through an austere observance of the demands of judicial self-limitation." But I am not satisfied with the entire austerity theory. For anyone to transcend his own convictions in the way Holmes is reported to have done would be more than human—and Holmes was always human. I am less impressed with Justice Holmes's austerity than with his shrewd Yankee sense of strategy. As a consummate artist, Holmes had a genius for economy of effort. He knew the extent to which a judge's constitutional doctrines were shaped by his social views, and his social views by his training and his sense of economic interest. He knew his brothers on the bench, and how their narrow lawyers' intelligences could play havoc with the broad demands of social growth. He knew how hard it was to hope for anything from a head-on encounter with them about social policy. And he must have known that, given the power of judicial review, the best way to keep them from meddling overmuch with the processes of social adjustment was to limit their activity as censors. Thus Holmes became the father of judicial self-limitation.

I am the more inclined to this view by several other considerations. One concerns the difficulty we have always had, on the premise of Holmes's uncompromisingly judicial austerity, of explaining the fault-line between his property decisions and his civil liberty decisions. The problem is this: how reconcile Holmes's toleration of legislative restrictions on property with his refusal to tolerate legislative restrictions on civil liberties? Mr. Frankfurter's resolution of this paradox is brilliant, but it stays within the limits of the austerity hypothesis. "Just as he would allow experiments in economics which he himself viewed with doubt and distrust," he says of Holmes, "so he would protect speech that offended his taste and wisdom." But surely that is either stretching austerity too far and making self-denial almost an end in itself, or shifting the ground from the principle of judicial self-limitation to the actual social values to be preserved, whether of economic experiment or intellectual experiment. I incline to the latter view as the more adequate, and I wish that Mr. Frankfurter were more consistent in holding to it. Holmes had a realistic way of keeping his eye on the object. He did not make a fetish of the policy of judicial tolerance because, in cases of legislative infringement of civil liberties, he found his colleagues all too willing to pursue such a policy. What was good strategy in regard to the economic restrictions because it led to good social consequences became bad strategy in the civil-liberty restrictions because it led to bad social consequences.

There were, moreover, cases even in the economic areas where Holmes dropped his protective mask of judicial tolerance and acted clearly in accord with his views of economic theory. These were, to be sure, cases where the question was one of interpreting rather than invalidating legislation; yet we all know that the Court has shown its power as much in its interpretation of statutes as in its veto of them. One instance was Holmes's opinion in the Northern Securities case. We can sympathize today with Theodore Roosevelt's rage over a line of reasoning which did so much to whittle down the effectiveness of the Sherman Anti-Trust Act. It is interesting also to read Holmes's opinion in the Dr. Miles Medical Company case, watch his floundering in the bog of Austrian economic theory, and see the similarity between his views and those which whittled down the effectiveness of the Federal Trade Commission. Mr. Frankfurter himself mentions some further instances of Holmes's archaic views of economic theory. All these cases added together remain marginal and do not reflect upon Holmes's greatness. Yet they indicate that Holmes was not wholly austere in his approach to legislation, that he had economic notions and applied them directly in his opinions, although most often he found it better strategy to let the legislature have its way, so long as it was safe to do so.

I do not want to press too hard this view of Holmes as a strategist. He was neither schemer nor dreamer. He was an aristocrat who cherished on the one hand little love for the *novi homines* of capitalism and on the other very few illusions about tender-minded sociologists and reformers. His decisions show scant sympathy for either. Yet he was caught in a dilemma. As an aristocrat he would not go out of his way to concern himself with mass welfare; neither, however, would he let the capitalists have things to themselves. The best gesture was at once generous and Olympian —to let the legislature have its way. He saw the uses to which he could put the philosophically aristocratic doctrine of judicial *laissez-faire,* and to give it substance he added to it the philosophically aristocratic concept of the reasonable man, borrowed from the common law of torts, changing it into the concept of the not unreasonable legislator.

He was not the greatest judge we have had on the Supreme Court. Marshall was more formative, and Taney. He had too much skepticism and too little fighting faith, was too little part of the emerging forces of our economic life, to be able to shape those forces with an unquenchable will. But he was probably the greatest mind and the most complete and human personality we have had on the Court.

If I have a quarrel with Mr. Frankfurter's masterly study it is for the tendency I have pointed out to take Holmes's rhetoric of austerity at its face value, and the tendency to deify him. I think I understand what lies behind this tendency. There is Mr. Frankfurter's own knowledge of the man, and his love for him. There is the fact that the Holmes method of judicial self-limitation, so long neglected by the Court majority, has come into the ascendancy in the present Court, and Holmes may be viewed somewhat as the judicial prophet now vindicated. Finally—for no work today can help being an *œuvre de circonstance*—there is the author's desire to hold Holmes up as a model of tolerance and social rationality in an irrational and sadistic world.

One may agree with all this and yet ask whether it is not time to bring Holmes down to earth. There he belongs and there, I think, he would prefer to be rather than in the godlike regions where men austerely transcend their social convictions.[8]

1938

---

[8] I must add in candor that some of those whose judgment I value most are most sharply in disagreement with me. Among them are Mr. Justice Frankfurter himself, who has told me that he is unpersuaded and impenitent; and Professor Harry Shulman, of the Yale Law School, who in private correspondence has expressed a low opinion of the view of Holmes I present here.

7

Mr. Justice Brandeis

The Social Thought of Mr. Justice Brandeis [1]

1

I N the judicial opinions of Mr. Justice Brandeis the realities of
social change confront the equally powerful realities of vested
interests and vested ideas. The result is as significant a mirror-
ing as judicial literature offers of the essence of the American national experience. With no other jurist are the issues that have
emerged from our economic development so clearly drawn or so
sharply presented. No other gives so immediate a sense of the
heroic and, as it sometimes seems, hopeless task that the Supreme
Court has wittingly or otherwise assumed—the task of directing
the chance and change of the economic process. Mr. Justice Brandeis has found himself in the thick of every battle involving important issues of statecraft. His name has therefore taken on in the
public mind implications in the realm of social policy as well as
in that of judicial opinion. The liberals have ranged him on the
side of the angels, the conservatives somewhat lower. For a surer
estimate one would wish to go beyond his reputation to the solid
fact of his written opinions, beyond that to the body of his social
thought, and finally to that integrated personal philosophy and
viewpoint which never fails to be impressive even when one disa-
grees with it.

But the difficulty of isolating and formulating the hard core of
Mr. Justice Brandeis's social thought can scarcely be overestimated.

---

[1] This essay was first published in the *Yale Law Journal* for November 1931, on the
occasion of Brandeis's seventy-fifth birthday. It was reprinted in the symposium volume *Mr. Justice Brandeis,* edited by Felix Frankfurter (1932). I have not sought to
revise it, except for the omission of a few superfluous footnotes. I have therefore not
included a discussion of Justice Brandeis's opinions in the intervening years, 1931–39.

He has nowhere mapped out his legal philosophy in the form of prolegomena to all future systems of judicial decision. Nor has he, like Mr. Justice Holmes, the gift of compressing a lifetime of thought into a single gleaming sentence that lights up and integrates everything else he has said. Mr. Justice Brandeis, it must be remembered, is specialized to advocacy and judicial decision and not to philosophizing. He is himself one of the most a-philosophical of jurists—a thinker whose thought is always directed to eventual action, a judge in the great tradition of the Anglo-American case law who proceeds from the facts of the concrete case to a particular decision, a social theorist whose "principles" are nine-tenths submerged in the form of preconceptions and crop out on the surface only as approaches to pressing issues in contemporary affairs. He has said of his own mental processes that it is only after he has found himself confronted by a specific set of facts and has thought his way through them to a conclusion that he has found it to coincide with some well-recognized philosophical "principle." [2] As for the received classification into schools of jurisprudence, it accommodates Mr. Justice Brandeis about as badly as it does Mr. Justice Holmes, or any other non-academic and non-imitative mind. Approaching the problem of law and society from an intensely activist viewpoint, Mr. Justice Brandeis has not been interested by the *Methodenstreit* of the schools. He has preferred to fight his battles on the fronts of social legislation and judicial decision rather than in the realm of method.

While this may be worth saying, it is at best only a set of half-truths. That men vary not so much in whether or not they are philosophers but in the extent to which their philosophy is articulate is a psychological commonplace. It is, in fact, one of the attractive paradoxes that emerge from a study of Mr. Justice Brandeis that with all his distaste for philosophy he is known as the judge with the most definite and coherent social philosophy, and that with all his apathy about method his greatest importance for the future may lie in the novel elements he has added to the traditional method of adjudicating legal controversy. The quest of the inarticulate major premise that Mr. Justice Holmes has inaugurated leads in the study of Mr. Justice Brandeis to consequences of some moment for legal and social theory.

---

2 Introduction by Ernest Poole to Brandeis, *Business—A Profession* (1914), xii.

There is of course the ever-present danger that the student will read his own preconceptions into Mr. Justice Brandeis's opinions.[3] And there is also the danger of his forgetting that the social thought of a judge cannot be estimated by the criteria that would be applied to a social theorist writing out of the plenitude of his experience and his imagination. We can scarcely expect—even if we might wish—a Supreme Court opinion to read like the *Communist Manifesto* or Sorel's *Réflexions sur la Violence*.[4] The judge cannot express an untrammeled economic or social philosophy. The facts and the issues of the specific case, the constitutional text he is seeking to apply, and the precedent he must to some degree follow all link him by a sure falconry to the solid ground from which he might seek to soar too far.

2

The earliest influence in fashioning the mind of Mr. Justice Brandeis—and perhaps therefore the deepest and least eradicable —was a strain of romantic liberalism whose essence was a gallant and optimistic struggle for certain supposedly primal human rights.[5] It was a liberalism compulsive enough in its emotional force to lead his parents to emigrate to America from Bohemia after the unsuccessful revolutions of 1848.[6] These revolutions,

---

[3] It is significant that most of the writers in the excellent collection of tributes to Mr. Justice Holmes (*Mr. Justice Holmes,* edited by Felix Frankfurter, 1927) find in him something to confirm their own faiths. Thus Mr. Justice Cardozo finds him a philosophical jurist, Frankfurter a legal statesman, Dewey a pragmatist, Cohen a lonely thinker, and Miss Sargent a gallant gentleman whose flame is fed by subterranean fires.

[4] This has, however, not kept some Supreme Court opinions from reading like Herbert Hoover's *American Individualism* (1922).

[5] For the biographical material on which the interpretation of Mr. Justice Brandeis's earlier career in this section is based, the writer has drawn chiefly upon Ernest Poole's introduction to Brandeis, *Business—A Profession, supra,* note 2. See also De Haas, *Louis Dembitz Brandeis* (1929), Norman Hapgood's penetrating "Justice Brandeis: Apostle of Freedom" (1927), 125 *Nation* 330, and Charles Beard's admirable introduction to Lief, *The Social and Economic Views of Mr. Justice Brandeis* (1930). The most valuable source material is to be found in the records of the Senate Judiciary Committee that held hearings on the appointment of Mr. Justice Brandeis in 1916. Since the present essay was written, Alfred Lief has published his very full biography, *Brandeis: The Personal History of an American Ideal* (1936), and Alpheus T. Mason has published *Brandeis: Lawyer and Judge in the Modern State* (1933) and *The Brandeis Way* (1939).

[6] The story of the emigration of the Goldmark and Brandeis families is recounted with considerable charm in Goldmark, *Pilgrims of '48* (1930).

aptly characterized by Trevelyan as "the turning-point at which modern history failed to turn," were in spirit constitutional, humanitarian, idealistic. They represented a renewal on Continental soil of the equalitarian ideals of the American and French revolutions. Carried back to the United States by the emigrant groups of the midcentury, they imparted a new freshness and vigor to the American tradition of civil and political liberties. Freedom and justice and democracy as home-grown varieties had wilted a bit in the hot climate of American experience; but when similar doctrines were transplanted from Europe they became vigorous and even beautiful growths. They were terms that still had a genuine and simple content for these naïve newcomers. Mr. Justice Brandeis grew up thus in an atmosphere of what might be called primitive Americanism.

This Americanism took the characteristic form, in the semi-frontier Kentucky society in which the Brandeises lived, of a deeply felt individualism. The complexion of such an individualism was as varied as were the sources of the sense of release from which it sprang. To be allowed finally to do what one in Europe had always dreamed of doing and what one had regarded as the marks of a freeman, to talk or criticize or worship as one pleased, to see an immediacy of relation between economic effort and economic reward, reinforced one's sense of the dignity and sovereign importance of the individual. There were also the slaves as intense and vivid symbols to sum up for a border-state abolitionist group what it meant to lack the liberties of an individual. Mr. Justice Brandeis recalls how violent his reaction was when, during a brief sojourn in Germany as a young man, he was reprimanded by the authorities for whistling at night. The reprimand was more than a personal reproof; it was an insult to a complete and cherished way of life.

One does not become easily disengaged from a way of life thus deeply learned. The whole early career of Mr. Justice Brandeis, with its hard work and study and success, runs in the best tradition of American individualism. In fact, all the events of his first forty years had conspired to make him an idealistic yet successful liberal and civic leader, whose conspicuous ability condoned his excess of zeal, and whose mastery of the hard facts of business showed that his somewhat tiresome sermonizing was not to be taken overseri-

ously. It is true, he showed at times a disquieting curiosity about
matters into which a Boston gentleman rarely pried; as when in
the eighties he began to talk with labor leaders, and to regard the
labor struggle from the worker's point of view. And he showed also
a somewhat unusual tendency to interpret the lawyer's function
as more than mere advocacy and to set himself up now as judge and
now as arbitrator. But all his offenses stayed within the limits of
tolerance.

The genuinely formative years of Mr. Justice Brandeis's mind
fell in the "social justice" period of American history, in the latter
part of the nineties and the first decade of the twentieth century.
They were years which witnessed on the one hand the rise of
powerful vested interests and the expropriation of American resources by capital acting under a *laissez-faire* philosophy of government, and on the other hand such movements as populism,
muck-raking, trust-busting, and the "new freedom." The vigor of
individual enterprise which had opened a continent had grown barbaric and piratical in the exploiting of it, and the pure metaphysical passion which had driven successive waves of migration to
America, were now transferred and transformed into an intense desire for purifying the body politic. To minds educated in the dialectic of liberalism it seemed obvious that the situation could be
best explained in terms of a dualism of conflicting forces. It seemed
clear that the captains of industry and the masters of capital, in the
exultation of success, would sweep away every landmark on the ter-
rain of American liberty. And it seemed clear also that the only recourse for liberals lay in a militant attack on all fronts—an attack
on bankers, on corporations, and on politicians corruptly allied
with them, a pitiless campaign of investigation and publicity.

It was amidst this planetary crash and turmoil that Mr. Justice
Brandeis's world took definite shape. It was in a sense inevitable
that he should have been caught up in the swirl of these forces.
For it is of the essence of his mind to be receptive to the aspirations
and conflicts of the world he lives in, and to desire participation
in them. Possessing little of Mr. Justice Holmes's transcendence of
any specific period, it is rather his genius to be immersed in his
time. After the critical struggle to establish a legal practice was
won, his mind, whose Hebraic sense of righteousness had been re-

inforced by his background of Continental liberalism, turned more and more to issues of social justice.

He found in the dominant temper of this populist-muckraking period that essential continuity with his own past without which no individual enters upon a revolution in his thinking. He found room in his new philosophy for the ideals he had learned as a boy, room also for the individualism that had dominated his youth. What this period added, in his case as in the case of other liberals, was a new perception of the changes that the coming of industrial society had wrought in the conditions of American liberty and American individualism. It was clear that the old ideals could no longer be pursued in the old way. That the ideals themselves were worth while and needed no replacement formed part of those first principles which the liberals of that day did not question.

In Louis D. Brandeis, the able Boston lawyer, the forces of liberalism gained no mean ally. I say ally, because a common, unquestioning soldier he could never be; stern individualist who cared more about the integrity of his personality than about anything else, he had to fight in his own fashion. He threw into the struggle all the resources of his mind—his amazing legal acumen, his persuasiveness, his mastery of the details and refinements of corporation finance, his unwavering sense of values, his eminently precise and constructive imagination. Equipped with every weapon of information one had reckoned one's own, he was a terrifying opponent to encounter. But if he spared no one else, he was most ruthless with himself. He worked indefatigably. He sacrificed his obvious interests. He dedicated himself with a monastic fervor to what he conceived to be the service of the public. He came to be called the "People's Counsel," and if there was a touch of asperity in the way the name was applied to him by opponents, he himself took it with a high seriousness. His ideal of citizenship was Periclean, but he pursued it with a religious intensity that was medieval.

He was effective. Of that there can be no doubt. The minutes of legislative hearings and investigations, the records of lawsuits in which groups of citizens, organized as a "league" of some sort or other, applied for court action against an encroaching corporation, the newspapers that reported his speeches and activities and the journalists who commented on them, all attest to his effectiveness. There was room in that struggle for every sort of talent—for a Bryan, a La Follette, a Roosevelt, a Steffens, a Hapgood, a Wilson. But when most of the brilliant legal ability of the country was being enrolled in the service of the corporations, the talents of a first-rate legal and statistical mind were worth more than the talents of all the politicians and journalists. Mr. Brandeis found himself at home with the sort of problems that had now to be mastered. His career, winding its way from one set of financial and political intricacies to another, takes on something of the fiber of the period.

In two important respects he stands out from the group of turn-of-the-century liberals with whom his name is associated. He had a passion for detail and concreteness where most of them dealt in invective and generalities. And he had a capacity for constructive achievement in the field of social legislation and social invention. An exposure of insurance companies was accompanied by a plan for reorganizing the industry and by a new form of savings-bank insurance; an attack on the railroads gave him a chance to launch on its career the principle of scientific management; a call to arbitrate a labor dispute resulted in the "protocol" and the "preferential open shop." And he knew not only how to create and state these ideas and plans; he knew also the technique of publicity and persuasion without which in the apathy of modern life they would have been ignored. But perhaps most important of all was the will to "follow through" an idea until it was functioning, and the infinite capacity for pains which saw to the details of organization. In the stress he laid upon social invention he was closely related to the Jeremy Bentham whom Graham Wallas interprets; [7] more closely even than was the administrative constructiveness which the Webbs were seeking to effect in London.

Yet even twenty years of unremitting effort in this direction would probably not have sufficed to rescue his name from the comparative oblivion of those who fight heroically in a hopeless cause. To say this is not to do injustice to either the seriousness or the effectiveness of Mr. Brandeis's public career before 1916. Whatever else happened, his place in the amazing history of those two

[7] "Bentham as Political Inventor" (1926), 129 *Contemporary Review* 308.

decades of American life would have been distinctive and secure. Nor is this the place to enter upon an extended critique of those with whom he was allied and their cause. From the vantage-ground of the present it seems clear that the cards were stacked against them. The forces they were fighting were too integrally part of a capitalist-industrialist society—part of the logic of its development and part of its psychological context—to be severed from it for separate destruction. None of them was either willing or ready to attack the foundations of the society itself. And to save the body while striking at the excrescences required a more subtle diagnosis of historic and economic forces and a more mature grappling with the complexities of the problem than the resources of those decades could command. If Mr. Brandeis stands out as a unique and heroic figure in the populist thought of that period, it is not for the raking fire of his cross-examinations, or for the brave assurance of his analysis of the Money Trust; [8] not even for that stubborn command of facts and figures which made men call him the mathematician of the movement.[9] It is rather because of the stress we find him laying, even in those days, upon the necessity for the continuous application of social intelligence to social problems, and upon the inadequacy of any solution which did not have behind it the creative will of the people.

But it was Mr. Brandeis's misfortune to try to fashion a social philosophy in the midst of a crusade. The pennons wavered for a moment, fluttered anxiously, but were immediately carried forward. He was himself caught up in their contagion, and since crusades never reach their goal, he might have remained merely one of the adherents of a "fighting faith" which had had its day and given way to another. But the fervor of the crusade had reached to the White House and when, on the death of Mr. Justice Lamar in 1916, President Wilson looked about for a successor his choice fell upon the Boston lawyer who had displayed such ability and courage and who, without holding public office, had already had a crowded public life.

Whatever the merit of the appointment, for us it changes the

---

[8] *Other People's Money* (1914). This originally appeared as a series of articles in *Harper's Weekly* (1913–14).

[9] See the reprint in Hapgood's introduction to *Other People's Money* of Hapgood's editorial for *Harper's Weekly* entitled "Arithmetic."

whole perspective of Mr. Justice Brandeis's work. It transformed him from a free lance into one of the ruling powers. It gave direction to his energies and meaning to the wide scattering of activities that had constituted his career. There is no need to underestimate the dramatic quality and the importance of that early career in order to see that as a result of the appointment its chief interest now lies less in its intrinsic qualities than in its having been an apprenticeship for an opportunity. We can see with some degree of clarity, with the detachment that the intervening years give, what that opportunity was and how effective was the apprenticeship. The entire focus of those two crowded decades changes, and they become pre-eminently a record of the education of Mr. Justice Brandeis.

Like any worthwhile education it consisted both of learning and of unlearning. It was comparatively easy for an energetic and responsive person amidst the social intensities of the period to unlearn the genteel tradition of restraint which tended to envelop one at Harvard [10] and the tradition of quietism in which the legal mind everywhere was wrapped. But it was harder to unlearn what had lingered over from one's liberal-romantic background—the faith that in a democratic society there was equality of liberty and opportunity, or some immediate relation between the functioning of government and the needs of the people.

From one point of view, Mr. Justice Brandeis's contacts with labor unions, corporations, and bankers, with the sweated workers and the vested interests, constituted an exploration of modern industrial society unique in the education of justices of the Supreme Court. He gained an understanding of the cleavage that lay between the haves and the have-nots,[11] and some notions of the implications of that cleavage for both. He grasped with some degree of realism the meager content of life for the vast armies of labor. He sought the answer to the riddle of how a society that gave its masses no leisure from the grinding hours of labor and no protec-

[10] For an account of this genteel tradition that can be set up in illuminating contrast to the turmoil of the "social justice" period, see Santayana's essay on "The Genteel Tradition in American Philosophy" in his *Winds of Doctrine* (1913).

[11] "We are sure to have for the next generation an ever-increasing contest between those who have and those who have not."—*Business—A Profession, supra*, note 2, at li–lii. This book is a collection of articles and occasional speeches by Mr. Brandeis.

tion from exploitation in the barbaric competition for profits, that took no measures to control how much they would be paid for their work or how much they would be charged for what they bought, and that made no provisions for them when they grew too old or sick to be profitable—how such a society could expect them to form the vital and intelligent units predicated in a theory of democracy. He saw the growing institutionalization of life as it was embodied in the corporation, the trade union, and the centralization of government, and the danger that amidst it the individual might be lost. But his education taught him also that there was invested in the American economic system more hard work and experience than any novel scheme of control could command, and that it was dangerous to drive beyond the bounds within which initiative and skill could be continuously exerted.

So balanced and mature an education could not have been acquired in a vacuum. Whatever Mr. Justice Brandeis learned or unlearned proceeded from that direct pragmatic context of exigency and action that seems always to have been so congenial to his mind. The fight he waged from 1896 to 1911 to keep the control of the Boston transportation system in the hands of the city gave him a notion of the political intrigue through which franchises are obtained. He delved deeper into public-utility economics in the struggle that he waged from 1903–5 for cheaper gas rates in Boston. His fight against the New England transportation monopoly of the New Haven railroad (1906–12) confronted him with the problem of the relation between inflated capitalization and railroad rates, and between monopoly and service to the community; and his appearance before the Interstate Commerce Commission in the series of railroad-rate cases (1910–13) made him think through the connection between the management of a railroad and its expenses of operation. His conception of the place of trade unions in American life came from direct experience in labor disputes. He waged a bitter fight in 1904 against the Boston Typographical Union, in which he discovered that unions no less than employers might be unscrupulous and irresponsible. But, though this caused him to think a good deal about the principles of trade-union organization, it did not make him an anti-unionist. He had found out at least as early as 1902 what despairs lay be-

hind the heroism of protracted strikes; [12] and he not only favored
the legislative objectives of the union in obtaining better wages
and more humane working days, but he regarded them as an insurance against the irresponsibility of employers. The year 1907
even found him at the strangely unjuristic task of tracing the possible consequences that a more-than-ten-hour day for women
workers in an Oregon laundry might have on their physical condition, their moral life, or the character of the future citizenry
they gave birth to.[13]

Perhaps the most impressive item that his labor contacts added
to his education came from his experience in arbitrating the strike
of the International Ladies Garment Workers in 1910.[14] Here he
was brought face to face with a strange group—intelligent, idealistic, bickering, embittered, exploited in the "sweating" system,
yet charged with tremendous vitality, through whom a rich and
alien culture imbued with European radical ideas was being transplanted to America. His studies in connection with the Ballinger
investigation of 1909, in which he had played so prominent and
dramatic a role, presumably as counsel for Glavis but in reality
as inquisitor for the public, had given him some notion of how
the natural resources of the country were disposed of. But here,
among the Jewish garment workers in New York, he found human
resources that called equally for conservation. He was successful
enough, tentatively, in evolving a technique for settling their disputes with their employers, just as he had been successful in 1905–
1908 in evolving a technique whereby, through savings-bank insurance, the workers of Massachusetts could get protection at rates
that were not excessive. But the thing that troubled him was that
ultimately these individuals—and all individuals—were at the
mercy of those in whom economic power resided, and that this
economic power went with the control of the fluid capital of the
country. His experience in the life-insurance fight had shown him

---

12 "If you search for the heroes of peace, you will find many of them among those
obscure and humble workmen who have braved idleness and poverty in devotion
to the principle for which their union stands."—Business—A Profession, supra, note 2,
at 84.

13 Muller v. Oregon, 208 U. S. 412, 28 Sup. Ct. 324 (1908).

14 See the account of this arbitration, its difficulties and consequences, in Lorwin,
The Women's Garment Workers (1924).

the degree to which the capital of the industry was concentrated
in the "Big Three" companies; and in his series of *Harper's
Weekly* articles in 1913–14 on the Money Trust he carried the
analysis further, making it embrace the entire financial structure
of the country.[15]

There was much, it is to be conjectured, that Mr. Justice Brandeis did not learn during those years of his crowded career. But
considering the blind chance that fits or misfits our haphazard
educations to the crucial tasks that somehow fall to us, the education of Mr. Justice Brandeis appears now as having been amazingly apposite. The social context within which, as a justice of the
Supreme Court, his thinking would have to proceed was more
complex than that in which either the Constitution or the body
of judicial precedent had been formed. A system of industrial organization so much more developed than that of the nineteenth
century as to take on the aspects of a second industrial revolution
had created also a "great society" that was unique in its problems
and temper. There were deep cleavages in social stratification and
obvious injustices in distribution. Above all else, American capitalism was going through a remarkable phase of concentration.
Power and control were being shifted and pyramided. The old
dichotomies between political power and economic activity were
rapidly becoming a matter of rhetoric rather than of actuality.
Here was a man who, beyond most others that might have been
chosen, was qualified by his experience to understand the processes of change and the instruments of control.

Enough opposition was raised to Mr. Justice Brandeis's appointment to make it something of a *cause célèbre*. Among those who
joined in the protest were leaders in American financial, legal, and
political life whose names carried great weight. The grounds advanced included infringements of legal ethics, unjudicial temperament, and even chicanery and dishonesty. There was an investigation by the Senate Judiciary Committee, in which some
fifteen hundred pages of testimony were taken, there were accusa-

---

[15] These articles, especially those on the size of the corporate unit and on the
failure of banker-management, are brilliant economic analyses that have scarcely
been surpassed in the literature. The title under which Brandeis published them
in book form, *Other People's Money,* has become a current phrase in economics and
journalism.

tions and defenses and recriminations, and there was finally an acquittal in the form of a ratification of the appointment.[16] At the time and since then the protest against Mr. Justice Brandeis has been sufficiently protested against. What was its significance? Can it be dismissed as the malevolent gesture of men whose hostility Mr. Brandeis had incurred? It is clear that such a judgment would be superficial.

There was much more in the struggle over the appointment than a matter of personal justice. There was a historical rationale in the utterances of the seven ex-presidents of the American Bar Association, the petition of the Boston men of affairs, and the editorials in the financial papers. The protest against the appointment of Mr. Justice Brandeis was a crucial recognition by the old order that the new order was threatening. There was a stiffening of the ranks, a closing of the gaps in the phalanx, a call for a united front. For half a century the possessing class in America had known the conditions under which they could operate and expand. The rules of the game, however advantageous they may have been, had been fixed. Surely, they could not now be revoked. A man who had formed and had expressed opinions on most of the great issues of national policy that were likely to come before the Court was dangerous, especially when those opinions were original, unconventional, and held with moral fervor.

The appointment was thus more than the filling of a vacancy. It represented a possible turning-point in the American judicial process. For whatever Mr. Justice Brandeis might or might not be expected to do, he could not be expected to cleave to the tradition that the whole duty of a Supreme Court justice was to maintain a decent ignorance of the world outside the Court.

3

In the fifteen years that have elapsed since the appointment of Mr. Justice Brandeis, he has become firmly entrenched in the public mind as a "liberal" jurist and one whose method of decision is "sociological." There is an essential soundness in this judgment, although both terms are shopworn to the point of vagueness and

16 U. S. Congress, Senate Committee on the Judiciary, Testimony Relating to the Appointment of Hon. Louis D. Brandeis (1916).

are more useful in embracing once significant similarities between jurists than in suggesting currently significant differences. Mr. Justice Brandeis has in common with other liberal jurists the fact that he has reacted against the rigor of a narrow mechanical jurisprudence which, containing within itself no principle of growth, applied old rules to new situations and ignored changing economic set-ups. But his unique importance is not summed up in this critical attitude but must be sought also in the positive logic of relationships between law and society that is implicit in his day-to-day opinions and dissents. In his case, as with other activists, it is the idea in action that pushes forward ideological advance.

On the Supreme Court bench it is Mr. Justice Brandeis who has made the sharpest break with the classical tradition. Whether it passed through a tory or a liberal mind, the classical tradition was concerned with the interpretation of the Constitution as an instrument of government. In the hands of Marshall and Story, Taney and Field,[17] it produced widely variant results, but it seems fair to say that the differences they revolved about were differences in political theory—the "narrow" or the "strict" construction of the Constitution, centralization or states' rights, the clash of sections. Fortifying each of these positions there were, to be sure, a social philosophy and the pressure of new or old economic forces.[18] But these remained in the rear. On the fighting-line were the competing political and constitutional theories. It is Mr. Justice Brandeis's achievement to have appreciably altered the basis and the terms of the conflict. He has been the first to face squarely and consistently the problem of the relation between social change and judicial action.

He is thus pre-eminently the jurist of a transitional society, in which change is the dominant, the obtrusive fact. His thought is geared to social change. Not that Marshall and Taney lived in a static world. But the realities they and their colleagues wrestled

---

[17] Mr. Justice Holmes has also in a sense broken with the classical tradition. But while he rejects the rhetoric of constitutional law as "a fiction intended to beautify what is disagreeable to the sufferers" (*Tyson v. Banton*, 273 U. S. 418, 446, 47 Sup. Ct. 426, 434 (1927), and has few if any "fighting faiths" of his own for time to destroy, his deepest attitude is still one of social skepticism. Few would accuse Mr. Justice Brandeis of making too ascetic a dissociation between his views of public policy and his opinions.

[18] See T. R. Powell, "The Logic and Rhetoric of Constitutional Law" (1918), 15 *Journal of Philosophy, Psychology and Scientific Method* 645–58.

with were the realities of constructing, consolidating, and reconstructing the foundations of the American polity. Where the principles of constitutional interpretation had themselves to be outlined, they occupied the foreground despite the social changes that accompanied the beginnings of industrialism in America. But the maturity of industrialism brought an unparalleled pace of change, opened new gaps between need and aspiration, revealed in startling outlines the logic of social institutions implicit in our system of economic organization. As the task of adjusting legal thought and institutions to economic development grew more difficult, it grew also more imperative.

It is this absorption with social change that chiefly differentiates the thought of Mr. Justice Brandeis from that of Mr. Justice Holmes. While the former has his eye fixed on the mutations in the life of society, the latter delights to observe the essential identities behind them. The curious uniformity with which the human animal behaves, whatever the century, runs like the hint of a theme through the entire body of Mr. Justice Holmes's opinions. But Mr. Justice Brandeis is concerned with the more immediate consequences of changes in social institutions and the traumata they reveal in our life.[19]

To adjust the body of legal rules to a world of bewildering change requires, to begin with, the fixed sense of social value and social need that accompanies a strongly functionalist way of thought. Institutions often develop their own principle of growth, not necessarily related to the need that brought them into existence, and the original need has commonly to be rediscovered and redefined. Mr. Justice Brandeis, with his Thoreau-like fervor for whittling life down to its essentials, is peculiarly qualified for such a task. Amidst the variety of conflicting practices regarding depreciation, he seeks the underlying function that a depreciation account serves;[20] in a case involving the abolition of private employment agencies he seeks to get at the functional purpose of all

---

[19] This is not intended to exclude other bases for comparison. For an admirable treatment of these two liberal figures, see Hamilton, "Mr. Justice Holmes and Mr. Justice Brandeis Dissenting" (1931), 33 *Current History* 654.

[20] *United Railways and Electric Co. v. West*, 280 U. S. 234, 266, 50 Sup. Ct. 123, 130 (1930).

labor exchanges; [21] in an investigation, before he came to the bench, of the insurance business, he analyzes aptly the social function of insurance.[22]

But a jurisprudence built around social change requires even more an intimate and realistic knowledge of economic organization. Without subscribing to the economic interpretation of the social process, Mr. Justice Brandeis believes that the forces that create new tasks for law are mainly economic. This belief and the insight of economic processes that he gained from his active career in handling business relationships give his thought its characteristic realism. Mr. Chief Justice Marshall also had a strong realistic sense, but it was of American political problems and processes; and Mr. Justice Holmes, with his mordant insight into human motives, is a consummate psychological realist. All realistic thought joins in the pursuit of the *élan* of the actual. It brushes aside form and fancy, and seeks the determining facts. Mr. Justice Brandeis's realism is chiefly economic; his thought evinces a mastery of the facts and processes of economic life hitherto unsurpassed on the Court.

It is chiefly concerned with effecting a *rapprochement* between law and the institutional life to which it is directed. Viewed typically and schematically Mr. Justice Brandeis's thought premises the process of public law as an interplay of relationships among three entities: the experience of society, out of which disputes and problems arise; some legislative body, acting alone or through administrative commissions it has created, which purports to crystallize social experience in its enactments; and the courts, which interpret the application of constitutional and common law principles to the specific case. His eye goes always beyond the superficial facts of the case to the matrix of need, maladjustment, or agitation

---

[21] *Adams v. Tanner,* 244 U. S. 590, 597, 613, 37 Sup. Ct. 662, 665, 671 (1916): "The problem which confronted the people of Washington was far more comprehensive and fundamental than that of protecting workers applying to the private agencies. It was the chronic problem of unemployment—perhaps the gravest and most difficult problem of modern industry. . . ."

[22] Among the changes that Mr. Brandeis recommended was "the recognition of the true nature of the life-insurance business; namely, that its sole province is to manage temporarily with absolute safety and at a minimum cost the savings of the people deposited to make appropriate provision in case of death. . . ."—*Business—A Profession, supra,* note 2, at 139.

out of which it arose; it moves from the object itself to the social landscape that gives it perspective. Such a method has a tendency to shift the venue of discussion and reorient the preoccupation of the Court. Anxiety about freedom of contract gives way to an analysis of wages and the conditions of labor, due process to waste and scientific management, discussion of principle to recital of fact. This shift of emphasis was marked dramatically by the "Brandeis brief" in *Muller v. Oregon* [23] but it runs through the body of Mr. Justice Brandeis's decisions as well as of his advocacy.

One of the consequences of such a conception of judicial interpretation is to allow greater latitude to the enactments of state legislatures and the rulings of administrative commissions than the characteristic trend of Mr. Justice Brandeis's thinking would have seemed to require. There is no inherent apotheosis of either the legislative or the bureaucratic process to be found in his philosophy. If anything, his experience with state legislatures in the years when he was fighting insurance companies, railroad companies, and trusts must have cast some doubt upon the disinterestedness of the ordinary legislator and the extent to which he represented the wishes of the "people." Nor does the broad tolerance, not unmixed with respect for the sovereignty of a morally self-sufficient group, with which Mr. Justice Holmes regards state legislative acts, occupy a central place in Mr. Justice Brandeis's thought. He is not a states' rights advocate, nor, with his distinctly humanitarian and reformist trend, does he have that skepticism about the superiority of one form of social action over another which might dictate a *laissez-faire* attitude toward legislatures. In him the tendency to relax the rigor of the constitutional limitations on state legislative action as hitherto interpreted seems to proceed from another source. The recent trend of legislative action, especially in the Western states affected by the populist movements, has represented the pressure of social change and social ex-

---

[23] *Supra*, note 13. This case involved an Oregon statute which limited the working day for women to ten hours. It is interesting to note that the mass of material which the brief presented as "the world's experience upon which the legislation limiting the hours of labor for women is based" was offered to the Court as "facts of common knowledge of which the Court may take judicial notice." Mr. Justice Brewer, for the Court, said: "We take judicial cognizance of all matters of general knowledge." The "economic briefs" were thus admitted into the mansions of the law through a side entrance.

perience much more adequately than have the legal concepts handed down in the common law. Forced to choose between the two, Mr. Justice Brandeis could have no hesitancy. In the test of reasonableness as applied to state legislation he has found an effective instrument ready at hand for some approximation toward a realistic jurisprudence.

The emphasis on the institutional context of a case is so characteristic an item in Mr. Justice Brandeis's method that "institutionalism" or "contextualism" might serve as readily as "realism" to describe the method. The context of a felt necessity for the particular legislative enactment is represented in a large number of his opinions—for example, the felt necessity of suppressing private employment agencies,[24] or of regulating unscrupulous steamship-ticket agents,[25] or of discouraging corporate business organizations by levying a state tax upon corporations.[26] The context of the case may even involve a prolonged agitation by interested groups to secure the enactment of the law, as in the account Mr. Justice Brandeis gives in *Duplex Printing Press Co. v. Deering*[27] of the legislative history of the Clayton Act. If the experience of a state in the administration of its weights-and-measures laws points to the advisability of legislating against excessive weights as well as against short weights,[28] if the excesses of cut-throat competition and the normal disorder that planless competition produces in the economic order suggest the pooling of trade information by a manufacturers' association in the lumber business,[29] if a state wish-

---

[24] *Adams v. Tanner, supra,* note 21, at 615, 37 Sup. Ct., at 672: "There is reason to believe that the people of Washington not only considered the collection by the private employment offices of fees from employees a social injustice, but that they considered the elimination of the practice a necessary preliminary to the establishment of a constructive policy for dealing with the subject of unemployment."

[25] *Di Santo v. Pennsylvania,* 273 U. S. 34, 37, 47 Sup. Ct. 267, 268 (1926).

[26] *Quaker City Cab Co. v. Pennsylvania,* 277 U. S. 389, 403, 410, 48 Sup. Ct. 553, 555, 558 (1928): "There are still intelligent, informed, just-minded and civilized persons who believe that the rapidly growing aggregation of capital through corporations constitutes an insidious menace to the liberty of the citizen; that it tends to increase the subjection of labor to capital; that, because of the guidance and control necessarily exercised by great corporations upon those engaged in business, individual initiative is being impaired and creative power will be lessened; that the absorption of capital by corporations, and their perpetual life, may bring evils similar to those which attended mortmain. . . ."

[27] 254 U. S. 443, 479, 41 Sup. Ct. 172, 181 (1920).

[28] *Jay Burns Baking Co. v. Bryan,* 264 U. S. 504, 517, 44 Sup. Ct. 412, 415 (1923).

[29] *American Column and Lumber Co. v. United States,* 257 U. S. 377, 413, 42 Sup. Ct. 114, 121 (1921).

ing to protect its workers from the arbitrary effects of the labor
injunction limits the use of the injunction in labor cases, except
against acts of violence,[30] or if wishing to protect its cotton-growers
from exploitation by the owners of private gins it grants special
privileges to gins owned by co-operatives,[31] it is the context of the
case that most seriously attracts Mr. Justice Brandeis's attention,
and he presents it with sympathy and with an engaging and sometimes passionate persuasiveness.

The elements in the social setting of a case that Mr. Justice
Brandeis inquires into in order to determine whether the legislation in question had reasonably weighed conflicting social values
are invariably significant ones. Half the task of realism is to ask
the right questions about which to seek adequate information. Mr.
Justice Brandeis's questions revolve about the ends sought to be
remedied by the legislation, the social need for it, the character
and extent of the public opinion behind it, the psychological
milieu in which it was passed, its possible consequences. "Nearly
all legislation," he says, "involves a weighing of public needs as
against private desires. . . . What at any particular time is the
paramount public need, is necessarily largely a matter of judgment." [32] Where the judgment is not demonstrably clear he appeals to the experience in other states or countries, to the consensus of practice within relevant groups, or to the consensus of
enlightened opinion.

The study of the context and the appeal to consensus, for which
Mr. Justice Brandeis is to a great extent responsible, are intellectual techniques holding out such great possibilities for the
judicial process that it is important to note their ultimate sub-
servience to the social philosophy of the judge. They aid him in
arriving at an opinion, but they are also almost inevitably themselves conditioned by an opinion already tentatively arrived at. For
the detached political psychologist there is little difference between
the pressures applied in an agricultural community in a time of
low agricultural profits to obtain privileged legislation for co-
operative associations and the hysterias that in time of war result
in criminal-syndicalism legislation or the suppression of radical

---

[30] *Truax v. Corrigan,* 257 U. S. 312, 354, 42 Sup. Ct. 124, 137 (1921).
[31] *Frost v. Corporation Commission,* 278 U. S. 515, 528, 49 Sup. Ct. 235, 240 (1928).
[32] *Truax v. Corrigan, supra,* note 30, at 357, 42 Sup. Ct., at 138.

agitation. Various individuals will sympathize with one type of legislation or the other depending upon their intellectual temper; a respectable array of social experience and a consensus of judgment could with discretion be marshaled for both. Yet Mr. Justice Brandeis has consistently upheld the reasonableness of legislation in the former type of case and consistently rejected it in the latter.[33] He finds it difficult to reconcile the deviation from sound judgment involved in what he considers an encroachment on fundamental civil liberties with any possible reasonableness in the legislation.

4

A significant social philosophy in the realm of law today must do more than eat away the lag between institutional change and legal development. That is, to be sure, of inestimable importance, especially in cases involving submerged groups such as labor whose interests have not been incorporated in the fashioning of legal rules. But it does not offer a technique for dealing with the problems emerging from the active development of business enterprise. The world that the Court operates in is a world of accomplished fact, with which one must come to the best terms possible. But it is also a world continually in the making, with many potential lines of development. To drive a wedge of direction through the flux of economic life and to turn it into socially accredited channels becomes the task of the modern state, and under our constitutional system pre-eminently the task of the Supreme Court.

In this sphere Mr. Justice Brandeis is easily our outstanding figure. He has stood firmly for holding business enterprise rigorously to its social responsibilities. He has kept himself sensitive to current trends in economic organization and has exercised the imagination of genuine statesmanship in envisaging their meaning for the future. He has applied on the judicial front the ideas developed in economic thought and has built up a technique of control that has appreciably added to the resources of our administrative law.

---

[33] See, for example, *Gilbert v. Minnesota*, 254 U. S. 325, 338, 41 Sup. Ct. 125, 129 (1920); *Whitney v. California*, 274 U. S. 357, 373, 47 Sup. Ct. 641, 647 (1926); *Schaefer v. United States*, 251 U. S. 466, 483, 40 Sup. Ct. 259, 264 (1919); *Pierce v. United States*, 252 U. S. 239, 273, 40 Sup. Ct. 205, 217 (1919).

There would seem at first sight to be a contradiction between such an instrumental conception of legal function and Mr. Justice Brandeis's well-known and fervent individualism. But the contradiction is resolved when it is recalled how far his individualism is from the quietistic attitude of *laissez-faire* economics. While he still borrows heavily from classical economic thought, he has discarded completely the Ricardian faith in the unassisted working of the economic order. He believes in competition as being good for the competitors, good for the consumer, and good for the industrial process. But he does not fall into the nineteenth-century error of believing that with competition as motive power the economic mechanism can be left to itself. He believes instead that only through the judicious intervention of the state under the proper circumstances can it function with its necessary smoothness.

It is clear that Mr. Justice Brandeis's philosophy of control could look to no comprehensive and continuous organization of economic life in terms of state power, no system of either planning or paternalism. He is entirely in accord with what he conceives to be the normal functioning of the present economic set-up; his animus is directed only against its pathology. The huge and unwieldly corporation, the industrial monopoly, the unfair competitor, the overcapitalized public-utility company, the pyramided money trust—these are the forces to be tamed. They represent unbridled economic aggrandizement and anti-social economic power. To Mr. Justice Brandeis they are not what they are to critics of capitalism—natural growths from capitalistic organization, and its characteristic products. They are rather excrescences—sinister growths in a world where no formula and no system can ensure perfection.

Mr. Justice Brandeis has had to work out his theory and technique of control in the course of interpreting the application of constitutional principles to the operations under the Sherman Act and the rulings of the federal and state administrative commissions. He has had to determine what the scope and the powers of the commissions were under the laws creating them, and in passing upon the validity of their rulings he has had to crystallize in his thinking the principles to be applied in the regulation of business.

At the base of Mr. Justice Brandeis's attitude toward the prob-

lem of regulation is his conviction that no rights are absolute.[34] In
the pitting of public welfare against property rights he insists that
there is no absolute right to make profits, just as there is no absolute
right to do anything else within the state. The state grants qualified rights in certain property, in return for which the corporation assumes corresponding obligations of charging fair prices, engaging in no discriminations or unfair practices, and allowing a
free field for all competitors. The resulting system is one of individualism, in the sense that it premises a regime of profits, competition, and private enterprise. But it is an ethical individualism
—one that emphasizes responsibilities and duties. When the conditions for vesting property rights are unsatisfactory in any situation, the courts must await legislative action by which a system of
regulation can be imposed.

Viewed from another angle, the rationale of Mr. Justice Brandeis's attitude toward control is furnished by his adherence to the
idea of competition. Wherever monopoly has taken the place of
former competitive units he wishes to restore and maintain competition; where, in a competitive situation, unfair practices
threaten the competitive equilibrium he wishes to curb them and
so maintain the plane of competition; where competition is impossible or undesirable owing to the nature of the industry he
wishes to pattern the system of control as closely as possible upon
the model of a putative competition. The first of these three spheres
of action for government control roughly parallels the operation
of the Sherman Act, the second the Federal Trade Commission,
and the last the Interstate Commerce Commission and the various
state public-service commissions. In all of them he projects the
competitive ideal into situations where it functions with difficulty,
even to the extent of introducing competition as a fiction, very
much as the social contract was a fiction, to rationalize regulatory
practices in the field of public utilities where in most cases it
would be drastic or impossible to maintain competition.

---

[34] The remainder of this paragraph is partly based on the able and subtle reasoning of Mr. Justice Brandeis in *International News Service v. Associated Press*, 248
U. S. 215, 248, 39 Sup. Ct. 68, 75 (1918). This case involved the copying of Associated
Press bulletins by the International News Service. Because the Associated Press had
unusual and even exclusive advantages in the gathering of foreign news, Justice
Brandeis felt that, in the absence of legislative regulation, no new property right
should be vested in news.

The adherence to the competitive ideal rests, in Mr. Justice Brandeis's thinking, not on an arid traditionalism but on a belief that competition best serves certain more fundamental social ideals. It keeps prices low and fair. It represents a phase of equality in that it gives the "little fellows" a chance. It advances the process of invention and fosters progress in the industrial and business arts. It keeps the business unit small enough to be manageable and creative. It prevents any concentration of economic power which might dwarf the individual and threaten liberty.[35] But while all these aims would be generally regarded as "idealistic," there is nothing of the doctrinaire in Mr. Justice Brandeis. Although he is always willing to see a "trust" smashed, he is keenly aware that a problem as complex and elusive as that of the control of economic development cannot be dealt with merely by militant and repressive measures. In interpreting the "restraint of trade" provision of the Sherman Act he points out the danger of an absolutistic approach to the problem.[36] He argues forcefully that "the Sherman Law does not prohibit every lessening of competition" nor does it "demand that competition shall be pursued blindly." [37] Whether a particular agreement is illegally in restraint can be determined only by reference to its context.[38] Thus a "call rule" on the floor of a commodity exchange does not restrain trade illegally; [39] price-fixing by the producer for the retail reselling of graphophones need not; [40] and even a manufacturers' association

---

[35] For an enumeration of the dangers of corporate control, see the eloquent passage in *Quaker City Cab Co. v. Pennsylvania, supra,* partly quoted above in note 26. The setting of the Sherman, Clayton, and Federal Trade Commission Acts in the history of American economic opinion is well presented in *Federal Trade Commission v. Gratz,* 253 U. S. 421, 429, 40 Sup. Ct. 572, 575 (1919).

[36] *Chicago Board of Trade v. United States,* 246 U. S. 231, 238, 38 Sup. Ct. 242, 244 (1917). See also *Federal Trade Commission v. Gratz, supra,* note 35, at 438, 40 Sup. Ct., at 578: "A method of competition fair among equals may be very unfair if applied where there is inequality of resources."

[37] *American Column and Lumber Co. v. United States, supra,* note 29, at 415, 42 Sup. Ct., at 122.

[38] *Chicago Board of Trade v. United States, supra,* note 36; *Boston Store v. American Graphophone Co.,* 246 U. S. 8, 27, 38 Sup. Ct. 257, 261 (1917).

[39] *Chicago Board of Trade v. United States, supra,* note 36.

[40] *Boston Store v. American Graphophone Co., supra,* note 38. See also Mr. Justice Brandeis's utterances on this question before his appointment; his statement before the House Committee on Patents, May 15, 1912 (excerpt in Lief, *The Social and Economic Views of Mr. Justice Brandeis* [1930], at 400–3); his article in *Harper's Weekly,* Nov. 15, 1913, at 10, attacking the opinion of the Court in *Dr. Miles Medical Co. v. Park and Sons Co.,* 220 U. S. 373, 31 Sup. Ct. 376 (1910), and *Bauer v. O'Donnell,* 229 U. S. 1, 33 Sup. Ct. 616 (1912) (excerpt in Lief, *op. cit. supra,* at 403–8); and his state-

among hardwood lumber mills organized to pool and distribute trade information regarding prices and business policy does not.[41] On the other hand, a tying clause, linking the purchase of jute bagging to that of steel cotton ties, does under the particular circumstances restrain competition.[42]

Mr. Justice Brandeis's opinions in the cases involving interstate-commerce and public-utility regulation represent in consummate form a combination of realistic knowledge of business, subtle and difficult economic analysis, skillful legal reasoning, and creative public policy. In the opinions bearing on the crucial question of the valuation of the rate base, he has pitted his mind against the most complex technical problem that has yet been encountered in regulation, and come away with distinguished success. The right and the wrong of the conflicting theories of valuation, while no doubt of great consequence to the nation, are less important to the present discussion than the method by which Mr. Justice Brandeis has arrived at his theories. He has passed first principles in review, inquiring into the grounds for rate regulation; [43] he has studied the intellectual history that lies behind the agitation for one rate theory or another; [44] he has assiduously sought guidance from economic thought [45] and business practice; [46] he has seen the process of valuation for what it is—not a single certitude, but a chain whose every link is a guess, an opinion, or an estimate; [47] he

ment before the House Committee on Interstate Commerce, Jan. 9, 1915, attacking *Bauer v. O'Donnell, supra* (excerpt in Lief, *op. cit. supra,* at 398–99).

[41] *American Column and Lumber Co. v. United States, supra,* note 29. For Mr. Justice Brandeis's views on this question before his appointment, see his statement before the Federal Trade Commission, April 30, 1915 (excerpt in Lief, *op. cit. supra,* note 40, at 411–15), urging it to take upon itself the function of spreading trade information.

[42] *Federal Trade Commission v. Gratz, supra,* note 35.

[43] "The investigator agrees, by embarking capital in a utility, that its charges to the public shall be reasonable. His company is the substitute for the State in the performance of the public service, thus becoming a public servant." *Southwestern Bell Telephone Co. v. Public Service Commission of Missouri,* 262 U. S. 276, 290, 43 Sup. Ct. 544, 547 (1922). It will be noted that this rationalization differs from that given above in which regulation is based on the competitionless character of public utilities.

[44] See the brilliant historical analysis in *Southwestern Bell Telephone Co. v. Public Service Commission, supra,* note 43.

[45] Especially in his attempts to find in economic theory a satisfactory definition of value. *Southwestern Bell Telephone Co. v. Public Service Commission, supra,* note 43, at 292, 43 Sup. Ct., at 548.

[46] Especially in his discussion of functional depreciation in *United Railways v. West,* 280 U. S. 234, 255, 50 Sup. Ct. 123, 127 (1929).

[47] Southwestern Bell Telephone case, *supra,* note 43, at 291, 43 Sup. Ct., at 547.

has finally sought to measure the consequences of the adoption of one rate base or another upon economic development. We are impressed by the erudition, technical grasp, and fine historical sense displayed in these amazing opinions; we cannot but admire the strategy with which, after having unsuccessfully defended historical cost against present value,[48] he retreats and takes up a new position with the theory of functional as against reproduction cost in the determination of present value.[49] But the significant fact here is not Mr. Justice Brandeis's strategy but the courage and resourcefulness with which he operates in a realm—that of economic statecraft—which must in the future increasingly absorb the energies of the Court.

In a real sense Mr. Justice Brandeis's conception of his task with respect to the control of industrial development has had as much in it of economic statesmanship as of judicial interpretation. In his scheme *stare decisis* has played a less important part than the effect of the decisions on industrial development and business initiative; and so far from hesitating to read his notions of public policy into the Constitution, he has deemed it his first duty to formulate a just and statesmanlike policy. To a degree there is an admixture of economic romanticism in his gallant wrestling with "these great issues of government." A less vigorous mind might have flinched from them and taken refuge in a safe judicial "objectivity." A more sardonic mind might have concluded that, amidst an economic welter such as ours, government can at best create an illusion for us and clothe with some semblance of order what are really the workings of chance and chaos. But Mr. Justice Brandeis, with his sense of the need of man's mastering economic circumstance, is interested even as a judge in the gigantic struggle we are waging here to subjugate every natural and human resource and turn it to the uses of the nation. And it is that which makes him our most important contemporary statesman.

5

Capitalism, itself a system of economic organization, reaches out beyond its economic confines. It entrenches itself in a system of

---

48 Southwestern Bell Telephone case, *supra*, note 43 at 292, 43 Sup. Ct., at 548.
49 In *St. Louis and O'Fallon Ry. Co. v. United States*, 279 U. S. 461, 488, 494, 49 Sup. Ct. 384, 389, 391 (1928).

legal rules and ideas that may be called capitalist jurisprudence.[50] It creates a social system and a way of life. This way of life has written itself into the history of constitutional interpretation as it has written itself into the history of the common law.[51] The opinions of the Supreme Court are composed in its shadow. It furnishes a body of first principles that remain unquestioned amidst the intricacies and the fierce battles of legal discussion. It constitutes the abiding set of preconceptions that demark the limits of judicial decision.

Mr. Justice Brandeis has not completely escaped the necessity of having to do his social thinking within the context of capitalist jurisprudence. To say that is not to set down the essential meaning of his career; one does not thereby, to use a phrase of Mr. Justice Holmes, "strike at the jugular vein" of his thought. Its real meaning lies elsewhere: away from rather than reinforcing the capitalist norms. Yet to understand his relation to capitalist jurisprudence is essential to perspective, for the charge of radicalism—shadowy word—has often been leveled at Mr. Justice Brandeis. Whatever his heresies may be they are not economic radicalism. Using that term in the only sense in which it has meaning for modern economic society—adherence to proletarian theory —one may say that it is incompatible with the task of judicial interpretation in a society whose legal foundations are capitalistic. "We must never forget," Chief Justice Marshall once admonished —and here we may give his remark a meaning he never intended —"that it is *a constitution* we are expounding." [52]

Justice Brandeis's animus, as has been noted above, is directed not at the normal functioning of a capitalistic society but at its pathology. He has so much respect for private property that he wishes it more equitably distributed, so much respect for capital that he wishes it to flow freely instead of being concentrated in a Money Trust, so much respect for competition that he wishes the conditions created under which it will be possible, so much respect

---

[50] For an interesting study of the relation between legal rules and capitalistic organization see Commons, *Legal Foundations of Capitalism* (1924). See also the chapter on law and politics in Veblen, *The Theory of Business Enterprise* (1904).

[51] The way of life that informs the common law is that of a rural and bourgeois society. But the ideas evolved in such a society have adapted themselves tolerably to the purposes of the successive stages of capitalist development.

[52] *McCulloch v. Maryland,* 4 Wheat. 316, 407 (U. S. 1819).

for profits as an incentive that he wishes it to operate unobstructed by the monstrous weight and the artificial power of corporations, so much respect for business enterprise that he wishes to make of it a responsible creative force. There is an almost idyllic freshness about the way in which he clings to the original content of economic institutions whose current form most of the rest of us accept in a somewhat jaded fashion. It is a freshness reminiscent of the manner in which the emigrant groups of '48 approached political democracy. He has thrown all his powers and all his passion into the problem of attaining freedom and justice and a fair chance for every individual to make a life within the framework of a capitalist society. To this end he uses law instrumentally, as a living organism of adjustment to a changing society, as a method for distributing power and control within that society.

Accordingly, within the framework of the present economic system Mr. Justice Brandeis's stand is for a courageous and enlightened meliorism strange and new to the traditions and convictions of the Supreme Court. He would soften the asperities of capitalism, humanize its rough competitive struggle, endow it with responsibility as well as with vigor. Mastering the field of social legislation, he has made it practically his own. He has fought, off the bench and on, for hours-of-labor legislation, a minimum wage, social insurance—all the points of contact at which the state intervenes to palliate the rigor of the economic process. He has championed the interests and defended the functions of the trade-union movement, but the support he has lent it has been far from unquestioning and uncritical enthusiasm. A trade unionism that had no sense of responsibility, that developed a sterile bureaucracy, or that used its power to advance petty interests received as little sympathy from him as a tyrannical and uncreative business aggregation.[53] He urged the merits of scientific management even against the opposition of labor.[54] He saw in it its possibilities for the cutting down of waste; and his was the broad humanism that added the cold precision of an engineer's viewpoint to the social

---

[53] *Dorchy v. Kansas*, 272 U. S. 306, 311, 47 Sup. Ct. 86, 87 (1926), where a strike was called "to collect a stale claim due to a fellow member of the union who was formerly employed in the business."

[54] "Organized Labor and Efficiency" in *Business—A Profession, supra,* note 2, at 37–50.

passion of the liberal.[55] Almost his principal concern has been the creation of sound conditions for the maintenance of a healthy system of business enterprise composed of small, independent individual units and achieving continuous advance in the industrial and management arts through the incentive of profits and the mechanics of competition. To this end he has favored the introduction of every device that made for efficiency, the dissemination of trade and market information, and the toleration of price maintenance. Just as he has seen in Big Business a dangerous and irresponsible force, he has looked to a business kept at its legitimate functions and proportions to take on the attitudes and the ethics of a profession.

All his efforts have been directed thus to the creation of a socialized, regulated welfare capitalism. One may discern that to achieve this ideal he has thrown his energies into two streams of direction: he has sought to socialize and ethicize business, and he has sought to gain for labor an equality of position at a bargaining level at which it could develop creatively its own contribution to the economic process. To do this he has had to work in two camps at once. Through his opinions there has crept into the body of judicial decision, to confront the philosophy of the entrepreneur and the stockholder, a new philosophy representing the aspirations and outlook of labor.[56] But running alongside of this there is a stream of thought in which the center of gravity of the economic system is not a militant and dominant labor group but a self-reliant body of independent businessmen.

That these two streams meet and flow strongly together in Mr. Justice Brandeis's own thinking is indisputable. But it may be

---

[55] At hearings before the Interstate Commerce Commission on a proposed advance in railroad rates in 1911 Mr. Brandeis as counsel for shippers introduced evidence indicating that the railroads could save $1,000,000 a day by "scientific management." This represented the first use of the term. For Mr. Justice Brandeis's views on the subject see his brief and argument at this hearing, January 3, 1911, and his foreword to Gilbreth, *Primer of Scientific Management* (1912). See also Drury, *Scientific Management: A History and Criticism* (1915).

[56] For a tantalizingly brief suggestion of the relation of legal status to class structure and philosophy see Alvin Johnson's review of Hoxie, *Trade Unionism in the United States* (1917), in 13 *New Republic* 319 (1918): "Existing law is the embodiment of one philosophy of life, a middle class philosophy. Labor is working out another philosophy of life. The laborer's conception of right locks horns with yours: labor is therefore the lawbreaker. Labor is the lawbreaker, for the present; as to the future, who knows what philosophies will prevail?"

doubted whether an economic philosophy that involves the balancing and synthesizing of such diverse tendencies will have any evocative power in a world that must take sides or grow apathetic. Above partisanship himself, Mr. Justice Brandeis runs the risk of appearing partisan to both extremes. He is little short of an Antichrist to the big corporations. And to many in radical circles his refusal, on ethical grounds, to intervene in the Sacco-Vanzetti case seemed equivocal.

Such contemporary opinion may be of small importance for what must be a long-run appraisal of the validity of Mr. Justice Brandeis's economic philosophy. And any point of view that has been forged in a lifetime of active thought and is the product of mature experience must seem equivocal viewed from the anxious passions at both the left and the right. But there is a significance in such disesteem, and it lies in its indication that the object of it, in pursuing the integrity of his own thinking, may have lost touch with the new emotional trend of his time; and the emotional trend of a period often comes close to being a reflection of its deeper institutional trends.

A very large body of American liberal opinion has made almost an idol of Mr. Justice Brandeis and acknowledges the leadership of his thought. But there are evidences that widening cleavages in American life may ultimately leave this body of opinion islanded and powerless. The crucial premise in Mr. Justice Brandeis's economic thought—that the things he is fighting are excrescences to be lopped off, pathological diversions of energy to be brought back to their normal channels—finds less and less confirmation in the *Spätkapitalismus* stage of American economic organization. Agglomerations of capital grow more monstrous, mergers have become the order of the day, the pyramiding of economic power goes on, the individual finds himself increasingly shut out. In the face of such tendencies Mr. Justice Brandeis's attempt to hold the balance scrupulously between what is legitimate in business enterprise and what is an encroachment upon the liberties of the individual seems somewhat indecisive; and his denial to capitalism of further increments of that power of which, as an interpreter of the Constitution, he could not divest them, seems a gallant but hopeless attempt to bridge two worlds.

This points to a deep strain of optimism to be found in the entire body of Mr. Justice Brandeis's social thought. Keenly sensitive to discords in the social system, his mind inevitably seeks to harmonize the jarring elements. From the enriching experience of his long career he has learned to approach every problem with a view to a constructive solution, and he falls thus easily into the constructivist's belief that no differences can defy the efforts of the human spirit to resolve them. Although he has at times pointed to the deepening cleavage between the "haves" and the "have-nots," it was essentially a note of warning that preceded a constructive and not a revolutionary program. With the contempt of a free and flexible mind for ideology and dogma he has steadily refused to see the social process in terms of the class struggle. There was no essential conflict, he felt, between capital and labor. It was at the worst a feud which could be settled by making each side see the stake it had in peace and the mutuality of benefit that lay at the base of their relationship. Although himself a hardened veteran in the wars against encroaching business interests, there is nothing *kampflustig* about Mr. Justice Brandeis. He has always been willing to sue for peace on fair terms, just as he has always been ready to fight in default of them. His technique has been to act as interpreter of one side to the other, and while urging each to resist the extreme claims of the other, to base a final solution only on that genuine meeting of the minds that proceeds from a recognition of common interests. It has been essentially the technique of conciliation. In fact, it is characteristic of Mr. Justice Brandeis's thought that his conception of the economic process is a judicial one.

Or perhaps it would be truer to say it is political, as the Greeks conceived the nature and the interests of the *polis*. Amidst the chaos of economic conflict and the pull of contending loyalties Mr. Justice Brandeis's final concern has been the quality and vitality of the state. Not the state as force has engaged his allegiance and his imagination, or the state as abstract idea, or even the state as justice. It is rather the state as summarizing and fostering the creative possibilities resident in every individual.

It is in the living context of this faith that the political ideals which have become stereotypes with most of us still keep for Mr. Justice Brandeis their original meaning and warmth. Much of his political thinking is polarized about democracy and freedom. But in the case of both concepts the original spirit is reinterpreted in terms of our changed society. His democracy is an apotheosis of the common man, but only of the common man viewed as a bundle of potentialities. And it is the sum of the conditions that enables him to develop these potentialities that constitutes Mr. Justice Brandeis's conception of freedom. These conditions are in our society mainly economic, just as the forces that threaten and dwarf our freedom are the outcome of our recent economic development.[57] Neither is his conception of democracy the traditional one —a principle set apart in government; it is part of every activity in the state, just as freedom is part of every activity. The greatest field for democracy today lies for him in the person-to-person working out of those daily economic relationships that we call "industrial democracy." It is in such workshops that the truly political attitudes are fashioned that go into the making of the state.

6

What ties this bundle of ideas together? More than anything else, Mr. Justice Brandeis's belief in the basic importance of experience. The experience of individuals is, for him, the great source out of which society draws its strength and its growth. Social institutions are the product and distillation of experience; laws are its expression; the judicial function builds from it. It is this absorption with the theme of experience that stamps the body of Mr. Justice Brandeis's judicial opinions as pragmatic jurisprudence.

Pragmatism is not new in law. In one sense, as hard-headed militant preference of fact to theory, as a steadfast clinging to accumulated experience, it informs the whole history of the common law. By its very nature a system of case law is unsystematic, anti-absolutist, capable of growth.[58] That same use of fictions which marks the reluctance of its changes to new conditions marks

---

[57] "The old method of distribution and developing of the great resources of the country is creating a huge privileged class that is endangering liberty. There cannot be liberty without financial independence, and the greatest danger to the people of the United States today is in becoming, as they are gradually more and more, a class of employees"—from Mr. Brandeis's argument at the Ballinger investigation, May 27, 1910.

[58] See Llewellyn, "Case Law" (1930), 3 *Encyclopaedia of the Social Sciences* 249.

also the fact of them. But what gives Mr. Justice Brandeis's pragmatism its character as innovation is the fact that the experience
on which it bases itself is the changing experience of the present,
not the accumulated experience of the past. A tory jurisprudence
has always the advantage of being evidently buttressed by past
realities; a liberal jurist, since he is advancing "new ideas," must
always face the charge that he is making the situation conform to
his idea of it. The body of pragmatic jurisprudence which, under
Mr. Justice Brandeis's leadership, is forming in America has given
a new prestige to the scanning of the contemporary horizon for
light on ancient legal principles.

The pragmatism of Mr. Justice Brandeis is in essence experimental. It sees two experimental processes going on at the same
time: the attempt of society to work out its problems and the attempt of the courts to find the right rule of law. The experimental
process going on in society is to Mr. Justice Brandeis generally a
blind one and often ignorant; the formulations that it presents at
any given time are tentative and imperfect. But they embrace the
energies and aspirations of men, and a "living law" cannot ignore
them.[59] The law is itself therefore in experimental flux, changing
with the changing configurations that society presents. Of the
"search by the court of last resort for the true rule," Mr. Justice
Brandeis has said: "The process of inclusion and exclusion, so
often applied in developing a rule, cannot end with its first enunci-
ation. The rule as announced must be deemed tentative. For the
many and varying facts to which it will be applied cannot be fore-
seen. Modification implies growth. It is the life of the law." [60]

In this philosophy of experiment and experience the individual
is the unit. Mr. Justice Brandeis believes, as Emerson did, in the
sovereign reality of individual experience. In common with more
recent psychological thought he believes that one can learn nothing except as it passes through one's own experience; every attempt
to impose artificial mechanisms results in failure. Whatever social
programs or techniques fall outside the ambit of the individual
mind are therefore sterile; the unit of organization should never be
made so large that the individual experience cannot compass it.
Mr. Justice Brandeis applies this principle to government, and

---

[59] Brandeis, "The Living Law" (1916), 10 *Illinois Law Review* 461.
[60] *Washington v. Dawson*, 264 U. S. 219, 228, 236, 44 Sup. Ct. 302, 305, 308 (1923).

emerges with a belief in decentralization. When he applies it to business organization it leads him to his well-known position that an overgrown corporate unit is wasteful and unwieldy, and that the men at the top of it are incapable of having that direct mastery and comprehension of its affairs that makes business enterprise a creative activity. A group of small units, each psychologically autonomous and self-contained, represents for Mr. Justice Brandeis the most satisfactory organization of any sphere of action.

Although Mr. Justice Brandeis's individualism is reminiscent, in its fire and conviction, of the fine nineteenth-century libertarianism of John Stuart Mill, it is far from being imitative of it. Where the English liberals feared the tyranny of political power, Mr. Justice Brandeis is solicitous for the liberty of the individual when confronted with the huge engines of economic power and large aggregations of capital. Where they wished to protect the individual from the state, Mr. Justice Brandeis invokes the state to protect him from menacing forces within it. "It was urged," he says in his opinion in *Truax v. Corrigan* "that the real motive in seeking the injunction was not ordinarily to prevent property from being injured nor to protect its owner in its use, but to endow property with active militant power which would make it dominant over men." [61] It is against this dominance of things over men that the whole force of Mr. Justice Brandeis's humanism is directed. Beyond the intent that this humanism embraces of protecting the individual from being hurt is its fear that he will be lost; that in a society in which things in themselves are invested with active power the initiative and creativeness of men will find no room for expression.

There is throughout Mr. Justice Brandeis's thinking an unmistakable ethical note. It keeps him, on the one hand, from a rule-of-thumb method of judicial decision; he does not decide cases atomistically but by reference to a deeply held code of valuations. On the other hand it keeps him from the doctrinaire mistake of dealing with concepts as undifferentiated counters. To him the autonomy of the individual is eminently desirable; but economic individualism as the nineteenth century conceived it, since it brings disastrous consequences in the modern situation, is a thing to be

---

[61] *Truax v. Corrigan, supra*, note 30, at 368, 42 Sup. Ct., at 143.

fought. It is not to be confused with ethical and psychological individualism, which involves responsibilities as well as liberties.

In this spirit Mr. Justice Brandeis refuses also to accept the validity of the issue between individualism and collectivism. Here again an ethical differentiation is necessary. The collective action involved in control of economic development is quite different in value from that involved in government ownership. Some collectivities, such as trade unions and co-operatives, are desirable; others, such as large corporations, are undesirable. But Mr. Justice Brandeis carries his differentiation even further. Corporations and trade unions may both be, in the specific instance, good or bad. What determines that is not an *a priori* ethical theory but an ethical judgment of their motivation and their consequences.

Amidst the difficult and technical legal reasoning in his opinions this ethical fervor might appear a gratuitous and harmless addition. But actually his moral earnestness does not merely run parallel to his legal reasoning. It interpenetrates it. It determines its course. It saves his amazing legal competence from becoming virtuosity.

7

Behind the uniform array of United States Reports reposing on the shelves of the law libraries a battle is being fought and constitutional history made. The dramatic quality of Mr. Justice Brandeis's career of advocacy has followed him to the bench, and as one of a militant liberal minority on the Court he has focused the attention of the nation. He has had to introduce his social philosophy into a milieu for the most part alien to its spirit and formulations, among justices whom the intellectual traditions of their class and period had educated to a conception of their tasks radically different from his own. Dealing with cases involving the gravest problems the Court has had to face since the initial period of constitutional interpretation, and in an atmosphere in which every legal doctrine has been charged with the emotional tensions of social struggles outside the Court, he has had to devote himself to a laborious exposition of the fundamental economic facts that determine the issues. He has had finally to contend with a conception of legal precedent that regarded the body of past decisions as something very like the *traditio divina* of the canon law.

In the face of a task of such proportions Mr. Justice Brandeis has been remarkably successful. He has not altogether kept the Supreme Court from appearing to liberal opinion as something of a Heartbreak House. But he has drawn the issues clearly, taken a positive and constructive stand, and polarized every liberal tendency in the Court. A more radical philosophy, a less statesmanlike attitude than his might have failed utterly. But Mr. Justice Brandeis's intellectual creed, although always clear-cut and decisive, contains that admirable balancing of tradition and innovation which represents the greatest assurance of eventual success. There has been no intent in it to break with the essential Supreme Court traditions. Mr. Justice Brandeis's doctrine of *stare decisis* is mature as well as flexible.[62] He has adhered to the American tradition of individualism, redefining it to suit the realities of the age. In his emphasis on democracy and freedom he has insisted that as a nation we bid fair to alienate ourselves from the psychological drives that have conditioned our history. The pragmatic cast of his thought, its ethical strain have set up responses in the American mind. His method—factual, experimental, inductive—strives only to assimilate law to those other procedures that already have those characteristics. He has advocated not the creation of new institutions but the instrumentalism that will use law to bring out the best implications of existing institutions.

It would be strange indeed if twentieth-century America, which has in almost every field of thought and art produced its characteristic expression, should fail to do so in jurisprudence. Mr. Justice Brandeis has admirably evoked and summed up contemporary tendencies in legal thought. It seems likely that the future of judicial decision lies with these tendencies rather than with those that have opposed them. But if that should prove true, will Mr. Justice Brandeis's work, in the phrase Fitzjames Stephen used of Bentham, "be buried in the ruins it has made"? To the extent that his thought merely merges with contemporary trends, that is likely. But there is permanence and distinctiveness in Mr. Justice Brandeis's conception of the "living law." His realistic method of shifting the

---

62 For Mr. Justice Brandeis's theory of *stare decisis* see *Washington v. Dawson, supra,* note 60; *Jaybird Mining Co. v. Weir,* 271 U. S. 609, 619, 46 Sup. Ct. 592, 595 (1925); *Di Santo v. Pennsylvania, supra,* note 25. "*Stare decisis* is ordinarily a wise rule of action. But it is not a universal, inexorable command."—*Washington v. Dawson, supra,* at 238, 44 Sup. Ct., at 309.

battle from the barren ground of precedent and logic to the higher ground of social function and social situation must prove an enduring contribution to the process of constitutional interpretation. Even the *epigoni* when they come will find it a technique which they can use.

1931

Brandeis and the Curse of Bigness [63]

B Y the very nature of his activity, Justice Brandeis has had to build the body of his thought out of the scattered fragments of articles, addresses, and judicial opinions. The luxury of the reasoned treatise or the philosophical essay has been denied him. The editor of the present book,[64] by the convenient grouping of topics, the exhaustive bibliographies under each heading, and the judicious selection of material to be reprinted, has performed an enormously useful task, therefore, in collecting the writings of Brandeis that round out his thought.

The book does not change appreciably the now familiar outlines of Justice Brandeis's thinking. If anything it sharpens them, because almost all these papers date back to the years before Mr. Brandeis became Mr. Justice Brandeis: the ideas of the People's Attorney were more boldly etched than those of the black-robed judge. The idealism of the Progressive Era breathes through these pages. The whole book is drenched in an atmosphere of light, but as we read it now the light is filtered through our experience with the war years and the boom years and the depression years. The call to businessmen, lawyers, and politicians to dedicate themselves to the public service comes to us tinged, if not with tragedy, then at least with a tragic irony. I find myself reading these masterly analyses of monopoly and railroads and finance, with their hard grasp of the facts of life in business, and wondering what it was that

---

[63] I have taken the liberty of consolidating in this essay two reviews in the *New Republic* and in the *Herald Tribune Books*.

[64] *The Curse of Bigness.* Edited by Osmond K. Fraenkel, as projected by Clarence M. Lewis. New York, Viking, 1934.

defeated this combination of the statistician and the prophet.

For there can be no doubt that he stands thus far defeated. The curse of bigness, which forms the overwhelming burden of his thinking, is still with us—in Mr. Roosevelt's America as in Mr. Wilson's. And Justice Brandeis's proposed policy of fighting bigness by breaking up the size of the business unit, regulating monopoly, loosening the death grip of the money power, is still with us as a program. In fact, it is still the political credo of the Midwestern and Far Western reformist groups who represent the Bryanism of today.

Justice Brandeis's own objection to bigness in the economic unit seems to rest not only on economic but also, and more basically, on psychological grounds. It is finally a question of the breakdown of dinosaur aggregates because of the limited capacity of the human mind. But this objection would seem to apply as well in the sphere of government regulation as in that of business enterprise itself. The very attempt to regulate monopoly leads to an administrative structure that cannot escape becoming a bureaucracy. Our generation today is asking whether the battle of the progressives was not fought on the wrong front: the real question seems to be not whether we shall have bigness or smallness, both in industry and government, but who shall control both and to what end. It is a question not of scale but of power.

It has become a truism for critics of Justice Brandeis to point out that he is seeking to turn back the hands of the clock. He is undoubtedly aware of the fact that the drift is all in the direction of economic gigantism. But for him this does not settle the issue. Unlike Archibald MacLeish's financier-hero McGafferty, Mr. Justice Brandeis refuses to succumb to the fatalistic view; fatalism is an amenity reserved for poets and philosophers of history.

Brandeis's central idea of the curse of bigness is not a popular one in a government whose great administrative effort is now directed toward co-ordinating further the many agencies huddled together in Washington but wielding a far-flung power. If this be taken as the core of Justice Brandeis's thinking—and there is every reason to believe that increasingly he regards it thus himself—the striking fact becomes not the identity of the Brandeisian thought and the New Deal, but their discord. Coming in to take control of a disintegrating economic structure, the New Deal necessarily involves pressure toward the center; Mr. Brandeis, on the other hand, calls for a "flight from the center." The New Deal has thus far, at least in the form of the NRA, meant the further consolidation of industries through trade associations and code authorities; Mr. Brandeis, with Senator Borah, is solicitous for the "small fellow." The New Deal, confronting a rapidly shifting economic picture, necessarily involves the continued delegation of power by Congress to the Executive; Mr. Brandeis insists that "we need more minds, not fewer."

The clash between the two finally came into the open in the decision in the Panama "hot oil" case. There Justice Brandeis was found voting with his more conservative colleagues against legislation framed by a liberal administration and drawn up by lawyers once nourished on his doctrines. There is no disaffection from liberalism here. There is no question of turning coat. It is merely that Mr. Brandeis is pushing his thought to its logical conclusion. His theory of the curse of bigness reinforces whatever constitutional arguments the lawyers for the "hot oil" companies may have used. The concentration of huge power is, he feels, unsafe, unwise, inefficient, even when it is vested in men with whose ideas he may in general agree.

The position that Mr. Justice Brandeis has taken on the Panama oil case and which he may take on other cases involving the constitutionality of the New Deal legislation [65] is foreshadowed in the present book. The important difference lies in the fact that the centralization against which the papers and speeches in this book are directed is in the field of business management and economic power, while the centralization against which his present thinking is being directed is in the field of government administration and political power. From all that can be gathered, Mr. Brandeis fears concentration of power in Washington on two counts: first, on the ground of efficiency, for to his mind a dinosaur government is no more feasible than a dinosaur corporation; second, because of the danger of fascism. The trend of thinking, in Washington at least, is against him. Whatever the solution for our business troubles, breaking business up into small units seems out of the ques-

---

[65] This was written before the Schechter and Humphries decisions.

tion—a part of the irrecoverable past. Whatever the dangers of a topheavy administrative structure, events have shown that there is no other agency or authority than the federal government capable of dealing at all with the problems of economic chaos. And European events indicate that fascism comes more easily when the central government is weak and incapable of dealing with the economic situation than when it is strong and resolute. Historically fascism is the outcome of drift rather than of mastery.

Thus Mr. Brandeis is not really the prophet come finally into honor in his own country. He is still in the opposition. He is the solitary militant figure he was in the early era of progressivism when he was fighting Mellen and Morgan. If anything, he is now more solitary and even more tragic. For a long time he fought the curse of bigness in business, and the industrial collapse seems to have justified him. But he cannot shake off the curse. He finds now that it has been transferred to government. And he is still fighting it. Which may make him, in the eyes of many, another Don Quixote—a gaunt and gallant but essentially helpless figure out of another era, earnestly tilting at windmills.

1935

Homage to Louis D. Brandeis [66]

WHOEVER is finally chosen to fill Justice Brandeis's shoes on the Supreme Court will have big ones to fill. With all the current talk of getting a Westerner for geographical and political reasons, we forget that there is no one who can be chosen, West or East, who will not seem at once magnified by the compliment and dwarfed by the comparison.

There is the usual crop of rumors about the reasons for the resignation, and as usual they are wrong. The fact is that at eighty-two Justice Brandeis has rounded out his career; and recent signs

[66] This was written on the occasion of Justice Brandeis's resignation in 1939, and before the appointment of Justice Douglas to take his place. It was somewhat condensed when published. I print it here as written, with the addition of several paragraphs from an earlier article, "Brandeis at Eighty."

of failing health have been warnings that he cannot keep up the demands on his energy that he has exacted, Spartan-like, since early youth. He will no doubt continue his interest in Jewish problems, as in other matters close to his heart. But it seems very unlikely at his age that he will take an active part, as rumored, in leading a world defense movement against anti-Semitism. His own career has been in itself the most galling reply to the Jew-haters, as well as to the haters of democratic practices and the liberal outlook. Given that, anything further would be anti-climax.

Since the World War the American legal world has had three outstanding names, fit to rank with the great ones of legal history. They have been Holmes, Brandeis, Cardozo. Of the three Brandeis is the last to lay his work down. The other two had more in common than either of them had with Brandeis. The literary flair, the philosophic sweep, the contrived simplicity, the flashing phrase, the sententious epigram, the articulateness about the nature of the judicial process—these are not notable in Brandeis. His opinions are not great writing. His philosophy is generally implicit. When he theorizes about democracy and the individual, and when he exhorts for new ethical codes in business, his exhortings and theorizings sound much like many others we have read somewhere. In themselves as writing they lack that personal imprint of greatness that stamps Brandeis's conversation, for example. Compare Brandeis at his civil-liberties best with Holmes in the Abrams case, or Brandeis in any social-legislation opinion with Holmes in *Lochner v. New York*. Read Brandeis's great economic dissent in the Southwestern Bell Telephone case and compare it—not in its economics but in its literary and intellectual impact—with Cardozo's dissent in the Jones case, under the SEC Act.

But this should not blind us to Brandeis's real greatness. His final effect on American law will probably be more substantial than that of either of his colleagues. Historically he has led the phalanxes that have brought the economic emphasis into legal thought. And he has evolved in the process a usable philosophy and a transmissible technique for generations of judges and lawyers to come. The philosophy is that individual rights and group claims are neither absolute nor unchanging, and that they must be weighed in terms of the need for checking and democratizing our corporate capitalism. The technique is to interpret the constitutional phrase and the legal doctrine as part of the living context of legislative history and economic fact out of which laws emerge. The philosophy has basic links with the whole tradition of American democracy since Jefferson. The technique is deeply rooted in our pragmatism and our hard-headed statistical bent. Together they have refertilized American law. Holmes and Cardozo will be read and quoted by eager students for generations, but their discipleship is limited by those gifts of sensitiveness, imagination, literary talent whose possessors are rare. Nothing is more horrendous than a mediocre disciple of Holmes or Cardozo. He turns the unerring simplicity into triteness, the flashing phrase into bombast. Brandeis on the other hand will live on by becoming part of the institutional fabric of the future—if we have a future.

What lies behind this enduring quality is a record that has written itself into the history of the American progressive mind. A boyhood in the individualist frontier society of Kentucky and a brilliant career at Harvard and as a young lawyer in Boston—many a life has started hopefully thus only to end up in a rut. But Justice Brandeis's did not. He would never take a case without turning it about in every direction, seeking to understand it. Similarly he could not live and work in a society without seeking to uncover its foundations. And the deeper he dug, the clearer became his conviction that it was the concentration of economic power that was responsible for the social blockage. It stood, a menacing giant, in the path of democratic action; it snuffed out the chances for a decent individual life.

He set himself, David-like, to fight this giant. The only weapon he had was his mind—concrete in a legal brief, swift and sure before a judge or an investigating commission, merciless with a witness—an architectural mind that laid brick on brick until the argument became a structure that could not be broken down. He mastered the intricacies of corporation finance because he saw that it was a key to the economic and therefore the social structure. From a few published figures and weeks of work he reconstructed the accounting system of the New Haven Railroad with such a deadly accuracy that the opposing attorneys thought he must have had access to the books. For twenty years, from 1896 to 1916, he fought the street-railway companies, the public utilities, the railroads, the life-insurance companies, the Money Trust. It was never a vindictive fight and never an aimless one. He had what Graham Wallas called "social inventiveness," and was always ready with a plan by which the railroads could be operated more efficiently or life insurance could be furnished to workers more cheaply. He took the causes that did not pay, and became the "People's Attorney." At sixty he was a public figure without having held public office—a living proof of how great a man can become if he loves justice and masters arithmetic.

There are two great and abiding facts about Brandeis. The first is that he has always been more than jurist. The second is that his thought flows out of action and is directed toward action. Alone among the Big Three of liberalism he had a notable non-judicial career before coming to the bench. That was why there was so great an outcry against his appointment in 1916, as there was to be against Black's appointment in 1937. He had laid his cards on the table. Brandeis was no radical, but it was clear that he would not abide by the fake rules of the game that the corporate financiers and the corporate lawyers had laid down. Hence State Street and Wall Street alternately groaned in agony and turned their eyes piously toward a heaven of professional legal ethics. But Brandeis's only sin was that he had beaten the corporation lawyers at their own game of amassing a fortune in legal practice, and yet was devoting an increasing portion of his time to the service of the common people in measuring and fighting the giants of monopoly.

So great has his work as a judge been, that we forget how great was his work as a lawyer. He transformed constitutional pleading through the "Brandeis brief." But he also transformed legal practice by becoming the successful symbol of a lawyer who does not have to lay his personal idealism and his practical social sense on the shelf while he is out making money. What Holmes was exhorting youngsters to do, in winged rhetoric at law banquets, Brandeis meanwhile went ahead and did. He became Exhibit A, and the profession will never again be the same because of it.

But he was more than a lawyer too. His 1907 testimony on the New Haven finance is a *tour de force* of statistical reconstruction. His 1913 testimony before the Pujo Committee and his *Other People's Money* (1914) together form one of the classic analyses of

American finance capitalism. These gave content at the time to Wilson's phrases about "the new freedom"—hence the historic justice in Wilson's appointment. On the Supreme Court Brandeis similarly geared his analysis to economic change and his directives to social action.

The theory underlying this social action has by this time been often stated. Brandeis is an individualist in his values without adhering to *laissez-faire,* a collectivist in his program without adhering to the bureaucratic state. His thought often becomes dizzying in striving to maintain this precarious balance. Its strength lies in its being compounded of a belief in the life of reason, an ethical fervor, a concrete and massive knowledge, enormous social inventiveness, an insight into the economic system—but above all, an insistence on our limiting ourselves to what is compassable.

But here too one may express doubts. Brandeis is against large administrative structures as he is against big corporations—because their size takes them out of the realm of the compassable. They don't work. The human mind cannot contain them. They become tyrannical. This explains Brandeis's opinion in the NRA case, which troubled many of his admirers; as it explains also his opposition to some of the recent New Deal trends. Yet the ironic fact is that if we ever achieve a planned economy, Brandeis will be shown as one of its forerunners. The crux of planning lies in the training of a body of officials and experts who give to public service the energy and devotion that are now given to business. If such a body is today growing in Washington; if the type-member of it represents a cross between the economist, the lawyer, and the engineer; if he combines an objective temper with an eye for action; if he is turning from a passive to an affirmative liberalism—then a large part of the credit must go to currents that Brandeis set in motion. And Brandeis's own career is proof that it can be done.

It cannot be done, however, if the Brandeises remain isolated thinkers and solitary fighters.

1936, 1939

8

Woodrow Wilson: the New Freedom and the New Deal

TWENTY years have passed since Woodrow Wilson in 1912, on the threshold of the presidency and at the height of his powers, wrote his whole social credo into the campaign speeches gathered in this book.[1] As the most open and defiant indictment that anyone in high public office has up to now made of the American plutocracy, the book has ranked as a cross between a classic and a museum piece, equally notable for the clangor of its sentences and the slightness of its results.

Wilson had, along with his iron-principled Calvinism, a sort of literary sensitiveness. He was forever sniffing the breezes of public opinion, forever finding "something new astir in the air." "We stand in the presence of a revolution," he announced to one audience, "not a bloody revolution—America is not given to the spilling of blood—but a silent revolution." Today when we are again talking of silent revolutions, the New Deal sends us not unnaturally back to the New Freedom, in a quest partly for origins but mainly for perspective.

The New Freedom was more than the phrase of a college professor turned politician. It was a fleeting gleam of vision caught by a whole generation of a way of escape from the intolerable oppression of the vested interests. Wilson was astute enough to snare the vision and to attach to it his political fortunes; he was phrasemaker enough to invest it with a moral fervor against which even the skeptical reader of today will not be immune. The formula that he evolves in these speeches is simple enough: smash the trusts, destroy special privilege, restore competition, let the full light of

---

[1] *The New Freedom.* New edition. New York, Doubleday, Doran, 1933.

publicity beat in on all the activities of business and government. And the strategy for effecting the return of this primitive economic democracy? "The way to resume is to resume," says Wilson, quoting Horace Greeley. Amazingly simple. Yet it elected a President and stirred his generation. In its day it was held to be desperately radical. But Wilson's radicalism was of the sort that took itself out mainly in after-dinner eloquence. "I do not say this," he warns, after one of his attacks on the plutocracy, "with the slightest desire to create any prejudice against wealth; on the contrary, I should be ashamed of myself if I excited class feeling of any kind."

Others of Wilson's time—Veblen, La Follette, Brandeis, and even the muckraking group—had gone far beyond him in making the age realistically aware of the power and the threat of the huge corporations. What Wilson did was to translate this awareness into terms of political thinking, and keep it from finding too dangerous an outlet in class feeling. Not for nothing had he read Burke and Bagehot and Gladstone. He saw the corporations as another government, superimposed upon and often displacing the regular government. The threat that he chose to see was the threat to the English ideal of political freedom. And his proud phrase, "Freemen need no guardians," was simply a diluted version of "Britons never shall be slaves." It would operate as cogently against government control as against plutocratic domination.

That is why in all fairness to Franklin Roosevelt—and despite certain gracious acknowledgments that he makes to his old chief in his own book of speeches, *Looking Forward*—the New Deal as a program must be clearly dissociated from Wilson's New Freedom. In fact, in the matter of control, the present Roosevelt stands in a more direct line of descent, in thought as well as in blood, from Theodore Roosevelt, who called specifically for monopoly control and for a differentiation between good trusts and bad trusts. Wilson's thought never departed essentially from the old competitive ideal of nineteenth-century England.

To say, as do some critics of the New Deal, that Roosevelt's recovery program is merely Wilsonian liberalism transferred to the present situation is to stretch the much abused term "liberalism" beyond all recognition. In place of *laissez-faire* we have a vigorous economic constructivism, in place of "government by discussion" we have a semi-dictatorship, instead of leaving freemen to their own desires and devices we regulate them through a highly centralized economic government in Washington, instead of the new freedom we have an approach to the corporate state.[2] The Wilson of these speeches would have been entirely out of sympathy with the New Deal. "I don't want a smug lot of experts to sit down behind closed doors in Washington and play Providence to me"— these words of his could be used to great advantage today by the coal and steel operators and by Henry Ford.

Despite these differences there is a real historical continuity between the New Freedom and the New Deal. Franklin Roosevelt has said of Wilson: "The problem he saw so clearly is left with us as a legacy." What he is referring to is "the concentration of financial power." It is the problem of an outward-moving finance capitalism which in Wilson's day had taken the form of enslaving the industrial system by monopoly and in Roosevelt's day has led to complete industrial collapse. Wilson's brilliant and yet somehow platitudinous phrases were the product of an era which could still personify the evil forces to be overthrown; Roosevelt's concrete administrative bulletins are an index of the agony of the capitalist state. But the two are bound in a real community by the fact that each represents for his own period the interests and the attitudes of the small man and his revolt against the dominance of the big fellow. And as both leaders set themselves to fight Big Business, so have they been loathed and feared by Big Business. The bitterness with which Wall Street hated Wilson on his entrance into office, even threatening to pull a panic on him, is matched only by the bitterness with which the captains of industry have been sabotaging the Recovery Act.

But the dialectic of history moves forward and carries with it the ironic compulsion of events. The Wilson who sat for eight years in the White House was a different Wilson from the one who had toured the country radiating moral energy. He never made any efforts to smash the trusts, but contented himself with establishing the Federal Reserve System and the Federal Trade Commission; his "government by discussion" turned into a uniquely despotic presidency; and his ideals of freedom were sadly squeezed out in the war which he had sought to avoid entering. The irony of the

---

[2] I now believe (1939) that some of the phrases in this sentence were overstrong. But I have allowed them to stand unchanged.

historical perspective that Wilson's later experience affords is that Little Business, which knows how to fight Big Business when the interests of the two diverge, knows also how to unite with Big Business against a common enemy. Wilson was led to draw his thunder, leaving the field to the Morgans and Palmers; Roosevelt may find on the other hand that only increasing coercion applied to labor as well as to capital can bring recovery and order.[3] In either case they strengthened capitalism in the very process of fighting it. For Roosevelt today, as for Wilson in its earlier phase, capitalism plays the role of Brahma in Emerson's poem: "When me they fly, I am the wings."

1933

---

[3] Here too I have allowed the sentence to stand, although I now think I misjudged the trend of the New Deal with regard to labor. The argument that follows, however, I still believe to be valid.

9

Thorstein Veblen

Recipe for an American Genius [1]

THORSTEIN VEBLEN came of Norwegian ancestry, of a land-hungry and land-tenacious tradition, with an intensely agrarian view of life. His parents had emigrated from Norway in 1847 and had settled on the Wisconsin frontier under conditions of enormous hardship. There Veblen was born in 1857. When he was eight the family moved to Minnesota, where his father took up a middling farm tract. The boy grew up in a clannish and culturally tight Norwegian community, well insulated against the more mobile life of the Americans around. He learned more of Norwegian speech than English. He was a queer precocious boy, prematurely skeptical and unpleasantly witty. At seventeen, because of his father's zeal for education, the boy was packed into a buggy and deposited at Carleton College, in Northfield, Minnesota, where he spent three years in the preparatory department, and finished the college course in three more, graduating in 1880. He suffered a good deal—a strange "Norskie" boy among Americans, with a scanty knowledge of English, lacking money and social standing, uneasy in the theological atmosphere in which the college was drenched. He had a lazy manner and a biting tongue that infuriated students and faculty alike; the only teacher who saw his promise and whom Veblen liked was John Bates Clark, at whose theory of distribution he was to aim his sharpest shafts years afterward.

But no college, however uncongenial, and no artificial textbook learning could keep Veblen's mind from developing. He read

---

[1] This biographical sketch I wrote originally for the *Dictionary of American Biography* and it is printed here with the restoration of a few cuts the editors found necessary. It is based largely upon the material gathered by Joseph Dorfman in his *Thorstein Veblen and His America*. The interpretation is, however, my own responsibility: I should not want Mr. Dorfman to suffer for any quirks of mine.

English literature, dabbled in poetry, delivered ironical orations, studied philosophy and economics, trifled with some of the radical doctrines then current, fell in love. After graduation he taught for a year and then, lured by the growing reputation of Johns Hopkins, he left for Baltimore to do graduate work. But the eastern university did not put itself out to welcome the gawky penniless Norwegian boy.

When he failed to get a fellowship at Johns Hopkins, he left before the end of the term to study philosophy at Yale with President Noah Porter and social theory with William Graham Sumner. Both men were impressed with him, and both his essay on "Kant's *Critique of Judgment*" and his history of the surplus revenue of 1837 (awarded the John Addison Porter prize in 1884) marked him as a distinctive mind. And yet his stay at Yale seems to have been unfruitful and frustrate. He had to struggle along, lonely, always in debt, earning his board by teaching in a military academy, regarded as a foreigner and an agnostic. When he took his Ph.D. degree in philosophy in 1884, he found that teaching posts were available only to the orthodox and acceptable young men with a divinity training. Disheartened, he took his useless Ph.D. degree back with him to his Minnesota farm.

The next seven years were probably the most miserable in Veblen's life. His education among Americans had unfitted him for the narrow life of a Midwestern Norwegian farmer, yet it had not placed any other way of life within his grasp. He seemed to disintegrate. While he read aimlessly and without stint he kept complaining of his health, railing at the parasitism of businessmen, mocking the sanctities of a conventional Lutheran community. He tried repeatedly for a teaching position, but always without success. In 1888, largely as a way out of a blind alley, he married Ellen May Rolfe, with whom he had once had a college romance and whose connections with a prominent business family held out some hope of employment. But an untoward turn of events shattered even that hope, and Veblen and his wife settled down on a farm in Stacyville, Iowa, waiting for something to turn up. Nothing did. Each year it became increasingly difficult to get a teaching job because of the embarrassment Veblen had in explaining his long absence from academic life. He finally decided to get back to some institution of learning as a graduate student and use that as a fresh point of departure.

In 1891, at the age of thirty-four, he turned up at Cornell, rustic, anemic, strange-looking in his corduroys and coonskin cap. J. Laurence Laughlin, who was worlds apart from Veblen and yet saw some of his quality, managed to obtain a special fellowship for him. Veblen's first essay, "Some Neglected Points in the Theory of Socialism" (*Annals of the American Academy of Political and Social Science,* Nov. 1891), contained many of the germs of his later theories. He seemed to spring into sudden maturity. And when Laughlin, called to be the head of the economics department at President Harper's new University of Chicago, took Veblen with him and secured him a teaching fellowship there (1892–93) at $520 a year, Veblen's long quest for some niche in the academic world seemed at last realized. Although he was never regarded with favor by the ruling powers at the Rockefeller-endowed university, the next year he became a reader in political economy, then an associate, in 1896 an instructor, and in 1900 an assistant professor.

Veblen dug down into anthropology and psychology and used them to focus a sharp new light upon economic theory. His mind had not brooded all those years to no purpose: it was crammed full of daring hypotheses and of significant detail quarried from a vast field of reading. Each essay he now wrote opened up whole areas for later exploration. The titles of his essays, generally published in learned journals, reveal the turn of his mind: "The Economic Theory of Woman's Dress," "The Instinct of Workmanship and the Irksomeness of Labor," "The Beginnings of Ownership," "The Barbarian Status of Women," "Why Is Economics Not an Evolutionary Science?" "The Preconceptions of Economic Science," "Industrial and Pecuniary Employments." His work as managing editor of the university's *Journal of Political Economy* (1896–1905, and in effect earlier) gave his thinking further range and depth. He met, either in the university or near by, a group of mature minds with which he could match his own: Jacques Loeb, Franz Boas, James H. Tufts, John Dewey, William I. Thomas, Lester F. Ward, Albion W. Small. At thirty-nine he began planning his first book.

The book that finally emerged was *The Theory of the Leisure Class,* published in 1899 when Veblen was forty-two. It gave him prominence overnight. Into it he poured all the acidulous ideas and fantastic terminology that had been simmering in his mind for years. It was a savage attack upon the business class and their pecuniary values, half concealed behind an elaborate screenwork of irony, mystification, and polysyllabic learning. The academic world received it with hostility. "It fluttered the dovecotes in the East," wrote a contemporary. "All the reviews . . . are shocked and angry. Clearly their household gods have been assailed by this iconoclast." The literary men, led by William Dean Howells, were delighted with its merciless exposure of aristocratic attitudes but missed its attack on the businessmen and the middle class.

Veblen now proceeded to a more direct analysis of business, and five years later, in 1904, he published his second book, *The Theory of Business Enterprise*, based on the material turned up in the nineteen-volume *Report of the Industrial Commission* (1900–2). It contains Veblen's basic economic theory—dealing with the effects of the machine process, the nature of corporate promoting, the use of credit, the distinction between industry and business, and the influence of business ideas and pressures upon law and politics.

It was almost a decade before Veblen published another book. In the interim he wrote essays on the methodology of economics for the professional journals. His life was disturbed by marital difficulties, and when, in 1904, his wife reported one of his relationships to the university authorities it became impossible for him to remain at Chicago. In 1906 he went as an associate professor to Leland Stanford University at the invitation of President David Starr Jordan. For a time he was reunited with his wife at Palo Alto, but soon the difficulties between them began again, and the two were finally separated. Veblen was relatively happy at Stanford. He spent part of his time in a mountain cabin, with a little farm around him. He made friends, had the esteem of the faculty, went his own way. But once more an unconventional relationship with a woman violated the academic *mores,* and he was forced to leave. He sought a Carnegie grant for an archaeological expedition to the Baltic and Cretan regions, and dug deep into the literature of the subject. But the grant was not forthcoming. Finally through the efforts of Herbert J. Davenport he was invited to the University of Missouri as lecturer and began his teaching there in 1911. About that time he secured a divorce, and on June 17, 1914, he was married to Anne

Fessenden Bradley, who also had been divorced and had two daughters.

Veblen stayed at Missouri for seven years. It was there that his most famous course, which he had already begun to teach at Chicago—"Economic Factors in Civilization"—reached its classic form. It was rambling, erudite, omniscient; it swept all history and all cultures. His classroom manner was casual and inarticulate to the point of despair. He cared little about teaching itself, and had no talent for it. But while he was never popular with the run of students he had many disciples and won their unstinted affection. He used all his courses as the basis for his writings, but the book which most nearly approximates the content of his principal course is his third, *The Instinct of Workmanship* (1914), which Veblen himself later called his most important book.

After 1914 the sequence of war, peace, revolution, and industrial collapse turned Veblen's interests from topics of professional concern to current issues. His writing took on a faster tempo and a more strident tone. His tenure at Missouri also became precarious, and finally in 1918 he burned his academic bridges and moved to New York, where he became first an editor of the *Dial* and then, in 1919, a member of the faculty of the New School for Social Research.

To this period belong his more revolutionary writings. Much of Veblen's appeal up to that time had lain in the fact that his most savage attacks on the social system had been made in the blandest manner. He had combined his uncompromising idol-smashing with all the intellectual qualities of the liberal mind—detachment, subtlety, complexity, understatement, irony. Now the urgency of Veblen's interests produced a progressive departure from this manner. His *Imperial Germany and the Industrial Revolution* (1915) has a bareness of structure not found in his earlier books, although it was still ambiguous enough to suffer the supreme irony of having George Creel's Committee on Information use it as grist for the propaganda mills while the Post Office Department held it up as subversive doctrine. Its thesis was that Germany's strength lay in the fact that she borrowed the industrial techniques from England, but instead of borrowing the English democratic procedure along with them she combined them with the unqualified feudal-militaristic institutions congenial to business. In *An Inquiry into the Na-*

ture of Peace (1917) Veblen made his meaning clearer by describing patriotism and business enterprise as having the common trait of being useless to the community at large, and analyzing them as the principal obstructions to a lasting peace. In *The Higher Learning in America* (1918) he leveled so bitter and direct an attack on the "conduct of universities by businessmen" that on reading an earlier draft friends had advised him to withhold it from publication.

Whatever its immediate subject matter, every one of Veblen's books was in reality directed at an analysis of business enterprise. In *The Vested Interests and the State of the Industrial Arts* (1919) he came closer to his subject, with a savageness of tone that repelled many of his disciples who had been accustomed to his subtler manner. He defined a vested interest as "a marketable right to get something for nothing," pointed out that the aim of business was to maximize profits by restricting or "sabotaging" production, and sharpened his now familiar antithesis between business and industry. During the "red hysteria" of 1919–20, Veblen, writing editorials for the *Dial,* described the passions aroused by the concern for the safety of capitalist institutions as a form of dementia praecox, contrasted the aims of Bolshevism with those of the guardians of the "vested interests" without discrediting the former, and wrote openly of the possibilities of a revolutionary overturn. In his papers collected in *The Engineers and the Price System* (1921) he sketched out a technique of revolution through the organization of a soviet of technicians who would be in a position to take over and carry on the productive processes of the nation. Veblen was no longer hiding his meaning.

Veblen's last years were lonely and his life tapered off. For a while he had plans, as the head of a group of technicians, for pushing further the investigation of the revolutionary role of engineers. But as with his other plans, nothing came of it: he had no talent for promotion or organization. His investigations for the Food Administration among the IWW for five months in 1918 had met with no official response. His attempts to become part of President Wilson's peace-conference mission had come to nothing. No one would furnish money for a trip to England to study British imperialism. In 1920 his second wife died. He felt tired, ill, rootless. Finally some ladies, solicitous for his health and admirers of his genius, took him into their home and watched over him. He had reached the stage of being greatly lionized and little understood. He moved about like a ghost among groups of liberal intellectuals, with his pale sick face, his sharp Vandyke, his loose-fitting clothes, his shambly gait, his weak voice so infrequently used, his desperate shyness.

His last book, *Absentee Ownership and Business Enterprise in Recent Times* (1923), was in a sense a summary of his doctrine. In 1925 an offer of the presidency of the American Economic Association, made after considerable opposition from within the organization, was rejected by Veblen because, as he said, "they didn't offer it to me when I needed it." In May 1926 Ellen Rolfe died, and Veblen returned to his cabin near Palo Alto.

Here he lived with his stepdaughter until his death in 1929, amidst furniture he made with his own hands, wearing rough clothes purchased through the mail-order houses, reading aimlessly, worrying incessantly about his losses through investment, watching the movement of events with a dull ache of bitterness and resignation. Six months before his death he said: "Naturally there will be other developments right along, but just now communism offers the best course that I can see." He died, presumably of heart disease, in Palo Alto, leaving instructions that his body be cremated and the ashes thrown into the sea, and that no memorial of any kind be raised for him and no biography written.

1937

Veblen and the Wasteland

BY some strange mutation there emerged out of the arrested energies of the nineties the most considerable and creative mind American social thought has yet produced. It belonged to Thorstein Veblen, whose paradox it was that, himself a product of Scandinavian stock which had for generations fought with the soil for life, he became absorbed with the surpluses of a leisure-class civilization; that, starting to reform professional economic theory, he made Americans aware of the wasteland of their contemporary social institutions.

After some *Wanderjahre* as a student and further years spent in desultory callings, Veblen came finally in 1892 to the glittering new University of Chicago as an instructor in economics. Into the group there—the first body of autonomous economic teaching in America—Veblen threw his startling generalizations about society, quarried from ethnological writings dusted off in the dark corners of the university library, or fashioned from a hint derived from conversations with John Dewey about philosophy or with Jacques Loeb about tropisms. But always, more coercive of his thought than anything else, there was Chicago itself, pressing its bulk and growth and tinsel wealth into his consciousness. Scarcely mentioned in his writings, it nevertheless polarized his thought and became a symbol of the society toward which his curious indirections were directed. And when on a battered Blickensderfer he had pounded out night after night the amazing pages of *The Theory of the Leisure Class* that society was for the first time made disquietingly aware of itself.

Veblen took as his theme the unproductiveness and inutility which become the ideals of a leisure class, and their psychological effects upon the whole of a society. He showed how, in such a society, prestige depends upon the flaunting of superfluous wealth through "conspicuous consumption" and "conspicuous waste," and through the "vicarious consumption" and "vicarious leisure" of the lady of the house and the corps of servants. He showed how the pecuniary values that dominated such a social structure informed every phase of life—religion, art, government, education; and in the tracing of the ramifications of leisure-class ideals through the whole of bourgeois culture he fulfilled the subtitle of the book— "An Economic Study of Institutions." Although his argument was unlocalized, we applied the moral to ourselves—to our *parvenu* millionaires and the ostentations of the gilded age—to the "common man" whom the previous decades had discovered and made a symbol of, and whom Veblen now showed to be exploited, accepting his status cringingly, subservient to those in whose pecuniary glory he hoped some day to participate.

With the writing of the *Leisure Class,* Veblen's energies were liberated and his thought flowed strongly into the channels of sig-

nificance that he found in modern life. He had waited for maturity
to write his first book (he was forty-two when it appeared) and
had in the interim crammed his mind full of hypothesis and conjecture about social institutions. Now in ten books, in the space of
two decades, he poured forth this stream of ideas, spilling over each
theme he treated; for he could never prune his thought or narrow
his emotion to his specific subject. The argument is considerably
repetitive and far from clear-cut. Veblen's writing is obscure, man-
nered, baffling; as Mr. H. L. Mencken has pointed out in one of
his wittiest and least sympathetic essays, it wastes much effort in
labored explanation of the obvious. But it encompasses the most
important body of social analysis in modern American thought.

Veblen's principal motivation lay probably in making economic
thought congruous with the conditions and spirit of latter-day economic activity. His brilliant series of essays on method, "The Preconceptions of Economic Science," in a manner which exasperated
because it was at once summary and elegiac, rejected not only the
prevailing economic doctrines but the unconscious premises behind them. These premises had emerged from the intellectual temper of their day, but they were out of accord with ours. Their world
had vanished. In its place there was a new world whose principal
economic outlines Veblen sought to sketch in *The Theory of Business Enterprise*. The small-scale entrepreneur had been replaced
by an absentee-owned corporation, the thrifty captain of industry
by the financier, the isolated machine by a well-knit and exacting
machine process, the higgling of the market by an all-pervading
price system, and competition by a set of refined and ingenious
devices for price control.

But the most important change of all was the broadening cleavage, in economic activity, between industry and business. Industry
was the thing-technique; it worked with things to produce things.
But at the helm, directing industry to its own purposes, was business, which worked with intangibles to produce money-values. This
dichotomy fascinated Veblen. It became for him something closely
symbolic of Balder and Loki—a dualism which in spite of his
detestation of moral valuations he could not help viewing morally.
His quest for the springs of human motive behind these two strains
led him to write *The Instinct of Workmanship*, at once the most

searching and perplexing of his books. It is an ambitious affair, full of provocative blind alleys, and at least half a splendid failure. Plunging morass-deep into "instinct" psychology, it emerges with the thesis that the "instinct of workmanship," deeply ingrained in man since savage times, has impelled him always not to waste his resources on alien and irrelevant purposes, but that it has been thwarted throughout human history by the piling-up of institutions which have run counter to it.

Veblen tended more and more to dwell on this monstrous conflict. As the steady pressure of science and technological advance beats the conditions of life mercilessly onward, and keeps forever changing the economic landscape and with it the contours of society, man finds himself ever farther away from the sense of economy and workmanship and social order that his primitive instincts called for. And as if to deepen the irony of his position, every attempt that he makes to adjust himself rationally to the new conditions of life is doomed by the nature of his own institutions. For an institution, while Veblen often thought of it merely as a pattern of social life—an organized way of doing things—was much more essentially for him the common way of thinking implied by it and growing out of it. And these ways of thinking—the belief, for example, in the "natural rights" of the individual—exercise their most tyrannical power when the patterns of life to which they were attached have been superseded. Out of their phantasmal world they reach the "dead hand of the past" to paralyze any attempt man might make to come to terms with his new world.

Inducted into a group of academic theorists who had exhausted themselves in warfare between rival camps, such an economics as this, with its airy rejection of all the stakes of conflict and its amazing vitality of thought, had an element of the grotesque, as if it were some exotic growth transplanted into dour and barren ground. Like all new doctrine, it had its trials at first. It was not even dignified by being called a heresy, but was dismissed as, whatever its merits, something other than economics—sociology, perhaps. But rapidly the younger scholars, those with energy and eagerness and a glimmer of daring, clustered around it. They became a school— the "institutionalists," from the conspicuous place in economic study that they give to the institutional patterns. And so Veblen's doctrine had its triumphs as well; and if it has not yet become orthodox, it ranks at least as a respectable heresy.

The generation which thus welcomed Veblen had been nurtured on a body of thought whose informing principle was that of a neatly arranged universe. In economics, physics, psychology, in art, morality, religion, political and legal theory, the prevailing attempt was to cling to a rapidly slipping sense of order. Veblen's principal achievement lay in his summary rejection of these dreams of social order. He saw a world in which the accumulated technical knowledge of generations of scientists and craftsmen—the current "state of the industrial arts"—was turned to the uses of an indifferent and even hostile system of business enterprise; a world in which there was a continuous "sabotaging" of industry by business whenever the aims of production threatened to clash with those of profit-making; and in which the natural resources of a country such as America had been squandered and exploited because, by our system of economic individualism, haste is especially profitable when it is accompanied by waste. In the realm of business he saw the growth of huge corporations under an "absentee ownership," where the most valuable arts were the refinements in manipulating items on a balance-sheet. He saw the incrustation of the "haves" into "vested interests" with a heavy stake in the maintenance of things as they are; and, exploited by them and subservient to them, an "underlying population" whose function as producers was to feed the "machine process," and as consumers to pay for their commodities a price of which the larger part went to items such as advertising and salesmanship and marketing. He saw in religion that the churches had become infected with commercialism, and in education that men had almost given up their strange task of domiciling the ideals of a disinterested "higher learning" in a society at the mercy of pecuniary values.

From what obscure impulsions in his brain Veblen's chugging polysyllables took their perverse direction can be left only to conjecture. But we do know that the advancing *Zeitgeist* was on his side. His thought, judged cynical and pessimistic by the generation that saw the publication of the *Leisure Class,* struck an accord with the mood of the generation that read T. S. Eliot. In its essential symbols Veblen's wasteland of social institutions corresponded with the world as it revealed itself to the more sensitive post-War poets and novelists. If Veblen in some respects anticipated their notation of the modern spirit it was because, while they had needed the personal experience of War to impress upon them the plight of the individual in a disintegrating society, Veblen had sensed this plight more easily because his mind was not turned in upon itself, but was always directed toward the volcanic play of social energies. His greatest appeal was to those for whom the neat garden-walks and trim hedges of contemporary social thought contained fictitious patterns, clipped of all emotional evocation and unfruitful of any satisfying analyses.

In a sense Veblen helped tide American social thought over a period of desperate transition. The optimistic world of the early stages of industrialism, in which the machine had been accepted as an absolute boon, was behind us. A not impossible world in which we shall have learned what to do with the things that the machine has put within our reach is still to come. In the confusion between these two certitudes it was Veblen's achievement to make articulate the desolateness of our position. He has shown us by what impalpable puppet-strings we are tied to our racial and cultural past, and yet how uniquely our economic institutions differ from any the world has seen. The fierceness of his intellectual processes was combined paradoxically with an unimpassioned appraisal of all our bigness and shrillness and showiness. By insisting on a realistic picture of our economic society, by himself isolating and analyzing the economic changes which were cutting away the ground under established ways of living and orderly habits of thought, he revealed transitional America to itself.

How effectively he did this is attested by the rapidity with which his analyses have become the customary and slightly worn currency of our thinking. Walton Hamilton has remarked that practically every vein of importance that is being explored today in economic thought may be traced back to Veblen. Not alone in the technical literature of economics but in so influential a lay theorist as Stuart Chase and so appreciable a figure in fictional social criticism as Sinclair Lewis, the influence is unmistakable. Known first as an eccentric who spun out labored ironies on what the reviewers were pleased to call our "social foibles," Veblen has suffered the most consummate compliment that can be paid to any thinker: in a few decades his ironies have become the basic material of economic discussion.

1931

What Is Usable in Veblen?

JOSEPH DORFMAN's important recent biography of Veblen,[2] with all its material on his life and writing and the America that he lived and wrote in, gives us at least the resources for taking a new measure of the man. We have none of us known what to make of his thought, and what meaning to extract from it for the dilemmas of today. It has been easy enough to see his glamour and succumb to it. Communists as diverse as Max Eastman and Mike Gold depart from their more drastic attitudes to do homage to him. Socialists and liberals see him on the side of the angels. Technocracy hitched itself to his name, and threatened for a season to become the tail that wagged the dog of his reputation. Yale University has hung his portrait in one of those buildings that were salvaged from the great bull market of the twenties. In Washington itself there are New Dealers high in government councils who use not only his phrases but some of his ways of thought; no doubt if there were any energy left among them for intellectual promotion it would be easier to found a Veblen society than any other.

The situation is a curious one, and not without a dash of irony. Does all this mean that the sallow Norwegian with his enormous intellectual effrontery, his desperate personal shyness, his total absence of our usual suavities, has become all things to all men? A "Norskie" eccentric, who had to eat for the greater part of his life the bitter bread of the alien and the heretic, is now seen as a home-grown product of the American soil. A scholar whose detachment made him a sort of symbol of "idle curiosity" is now talked of as a major influence in economic policy. It is as if history had staged this last theatrical trick to add to the already overgrown Veblen legend.

---

[2] *Thorstein Veblen and His America.* New York, Viking, 1935.

At the core of the Veblen legend is one of the most tangled and baffling personalities in American history. By the side of it Henry Adams is a study in simplicity. The legend has several phases. One has to do with Veblen's sea-green aloofness from the ordinary concerns of life, as of waters coldly lapping the shores of the world but never mingling with the swift currents. Another has to do with the feckless professor, unintelligible to his classes and his readers, writing on interminably in impossible sentences. Still another depicts the savage ironist who could impale a whole civilization on one of his phrases.

Added to these threads of legend was the mystery of Veblen's personal life—his amazing clothes, his home-made furniture, his notions on domestic economy (so much more drastically original even than those on political economy), his unmade beds, his dirty dishes packed high in a barrel waiting for the garden hose, his monogrammed cigarettes, his unstable ménages ("But what is one to do if the woman moves in on you?"). The dry talk of the faculty lunch tables was fanned into something like a glow when a new Veblen story was recounted. Here and there on academic campuses young men walked about dizzy with a peculiar and recognizable intoxication, their usually plodding wits reeling because somehow a Norwegian farmboy-turned-scholar had blundered into magical English polysyllables. For many of the generation that came to maturity between the War and the crash Veblen was more than a thinker. He was, like Marx and Nietzsche, a symbol by which men measured their rejection of the values of the established order. And when they found such a symbol their myth-making faculties worked overtime. Mr. Dorfman, by his massive piling-up of the details of Veblen's life has, without diminishing Veblen's stature or complexity, brought the legend down to earth.

But, legend aside, measure Veblen's meaning for today and you will be forced to conclude that his role was not directive but chiefly disillusioning. Read him for direction and you will, as Samuel Johnson said of the plot in *Clarissa Harlowe,* hang yourself first. His own starting-point was that of disillusionment with the orthodox systems of economic thought. For almost two decades he was preoccupied either with speaking his mind on the economic theory of Ricardo, Jevons, and their followers or else with making up his mind about the economic and social theory of Karl Marx and his followers. He was infinitely more successful in achieving the first than he was the second. Orthodox economic theory is probably deader today in America than it is anywhere else in the capitalist democracies. Ask for its whereabouts and you will see only the frayed fragments of its graveclothes, peeping out at two or three universities.

But for all his cocksureness about orthodox economics, Veblen had on the subject of Marxism only a painful indecisiveness. He had the hatred that any original mind has for every theoretical system except its own. Even had he accepted Marxism it would have been with a saving skepticism. But he wrote on socialism with a caution and canniness unusual even for him. His first important article, "Some Neglected Points on the Theory of Socialism," was hailed by his associates at Cornell as having nothing to do with the actualities of the class struggle and as being only "a metaphysical disquisition." On the basis of it Veblen got a fellowship the next year. His lectures delivered some years later at Harvard (at the invitation of Professor Taussig) on "The Socialist Economics of Karl Marx and His Followers" were such as to strengthen any doubts about Marxism that may have crept into the minds of his Harvard listeners.

Veblen can never be accused of cowardice. It would have been suicidal for him, desperately dependent as he was for a job upon the good-will of Laughlin and the other academic moguls, to show too much warmth for Marxism. He was writing in the midst of a red scare. No one who reads Mr. Dorfman's book, with its story of the bitterness of Veblen's life until he succeeded in getting some small academic foothold, can wonder that even when his own thought was closest to the Marxian categories he chose to clothe them in other terms.

This is of vast consequence in Veblen's thought. For one thing it means that Veblen's response to the conditions of American life had to be tortuous and indirect. Mr. Dorfman sketches in, as the backdrop against which the amazing enactment of Veblen's life took place, an excellent picture of Veblen's America. But for all the talent and research that he lavishes upon it, much of it is finally indecisive. Veblen lived a remote and abstracted life, never in the thick of things. He took part in no movements, traveled little,

shrank from conversation, refused to vote. Even Thoreau was stirred
by John Brown's death, but neither the Homestead strike nor the
Haymarket trials seem to have left any direct traces in Veblen's
writing. Amidst riots and judicial assassinations Veblen was writing
"The Economic Theory of Woman's Dress," or framing metaphysical refutations of the marginal-utility school. At least during
the first part of his writing career the effect of the American turmoil
on Veblen was chiefly negative. The Veblenian irony is a way of
saying things and yet not saying them, the Veblenian mystification
is a form of protective coloration, the Veblenian vocabulary is triple
armor against the charge of agitation, the Veblenian erudition in
ethnology and archaeology gives perspectives of the past but never
dangerous projections of the future.

But these very qualities have formed the basis of Veblen's acceptance. He was a godsend for the college instructors and other
liberals who did not yet wear the stuffed shirts of capitalist apologists
but who sought escape from the stridency of populism. He gave
our taut generations relief from having to make a choice between
brusqueness and passive acceptance. He was a new kind of experience for the American mind. You could discuss the economic
problem in his terms without having to take sides. His intellectual
method included most of the qualities that have since become the
sacred cows of liberalism—disinterestedness, complexity, subtlety,
irony, elusiveness, indecisiveness, realism, an awareness of one's
own preconceptions, and an emphasis on "institutions" (harmless
but magic word). Armed with these qualities you could transvalue
all values and lay bare the desolate and jangled wasteland of economic life, but the blessed thing was that you could free yourself
thus from bondage to your society without having to do anything
about it.

Not the least attractive thing about Veblen is that he has been
regarded as native American stuff. He is one of the writers most
relied upon by liberals who insist upon an "American solution"
to our economic problems, and radicals who would rather point to
a nativist revolutionary tradition than a Marxian one. Actually the
only one of Veblen's books directly addressed to the "case of America" is *Absentee Ownership,* written at the end of his life. In his
other books, as far back as the *Theory of the Leisure Class,* he
uses the American scene merely as a convenient ledge on which to

perch while surveying the human comedy. His strength lay not in that he concentrated on American life but in that he enlarged the perspective in which American life could be viewed. He was not one of the American mind and American essence hunters. In fact there are few instances in American thought of such complete isolation from other American writers. Veblen seemed to come from nowhere.

If his mind took its temper from any tradition it was, as Mr. Dorfman convincingly points out, the hard-bitten, land-tenacious tradition of Norwegian agrarianism rather than anything uniquely American. Most of his reading and ideas derived from European sources—chiefly the Marxians and the anthropologists. His originality lay for us in his application of these European perspectives to our own life, and his canniness in seeing that the crucial time had come for transforming economic theory by recasting it in terms of the newer anthropology and psychology. His drive was toward economic realism, and he preferred to construct his theory of business enterprise from the United States Steel Corporation rather than from David Ricardo. If ever a government investigating commission justified itself, the Industrial Commission of 1900–2 did because of the use Veblen made of its *Report*.

And yet his greatest theories were brilliant intuitions rather than careful inductions from American material. He was not one of your statistical economists, and he was rather horrified at the prospect that economics "in the calculable future" would consist mainly of detailed factual monographs on business practices. As often as not, in reading Veblen, when you are just at the point where a factual survey would clinch the analysis you find that he has retreated to neolithic times.

With the outbreak of the War a change seemed to come over Veblen's life. It had never been a life sensitive to outward changes. Veblen's first book already reveals his distinctive traits of thought and tricks of style, and for fifteen years after it there are no marked changes in either. But the sweep of events after 1914—war and peace and revolution—added to the final loss of his academic posts, combined to fashion a rather new Veblen. He became less of a recluse, he came to New York, he mingled (although always ill at ease) in intellectual circles, he wrote for the journals. The tempo of his writing quickened and a succession of books flowed from his pen. To the period between 1915 and 1921 belong *Imperial Germany, The Higher Learning, The Nature of Peace, The Vested Interests, The Engineers and the Price System.*

The tone of Veblen's writing grew more bitter and more direct, while retaining much of its elaborate ironical apparatus. The first draft of *The Higher Learning,* finished in 1916, out-Marxed the Marxians in its analysis of direct business pressures upon education and drew from one friend the comment that people would think Veblen had gone mad. *The Vested Interests* repelled many Veblen disciples because of the savageness of its tone: their liberal sensibilities were ruffled. *The Engineers and the Price System* went so far as to suggest the only line of strategy Veblen ever advanced— a general strike of the technicians and the formation of a technical soviet, which with the aid of an economic directorate would carry on the productive processes of the nation after the seizure of power.

With his expulsion from the University of Missouri Veblen had definitely burned his bridges. He no longer needed to hide his meaning behind elaborate anthropological analogies. His irony was still there, but it was soaked in vitriol. His appearance of detachment, which he probably maintained more out of habit than policy, seemed almost gruesome now amidst his talk of war and revolution and collapse. It was like a plague-stricken group out of one of Poe's stories observing the punctilios of a formal evening party.

This was no complete and abrupt change. Veblen's writing had always contained revolutionary implications, and there remained in it now a good part of his liberalism. In the mixture of these two elements lie both his confusion and his richness, his lack of direction and the incalculable possibilities of his thought.

Out of all the welter of his thinking we can extract certain ideas that are still usable. Their value goes beyond the excitement or consolation they may have offered to Veblen's readers over the span of a quarter-century. They still retain some validity for understanding and confronting the dilemmas of our own day. Set down categorically they are:

1) *The rigor and potentialities of the machine process.* Veblen showed the insurmountable barrier that every system of economic

organization must face—the fact that the physical necessities of a complicated industrial civilization must be produced by a method dictated by the machine and its rhythms rather than by us and our own rhythms. The implication is that no program can turn its back on the requirements of an industrial technology. But an equally far-reaching implication is that we are living in an economy of potential plenty.

2) *The antithesis between industry and business.* This was probably the basic cadre of Veblen's thinking. The machine process and the pecuniary structure that has been erected upon it look toward entirely diverse purposes. One is concerned with the fulfillment of needs, the other with the creation of money values. The tragic irony of such a collapse as we are now suffering is deepened by the fact that the recovery and extension of industrial efficiency must wait upon the rebuilding of the pecuniary structure.

3) *The anti-social tendency of business enterprise.* The essence of business enterprise lies in the restriction of production in order to maximize profits. Veblen found in business rather than in labor the real sabotaging—the "conscientious withdrawal of efficiency." For many of his disciples this has led to a declaration of the need of a program of social control of business, so that this inherent tendency may be restrained, and profits maintained by maximizing production and lowering prices. Veblen's own thought, far from bolstering such a hope, constitutes rather a denial of the possibility of its realization.

4) *Legal and political institutions as the vesting of economic interests.* Veblen defined a vested interest as a "legal right to get something for nothing." He saw law and politics as primarily molded by the drive to create and maintain these rights. The current radical analyses of the trend of Supreme Court decisions owe much to this view. Any program of social control of business, since it operates through the same legal mechanisms, must face the valuation of the extent to which it entrenches existing vested interests or creates new ones.

5) *The compulsive force of idea-patterns.* Veblen's explanations of the origins of institutions tend on the whole to run on the technological plane; his explanations of their persistence tend to run on the ideological. By his stress on the latter he focuses our attention on the basic importance of ideas which, however outworn and archaic, still move men to action or inaction. Here lies much of the explanation of middle-class inertia in the face of widespread economic collapse, and here also the sources of strength on which the industrialists who propel fascist movements may rely. Through his stress on the com-

pulsive force of ideas Veblen can explain a good deal of the power that pecuniary values have upon our lives that cannot be explained by a theory of direct business pressures or even of vested interests.

6) *The bankruptcy of leisure-class (business-class) values and of a culture dominated by them.* Here Veblen has added much ammunition to the attack on bourgeois values along the cultural front.

Granted that all this in Veblen is still usable and even powerful, the pressing question is: Where do we go from Veblen? Here, in his lack of direction, lies Veblen's greatest weakness. Veblen's followers have been uniformly mobile and footloose in their economic allegiances. Many of them entered the Wilson war administration and either helped determine policy behind the lines or sought to implement the peace through research. There is a special irony in the fact that *Imperial Germany* was deemed by one branch of the government good grist for the propaganda mills at the same time that another branch of the government sought to censor it. In fact, this symbolizes Veblen's entire position. He was too well aware of the weaknesses and paradoxes of the existing economic structure to desire its continuance; yet he saw too clearly the tenacity with which the ideas and habits flowing from that structure hold onto our lives to have any hope of realizable radical change. He was finally forced to locate the revolutionary process in that most unlikely place, the minds of engineers and technicians, hoping that in them the force of business values would be more than counterbalanced by the force of the values and habits flowing from the machine process. The tenuous character of this hope is the measure of Veblen's confusion. It was ultimately as great, although on a more subtle plane, as the confusion of the wasteland generation whose plight he so clearly revealed.

Veblen's disciples have given a more straightforward answer to the question of direction. Their answer is embodied in much of the rhetoric of the New Deal. I say rhetoric rather than logic, because the essential logic of the New Deal flows still (1935) from the *modus operandi* of American business enterprise. The NRA embodies a further limitation of production in a business system already founded on the principle of a "conscientious withdrawal of efficiency," while the AAA extends the same principle outside the business system proper into agriculture. Industrial self-government through the code authorities and the control of each code by the largest operators involve a further handing over of business power to those whom Veblen called the "guardians of the vested interests."

But a few of the New Dealers are still sincere Veblenians, and it may be said that in so far as there are forces in Washington working in a liberal direction they owe as much to Veblen's ideas as to those of any other thinker. Their central idea is one not found explicitly in Veblen but implied in his writing—the idea of social and legal control of business enterprise. The final aim is the curtailment of the limits of a profit economy, a tempering of the extravagances of the pecuniary system, a clearing of the way for technological efficiency, and an eventual controlled capitalism. The aims themselves are to be found fitfully stated throughout the history of the New Deal; genuine adherence to them is probably restricted to the liberals. The idea of social control itself, while its economic roots are chiefly to be found in Veblen, is really a composite of his work and that of other American theorists. Its social theory traces back to Cooley and Ward, its philosophy of experimentalism to Dewey, its legal technique to Brandeis.

But a New Deal, even if it were a genuine one, is only one of the several programs that could be founded on Veblen's thinking. He would himself undoubtedly have found most of the features of the administration program obnoxious to his deepest intellectual drives. His skepticism would have eaten through the very rhetoric of the New Deal that to such an extent derives from him.

A final judgment on the force of Veblen's ideas in American history will not be possible until we see what happens to the Roosevelt program. Veblen's thought has gradualist elements that will be confirmed if that program succeeds; it has also revolutionary implications and consequences that are still suspended in the context of history. If the middle road of the New Deal should prove impossible or should finally deviate too far from the middle, in every one of Veblen's basic ideas there is dynamite that may burst asunder the whole fabric of institutions and habits that capitalism and the capitalist state have built up. Veblen himself just before he died admitted that he saw no other way out than communism. The conclusion that he drew from his own thought can be drawn by others, but it will need a new generation of Veblenians to draw it. Veblen's tragedy is not only that his intellectual system lacks a program and a strategy; it lacks also a clear historical analysis that would have indicated the direction of further development in the "calculable future." His fate as a thinker is thus concealed in that very chamber of history-to-come for unlocking which he furnished no key.

1935

Veblen's World

WESLEY MITCHELL's anthology of Veblen's writings [3] reminds us, if we needed to be reminded, that Veblen has already become a classic. In this "Norskie" farm boy who grew up to be a college professor America has produced its most considerable and most acid intelligence in the realm of social thought. In these lumbering six-syllabled sentences, with their devastating understatement and their poisonous indirections, America has produced a unique literary manner. In this man at once fierce and desperately shy, rooted in the soil like a giant in the earth and yet wandering nomadically from one university to another, turning his "swift wit and slow irony" on you so that you recoiled in fear, mumbling his lectures incoherently yet gathering disciples wherever he went— in this curious personality America has produced one of its complex and legendary figures. The five hundred pages selected from his twelve books and the definitive essay on Veblen by the editor constitute a gateway to Veblen's world.

What sort of world is it? Its outlines have the essential unity of any great theoretical system. It is a fluid unity, however—not, like that of Marx or Kant or Herbert Spencer, one in which all the pieces fit, or can be made to fit, together, but rather a *Gestalt* that comes into being after you have soaked yourself in Veblen's writing and approached with him, by roughly the same paths, one problem after another. For there can be no doubt that Veblen is repetitious to the point of despair. He traverses and retraverses the same ground, from *The Theory of the Leisure Class* in 1899 to *Absentee*

[3] *What Veblen Taught.* New York, Viking, 1936.

Ownership in 1923. In a sense the core of his entire body of thought can be found in his early essays and his first book. The rest was elaboration, sharpening, strengthening.

Partly this is to be accounted for by the fact that Veblen waited until he was forty before he wrote his first book. When he first flashed through the American heavens he was a meteor already fully formed, with all his strength and brilliance gathered and tightly knit. Partly also it is to be accounted for by the fact that Veblen lived so secluded a life that he was able to create an intellectual world with unmistakable features of its own. It has its own land-scape, its own heaven and earth, its own seasonal moods, its own mythology and demonology. He buried himself in his reading and his brooding. He read the economists, the anthropologists, the so-cialists—and the nineteen-volume *Report of the Industrial Com-mission*. While Veblen knew America and seemed able to breathe a sense of America into his pores, he lived insulated against its pass-ing fashions and follies. His greatest generalizations were brilliant intuitions or uncompromising deductions from daring premises. The unity that his thought has is a unity not so much of structure as of mood and method.

Since Veblen does not have a "system," the body of his thought defies any easy analysis. The key idea is generally held to be the antithesis Veblen finds between industry and business—the one concerned with satisfying human needs, the other with creating artificial pecuniary values. Industry is with Veblen a continuing evolutionary process, starting with the savage state of the industrial arts and coming to its present climax in the modern machine tech-nology. Business is the art of getting something for nothing—also an evolutionary process, starting with the predatory barbarism that followed the peaceful savage state and ending with present-day corporation finance and the techniques of the holding company. Industry and business are the economic forces operating in a psy-chological medium—in a world of instinct and habit. The deep unrests in our life now arise from the fact that the habituations of the industrial process, based on the instinct of workmanship and the parental bent, are moving ever farther away from the "idiot" institutions of our society maintained by the vested interests. When the gap has become so great that it has strained the limits of toler-ance of the engineers and the workers, we may expect a change.

Meanwhile there is still a considerable social lag which limits "the prospects of an overturn."

Thus, despite Veblen's delvings into neolithic times and his wanderings in the morass of instinct psychology, there is a Veblen who has meaning for today. And he belongs to the present for the reason that he has so searchingly explored the past and analyzed the economic and psychological roots of our modern being. I have pointed out elsewhere [4] that there are two Veblens rather than one. There is Veblen the liberal, with his fetish of disinterestedness, his awareness of his own preconceptions, his lingering irony, his Olympian detachment from the real struggles of a real America. This is the Veblen who offered, and still offers, consolation to those unwilling to take sides in the planetary turmoil of an era of finance capitalism, yet eager to liberate themselves from the values of a leisure-class society. There is also the second and more revolutionary Veblen, implicit in the first from the very beginning, yet emerging with ever-greater clarity after the outbreak of the War and the coming of peace. This was the Veblen who began to think in terms of the collapse of a decaying world and the seizure of a power. My only quarrel, if I have one, with Mr. Mitchell's anthology is that he overvalues the interest that the earlier Veblen—especially Veblen the destroyer of the idols of classical and hedonist economics—has for us, and undervalues the real interest of our generation in Veblen the revolutionary thinker.

Apply Veblen to the issues that confront us today and you get some notion of his continuing vitality even for a world that is no longer agitated by Darwin and Spencer. In a sense Veblen was part of the movement of populist thought in the first decade of this century and therefore part of the progressive tradition in America. Yet in a curious way he seems completely out of place amid the writings of the Progressive Era, at once strident and indecisive. By the same token his approach to the problems of this generation would be quite different from that of the other progressives and radicals. He would not so much rail at the patrioteers and the Liberty League as calmly destroy them by detached analysis of how closely their mental temper corresponds to that of dementia praecox. He would seek the roots of fascism not only in the immediate

---

4 See above the essay "What Is Usable in Veblen?"

struggle for power but more searchingly in the entire history of the predatory barbarian tradition. He would understand why it is that middle-class patterns of ideas still linger sufficiently in the minds even of our workmen to make a united labor party a thing of long-run rather than of immediate concern, and he would stress the peculiar need for an alliance between the workers and the technicians. On the issue of neutrality and the war he would get away from the immediate debates sufficiently to analyze the character of the dynastic state under capitalism and its compelling urge toward war. And when he came to the Supreme Court he would probably analyze it not so much as a judicial agency as in terms of its economic utility or wastefulness, much as he did in his unparalleled economic evaluation of the churches, which may be found in a long footnote in *Absentee Ownership*. I am sorry that Mr. Mitchell did not find a place for this passage, which represents Veblen at his maddest and best.

None the less, most of the famous Veblen passages are in this book, and one comes upon them with a delight that can be explained only by the fact that Veblen is stylist as well as thinker. You will often have someone come up to you in an exasperated sort of way and ask why it is that Veblen is so unintelligible. The answer is that he is not. The manner of his writing is one that was beautifully calculated to achieve the purpose of his thought. He has, to be sure, a vocabulary of his own, but it is not merely an erratic vocabulary. Such phrases as "conspicuous waste," "absentee ownership," "vested interests," "leisure class," "invidious distinction," "calculable future," while not always of his own coining, have been given his peculiar stamp. They have worked themselves into the texture of our own vocabulary in a way that shows the enduring appeal of Veblen's writing. He had to create a new style because he was dealing with a range of ideas which completely cut under the prevailing range of ideas in America. The important thing about his style is that his entire intellectual method, with its satire and its detachment and its indirection, is implicit in it. Any anthology of American prose in the future and any history of American literature will ignore Veblen at its peril.

1936

10

The Social Thought of Hadley of Yale

ARTHUR TWINING HADLEY, who has come down as "Hadley of Yale" because of his long association with the university, occupies a not inconsiderable place in the history of American economics. From an academic family environment and a Yale training Hadley went to Germany, where he studied for two years (1877–79) under Adolf Wagner at the University of Berlin. He returned to a career of Yale teaching somewhat affected by the historical approach in economics and especially by the work of Knies, Cohn, and Sax on transportation.

His first book, *Railroad Transportation: Its History and Its Laws* (New York, 1885), was notable for its use of the comparative method, its clarification of the theory of railroad rates, and its orientation in regard to the question of "state interference." Hadley had become acquainted with the state-socialist position in his studies with Wagner, but his own conclusion was in favor of the maintenance of the individualistic principle bolstered by the development of responsibility within the industry. This view was retained and strengthened in the course of Hadley's subsequent contacts with the railroads: in his testimony before the Cullom Committee on the Interstate Commerce Act (1885); his experience as associate editor of the *Railroad Gazette* (1887–89); and his service as chairman of the Railroad Securities Commission created by the Mann-Elkins Act (1910), whose work foreshadowed the Railroad Valuation Act of 1913.

Hadley further explored the problem of the province of government in his second book, *Economics: An Account of the Relations between Private Property and Public Welfare* (New York, 1896). In scope and emphasis this general exposition of economics responded less to the prevalent interest in marginal introspective theory than it did to the intense economic stress of the period. Hadley wrote it at a time when the exploitation of national wealth under private property was being increasingly challenged, while populism on the one hand and socialism on the other were attacking capitalist enterprise. Although a textbook in form, this work was in reality as intelligent an apologia and as judicious a defense of the economic institutions of the day as the American literature contains. Its approach was not from a theory of distribution, as was, for example, J. B. Clark's, but rather from what Hadley called a theory of prosperity. Conceding imperfections in the existing organization of economic individualism, Hadley regarded them as departures from a norm or an ideal which in itself represented a tremendous advance in human history.

Hadley was now led by the logic of his position from an economic to a preponderantly ethical and political approach. He had to reconcile his reluctance to admit radical social change with his rather realistic perception of the extent to which the institutions of competition and representative government had broken down. He was first forced into denying the importance of all institutional constructions, asserting that men are saved "less by their institutions than by their characters" and treating institutions as merely scaffolding or machinery. Seeking some ultimate base for his thought —an *inconcussum quid* on which it could come to rest—he found it in the standards of morality and the public spirit which give substance to the scaffolding of institutions and furnish the power for the administrative machinery (*The Relation between Freedom and Responsibility in the Evolution of Democratic Government*, New York, 1903; *Standards of Public Morality*, New York, 1907).

Hadley's investigation in what we may call the dynamics of institutions took two directions. He studied the wheels and pulleys of the actual controls in society (*Undercurrents in American Politics*, New Haven, 1915). In another direction and in a more hortatory mood he considered how these controls might be ethicized through the education of public opinion. This was his principal concern in all his writings and in his tenure as president of Yale University (1899–1921). His theory of education oscillated between the principle of freedom and the principle of responsibility as between two poles.

On the whole, however, as a true follower of the tory tradition of Burke, Alexander Hamilton, and Walter Bagehot, his sympathies lay with social cohesion rather than with individual or class freedom, with tradition rather than with innovation. The worst form of irresponsibility was to Hadley's mind the pushing forward of the interests of a class or group to the detriment of the interests of the community (*Economic Problems of Democracy*, New York, 1923). In his presidential addresses before the American Economic Association in 1898 and 1899 he advanced the thesis that, since political representation had become particularistic, the true function of the economist lay in representing the widest interests of the public. A rejoinder by John R. Commons emphasizing the essential class basis of prevalent economic conceptions was an indication of the body of thought that was coming increasingly to challenge the thought for which Hadley stood.

1932

11

The Legal Economics of
John R. Commons

A BOOK by John R. Commons is likely to be not so much an ordered end-product as a chance offered to the reader to follow a profound and tortuous mind as it winds its way into a subject and cuts a path across the received modes of thinking. This bulky and close-packed volume [1] is no exception. Although it stands as the culmination of a line of distinguished books extending over a period of forty years, there are few finalities in it and many beginnings. As a book it eludes definition. It combines aspects of a treatise on economic theory, an exploration of contemporary institutions, a set of essays in the history of economic thought, an approach to the Supreme Court, and a running critique of types of economic policy. Its interest for lawyers lies in its being the sequel, published after the interval of a decade, to the author's searching study of *The Legal Foundations of Capitalism* (1924). The central preoccupation is with the convergence of economics, law, intellectual history, and the programmatic elements of governmental policy in those "going concerns" that the author calls "institutions."

Any treatise with the title *Institutional Economics* immediately invites analysis of its concept of institutionalism. During the past quarter-century, institutional economics has been the storm center of methodological discussion in American economic thought, much as the sociological-realistic schools occupy that place today in American legal thought. The German "historical school" as such never took very deep root in America. We skipped directly from neo-classical and Austrian economics to institutionalism. The latter came into prominence as a dangerous heresy and is even now little better than a tolerated heterodoxy. It came in as part of a general

---

[1] *Institutional Economics*. New York, Macmillan, 1934.

complex in social theory that included pragmatism in philosophy, instrumentalism in logic, behaviorism in psychology, and functionalism in law. Its great founder was Thorstein Veblen; it drew heavily from Cooley in sociology and Dewey in philosophy; its leading contemporary exponents in economics are Wesley Mitchell, Walton Hamilton, John M. Clark, and John R. Commons.

But like the historical school in German economics, while it has had a lineage and has able expounders, institutional economics has never successfully answered the challenge hurled at it by its opponents that it cannot construct a coherent body of principles. The tendency of the institutionalists hitherto has been to reply that they are less interested in constructing a tight and consistent system of thought than in perfecting an instrument for analyzing economic problems and directing economic policy, and that the inherent emphasis of institutionalism upon social change precludes them from laying down invariant laws. I take it that this volume by Professor Commons is the first important attempt to go beyond this position and meet the challenge of the orthodox critics squarely by constructing a body of principles. The very title he uses, *Institutional Economics, Its Place in Political Economy,* is significant of his intention to fit the new institutionalism into the traditional framework of economic theory.

In doing this Professor Commons has run the risk of drawing heavy fire from all directions. He admits frankly that his view "may or may not fit other people's ideas of institutional economics." But while this is disarming, it will not be considered by the main body of the institutionalists as meeting the issue. Methodologically, Professor Commons belongs in what may be called the right wing of institutionalism, far removed from the left wing of Veblen and his more direct followers. In fact, a more or less confirmed Veblenite like myself experiences, among the press of concepts in these pages, a sense of having been transported to an intellectual never-never land, where terms like "futurity," "scarcity," "security," "efficiency," "input-output," "outgo-income," "exchangeability," "interdependence," "supply and demand," and "fair value" create a dreary landscape at once familiar and strange—familiar in that it brings back many of the concepts that Veblenian economics had sought to discard, strange in that it invests them with novel meanings.

It is for the latter reason that Professor Commons will draw fire from the right as well. His discussions of Böhm-Bawerk, Menger, Wicksell, while sympathetic, are not the discussions of a disciple but of one concerned to select, reject, discriminate, and recombine. The direct line of neo-classical economists will be horrified at the results; even the Austrian line, accustomed to the psychologizing of the old concepts, would not recognize his conclusions. To purchase his originality, Professor Commons has been willing to run the risk of seeming to be merely eccentric and unintelligible.

What he has sought essentially to do is to find a way of reconciling the economics of the market with the economics of Veblen and his followers. That means to take a set of static and constant concepts and reconcile them with a set of evolutionary and contingent concepts. It means to take concepts that interlock with mechanical precision in explaining price determination and reconcile them with concepts stressing psychological habits and attitudes in the market. It means to take concepts that assume certain conditions of property distribution and reconcile them with concepts that aim to study property distribution and the behavior of economic groups in various types of societies.

I do not say that such a reconciliation is impossible; in fact, to compass it is in a sense the major task of economic theory for the next few generations. I do say that Professor Commons is far from having effected such a reconciliation. He has rather given us a *mélange* in which Malthus, MacLeod, Marx, and Veblen rub shoulders with Walras, Menger, and Cassel, in which "negotiational psychology" and the judicial process are somehow scrambled up with the theory of money and credit, in which the "scientific pragmatism" of Charles S. Peirce and the Gestaltism of Wertheimer, Köhler, and Koffka are made to fill up the chinks left by the logic-choppers of the great tradition of economists. Many times as I read the book I had the feeling that, while Professor Commons had not effected the reconciliation, he had taken the greatest step toward it since Marx's effort to mix indifferent Ricardianism with good social theory. But each time in the end this sharply stirred expectation was forced to give way to a desperate exertion to piece together an intellectual universe of incomparable dimensions and unassimilable material.

I do not wish to be unjust to Professor Commons's own modest intentions. He does not pretend to great originality; in fact, he rather implies that the drive toward an exclusive originality has been one of the banes of economic thought. His method is throughout critical and judicial. He conceives his function as that of an arbitrator who has to judge between conflicting interests and principles which "must be made to work together peaceably, if possible." Such a procedure jibes with his own earlier life, when he was active as conciliator between capital and labor and thought markedly in terms of class collaboration. Defining an institution as "collective action in control of individual action," he proceeds to retranslate the history of economic thought in terms of the contributions toward such a concept of institutionalism. "The problem now," he writes, "is not to create a different kind of economics—'institutional' economics—divorced from the preceding schools, but how to give to collective action, in all its varieties, its due place throughout economic theory." This he proceeds to do by an examination of thinkers from Locke to the most recent exponents of communist and fascist economics. By thus minimizing his own contribution, Professor Commons forms a striking contrast to Veblen, whose every sentence implied a Copernican revolution in economic thought. If the Commons method results in certain distortions of perspective—as when he magnifies the creative place of MacLeod in introducing the concept of the salability of a debt, or when he reduces Veblen to a link in the chain of the theory of reasonable value—it has the merit of broadening the base of economic thinking and of seeking to construct an economic theory out of the history of economic theory.

Commons's sociology is the sociology of conflict and co-operation. Conflict underlies individual action and arises inherently from the scarcity of goods; co-operation is essential to social survival and is the purpose of all collective action. The unit of economics (as indeed it is "the ultimate unit of economics, ethics, and law" [2]) is not the classical conception of the individual (in Veblen's phrase) as "a lightning calculator of pleasures and pains," [3] but the transaction. Transactions are "the alienation and acquisition, between

[2] Commons, *The Legal Foundations of Capitalism* (1924), 68.
[3] *The Place of Science in Modern Civilisation* (1930), 73.

individuals, of the *rights* of future ownership of physical things, as determined by the collective working rules of society." The transaction implies thus not only the interested bargaining, working, managing individuals, but also other individuals in the society who in a competitive sense might potentially supplant them in the relationship; and always the ruling authority is in the background ready to decide disputes and to resolve conflict into co-operation and order. Transactions in turn combine in larger categories called "going concerns"—e.g., "the family, the corporation, the trade union, the trade association, up to the state itself." "It is these going concerns, with working rules that keep them agoing . . . that we name institutions."

Thus Professor Commons seeks to fuse an individualistic economic psychology with a "negotiational" social psychology; and thus also he seeks to bring the state and its sovereignty and its ever-present sanctions into the economic picture. It does not appear as "government interference," or as a *deus ex machina* intervening from without, either benevolently or malevolently, or as a regulatory force the limits of whose province must be clearly determined, but as an integral and inherent part of every economic transaction, forming the very core of the basic unit of economic activity.

This knitting of state authority into the texture of accepted economic material constitutes the real significance of Professor Commons's work. While his framework is large enough to include all forms of "collective action in control of individual action," he actually concentrates on the legal sanctions. He forms in this sense a contrast with Veblen, who was most at home in the realm of the mind where the instinctive dispositions of men interlocked with the compulsions of socially conditioned habits, and who interpreted modern economic society in terms of the cumulative force of these habits. Veblen's contribution to legal and political theory lay in revealing the extent to which political action is conditioned by the process of economic development and the habits it engenders, and the extent to which legal sanctions represent the formal vesting of interests created by economic predacity and business sabotage. But the real crux of his thinking was not to be found in the legal realm. In the work of Professor Commons, on the other hand, law is of central importance as the core of the "transaction," and the entire theory finally builds up to the determination of "reasonable value" by the Supreme Court.

The implications are far-reaching for students of economic policy and constitutional law. It should be clear on reading the reports that the Supreme Court is moving in two universes of discourse, the legalistic and the economic. Commons has sought to build a bridge from the one to the other. First, in *The Legal Foundations of Capitalism,* he started on the legal side and threw out a span that went half-way across the chasm. The book was a brilliant piece of legal and social history, exploring the extent to which capitalist development, especially in England but also in America, was conditioned by the development of "working rules" through the common law and the court system. The role of the courts was to select certain working rules for legalization. It left the analysis hanging in midair, however, since the question remained as to the principles of selection that the courts followed in sanctioning certain working rules but not others, in developing certain legal concepts and not others. In short, a dynamic had to be found for the development not only of capitalism but also of law itself.

I had hoped that this second volume would supply it and that we should be given a volume on *The Capitalistic Foundations of Law.* I had hoped, in short, that Professor Commons would go over to the economic side of the chasm and throw out a span which would meet his first.

But he seems too committed to the ideological emphasis to have done this. He has instead shifted from capitalist development to economic theory, and written what amounts to a book on *The Legal (and Other Institutional) Foundations of Economic Thought.* I can explain this only by the decisive impetus that Professor Commons's early studies in Austrian theory and hedonic psychology gave him toward solving the basic dilemmas of economic theory. But I fear this deflected him from the essential task that remained when he wrote his book ten years ago—to find a set of forces that will rationalize the development of law and legal theory in terms of the economic stuff of life with which law deals. He has been too intent on reconciling the utterances of judges with the ideas of economic theorists and too little intent on discovering the sources of both in the flow of economic and social reality. The task may prove to be not one of reconciliation (so dear to one who, like Professor Commons, has his roots deep in the technique of industrial relations), but one of discovering and tracing the complex inter-conditionings within the realm of legal and economic actuality.

One word remains on the moot question of Professor Commons's language and style. Gerard Henderson once objected to the essentially *verbalistic* character of much of the author's work. The stricture still remains. In the realm of economic theory itself, Professor Commons is more at home than he was in the legal realm in his earlier book. But the result is an even greater absorption with problems of words. Often, one suspects, the author begins with a genuine reorientation in theory, is forced to find a new term to express it, and, having found it, is carried by the zest of his exploratory impulses much deeper into merely verbal territory and farther away from his intellectual supply-base than he had planned.

To add to the difficulty, Professor Commons has set himself not only the task of a reorientation in economic theory but also that of bringing into line the related social and philosophical disciplines. His work involves a confrontation of deep-reaching problems in psychology, ethics, and epistemology. Fortunately he does not flinch, as so many of our American legal and economic thinkers have done, from the necessary metaphysics of his problem; nor does he seek to carry his freightage of learning lightly for fear of being called academic. But the consequence is a continuing sense of turmoil throughout the book. The reader feels that he has been a-journeying even when he cannot describe what he has seen. Like Tristram Shandy's father, one has the heady sense of having done a lot of thinking.

All this is not to deny either the profundity of the basic thesis of the two books or their importance in the history of thought. It is merely to point out the heavy price that must be paid for such achievement in the present state of social thought.[4]

1935

[4] I am deeply indebted to two articles by Wesley C. Mitchell, "Commons on the Legal Foundations of Capitalism" (1924), 14 *American Economic Review* 240, and "Commons on Institutional Economics" (1935), 25 *American Economic Review* 635–52.

12

Charles A. Beard

Beard's Economic Interpretation [1]

AT Columbia about a quarter-century ago, crowded classrooms were listening to an assistant professor in his late thirties expound strange doctrine. His name was Charles A. Beard and he was a tall, rangy young man, with a sharp aquiline profile, looking half farmer and half Roman philosopher. When he talked he threw back his head and half shut his eyes, but his doctrine was such as to cause the ghosts of generations of Constitution-mongering professors to hover uneasily over his classroom. The study of the Constitution, he said, was cluttered with myths that had more relevance to filial piety than to the real past. He was concrete. Instead of repeating Bancroft's sunny banalities on the guiding hand of Providence in the affairs of the young republic, which led to the conclusion that the Almighty must have been a Federalist, he analyzed a batch of Treasury statistics, or dug up some pamphlets by John Taylor. He was unafraid to incur the charge of irreverence. He refused to convert his job into a pastorate for a herd of academic sacred cows.

Every great thinker stands between the dying and the being born, between old bones and new stirrings in the realm of thought. Beard in 1913 could see the disintegration of the filial historical school. In constitutional history the great names were still Bancroft, Schouler, von Holst, Fiske, and McLaughlin, but their authority had worn thin. By the dominant tradition American history was still written and taught with a mixture of formalist logic-chopping and the star-spangled manner. But fresh work was getting done. Tur-

1 Originally published in the *New Republic* series, "Books That Changed Our Minds," this essay is to form part of a book under that title, edited by Malcolm Cowley and Bernard Smith.

ner's frontier theory, first broached in 1893, represented an economic emphasis. In the year that Beard took his doctorate at Columbia, 1904, Thorstein Veblen at Chicago published his *Theory of Business Enterprise* which was to remake American economic thought. Among Beard's own colleagues at Columbia, a genuine intellectual renaissance was in process: John Dewey was making philosophy democratic and pragmatic and James Harvey Robinson was extending the boundaries of history to include the whole realm of the history of ideas.

But the strongest impulses were coming from the new jurisprudence. Holmes had struck in 1905 in his dissent in *Lochner v. New York* the high pitch of American juristic thought. And in 1908, Louis Brandeis, the "People's Attorney" of Boston, had presented his famous *Muller v. Oregon* brief with two pages of legal argument and several hundred pages of economic statistics—and had won the case. The same year that saw Beard's book on the Constitution published saw also Brooks Adams's *The Theory of Social Revolutions*—a merciless analysis of the Supreme Court decisions and the history of our constitutional law from the viewpoint of the historical materialism of an eccentric Bostonian aristocrat.

The fact is that Beard's book was no literary mutation. The intellectuals were writing in response to new movements for social justice—populism, trade unionism, socialism, muckraking, the "new freedom," the "new nationalism." And these movements were themselves a response to the powerful compulsions of the new technology and the new system of class relations. Thus Beard's book was not so much influenced by Turner, Veblen, Holmes, Brandeis, Robinson, Wilson, T.R., Brooks Adams; rather were they outgrowths of the same social soil and intellectual climate. Beard was to write (with his wife) in his *Rise of American Civilization* in 1927 a Veblenian chapter on the intellectual history of this period which he called significantly "The Machine Age."

Once the juristic wall was breached, a search began for the springs of motive that induced individuals and groups to take part in the governing process. . . . As fitted the machine age . . . the search for such origins opened a way into the realm of economic enterprise. When that departure was made, no sanctum could elude intruders; no department of government, legislative, executive, or judicial, could avoid the light of scientific criticism.

Thus did the Beard of 1927 describe the forces that led the Beard of 1913 as a scientific "intruder" into the "sanctum" of the economic motives of the Founding Fathers.

The book that was the product of the intrusion was *An Economic Interpretation of the Constitution*. The title itself was enough to startle the academic and political tycoons: the very juxtaposition of our great Sacred Writing with so secular a phrase as "economic interpretation" conveyed to many the suggestion of outright blasphemy. And the book pulled few punches. It set out to explain the formation of the Constitution and the founding of the new government, not on the doctrinal plane of the "federal" as against "states' rights" doctrine, or on the traditional plane of "compromises" between geographic sections and between small and large states, but on the plane of economic interests.

The sheer masterful structure of the book has nowhere had adequate justice done to it. Beard must have had a premonition of the desperate resistance he would run into. He made his book a magnificently planned battle. He reconnoiters the enemy, surveys the ground, deploys his troops, opens fire, brings up his heaviest guns, and then systematically mops up and consolidates his position. Most great books require a creative act in the very summary of them. That is not true of Beard's. Its argument is patent for anyone who will take the trouble to read it, as so few have done. There is little in it of marginal suggestiveness—in fact, as literature that is its principal weakness. You get what the author is driving at in the very first chapter; after that, the interest of the book lies in seeing how he elaborates and defends his thesis. It is all a bit like a demonstration of a mathematical theorem. You feel like writing Q.E.D. at the end or else "not proven." It is almost as if the author had set out with a deliberate severity to strip the book of every adornment, on the theory that a plain woman would be less suspected of being a wanton than an attractive one.

But if the manner is severe and geometrical, the matter must have been to the generation of 1913 brash and daring. Instead of proceeding with Bancroft on the hypothesis that American history had been determined by the "higher power" that operates in human affairs, or with the school of Herbert Adams and John Fiske on the hypothesis that the presiding power had been the genius of

Teutonic tribal institutions, or with McMaster and Rhodes on the hypothesis that no hypothesis was necessary and that fact-gathering from archives and newspapers was enough, he proposed to proceed on "the theory of economic determinism"—which, he remarked, "has not been tried out in American history, and until it is tried out, it cannot be found wanting."

The book became thus an inquiry into the proposition that "the direct, impelling motive" in the formation and ratification of the Constitution "was the economic advantages which the beneficiaries expected would accrue to themselves first, from their action." To test this he set about making a survey of property interests in 1787, both in realty and personalty. It led to the hypothesis of an opposition of economic interest between the small farmers, the debtor class, and the unpropertied urban dwellers on the one hand, and on the other the landed proprietors (Hudson Valley patroons and Southern slaveholders) and the groups with personalty interests (money loaned or seeking investment, state and Continental paper, manufacturing, shipping, and trading, and capital speculatively invested in Western lands). The interests of the propertied groups often clashed. But, whatever their differences, on one thing they were agreed: if they were to survive, then what was needed was a strong central government that would check radical state legislation, put down open insurrections against property, create a unified tariff and monetary system, and set up checks upon the action of the majority.

The political leaders of these propertied groups were compelled to resort to an extra-legal coup—a Constitutional Convention which adopted a revolutionary program and put it through in defiance of the provisions for amendment in the Articles of Confederation. The groups representing important personalty interests in the state legislatures quietly and carefully engineered the selection of their own delegates to the Convention. In the amazing Chapter V on "The Economic Interests of the Members of the Convention," which is the heart of the book, Beard examines in detail the economic interests and experiences of each delegate and concludes that "not one member represented in his immediate personal economic interests the small farming or mechanic classes," while at least five-sixths (including the Convention's leaders) "were immediately, directly, and personally interested in the outcome of their labors at

Philadelphia, and were to a greater or less extent economic beneficiaries from the adoption of the Constitution."

The document they constructed, for all that it was couched and
defended in terms of political doctrine, was in all its implications
and in its deepest meaning an economic document. The state ratifying conventions were chosen, because of property disqualifications
or indifference, by a vote of not more than one-sixth of the adult
males. They were certainly in their leadership representative of the
same economic groups as the members of the original Convention.
The whole process of ratifying this document had the same aspects
of a deliberately maneuvered coup by the propertied interests as
the calling of the Convention itself. Hamilton and Madison both
justified their procedure ultimately on the right of revolution, i.e.,
counter-revolution.

One need scarcely say what an anguished cry arose when the book
appeared in July 1913, from the masters of property and their lieutenants in politics, in law, in the press and the academies, among
the professional patrioteers. William Howard Taft and Elihu Root
both attacked it, and Taft, just become ex-President, not only mentioned it slightingly in his valedictory book *Popular Government*
but went out of his way to make a speech against it. A self-formed
committee of the New York Bar Association summoned Beard to
appear before it and defend his thesis; "and when I declined . . ."
Beard wrote later, "they treated my reply as a kind of contempt of
court." Some of the reviewers showed a sense of injured national
pride amounting to hysteria. Albert Bushnell Hart, the mogul of
the historians, set the tone in his article "Baseless Slanders on Great
Men." The *Dial* said it "tends . . . to foster unjustified class antagonism." J. H. Latane, in the *American Political Science Review,*
wrote: "It will require more convincing evidence . . . to upset
the traditional view that the members of the federal convention
were patriotic men earnestly striving to arrive at the best political
solution of the dangers that threatened the republic." The *Nation*
reviewed it rather favorably when it appeared, but a year and a half
later—perhaps when the editors had had a chance to digest the
general hysteria—it published a scathing editorial called "Muckraking the Fathers." The Seattle high schools, no doubt partly in

response to the current local agitation over the IWW, took the trouble to ban the book outright.

There were other and divergent voices. O. G. Libby (who had helped clear the ground on which Beard built) and William E. Dodd gave it courageous reviews. What happened in the New York *Times* was curious. It did not get a review there at all for four months; then, on November 23, a week before the publication of the *Times* list of the "100 Best Books of the Year" (chosen by an independent group of critics), there was a fair and cordial review; the next week it was one of the list. Parrington has written about Beard's thesis, in the third volume of his *Main Currents,* that "the really surprising thing is that it should have come as a surprise." That would be true, if one could premise on the part of people a knowledge of what they ought to know if they were rational and sensible. Actually, given the way in which the book tore aside the veil of patriotism that clothed the role of big property in American history, the surprising thing is not that there was so much anguish when the book appeared, but that there was not more. That it was not unanimous testifies to the strength of the forces that had in the first instance brought the book to fruition.

What was maddening to those who raged against Beard was that he could not be ignored. Something a good deal like his thesis had appeared two years earlier (1911) in A. M. Simons's *Social Forces in American History* and a year earlier (1912) in Gustavus Myers's *History of the Supreme Court,* but they were Socialists and could be dismissed as such. The connection between corruption and Big Business, between political action and economic interest, had been shown in contemporary terms by Lincoln Steffens's *Shame of the Cities* and the writings of the other muckrakers, but they were, after all, muckrakers. Here was someone who was neither Socialist nor muckraker. He was American to the core, laden with degrees, drenched in teaching. Professor J. Allen Smith had published, in 1907, a strikingly original book—*The Spirit of American Government*—which opened up many leads that Beard followed. But where Smith was suggestive, Beard was thorough and systematic. What was galling about him was that he used all the paraphernalia of scientific method, which had been considered a monopoly of smugness and the *status quo.*

There is a tradition to the effect that he had started with the intention of doing a biography of Alexander Hamilton and, while quarrying among the musty archives in the basement of the Treasury that had not been touched for a century, he saw the more dramatic possibilities that these documents and the state financial records disclosed for a study of the political role of the holders of government paper. At any rate, the research he did was a real *tour de force;* it could put to shame on the level of sheer scholarship anyone who sought to challenge it from his Olympian heights. The technical flaws that could be picked were few and unconvincing. The citations, where they were not from primary statistical sources, came from the utterances of the Founding Fathers themselves, from the *Federalist Papers* (especially Madison's famous No. 10, whose importance in the theory of economic interpretation Beard was chiefly responsible for pointing out), from such writings as John Marshall's *Life of George Washington.*

What could you do with a man like that? You could not ignore him. You could only rage against his indecency, question his patriotism, accuse him of fomenting class hatred—and bide your time.

The time came, four years later. Beard had been watching the progress of the European war with enormous anxiety, alarmed at the submarine campaign, fearful of the danger of Prussianism to the world, making periodic statements to strengthen Wilson's hand in dealing with Germany. Then, on October 9, 1917, the front pages ran the story of his resignation from Columbia, immediately as a protest against the dismissal of Professors Cattell and Dana in the patriotic hysteria that followed our entrance into the war, but basically—as he explained in the *New Republic* of December 29, 1917—as a protest against business control of university educational policy and the "doctrinal inquisition" of himself and others on the faculty by the trustees. The letter to President Butler that accompanied his resignation is a classic of American university history:

The University is really under the control of a small and active group of trustees who have no standing in the world of education, who are reactionary and visionless in politics, and narrow and medieval in religion. . . . As I think of their [his colleagues'] scholarship . . . and compare them with a few obscure and willful trustees who now . . . terrorize the young instructors, I cannot repress my astonishment that America . . . has made the status of the professor lower than that of the manual laborer who, through his union, has at least some voice in the terms and conditions of his employment.

If his book on the Constitution was his *Theory of the Leisure Class,* this was his *Higher Learning in America.* His own attitude was patriotic enough, but in his generosity and his belief in freedom he could not tolerate the gagging of others, and in his "Olympian anger" he had to speak out. He had been hounded ever since the publication of his book by sometimes silly and sometimes vicious annoyances and pressures. But the climax was reached when President Butler failed to shield him from a stupid grilling by two of the trustees, Bangs and Coudert, about "teachings likely to inculcate disrespect for American institutions." The pay-off came in a *Times* editorial the day after his resignation was announced. It was called "Columbia's Deliverance," and was an answer at once to his resignation, his letter, and his book:

Columbia . . . is better for Professor Beard's resignation. Some years ago Professor Beard published a book in which he sought to show that the founders of this Republic and the authors of its Constitution were a ring of land speculators who bestowed upon the country a body of organic law drawn up chiefly in the interest of their own pockets. It was pointed out to him at the time, with due kindness but frankly, that his book was bad, that it was a book no professor should have written, since it was grossly unscientific. . . . It was the fruit of that school of thought and teaching . . . borrowed from Germany, which denies to man . . . the capacity of noble striving . . . that seeks always as the prompting motive either the animal desire to get more to eat or the hope of filling his pockets. If this sort of teaching were allowed to go on unchecked . . . we should presently find educated American youth applying the doctrine of economic determinism to everything from the Lord's Prayer to the binomial theorem. . . . If colleges are not to become breeding grounds of radicalism and socialism, it must be recognized that academic freedom has two sides, that freedom to teach is correlative to the freedom to dispense with poisonous teaching.

It had taken a long time, but American capitalism had finally published its review of Beard's book.

Beard is the only American historian since Turner whose historical method has been widely recognized as taking the shape of a "theory" or a "thesis." [2] This may be because he has always been more than a historian. He has always had one foot, and the firmer one, planted in political science—which may prove the meaninglessness of both labels or may prove Robert Lynd's contention (in his *Knowledge for What?*) that a historian is always a better historian when he is something else to start with. We see now that Beard's inquiry into the origins of the Constitution was only the first of a series of panels on the theme of the role of the economic in American culture. The second was *Economic Origins of Jeffersonian Democracy* (1915), a study of party beginnings which I hold the maturer and meatier book, one of the neglected American classics. The third was his theory (best found in *The Rise of American Civilization*, 1927) of the Civil War not as a struggle over the slavery doctrine but as "the second American Revolution" of the capitalists against the planter class; and, in sequel, the view of the Fourteenth Amendment as an ingenious "conspiracy" which was none the less the logical outcome of the war in insuring the ironclad protection of capitalist enterprise by the courts.

Such doctrine, quite apart from the initial shock it gave in 1913, could not help leaving a more continuing mark on American thought. It was for many a harsh awakening from a fake American Dream. The premise even of the muckrakers had been of an original Eden, and a fall from grace—to be remedied by the atonement of reform. But Beard laid bare the basic struggle between democracy and capitalism and traced it back to the origins of the American state. Eden had never been Eden. The triumph of the oligarchs that Beard's contemporaries were witnessing was thus not contrary to the spirit of 1789 but a logical culmination of it. And what was true of the origins of the government was true of later crises in its history. The slogans of the propertied groups took on for many people a new meaning. The Supreme Court issue was especially affected. For if it was true that the Constitution itself was the product of class interests, it would follow *a fortiori* that the same interests were operative in its interpretation. Then what became of the

---

2 For further discussion of Beard's theory of history, see the two essays on him that follow. Readers interested in following through the theme of historical theory in this book may wish to go from these essays to the essays on Veblen, Becker, Lynd, Lenin, and Pareto, in Parts II and III; and to "Materialism and History," "The Theory of the Social Process," and "The Supreme Court and American Capitalism," in Part IV.

divine right of judges and their Lucretian place above the mortal battle? Nor were the Socialists, despite Beard's protestations, slow to make their deductions. The book, writes Joseph Freeman in *An American Testament*, "was a byword among Socialist agitators who liked to quote established intellectual authorities. . . . [It] established beyond question the socialist contention that the United States was a class society whose fundamental laws are class laws for the benefit of the bankers and manufacturers as against the workers and farmers."

Beard has often disavowed this claim that his book proved the Socialist thesis. While I think he has underestimated the effect of Marxism on the climate of opinion from which he drew his doctrine, he has undoubtedly been accurate in distinguishing between Marxist thought and his own. He has traced his own intellectual genealogy back to Madison, Hamilton, Webster, Calhoun, and Emerson, and beyond them to Harrington and Aristotle (see his *Economic Basis of Politics* and his new introduction to the 1935 edition of the *Economic Interpretation* [3]). There has been, he contends, a tradition of economic emphasis in native American political thought. This is a healthy reminder for those who equate "economic" with "un-American." Under the stress of the attack on him, Beard has increasingly underlined this dissociation. And actually one may trace in his writing a decided attenuation of the economic interpretation of history—if one begins, for example, with his statement in his 1913 book that "until it [the theory of economic determinism] is tried out, it cannot be found wanting," then goes on to the explanation in his 1935 edition that he meant merely that the economic factor must be included among other factors in history, and ends with his treatise on method in history, *The Discussion of Human Affairs* (1936), in which he concludes that the whole problem is really very difficult and full of intangibles.

The fact is that Beard, like other social thinkers in his tradition, has never made up his mind on the central problem of the role of the economic in history. His book on the Constitution was the closest he came to a formulation. In some ways it was oversharp, in others not sharp enough. It was oversharp by making the economic interpretation a theory of men's motives rather than of men's ideas.

---

[3] For a discussion of this introduction, see the essay below, "Charles Beard Confronts Himself."

Spurred no doubt by a desire for definiteness and precision which is not to be found in the history of ideas and by a need to protect himself against the charge of vagueness, Beard cut out for himself too big a job—to show that the members of the Convention stood to gain in immediate and personal economic advantage by the outcome of their work. This was an unnecessary *tour de force* of research. It is as if, in seeking to explain the anti-New Deal rulings of the Supreme Court majority during the constitutional crisis of 1935–37, one were to seek to show that their own investments were at stake. What was relevant in a theory of economic conditioning was the relation between class and group interests on the one hand and ideas and behavior on the other. What was relevant was not the property *holdings* of the members of the Convention but their property *attitudes*. To be sure, their attitudes might be inferred from their holdings, but it was a roundabout procedure and one that laid Beard open to the charge of stressing the crass aspects of men's motivations. His enemies made the most of it.

Here a more Marxian approach, rather than a straight Madisonian one, would have been helpful. For on the plane of the history of ideas, the Marxian view stresses attitudes as outgrowths of interests; and the attitudes of a particular individual need in no sense be related to his sense of a direct economic interest. They may be only his borrowings from the prevalent climate of opinion, which in turn, but at a remove, rationalizes class interests. Had Beard taken such a view he would have been able to solve the basic dilemma in his book of being caught between a denial of the disinterestedness of the Founding Fathers and a denial of their patriotism and sense of national interest. Again and again Beard talks of the "wise" Fathers, yet most of his readers must have been puzzled as to how they could be selfish and "wise"at the same time—unless one premised a sort of enlightened selfishness such as may be found in Adam Smith's "economic man." One answer is that many of them felt, and could afford to feel, unselfish and patriotic; for there was no fault-line between their sense of class interest and the prosperity of the new nation. And when that prosperity came it ratified their wisdom whatever their intent, and made saints of them.

It is significant that when Beard published his sequel on Jeffersonian democracy, no comparable cry of anguish arose from the propertied groups and their spokesmen. He had moved away from the Fathers to the less sacred precincts of Jeffersonian politicians and theorists. And it is also significant that when Beard came to discuss the framing of the Fourteenth Amendment he should have seen in it, as Louis Boudin has recently pointed out, a "deep purpose" in the nature of a conspiracy. A theory of direct economic motivation leads quite naturally to a penchant for seeing conspiracies.

But these criticisms should not blind us to the importance and influence of the book. Its importance lay in the directness with which it cut through the whole tissue of liberal idealism and rhetoric to the economic realities in American history—and therefore in contemporary American life as well. Its influence is not to be measured by its sales, which, after the initial flurry on publication, dribbled along year after year until new interest was awakened by the New Deal constitutional crisis. Beard's book on the Constitution is one of those books that become a legend—which are more discussed than read and which are known more for their title than their analysis. But in a quarter-century its thesis has increasingly seeped into our history writing, although a recent study shows that most of the primary and secondary school textbooks either ignore it or mention it only for refutation. It is not hard to guess that this is because school supervisors are still fundamentalists.

1939

Charles Beard Confronts Himself

WHOEVER knows Charles Beard or has heard his lusty sallies against Hearst may resent my going back to a book of his written in 1913. Any attempt to place a man's past work in perspective is always a more or less elaborate process of embalming. And if there is any question of embalming, remember those flashing eyes of his, the kindly yet pointed wit; recall what Randolph Bourne once called Beard's "Olympian anger"; watch him in action at some Senate hearing on railroad reorganization or hear him talk about the regime of the drill-sergeant in Nazi Germany. I had meant to call his great book on the Constitution a classic, and the appearance of a new edition [4] (which has received all too little notice) gave me, I thought, both occasion and excuse for it. But to speak of a man's having written a classic may seem like saying of a French writer that he belongs in the Academy or of any writer that he has become a museum piece. So I shall say instead that Mr. Beard's book not only deals with history, but has made history. The new edition, with an immensely interesting introduction, comes with a sharp significance at a time of constitutional crisis even greater than when the first edition appeared.

The book was an inquiry into the economic interests and pressures behind the framing and ratification of the Constitution. It was a *tour de force* of historical research. Into it Mr. Beard distilled the debates of the Constitutional Convention, the musty and neglected Treasury records, the yellowed files of contemporary journals. He piled up massive evidence to show that the Constitution was an "economic document"; that it was supported by "substantially all the merchants, money lenders, security holders, manufacturers, shippers, capitalists, and financiers, and their professional associates," while on the other side were the non-slaveholding farmers and the debtors; and that the political doctrines which shaped the Constitution were themselves shaped by the economic interests of the Convention members. The very title of the book, thrust into the atmosphere of theology which covered the thinking of the day like a pall, showed that a new higher criticism had come into existence. For Mr. Beard dared defy all the myths and taboos of the historical scholarship of his day. He dared say that the Founding Fathers may have been businessmen as well as patriots and that the Constitution, instead of being of divine origin, had been born of the earthly travail of economic interest and economic conflict.

Naturally the book made a stir. A campaign had been on just the year before, and its effects were still felt. Theodore Roosevelt, who as President had thwacked the trusts with a resonance intended to impress the common people and, incidentally, his own sense of rectitude, had just been seeking as candidate to thwack the Supreme Court with similar intent. Mr. Taft, on the other hand, had been making speeches in which he averred that there would always be a special niche in heaven for judges. Although on a historical subject,

---

[4] *An Economic Interpretation of the Constitution of the United States.* With a new introduction. New York, Macmillan, 1935.

the book by the young Columbia professor of politics became of contemporary moment. Much of what supported the sanctity of the Supreme Court, at that time as today, was the sense of the sanctity of the Constitution. A shattering of constitutional mythologies might mean thus a shattering of judicial mythologies. The book caused a fluttering in the academic dovecotes. Albert Bushnell Hart called it a little short of indecent, and other scholars called it Marxian— which served the same purpose. Mr. Beard in his new introduction insists it was neither.

The introduction is of importance, because it brings the Charles Beard of today face to face with the Charles Beard of 1913. Mr. Beard confronts himself and tries to explain his stand on the theory of history. In the process he almost explains it away. He insists that his economic interpretation was not Marxian but Madisonian. There can be no quarrel with any label he may wish to choose. A number of thinkers from Aristotle to Bentley and Veblen had seen the power of economic interests in the province of government, and its most sensational expression in the American tradition was by James Madison in the famous passage in No. 10 of the *Federalist Papers*, where it was used to defend the system of checks in the Constitution. And yet, unless it be on purely tactical grounds in order to confound the professional patrioteers, I do not see the cogency of avoiding the Marxist stigma as if it were leprous. Let us say that the sources and impetus of Mr. Beard's thought were primarily in the American tradition. That does not prevent its import from being Marxian, especially since the economic interpretation is in Madison a set of brilliant *aperçus,* but in Marx an intellectual system.

What its place is in Mr. Beard's thinking is difficult to say with any definiteness. When his book was first published there was a tendency to regard it as the lustiest American blast for the economic interpretation of history. But Mr. Beard today evidently has a horror of being thought to dwell too exclusively on the economic aspect of history. "Since this aspect had been so long disregarded," he writes, "I sought to redress the balance by emphasis. . . . I simply sought to bring back into the mental picture of the Constitution those realistic features of economic conflict, stress, and strain which my masters had . . . left out of it, or thrust far into the background as incidental rather than fundamental." Mr. Beard seems to see his work, therefore, as part of a pendulum process in which an equilibrial correctness is achieved by going from excess to excess. He seems thus less in the tradition of the economic interpreters than in that of the "multiple-causation" school of American sociology, which sees history as the product of a vast variety of factors none having priority over the others.[5]

He does not, to be sure, travel the whole road in that direction. "In the great transformations in society," he writes in his introduction, "such as was brought about by the formation and adoption of the Constitution, economic 'forces' are primordial or fundamental, and come nearer 'explaining' events than any other 'forces.' " But surely the whole historical process is one of social transformation. Taken with any precision, Mr. Beard's statement would mean that he restricts the economic interpretation to revolutionary periods, and that for more normal periods he would switch to some "broader" interpretation.

All these twistings and turnings may be explained by Mr. Beard's desire to escape any form of determinism in history. He says repeatedly that the economic factor cannot explain history, that all of history cannot explain life. He has a horror of the history writing that was drenched with spiritual unction. In fact, I suspect that much of the reason why Mr. Beard and many of his generation were once attracted by the economic emphasis in history is that it gave them a sweet and secret iconoclastic sense. Like the village atheist, they got a kick out of destroying the theological and pseudo-spiritual myths.[6] Mr. Beard has, in the quarter-century that has elapsed, continued his economic emphasis, although with something of a diminuendo. More and more his economic interest, never strongly rooted in an economic philosophy of history, has become an interest in economic problems and economic policy, such as foreign trade. His basic philosophy has become, as perhaps it always

---

[5] For the multiple-causation school, see the essays in Part IV below on "Materialism and History" and "The Theory of the Social Process."

[6] Mr. Beard has several times since the publication of this essay objected strongly to my use of the phrase "village atheist" in this connection (see his "Historiography and the Constitution," in Conyers Read, ed., The Constitution Reconsidered, p. 159; also his review of Allan Nevins's Gateway to History in the Nation for Sept. 24, 1938, p. 300, and my reply in the Nation for Oct. 22, 1938, p. 436). Mr. Beard seems to lump me with those who object to his economic interpretation for its irreverence. My objection is rather to its lack of precision and discrimination.

was less explicitly, a philosophy of voluntarism and contingency. More and more he dwells upon the role that chance and human will play in fashioning history. More and more he admonishes us to "walk lightly," lest with our crude and unthinking tread we destroy the fragile web that history weaves. More and more he fashions a philosophy of the bewildering unexpectedness of the contingent.

I can agree with much of this. I can agree with Mr. Beard that the economic interpretation is broader than Marx, and that Americans have contributed to it. I can agree with him that no formula will "explain" history, any more than a formula will explain life. But having said this we must get on. I can agree with Mr. Beard that chance (*fortuna*, he calls it, after a formula which he borrows from Machiavelli) plays an appreciable role in human affairs, and that the human will (*virtù*) may within limits be powerful. But what are those limits? And how can the human will ascertain the unyielding trends of history (*necessità*) so as to work with them rather than to spend itself against them?

We do not want final explanations. What we want is an approach to the movement of history, a way of interpreting it. What we want above all else is an instrument of analysis. One asks not only how fundamental are the economic forces, but what dynamic is there that they use and that uses them in the processes of history? The Marxians have an answer—the materialist dialectic, the shifting technologies creating shifting class relations and class conflicts in such a way that each era and each social system, out of its own energies and tensions, fulfills itself and gives way to the next. It may be an incomplete answer, it may be too sweeping or dogmatic. That remains to be determined as serious attempts continue to be made to apply it to the task of historical interpretation. But it does give philosophic roots to the emphasis on economic factors. I fail to find in Mr. Beard's system of thought any relation between his economic emphasis and his basic philosophy. Instead, I find a curious sort of split which seems to have widened with time, and which serves to account for the earlier self.

Mr. Beard's plight, if it is one, is the more illuminating because he is one of the few progressive thinkers active today who span the entire period since the pre-War days. He has lived through the American imperialist venture, a world war, revolutions and threats of revolution, the terrible reality of fascism. He is thoroughly alive to the dangers that surround the human spirit—fearful lest amid the barbarities that encompass us it may be snuffed out. He represents, in short, the linking of past progressivism with present agonies. Out of the past progressivism comes his realistic economic strain; out of our present agonies comes his tortured plea, as he expressed it in his recent article in the *Nation* on the Constitution, to "walk lightly. Things are not so simple." [7] He is fearful lest our civil liberties and our entire social heritage be wiped out by hasty action whether with respect to the Supreme Court or the deeper problems of our economic organization. He knows the evils we suffer, but he is unwilling to fly from them to evils he knows not of. The only positive program he has linked his name with is one for American economic isolationism, as a way of avoiding the struggles for foreign markets and the complications of foreign wars. He wants to escape the tensions and contradictions of an era of corporate capitalism by a concentration on the home market and an admonition to walk lightly. Caught in the tangles not only of a world economy but of world-wide social forces that are convulsing every nation, he leaves us with a "Look homeward, Economic Angel."

We can learn a good deal from Charles Beard, from his courage, his amazing vitality, his luminous influence upon American history, his humanizing influence upon American scholarship—even from his mistakes. We can learn that people do not act—as, all too mechanically, he made the members of the Constitutional Convention act—from direct economic pressures and interests. For we know that the subtlest way in which class interests influence the course of history is through affecting the climate of opinion: often the people who are most enslaved to the going ideas are those who have no direct economic interest in the maintenance of them. We can learn from Charles Beard what the Marxians have thus far not taught us sufficiently but what Veblen did emphasize—a sense of the play of these conscious and subconscious psychological factors in retarding and even distorting the play of economic factors. But we must also learn that the economic interpretation of history cannot be merely a vague emphasis on economic factors. It must be part of a deeply rooted philosophy which makes room within the

---

7 "What about the Constitution?" (1936) 142 *Nation* 405–6.

framework of economic forces for chance, contingency, and human effort.[8]

1936

Midpassage—toward What?

"NEL mezzo del cammin di nostra vita" is the motto that Charles and Mary Beard prefix to their huge history of the last decade in America. "In the midpassage of our life": this hint from Dante of epic sweep and of reminiscence fraught with a sense of fatality is exactly the note to which the whole *Rise of American Civilization* has been keyed. The present volume,[9] the third in that already classic work, is a striking achievement in contemporary history. Yet whether they are writing of the distant past or of only yesterday the Beards always write impassioned prose in the grand manner. They may be dealing with the onward march of a triumphant capitalism in the midcentury or with the intellectual bankruptcy of the Lords of Creation under Herbert Hoover. They may be examining the economic forces behind the Jacksonian revolution or the economic implications of the New Deal program. But always they write with an unflagging magisterial air, and always they marshal their materials within a frame that keeps a sure tension between a detachment about the facts and a concern about the values of American life. Charles Beard's basic philosophy and method have been challenged time and again by some of the younger men. Yet as working craftsmen he and Mary Beard have no equals today in the field of American history, whether among old or young.

An analysis of that craftsmanship is no easy task, for Charles Beard's whole philosophy of history is elusive, his master theme of the dominance of the economic in the stream of history has been a shifting affair, his process of synthesizing the major forces in history is at once bold and subtle. Add the fact that the Beards have by now

---

[8] For an interesting attack on this essay, see Fred Rodell's comments on it in the course of his review of Beard's book, *Yale Law Journal*, vol. 45, p. 1327.

[9] *America in Midpassage.* Volume III of the *Rise of American Civilization*. New York, Macmillan, 1939.

developed a style which is as much their characteristic creation as that of Parkman, Gibbon, or John Fiske—a style that is a blend of Olympianism and the concrete, and that is complete even down to the mannerisms of a favorite vocabulary and a repetitive pattern of rhythm and sentence structure. The Beards have become literary artists without ceasing to be good historians, hence the impressive popularity of the *Rise of American Civilization*. Beside these volumes the "epics" of James Truslow Adams, which once had great popular vogue in the decade that this book covers, seem thin and amateurish. Here is no genteel tradition, no dilution of the strong stuff of history. Here are sweep, learning, depth, toughmindedness.

I could document this judgment at length, but the Beards do not need such praise. More important for historical scholarship in America are the problems of method and philosophy that the book raises. One set of problems relates to the technical premises on which the Beards' *Kulturgeschichte* rests. The second concerns the basic premises of their social analysis.

I call their work *Kulturgeschichte* because the authors have attempted to trace the whole moving stream of American culture through time. They recognize nothing as outside of their scope. Three-fifths of the present volume of close to a thousand pages is devoted to phases of American life beyond the political and the economic. To write this kind of history the historian today must equate the scope of his interests and the range of his talents with the whole bewildering variety of American life. He must be economist, politician, administrator, military- and foreign-affairs expert, geographer, educationist, sociologist, lawyer, scientist, literary and artistic critic; and he must finally be part of and yet detached from the ways in which the American masses spend what we call by a euphemism their income and their leisure. To do this well is the privilege of only a very few. Some must be excluded because they lack the gusto for it, others because they are not well enough rounded. To say that the Beards fall down at some points is therefore not a damaging criticism. What is amazing is not so much that they show some faults in their chapters on foreign policy, literature, and aesthetics, but that on the whole the competence of any authors should be so well sustained.

The weakness in the foreign-policy chapters is not one of *ex-*

pertise but one of perspective. Here is a problem that touches the
authors so deeply that the advocate elbows out the narrator and
critic. The chapters on the New Deal foreign policy are only brilliant pamphleteering. It is interesting, for example, to compare the
way the authors handle the debate over radio control and the debate
over foreign policy. Their discussion of the first ends with a set of
questions. Their discussions of the second consists to a great extent
of a series of affirmations. The reason is probably that the Beards
have no particular emotions and no finality of belief on radio control, while in foreign policy they are vigorous isolationists, and
every effort toward historical detachment melts away under the
fierce fire of their indignation.

With respect to the literary and artistic history of the period,
the problem is a different one. I am not sure that the Beards have
decided here whether the function of the historian is to be that of
chronicler or critic. The result is that they are sometimes one and
sometimes the other. I assume that there is a difference between
literary history and literary criticism. Literary history as part of
cultural history is concerned with popular themes and tastes, with
fashions in ideas, with formative literary movements and their relation to the culture as a whole. Literary criticism is concerned
with aesthetic and social values. In dealing with the movies as entertainment and as molders of the mass mind the Beards do a stun-
ning historian's job. But in dealing with the "ranges" of literature
during the period they fall on the one hand to cataloguing and read
at times like a digest of weekly book reviews, and on the other hand,
when they make sorties as literary critics, they are not always felici-
tous. I doubt whether Kay Boyle's *My Next Bride,* for example,
deserves three pages whether as literary art or social documentation
as compared with a short paragraph for William Faulkner; or
whether if one poet only were to be quoted in addition to Edna
Millay, Archibald MacLeish, and Carl Sandburg, it should be
Phyllis McGinley. The chapters on literature, aesthetics, and science
lack the sense of authority which, for example, the chapter on social
thought possesses.

All these "cultural" chapters, moreover, suffer by being segregated from the rest of the book and thus abstracted from the current of events. For example, if the brilliant chapter on "Frames of
Social Thought" had been worked into the account of the develop-

ment of the New Deal, it might have been given an added significance. There would thus have been that mutuality of relation—what Engels calls *Wechselwirkung*—between the economic and ideologic which would illumine each. Perhaps I am setting up an unattainable objective. But, sliced as it is into cultural segments, the book tends to fall apart, somewhat after the manner of a symposium, except that this is a symposium written wholly by the same hands. There still remains for us the problem of narrating cultural history so as to present the whole moving stream of it.

I turn finally to the implications for social thought of what the Beards might call their "overarching conception" as expressed in the title. Many times in the book a phrase like "in the strange times of the midpassage" occurs. Clearly the Beards are trying to give the recent decade of American life a definite stamp of a transition period. But "midpassage" can mean nothing unless we know to what. The present volume ends on a gallant note, with a chapter on "Reconsideration of Democracy" whose thesis is that the best currents of American life have always moved toward a "humanist democracy" and that the New Deal must be seen as a reassertion of those same impulses. But unless this chapter be set down as mainly in the nature of peroration, a final flight into the hortatory realm after the grime and muck of actual history, it is fair to ask whether the rest of the book bears it out. If the economic rulers of America are as morally bankrupt and politically blind as the Beards convincingly make them out to be, if the New Dealers are as blundering and militaristic, labor as uncohesive, the Marxists as dunderheaded, and the middle class as capitalist-minded, then how shall we ever achieve a humanist future? One does not demand of historians that they chart the path toward the future, but one may well ask those whose whole concept is that of "midpassage" by what favoring winds and through whose oar-power and seamanship they hope to reach the fair haven.

To speak of midpassage given the present strong undertow of reactionary opinion in America would be but a grim sort of jest, unless one were to seek to discover the potentials of a democratic renaissance. But it is hard to find them in this book in any convincing form. There is no analysis of the economic imperatives that would lead to democratic survival within a planned economy, and no indications of how the New Deal economic effort can be salvaged, short of planning. There are no world movements that can offer hope, if the Beards' contention be true that America's destiny is solitary. What analysis there is of class contours, chiefly in the chapter on labor, shows labor and agriculture and the middle class at swords' points, with the middle-class mentality as the one dominant force. There are some fine notes of affirmation, as in the discussion of the TVA, the Federal Theater venture, and the CIO leadership, but they are isolated and unconnected. The very qualities which give the book its distinction—a prevailing judiciousness of tone, a tentativeness of judgment, a fine balancing of opposed forces —are the qualities that make it unlikely that the authors will uncover in the last decade those energies of idea, of economic thrust, of class, of social movement, out of which the American future must be forged. I say "must" and should add: if it is to be tough enough to survive and humanist enough to be worth survival.

Lacking this firmness of analysis, there is a danger that the "midpassage" concept will be for the American historian what the "social process" concept has been for the American sociologist—a way of indicating motion and change without indicating its quality or direction. Lacking it, this brilliant book remains, for all its talent, truncated—an ironically expressive monument to a decade that presumably has not known where it is going or how it will get there.

1939

13

John Reed: No Legend

O NE of the best ways to damn a man, if you cannot ignore him
or vilify him outright, is to build a legend around him.
That makes him a hazy and unreal figure and takes the edge
off whatever sharp meaning his life might otherwise have. John
Reed was a dangerous man. His life traced a pattern which, if it
were followed by other middle-class lives, would burst the bounds
of our entire present social system. And so those who have feared
him, unable to fight his influence in any other way, have welcomed
the chance to make him incredible. They have called him wild,
irresponsible, reckless; dubbed him—and the name has stuck—a
playboy; underscored his pranks and amours; mocked the bewildering succession of his plans and projects; damned him not with
faint but with exaggerated praise for his versatility, so that the
versatile passed by innuendo into the superficial; marveled at his
all-seeing reporter's eye, the implication being that what was all
eye could scarcely be much brain; endowed him with seven-league
boots for bestriding all the roads and oceans of the world; conde-
scended to his Faustian thirst for life. Thus they have made of him
an unreal mythical figure instead of a lusty life-sized man. Walter
Lippmann set the pattern as early as 1914, four years after they were
both out of college, in his article on "Legendary John Reed," and
Reed's enemies have followed the pattern, as his friends have often
stumbled into it.

Granville Hicks has now written a biography of Reed [1] which has,
among many merits, that of making him credible. It required restraint to do this, for the legend is deeply rooted, and Reed's life
was indeed fertile soil for such a growth. An Oregon boy of good
family and considerable means, one of the possessors of the earth,

---

[1] *John Reed: The Making of a Revolutionary.* New York, Macmillan, 1936.

educated at the fashionable private schools and at Harvard—such
a boy becomes a rough-and-tumble war correspondent, labor journalist, radical poet, war resister; and after witnessing and describing
the "ten days that shook the world" in the October revolution, he
stands trial for sedition in America, helps organize an underground
American revolutionary party, and finally at thirty-three dies of
typhus in Moscow and is buried with honors in the Kremlin.

What made it an important as well as an exciting life? Not merely
Reed's unquenchable desire for experience. Through all its apparent gyrations it had order, sequence, an inner logic. Actually it
was one of the most deadly serious attempts ever made by an American to organize his experience into something that had meaning
and stature. If Reed's story is seen that way—the story of a middle-
class boy and of how he is educated by events, how he is led by an
unswerving instinct to break with his class and his past, how he
explores every channel of rebellion and innovation until finally he
throws his lot in with a workers' collectivism—it takes on a meaning that places it high in the history of the American consciousness.

Reed had to an enormous degree a life-affirming quality. He was
a long time in discovering it, as he was in finding himself at all.
He had first to pass through the phase of negative rebellions against
the culture around him. Then came a period of crisis and uncertainty, precipitated by the war. And finally, in his last and revolutionary phase, came a sense of peace and discipline. But throughout
his life the pattern that we may trace is the growing affirmation of
joyous, human values. Prodigal in his own talents and resources and
prodigal in spending himself, he felt stifled in a world where the
sort of freedom and experience he wanted was not accessible to all.

It was probably at Harvard, at once the citadel of social orthodoxy
and the breeding-ground of intellectual dissenters, that Reed first
became restlessly aware of the cleavage which it would take the rest
of his life to heal. And yet he left college essentially unscarred,
and his cattle-boat trip to Europe, his adventures in Paris and Spain
brought him back to New York determined to make a million and
get married. His discovery of New York was what every Western
boy and every Harvard poet have re-enacted—the warm polyglot
life of the city, the sweet sense of personal freedom, the reckless
spending of oneself in its pursuit. But he discovered also social
misery and oppression, and his energies took the form of an in-

creasingly bitter indictment of middle-class culture because it stifled life. It was this that led him inevitably to break with the successful New York literary groups, join the staff of the *Masses,* turn with sympathy to the Mexican peons whom he learned to know as a war correspondent. But the more nomadically he wandered about the world, the more restlessly he explored the possibilities of love and adventure, the more doubtful his solutions and successes seemed to him.

Contact with the labor movement was not enough. He was still, even as master of ceremonies at the Paterson pageant in Madison Square Garden, essentially the John Reed who was cheer-leader at Harvard the year when Hamilton Fish was captain of the football team. He had got a sense of the possibilities of the common man from his experiences with Villa's *jacquerie.* He had been labor journalist as well as war correspondent, and the Ludlow massacre had left its mark on him. But it was not enough. The American entrance into war found him troubled, indecisive, discouraged— world-weary at twenty-nine.

To a considerable extent the Russian Revolution resolved his personal crisis. What had been troubling him was that, despite his clear recognition that capitalist culture was life-denying rather than life-affirming, he could not get any conviction that the workers were any better or different. He ate his heart out at their lack of courage and spirit, at the docility with which they allowed themselves in every country to be herded into the war-pens and butchered there, at the bewildered way in which they accepted conscription in America, at their fear of finding out how hard a policeman's club could really hit. But in Russia he found that it was the workers and the soldiers and the peasants who stood fast in the great emergencies of those ten days and who won the revolution.

Thus through all his wanderings and explorations Reed was led, by some hard and uncanny inner sense, to discover truths and solutions that remained hidden from wiser minds than his, such as Lincoln Steffens's, and from subtler minds, such as Walter Lippmann's. He often got the right answers on the basis of the wrong reasons. Part of his genius lay in his being so terribly unfooled. "This is not our war," he kept saying, when everyone else was getting lost in a maze of sophistry and propaganda. He was no thinker but a man of action. But it was his good fortune to be led to the

most desirable of all fates for a man of action who is also a writer
and a poet—the chance at once to write history and to make it.

It is this emphasis on freedom and action and joyousness—almost
this obsession of Reed's with them—that gives his life its importance for us and makes the incidents of it credible. Reed died thinking he had found in communism a solution not only for himself
but for the workers and the creative everywhere. How deep his
communism was is a question that is difficult to answer. He probably understood communism only as he understood everything else
—as a verifiable part of his own experience. Whether he would have
stayed with communism is an even more difficult question. Could
his restless spirit have disciplined itself to withstand the weariness
and the bitter disappointments of the years that have elapsed since
his death? That question need not be answered. His experience
went deeper than communism. It raised, without answering in
any final way, the basic question of how to secure the generous
and expansive values of life for all men—a problem in solving
which communism may prove, as individualism has proved, a historical episode.

John Reed was a great journalist and, when he could be genuinely
a part of all that he met, a first-rate writer. Already he has become
for the thinking minority of our young people in and out of the
colleges the most evocative figure we have produced—terribly close
to them, moved by their impulsions, confronted by their dilemmas.
Mr. Hicks's book should get the Pulitzer prize for biography; for
its theme and for the moving yet scholarly and restrained way in
which it is handled, for the mastery with which the author shows
Reed coming to maturity amid the attractions and tensions of life
in a bewildering era. It should get the prize, but it will not. That,
too, is part of John Reed's story.

1936

14

The Liberalism of O. G. Villard

M R. VILLARD'S book of memoirs,[1] compact of militancy, indignation, and an underlying sense of failure, lights up a whole period in the history of American liberalism. It does not to the same degree delineate a personality. There is little in it of the interior writing that has marked the creative tradition in modern autobiography, from Rousseau to Henry Adams and Lincoln Steffens. The category it falls into is "this I remember and this I did," rather than "this is how I shaped my view of life." Despite the warm chapters on the author's childhood years, on his Harvard days, on his early experiences as a reporter in Philadelphia, there is a poverty in the book of education in its deepest sense. Mr. Villard is not interested in the painful and experimental unfolding of a personality. The focus is always on an impassioned view of the external rather than on a detached view of the internal world. The crowded pages form a portrait gallery of public figures whose lives impinged on that of the writer—Presidents, Prime Ministers, Cabinet officials, generals, journalists, reformers, adventurers. But while Steffens's first question about a man was always: "How can I learn from him what makes the world tick?" Villard's was always: "How far do his ideals conform with mine, and how can I influence his action?" While Steffens, like Henry Adams before him, was primarily interested in the search for truth and saw life as an unending quest, Mr. Villard is primarily interested in the propagation of truth and sees life as an unending battle.

There are three things about the book that will give it interest for many readers. One is its magnificently concrete sense of incident and personality. Mr. Villard has the quick eye of the journalist for the telling detail: there are few complete portraits in the book,

---

[1] *Fighting Years: Memoirs of a Liberal Editor*. New York, Harcourt, Brace, 1939.

but there are few men mentioned to the outlines of whose personality Mr. Villard does not add a specific touch from first-hand acquaintance; and there are many amusing incidents in what is nevertheless an essentially humorless book.

The second is the journalist's frankness and iconoclasm in dealing with prominent public figures. President McKinley was "dishonest." General Leonard Wood was "blindly ambitious," mixed up in shady deals, and "were he living today he would be the ideal fascist leader." All the Roosevelts have had a "propensity for not telling the truth when it served their purposes," but T.R. was, according to Villard, a liar and a craven many times over; despite T.R.'s denial that he had solicited funds from Wall Street for his 1904 campaign against Parker, Villard quotes conversations with two Wall Street men, one of them Henry C. Frick, asserting flatly that T.R. in a panic about his campaign had sent for Frick, Harriman, Twombly, Lamont, and others to come to the White House, and asked and got from them a quarter of a million dollars in return for a promise to leave Big Business alone in his second term. "He got down on his knees to us," Frick told Villard; "we bought the son of a bitch and then he did not stay bought." Charles E. Hughes was "narrow, obstinate, and opinionated." Taft was "extremely lazy and a great procrastinator." "Fighting Bob" La Follette, like Senator Norris, is praised for his anti-war stand, but his great 1912 speech on monopoly—one of the classics in the movement against the power of concentrated wealth—is dismissed with the explanation that its long, rambling, and vituperative character was due to the speaker's "being under the influence of liquor." Wilson comes in for an extra measure of condemnation. His sharp shift from a conservative New Jersey Governor to a radical candidate for President already augured his later treachery about war and peace; his career was a "long series of broken friendships"; "he was inordinately wrapped up in himself and his future"; he was "extremely penurious"; he was narrow and cowardly on the Negro problem, weak and deceitful about the war issue, caught up in the war madness, unwilling to lift a finger to restrain the suppressions of freedom of press and the cruelties inflicted on conscientious objectors, invariably ungrateful, inexplicably rude, crassly opportunist.

The third appeal of the book lies in its giving a historical framework for pacifist liberalism today. Mr. Villard speaks early in the book of the passion that led his grandfather, William Lloyd Garrison, to close his mind to every other consideration where the question of Negro freedom was involved. Mr. Villard devotes the same obsessive energy to the World War and the peace that followed it. Increasingly it has come to occupy the center of his thinking, to organize his memories of the past and his perspective of the present. His most memorable experiences were those of a leader of the opposition to America's entrance into the war. As a result, he was ostracized by his own social group, was hounded by mobs, and came close to being tarred and feathered in Cincinnati. That sort of experience is not easily forgotten, and Mr. Villard has not forgotten it. His most stirring chapters are on Paris during the Peace Conference and on Munich and Berlin during the days of armistice, revolution, assassinations. The emphasis throughout is on the blundering entrance into war, the dictated peace, the blind ruthlessness of the Allied diplomats and their outmaneuvering of Wilson, their refusal to recognize that they were sowing the seeds of revolution and reaction in Central Europe.

It is here that his meaning for the history of American liberalism lies. His best fighting years were the years of fighting against an imperialist war and a Carthaginian peace. He reached the height of his powers between 1914 and 1920, the beginning of the war and the end of the peace, during his last years on the *Post* and his first on the *Nation*. This was liberalism's Heartbreak House. In it Villard could vent his bitter indignation at the insolence of office, the pride and treachery of power, the tyranny of the unthinking mob. This lashing indignation reached thousands of homes, and brought with it a comforting sense of the community of the little band of high-minded in the desert of American life.

But however well Mr. Villard may have summed up the frustrate energies of pacifist liberalism, its philosophy was a woefully inadequate weapon with which to confront a ruthless and planless corporate capitalism. No clear outlines can be found in the entire book of a conception of social causation, a theory of history, a program of action. His notions about society have neither body nor precision. His career spans the period from the 1890's to the present, more than forty years of the mightiest industrial concentration and the sharpest social clash in our history. Yet one searches the book in vain for evidences of an understanding of the class interests and tensions that were changing the face of America. This may account for the feeling the reader gets of being in contact with an instrument, a lens that makes some outlines terribly sharp and leaves others distressingly fuzzy. The sharpness proceeds from the journalist's eye, the concentrated passion of a reformer who was not content to rest on his inherited wealth but made out of his life one long cry of indignation at man's inhumanity to man. The fuzziness lies in the vaguely moral approach to politics and economics, the uncritical acceptance of a set of liberal doctrines that were as little based on logic as the reactionary doctrines of the day. It lies above all else in the blurring that occurs when an absolutist dream impinges upon the area of social possibility.

Mr. Villard's name has been widely linked with "liberalism," and his book abounds in vague identifications of himself and his group with the liberal movement of the day. One feels almost as if liberalism had been handed down to him as a family heirloom. In a sense, of course, it had. His mother was the daughter of William Lloyd Garrison. His father, Henry Villard, had brought with him to America the aspirations of the German libertarian movement of the 1840's. He was an admirer and follower of Edward L. Godkin, who had founded the *Nation* and become editor of the New York *Post,* both of which Henry Villard bought and merged. Godkin used to complain of the dearth of good writers in America; and Villard, visiting London in 1918, looked enviously at the roster of great writing names that H. W. Nevinson had gathered around him on the *Nation* at London. He sets down Nevinson's abundance to the British university system. But that is a surface explanation. Actually English liberalism was more homogeneous than the American; it was concentrated in the intellectual Fabian-Liberal-Labor circles in London. But it would be dangerous to get the impression that the New York Mugwumps and the Cambridge Brahmins had a monopoly of American liberalism in Godkin's day. There were other liberal strains, if only an important journal had found it worth while to quarry for them. From Henry Demarest Lloyd and Edward Bellamy to Bob La Follette, from Thorstein Veblen to Charles Beard, there were rich and strong currents in American liberal thought in the quarter-century before the World War. But they passed by Godkin and Charles Eliot Norton and Paul Elmer More marooned on the *Nation*.

This is important if we wish an insight into Mr. Villard's liberal mentality. For all the changes that he made on the *Nation* after he took it over in 1918, the liberal tradition he himself followed was still mainly that of Godkin. Other brands found their way in, through some of the brilliant young editors whom he gathered around himself from 1918 to 1933 and who helped so largely to make the *Nation* the progressive force it has become. But Mr. Villard himself has never shown a strong curiosity about the creative strains in American progressive and radical thought, and his book shows no traces of it.

There is a brilliant analysis of Godkin's outlook in the third volume of Parrington's *Main Currents in American Thought*. He was at heart an aristocrat who devoted his life to a vision of a democracy led by a cultured élite. He took the already frayed garment of Manchesterian liberalism and threw it around his shoulders when he went forth to battle the elements of American political and economic life in the Machine Age. His political creed was honesty in government and his basic political assumption was that no governing group could be honest. He was horrified at the new surging forces of American life—at the crude strength of the labor movement and the sense of awakened power in the financiers. His ignorance of economic theory did not prevent him from making the most magisterial declarations in his editorial columns upon economic policy (Mr. Villard calls him "the greatest editorial writer the American press has ever produced"). His creed was a free market, free trade, sound money and a Civil Service, and he clung to them the more desperately as they became ever more futile amidst the wrack of his world. "His later comments," Parrington writes, "tended to become ever thinner and shriller—not criticism at all, but the sharp expression of aging prejudice."

This is the tradition in which Mr. Villard was steeped and which he inherited. I have had the experience, during random hours of browsing through old volumes of the *Nation,* of coming upon editorial leaders in the margin of which was penciled "E.L.G." and of recognizing with a start the ring of familiarity that linked them with some current page of "Issues and Men" that I had been read-

ing only a few hours before. In several respects Villard has modified
the Godkin tradition. His fight for Negro rights was already implicit in Godkin's first editorial statement in the *Nation* of July 6,
1865, yet it has been waged with a courage and an explicitness that
have made it one of Villard's great crusades. His fight for the
economic, political, and sexual emancipation of women would have
horrified Godkin. He has been far more sympathetic to trade unionism, yet his readers will remember the way in which he joined the
outcry against labor "violence" during the organization of the CIO,
and helped to lay the foundations for the present campaign against
the Wagner Act. He has been sympathetic, where Godkin never
was, to the less drastic forms of governmental economic control, yet
his readers will remember that the New Deal has not found in him
one of the stanch supporters of its major reforms. He has been
vigorously anti-imperialist and anti-militarist, and has always spoken
out against oppression. Yet all these have tended to modify the
tradition rather than transform it.

He has not sought to transform it, I suspect, because like the
other liberals of his brand he has been unwilling to face the consequences of victory for a transformation of the economic structure.
The most significant thing about Mr. Villard's book of memoirs is its omission of almost every strong movement, whether political or intellectual, toward genuine economic reform during the
"fighting years" that it covers. The emphasis is always either upon
foreign policy or upon the marginal movements for civil liberties
or women's suffrage. Trade unionism, farm revolt, muckraking,
trust-busting, the researches of Beard into constitutional origins,
of Brandeis into financial concentration, of Veblen into the nature
of business enterprise—all are conspicuously absent. There was a
phase of T.R. that was not just histrionics and evasions—something
called the "New Nationalism" that did much to educate people to
the need for federal economic control. There was a phase of Wilson
that was not the betrayal of pacifism—something called the "New
Freedom" that left a genuine deposit of economic reform. There is
a phase of F.D.R. that is not just war-mongering—something called
the "New Deal" that has put America today in the forefront of
progressive governments. It is significant that while half the book
is devoted to Wilson's dallyings and adventures with war and peace,
three paragraphs dispose of the domestic achievements of his first

administration. It is even more significant that Mr. Villard has almost nothing affirmative to say of the three recent reform Presidents —Wilson and the two Roosevelts—without whose concrete achievements the liberal slogans in America would today be far emptier and the prospects of democracy far bleaker than they are.

I suspect that at the root of Mr. Villard's hatred of the reform Presidents there is the absolutism of the crusader for lost causes. The New Dealers and their labor allies have been taunted for their "neo-liberalism," and Mr. Villard has many times expressed indignation at their betrayal of the liberal tradition. Thurman Arnold has countered in his *Folklore of Capitalism* by gibing at the professional liberals who would rather lose and cling to their "ideals" than win by adapting them to a real world.

The sickness of paleo-liberalism goes deep. It seems to contain a fatality for failure. Mr. Villard, for example, has a sort of obsession with lost causes. It is significant that he has never been on the side of radical economic reform except when it has represented a lost cause. He is the great apostle of the "protest vote," having been for Debs in 1916 and for Norman Thomas in 1936. He was for Wilson until it looked as if he meant business in his fight with Wall Street; then he adopted Thomas Lamont's viewpoint of the unreasonableness of Wilson's attitude toward the House of Morgan. He was for F.D.R. until it turned out that he meant business with the New Deal and the political mobilization of labor and the reform of the Supreme Court; now he is writing in Frank E. Gannett's magazine, *America's Future,* along with those other liberals, Gannett and Amos Pinchot, and that Indiana statesman, ex-Representative Pettengill. I do not say that he shares their economic and social outlook. Most of what he shares is their bitterness against Mr. Roosevelt. He does not direct that bitterness point-blank at his economic and political program. He clothes it in the indignation of the pacifist with Mr. Roosevelt's militant foreign policy, in an austere Plutarchian view of what he considers Mr. Roosevelt's ambition, mendacity, treachery. But while he approaches the anti-Roosevelt encampment by a different entrance from the anti-New Deal and isolationist reactionaries, he comes out at the same door.

Ideas are weapons, but the ideas that Mr. Villard's liberalism marshals have long since lost their cutting edge in the struggle against the real enemies of a humane American civilization. The Godkin tradition of liberalism began with the aloofness of an élite that considered the actual fight for power beneath its dignity, and its alienation from power has been so enduring that it has ended in an incapacity to envisage the implications, consequences, and responsibilities of power. That is why it has always been a minority movement and has turned away in horror from the give-and-take of majority politics. That is why, for all its rhetoric and indignation, it has been in actual practice a passive liberalism. That is why Mr. Villard, cut off from the mass movements that make history, has been forced back on what Charles H. Cooley once called the "illusion of centrality." That is why his book never deals with the problems of class structure, economic planning, economic realignment, the struggle against reaction. That is why his comments on politics are personal, marginal, obsessive.

Mr. Villard has fought the good fight according to his own best lights. But the liberalism to which his fighting years have been devoted is an inadequate weapon. Pacifism and passivism are not enough.

1939

15

Walter Lippmann

Lippmann Agonistes

"THE GOOD SOCIETY"[1] marks Walter Lippmann's renunciation of the earlier Lippmann and his consolidation of the latter-day Lippmann. It marks also his renunciation of the latter-day liberalism and his plea for a return to the earlier liberalism of the Western world. There are thus a pair of dialectical processes at work in the book simultaneously. The author is fighting the new order and arguing for the Golden Age of the old order; but he is also and at the same time arguing against the premises of the younger Lippmann and making explicit a new set of premises for the older Lippmann. It is no accident that the book bears on its title-page a text from Milton's "Samson Agonistes." Where could one find a better prototype than in Samson the Wrestler for the man of godlike strength who has known happier days, who now finds himself in the philistine world of collectivist principles, and who out of an inner clarity of sight finds the strength for a last and mighty single-handed effort to tear down the pillars of the totalitarian temple? The whole mood of the book is that of the Hebrew prophets. It begins with a devastating attack upon the collectivisms of the day as the Sodom and Gomorrah that have brought mankind to its present pass. It continues with a passionate defense of the older liberalism ("If I forget thee, O Jerusalem . . ."). And it ends in an apocalyptic vision of a future society in which men are once more free.

At forty-eight Mr. Lippmann has behind him a quarter-century crowded with writing and political activity. He divides his career into three parts: the years before the Great War, when he assumed "that in a regime of personal liberty each nation could, by the in-

---

[1] *The Good Society*. Boston, Little, Brown, 1937.

creasing exercise of popular sovereignty, create for itself gradually a spaciously planned and intelligently directed social order"; the years of "blundering improvisations" of "a rather bewildered man" that followed the war; and the present period, in which the direction that the collectivist movements have taken has forced him to re-examine what he believes and state it, as he does in this book, with finality.

A man should be allowed his own autobiographical schema, and I shall not quarrel with Mr. Lippmann's. But to think and to say that one has achieved a final clarity is not the same as to have achieved it. Mr. Lippmann clothes incredibly naïve statements with a magisterial solemnity; he takes the platitudes of individualist capitalism and dresses them up in fine verbal raiment until they almost look like something else. A mind moving toward maturity must learn to make distinctions before it makes syntheses; it must learn to discriminate before it condemns, and to be realistic before it affirms. Yet Lippmann has in the course of his writings extended the sphere of his aversions and antipathies until he labels everything he does not like as "totalitarian." He has stripped himself of most of what he once knew about the fatal lesions and contradictions of *laissez-faire* capitalism, until he has now come to equate it with the eternal values of human freedom. The intellectual world in which this book moves is arid, mechanical, and in a final sense reactionary.

Lippmann's basic premise is that no human being or group of human beings can know or grasp their social world—the Great Society. He finds the thought of the complexity of government today overwhelming. And in his recoil from the coercions of political power that he sees around him he flees to the Nirvana of political inaction. His remedy for the social chaos which the regime of individualist capitalism and the free market have brought in their wake is a homeopathic one—more of the same thing. Like the Manchester Liberals to whom he looks back with an eloquent nostalgia, he has a horror of governmental power, and a belief in a "higher law" and some mystical guiding hand that will bring order out of chaos. When Lippmann seeks to translate the Great Society into the Good Society, his basic program is to make all governmental power judicial power; even legislators would be essentially judges, and litigation would become the normal mechanism of government. Carlyle had a term for such government when it was advocated by the Manchesterians. He called it "anarchy plus a constable."

There are two antiphonal strains in the book. One is the dissection of collectivism; the second is the defense of liberalism. Mr. Lippmann manages to bungle both jobs woefully. In the first one he is never quite certain whether he is talking of dictatorship, economic planning, or the various partial forms of government intervention in the economic process. To attack political dictatorship is one thing; to attack a planned economy quite another; to link the two explicitly is a writer's privilege, if he can defend his thesis; and to bring every form of government control of industry into the same picture would be to fashion a political theorist's nightmare. But when Mr. Lippmann shuttles back and forth from one type of collectivism to another, treating them all as qualitatively alike and attributing—by implication—fascist brutality and militarism to the U.S.S.R. and the scope of Soviet economic planning to the mild measures of the New Deal, one can only gasp at the shambles of undistributed middles.

What Mr. Lippmann is in effect doing, whether he knows it or not, is to brand with the fascist stigma every attempt of mankind to carve out a good society for itself by conscious social action. By presenting as the only alternatives a totalitarian dictatorship on the one hand and an individualist capitalism on the other, he consigns the future of mankind to the terribly weak props of a *laissez-faire* economy. Since those props are certain to collapse, the final prospect we are confronted with is fascism. Actually, man's fate lies with a whole variety of socialisms and partial collectivisms that are yet unexplored.

It is in the second of his antiphonal strains, his discussion of liberalism, that Lippmann is weakest. He regards all of human history as a preparation for the century between Adam Smith's *Wealth of Nations* (1776) and the British social-welfare legislation beginning in the 1870's. Before Smith wrote, mercantilism exercised a tyranny over men. After 1870 a new form of mercantilism reasserted its tyranny. The century between becomes thus an all too brief interval of liberal light between two darknesses. The world presumably took the wrong turn in 1870 and has been going in the

wrong direction ever since. Mr. Lippmann offers no explanation of
the wrong turn. If he were not writing a tirade against Marxism,
he might have seen that the century he speaks of was the century of
an expanding industrial capitalism in England, when England became the center of the world market and the distributing point of
goods to countries with inferior industrialisms. When the other
countries developed their own industrial technique, the world
market began to break down; and meanwhile English capitalism,
entering a contracting phase, had to be bolstered and regulated by
state action. The social-service state succeeded the *laissez-faire* state,
and Mill's partial socialism succeeded Ricardo's individualism.

It should be noted that Mr. Lippmann is not against social control as such. The "good society" he depicts is riddled with social
controls and cluttered with legal controls through litigation; all
that it lacks is governmental control in the economic sphere. I can
only assume that Mr. Lippmann, in his proposal for stripping away
all governmental controls except those of the common law, is writing with a naïve innocence of legal history. Otherwise he would
know that what he proposes is exactly what has been tried and has
failed. The history of the common law is the tragic record of the
attempt to build a system of economic order in an industrial society
on a system of legal procedure meant to catch petty thieves and dishonest hucksters in a pre-capitalist economy. It was because the jury
and the writs and the injunctions were a complete failure that we
have had to build up our complex body of administrative law.

The author pleads his case, let it be added, with integrity. I do
not subscribe to the theory, held by some of my contemporaries,
that Walter Lippmann has "sold out." It is a foolish theory, unless
it is used in so unconscious a sense as to be stripped of meaning.
Lippmann has not had to sell out. He has been able to adhere to
the ideals of his liberalism and the idols of the marketplace at the
same time, for the two are good companions. The compass of his
thinking has swung round under the pressure of events from the
liberalism of the left to the liberalism of the right; the catchwords
have remained the same, but the content is the opposite of what
it was.

Mr. Lippmann is a rich man; his friends are the possessors of
the earth; he is their prophet. What obscure psychological bolster-

ing he finds in them it is beyond my competence to guess; they find in him, as the possessors of the earth have for centuries found in the liberalism of the right, a rationalization of their economic claims and their political fears. Mr. Lippmann's brand of liberalism is the intellectual garment of capitalist power; it is the liberalism of the Supreme Court majorities, of the businessmen who call for a determined but muted predacity, of the professors and editors and lawyers who want at the same time to preserve the *status quo* and their self-respect. It is not the dishonest intellectuals who are the best servants of bankers and industrialists today. It is those who cling with the fiercest sincerity to a body of principles that represent the death's-head of capitalist power dressed up in its Sunday best.[2]

1937

Lippmann and the Supreme Court

FOR two weeks I have followed anxiously the serialized account of Walter Lippmann's hopes and fears for the Constitution.[3] I had two motives for my religious pursuit. Here, I felt, in these flowers plucked from Mr. Lippmann's corner of the *Herald Tribune's* crannied wall, I should get at the secret of his whole universe. And here too I should find summed up the mature thinking of conservatives on the constitutional issue.

In the first I was not disappointed. I found everything in Mr. Lippmann's career rolled up in these six articles as in a single ball. Something in his subject had clicked with him as never before. I found spread out before me the entire anatomy of his mind —his easy expository tone, his dialectical skill, his genius for clarity to the point of bareness, his rhetoric which is always just on the point of becoming eloquence, his magisterial air, his talent for open-

---

[2] For a further discussion of Mr. Lippmann's thinking, from a somewhat different angle, see "Do Free Markets Make Free Men?" Part IV below.

[3] This was written in the midst of the struggle over President Roosevelt's reorganization plan, and is a critique of a series of articles on the plan published by Mr. Lippmann in his syndicated column, and later gathered into a pamphlet under the title *The President and the Supreme Court*.

ing his mind to no more of his subject than for the moment he cares to admit, his tone of fairness, his capacity for concealing the impulsions of his thinking while laying bare its framework, the confidence about his own motives and the attribution of dishonesty to others which I can only describe as a moral megalomania. And I found in addition what one finds when the usually cold Mr. Lippmann gets really excited—a sort of glacial hysteria that fascinated me by its union of opposites.

The second part of my quest was disheartening. Clearly Mr. Lippmann is heir to the whole tradition of American political thought. What use does he make of it? Confronted by President Roosevelt's plan for reorganizing the Supreme Court, he calls it dastardly, dishonest, reactionary, "audacious, ingenious, and at bottom stupid"; an act of "usurpation," a "bloodless *coup d'état*" which strikes at "the moral foundations of the republic."

This leaves one a bit breathless and stunned. It is possible to discuss the President's proposal on three planes—the plane of legality, the plane of morality, and the plane of the mechanics and dynamics of government. On the score of legality, Mr. Lippmann can have no quarrel with the President, except to say that the legality is only a cloak for dark motives and something morally sinister. On the score of morality I can have no quarrel with Mr. Lippmann: he is welcome to his own moral canons, provided he will let others have theirs. Mr. Lippmann should remember that "moral foundations of the republic" is one of those stereotypes which he so admirably analyzed years ago in his book *Public Opinion,* and which is chiefly used as an emotional substitute for thought.

Let us stay on the plane of political analysis. Mr. Lippmann's chief fear is that the measure will destroy the independence of the judiciary. He sees the Court as being "packed" with "young henchmen" of the President, political hacks responsive to his desires. And then, by a parade of imaginary horribles, he converts a statute for retiring justices at seventy into a *coup d'état.*

What is not fantasy in this analysis is based upon faulty history and naïve political theory. The independence of the judiciary does not go beyond the constitutional safeguards. It does not extend to non-partisanship. Every President "packs" the Court when he appoints a justice. Presidents have always wanted men of their own persuasion on the bench. Our greatest judges—Marshall and Taney, outstandingly—have been men of political and economic convictions, deeply embroiled in politics before their appointment. Surely Mr. Lippmann has read the letters between the earlier Roosevelt and Senator Lodge on the question of whether one O. W. Holmes, Jr., had the right sort of economic views. By accepting the myth of judicial neutrality Mr. Lippmann misreads history. By charging the President with seeking to change the Constitution he misreads judicial theory. The fact is that every important decision of the Court changes the Constitution. It was a realistic tory lawyer who described the Supreme Court as an "adjourned session of the Constitutional Convention." Under the new plan the "independent judiciary," which has never been independent of Big Enterprise, would merely continue its work within new limits on age and numbers legally set by Congress.

So much for the critical portion of Mr. Lippmann's articles. There remains the constructive part. Mr. Lippmann admits that some of the Supreme Court decisions have distressed him. But he fears to limit the Court's power to render such decisions, and he fears also too extensive a grant of power to Congress. After teasing our appetite, Mr. Lippmann finally advances his own proposal. He favors a *specific amendment* each time a new specific power is needed by Congress and refused by the Court. But the amending process, he knows, is fearfully difficult. His answer is to amend the power to amend, with respect to the commerce clause only (with a six months' limit for ratification), and to leave the rest alone.

It was here that I really gasped. Commerce clause indeed! Surely anyone with Mr. Lippmann's background does not need an education in the obvious. He does not have to be told that there is more in the heaven and earth of the Supreme Court than is dreamed of in the commerce power. *Hammer v. Dagenhart* (the child labor case) is based not only on the commerce clause but on the Tenth Amendment. The Adair case and the railroad retirement pension case are based not only on the commerce clause but on the due process clause. The briefs in the Wagner Labor Act cases are built not only on the commerce power but on the First Amendment and the Fifth Amendment as well. In killing legislation the judges have been equipped with a whole quiver of arrows, any of which they could draw as the occasion demanded.

With his proposal Mr. Lippmann lets the cat out of the bag. He does not want to achieve real legislative flexibility. He thoroughly distrusts Congress, as he distrusts every organ of the people. He wants to entrench minority rule. He wants to consider the Constitution as a grant of *specific* powers, and he wants each additional specific power (that is, every important piece of new social legislation) to run the gantlet of a two-thirds vote of Congress and a three-quarters vote of the states. This would be minority rule with a vengeance. And it is a tribute to Mr. Lippmann's intellectual athleticism that he can glorify minority rule in the name of democracy.

1937

16

Thurman Arnold

Capitalism as Magic

WE are a perverse lot. Thurman Arnold has written a witty, learned book,[1] full of principles and examples, to prove for all time that learned books full of principles and examples are feckless and insubstantial things—mere symbols to mediate between our lingering illusions and the advancing world of reality. And having been told that learning and theorizing are so much eyewash, we flock in hordes to buy and devour this particular offering.

This is Mr. Arnold's second book, his first, *The Symbols of Government,* having had little more than a *succès d'estime.* He pursues pretty much the same theme in both books, for Mr. Arnold is a tenacious sort of fellow who has got hold of some ideas that are good things; and with these ideas he has been poking about, like a photographer with a good camera and a remarkably fresh eye, in all sorts of corners and emerging with pictures of men, their minds, and their society that have been shot from startling angles.

It is rather characteristic of the book that one's first impulse is not to tell what it says, but to give examples. The book is molecular. It mounts up by aggregation, like Burton's *Thousand and One Nights,* rather than by systematic exposition, like John Stuart Mill's *Principles of Logic.* The beautiful thing about it is that the author has violated every rule on how to write a treatise—which may account for his brilliant achievement. I nominate him for whatever prize, from the Pulitzer up, is awarded to the man who best succeeds in being the *enfant terrible* of his craft and in standing our world on its head.

The total effect is joyous. To give a connected account of the theme of the book would be, therefore, like giving a solemn report

---

[1] *The Folklore of Capitalism.* New Haven, Yale University Press, 1937.

on a gay and buoyant Mardi Gras one has just come away from. It
is not so much what happened that counts as the general spirit of
the thing. Everyone was dressed in costume, and there was a lot of
snatching off of false faces, and Dorothy Thompson and Westbrook
Pegler and Walter Lippmann looked rather sheepish when theirs
were torn off, but no one could feel upset about it because eventually it happened to everyone. The place was a veritable shambles
before you got through, with punctured windbags going off everywhere and shirt-stuffing lying about inches thick.

But there is far more in the book than wit and paradox and
iconoclasm. There is a heroic attempt to see our economic system
and our ideas about it in anthropological terms. Mr. Arnold adopts
what Kroeber has called the "anthropological attitude" toward our
own culture. He watches us much as an ethnologist might watch a
ceremonial dance among the Hopi Indians, with the same detachment and lively curiosity. His basic thesis is that the "society" we
live in is actually a whole set of smaller social organizations within
larger social organizations, like boxes within boxes—family, club,
church, business firm, university, government; that these organizations have in common certain creeds, rituals, and mythology; that
the so-called "sound thinking" of law and economics and political
theory is in itself so much folklore, used in order to give the members of the tribe a sense of tribal unity; that in expounding this
folklore the high priests of scholarship and opinion in university
and editorial room start with pictures of the world, already formed
in their heads, which obscure their vision of the things they are
trying to describe; that the result is that corporations are treated
like glorified persons, the economic system as if it were an assemblage of hucksters instead of an army of industrial organization,
government as if it were the malignant monster which tribal tradition says will eventually destroy the tribe; that the real function of
the folklore of capitalism is not realistic accuracy, but consolation
both to the thinker and the mass, and the shutting out of the un-
pleasant things that the encroaching world of reality is always trying to force on our consciousness; that our thinkers—radical,
liberal, and conservative alike—are so obsessed with the ceremonial
of logical consistency that they would rather be ineffective than
follow the wrong ceremonial; that the best platform for an observer
of government and society is to see the whole thing as a dramatic

spectacle with a religious theme—a sort of miracle play, with opposing devils, angels, and gods; but that the art of political dynamics
is secular and not theological, that it must deal not with logical
systems and eternal verities but with functioning social organizations which yield to the skilled compromiser far more than to the
scholar or the martyr.

As I reread this summary I know that I have not done the book
justice. I shall attempt a very different sort of summary on another
occasion,[2] for Arnold's mind is so supple, so full of all sorts of
marginal meanings, that you cannot make your full reckoning with
it at once. He has been given some pretty lavish praise in the reviews, Fred Rodell comparing him with Karl Marx—to Marx's
disadvantage; Alfred Bingham saying that the book will rank with
Darwin's *Origin of Species* in the history of human thought; Stuart
Chase seeing him as the new Machiavelli of our age; and Ralph
Thompson calling the book the most penetrating political study in
America since Thorstein Veblen's *Theory of the Leisure Class* in
1899. I think I see what they are driving at, but those are large
orders. Mr. Arnold does not pretend to be, like Machiavelli, Marx,
and Veblen, a system-builder, an articulator of a new world consciousness. But his book is one of the most hopeful signs I have seen
in some years of the vitality of American social thought.

That vitality has stemmed from the very thing that Mr. Arnold
says the universities are not doing—the transcending of the boundaries between social disciplines. In fact Veblen's importance, forty
years ago, was that he broke down the fences between economics,
politics, anthropology, psychology, and law. Arnold himself is, as
the reviewers say, "a phenomenon"—a Wyoming lawyer, formerly
Mayor of Laramie, Dean of West Virginia Law School, now teaching law at Yale, a man who has brought some of the Wyoming horse
sense into the pomposities of the academic disciplines. But that
"phenomenon" cannot be understood unless we remember that
Mr. Arnold is part of a whole movement of thought that has been
indigenous to America—the "realist" school in law, the "institutionalist" school in economics and social theory, the "psychological"
school in politics. What he has done has been to set down the in-

[2] This was written, and is printed below: "The Shadow World of Thurman Arnold."

sights of those schools, along with his own wit and sense of paradox, in the most sustained study of existing ways of thought that we have had in the post-depression years, of whose disillusionments it is to some extent a product.

Its weaknesses, like its strength, flow from the weaknesses of the institutionalist, realist, psychological schools. It is basically anti-rational, anti-intellectual, atomistic; it takes what is at best a meta-phor—that society is a drama or a battle—and extends it until it becomes the basic method of analysis; it fails to see that the enormous strides that men have made since their beginnings have been due to the rational thinking about themselves and their world which is science, technology, social science; it concentrates on the words and ideas that we use, while in the tensions of our day we have a more dire need of understanding the economic realities. Nowhere does Mr. Arnold differentiate between the levels of symbolism—between the symbols that are mere abbreviations and those that are powerfully evocative ways of thought hard to displace. Nowhere does he distinguish between the over-rational symbols of law and economics and the too little rational symbols of popular opinion. Nowhere does he set the folklore that challenges the *status quo* against the folklore that hems it in and defends it—both systems of folklore, but how different in their class base, how vastly different in the resources of social power that are brought to their support! And nowhere, finally, does he make us understand that the battle of the symbols is not a bloodless battle of categories, and that history will be decided not by symbols alone but by the strength of what they stand for.

I have no objection to brilliant talk about capitalism as magic, and I get a lot of fun out of it. But I want more light on how capitalism works or doesn't work, and how to control it or displace it. The emphasis of the recent stream of books on the tyranny of words and the folklore of ideas is a healthy emphasis. We need to sharpen our tools. But the basic jobs still remain.

1938

The Shadow World of Thurman Arnold

I. Literary Anthropologist

THURMAN ARNOLD'S *Folklore of Capitalism* has received so much acclaim that the task of criticism is no longer to recommend it for its wit and novelty,[3] but to probe its weakness as well as its strength, and seek to place it in American social thought. It has been compared, with reviewers' exuberance, to the great ones of the earth—to Machiavelli, Darwin, Marx, Bentham, Veblen. It has also been dismissed, typically by Mr. Henry Hazlitt in the New York *Times,* as a set of bad jokes on capitalism or (what is evidently even worse) an *apologia* for the New Deal. Clearly it is none of these things, nor even what the author himself would have us believe—a detached and impersonal dissection of capitalism. It is a spirited foray into our current ways of thinking, written with wit and acumen, and containing a social philosophy which the reader will discover if he doesn't get too distracted by all the signs labeled "Laboratory" with which the author has cluttered up the place.

I am frankly skeptical when people working on the study of societies begin arming themselves with scalpels, slide-rules, and test-tubes. For they are promising more than they can possibly fulfill. The protestations of complete objectivity that we have been hearing from students of society in the past quarter-century have taken on a religious note. That is why I feel disturbed when I find as sensible a person as Thurman Arnold talking in terms of the laboratory and the dissecting room, and making them—in his reaction against "ideals" and "inspirational philosophies"—his protective symbols. I suspect that Arnold assumes his attitude of "detachment" mainly as a literary device. For he must know that the realm of society cannot be charted with the inhuman precision that we apply to physics or chemistry or astronomy. It is capable at best only of the sort of scientific humanism that is involved in clear thinking and factual knowledge, such as Lancelot Hogben has recently called for in his *Retreat from Reason.*

It is as a prelude to such a scientific humanism that Arnold's book

---

[3] This I have already done; see above, "Capitalism as Magic."

is chiefly valuable. It belongs in the category of corrosive books, which eat away the past complacencies without whose removal future constructions are impossible. It is in that sense part of a pre-revolutionary era. For the significant literature in a time of social tension such as ours falls into three categories. One is the literature of social protest. The second is the literature of salvation, of "the way out," ranging from the great revolutionary proposals, through ingenious devisings, to messianic or merely crotchety schemes. The third is the literature of corrosive "detachment," whether critically contemplative or satiric. And it is of this third category that I want to speak.

Its habitat—like that of its dry-as-dust brother, "sound" orthodox thought—is often the university, but more often the modest quarters of the free-lance writer. But in either case its habits are prowling and destructive. It is given to preying on the substantial citizenry of the intellectual world, counting everything fair game that is smug, stuffy, traditional, obese. The writers in this category do not wholly escape the contagion of protest or salvation, since the one is needed as an impulsion to analysis and the second is the inescapable sequel of it. Yet their weight is not thrown on these. Their thrust is always at the underlying assumptions of a social order—questioning, assaying, mocking if the mood to mock is on them, but always undercutting the accepted first principles and taboos of their society. They are the sappers and miners of a social order; dangerous men because they belong to the breed of anthropologists, and anthropologists are always more dangerous when they study their own culture than when they dose themselves with quinine and deck themselves out in mosquito netting to study a savage culture. If the anthropologists who study primitive tribes are the forerunners of missionaries and traders, those who turn to their own cultures are the forerunners of revolutionists.

I have only to mention a few names and books of the past to convey the importance of this sort of writer, whom I should call a literary anthropologist. Think of Swift's *Gulliver's Travels*, of Voltaire's *Dictionnaire Philosophique*, of Montesquieu's *Lettres Persanes*, of Nietzsche's *Jenseits von Gut und Böse*, of Sorel's *Réflexions sur la Violence*, of Veblen's *Theory of the Leisure Class*. What all of them have in common is a capacity, through a heroic effort of the imagination, to stand aside from one's own culture and examine it with a devastating effect. Their anthropological attitude is a literary, not a scientific device—but it is none the less effective.

These books are epoch-making, as Arnold's is unlikely to be, because it lacks both their clarity and their depth. But their mood is his mood, as it is also the mood of such contemporary books as James Harvey Robinson's *Mind in the Making,* William Bolitho's *Camera Obscura,* Karl Mannheim's *Ideology and Utopia,* the Lynds' two books on *Middletown,* Stuart Chase's *Tyranny of Words.* All of them involve turning the searchlight on the basic institutions, premises, and attitudes of our own culture. And it is with this company that Thurman Arnold belongs. He brings into their midst a verve, an exuberance, a sharpness of intuition, a histrionic capacity that give him a quality of distinctiveness even when his ideas are not markedly different from the rest.

II. By Way of Summary

I want to set down what I take to be the argument of Arnold's essay in the anthropology of our contemporary attitudes. It is not logically presented. It grows not by a sequence of syllogisms, but by an aggregation of examples. Yet some of the reviewers, in emphasizing its chaos, have done less than justice to a certain structure it possesses. As I read it, it falls into four parts. The first (Chapters 1 and 2) is an introductory statement of the author's approach; the second (Chapters 3–7) discusses the prevailing academic folklore in economics, and contrasts "polar" thinking with that of the "fact-minded observer"; the third, the heart of the book (Chapters 8–12), discusses in concrete terms five phases of our economic and legal folklore, being principally popular opinion about corporations and the government; the fourth (Chapters 13 and 14) represents a bold attempt on the author's part to outline his own "principles of political dynamics."

From all these one can extract a certain point of view about society. In trying to set it down, I shall incur the risk of setting down not only what I have read in Arnold but also what I have read into him. But since much of the effectiveness of the book lies in its marginal suggestiveness, the risk is worth taking.

Arnold considers most social thinking, along with much of social activity, as ritualistic. Its function, that is to say, is not that of the laboratory but that of the theater, not description but consolation. Arnold implies—although it would be better if he said it clearly—that most of us dare not face the Medusa-head of social reality: it would turn us to stone. Nevertheless, there is in us somewhere a drive to make sense of our experience, even though that experience is a welter of nonsense. And because, along with all the irrational impulses on which our behavior is actually based, we have this desire for making rational order out of our chaos, we build elaborate structures of rationalization that we call legal and economic thinking. These structures are our ideals, our folklore. They are called "sound thinking." They are cast in an abstract form by our university professors; they find their way into current popular thinking as unanalyzed assumptions, through the ministrations of columnists, editors, and professional oracles. What these two groups, academic and non-academic alike, have in common is that they are the high priests, the shamans, the ritual-makers of the tribe—the fashioners of the tribal folklore. This folklore, or ritual, finds its way down from the basic social organization of government and business, into the whole set of institutions and social organizations in which we live—the family, the church, the club, the school—so that they all take on the same symbolism and the same pattern of "sound ideas."

The function of folklore is, for the individual, consolation: to be shored against the advancing tides of reality by ideals one may cling to. For the group as a whole it is social cohesion and a sense of unity. But actually there is no correspondence between the ideal formulations and the actual practices in business—no correspondence, that is, between the folklore of capitalism and capitalism itself. Our folklore is a body of slogans and symbols intended as a form of social therapy. They are healing and consoling to us, because it would be intolerable to all our impulses and traditions to allow the practices of capitalism to continue if we understood their naked meaning. So we interpose between ourselves and the real world certain "little pictures" (what ingenuous effectiveness in that adjective!) of the world, in the form of ideas and ideals—neat, tidy, trim, and simply not true. All of us have our varying sets of pictures, and the difference between liberal, reactionary, and radical is the difference between the pictures that obscure their vision of reality. But all the pictures are neat, and all of them posit a "thinking man" who is far less irrational than men actually are and who will somehow make a deliberate choice between systems of social organization.

Having come to reality with our pictures, we come away again with them and nothing else. We have not seen anything because we have rejected everything in the real world that did not conform to our pictures. The result is that we see the economic system, which actually operates as a far-flung army of industrial organization, penetrating and occupying every nook of our lives, as an assemblage of hucksters in the marketplace of an economy of petty trade. We see the huge corporations, which dominate our lives, as persons whose privileged position must be protected by the courts against government and labor, much as might the civil liberties of an individual. Where the landscape is filled with looming monopolies, growing out of the compulsives of the new technology, we talk of enforcing the anti-trust laws, and we content ourselves with such talk because it will not interfere with the onward thrust of the monopolies. When the government seeks to recognize the compulsives of technology, and supply the people with light, with power, with housing, with credit, we cry out that this is tyranny. The reason is that we associate the government with the symbol of taxation, and what we pay as consumers for its services seems to us in the nature of forced contributions. But when the corporations extract the same levies from us—or even more—in the form of inflated prices for their products, we do not think of it as taxation; we think of ourselves as protected by an automatic price mechanism even where it does not exist. And when the inefficiency and depredations of the big corporation have gone too far, and it breaks down under its own weight, our folklore helps it rebuild itself. We construct a ritual of corporate reorganization, as highly stylized as a Chinese play—a mysterious texture of law and economics, which is used as a screen behind which debts are written off, shrewd horse-trading goes on, and all sorts of financial juggling are accomplished. And when this vicarious atonement for past sins has been complied with, the corporation is ready to proceed with further depredations —that is, with business as usual.

Thus does the shadow world of symbols mediate between our lingering illusions and the advancing world of reality. Arnold sees the whole process of government and society as a dramatic spectacle with a religious theme—a miracle play with devils, angels, and gods. He has a healthy contempt for all professional spokesmen, especially the liberals. They are so influenced by a worship of the proper intellectual ceremonial that they are like the king of France whom Veblen describes in *The Theory of the Leisure Class:* the king was burned to death because the proper functionary was lacking to move him from the fire. But, Arnold concludes, there is an art of political dynamics which deals with organization while it takes account of ceremonial. Its prime purpose is not the construction of logical systems but the building of effective social organizations. And for that task one must have not the weaver of eternal verities but the skilled and slightly cynical compromiser.

III. The Heaven of Realism

Arnold has put his own personal stamp on his book. He has written it with such vividness that no one who writes either of capitalism or of symbolism from now on will write the same for the fact that this book has been written. In an age of timidity, he dares to be himself. His flashes of wit and paradox are being worn thin as they pass current in dinner-table conversation among the intellectual élite. When that happens to a book, its real meaning is likely to be narrowed down to a particular angle of refraction that has caught the popular eye. This chances to be the joyousness with which Arnold deflates the current gasbags, and the abandon with which he lays about with his cudgel thwackingly and resoundingly.

Yet no man spins a book purely out of his own innards. If this one is important, it is because it comes out of the main streams of American thought today. And, as with most books that achieve popularity, its deeper appeal lies not in its originality but in the sharpness with which it says what others have been trying to say for some time, and what they have therefore prepared us to listen to. A popular writer is one who passes with flair and resplendence along a way already beaten out for him, while an original writer must too often prepare the road along which he will eventually be met.

Arnold stands at the crossing of four strains in our thoughts, all of them characteristically American: first, "common-sense" *realism;* second, *psychologism* as applied to political man, with its overtones of anti-rationalism and anti-intellectualism; third, *institutionalism* in economics and social theory; fourth, *middle-class radicalism* in program and tactics. I want to consider each of these in the sections that follow.

It is the realist's boast and fond dream that he is, in William James's phrase, tough-minded rather than tender-minded. There are few contemporaries that exceed Arnold in striving for toughness. And this takes most characteristically the form of an anticonceptualism. I have said elsewhere [4] that he observes our social attitudes with the detachment and lively curiosity of an ethnologist watching a ceremonial dance among the Hopi Indians. This is undoubtedly the effect he intends. But on reflection I want to qualify the comparison. For Arnold has more at stake in his observations than the ethnologist has. There is an animus with which he starts—an animus against all intellectual constructs and a contempt for the virtues of logical consistency, an animus which does much to give his writing its quality of irony and irreverence. He is always concerned with the illogic of logical thinking, the unreality of abstract principles, the futility of intellectual system-building.

As I understand it, this is one of the oldest and newest themes in the history of thought. For all the fervor with which Arnold clothes his assaults, there have been Prometheans before who have raged against the vested interests of the reigning intellectual divinities. He has chosen to tackle one of the most persistent problems in the realm of thinking—the problem of illusion and reality, of certitude in our minds and change in the world outside of them, of intellectual structures and functioning social organizations, of hierarchies of moral values and the twisting, elusive thing that we call social fact—in short, of the reality of the world and our apprehension of it.

I suspect that Arnold will not enjoy my saying that the question he is absorbed with was once the deep concern of the medieval Schoolmen. It furnished the core of the struggle between the Realists and the Nominalists, and was the essence of the "battle of the universals." For the medievals too were concerned with the question whether the concepts that we use for the generalizations in our thinking are only convenient and fictitious labels, or whether they have a real existence apart from the particulars in which they ap-

---

4 See above, "Capitalism as Magic."

pear. I need scarcely add that the Nominalists in the Middle Ages took the position that Arnold and the realists take today, and that this position distressed Church and State no end. For it robbed both of them of their most secure claim to allegiance—their claim to a continuous and universal existence. It reduced Church and State to mere bundles of human beings, building institutions useful for the purposes of the day, but giving way to other institutions when their utility was ended. And the authoritarians of the day sought to demolish this heresy, much as the Hutchinses and Adlers at Chicago today—Realists in the medieval sense—regard the heresies of Thurman Arnold as dangerous.[5]

I have gone to some length to point this out because I believe in the continuity of Western culture, and I feel it is a mistake to separate ourselves too sharply from our past. We shall never escape the lot of having to deal with age-old problems, and our only hope is to deal with them in a fresh way. But I fear that many of Arnold's successes in demolishing concepts are set-ups, achieved by premising the hollowness of all concepts. We make a drastic error if, in fighting certain over-artificial intellectual concepts, we forget that we can fight them only with other intellectual concepts, not with bare knuckles and mother wit.

Arnold has done an exhilarating job in knocking the stuffing out of all sorts of sawdust-laden minds. For that, all honor to him. But he is doing us a disservice by his fierce atomism—by implying, as his book seems to, that all rational and conceptual thinking necessarily consists of sawdust, or even that its main effect is to hamper social constructions. For he must know what immense new constructions of the Western world stem directly from the rational systems of the English seventeenth-century political theorists and the French eighteenth-century *philosophes*. He must know that the new social organizations of the fascist states—whatever we may think of them—derive largely from the writings of Nietzsche, Bergson, Spengler, Sorel, and Houston Stewart Chamberlain, and that Hitler's foreign policy, step by step, may be found charted out in the pages of *Mein Kampf*. He must know that the social construc-

---

[5] John Chamberlain reports that Hutchins remarked to him: "Yes, Thurman Arnold is unique. So is a rattlesnake unique." I fear that in both cases he was doing an injustice to his own Realist medieval doctrine. See Chamberlain, "The Folklore of Reviewers," *Saturday Review of Literature*, March 12, 1938.

tions of the future cannot help owing a great deal to the logical system-building of Marx and Engels. Actually Arnold disproves his own thesis. For after a scathing attack on "abstract ideals" and logical systems, he devotes his last two chapters to "the social philosophy of tomorrow" and "some principles of political dynamics." Clearly the other fellow's "abstract ideals" become one's own "principles of political dynamics."

Along with a fierce atomism, there is in Arnold a fierce pragmatism. He wants to know what things work or fail to work in society, why certain programs succeed while others fail, what stands in the way between social thinking and social effectiveness, what are the rules of action for the men and groups who win out in the fierce struggle for a place in the sun. He is not content with threshing over the dry straw of other men's intellectual disputes. His concern is with what works as against what is only logically consistent—a concern possible only in an age in which the rational technology of industry has yielded place to the manipulations of corporate finance, the propaganda machines of nations in mortal combat, the power-diplomacy of fascist adventurers. And I suspect that in this contempt for the geometry of reason and in his fervor for the instrumentalisms of the contemporary world, Arnold is not merely expressing some personal experience of disillusionment. He sums up tragically the consciousness of a generation which thinks that the social good which it has failed to achieve by rational effort can be won by being fragmentized and pursued with a desperate immediacy.

I think I can understand Arnold and sympathize with his animus, because I belong to the same desperate generation. Nevertheless, I cannot find any comfort in a heaven of realism from which, because concepts have grown old and stuffy or been captured by the enemy, we would eject all concepts—even those that are necessary to defeat the enemy or give meaning to life. I know that Arnold will say at this point that the terms "enemy," "meaning," betray me, for they are in his terminology "polar words" and as such have no place in the vocabulary of the "fact-minded observer." But one of the revealing things about his book is this very insistence not only on distinguishing between observation and value-judgments, but on excluding all values from his system. What would be left if he succeeded in doing this—which, of course, he does not—would be a chaos of atomistic "facts," unrelated and meaningless, powerless even to cluster themselves into those "principles of political dynamics" upon which Arnold is finally thrust back. Like Satan who carried Hell with him wherever he went, Arnold cannot escape the abstraction. The "fact-minded observer" is himself an "abstract ideal," "a polar word," a fictitious refuge from Arnold's own passionate fear of values. So also is his other favorite, the "organizing man." By the realism which refuses to face the need for abstractions, Arnold succeeds only in admitting them by inadvertence and thus becomes the more readily their victim.

My guess is that Arnold's fierceness against concepts comes chiefly from his training in law. It is in law that concepts, long after their vitality is gone, linger on as fictions and rituals. And it has become the tradition of the school of legal realists to aim their sharpest javelin thrusts against the rituals and formalizations of the law. The realist believes that there is something more "real" than these rituals, and he goes off in pursuit of that something. The interesting thing about Arnold, on the contrary, is that he finds the real meaning and force in the law exactly in the ritual itself. For he sees that the ritual holds a subjective sway over men's minds, largely because of its correspondence with their desire for the dramatic and the symbolic. I think it may be said that the school of legal realism has two divisions. Both start with the discrepancies between our pictures of the law ("the law in books," etc.) and the law as it is ("the law in action"). But one branches off to concentrate on examining the latter, while the second, including Arnold—through the fascination that symbols hold for him—is mainly interested in the former.

Let us follow him into his world of symbols and myths. For if there is anything to bolster his uncompromising realism, we must seek it in the picture he draws of psychological chaos in human beings.

IV. The Dance of the Symbols

I have dealt in the last section with the over-rationality (in Arnold's scheme) of legal ritual and other symbolic constructs. I want to deal now with the under-rationality, or irrationality, of the minds on which those symbols impinge. Arnold has been deeply affected by the psychologism of modern thought. He learned much from contact with the restless and pioneering mind of Edward S. Robinson, with whom he collaborated in a seminar on law and psychology. But his handling of the psychological schools is still that of the brilliant amateur. One finds in the present book a measure of behaviorism, a dash of *Gestaltism,* a bowing acquaintance with the experimental techniques, a large admixture of psychoanalysis and psychiatry of various brands, and a liberal dose of the social psychology of crowds. The result is a generous eclecticism which, while it may bewilder or even appall the reader, produces at least an intense intellectual ferment.

What these various psychologies finally boil down to as a residue is the complete and utter irrationalism of man as a political animal. Just as he has a dislike for concepts, so Arnold has a distrust of reason. The "reasonable man" or the "thinking man" is one of his dearest objects of ridicule. Through the entire book Arnold parades man as exactly the opposite—incapable of grasping more than the stereotypes of politics, hungry for drama and display, ridden by myths which he is incapable of examining in any critical fashion, narcissist in his desire to dress himself up in various roles and parade through his own imagination, incapable of creating except through great leaders and organizers, herdlike in following the leader's aim and the mass emotion. I do not believe I have overdrawn the picture, which I have had to piece together from various parts of the book.

Clearly such a psychological conception is a sharp instrument for puncturing many pretensions, effective in probing for obscure motivations and for uncovering hidden ideologies. Arnold sees politics, in a sense, as a histrionic release from the intolerable burden of having to live and think like rational creatures on the basis of an irrational psychic endowment. It is this fault-line between the pretensions of rationality and the facts of irrationality that does much to give the book what elements it possesses of high farce. For in the most serious sense, such a confronting of discrepancies is an exploration of the comic. What a Teutonic scholar such as Mannheim [6] does in a lumbering way to uncover and lay bare the thrusts of impulse and interest behind the formal edifices of reasoning, Arnold accomplishes with wit and *esprit,* if with a good deal less

---

[6] Mannheim, *Ideology and Utopia* (1936).

of method. What the Marxians do to economic interests on the assumption that man is a rational animal, Arnold does to the Marxians and other system-builders on the assumption that man is quite
irrational. And as for the unveiling of the hypocrisies, the blind
aimlessness, the feckless shams of business practices, no one since
Veblen has done it with so savage a gusto or so devastating an effect.

But granted these rich values, Arnold's method and conception
have their grave limitations. The first lies in the use of the symbolic
instrument itself. Arnold fails to differentiate between the levels of
symbolism. There are symbols that are merely abbreviations, without which life would grow too complex for survival. There are also
symbols that are short-cuts to emotion, ways of revealing or obscuring the meaning of society. There are symbols by which some
men achieve and maintain a hold over the rest of mankind. There
are finally, as Arnold might have learned from Whitehead,[7] whole
symbol-clusters that are evocative ways of thought and patterns of
life. Man as we find him is irrational enough; but Arnold adds to
this irrationality by attributing the distorting effects of symbolism
even to the situations where symbols alone give life meaning and
where they clear the path for, instead of blocking, social construction. He lumps all the symbolisms of men's actions together, without getting at the purposes of those actions, without getting at the
for whats? An irrational symbol for one purpose may be a perfectly
rational symbol for another. It is Arnold's incapacity to say *for
what?* to his symbols that is at the root of much of the book's confusion. When you see everything as undifferentiated symbols, then
the symbol ceases to have meaning, but takes its place only as a
senseless particle in a mad dance.

The second difficulty, however, lies in the anti-intellectualism
and anti-rationalism toward which Arnold's position inclines him.
I say "inclines," because Arnold may well answer that he is not
necessarily anti-anything, whether rationalism or irrationalism—
that he is merely describing men as irrational. That is strictly true.
Yet with only a limited number of conceptions of man's rationality
available, the one you choose for describing the world is also the
one you use for evaluating it. And Arnold is throughout the book
betraying his scheme of valuation. He depicts thinkers as stumbling

---

[7] Whitehead, *Symbolism: Its Meaning and Effect,* 196.

along ineffectually while the decisions of the world are left to men of little logic and ruthless purpose. The intellectual, in the book, is always flouted in favor of the hard-boiled practical politician and the organizing genius. Arnold displays a faith in the latter almost akin to the sentiment the eighteenth century felt for the "noble savage." And as a corollary to the esteem he feels for the big doers, and the leaning toward the great-man conception of the historical process, there is a tendency toward anti-massism in the book. After expanding on the irrational blunderings, hypocrisies, slavishnesses of most men, Arnold singles out as the agents of social construction "men without moral illusion who are able to create great organizations through the sheer use of power." He has in mind, in this context and others, men such as Hitler, Mussolini, Stalin, Henry Ford, John D. Rockefeller, John L. Lewis.

Arnold is motivated, I suspect, by a reaction against the centuries of reason, much like his animus against abstract ideals. He is disillusioned about them. If one understands that disillusionment, one understands also the climate of opinion in which the luxuriant growths of recent irrational philosophies have sprung up and the quest of symbols has flourished. Take a generation which intellectually spans the post-war and post-depression periods, both of them filled with hypocrisies which have made the most significant American expressions of our time "Oh, yeah?" and "It's a racket." What such a generation tends to develop is not so much a philosophy as a reaction against the intolerable humiliation of having been "let down." Out of this comes the impulse toward "debunking" —the inevitable sequel of a sharp disenchantment with once cherished values. The most important influences in the thinking of this generation have been the experience with war propaganda and the study of the techniques that the fascist and communist movements have used in manipulating the effective symbols for mass persuasion, both separately and in their mutual conflict. The effect of these influences on our political and psychological thinking can scarcely be overestimated. They are comparable to the effect of capitalist collapse upon our economic thinking.

Given this climate of opinion, it explains but does not validate the anti-rationalism of Arnold. For in his reaction against the centuries of the great hope, he fails to see the strides that men have made through their tireless perfection of what little wit nature has given them. Despite his exaggerated use of the symbolism of the laboratory in his own behalf, Arnold is very grudging toward science. He fails to see that men have moved forward through the rational thinking about themselves and their world which is science, technology, social science. While science may be a symbol, it is also an objective fact in human history. And unless men can learn how to use this symbol, or fact, for new social constructions and for the creation of new symbolisms, they may well end up not in the relative decency that Arnold in his final chapters foresees for them, but in complete barbarism.

There is a curious blindness in the book with respect to the potential value of revolutionary and reconstructive symbolism. Arnold does not distinguish between the folklore that challenges the *status quo* and the folklore that hems in and defends it. The only emerging philosophies that he alludes to are those of the New Deal and the nationalist dictatorships, but they are all lumped in their treatment with the philosophy of present-day capitalism. Yet the revolutionary philosophies are completely different in their class base, their purposes, the resources of social power they bring to their support.

V. INSTITUTIONS AND LAG

There can be no analysis of folklore without an analysis of the social structures from which it grows, no theory of capitalism without a theory of institutions. In his discussion of capitalism, Arnold follows in general the lead of the institutional economists. Among them he seems to have been most deeply influenced by Thorstein Veblen, Walton Hamilton, and A. A. Berle and Gardiner Means. It is not surprising that he should cultivate their company, for the essence of institutional economics is revolt against the too austere and abstract formulations of the classical old masters. And in its revolt, it succeeds also in breaking down economics itself as a category so that it becomes merely the most significant point at which law, custom, technology, psychology, and property relations meet and cross.

In such an economics, Thurman Arnold is clearly as happy as a professorial cow that has kicked down the fences and found succulent pastures to roam in. It is where law meets economics, rather than where law meets psychology or metaphysics, that Arnold finds the best grazing and the greatest felicity. His most masterly chapter is easily, and by a quite general accord, the one on "The Ritual of Corporate Reorganization." Those on taxation and the anti-trust laws are runners-up in interest. He is at his best when he is dealing with operative legal and economic techniques, and never so effective as when the ostensible purpose of the techniques is far removed from their actual function.

For Arnold's most fruitful thinking is based on the lag. That is one reason among many good ones why he will never be a Marxian. For Marxian social thought is built on the conditioning relationships between the several parts of a hierarchy—between the material base, the class structure, the secondary social structures, the idea systems of a society—and on the laws of movement and change from one hierarchy to another in time. Institutional thought, on the other hand, is built on the distances or lags between the various elements in a social complex. And Arnold glories in the lag. He approaches a problem at the point where he can find the most striking discrepancy between the going technology and the pace of industrial change on the one hand, and, on the other, the legal rituals and popular symbols through or despite which the technology is finally translated into consumable goods. What interests him, in short, is the distance that separates economic reality from economic and legal opinion and emotion. That distance is spanned by the folklore of a culture.

But more than with the lag itself, Arnold is concerned with the mechanism by which men are kept more or less unconscious of its existence, and the mechanism by which the fact of the lag facilitates a rough adjustment to an imperfect world. Let me illustrate by Arnold's chapter on the anti-trust laws. The economic reality is the large-scale industrial technique, demanding large-scale methods of distribution. The lag is the distance that separates such a technique and its demands from the prevailing economic opinion favoring the small productive unit and the competitive market. The mechanism of the anti-trust laws, says Arnold, satisfies our ideal of the preservation of competition; at the same time it also satisfies the compulsives of the industrial techniques. It can do both by the fact of being on the statute books and being the subject of a vigorous campaign, yet remaining essentially unenforced because of the enormous difficulty of enforcement and the clumsiness of the machinery. Our censor is, so to speak, lulled into unawareness of the continued existence of the lag; and under cover of that unawareness, business enterprise is built up to monopoly form, and a rough adjustment is made to the compulsives of the new techniques.

Arnold's theory is neat. But it has several difficulties. One is that there is nothing in it that indicates why the lag arises in the first place. The second is, that it does not indicate why, having arisen, the lag is maintained, and why it is not resolved. The third is that when the theorist turns actor the theory has to be tempered.

Arnold does not explain why the lag arises, because his theory does not carry him beyond the recognition of a certain static quality in opinion which does not allow it to keep pace with the pace of social change. Yet the fact of the inertia of ideas is not enough, for ideas do change—often at a revolutionary pace—when the conditions are right for change. What is needed in addition is a theory of vested interests and vested ideas, which puts a premium on conformity in thought even while it places a similar premium upon advance in technology. And once the lag arises, it is maintained for the same essential reason. It continues because the machinery of political power and the control over the channels for forming public opinion are in the hands of the group that wants monopoly and sees that it can best achieve it by maintaining the fiction of competitive units in a petty economy. In short, the changes in technology are not translated into corresponding changes in property relations or the relations of class power, i.e., not translated into corresponding institutional change.

I have said that when the theorist finally turns actor the theory has to be tempered. But that will best introduce another phase of Arnold's thought.

VI. TACTIC—FOR WHAT?

As I write (1938) the United States Senate, through a subcommittee of its Committee on the Judiciary, has just had a tussle with the meaning of Professor Arnold's book and the validity of his thinking. Book and author have come out the victors, but I ask myself whether it is not a Pyrrhic victory. Arnold got the recommendation confirming his appointment, but I am half inclined to the view that he left his theory behind on the field of battle.

By one of those ironic twists of fate, Arnold was nominated to be

Assistant Attorney General in charge of anti-trust law enforcement, to succeed Robert H. Jackson.[8] With a coolness that does justice to his courage, he accepted the nomination, and faced Senator Borah, whom he had in his book called (in effect) the high priest of the folklore of the anti-trust laws. The newspapers were quick to see an opportunity for exploiting some of their own folklore, and making some anti-New Deal capital, and for several days the editorial pages carried succulent excerpts from the chapter on the anti-trust laws. Would the author of *The Folklore of Capitalism*, they asked, have his heart in the job? But the campaign died down. Arnold was obviously so well qualified for the post by gifts and training that blocking his nomination would be fantastic. Their own hearts were not in the job of hounding him.

I am certain that Arnold will make a first-rate man for his post. Yet the irony of the appointment remains—except that it is an irony directed back toward the book. One who reads the account of the Arnold-Borah encounter in the committee room cannot but feel that the temper of Arnold's replies to Borah was not quite the temper of the book. There was more restraint in it, less joyousness, less certitude, less of the sharp quality of the dissecting room. The moral, of course, is that you don't take your dissecting instruments into the Senate chamber—it would clutter up the place and get in the way of the Senators. Yet it is a moral worth remembering. Here was the historian who was given a chance not only to write history but to make it; and he failed to carry over his historian's techniques. Here was the philosopher become king, acting every inch the king but somewhat less the philosopher.

This raises the entire question of Arnold's "principles of political dynamics." The tactic that Arnold builds up in his concluding chapters is a tactic of accommodation and compromise; Arnold has been compared with many great writers of the past, but in this respect the best comparison is with John Morley's *On Compromise*. The heart of the book seems to me to lie in the new tactic of capitalist progressivism that it proposes.

There can be no doubt that a new movement of what we may call middle-class radicalism is arising in America. To my mind, Arnold

---

8 Mr. Jackson became Solicitor General, although by not too wide a margin of confirmation. He writes no books, but—what is almost as dangerous—he makes speeches.

—more than any man who has appeared on the landscape so far—is
its philosopher: he rationalizes both its thought and its tactic. The
possible exception is President Roosevelt, who is a good tactician
but no philosopher, and who is better counted as a datum for Arnold to rationalize. There is a deep nativist streak in Arnold's thinking, which shows itself in an isolationism both as to foreign policy
and foreign thought. There is something of the spaciousness and
exuberance of the American plains in him, as also in a politician
who comes very close to Arnold's ideal—Congressman Maury
Maverick of Texas. Arnold writes of the "rise of a class of engineers,
salesmen, minor executives, social workers" as the significant emergence of the immediate future. His chapter on "The Social
Philosophy of Tomorrow" is a vague but provocative forecast of
the coming of something that is neither communism nor capitalism,
but something else in its own way just as thorough going—that
tertium quid, an American radicalism. Its tactic is to be gloriously
opportunistic, something very close to a shrewd and intuitive dema-
gogism.

This is, of course, not Arnold's own program: he is again describing what he sees ahead, not advocating anything. Yet we have
learned from Veblen's example that description, if persistent and
exclusive, may be held *faute de mieux* to take the place of advocacy.
Perhaps that is doing Arnold an injustice. But there can be little
doubt that all this jibes pretty well with the principles of political
dynamics that he confesses to. It has given rise, among certain critics,[9] to the warning that there are elements in Arnold's thinking that
run parallel to elements to be found in fascism. I think that's going
it strong. But Arnold's anti-rationalism, his anti-intellectualism, his
radical pragmatism, his cult of the survivor, his deification of the
practical man and the organizing genius, his emphasis on the discovery of effective techniques, his opportunism, his leaning toward
middle-class radicalism, his mob-psychology conception of the
masses—all these, if torn out of the context of Arnold's own pattern,
could be fitted into a pattern that would begin to look sinister. I say
this not because I feel that anyone as sophisticated about politics as
Arnold is needs any admonition. I say it because it is always worth
while for us to remind ourselves that as political thinkers, no less

[9] *Cf.* James Burnham, book review, *Partisan Review,* March 1938, 50–53.

than as political administrators appearing before Senate Committees or as editors or as teachers, we owe a responsibility to our ideas. And that responsibility is to think of them in the context of our time, and in the light of the tendencies rampant in our world. Direction and consequence are as much part of ideas as origin and innate quality.

Yet my guess is that the real criticism of Arnold is not in the fact that his ideas tend to form any sort of pattern, but that there is too little pattern in them. In his almost obsessive desire to steer clear of ideal values and moral judgments he has had to concentrate on tactics and techniques exclusively. His last chapter tells you how to get things done in politics; what you may want to get done is your own affair. Now, I have no stomach to reprove a man for not doing what he does not set out to do. Arnold has not chosen to write a program, or a theory of moral or political values. Yet that is in itself a deeply significant thing. He gives us a tactic—but for what? Means have no import without ends; yet when you get to the question of ends, Arnold is maddeningly elusive. It is deeply significant that we find in him no real economic philosophy or program, other than a vague allegiance to the amorphous experimentalism of the New Deal; no political tactic that goes beyond techniques to programs or values; no philosophy of industrial change that goes beyond a grasp of the importance of technology and its compulsive character.

VII. BEYOND MYTHS

Do what you will with Thurman Arnold, you cannot ignore him. He has placed himself squarely in the path of our attention, as few social thinkers have done in this decade; and his book is one of the best warrants of the vitality of our thought. There is in him a daring and an irresponsibility that go with singular creativeness. He takes intellectual risks that the more cautious and cloistered of us would consider dizzying. He is volatile, shifting, contradictory—but he is alive, and so is his book. Its confusion is a mirror and index of the confusion of our social system and our whole intellectual world, but its acid is the expression of a corrosive force in our culture which may yet dissolve those confusions and make new social constructions possible.

And yet I cannot suppress the feeling, for all of Arnold's realism,

for all his shrewd insights into men's motives and foibles, for all
his tough-minded grasp of the dynamics of political life, that the
plane on which he does his thinking is the shadow world of two-
dimensional symbols, which do not reach to the substance of social
reality. "Men believe that society is disintegrating," he says in one
place, "when it can no longer be pictured in familiar terms." True
enough, and a good truth on the symbolic plane. But let us go
beyond symbols, beyond myths, beyond what men believe, to society itself as an objective fact. When *is* society disintegrating? But
to answer this, Arnold would have to have not a philosophy of
symbols, but a theory of society and of history. Perhaps one answer
is that society is disintegrating when its thinkers no longer ask
when it is, but only when men believe it to be.

But that is only a surmise, not a theory. The fate of societies, we
may be certain, will be decided not by symbols but by the strength
of what they stand for.[10]

1938

---

[10] Readers interested in the essays in this volume bearing directly on legal theory,
in addition to this analysis of Arnold, are referred to the studies on Cohen and
Corwin in Part II below, and to "The Jungle of Legal Thought" and "The Supreme
Court and American Capitalism" in Part IV.

17

Morris R. Cohen: Law and the Life of Reason

WHATEVER the chance that first led Professor Cohen to turn his fine philosophical gifts to "the meaning of law in the lives of men and women," we have it to thank for a vast amount of both light and dynamite. To parallel the importance for American legal philosophy of his volume of essays [1] one goes back quite naturally to 1920 and the appearance of Justice Holmes's *Collected Legal Papers*. Like that extraordinary book, this collection of essays and reviews, despite the adventitious character of its contents, possesses none the less the inner symmetry that flows from an ordered and deliberately held view of life. The similarity between the two minds is primarily one not so much of theory as of temper. There is the same disinclination to join schools and run with the scholarly herd, the same tight sanity amidst the fluid doctrines of the day, the same acrid and canny capacity to pierce intellectual pretensions, the same final dignity of thought.

The writings span a period of twenty years. The amazing thing is how well they have stood the intellectual buffetings of those years so filled with movement and stir. Hardly a line dates. And whole pages written fifteen or twenty years ago contain fresh-minted the intellectual currency that is only now circulating freely. During those intervening years many other legal philosophies that reared their heads bravely and made more noise have gone down. The structure of Professor Cohen's thought, whatever its shortcomings, has had the enormous merit of durability. It is as if he had stripped his thinking of everything faddist and impulsive before he ever set pen to paper. He has managed somehow to see law steadily and see it whole.

---

[1] *Law and the Social Order.* New York, Harcourt, Brace, 1933.

I do not mean that he has avoided the polemical and kept himself above the battle, or that he has mastered the perhaps unattainable art of equating a mordant, critical insight with a scrupulous fairness to opponents. Part of the excitement of reading these pages comes from the joyous militancy with which Professor Cohen defends every position. This book has the same stinging quality of thought and style that marked the author's *Reason and Nature* (1931). At times, as in the essay on "Philosophy and Legal Science," his sense of workmanship in dispatching an opponent becomes so completely the center of the show that everything else fades out. But the thing that is disconcerting about Professor Cohen as a polemicist is that he is often to be found smiting right and left in the name of a victory not envisaged by either side. He makes at best but a dubious champion. After having laid your enemy low, as like as not he will turn about and administer as severe a drubbing to you. He is as averse to accepting the traditional statement of issues as he is loath to take the fashionable position in regard to them. To every one of the going "schools" he deals out criticism with unsparing but even-handed severity.

There is nothing here that is merely whimsical. It is safe to say that no more integrated position than Professor Cohen's exists today in American legal thinking. But, as in his larger philosophical structure, the integrating principle in his legal philosophy is one of criticism. No scalpel is defter than his in laying bare a half-truth or an overstated truth, or in probing the intellectual insolvency of some brave array of argument. It is because of this approach that much of his best work proceeds chiefly by a critical review of the existing theories and "a sifting of the valid from the invalid elements in them."

Such a procedure, which might in someone else be only a formal if necessary clearing away of past debris, becomes in Professor Cohen's hands an instrument of affirmative statement. It is given this significance by the principle of polarity to which he calls attention in his preface, and which is set forth explicitly in his *Reason and Nature*—the principle that in any situation metaphysical categories which are generally believed to be opposed to each other (Professor Cohen instances such categories as "unity and plurality, the fixed and the flux, ideal and real, actual and possible . . .") actually involve and determine each other "like the north and south poles of a magnet." [2] While throughout life and thought the inherent tendency with regard to any issue is to push to one extreme pole or another, the function of the critical intelligence is to find, beyond the apparent strife and contradiction of categories, the essential and integrating principle. This is to attribute to criticism not merely the preliminary and negative function usually accorded it, but to invest it with a creative capacity which has usually been considered outside its scope.

Wrenched out of its philosophical context Professor Cohen's entire critical method may have a ring of the obvious. But give such an instrument to a closely reasoning mind, endowed with critical insight of the first order, and apply it to the welter of forced and extravagant statement in contemporary legal thought—and the result is this book. American legal scholarship has been for the most part crotchety and provincial, untutored in the larger reaches of social and philosophical thought, disposed to veer from extreme to extreme in the desperate search for the emphatic. It has, in short, been not unlike the whole vast area of American life. In the past quarter-century especially we seem to have touched the outermost limits of the worship of the empty abstract principle on the one hand, and of the blind concrete case on the other.

To create synthesis out of confusion Professor Cohen is led by his method to administer a critical spanking to both parties. His essays fall thus into two groups. In the first, in which he is a critic of Toryism in the law, belong roughly the first two of the four sections into which the book is divided—"The Social Scene" and "Law and the Social Order"; in the second group, in which he becomes a critic of contemporary Whiggism, belong the last two sections, dealing with "Law and Reason" and "Contemporary Legal Philosophy."

It is more than an accident that all but one of the writings in the entire first group appeared originally in the *New Republic*. They were published in the years between 1914 and 1923, when Herbert Croly and his fellow-editors were gallantly seeking the promise of American life in the disheartening desert stretches of actual American society. A journal of liberal opinion was wise to welcome the aid of these acrid, pungently phrased essays and reviews which were

2 *Reason and Nature*, 165.

more devastating in their philosophical deliberateness than all the brash and indignant crusading articles added together. The immediate targets in some of the reviews happened to be Mr. Hoover, Mr. Root, Mr. Guthrie, and Judge Emery; but though they were thoroughly riddled as targets it was always clear that they were chiefly symbols, and that beyond them lay the smugness of the contemporary legal attitudes and the brutal incidence of the existing legal machinery. And the attack on these is not only the dominant theme of this first group of essays, but in a sense represents a facet of Professor Cohen's entire legal thinking.

Yet I cannot feel that it is the more important facet. The other, which finds its principal expression in the last two sections of the book, comes much closer to the center of his interest. It is concerned primarily with the metaphysical foundations of legal thinking—in Professor Cohen's own phrase, with "law and reason." What he is fighting here is not social Toryism but intellectual Whiggism, not the worship of tradition but the flouting of it, not a concept-jurisprudence but the denial of all principle in the law, not legal authoritarianism and the "phonograph theory" of the judicial process but legal anarchy and some excessively individualistic theory of the judge's function, not the rigidification of logic but the refusal to admit that it has played any part at all in the growth of the law, not the blindness to the facts of society but the blind empirical reliance on experience alone. To write these essays required the greater courage because they involved a disassociation from those by whose side Professor Cohen had been fighting the reactionaries. Yet despite this—or perhaps because of it, for Professor Cohen is at heart a lone fighter—these are his best essays and the enduring things by which he will live in the history of legal philosophy. These —and not his liberal excursions in attacking economic individualism and other idols of the marketplace. For here he can defend the values he holds most dear: order, reason, principle. And I for one can never escape the suspicion that Professor Cohen is more concerned to annihilate those who deny scope to logic than he is to attack those who claim too pervasive a scope for private property.

This second group of papers also bodies forth most clearly the rationalism and realism which are at the base of Professor Cohen's philosophic position. Into the muddle and irrationality of contemporary legal thinking he wishes to introduce the principle of

order and the life of reason. As he had done in his earlier book with
respect to the entire intellectual field, so here in the domain of law
he asserts the primacy of reason and rejects whatever substitutes
have been proposed for it, whether on the side of legal authoritarianism or of social experience. And in the long-drawn-out controversy in legal philosophy between the particular and the universal
the stress that has been currently laid on the first causes him to
throw his own weight heavily toward the second. This attitude of
his in affirming the existence and validity not only of the concrete
case but also of the abstract principle rests ultimately on the realist's
affirmation of the object of knowing. It is "realism" not in the sense
in which the word has been used in the recent revolts against formalism and conceptualism in law—Professor Cohen points out that
these revolts are in the strict philosophic meaning nominalistic—
but in the sense of medieval realism, which affirmed the reality of
universals.

Such a position, projected into American legal philosophy, finds
itself in a somewhat alien world. Aside from the period in which a
lip-service to "natural law" was convenient to the purposes of a
capitalist legal system, American legal thought has been skeptical of
general principles. The whole tradition of Anglo-American case
law is tough and empirical; the wider tradition of Anglo-American
thought shows a skepticism of values that are primarily intellectual.
The real tradition from which Professor Cohen derives belongs to
the philosophers of the realm of essence; the legal philosophy with
which he seems most in agreement is contained in the brilliant work
of Demogue. In fact, despite the specifically American locus of
much of Professor Cohen's subject matter, we find ourselves moving
throughout his pages in a world much closer to Continental thought
and to the system of civil law. And in the perspectives of Continental thought it is easier to understand his stress on the invariant elements underlying flux in law, and on the persistence of the ultimate
and unchanging through all the historical mutations of legal institutions.

The central question that the book evokes is whether such a
philosophical emphasis as this can be genuinely fruitful for a theory
of law and social order. In legal study, as in all fields of thought, the
trend has been so strongly to social values that every important

legal philosophy must inevitably be examined from the viewpoint of social thought. Professor Cohen, by giving his "essays in legal philosophy" permanent form under the title of *Law and the Social Order,* has given his assent to this position. His title implies that while his chief concern has been legal philosophy the orientation of that philosophy has been toward the problems of society.

Appraised thus, the book, especially in its first two sections, is not without a good deal of valuable and penetrating thinking on the relation of law to society. There is the suggestion that the existing legal system weighs more heavily on the poor than on the rich; that no theory of the social order which separates the individual from society can form a proper basis for legal thought; that economic individualism, operating through its legal machinery, has consequences which destroy rather than foster the real autonomy of the individual life; that constitutional myths such as the bill-of-rights theory, historical legends such as Magna Charta, and ingrained attitudes such as that which conceives the judicial process as being completely non-legislative, can be used to cloak and condone the injustices of the contemporary legal system; that the chief encumbrances in the way of legal reform are likely to be the outworn but persisting attitudes toward the law; that a legal institution must serve some desirable social end; that the institution of inheritance is defended by an array of moral and intellectual arguments which are only a system of apologetics, and that its real basis is "our established habits and prejudices"; that such institutions of private law as contract and property may have more important relations to state sovereignty and power than to doctrinal symmetry or moral purpose.

But a scattering of social insights does not make a social theory. The essays on contract, on property, on judicial legislation, on the bill-of-rights theory are brilliant and suggestive, and some of the other articles and reviews contain a host of illuminating asides, but they lack the coherent theory which his essays on the rational methods of legal thinking contain. The truth of the matter is that the analysis of law in the social order is not the real focus of the book.

The integrating principle is rather in the philosophical realm than in the realm of social thought. This is perhaps deliberate on Professor Cohen's part. In one of his essays on Dean Pound he draws a distinction between a philosophical jurisprudence and a philosophy of law. He says that Pound "has sought to make the science of law as philosophical or reflectively rational as possible rather than to answer the questions that one primarily interested in philosophy would ask concerning the role of law in a unified theory of human life and natural existence" (p. 327). Similarly Professor Cohen may think of his own book as geared to these more fundamental questions rather than to a theory of law in society. If it were so, it were a grievous truth, for it would strip the book of much of its significance for a generation which must at its peril discover the relation of law to the whole play of social forces.

I shall confess that I am a bit perplexed as to what Professor Cohen intends to convey on this issue. The preface, where an author of essays written over a period of time and in diverse subjects has a chance to indicate his emphases, does not remove my confusion. For while he dwells principally on the theme of law and reason, he describes the second of his four sections as surveying "the part played by fundamental legal institutions in maintaining the present social and economic order and in blocking the road to a better one" (p. viii). I cannot feel that the essays to which this refers carry the analysis very far in the direction it indicates. But aside from that, such a statement carries with it very serious intellectual responsibilities. For it reaches to the heart of what is perhaps the crucial issue in a social philosophy of law—the reciprocal relation of legal and other social institutions in the realm of power. And such an issue cannot be dismissed with a simple statement, but must be the subject of a complex analysis. We are left in doubt as to whether Professor Cohen means his statement as a description only of the role that American legal institutions are currently playing or as a generalization about the nature and function of all fundamental legal institutions in any institutional system. We do not know what elements in the present social and economic order are thus maintained, or what principle explains the tie-up. Nor do we know whether the reciprocal of Professor Cohen's position is also true— that our legal institutions are maintained by the elements of economic power in our social system; and we are left somewhat in amazement as to how to reconcile the startlingly revolutionary implications that would flow from Professor Cohen's statement with his expressed rejection of an economic interpretation of law or of a Marxist view of history.

It is doubtless unfair to expect a group of scattered essays and reviews to yield an articulated or comprehensive social theory of law. It seems less unfair to expect somewhere, in a book oriented toward a consideration of law and the social order, a direct wrestling with the problems and the implications of the major issues in the social analysis of law. Professor Cohen, by a remark in the preface, leads us to hope that he will eventually publish a connected treatise on legal philosophy.[3] There is no one in the field who would not await such a treatise eagerly, all the more so if it would tie up the author's known views on method in legal thinking with his integrated theory of the social order. Meanwhile it may not be amiss to sketch out some of the further problems that such a theory would have to face.

No legal philosophy of the generation on which we are now entered will have a prospect of adequacy unless it starts from a theory of social change. Unfortunately Professor Cohen has advanced no such theory, unless we are to assume that his principle of polarity has historical implications as well as metaphysical, and that the "perpetual and cruel swing from one extreme error to its opposite" is an inherent part of the historical process. That would imply either a pendular or a cyclical theory of intellectual change, but it would still provide for no coherent theory of the social process. For lack of such a theory a philosophy of law will be found to move chiefly on the ideological plane, a danger to which any rationalist philosophy exposes its holder and against which Professor Cohen himself utters a warning in his essay on Dean Pound.

In an adequate theory of law in society the movement of legal ideas, the formation and the contours of legal institutions, the shifting alignments of economic and political power, and the entire play of forces in the world of social thought and social fact would have to be related. Which is to say that, among other things, such a theory would have to tackle deliberately and with all the resources available the vexed problem of the determination of legal ideas and institutions by outside forces, whether economic or more broadly social. It would have not only to fix the extent and boundaries of whatever determinism existed, but also to analyze the elements of

---

[3] This has not yet (1939) appeared.

autonomous development, and in terms of both seek to account for the amazing diversity, lags, and inconsistencies of legal institutional forms. It would have to examine the relation between the structure of law and the ramifications of economic activity on which it rests. It would have to show the tie-up between the judicial process and the social process, analyze the agencies on which the growth of the law depends—judicial, statutory, administrative, or extra-governmental—and account for the shift in emphasis and creativeness from one to another. It would have to deal with the historical logic of the rise of important legal doctrines and institutions, the social logic of their persistence, and the social consequences of their functioning. It would have to use all the sophistication and all the hard grip of fact at its disposal in studying the actual set-up of legal procedure and legal machinery, and its meaning in the known context of the legal profession and under the bewildering impact of all the forces loose in modern life.

This is a partial statement of a huge and complex task—a task for a whole generation rather than a single mind. With some aspects of the issues raised Professor Cohen has dealt brilliantly; on other aspects some of our best legal thinkers are now at work. None of them will ever achieve a complete and articulated theory, but we may hope that each tentative synthesis will carry us farther toward clarity and adequacy. But the whole line of movement toward a social orientation in law represents a shift of axis—a shift which Professor Cohen, with his eye primarily on the philosophic traditions, may be the less mobile in making. All around legal theory, in the social sciences, are rich theoretical resources waiting to be assimilated to its uses. But Professor Cohen, with his austere rejection of whatever is unfinished and overaccented, with his rationalist philosophy and his metaphysical interests, will probably have but small appeal for a generation determined to hew a social theory out of these resources. Despite the admirable manner in which he applies the principle of polarity, Professor Cohen's inherent preference as a rationalist is for the invariant and abiding realities of life rather than for the contingent and the changing institutions. But the impelling needs of the present are for change and its mastery, and out of the materials of our shifting social world we shall have to fashion as best we can a social theory of law.

In the attainment of that task we shall not be able to dispense with much of the intellectual equipment which Professor Cohen offers us in this book. Nor should we need any longer to attack the errors he has here so effectively exposed—the smug rejection of metaphysics, the blind worship of immediate experience, the atomistic emphasis on the individual case, and the short-sighted concentration on the individual judge. Our thinkers will, moreover, have to proceed in something like Professor Cohen's temper—his exacting mind, his circumspectness about inflated claims, his social sympathy and passion for social justice, his courage in embracing moral values and in not shrinking from the intellectually rigorous, and his wisdom in never making a method an end in itself. The book should thus serve as an intellectual challenge to the proponents of drastic experiment and revaluation in the law—a challenge to them to keep their powder dry, to understand that no lasting change in society or philosophy can be brought about without an exactingly considered orientation. It is here that Professor Cohen will leave his enduring impress. He will have taught us the importance of philosophic values and scientific method in legal thinking, no matter with what materials it works or toward what objectives it drives.

1933

18

Corwin and the Judicial Power[1]

WITH his book *Court over Constitution* Professor Corwin consolidates his position as our foremost student of the doctrine and dynamics of judicial supremacy. Ever since his first book a quarter-century ago on *The Doctrine of Judicial Review* and his early articles on the concepts of "vested rights" and "higher law" in American jurisprudence, his writings have tended to keep pace with the changing forms that the Supreme Court's power and its doctrinal defenses have taken. Having come to Princeton as one of the young preceptors recruited by Woodrow Wilson when he sought to vitalize politics and history under his university administration, Corwin has clung to a faith in popular government as against judicial supremacy ever since. Just as his social outlook spans the distance between Wilsonian idealism and the militant democracy of the New Deal, so his interest in the Court spans the distance between the furor raised by the judicial-recall proposal of the first Roosevelt and the Court reorganization proposal of the second. Increasingly his writings have taken on greater relevance for us. They have become less purely studies in the history of ideas (although so recent a book as the 1934 *Commerce Power versus States Rights* was to a degree an exercise in syllogistic sequences) and more strikingly expressions of that sense of the modern instance backed by an immense historical erudition which has given him his characteristic quality.

Court over Constitution [2] (Professor Corwin has not been happy in the choice of some of his recent titles) is a collection of five more or less independent law-review articles and lectures. None the less it has elements of a real unity. According to the subtitle, they are all

---

[1] This paper was published in an abbreviated form in the *Harvard Law Review*. The original paper is here given.
[2] Princeton University Press, 1938.

concerned with "judicial review as an instrument of popular government." This subtitle should, however, not be taken as descriptive of either the functioning or function of judicial review, but as an expression of the author's critical position toward it. Given some sort of judicial review, he feels that it ought to be used and presumably can be used as an instrument of popular government. And he offers this as a yardstick against which to measure the actual historical role of judicial review.

That role turns out to be anything but glorious. As judicial supremacy the Court's power is not doctrinally defensible when it is set over against the power of Congress (Chapter I); nor is it organically related to the Constitution (Chapter II); nor is it, except by a liberal interpretation of the congressional spending power, compatible with an effective functioning of the federal system (Chapter III); moreover, the judicial power at its worst, as proved by an intensive study of the Pollock income-tax case, operates in defiance of jurisdictional rules, history, logic, precedent, public opinion, national policy, and even the formal doctrine of judicial review (Chapter IV); finally, in so far as it has thrived on and helped build up the myth of the divinity of the Constitution, it has set a fetishized Constitution (and incidentally its own interpretation of it) over the interests of a developing nation, and frustrated that final test of a democratic Constitution—the test of serviceability (Chapter V).

Professor Corwin's hand has not lost its magic in the area of doctrinal history written à clef. His defense of the Jeffersonian "departmental" theory of the equal power of each of the three departments to interpret the Constitution, as against the "juristic" theory of the binding finality of the Supreme Court's interpretation, is brilliantly learned and persuasive. While actual constitutional practice seems, despite the battle of the scholars, to have settled the moot question of the validity of judicial review as an institution, Professor Corwin points out that neither history nor doctrine has in any sense settled the problem of its scope and finality—that is, of judicial supremacy as distinguished from the valid functioning of the judicial process. The departmental theory, which in effect means legislative supremacy in the legislative field, "still offers a viable alternative." Actually judicial supremacy has been able to maintain itself chiefly through the role of the Court as a constitution-maker.

And the Court has fulfilled this role not by reading certain phrases in the Constitution but by reading certain doctrines into it. Nowhere has this creative function of the Court in manufacturing synthetic constitutions been more brilliantly elaborated than in Corwin's second chapter. If you ever doubted that doctrines had an autonomous existence of their own more or less independent of the Constitution, read this essay.

But this very role of the Court as doctrine-maker, doctrine-user, and doctrine-manipulator may have its compensations and contradictions. Corwin's third chapter, the most optimistic in the book, deals with the doctrines that have clustered about our federal system. If Corwin is correct, the history of constitutional ideas and practices may be read as the record of a struggle between the "co-operative" and "competitive" conceptions of federalism, with the balance in favor of the former. The framers had in mind the possibility that "the national government should utilize the states as subordinate instruments of its powers." Even under the states' rights theory this was modified only to bring in the precondition of the consent of the state. Today we are proceeding rapidly to gear the two sets of powers together in a single governmental machine. One method is by using the power of the national government over commerce and communications to help enforce desirable state policies (e.g., lotteries, white slavery, convict-made goods, child labor). The other method is through grants-in-aid, used to induce state governments (some would say "bribe" rather than "induce") to follow certain national policies.

Corwin sees in the functioning of the co-operative federal concepts the possibility of "effective" government. He argues, at least by implication, that it is only thus that we have managed to survive. One might answer that we have never had really effective government, and that we have survived in spite of the obstructionism of the competitive concepts of federalism that we have on the whole followed. Nevertheless his essay offers a fresh interpretation of the arid controversy between states' rights and nationalism. And he does make out as persuasive a case as I have ever seen for the constitutional, administrative, and moral validity of a system of grants-in-aid.

What is not so persuasive is his optimism that such a co-operative concept of federalism will be held constitutional by the Court. It will be recalled that Professor Corwin expressed a similar optimism about the constitutionality of the New Deal in his *Twilight of the Supreme Court,* only to have the Court play ducks and drakes with his title and thesis while the ink was scarcely dry on his book. Professor Corwin's book became thus not only a commentary on history but also, in a sense, a part of it—as much a victim of the Court majority's expression of its class view as was the AAA. Professor Corwin was correct in his doctrinal analysis: the Court could very easily have held the New Deal constitutional. But it chose not to. That is to say, Professor Corwin miscalculated on the time element and on the dynamic which would lead the Court to see the light. The Court became a good deal more powerful before it became a good deal less powerful. And it became less powerful not through recognizing the national need, but through a test of strength with the President.

There is a similar confusion in this book with regard to timing and dynamics. Professor Corwin says that the Court has "beat a re-treat from certain out-of-date positions regarding national power, thereby emphasizing anew its recognition that judicial review is a process of popular government" (pp. 175–176). In the first place, I doubt that the Court's retreat ever embodied such a recognition. It was a stubborn and reluctant retreat. The Court's liberalism after the Jones and Laughlin decision was a shotgun liberalism; and now it has chosen, so far as labor cases are concerned, to annul the mar-riage into which it was thus precipitately thrust. Whatever was valid in Professor Corwin's sentence in the heyday of the Court's liberal phase is no longer valid after the new Labor Board deci-sions.[3] Professor Corwin will have once more to revise his timing.

I think the confusion in the sense of timing is linked with the confusion with respect to dynamics. As long as we rely on the Court's own self-restraint to furnish the motive force, judicial review can never become an instrument either of popular government or of effective government. That is to say, no governmental institution that consists of a group of legal technicians appointed for life can ever hope to cope with, much less solve, the exigent problems of our polity. If Professor Corwin had chosen in this book to dig more

---

[3] I refer here and below to the 1939 decisions in the Consolidated Edison case and the Fansteel, Sands, and Columbian Enameling cases.

deeply into the class roots of the Court's exercise of power, he might have laid bare the failure of the Court to give us effective government and its unwillingness to give us popular government.

It is apparent why Professor Corwin and others like him should feel that judicial review is not incompatible with popular government. Every analyst of judicial review confronts a basic polarity in it. On the one hand it may be the instrument for the exercise of arbitrary power by a small group; on the other hand it may offer an instrument flexible enough to adjust itself to the needs of the country and the will of the majority. Through the historical interplay of divergent social forces and varied judicial personalities upon the same constitution and the same body of judicial doctrine, the Court in any crucial case has two alternative roads to follow. In the New Deal cases, for example, as Professor Corwin has several times pointed out, the Court might have followed a broad interpretation of both the commerce and the spending powers instead of a narrow one. It deliberately chose the interpretation least favorable to Congress and the administration. But the important fact, for Professor Corwin as for others, is that the two alternative roads were always there. "The road not taken," to use one of Robert Frost's phrases, in the Carter Coal case, became the road that was taken in the Jones and Laughlin case.

Professor Corwin is right in stressing the extent to which the Court's role as a doctrine-maker and therefore a constitution-maker may give flexibility to the Constitution and the body of doctrine it is interpreting. The very thing that creates the Court's power leads also to a way of egress from it. Thus also the very independence of the judges from the constitutional documents they are interpreting may lead to the use of the Constitution as an instrument for an effective national policy, as was so notably illustrated in Marshall's judicial career. For if the Constitution were hardened and formalized into something rigid, there could be no escape. What offers escape is the fact that "judicial review contributed to the survival of the Constitution . . . largely by displacing it"—that is, by displacing it with a vague and synthetic body of constitutional doctrines. And when that entity is unformalized and is to be found only in a large mass of judicial decisions and there often only by implication, there is a chance to follow one doctrinal road rather than another.

This is, one might say, the dialectic of the judicial process in the United States. But in recognizing this polarity within the judicial power there is a danger that one will grow confused and shuttle unceasingly between the two poles. Professor Corwin has not made up his mind that it is the judicial power itself which stands in the way of effective popular government. To him it is still only the misuse of the judicial power; hence hope for a liberal Court interpretation of the national powers and of a co-operative state-nation federalism springs forever in his breast. The weakness of this hope lies in the fact that no objective mechanism is provided by which the chances of effective popular government are removed from the subjective plane of the will and the self-restraint of the judges themselves.

Actually this whole question of what mechanism we shall use to translate judicial review into popular government has never been rigorously analyzed. Mr. Dooley, who has in this field been elevated to the rank of a profound theorist, says it is the "election returns" which furnish the mechanism; and much of the defense of the recent reactionary Labor Board decisions of the Supreme Court run in Dooleyesque terms. Mr. Charles Warren and his school rely on the judges' sensitiveness to the currents of public opinion and the fact that the appointments to the Court in the end follow that public opinion, although with an intervening lag. Justice Holmes and President Roosevelt have both agreed that the only safe mechanism is for the judges to follow the legislative and executive mandate by a hands-off policy on the part of the Court; unfortunately this means in actual terms that we are asking the judges to use their self-restraint in giving priority to the legislative and executive mandate. It was Justice Stone who remarked in his AAA dissent that "the only restraint we have is our self-restraint"; and now in the recent Labor Board cases we have had a chance to see how closely similar the operation of Justice Stone's self-restraint may be to that of Justices Hughes and Roberts. The whole history of the Court indicates, to use an antithesis that Professor Corwin himself quotes from Alexander Hamilton, that the judges have tended to exercise *will* rather than *judgment*. Why should we expect them to stop now?

I think that Professor Corwin would, for the most part, agree with this analysis. Yet he has allowed himself at times to fall into a position that is incompatible with it. I think he has been led, by the very clarity with which he sees the alternative doctrinal roads that the Court might have taken, to fall into the belief that the judges have only to see those alternatives with equal clarity in order to follow the better road. There is no basis for believing that the problem of judicial supremacy can be settled in any way except by eliminating judicial supremacy. Professor Corwin's book would have been richer and stronger if he had followed out the implications of his own analysis.

1939

19

Carl Becker: Historian of the Heavenly City[1]

HERE is a book so simple, so light, so clear, that one feels didactic in pointing out that it is really a scholarly study in the history of ideas, and a bit ponderous in assessing it (as it must none the less be assessed) a classic. It is cast unmistakably in an enduring mold. Into it a lavish scholarship has been poured, but with a hand so deft as to conceal everything except the significant. Those who seek the tortuous in thought and the magisterial in style will do well to avoid this book. They will be cruelly duped by its effortless clarity and will conclude that what is so smooth in the reading cannot have been weighty in the writing. For Mr. Becker has attained here that final simplicity by which the idea and the word are but phases of each other and move to a seemingly inevitable rhythm. In this book he reveals more fully even than in his previous writing a maturity and a wisdom that flow lightly from his experience but for which the rest of us must sweat. He has achieved that most difficult of all victories for the scholar—a knowledge of what to omit as well as what to include. Here is no mere emptying of notebooks but the distillation of a mind.

And since it is a distinctive mind, we may be grateful that through it the author has written his world, his generation, himself into this account of the ideas of the eighteenth-century Philosophers. Reading the book one is impressed with the truth of Maitland's remark that the best history is written backward. The author starts with the preoccupations of his contemporary world; in the light of them he has turned the ideas of the Philosophers about in his mind until they have revealed exactly those facets that hold the greatest interest

---

[1] *The Heavenly City of the Eighteenth-Century Philosophers.* Storrs Lectures, 1931. New Haven, Yale University Press, 1932.

for our own generation. This brilliant, heroic and slightly ridiculous band of Philosophers—Rousseau, Diderot, Hume, Herder, Gibbon, Voltaire, and the others—who have undoubtedly changed the shape of our thinking and therefore of our history, has been written about copiously and in a variety of ways. Be certain that wherever you have seen some glowing and plentifully capitalized account of the Age of Reason, or the Enlightenment, or the great Humanists, or the growth of Freedom of Thought, or the Increase of Tolerance, or the history of Progress or of Liberty, you have come unavoidably upon their names. And they have been invested therefore with that somewhat unctuous association that comes from always being found on the side of the angels, especially when those angels are nineteenth century and Whig. There was indeed a period in which a slight tang of scandal still attached to them, the scandal of being atheist and revolutionary and mostly French; but that was before the full effects of the libertarian influence of Auguste Comte and John Stuart Mill had been completely felt. And there has been a period more recently in which we have stipulated a dissent from their theories of natural law before we could quite accept the rest of their doctrine. But in the main our valuations of the Philosophers have incorporated and expressed nineteenth-century intellectual experience, and have been curiously unreceptive to the tremendous change that has come upon our thought since the World War.

Mr. Becker is far from being an intellectual Whig, although I have read somewhere else his expression of his political faith as a liberal. This is, I take it, one aspect of the importance of his book on such a subject, aside from the sheer delight of it. The detached, remote, slightly acidulous manner in which he inspects the Philosophers and their entire baggage of ideas—their execration of priests and kings, their attempts to become harmonious with Nature, their theories of progress, their eager glances at Posterity—flows not only from the author's shrewd insight into the springs of human conduct; it is the product of our entire present generation, one which has not only learned to question existing institutions but, whether out of philosophy or out of despair, has become skeptical of the very questioning itself. The author's approach to the eighteenth century is not therefore that of the attack direct. He achieves a more telling effect by raillery than he could have achieved by heavy artillery. Instead of blowing the age to smithereens he stands it gaily on its head. His central thesis, expressed also in his title, is a paradox: the Philosophers, who thought that they were using reason to destroy faith, were really constructing a faith of their own, and found finally that they had reared for themselves a new and gleaming City of God.

It is all a little like the two sides of a man's face that are supposed to reveal contrasting aspects of his character: look at one side and it is reason you see, look at the other and it is faith. This dual visage in the system of the Philosophers the author presents with a skill that is at once our admiration and our despair, so subtly has he worked out the logical—or perhaps we should say the psychological —development of their thought.

They are shown as a group of men intent on setting things right; to do this they find it necessary first to remove the obstacles that have stood in the path of human development; they find those obstacles to be chiefly superstition, ignorance, and authority. Accordingly they deliver a frontal attack on Church and State, on priests and kings; they expose to the merciless scrutiny of their intellect institutions which God and man had taken centuries to build up; they find their most effective weapon in the cold power of reason. But in the process the very coldness of their reasoning becomes an enthusiasm with them, their hatred of priests and kings a demonology, their love of humanity and their projects for its reform a religion. They find in the concept of Nature a satisfying mechanistic explanation of life, which makes unnecessary the old theological explanations; they embrace it eagerly, try to come into harmony with it—only to find that they have replaced an old God with a new one. When they try to follow their naturalistic theories to a logical conclusion, they come squarely up against atheism and immorality; trapped, they have recourse to distinctions, and proceed to separate what is essential and noble in Nature from what is base and degraded. They set out on a magnificent research of history, in quest of the something that is essential to human nature, so that on the basis of it they may reconstruct human society. They find in the past certain intervals of lucidity, especially the *quatre âges heureux*, but in the main they find only a wasteland dominated by "the triumph of barbarism and religion," for "in a very real sense they never pass the frontiers of the eighteenth century"; they have only projected their own reformist scale of values into the past, and their "new history" has been "philosophy teaching by example." Having thus ransacked the past for Hell, they turn to the future for Heaven. They find that to fight the Christian religion they must construct a picture of human life as dramatic as the Christian story, for "it is true of ideas as of men that they cannot fight unless they occupy the same ground." Accordingly they evolve the concept of social progress, to which they dedicate themselves; and in the process they discover "the uses of posterity," for the martyrdom suffered in the struggle for refashioning society is rewarded by immortal life in the memory of succeeding generations.

This picture of the eighteenth-century mind as the author draws it before our eyes in vivid strokes is, some will fear, perhaps too brilliant to be fair and too pat to be sound. The direct question of its authenticity as an analysis would require a far more immediate acquaintance with eighteenth-century writings and the personalities of the Philosophers than most of us would be able to muster. But more important perhaps than the authenticity of the analysis are its implications. And it is these implications that cut completely across the boundaries of academic specialties, and make this as fitting a volume for the Storrs series of lectures at the Yale Law School as any of the earlier volumes which have confronted directly the problems of legal philosophy. Of the rich mass of these broader issues that the book raises, for law as for other social studies, we may select three groups that seem most significant.

The first has to do with the method that the book presents for the study of the history of ideas. That method is not the traditional one. It has been, as we all know, too true in the past that the history of ideas has been written genealogically, in the manner of Deuteronomy. It has been for the most part an exercise in chain-making: link has been added to link in tracing the "development" of some doctrine or theory, each great thinker being represented as having just so much sounder a view than his predecessors and passing on his accumulated advantage to his successors. And the entire development is generally traced within some group of ideas in economics or law or politics. What Mr. Becker succeeds amazingly in doing is to capture the mind and mood of a whole age. He compasses this partly by his skillful use of the concept of the "climate of opinion," partly by his subtle understanding of the anatomy of an entire system of thought and the interplay within it of emotional and intellectual elements. He develops the idea of the climate of opinion by contrasting the things that seem obvious and the things that seem strange to an ordinary man in the day of Aquinas and Dante, in the day of Voltaire and Hume, and in the day of Einstein and H. G. Wells. The enormous advantage of such an approach in the history of ideas is that it enables the author to deal with things unseen as well as things seen, to discuss for an age those preconceptions which may be more important than its expressed beliefs. Mr. Becker charts not only the things the Philosophers thought and talked about and the ideas they were obsessed with, but also the things they did not talk about, either because they deemed them too obviously true to need discussion or statement, or because they had not yet glimpsed them as separate entities.

Related to this is the chance that such a method offers of studying the entire *Zusammenhang* of an age—the relation of its literature and its law and its religion and its philosophy and its politics. Not in the hands of every writer will this relation be presented as artfully as in this book; there is of course the danger that where the learning is carried less lightly it will lead to the introduction of a horrendous apparatus. But it is a valuable technique, and in the history of legal ideas especially its organic quality will be useful. For legal history is notoriously tortuous, paradoxical, erratic; to try to trace it outside of its integral relations with the rest of the climate of opinion will make it merely whimsical; and to sever the crabbed logic of its development from the rich emotional growths of its time will make it what it was never intended to be—merely a black-letter study.

Mr. Becker's own handling of this method in his book is so effective that it may seem carping to quarrel with it on some scores. But I feel that he would have given his picture of the eighteenth-century mind a greater air of conviction for us if he had introduced into it some of the roughnesses and loose ends that we see around us in our own age, and had been less insistent in making out of it a paradox within a unity. Such an oversimplification is probably the price we should have under any circumstances to pay for the precision of the analysis. But it is emphasized by several further facts. The system of the Philosophers is, quite rightly, constructed from materials scattered over the century, from Bayle and Fontenelle to Robespierre and Madame Roland. These people span several generations; they were addressing their thought and their words to widely variant situations; and unless these situations are expressly taken into account, the unity of the thought is attained at the cost of some dislocation. Moreover, they were only intellectuals, and the sum of what intellectuals think does not—as some of us have learned to our sorrow—add up to the mind of an age. When you talk of "the age," says Emerson in his essay on "The Times," you mean your own platoon of people. The Philosophers undoubtedly labored under a similar delusion. They were indeed the men of letters, the men of learning, to some extent the "men of sense" of the age. But they represented only themselves, and perhaps also the middle class whose road to power they were smoothing. They did not represent either the classes whom they were seeking to depose or the masses whose plight they could scarcely estimate. And it is here that we reach the gravest criticism that may be made of Mr. Becker's method. He leaves out of account the whole play of economic and political forces out of which ideas grow. He is so concerned with giving us the climate of opinion that he forgets about the soil of opinion.

The second group of issues that the book raises has to do with the theory of natural law. Nature is of course the principal protagonist in the intellectual drama built around the Philosophers: it is in a sense both the hero and the villain of the piece. The Philosophers, says Mr. Becker, were through all those years putting God on trial: "the affair was nothing less than the intellectual *cause célèbre* of the age." In the same way we may say that throughout the book Mr. Becker is putting Nature on trial, and in this he is also reflecting the contemporary suspicion of natural law and the whole concept of the natural. From this angle the experience of the Philosophers with "the laws of Nature and of Nature's God" is of real relevance to our own situation. The appeal to natural law by the eighteenth century was an appeal from the positive law of Church and State, which was held to be impeding cultural progress. In the American experience of the last half-century the appeal has also been from the positive law, although it has been made not in the name of cultural progress but in the name of stability, and it has been used by the Supreme Court against the more democratic legislative programs of the states and of Congress.

But Mr. Becker points out an extremely significant progression in the intellectual odyssey of the Philosophers. The natural law that they finally arrived at did not belong to the Nature with which they started. That Nature they took from seventeenth-century science, and its spirit was matter-of-fact and non-ethical, much like our present science. But when they followed up its implications it led either to a complete acceptance of what is, which would have defeated their reformism, or to the denial of morality which would endanger the whole social fabric, including any new one they might construct. They retreated, therefore, to a natural law that was founded upon human nature in its best aspects—something essential to man which they hoped to discover by their historical research. This was, Mr. Becker points out, far from the complete atomism involved in Locke's denial of innate ideas; it was rather the rediscovery of medieval "realism"; and "the innate ideas which Locke had so politely dismissed by way of the hall door had to be surreptitiously brought back again through the kitchen window."

Does this have some relevance to our own situation? The social effects of the application of natural law concepts by the Supreme Court have produced such a revulsion among our jurists and other intellectuals that they have fled to an atomism which would deny that there is anything at all "essential to man" by which positive law must be judged. Can we too rediscover something approaching medieval realism and believe in it? Thus far in our quest for man in general we have had to rely on a psychology no further advanced in this respect than that of Locke and Hartley, and a real natural law must first of all await an adequate psychology. From another direction, the possibilities of the Marxist historical analysis for jurisprudence have not yet been incorporated into our thinking, but one may read between Mr. Becker's lines the warning that is implied in the fact that in a somewhat similar historical research the eighteenth-century Philosophers never once stirred from the closed chamber of their own minds.

The book raises finally a group of issues that is tied up with the problem of social change in the eighteenth century and in our own time. The period of the Philosophers was a period remarkably like the present. It was an age of intense disorganization, of changing intellectual horizons, of preparation for a social upheaval. The book, being a study of the minds most active in this context, is therefore most significant as a study in the dynamics of intellectual revolution. And our attempt to appraise the revolutionary thought of an age so like our own, to examine its consistency, to see to what extent these thinkers were gigantic minds and to what extent they were merely deluding themselves with dreams of a heavenly city, is in reality so much more than history: it is an attempt to orient ourselves with regard to our own intellectual instability.

Mr. Becker's scalpel lays bare two principal weaknesses in the anatomy of the Philosophers' thought: the religious, almost messianic, character of their rationalism, and the fact that, although they affected to despise morality and religion, when they found that their fight might lead through the assault on these to the destruction of the social fabric, they pulled their punches. With the first of these the author deals the more effectively. In a very significant section in the last chapter he points to the religious ritualism of the French Revolution as the logical sequel to the heavenly city of the Philosophers, and then turning to the communist movement and the Russian Revolution he shows the fundamentally religious character of Marxist agitation and thought and the religious symbolism involved for example in the apotheosis of Lenin. This is of course entirely true, but it may be pointed out that Mr. Becker's analogy between the Philosophers and the communists is too closely drawn. The enthusiasm of the first was largely *Schwärmerei;* it was the sort of day-dreaming and project-making that intellectuals have always been prone to, and on which incidentally the best of our intellectual achievement has been built. But the religious fervor of the communists has a mass base; it springs, as all of us recognize, from the passion arising out of a desperate economic situation.

It is for that reason that Mr. Becker's second indictment of the Philosophers—that in the crucial moment they pulled their punches —is even less applicable to the present revolutionary movements. The Philosophers were interested enough in an intellectual revolution, so long as it did not involve a real break with the social heritage. But they stopped short of social revolution because they were themselves an integral part of the world that would thus be destroyed. Hume locked his *Dialogues* up in a desk because he shrank from the moral depravity that might flow from his strictly logical theses; Franklin abandoned his youthful atheism because, as Mr.

Becker remarks, it was "not very useful to him, a respectable printer and politician living in Philadelphia." For was he not Poor Richard, the best bourgeois of them all, dependent for his career to swim on the rapidly mounting tide of middle-class power? Here again a closer inquiry into the economic soil of eighteenth-century ideas would have clarified and corrected some of the implications of the book. For while communist Russia is keeping a good part of the capitalist social heritage—our entire technological system, our money mechanism, our militarist and international tactics—its driving revolutionary strength is far from the compromises of Hume and Franklin and Diderot. And that strength is, we may guess, derived from an entire economic class, and not from philosophers.

1932

20

Roosevelt and History

THE American people, Mr. Dooley once reminded us, build their triumphal arches out of bricks, to have missiles handy when their heroes have fallen. So with Franklin D. Roosevelt, who has had his taste of Carlylean hero-worship and is now (1938) experiencing one of the fiercest lynching bees in our history. In this context the annotating and publishing of five volumes of the President's state papers [1]—one for the years of his governorship and one for each of the years of his first term, with volumes for the later years to follow—is an act of historical consciousness. Mr. Roosevelt is making his appeal from the distortions of the day to the perspective of the generations.

His volumes deserve that sort of perspective. They represent a significant event both in the art of history and in the history of publishing. One could devote considerable comment to such things as the excellent format; the order and clarity of the editing by Judge Samuel Rosenman, who was the Governor's counsel and has been the President's literary aid and adviser; the dramatic story the speeches and messages tell of political conflict and national crisis and vast administrative effort in dealing with it; the light that the President's prefaces and notes and the excerpts from press conferences shed on the inside history of some of the major events and on future policy. But these are not volumes to be reviewed briefly for either text or gloss. It takes a week of reading merely to hit the high spots of the 3500 pages, a million and a half words; one would need a small volume for adequate comment and criticism. I prefer to meet the President's courageous gesture toward history by a more foolhardy gesture, and risk setting down a few reflections that the

---

[1] *The Public Papers and Addresses of Franklin D. Roosevelt.* New York, Random House, 1938.

volumes evoke on Mr. Roosevelt's place in what Justice Holmes has
called "the campaign of history."

I use the Holmes phrase deliberately. For there can be no doubt
that Mr. Roosevelt would be but small shakes if history had not
conscripted him to its wars. The figure of him that emerges even
from these relatively formal pages is a warm and human figure, with
a lusty talent for both talk and action—but it is not that of a superman. Had he come to the presidency at another time—say in 1924
instead of 1932—he might never have emerged as more than a
skillful politician, with a sharp mind, an expansive manner, a sense
of command. The first volume of these papers, dealing with his
years as Governor, is entitled *The Genesis of the New Deal* only as
a historical afterthought. It needed the years that his sickness gave
him of enforced isolation and brooding reflection to develop in the
Roosevelt of the 1920's a sense of mastery over himself and others;
but it needed the tensions of the Great Depression to evoke that
mastery and give it a historical framework within which it had an
impact on events.

Roosevelt was an able officer whose generalship would never have
emerged except in a war atmosphere. It is no accident that the
metaphors throughout the volumes on the presidency are war metaphors. An intense, embittered, twisted personality such as Napoleon or Hitler carries war within him wherever he goes and imposes that war on the world. But a man like Roosevelt, whose energies are closer to the surface, needs the outer compulsions of
economic collapse and social crisis to mobilize those energies and
evoke the martial in them.

But what has been the character of this war? It started as a war
against the depression; it has been transformed, by the inescapable
logic of events, into a war between an entrenched minority and an
awakening majority. I doubt that this trend was either conscious or
deliberate. One can read in the successive volumes the President's
struggle against it, the conflict between his inherited traditions of
thought and action and the coercion of events. There is agony to be
read in these volumes. For Mr. Roosevelt was not born to lead the
democratic phalanxes. History will see in him the paradox of a
landed aristocrat and gentleman farmer, a *rentier* living on funded
income, who had to place himself for a period at the head of the
urban and agrarian masses. He has always conceived of himself as

making the minimum necessary adjustments to the conditions of capitalist collapse; but even that minimum has been fought so bitterly by one of the blindest ruling classes in history that Roosevelt had to become the conscious leader of the majority forces in order to save capitalism despite the capitalists.

In one important sense his class roots have enabled him to assume this role. Had he come from the lower middle class he might have turned out a Hitler; had he come from labor, a Ramsay MacDonald; had he come from the financial group, a Neville Chamberlain. But coming from the landed gentry, with a tradition that had always included a distaste for money-making and not much of a knack at it, he has had a detachment from the economic rulers of America that a man who was one of them or a man who envied them and panted for their position could not have had. Only a member of an old family, a little amused at the fierce pecuniary and speculative absorptions of the *novi homines,* could have had the courage to break with them and take the punishment.

In considering a final estimate, one must remember that the war is still going on and history is written by the survivors. A historian in a fascist America will set Mr. Roosevelt down as weak, indecisive, degenerate, a prisoner among reckless socialist theorists, a dreamer bemused in a humanitarian dream. A historian in a socialist America will see in him a confused but well-intentioned forerunner, who saved America from the anarchy of *laissez-faire* but brought it close to collapse by his failure to carry through the logic of his own premises. Mr. Roosevelt himself does not have, and these volumes do not reveal, a clearly articulated social philosophy. He learns rapidly but retains slowly; he is a brilliant improviser but not a cogent thinker; he is a tactician without being a theorist. Yet he has a constant sense of historical perspective. He knows that we are living on the thin edge of history; he has no illusions about an individual's capacity to rule the forces of the historical process; far more than Lincoln or Andrew Jackson he is aware of his relation to the upsurging movements of American democracy, and of the strength and purposes of the opposing forces.

There are certain things that history will concede his having accomplished toward survival—a framework of social-security legislation, a basic code for labor bargaining that has given organized labor a chance to double its numbers, a set of cushions against precipitous bank panic, a gentleman's code for the marauders of the securities markets, a start toward public control of the utilities and other big business, a liberalization of the Supreme Court and an advance in popular education about the judicial process. Above all else his role has been that of the educator who has had an enormous influence in changing the premises of popular thinking and political discussion. But will that prove enough? Twice he had a chance to go beyond this framework of achievement—once in 1933 in the midst of the general panic, when he could have nationalized the banking and credit system; a second time after his re-election in 1936, when instead of deflecting his energy on a constitutional fight he could have spent it on driving through a decisive program of economic planning. He muffed both chances.

If, as I suspect, Roosevelt's failure turns out to be like that of other reformers who have willed the ends without daring to will the means, he will be better remembered for his inadequacies than for his achievements. Yet whatever the outcome, he will be remembered also as a man who, without being of the people, was able to come near them; who, without being a scholar or an artist or a great master of words, was able to grasp and to some degree communicate what the common man dimly felt. The needs and hungers and aspirations of the ordinary man and woman speak, in all their confusion, through these volumes as they have never spoken before in the state papers of an American President since Lincoln. If these voices eventually will have to find far different channels for expression, it will be because the human vision of the reformers is clearer and stronger than their economic grasp and their political tenacity.

1938

21

Jim Farley: Soldier and Artist

O
URS is a relatively literate administration. Several of the
Cabinet, including Mr. Ickes, Mr. Wallace, and Mr. Cum-
mings, have turned authors; and of the Little Cabinet,
Thurman Arnold and Jerome Frank and Harry Hopkins, in addition to throwing minor frights into dowagers every morning at
breakfast, write books that give the whole family a major scare periodically. And, of course, there are the writing Roosevelts, husband
and wife. But Jim Farley as author is something novel—and de-
lectable. Jim has been, on and off, the biggest breakfast bogy of
them all. He has been damned by the radicals and intellectuals for
a hand-shaking Babbitt. He has been scorched by the reactionaries
as a grafter and a tyrant. And the liberals have pointed their finger
at him as the sinister side of the New Deal. Now Jim has dared write
a book,[1] and has placed his life in our hands.

It is an engaging book and an engaging life. It is the sort of book
that would have delighted Lincoln Steffens. For whatever else may
be said of Jim Farley, he has not a tithe of the hypocrisy of the
Republicans who attack him, and he lacks the smugness and cant
of the reformers. He is proud to be a politician. He delights in re-
counting his methods and his rewards. He knows he has come far
in the world. A poor Irish boy, of a line of peasants and day-laborers,
a boy who worked in the brickyards and tended bar in his mother's
saloon and later got eight dollars a week as a bookkeeper, is now a
dispenser of jobs and patronage to hundreds of thousands. The
political heeler who started by ringing doorbells at Grassy Point,
New York, and who trembled when he reached the heights of an
audience with Al Smith or Boss Murphy, is now a political mover
and shaker, creator and confidant of Governors, Senators, Presi-

---

[1] *Behind the Ballots: the Personal History of a Politician.* New York, Harcourt,
Brace, 1938.

dents. Jim Farley has made good, and this book (whoever may have helped write it) is his utterly unself-conscious success story.

It is the pre-convention campaign of 1932 that looms largest in his mind and book. In 1930, when the Roosevelt forces began preparing the presidential build-up, Farley was New York State Boxing Commissioner, and a second-string politician. In 1932, after the convention, he was the acknowledged field-marshal of the national Democratic forces, hailed as an organizing genius by veteran politicians. The credit for the 1932 victory, both at the convention and at the polls, must go to one of the greatest trio of generals in the history of campaigning—Roosevelt, Farley, and Louis Howe. There never was a stranger assortment than these three made—the smiling and confident patrician who knew how to reach the common man, certain of his star even when he was hazy as to what he would hitch to it; the tall, massive, Irish building-supply salesman who could talk to the run of political heelers and "leaders" because his mentality was theirs, only raised to the nth power of shrewdness and drive; the gnome-like little newspaper reporter, his hundred pounds of body racked by asthma, devious, cunning, a Lilliputian Warwick dominated by the single idea of making his "Franklin" President. In a sense, of this trio, one was the front-man, one the leg-man, one the behind-the-scenes man.

The most important story in the book is the account of the way in which the Garner delegations in Texas and California, which held the key to the 1932 nomination, were won over to Roosevelt. Farley says everything was aboveboard, that there were no "deals," that Hearst had nothing to do with it, that Garner feared to jeopardize the Democratic chances by continuing a bitter-end deadlock in the convention, and released his delegates through Sam Rayburn without any promise having been made about the vice-presidency. The ingenuousness of this is relieved somewhat by Farley's admission that there was a tacit "understanding" about the vice-presidency between Rayburn and himself, although no words passed to confirm it. Logicians interested in intuition and the transcendental would do well to make a study of convention politics.

There is a good deal more "inside stuff" in the book. I suspect that for every decision to tell all, Farley made five more to keep his peace and to convert the book (in Mr. Dooley's phrase) into "a hitching-post for his silences." But what there is makes a rich enough harvest: that Al Smith, for example, never said: "Hello, you old potato" to Roosevelt in the 1932 reconciliation scene, but that the phrase was contributed gratis by a reporter; that Roosevelt and Martin Conboy, his counsel, had not reached any conclusions about Jimmy Walker's guilt or innocence when Walker resigned; that Paul McNutt fought Roosevelt bitterly at the 1932 convention and was not scrupulous in his methods; that Huey Long was the *enfant terrible* of the Roosevelt forces at the convention, almost wrecking them by his exuberance; that his plan for his own role in the campaign was to be given a special train, equipped with loud-speakers, and swing around the forty-eight states promising immediate payment of the soldiers' bonus. The best story in the book is the one about Huey Long's hat. Huey was chafing at the delay in getting his share of the spoils in the form of federal appointments for his men. He determined either to break the President or to break with him. The climax came at a White House interview, during the better part of which the blustering Kingfish kept his bright-ribboned straw hat on in the President's presence. The President was cool, smiling, perfectly aware of what was going on, and quietly firm. Finally Huey took his hat off and kept it off. At the end of the interview he said to Farley: "What the hell is the use of coming down to see this fellow? I can't win any decision over him." Yet before Long's death Roosevelt was worried enough about him. Farley conducted a secret poll indicating that Long would get between three and four million votes running as an independent, fairly well distributed over the country and enough to hold the balance of power in 1936 and elect a Republican. And he learned also that there were "Hate Roosevelt" financial moguls who were ready to put up the money for Long's campaign.

There are other items as interesting, if less momentous: that when the "philatelic scandal" broke and Farley was accused of handing out special stamp issues to friends he could have shown from Post Office records that Republican bigwigs had always got valuable stamp handouts, but decided it was more generous and also better politics at the time to keep quiet; that Roosevelt draws sketches for many of the stamp designs himself; that the Mother's Day stamp was drawn by him, with Whistler's picture as a model, but that in the process of revision at the Bureau of Engravings a vase of flowers had to be added and the mother's feet subtracted, bringing irate letters from Whistlerites on both scores; that Emil Hurja, the wizard ballot-sampler of the Democrats, was way off in 1936, predicting only 376 electoral votes, while Farley guessed dead right; that Roosevelt asked Farley to assure Senator Robinson in the midst of the Supreme Court fight that the Van Devanter vacancy was his but that the appointment could not be made immediately; that the President has not made up his mind about a third term, and is too smart to talk about it now.

Farley loves politics, and is almost a pure artist at it. I call him a pure artist because his art is unobscured and unhindered by considerations of substance. It was sheer and ironic accident that made him the political generalissimo of the New Deal. Had the cards fallen differently, he might with greater comfort have devoted his talents to a Republican or a conservative Democrat. For there is scarcely a breath in the book of the substance of politics—of program and social forces, of revolution and reaction, of labor and capital and the middle class—what the younger group around Mr. Roosevelt calls the "politics of principle." Farley is sometimes likened to Mark Hanna, but in one respect the similarity falls down. It is true that Farley, like Hanna in his day, modernized the political campaign and applied business methods to it—the build-up, the "deals," the salesman treks across the continent, the systematic coverage of minor "leaders," the large-scale "personal touch," the sample polls, the network of reports and communiqués, the elaborate espionage system. Yet in Hanna the capitalist outweighed the politician. His politics was in his own sense a politics of principle—capitalist principle. Farley's is much more a devotion to forms and traditions of the political game.

It is all mimic warfare for him, like the battles of the Norse gods in Valhalla: after the day's fighting their wounds were healed and they all sat down amiably to supper. Farley's politics has the same sporting spirit—like football or boxing. His words indicate that he actually thinks of himself as a prize-fight manager, and of the President as the most valuable fighter in his string. His conception of convention politics is in the sporting tradition; it is chessboard politics, requiring concentration and finesse, but the counters that are moved about have only the symbolic value that attaches to victory or defeat (I am not forgetting the patronage system, which

Farley is frank in defending—but he is not venal), and none of the substantive values upon which in the social struggle victory and defeat themselves depend for meaning. Set his account, for example, beside the account of a Democratic convention in Matthew Josephson's *Politicos* or Herbert Agar's *Pursuit of Happiness;* being moralists, they see the formal hollowness and the hidden social meanings; being a political technician, Farley sees the formal beauties and does not look beyond.

It is from this angle that we may approach two present facts, otherwise paradoxical, about Farley's relation to Roosevelt and his loyalty to the President and his increasing coldness for the New Deal. Farley has been a good soldier persistently. He has followed orders, and often taken the "rap." Bryan had no Farley, nor had Woodrow Wilson, and the measure of their lack was in part the measure of their failure. A Farley is an essential transition figure. No party can move toward the democratic collectivism which is America's manifest destiny without keeping its rear protected and its lines of communication with the past well open. Farley, with his middle-class mentality added to his craftsman's sense of the job has filled that function.

But that same middle-class mentality and that same craftsman's sense are now elements of danger to the New Deal. Farley, for all his discretion in the book, is plainly anguished by the President's drastic persistence in his reform aims. Surely Mr. Roosevelt and his advisers are too much in earnest to play the game well, are taking risks disproportionate to the political rewards, are even endangering Farley's big sacred cow—Party Unity. The story of the past few years is tossed off with a casualness, a discontinuity, a studied aversion to saying much, that show clearly Jim's heart is not in it. The mood of the last pages betrays a sense of almost tragic conflict—between the demands of the good soldier which tell him to remain loyal, and the demands of the craftsman in politics which tell him that Roosevelt and his advisers are allowing considerations of social policy to intrude themselves into the domain of pure politics.

If Farley should follow "Jack" Garner, whom he fervently admires, and break with the administration, what would be the consequence? In one sense, he is already part of the past. The New Deal has also a new politics, which every future administration will have to copy. It is the politics of the deed. In place of Farley's classical allegiance to the patronage system as he has always understood it, there is the politics of relief and the WPA and social security and labor legislation, and grants-in-aid to the states, and farm subsidies and public works. There is little in the book about this politics, for Jim Farley was not brought up to it. Events move fast. Six years ago he was an innovator. Today there are new men for new methods— a Hopkins, an Ickes, a Wallace, a Lilienthal, above all a Corcoran. What Jim Farley must think of these *novi homines,* and how eloquent are his silences about them! His place in history will be most clearly understood when an attempt is made to find a Farley for the new politics. But before that happens much else will have happened that Jim Farley will never understand.

1938

22

Mr. Justice Black

Hugo Black—a Personal History

I WAS on the revenue cutter off Norfolk, along with about seventy-five reporters and photographers who had converged on the pleasant Virginia seaport to surround a man finally trapped. I marveled at how little rancor the quarry showed when he met the newspapermen. In the cabin, before he went on deck to confront the cameras and notebooks, he told me with amusement how he had been hounded in London by American reporters. That very morning I watched his unperturbed cheerfulness survive even the efforts of a photographer outside his cabin to poke his camera between the slats at the bottom of the door; he wished, I suppose, to preserve for posterity a pictorial record of the legs of those inside. Although in his statement Justice Black hit at the distortions of the press, he somehow made the reporters understand that his quarrel was not with them but with their bosses. And two days later he made his radio audience of some thirty million understand why he was talking directly to them. The idea of using the radio was one which had come to him on his way across the Atlantic. It was a sound democratic instinct. And because he followed this instinct, he turned what might have been, in a sense, a lynching bee into something like a triumphal homecoming.

I shall not easily forget an extended conversation with Justice Black on the evening following his arrival. Journalists learn to be skeptical of the drama of events, and yet there are moments when man and occasion combine to leave an ineradicable mark. This was one. Justice Black's biography, as I have pieced it together from this and other sources, is one of the most moving and contradictory records in our history. Since the sources were sympathetic, the record I am setting down may contain a degree of bias or rationalization. I offer it not as a final critical account but as a personal history, in which I have sought to view the action as the actor might have viewed it.

Hugo Black was born in 1886 on a farm in Clay County, Alabama, the youngest of a large family of a desolately poor farmer. He was of Scotch-Irish and English descent, and his Irish ancestors had been driven out of their country for their religious beliefs. When Hugo was five, his father moved to the county seat at Ashland, bought a small store, and became a tolerably successful merchant. The county was poor; it had neither bank nor hospital, but it did boast a primitive sort of academy called Ashland College, which provided the boy's schooling from six to sixteen. He studied medicine for a year, but he had always had a hankering for law, and so he left medicine to complete a two-year law course at the University of Alabama. In 1907, at the age of twenty-one, he settled down to a career as a Birmingham lawyer.

There followed intense work at law, reading crowded into the night hours, rapid political success. Birmingham was the school that taught him. He made close connections with the trade unions; in 1909 he represented the miners' union in its first Alabama strike; later he was attorney for the carpenters' union in another important suit. He loved the techniques of the law, mastered its procedure, began to build a state-wide fame. This led naturally to politics, and Black was elected police judge in 1910, at twenty-four, and prosecuting attorney in 1914. He had been absorbed with politics ever since he could remember; he recalls staying up all night as a boy of ten to listen to the election returns for probate judge. He was a hard and tireless campaigner; for the 1926 election he campaigned for thirteen months, dropping all his work, covering every county in the state, some of them twenty times. His opponents learned to fear him, because his appeal was that of one who knew his audiences and loved to match wits with them. In fact, as I talked with him I had a notion that when he came to make his radio statement he would feel isolated before the microphones. He would, I think, have preferred to carry his answer to actual audiences all over the country, face to face with the people to whom he responded and who responded to him.

That a man like Black should have come to join the Klan is one of those facts monstrously hard to grasp until you approach it not as a moral problem but simply as a piece of political behavior. Black's career was that of a progressive in politics, and in the South in the decade after the World War such a career inevitably crossed that of the Klan. For the Klan had not inconsiderable roots, although twisted ones, in the mass mind. Its superpatriotism fitted the anti-radical mood after the war; its law-enforcement plank went strong in the period of Prohibition racketeering; in regions of economic distress its nativism seemed an insurance against the competition of immigrant labor; amid the decay of religious faith its mystical religionism had an appeal; its attitude toward the Negroes was integral to the Southern psychosis of "white supremacy." In such a soil the Klan grew with an intoxicating speed that seemed its own sanction. Many of the younger Southern leaders felt helpless before it. They must either ride the whirlwind of the Klan or surrender, and they had no thought of surrendering.

It is easy to call their point of view contemptible. It was a tragic mistake, and it is clear that Justice Black thinks so now. But it is easy to be wise after the fact. In Alabama at that time not only the farmer and merchant were Klansmen; 90 per cent of organized labor in Birmingham was enrolled. The common people had been captured by the Klan, for it buttressed them against problems they could not understand with principles that seemed eternal. The Klan assumed, moreover, a radical attitude on many specific issues which appealed to the progressives. Like the fascist movement in Germany, it combined a spurious radicalism with terrorism. Those who leaned toward the first were often able to shut their eyes to the second. But as the Klan madness took its swift and terrible course, and as it became the prey of racketeers and hoodlums, its fascist character grew ever clearer. Before that process had gone far, Hugo Black had left the Klan, but he could not escape the shadow of it.

He was from the very beginning a "joiner." Even before he was of age, he had put in his application for the Knights of Pythias and the Masons. He had a youthful fervor for these secret societies. Somewhere around 1920 he was approached to join the Klan. He pleaded lack of time; he was then Grand Chancellor of the Knights of Pythias and an officer of his Masonic lodge. He was skeptical of the Klan's exclusion of Jews (the Masons admitted them), eager to know the character of its members, suspicious that they might take the law into their own hands. The matter was dropped, but soon a close friend approached Black again, and this time overcame his objections. But it was not until two years later that Black actually attended a meeting and paid dues. He went to very few meetings, and when he spoke it was to warn against lawlessness and religious intolerance. Finally, on the eve of the Senate race, he resigned altogether.

He resigned, but he did not openly repudiate the Klan. To have done so would have taken greater political hardiness than Black possessed. And he accepted in his election the support of the Klan people, because he needed the votes of the workers and farmers who made up its members. In 1926, after the election, he was invited by Esdale, the head of the state lodge, to address a meeting at Birmingham at which Governor-elect Bibb Graves was also to speak. He went to it, as he went to similar meetings of other societies. He was in a jubilant mood after his victory, and he thanked the audience for its support as he had thanked many other audiences. His speech, if the Sprigle version of it is correct, pulsed with a vague religionism and an overaccented brotherly love, but little more. After that, he never attended another Klan meeting, and his relations with the Klan grew steadily worse. In 1928 his support of Al Smith went directly counter to the Klan's policy. In 1930, when Heflin (who had been read out of the party for bolting Smith) ran for the Senate, Black stumped the state against him, further embittering the Klan, which was openly backing Heflin. And it was Black's opposition that defeated Heflin and elected Senator Bankhead, as Heflin has himself admitted.

Hugo Black is no Klansman. Everything that he has stood for in his eleven years in the Senate runs counter to what the Klan has stood for. The Klan itself hates him bitterly now, as the Alabama employers hate him, and it has evidently lent its records with great willingness to the "investigators." Black has supported human rights in their crucial aspect in the America of today—the right to have a job and get decent wages and not work excessive hours; he has fought for adequate relief for the unemployed from the ravages of the depression; he has fought to give Negroes in the South the same economic status as whites, and to save them from discrimination in the provisions of the wage-hour bill; he has fought for the consumer of public-utility services; he has fought for the liberation of the common man from the oppressive weight of the giant corporation lobbies, which have hitherto kept him from thinking freely or freely exercising his political privileges. Black has throughout his Senate career been more than the politico who pays lip-service to the tenets of liberalism. He has been a passionately sincere humanist, guided throughout by his understanding of the fundamental truth of the new militant liberalism—that the basic approach to human rights lies in securing for the individual that economic freedom on which alone the dignity of the individual can be based.

Hugo Black was not born to this knowledge. He was no New England Brahmin, no Western Populist, no New York intellectual. He did not have in his blood and at his command the traditions of intellectual enlightenment that Justice Holmes, Senator La Follette, Justice Cardozo inherited. For what he is, he has had to sweat and fight. He has come up from the ignorance and bigotry of the Southern masses. He has fought his way from a rudimentary schooling and a small-town law practice into national prominence. He has had no one like Emerson near him to discuss Plato with, as Holmes did, no Harvard training as Brandeis did. He has had to grope his way unaided through books, see through their platitudes, get at their truths. On his visit in London the man he sought out was Harold Laski, the place he sought out was Toynbee Hall, the books he looked for in the bookstalls were a volume of Grote's *Aristotle* which was missing from his collection, and Thucydides' *History of the Greek Wars.* Between the philosophical radical of today and Black's origins in the little town of Ashland, Alabama, stretches an enormous span. The story of how that span was built is the story of the education of Hugo Black. And in that education the Klan incident was an episode, blunderingly entered upon and now being bitterly paid for. But the results of that education hearten us with a renewed belief in the possibilities of American life.

Black's Senate record was such as to wipe out, in his own mind as in the minds of those who valued his liberalism and humanity, all concern with, if not all memory of, the brief Klan years. When the nomination to the Supreme Court came to him, he accepted it as a recognition of his work as Senator. If he did not mention to the

President his former Klan membership, it was because by the side of his Senate career it seemed irrelevant. We may regard such a judgment as an error, but it was understandable.

There are some who feel more strongly about his failure to tell the Senate about the Klan connection when the issue was raised. But the same sense of relative unimportance would have operated in Black's mind with respect to the Senate. There would be, in addition, his unwillingness to involve the administration in a row over an episode which seemed to have lost all meaning, the fact that no Senator questioned him on the subject, and finally a feeling of pride that the least his own colleagues in the Senate could do would be to judge him on the basis of their association with him.

When the Sprigle series broke, Black was in London. He knew that groups similar to those behind these articles had, in both his senatorial campaigns, sent agents and investigators to Alabama who had scoured the state to find something they could use against him. In fact, the Sprigle material itself was not new, except for the stenographic records; the letter of resignation and the "grand passport" had both been made public in Alabama during the last Senate fight. Knowing this, Justice Black was inclined to give the American people more credit for keeping their heads than we turned out to deserve. When he found that the articles were raising a storm, he had to face a bitter choice between making a statement and remaining quiet. But it is clear that to put the charges in their true perspective would have been impossible from across the ocean; the only items to survive transatlantic passage and the mercies of the newspaper moguls would have been the admission that he was once a member of the Klan. And Hugo Black has had as good a training in political tactics as the next man. He knows that when you are unscrupulously attacked, instead of answering at a disadvantage, it is better to wait until it is your show, and then strike dramatically and hard. Hence the wait and the eventual radio speech, although as a speech it must be admitted that it lacked the candor and fullness his friends would have liked.

There are several ironies about the whole episode. The obvious one is that so militant a New Dealer should be accused of being a reactionary. Another is that this man, charged with hostility to Negroes, would have faced defeat in another senatorial contest because he had fought too strenuously for raising the wages of Negro mill hands and lumber workers. But the greatest irony is that the most fervent Senate admirer of John Stuart Mill and the liberal tradition should be charged with being a bigot and an enemy of civil liberties. Mill's *Autobiography* and his essay *On Liberty*, Plato's *Dialogues,* and Grote's *Plato*—these are the books on which his mind dwells. But there are two authors whom he has read even more assiduously: Jefferson, whose set of writings in his library is completely marked up; and John W. Draper, whose highly libertarian *Intellectual Development of Europe* he has read four or five times. The curious may even now turn to the *Congressional Record* for 1929 and read Black's fervid speech against the Treasury bill for censoring books from abroad, in which he quoted Draper's account of the burning of the Alexandria library; and then compare it with Heflin's speech on the subject.

I do not mean to say that Justice Black is all of one texture. In fact, the remarkable thing about him is that he is so full of contradictions. He is not a simple man to understand. His critics have called him slippery, but that was not the best word I found to fit him. I found a man who was confident of his strength. I found a quick and elusive intelligence that defied whatever rules I had built up for putting people in their proper niche in my own mind. Here was a man who had toiled day and night over his law books and had still kept an open mind for ideas; a man of limited education and sectional outlook who had managed to become a statesman as well as a tactician; a progressive who was also a Southerner, and who believed that the problems of progressive democracy in the South had to be approached differently from the same problems in the North; a lawyer and politician who knew more about economics than almost anyone in the Senate, and who had dug beneath the political forms of today to their economic realities.

Such a man could do much to vitalize the Court and to broaden himself further in the process. He is on the Court now and he means to stay. He knows that he belongs there, and he feels that the majority of the people want him there. The impression has been built up that he is not of good legal caliber, and that his talents are only those of the police judge and the prosecutor. That is not true. It is true that he never had a Harvard Law School training and never was an operative in a New York law factory. But he has come up against the smart lawyers and the corporation lawyers, both in his practice and in the Senate; and the encounters have not left him with a feeling of inferiority. He probably does not know much about admiralty or patent law, but neither, I should venture, does anyone else on the present Court; both those subjects should long ago have been segregated in a special court of experts. Justice Black is no backwoods lawyer. For years before he came to the Senate he had a large and brilliant law practice in Alabama, which had begun to net him an income of some $40,000 a year. And as for the "certioraris"—those voluminous writs over which the justices exhaust themselves during the summer—time and a quick eye and a nimble intelligence have proved sufficient equipment for other justices.

Technical questions aside, we must recognize that the Supreme Court justice of today must have more than law courses and fat corporation fees to his credit. He is right in the center of the formation of economic and social policy. He must combine technical ability with economic realism and philosophic grasp. Justice Black does not have either the philosophy or the style of Justice Cardozo. But more than anyone else on the Court he resembles his close friend Justice Brandeis, if not in moral fervor at least in the combination of legal acumen and economic knowledge. He may yet write Court history, as he has already written Senate history.

1937

Mr. Justice Black, Dissenting

"THE man who wrote that opinion," I heard a legal friend say of one of Justice Black's dissents, "is a damn good lawyer." And he smiled broadly and knowingly. I did not smile back at the innuendo that Justice Black did not write his own opinions. The remark summed up the peculiar dualism of attitude of the anti-Black people now that he is writing his name large in the Court's annals. They cannot help admiring the courage and ability shown in his decisions; yet the censor that watches over our self-esteem will not permit them to confess that they were wrong about him in the first place. The result is the conclusion that, since the opinions are good ones, it must have been a couple of other fellows who wrote them.

Whoever wrote them, they have set the legal world on its ear. There were many among Justice Black's friends who wanted him to go slow when he came on the Court, wanted him to establish his position before he began applying his drastic progressivism to the judicial process. This applies to several of Black's friends on the Court itself, who received him with a mixture of welcome and trepidation. They regarded him much as a Social Registerite might regard a protracted visit by a relative fresh from the sticks, talented and high-spirited, but uncouth, unpredictable, and a questionable addition to formal parties. They wished he would give himself a chance to mellow. Several are reported to have said that given five or ten years in which to master the lore of the Court and steep himself in its traditions and spirit, Black would make a great justice.

But Black didn't intend to wait that long. Outwardly he proved malleable enough. His relations with his colleagues have been personally cordial. The Chief Justice went out of his way to be friendly. Only Justice McReynolds is still hostile; he regards Black as a renegade Southerner. And well he may, for their two social philosophies are as widely removed as the antipodes. Responding to the friendliness of the other judges, Black has been almost hypersensitive to the Court tradition about personal discreetness. He surrounds even his casual contacts with elaborate safeguards. He is still suffering from the trauma of having people forever on his trail during the agonizing weeks of his *cause célèbre*.

But while eager to play the game in all personal matters, Justice Black has challenged the rules of the game so far as constitutional law is concerned.

Of twenty opinions in which Justice Black's name has thus far (1938) appeared, six have been dissents and six have been concurring opinions in which he disagreed with the Court's reasoning but agreed with the conclusion. In eight he wrote the Court opinion. This is a high ratio of divergence, especially for a new justice. I shall pass over the cases in which Black has written the Court's majority or unanimous decision, because the cases assigned to him have been relatively unimportant. It is as a dissenter that he has most sharply broken the Court's patterns of thought and most distressed even his liberal colleagues.

The case involving the "obligations of contracts" clause (*Indiana ex rel. Anderson v. Brand*) does not at first sight reveal the importance that it possesses. The Indiana legislature in 1927 passed an act establishing a certain tenure for teachers, and then in 1933 it passed another act excluding township schools from the tenure provisions. A teacher in a township school who had lost her job sued on the ground that the 1927 act established a contract whereby she could not be discharged except under certain conditions, and that the 1933 act had impaired the obligation of the contract and was invalid. The Supreme Court, reversing the state court, held with her, but Black dissented. A comparison of his opinion with the majority opinion by Justice Roberts shows disagreements as to the construction both of the state legislation and of Indiana precedents. But basically the disagreement was over the extent of state sovereignty as against the overriding sanctity of contracts. And there, for Black, is the nub of the matter. He believes in legislative supremacy, state or federal, as against judicial supremacy and the rigid hold of contract doctrine. Intellectually he knows where he stands in the struggle, begun in America more than a century ago with *Fletcher v. Peck* and the Dartmouth College case, between those who would freeze our order through property institutions and those who would keep it fluid through legislative change.

But the struggle over the contract clause is more an echo of past battles than an expression of present conflicts. More central in Black's judicial career are his opinions in the utility cases. Two of them stand out—a dissent in *McCart v. Indianapolis Water Company* and a concurring opinion in *United Gas Public Service Company v. Texas*. The Indianapolis Water dissent created a flurry in legal circles on procedural grounds. For Black did the unprecedented thing of dissenting from a *per curiam* decision, in which the Court speaks as a whole rather than through any particular justice. With a sharp, clipped severity the Court held that the lower court, in upholding the state commission's schedule of water rates, had erred in not allowing for an upward trend of prices between 1933 and 1935. The rates had been held not confiscatory in 1933; but— the *per curiam* opinion argued—they might have become confisca-

tory by the time the 1935 decision was handed down. Black's answer
to this decision forms the best opinion he has thus far written. It is
full, detailed, statistical in the best Brandeis manner; it is powerful
in its irony at the fantastic delays of due-process procedure; it cuts
through the overgrowths of legal jargon which screen the fact that
ultimately it is the consumer who pays for the impotence of the
regulatory system and for the luxury of shuttling cases back and
forth between courts. It had taken six years for the Commission's
order to reach the Court; it was now being remanded; at the same
rate, it should be back in the Court again in 1943. Black preferred to
settle it then and there. And he does so on the basis of the prudent-
investment principle which Justice Brandeis had developed in his
classic dissents. In the process he writes a severe condemnation of
the whole practice of the Court, since 1890, of invalidating state
regulation of utility rates.

The Texas gas case was the second round of the utility fight between Black and the Court. Here again he pulled no punches. In a
separate concurring opinion he pointed out that the company is an
affiliate of the Electric Bond and Share, that the salaries paid to the
holding-company officials are set down to operating expenses for
the subsidiary and are paid by the consumer in the form of inflated
rates. This opinion is notable also for its defense of the jury trial as a
method of fixing the validity of commission rate-setting (Justice
McReynolds, in one of his *ex tempore* speeches from the bench,
called it "little more than a farce").

But the dissent which has proved most breath-taking is the one on
the corporation as a person (*Connecticut General Life Insurance
Company v. Johnson*). The California legislature laid a tax on re-in-
surance premiums which was aimed at corporations from other
states. The Court overruled it as violative of the Fourteenth Amendment, which provides that "no state shall . . . deprive any person
of life, liberty, or property without due process of law, nor deny to
any person . . . the equal protection of the laws." Black says quite
simply: "I do not believe that the word 'person' in the Fourteenth
Amendment includes corporations." And thus he sweeps away fifty
years of Supreme Court history and strikes at one of the props of
corporate power.

But he does so only after an interesting survey of the legislative and judicial history of the amendment. I believe he is on solid ground so far as history is concerned. There has been for some time a controversy among American historians as to whether those who framed the amendment intended it as a protection of corporate property rights. That such was their intent was the argument of Roscoe Conkling, one of the members of the congressional committee which drafted the amendment in 1866, when he appeared before the Court in the San Mateo case in 1882. This would imply something of a plot or conspiracy on the part of the committee, for the purpose of the amendment was clearly the protection of the newly granted rights of Negroes against hostile state legislatures. Conkling's thesis was accepted as Court doctrine in 1886 in the Santa Clara case. Black challenges it as irrelevant. Whatever individual members of the committee may have thought or intended, he points to the undoubted fact that the Congress that passed the amendment, the states that ratified it, and the people in whom the amending power rests were told that it was to protect Negroes and not to remove corporations from the regulation of state governments.

Black's argument is good. There are, however, three things that trouble me about it. One is that in the face of fifty years of Court history it is never likely to be more than a courageous gesture. Nor is it merely the time that has elapsed; it is the fact that the personality of the corporation has become an integral part of our constitutional law—right or wrong. The second is that his opinion would have been more complete if he had taken account of the fact that where "person" has been used previously in the language of the law and of lawyers, it has also been construed to include the corporation. The third is that the more strategic line of attack on the abuse of power by the courts would have been to insist that "due process" should be interpreted only to mean procedural safeguards and not substantive determinations of social policy. That was the direction of the Holmes approach, and an economic realist such as Black could carry it out even more completely.

There remains the question of Black's impact on the future. He is not the sort of person who, like Holmes or Brandeis, can build a liberal minority around himself. His liberal colleagues are not ready to go with him; he is too acid, too impetuous, too downright; he ruffles judicial sensibilities. Like the child in the story he cries

out that the king is after all naked, and it has been the whole function of constitutional law to weave imaginary garments for the
nakedness of corporate power. Added to that, there is the fact that
while his decisions are clear and well written they do not have the
brilliance of phrase and the sure legal touch that Holmes had, or the
scrupulous solidity and genius for procedure that Brandeis has.

All of which means that Black has become a judicial crusader
before he has come to maturity as a judge. His strength lies in the
things in which he was strong as Senator—his feel for economic
realities, his intrepid belief in popular democratic government as
against any sort of oligarchy. He seems to belong in the Jacksonian
period of the Court, when the democratic upsurge brought to the
bench tribunes of the people who had fought for them in the legislatures. Black has proved himself, in the deepest sense, a tribune of
the people—ever watchful of their interests, zealous in protecting
legislative power, reducing utility cases to the final problem of the
interests of the consumer, zealous for government regulatory power
over corporations. What remains is to see whether he can add to his
other capacities that of patience, and whether he can discipline
himself to make possible a common base for all the Court liberals.
For the time will come soon when the constitutional crisis will again
be acute, and Black's dissenting doctrines will be put to the acid test
—whether they can be translated into majority doctrines.

1938

23

William O. Douglas: Diogenes on Wall Street[1]

Lᴵᴷᴇ any body of men that makes prowess and luck its *summum bonum,* Wall Street personalizes the forces with which it has to deal. Since 1934, when the Securities and Exchange Commission was created to watch over the men who manipulate other people's money, its chairmanship has, for the Street at least, ranked in interest beyond most Cabinet portfolios. The first chairman, Joseph Kennedy, was definitely "one of ours"—a boy from the Wall Street slums who had somehow grown up in that financial Dead End without succumbing to its gangsterism, but who was nevertheless known and trusted by the big shots on the Street. His successor, James Landis, being a Harvard law professor, a former Frankfurter disciple, a drafter of the Securities Act, and seemingly a brash young man, aroused Wall Street fears at first, but soon managed to allay them. Now comes, as the new chairman, William O. Douglas. And Wall Street wants to know, in his own words, "what kind of a bird" he is.

Apparently the Street has some basis for its jitters about Douglas. His record thus far is that of the most uncompromising member who ever sat on the commission and, despite Kennedy's belief in him and support of him, Wall Street fought his selection as chairman with every means it knew how to employ. Now, nervous over the stock-market slump, aware that the first two chairmanships of the SEC were merely preparatory and that this one is likely to be crucial, it wants to know how "safe" its new mentor is.

---

[1] This was written on Mr. Douglas's selection as chairman of the Securities and Exchange Commission in 1937, and deals only with his career up to that time. It is written in the present tense as of that year, and I have allowed it to stand thus. In 1939 President Roosevelt appointed him to the Supreme Court.

Whatever he is, whether radical or conservative, Bill Douglas is the West Coast brand. At thirty-nine he has not lost the look of the Western college boy, lanky, sandy-haired, earnest, able, who has come East and made good. The first impression he makes is bucolic —a big fellow, very blond, with light eyebrows and childlike blue eyes—a slow-moving fellow, low-voiced and deliberate in speech— a simple sort of fellow, with slouching ways and carelessly chosen clothes. As you get to know him, however, you discard any notions you may have had of his being either bucolic or simple. He has one of the sharpest and deftest minds in Washington, a capacity for handling people and a calculated skill in winning them over or shocking them, as occasion may require, a sense of strategy, and an air of quiet authority. You begin to see him tentatively as a man of immense native ability, who has fitted the standards of an American university training and the skills acquired in the world of law and finance into the ideals of the Western lower-middle class.

Douglas's boyhood was nomadic in the best frontier tradition. His father, who was a home missionary, moved from one Western small town to another. After the father's death, the family finally settled in 1903, when the boy was five, at Yakima, Washington. Yakima was a small town, with the narrow conservatism only a small town can show. In fact, the whole state had been little affected at the time by the radical agrarianism of its sister-state, Oregon. And yet signs were not wholly lacking of new and native radicalism, based on a dawning consciousness that the natural resources of the state had been rifled by predatory finance.

High school was for Douglas an intellectual awakening, chiefly because of good teachers. They made dents in the armor of his conventionality—so much so that the claim made a short time ago by the Yakima *Republic,* a stalwart Republican daily, that "the Yakima school system should not be held responsible for the career of the infant prodigy who seems destined to become chairman of the Securities and Exchange Commission" was by no means warranted. At Whitman College, in Walla Walla, young Douglas majored in economics, but the principal impressions made on him came slantwise from unlikely sources—from an English professor who, apart from his subject, was a great stirrer-up of young men, and from a professor of geology and physics whom Douglas considers the greatest teacher he has ever met and of whom he still speaks with fervor. As for books, Douglas was too busy working outside class hours to read any. One still gets from him the feeling of a man who has never had leisure and wouldn't know what to do with it. During the harvest season he went into the wheat fields with the casual laborers, mostly IWW's, and after work he sat around with the "wobblies" on sacks of wheat, while they talked of their experiences and their prowess and the dream of revolution. Curiously, Douglas seems comparatively untouched by their social doctrine. I have rarely seen a man regarded as a radical, even a Western radical, who had less interest in labor or revolutionary doctrine.

How Douglas made the transition from all this to his present place has become by now a set of minor myths. He wanted to study law in the East, but he had no money. He taught Latin and English for a few years at the Yakima high school and coached the debating team, but most of what he saved he lost through an unlucky insurance venture. Finally in 1922 he set off desperately for New York. How he took charge of a herd of sheep as far as Montana, rode the rods the rest of the way into Chicago, and then spent his last dollar on railway fare to New York has been told several times. What has not been told is how miserable this Western boy felt when he first encountered New York. He found none of the warmth of the West; he found only cold, reserved men, intent on success. He could get no work, failed to pay either his room rent or his tuition, and was put out of his dormitory room. He soon managed, however, to pick up about $600 by taking a correspondence-school textbook on commercial law and fitting each lesson out with an armory of actual cases, and it tided him over his difficulties. But the study of law still seemed to him heavy, dogmatic, and stultifying. He felt he had made a mistake to come East at all, but he stuck the year out. The last two years of law school were, however, transformed for him by the work on the relation between law and business that he did with Underhill Moore, whom he regards as the best teacher in the entire field of law.

For two years after graduating from law school, Douglas went out, like an anthropologist, into Wall Street to study the facts of law and life among the natives. He interviewed the high-powered lawyers in the financial district, right down the line. It was hard not to succumb to the magic of the power that surrounded them, and for a moment at least—so Douglas confesses now—he had a vision of becoming one of them. The firm he entered was Cravath, de Gersdorff, Swaine, and Wood, and what he found in his new work was something he had been entirely unprepared for. It was not so much law as corporation finance, intricate, subtle, compelling. He threw himself into its mysteries and how well he mastered them many a lawyer and broker has since ruefully acknowledged. He was apprenticed to a good craftsman—Robert T. Swaine, one of the crack corporation lawyers in the country. By a curious twist of irony, Douglas years later was to have Swaine on the stand in the course of his protective-committees investigation for the SEC, to hammer away at him for five days in his inquiry into the Frisco and the Paramount-Publix reorganizations, and, as the record shows, he did not come off second best.

A bright future beckoned Douglas if he stayed with the firm. The boom market of the twenties was in full swing, his contacts with the Exchange were numerous and intimate, his friends were all playing the market. But a single plunge, although it netted him a profit, proved enough for him. He never went in again; it was too much like rolling dice. Despite the temptations to stay in Wall Street, Douglas managed to build up a curious detachment about the whole business. Moore, who was a Veblen enthusiast, had introduced him to *Absentee Ownership*, which made a deep impression on him, and evoked that mood of pitiless aloofness that gave Veblen's thought about business its strength and its stringency. He was even more impressed by Brandeis's *Other People's Money*, phrases from which still keep cropping up in his speeches. So, in 1927, he left New York and went back to Yakima to hang out his shingle. He had a strong feeling for the Western country and was sure his roots were there. But arrived at Yakima, he found he was one of sixty-five lawyers in a town of 20,000. After ten days he came back to Columbia to teach and he has been teaching law ever since. Even now, as chairman of the SEC, he is on leave of absence from the Yale Law School.

Douglas came to the SEC in October 1934 as head of its investigation of protective committees, held hearings for fifteen months, established a reputation as an unyielding and infrangible inquisitor, and was on the point of writing his report in January 1936 when Kennedy resigned from the commission and Douglas was appointed to succeed him. It is one of the anomalies of his personality that, radical as he seems, he always got along with Kennedy. Philosophically the two men have some area of common ground—one could even take the now famous Bond Club speech of Douglas's and find its essentials stated in various memoranda that Kennedy has left in the SEC files—but where they differ is that in action Kennedy has usually yielded to Wall Street, whereas Douglas's compromises still lie in the future.

Douglas has worked out a formula about the history of the commission which is tactful yet fairly true. Kennedy's chairmanship he sees as the period of consolidating the legislative victory of the Securities Exchange Act, when everything depended on good relations with Wall Street; Landis's chairmanship he sees as the period when the tools were sharpened with which the commission would have to work; but both periods took too long, he adds, and it is high time now that the commission got things done.

Whether he will be able to get anything done depends on a good many factors. He has to reckon with opposition from the financial community. He has, secondly, to do his work within the frame of Washington politics, both sacred and profane; that is, he has to deal with Morgenthau of the Treasury and Eccles of the Federal Reserve Board, as well as with Farley and Congress. Finally, he has in the membership of his own commission a still unknown quantity.

Beyond the commission itself, the problem of personnel is almost insuperable. The staff of the SEC is recruited largely from money-minded men who come to government work because they will be able to capitalize on it when they go back to Wall Street later on. Even with an ideal commission, the energy for regulating the exchanges and the utilities effectively would have to be transmitted through the whole staff. And it has been the fate of every agency that has set out to regulate Big Business that its staff has made it in the end an intellectual suburb of Wall Street. Douglas knows this. He is not naïve about either economics or administration. When he says, then, that he wants action, what sort of action does he mean, and how does he intend to get it?

His purposes seem to involve a pretty complete reconditioning of the financial structure of the country. That will sound to most Wall Street men, and even to most liberals, sweepingly radical. But when stress is laid upon the word "reconditioning," it becomes clear that if his plans are radical, it is only in an ethical sense. Douglas is both ironically and genuinely honest when he calls himself "a conservative of the old school." What he is driving at is that, given a capitalist structure, there is nothing wrong with the conservative theory of finance. What is wrong is the wild and unscrupulous departure from that theory in actual practice. And he knows as well as anyone in the country what excesses that practice has involved. For years he conducted a bankruptcy clinic at the Yale Law School. During his three years with the commission he has spent most of his time studying reorganizations. He has become a specialist in ruins, and as a result there has crept into his thinking the macabre moral note that you will find in most undertaking establishments. In fact, the reason his speeches have been so frightening to those high financiers who live by respectable crookedness is that he takes their professions at face value and demands that they be translated into action. And that involves, of course, not a new framework of ideals but a change in behavior.

The infuriating thing from Wall Street's viewpoint is that Douglas has taken an impregnable position. All that the big fellows can do is to rage privately and seek through subterranean channels to sabotage whatever program he may seek to put through. Publicly they can only agree. He is in a beautiful strategic position when he sits back and says that, as Wall Street's mentor, all he wants is honesty on the Stock Exchange—the simple honesty by which customers' men will not try to sell clients the stock in which their own firms have heavy interests, by which commercial banks acting as trustees will not feather their own nests in the process, by which lawyers and bankers will not first wreck a corporation to their own advantage and then reorganize it so as to perpetuate their control. And when, as in his Chicago University speech a year ago, he called the dishonest people on the Street "financial termites," eating away at the structure of sound finance, business might have been appalled at the phrasing, but the sentiment was impeccable.

As for methods, Douglas is a thorough realist. He is keenly aware of the difficulties of his job. "A fellow like me," he says, "starts with

100 per cent, and he'll be lucky if he gets 51 per cent." Since his whole program runs in terms of the enforcement of honesty, this means that the best you can expect from finance is an honest deal about every other time. On the commission itself the new chairman will prove a shrewd bargainer. He has an engaging and deceptive frankness, a knowledge of how to hold a couple of deuces in his hand without betraying the fact, and a quality of will that retains a good deal of steel. He knows how to handle men, how to work with them and get their loyalty; he knows the importance of backing up a subordinate when the heat is put on him; and he has the patience and the stamina to drive a job through to its end.

And yet I am by no means optimistic about his getting even his 51 per cent. Basically, the job he has undertaken can be handled for better or worse, and he is definitely on the better side; but it cannot be handled thoroughly. What the commission confronts is not merely a few moral foibles or a few criminal acts in a general structure that is in essence sound. Douglas has been influenced, as I have said, by both Veblen and Brandeis, but I cannot see that he has ever really understood Veblen. For Veblen's theory was not an ethical one, of seeing high finance as socially vicious only when it departed from a sound norm. To Veblen the norm itself was predatory, exploitative, and hollow; finance, as distinguished from industry, was "the art of getting something for nothing." And from this viewpoint to ask high finance to be constructive and honest is to ask it to commit hara-kiri and rid itself of its own essence.

We are dealing with an economic and legal set-up in which our whole industrial system is a satrapy of high finance. To attempt to do away with banker control of industry is impossible short of socialism—and Douglas is nothing of a socialist. He knows that the power of finance over industry is a fact. The question for him is where it shall be permitted to concentrate. There are two schools of thought on government regulation—one holding that if the financial power is concentrated in a few hands it is more subject to government control than if it is driven underground, and the other maintaining that it is more easily controlled if it is decentralized. Douglas goes with the latter. That is, of course, the Brandeis school of thought, and the nation may well expect that Douglas will drive in that direction as hard and as skillfully as he can. His vision of the financial structure is one in which the rules of business conduct on the exchanges will be enforced instead of being ignored in a gentlemanly fashion, in which the number of commission-hungry mouths will be reduced so that there will be enough commissions to go around, in which the conflicts of interest which make a broker or banker or dealer or underwriter seek to serve more than one master will be disentangled and resolved. He envisages, in his inmost mind, a neat and tidy financial universe with a perfect division of labor, each group performing a single function and getting for that function the reward that goes to the honest serving of industry and the assumption of risk—and only that reward.

It is a fine and courageous ideal. But it will be fun to watch what happens to an intelligent and militant public official when he discovers finally that it cannot be realized.

1937

24

<hr>

Robert S. Lynd: the Revolt against Quietism

ADD to the revolt against quietism Robert S. Lynd; in fact, put him at the head of the rebels. Here [1] is a portrait in acids of American social scientists keeping placid amidst disaster—"seismologists watching a volcano," he calls them. The figure he uses is almost as good as the one in the phrase he quotes from Auden: "lecturing on navigation while the ship is going down." His colleagues in the academies will doubtless refuse to face the fairly patent fact that the "detachment" and "objectivity" that they have exacted of themselves have been excuses for keeping quiet, dodges to avoid thinking, devices for saving their skins. Nevertheless, every working social scientist in America should get this book and wrestle with it as with his own naked conscience. For while Lynd has written the most searching volume in the annals of self-criticism in American social science, he has also staked out the most spacious claims for the possibilities of social thinking—nothing short of the reconstruction of our culture. I like this sort of book. I find in it exactly the right mixture of the humble and the arrogant—humility about our achievements as thinkers, arrogance about the world we may yet win.

After the writing of *Middletown* Robert and Helen Lynd might have coasted in ease along the academic runway. But *Middletown in Transition*—a tighter, tenser, franker book—showed they had no intention of coasting. *Middletown* made Lynd a Columbia professor of sociology. But instead of becoming safely oracular, he proceeds to ask in this book the simplest and yet the most disquieting questions. Why do our social scientists still lock themselves in air-

<hr>

[1] *Knowledge for What? The Place of the Social Sciences in American Culture.* Princeton, Princeton University Press, 1939.

tight compartments? Why don't they fashion a culture concept which will follow the actual contours of American life and give cohesion to their work? Why don't they get down to the *cui bono* of their thinking and research—ask what their knowledge is for and what values it serves? Why don't they use the social sciences as tools, as ways of testing hypotheses which if acted upon might help build the sort of society in which alone free social thought can survive?

The questions are so direct that the "subtle" minds among social scientists have failed to see them and the "neutral" minds have scorned to ask them. We have had, of course, all sorts of coroner's inquiries into social science: we have had countless meetings of research experts, foundation moguls, tycoons of methodology, all of them adept at the art of raising and spending money so that two monographs will grow where one grew before. Lynd makes little pretension to originality and none to neutrality. What he has brought to his thesis is a capacity for sharp analysis, a rich and massive documentation, a forthrightness—and, above all, a heap of courage. He has put things into his book—things about the incidence of capitalism, the relation between thought and action, the need for planning, the meaning of the Soviet experience—that give me pleasure with an added ironic twist because they are uttered by a Columbia professor in a course of Princeton lectures. And I suspect he will be listened to. He has shown in his previous books a craftsmanship that must win him an audience when he talks about method in social science. He has shown the falsity of Shaw's remark that "those who can, do; those who can't, teach." Lynd now adds precept to example.

There will, no doubt, be sharp protests from the academies. Julien Benda once wrote a book which he called *La Trahison des Clercs,* and there will be many to echo Benda's contention that any departure by the intellectuals from the medieval ideal of scholastic seclusion is treason. Crane Brinton, in the *Saturday Review,* says that social science like the physical sciences must grow by numberless small accretions of knowledge, and that, presumably, what happens to this knowledge is the concern not of the science of social study but of the art of social action. Lynd, he says in effect, has forgotten the condensation of accretions which is the social-science tradition. Look at his index, he says; he does not mention the right people—Weber, Pareto, Henderson, Elton Mayo—with proper reverence; you will find in the index not the great names but a whole host of *minusculi,* fellows who write for the *New Republic* and the *Nation.*

I am glad Brinton has sharpened the issue. The question is not whether someone else tackling the same task might have had different names in the index; I should myself, from the viewpoint of effective analysis, have preferred to subject to the scalpel the solider treatises and the more massive reputations. But while a fault in Lynd, it is no grievous fault. His whole point is that social science cannot recognize boundaries between the professional and amateur status, between the sacred and the secular in the tradition. It cannot survive as a closed union with jealously guarded jurisdictional divisions. It must be a fellowship into which anyone can enter who can show results—a capacity to use his tools so as to illumine the nature, conflicts, problems of his culture. Lynd himself has read widely and, what is more important, marginally. In his book the newer social sciences—anthropology, psychology, psychiatry—come into their own and thrust older ones such as history, economics, politics, law, into the background. And the new studies bring with them new and unhallowed names.

For myself, I salute these names. In fact, I could wish that Lynd's probings into the recent social-science literature had been more comprehensive and less haphazard. And I salute also the newer spirit of an unashamed instrumentalism in social science. There can be no piling up of increments of social knowledge in the dark. Lancelot Hogben has shown, in his acute little book *The Retreat from Reason,* that the cleavage between our intellectual habits and our patterns of living leads to the destruction of both. And the German experience has shown that while the scholars wait for increments of knowledge to pile up and find their own uses, there are other forces at work that are neither so patient nor so scrupulous. A social science in blinkers can lead only to social scientists in uniform.

There are passages of sheer writing brilliance in the book. In speaking of a return to *laissez-faire* or of "casual minor repairs in the machinery," he goes on: "If praying to the gods for rain does not increase the fertility of our fields, it avails little to redouble our prayers or to make alterations in their wording; we would better turn our energies to the techniques of agriculture." Or take this passage: "Alternatives to capitalism deserve careful analysis as well as ways of improving the operation of capitalism. One of the things that social science knows most surely today is that no culture can be realistically and effectively analyzed by those who elect to leave its central idols untouched; and, if fundamental change is required, it does no good simply to landscape the ground on which these idols stand." Yet the man who can write such sentences can also be guilty of long passages of an insistent hammering rhythm, or jargon such as: "it is necessary to structure into a complex culture like ours a congruent hospitality to change in all institutional areas." I fear that while Lynd has liberated himself from the deadly indecisiveness of the American sociological tradition, he is still partly under the spell of its terminology. The reader will not find the book all easy going; but it is fertile with fresh leads into social inquiry.

It could have been even more fertile if the author had shifted his emphasis a bit from the theory of the culture pattern to the theory of social change and its class foundations. If we are to use the social sciences as tools, he says, we must have cohesiveness in our thinking. But when he tries to state where that cohesiveness may be found, he tends to do it on a one-dimensional plane of a theory of human nature and a theory of the culture pattern—the personality in the culture and the culture in the personality. I call this one-dimensional because I should have liked to see much more stress on the developmental sequences in a theory of social change. In a final magnificent chapter, "Some Outrageous Hypotheses," Lynd does deal time and again with the problem of social change, and poses the question of how sufficiently thoroughgoing change can be achieved. Yet it is significant that the social sciences that he stresses in the rest of the book are the pattern-sciences—psychology, anthropology, sociology. His treatment of recent developments in political science is inadequate, he is not strong on economics, he neglects almost wholly the brilliant recent work in American legal theory, and —most important of all—he considers history as ready for the discard.

From the viewpoint of an inquiry into personality in culture and culture in personality his emphasis is the right one. From the standpoint of an inquiry into the theory of the nature, sources, dynamics, and consequences of social change, it needs extension. The pressing social inquiries today must be those turning on how power is captured and consolidated, why economies break down and how they can be made to work, how men think and how their thinking is manipulated, what new legal and administrative formations are emerging and how they can be used for human purposes, what revolutions are, why and how they occur, and how the revolutionary energies can be harnessed and channeled. In short, so far from discarding history, we need to focus our attention on an adequate theory of history—which is to say, an adequate theory of social change.

I want to make clear that my quarrel with Lynd is not a basic one, but a matter of emphasis. The things I have mentioned are in the book, but I should have preferred to see the book built around them. With Lynd's major thesis and his general direction I agree wholly. And I agree also with the stress he lays on the enormous task that confronts social science. "There is no other agency in our culture," he says, "whose role it is to ask long-range and, if need be, abruptly irreverent questions of our democratic institutions; and to follow those questions with research and the systematic charting of the way ahead." Today research and planning of this sort are left to the foundations to organize, that is, to men whose thought-processes have already been shaped in the image of the power formations of the day. If our democracy were worth its salt, it would create a Research and Planning Commission to take over the functions of the foundations. And on it would be men like Robert Lynd.

1939

25

Sinclair Lewis, Caliban, and the Federal Power

I WENT to see the Federal Theater put on *It Can't Happen Here* at the Adelphi. I found it a good show, although a bit pedestrian. It was cleanly etched without being memorable, onmoving yet not swiftmoving, hard and concrete yet lacking the novel's merciless piling up of detail, intense but without the passion that Sinclair Lewis himself, speaking in his own medium, was able to muster.

But that is not what I want primarily to write about. For the merit of the play is, in my mind, sandwiched in between two vastly more important questions, one raised by the novel, the other by the play's producers, the United States Government. Both questions are really political rather than dramatic, but they are worth asking because they are the sort of political questions with which the destinies of the drama may be tied up. The first is: How credible is Sinclair Lewis's picture of fascism in America? The second is: What is involved in the production of a political play by a government theater? And the questions have important links with each other.

My own feeling is that Mr. Lewis's picture of fascism is, with minor qualifications, credible enough. It emerges more strongly in the book because there the author has room enough for his indignation. But both book and play have the same shrewd understanding of the American native quality, the same insight into the aspects of our life that are already potentially fascist and need only something to precipitate them.

For the truth is that Sinclair Lewis has rewritten *Main Street,* only he has put Caliban in. In any complete picture of America

both Caliban and Carol Kennicott belong, and Carol is here again
in the form of Doremus Jessup, with his ineffectual idealism and
his tragic reliance on the "free inquiring spirit" of liberalism. But
Doremus loses to the Caliban of fascism, and the free inquiring
spirit is snuffed out by the brutish cruelty of Effingham Swan and
Shad Ledue. Fascism is one phase of our life even today—an organic
part of our culture, with its baiting of foreigners, Negroes, radicals,
and Jews, its fear of the labor movement, its tissue of hatreds and
inferiorities that will clutch at any instrument, its gullibilities, its
selfish and unthinking capitalism that will put itself in the hands
of brute force rather than make any concessions at all. This is the
Caliban in us, and when Mr. Lewis places him on the other side of
Main Street he is dead right.

Mr. Lewis saw a danger. Having some humanity in him he
wanted to warn his fellows of that danger. He wrote his book passionately, eloquently, as Upton Sinclair wrote *The Jungle,* Edward
Bellamy *Looking Backward,* Harriet Beecher Stowe *Uncle Tom's
Cabin.* But a book is a limited instrument for influencing opinion.
It takes years to penetrate, and in the fight against fascism time is
everything. Moreover, a book's audiences are limited. Destiny in
politics may lie with a whole succession of layers of opinion that a
book never reaches. That is why it was so important when Hollywood put *It Can't Happen Here* into movie form, and that is why
its suppression created such a furor.

Second step: the play. Scene: important political document meets
Federal Theater. And what a meeting that is, my countrymen! For
the Federal Theater, flung up out of the depths of the American
depression needs, is the most important development in the power
structure of the theater world since, back in the nineties, the star
system and the Theater Syndicate made theater production part of
Big Business. It has a far-flung chain of theaters the country over.
It has put twelve thousand people back to work in the theater arts.[1]
It has, since August, played to audiences of close to five million
people. It can put twenty-one different companies into the field
simultaneously in eighteen cities, running twenty-one concurrent
versions of the same play. Being subsidized, it can charge small admissions or no admissions. Being non-profit-making it can venture

---

[1] This was written in 1936.

on uncommercial themes. Being independent of the tyranny of the metropolis, it can meet the local and regional needs wherever it plays, and build its productions integrally into the regional speech and the regional ways. Put a play like this and an organization like this together, and all sorts of vistas open.

To some, these vistas will prove frightening. Before the coming of the Federal Theater, the theater world was built on *laissez-faire* in ideas and private enterprise in profits. Most of the plays, of course, have not dealt with ideas, except in their usually unconscious acceptance of all the premises of the existing order. But those that have dealt with ideas have had to sell them in the marketplace, make them commerciable. The only exceptions were the Little Theater groups, which solved the problem either by producing on next to nothing or by getting subsidies from private sources. Now the Federal Theater cuts under both of the premises of the theater world. It offers some fairly effective economic competition to the private producers. And it breaks down the *laissez-faire* of ideas by bringing the government into the business of spreading ideas through the theater.

Whatever you think, the fact itself is clear, and there can be no advantage in refusing to face it. It is as clear as the fact that the government through its operations in the TVA has cut under *laissez-faire* and private enterprise in electric power. There is an engaging similarity between the two situations. Both the TVA and the Federal Theater are depression agencies. Both of them, by the logic of putting people to work, were pushed willy-nilly into the position of competing with the established powers. Both have tried desperately to minimize the degree of that competition and limit its scope. Both have hedged themselves about with constitutional limitations: the TVA bases itself on the national defense power and the irrigation power of Congress; the Federal Theater puts on its programs, "the viewpoint expressed in this play is not necessarily that of the WPA or any other agency of the government." Both of them have come into situations where there is nominally a free field for everyone, but where actually there are entrenched interests that weight the scales inexorably in the direction of the *status quo*. Both of them have succeeded in bringing their commodity (plays, electric power) to consumers who have never had a chance at it before, and have thus done less in the way of direct competition than in bringing idle resources into use and raising the standards of living. Both have set up a yardstick of cost and accomplishment which will affect the rest of the industry. Both have encouraged regionalism and changed the way of life of the people they have touched. And finally neither must be regarded as going further than it does: the TVA is not socialism, but regulated capitalism; the Federal Theater is not a government propaganda agency but it does bring the government as a powerful factor into "the competition of ideas in the marketplace." [2]

One thing is clear. This new role of the federal government is a double-edged sword. Today a progressive government is lending its strength in the fight against ideas hostile to democracy. Tomorrow a reactionary government may turn about and do exactly the opposite. The precedent is set. The habit may be created. I feel we must be aware of this possibility. Yet to say, as many do, that this is fascism is of course absurd. The Corpo government in the play sends its storm troops about smashing radios, so that Trowbridge's broadcasts from Canada may not be received. That is real suppression. For the Federal Theater to produce *It Can't Happen Here* does not suppress anyone or anything. It is an attempt to dramatize what would happen if we had a government bent on suppression. And it can never mean anything more than another competitor introducing ideas into the marketplace.

What we are faced with is the fact that in fighting fascism the traditional liberal doctrine is not enough. *Laissez-faire* in economics, unlimited and unqualified, brings about an economic chaos that leads straight to fascism. And Doremus Jessup found out that the hands-off policy of the liberal in the realm of ideas and political action led straight to Buzz Windrip and Effingham Swan. In rejecting the chance to have a single, chaste, and aesthetically perfect production of his play on Broadway and preferring the eighteen productions of the Federal Theater, Sinclair Lewis has gone a step beyond his hero in political sophistication. And the government,

---

[2] I have developed a similar theme at greater length in the chapter above, "Freedom in the Opinion Industries."

in taking the play on, has shown its understanding that, if a people is not willing to use ideas to defend itself and its culture, it has lost the strength for survival.[3]

1936

---

[3] As I go over the essay, preparing it for the press (August 1939), a reactionary Congress has legislated the Federal Theater out of existence. There can be little doubt that this was not an action prompted by economy, despite the talk of budget-balancing, but a recognition of how powerful a weapon a Federal Theater can be in the realm of opinion.

26

The America of John Dos Passos

O NE'S impulse is to write about John Dos Passos as he has himself in his novel-trilogy written about other Americans. That is to say, to write a prose poem telling of those early impressionable days when he was carted around the world in the shelter of a well-to-do family, his dawdling at Harvard, his "one man's initiation" into the disenchantment of the war, his attempt to apply a novelist's scalpel to murder on an organized scale in "Three Soldiers" and to the entire anatomy of a diseased social system in the more firmly wrought novels that have followed. One would set down the contradictions of a sensitive (almost shy) personality, an acid intelligence, and a gusto for life which scoops up experience with both hands.

His talent is expansive rather than concentrated. There is little of the creative frenzy about him. There is no tone of philosophic brooding about his books, and few of the flashing insights by which Malraux, for example, can distill a lifetime into a phrase. But there is a massiveness about Dos Passos's work, as about that of Dreiser or Lewis, that places it squarely in the path of our attention.

His aim has been to capture in three novels [1] the whole spirit and movement of American life from the beginning of the century to the end of the boom period of the twenties. There is a central group of characters that runs through the whole trilogy. There are interlacing individual lives and destinies, but the central theme and destiny belong to America itself. The first book, *The 42nd Parallel,* shows America in a mood of nascent strength and recklessness, with business enterprise finding itself and expanding into new domains, with labor going through the adolescent crudeness of its

---

[1] *The 42nd Parallel, 1919,* and *The Big Money,* later gathered together under the title *U.S.A.* The present essay deals with the trilogy as a whole, but principally with *The Big Money.*

IWW phase on the one hand and its dreams of capital-labor co-operation on the other, with the whole complex of American life rushing into the World War. The second book, *1919*, deals not with the war itself but with the fringes of it, for the author's concern is not with what happened to the cannon-fodder, but with the war as a phase of our culture. It is a study in individual rootlessness and group hysteria, and it is only at the end of the book that the magnificent lyric on the Unknown Soldier hurtles us back ironically into a consciousness of what price we had paid as a culture for the dalliance of our Eleanor Stoddards and our J. Ward Moorehouses and our Eveline Hutchinses in Paris. The last book, *The Big Money*, deals with the sequel of the war in the period of boom capitalism in the twenties. It is the era of stock speculation, mushroom real-estate values, advertising and marketing, paradise on the installment plan, the flowering of junior vice-presidents. Dos Passos has caught unforgettably the flow of American life at its high point—just before the Ice Age of the depression set in. The three books together form as complete a record as we have in fiction of the crest of American capitalist culture. If America is ever destroyed by war or overwhelmed by fascist barbarism, later generations may dig up these books and read what manner of lives we led.

Dos Passos, as is well known, is not an anatomist of the individual but a historian of the collective mentality. What he seeks to build up always is the climate of opinion—the milieu of emotion, aspiration, and shibboleth in which individuals move. This is what gives unity to each of the books. In *The Big Money* the dominating mood is the feverish desire to be where the sluices of wealth are running free and strong. The principal characters—Charley Anderson, Mary French, Margo Dowling, and Richard Ellsworth Savage—are either possessed by this desire or have to reckon with it. Charley Anderson will be remembered as the Western boy whose mother ran a railroad boarding house and who had roughed it about a good deal before going to war. He comes back restless but determined to get at the big money, turns his mechanical sense to aviation, grows wealthy, marries a banker's daughter. But though he boasts of being mechanically "the boy with the knowhow," the boys at the pecuniary end outsmart him; he is stripped of most of his money, and the only love and pleasure he gets are what he buys. His tragedy is the tragedy of the technician in a money age, and of fine impulses in a shoddy culture. In fact the whole character may be regarded as a footnote to Veblen's *The Engineers and the Price System*. Dick Savage does, on the surface at least, a good deal better. Harvard-bred, he comes back from a soft berth behind the lines in France to become J. Ward Moorehouse's right-hand man in the publicity racket. He is cruelly drawn. His life, no less than Charley Anderson's, is stripped of any real satisfactions—a sacrifice to the Moloch of the big money. But while Charley Anderson in going to his ruin adds something at least to the industrial arts, Savage adds nothing except marvelous ideas for getting Bingham's Patent Medicines across to the country.

There is a similar contrast between Mary French and Margo Dowling. Mary, after a middle-class girlhood in Colorado, wanders into social work, meets up with some steel strikers, falls in love with a succession of radicals and near-radicals, and learns that love can be just as frustrate on the fringes of the revolutionary movement as anywhere else. But despite the frustration she does throw her energies into organizing work which may some day have meaning for America. Margo Dowling on the other hand throws hers into building the illusion of glamour on the screen. She is the ruthless career girl on whom the boom decade smiles most kindly. She learns how to sleep her way to success, and her path carries her to Charley Anderson's arms, to the Miami land boom, and finally across the country to Hollywood, where her smooth heartless face makes her exactly the person for director Sam Margolies to exalt to stardom.

To portray the collective mood and the mass culture requires technical innovation in the novel. To my knowledge Dos Passos has never formulated a theory about it, as Jules Romains has done with his *unanisme*. But it is clear that he has in the realm of the novel-form what H. G. Wells has called in another connection the "skepticism of the instrument." He has played havoc with spelling and his punctuation has given the traditionalists among the critics some acute distress. More important, he has selected out of the stream of American living speech a new American language which for its vitality and usableness should delight Mr. Mencken. Most important, he has contrived a film technique for giving perspectives, close-ups, rapid sequences difficult for the orthodox narrative.

The problem was this. Here are people neither sensitive nor

complex, living a good part of their lives not far from the level of animal behavior. Here is a culture shot through with complex currents and cross-currents of influence which touch the lives and destinies of even the simplest people. Experience is no longer the tidy unity it was once believed. How can the author catch up the splintered fragments of experience and hold them up to view while at the same time getting something like a total effect?

The answer was a fourfold technique. The *narrative* of individual fictional lives is told in an unadorned hard-surfaced manner—a modern picaresque that gives the barest details of overt behavior. The *newsreel*, made up of newspaper headlines, speeches, popular songs, tries to depict the mass consciousness and furnishes a backdrop against which the individual lives are enacted. The *biography* deals with historical Americans who summed up and expressed in their lives the main forces of their day. Finally, the *camera eye* turns the searchlight of the author's own intense brooding gaze at the set of events being discussed: it is a chaotic flow of consciousness, strangely subjective and lyrical amidst the expanse of objectivity elsewhere in the book, warm and intimate with the remembered rush of personal incident. Mechanically used, these four devices may merely make the problem of communication so much more complex. Skillfully interwoven they may go to form a unity that does not simplify, and hence falsify, the reality. There is a good deal of both —mechanical and skillful—in the trilogy. But in the last book Dos Passos has written with a passion that welds his material together as never before. The improved cunning of his hand is governed by a real heat of the brain. This book is therefore easily the best of the whole series.

The America of John Dos Passos that is presented in these pages is not a lovely America. How could it be? Dos Passos is one of the few novelists writing today who are truly literate. He knows things. He knows the force of institutions and mass ideas, he knows by what impulsions people are moved, he knows what things are first things in a social system and what things are derivative, he knows the ways and the speech of common people. He is part of the America that he depicts, and he bestows upon the portrait that desperate tenderness that can flow only from love and solicitude turned into satire. His social analysis owes much to Marx, but essentially he is the Veblen of American fiction, sharing Veblen's rebelliousness, his restless questing mind, his hatred of the standardized middle-class culture and of the leisure-class aesthetic, his insight into American traits, his divided feeling about the underlying population. But beyond social analysis he has the qualities of the great novelist—tenderness, humanity, fertility. He is never at a loss to people his world, and already his world has come to have an existence of its own in the reader's mind, apart from the America it depicts.

One thing is certain—he will keep moving. His social beliefs are still fluid, his sense for innovation still has a sharp edge. But what will carry him farthest is his belief in American life. A sentence from one of his camera eyes contains affirmation as well as irony: "I go home after a drink and a hot meal and . . . ponder the course of history and what leverage might pry the owners loose from power and bring back (I too Walt Whitman) our storybook democracy."

1937

PART THREE

Some European Thinkers

1

Jonathan Swift: Literary Anthropologist

SWIFT ranks among the great satirists of all literature, but since he was primarily a pamphleteer, his art, even when most universal, is integrally related to the political preoccupations of his day. Born of the faded gentry, penniless and yet consumed by ambition, he chose the Church as a career and party pamphleteering as the shortest road toward ecclesiastical preferment. He served a literary apprenticeship as secretary to Sir William Temple and through him became embroiled in the current controversy over the respective merits of the ancient and modern writers; from his brief sortie into this field emerged *The Battle Fought between the . . . Books* (1704), the most brilliant of the products of the controversy, which already revealed Swift's Tory leanings.

An unsuccessful mission to London in behalf of the Established Church in Ireland taught him the difficulties of political intrigue in what was perhaps the most corrupt period of English politics and gave him, moreover, a taste for it. He began as a moderate Whig, and wrote his *Dissensions between the Nobles and the Commons in Athens and Rome* (1701) for the Whigs. But his discontent with the treatment they accorded him ("Rot 'em for ungrateful dogs; I will make them repent their usage") and especially his sense for Church statesmanship, his preference for order and authority, and his dislike for the new merchant class finally threw him in with the Tories.

He played an important role in bolstering the Harley ministry (1710–14), being most effective as the editor of the official party newspaper, the *Examiner,* which was the spearhead of Tory opinion. He ranks therefore, with Addison and Defoe, as one of the founders of English journalism. He was quite conscious of the possibilities for power that journalism offered in a parliamentary system increasingly dependent on the opinion of the electorate. His writings reached the wits of London and the aristocracy and especially the plain people in the country parishes; but, unlike Defoe, he scorned to appeal to the growing class of merchants, shopkeepers, clerks, and apprentices. He relished his part in the councils of the great, and in return he served them powerfully in his articles and pamphlets. The most important of these politically, *The Conduct of the Allies* (1712), was an attack on the military and diplomatic logic of British participation in the War of the Spanish Succession, and it made European history.

Despite his repeated pleas for preferment and his obvious panting for a bishopric, Swift had finally to be content with a deanship in Ireland. The tragic frustration of his ambition must be laid to his irresponsible pen, which in *A Tale of a Tub* (1704) had treated religion somewhat cavalierly; and in a succession of poems and pamphlets he had lashed out so furiously at persons in high place as to make him powerful enemies. But it is to this same irresponsibility that Swift's political pamphlets owe their greatness. The best of them, to be sure, such as *The Sentiments of a Church of England Man* (1711) and the *Letter . . . concerning the Sacramental Test* (1709), are measured and cogent expositions of his political and ecclesiastical theory. Swift was shrewd enough to see that the Tories and the High Churchmen had to abandon their divine-right theories and rest their claims upon the strength of traditional institutions; he sought to adapt the Tory position to the *fait accompli* of the Revolution of 1688 and went so far as to claim for the Church of England as against the dissenters the important part in that revolution.

Swift is thus, with Bolingbroke, a crucial figure in the readjustment of Tory thought. But there is a desperate strength in his polemics. He had attached himself to the Tory party in its brief interval of power before its final decay. It was part of his ironic destiny to spend his fine gifts upon a losing cause and in defense of a dying class. Like the great Latin satirists he was defending an old order against the encroachments of a callow bourgeoisie and a rising money power.

Swift in Ireland, banished as he felt from a life of action, looked back with nostalgia upon his brief years of power, brooded over his grievances, journeyed through the countryside, and was further embittered by the poverty and degradation of the life of the Irish masses. When the English crown sold the Irish coinage monopoly in a manner flagrant even for an age of political jobbery, Swift's accumulated resentment flared up in the *Drapier Letters* (1725), whose importance lies not so much in their somewhat questionable monetary doctrine and value theory as in their ringing challenge to British imperialism and in the basis they laid for the later agitation for Irish independence. In *A Modest Proposal* (1729) he reached the most relentless *reductio ad absurdum* of English policy, in his suggestion that the Irish economic problem could best be met if Irish children were sold as tender meat.

But the climax at once of his social thought and of his writing art was reached only in *Gulliver's Travels* (1726). Using the contemporary literary form of the imaginary voyage, he achieved thereby an anthropological attitude which enabled him to gain an inhuman perspective in measuring human character and social organization. Toward this end he sought heroically to master a wide range of devices—increasing the size of man (Brobdingnag), decreasing it (Lilliput), making him live forever (Struldbrug), making him all intellect (Laputa), making him all bestiality (Yahoo). Into the early voyages Swift poured his entire experience with English government, so that the satire is chiefly political. But at the time he wrote the later voyages he was more concerned with Irish social conditions: the satire broadens in scope, reaching to the institutions behind politics and the essential human character underlying both. He launches a frontal attack upon the entire apparatus of civilization—upon war, capitalism, property, trade, kingship, the court, education, and imperialism. He had in the second voyage described men as "the most pernicious race of little odious vermin that Nature ever suffered to crawl upon the face of the earth"; in the fourth, which has been quite generally repulsive to critics, he goes beyond invective into symbolism, and by setting off the Yahoos against the Houyhnhnms he portrays at once the most degrading traits in human nature and the possibilities for a rational ordering of social life.

It is a mistake to regard his doctrine as all cold hate. His corrosive mind ate away the Augustan complacencies of the England of his day. Living in an age of expansion, at the crest of the commercial revolution and the beginning of the industrial, he saw clearly that man's increasing power was being crystallized in stupid institutions, vested in a grasping new class, entrusted to an animal who, in Swift's own words, was not by nature *rationalis* but only *rationis capax*. He died raving and insane, but an even greater doom has been society's revenge in interpreting his criticism as either spleen or absurd imagination, and consigning it to the entertainment of children.

1934

2

The Paradox of Adam Smith

LIKE all great books, *The Wealth of Nations* is the outpouring not only of a great mind, but of a whole epoch. The man who wrote it had learning, wisdom, a talent for words; but equally important was the fact that he stood with these gifts at the dawn of a new science and the opening of a new era in Europe. What he wrote was the expression of forces which were working, at the very time he wrote it, to fashion that strange and terrible new species— *Homo oeconomicus,* or the economic man of the modern world.

I use that term not in the sense of the lifeless abstraction which economic theorists have invented to slay any proposals for social change, and which has in turn slain them. I use it rather for the very living and human businessman, in defense of whom the economists have written and in whose interests they have invented their lifeless abstraction. All the forces which were at work in Europe creating the businessman, and the society he was to dominate, were at work also creating the framework of ideas and institutions within which Adam Smith wrote his book. And that book, as though conscious that one good turn deserved another, became in its own way a powerful influence to further the work of those forces. Thus it is in history. A new society, emerging from the shell of the old, creates a framework within which a great thinker or artist is enabled to do his work; and that work, in turn, serves to smash finally the shell of the old society, and to complete and make firmer the outlines of the new. Thus it has been with Machiavelli's *Prince,* with Adam Smith's *The Wealth of Nations,* with Karl Marx's *Capital.*

That is why the arguments of all the scholars who have been thrashing about, seeking to determine how original Adam Smith was, are essentially futile. No first-rate mind whose ideas sum up an age and influence masses and movements to come is in any purist sense original. *The Wealth of Nations* is undoubtedly the foundation-work of modern economic thought. Yet you can pick it to pieces, and find that there is nothing in it that might not have been found somewhere in the literature before, and very little that comes out of it that has not to a great degree been punctured by the literature that followed. What counts is, of course, not whether particular doctrines were once shiny new, or have since stood the ravages of time. What counts is the work *as a whole*—its scope, conception, and execution, the spirit that animates it, and the place it has had in history.

Here,[1] then, is the thing itself: a strange mixture of a book—economics, philosophy, history, political theory, practical program; a book written by a man of vast learning and subtle insights—a man with a mind that was a powerful analytic machine for sifting out the stuff in his notebooks, and a powerful synthetic machine for putting it together again in new and arresting combinations. Smith was sensitive to the various elements on the intellectual horizon of his day. Like Marx after him, he was no closet scholar, shut off from the world; he was all antennae, reaching out for and absorbing everything within reach.

He wrote at the end of the break-up of feudal Europe, at the beginning of a modern world in which the old feudal institutions were still holding on with the tenacity that the vested interests have always shown. It was against these vested interests that he wrote. And the result is that his book has not been merely for library shelves. It has gone through many editions, and has been translated into almost every language. Those who read it were chiefly those who stood to profit from its view of the world—the rising class of businessmen, their political executive committees in the parliaments of the world, and their intellectual executive committees in the academies. Through them it has had an enormous influence upon the underlying populations of the world, although generally all unknown to them. And through them also it has had an enormous influence upon economic opinion and national policy. It has done as much perhaps as any modern book thus far to shape the whole landscape of life as we live it today.

---

[1] This chapter first appeared as the Introduction to the Modern Library edition of *The Wealth of Nations*.

Who was the man who could do all this? At first glance Adam Smith appears only as a mild Scottish professor of moral philosophy, retiring and absent-minded, a gentle sage with dynamite flowing from his pen. His career had nothing extraordinary in it, except that at three he was carried off by a band of gypsies, and only with difficulty restored to his family. But whatever other adventure the rest of his life held for him was to lie in the dangerous voyage of the mind rather than in the glories or disasters of an adventurous outward career. He had the traditional Scottish boyhood in a frugal family; spent the traditional years at Oxford—years which served as the basis for the caustic attack on universities which is to be found in these pages; cooled his heels for the traditional period while he waited for a suitable university appointment; was made professor of logic and then professor of moral philosophy at Glasgow, giving lectures on theology, ethics, jurisprudence, and political economy, to students who probably cared more about their careers in the rising merchant class than they did about moral philosophy; wrote a book called *The Theory of Moral Sentiments,* which made something of a splash at the time, and since it explained the social psychology of human behavior in terms of the sentiment of sympathy, got itself much talked about and read in polite circles throughout the British Isles; gave up his university post to go as traveling tutor to the stepson of the famous colonial-baiter Charles Townshend—the young Duke of Buccleuch—and spent a year and a half at Toulouse and a year at Paris with him; began, while on the trip, a treatise on economics, completing it ten years after his return to Scotland; finally published his treatise in 1776 under the title of *The Wealth of Nations;* and spent the rest of his life as commissioner of customs at Edinburgh, living quietly with his mother and a maiden cousin.

That is one version of Adam Smith, and it is true enough—for a half-truth. But there is another half-truth needed to complete the picture. Adam Smith was always alive to what was going on in the world. He was heterodox enough to remember with passion the futility of the ordinary university teaching, as he had experienced it at Oxford. In his own teaching, while he had no eloquence, he could communicate to his students his own fervor for ideas. Of his lectures on jurisprudence, John Rae, his biographer, tells us that the course "taught the young people to think. His opinions became the subjects of general discussion, the branches he lectured upon became fashionable in the town . . . stucco busts of him appeared in the booksellers' windows, and the very peculiarities of his voice and pronunciation received the homage of imitation." The doctrine that he was teaching was, it must be remembered, new doctrine— that of economic liberalism and freedom from governmental interference. To it were attached therefore at once the obstacles and advantages of new doctrine; it met with the hostility of the entrenched and the salvos of those who stood to gain by innovation. Smith himself was by no means a recluse. The tutorship that was offered him was lucrative, and yet there was a gamble in leaving his university chair. That he did so is evidence of his restless desire to explore the bounds of the new European society. He was a friend of Hume, and in France he found in addition Quesnay, Turgot, d'Alembert, Helvétius—the physiocrats who were fashioning a new and exciting economic science, and the *philosophes* who were constructing out of the materials of the rational life instruments for shattering encumbering and irrational institutions.

Smith kept his eyes and ears open; he kept his notebooks ready; he kept his wits with him. He started to write up his lectures on political economy, as he had formerly written up his lectures on moral philosophy. But this was a different matter. It wasn't merely the business of going back to first principles, and then spinning the rest out of one's philosophic entrails. Here was something that gave order and meaning to the newly emerged world of commerce and the newly emerging world of industry. Here was something that could be used in fighting the clumsy and obstructive vestiges of a society governed by a feudal aristocracy. Smith trembled with anticipation, and could not help communicating his excitement to his friends. They too trembled—and waited. Smith took ten more years. He could not be hurried in this task. He had to read and observe further. He poked his nose into old books and new factories. He got led off on long excursions into the history of silver coinage, the economics of ecclesiastical institutions, the whole cultural history of Europe. He had to polish his style, but, more important, he had to fashion and carry through consistently a new way of looking at things—the hard-bitten economic viewpoint. He had, above all else, to avoid making his book merely a theoretical construction; it must deal with the burning issues of national and international economic policy of his day. When the book was finished, therefore, it was more than a book; it was the summary of a new European consciousness.

You will find the basic principles that Smith embodied in his book explained in all the histories of economic thought. What you will not find is the skill, the charm, the greatness with which he wove them into the fabric of his chapters. The principles are simple. First, Smith assumes that the prime psychological drive in man as an economic being is the drive of self-interest. Secondly, he assumes the existence of a natural order in the universe which makes all the individual strivings for self-interest add up to the social good. Finally, from these postulates, he concludes that the best program is to leave the economic process severely alone—what has come to be known as *laissez-faire,* economic liberalism, or non-interventionism.

All this is now familiar enough. Largely through Smith's book it has made itself a part of the structure of our often unconscious beliefs, and is only now beginning to be dislodged. Of Smith's first postulate it must be said that while it is largely an abstraction from experience, as the institutional school of economists has delighted to point out, the experience from which it is abstracted does much to verify it. The view which makes of man an economic automaton is obviously oversimplified. But the view which makes out of him a hard-headed and predatory seeker of his own gain is, as we look back at the history of business enterprise, largely justified. What we have learned, of course, is that it is not an inherent or universal trait, but part of a historical method of organizing economic life.

As for Smith's second postulate, that there is a "natural order" whereby the pursuit by each individual of his own self-interest contributes ultimately to the social welfare, that must lie outside the realm of science or of historical verification, and must be set down as a cardinal principle of the faith of the age. As Carl Becker has pointed out, the "natural order" which the eighteenth-century philosophers postulated in order the better to fight the ecclesiastical institutions and the political obscurantism of their day became itself a source of a quasi-theological faith and of obscurantism.

The conclusion that Smith drew from these postulates was simple enough. Since a natural order exists whereby the enlightened self-ishness of all men adds up to the maximum good of society, since there is a "divine hand" which guides each man in pursuing his own gain to contribute to the social welfare, it must follow that government is superfluous except to preserve order and perform routine functions. The best government is the government that governs least. The best economic policy is that which arises from the spontaneous and unhindered action of individuals. We recognize this, of course, as the unregulated and individualistic capitalist economy—what Carlyle has unforgettably termed "anarchy plus a constable."

One warning is necessary. We must not conclude, because Smith's intellectual system can be presented in an orderly sequence from postulates to conclusion, that he arrived at it by the same sequence. It is much more likely, as with almost all intellectual constructions, that instead of Smith's program flowing from his principles, it was his principles that flowed from his program. He did not start with truths about human behavior and the natural order, and arrive at economic liberalism. John Maurice Clark suggests that his system can be best understood in terms of what he was reacting against. And it is true that Smith's system of thought took its shape from his intense reaction against the elaborate apparatus of controls which the surviving feudal and mercantilist institutions were still imposing on the individual. The need for removing these controls was Smith's underlying theme. And it was the response which this theme met from the mercantile and industrial class of Europe that gave *The Wealth of Nations* its enormous impact upon Western thought and Western institutions. Harold Laski has demonstrated, in his *Rise of Liberalism,* how Smith's arguments fitted in with the prevailing middle-class temper in Europe. The businessmen were delighted. "To have their own longings elevated to the dignity of natural law was to provide them with a driving force that had never before been so powerful. . . . With Adam Smith the practical maxims of business enterprise achieved the status of a theology."

But there is another side of the shield. Smith was, to be sure, an unconscious mercenary in the service of a rising capitalist class in Europe. It is true that he gave a new dignity to greed and a new sanctification to the predatory impulses. It is true that he rationalized the economic interests of the class that was coming to power in such a way that he fashioned for that class a panoply of ideas behind which they are still protecting themselves against the assaults of government regulation and the stirrings for socialization. It is true that Smith's economic individualism is now being used to oppress where once it was used to liberate, and that it now entrenches the old where once it blasted a path for the new. But it must be said for Smith that his doctrine has been twisted in ways he would not have approved, and used for purposes and causes at which he would have been horrified.

Adam Smith was, in his own day and his own way, something of a revolutionary. His doctrine revolutionized European society as surely as Marx's in a later epoch. He was, on the economic side, the philosopher of the capitalist revolution, as John Locke was its philosopher on the political side. His own personal sympathies were not entirely with the capitalist. Eli Ginzberg has pointed out, in his *House of Adam Smith,* how there runs through *The Wealth of Nations* a strain of partisanship for apprentices and laborers, for farmers, for the lowly and oppressed everywhere, and a hostility to the business corporations, the big businessmen of the day, the ecclesiasts, and the aristocrats. Read the book with an eye for these passages, and it becomes a revealing document showing Smith's concern for the common man. Far more important, of course, than any of these more or less sentimental expressions of sympathy, is the doctrine of labor value which is at the core of Smith's economics. In enunciating for the first time the doctrine that labor is the sole source of value in commodities, Smith became the forerunner of Bray and Hodgskin and eventually of Marx. As an originator, Smith developed this doctrine clumsily. It remained for Marx to refine it, convert it into an instrument of analysis, extract from it the revolutionary implications that were inherent in it from the beginning. This leads us, however, much too far afield. On Smith's relation to the labor theory of value there is a large and polemical literature. On the validity or confusion of the theory itself there is a literature even larger and more polemical.

All that concerns us is to see the curious paradox of Smith's position in history: to have fashioned his system of thought in order to blast away the institutional obstructions from the past, and bring a greater degree of economic freedom and therefore a greater total wealth for all the people in a nation; and yet to have had his doctrine result in the glorification of economic irresponsibility and the entrenchment of the middle class in power. A reading of Adam Smith's work and a study of its place in the history of ideas should be one of the best solvents for smugness and intellectual absolutism.

1937

3

Walter Bagehot: a Credible Victorian

Outwardly he was not very different from those English patriarchs of his day—Mill, Gladstone, Bryce, Morley. He led one of those curiously rich and exemplary lives that make the English gentleman-scholar of that epoch the consummate product of the Western world. Which is to say he had good parentage and a scrupulous home life, was educated in the classics, mathematics, and the moral sciences, wrote long letters on theology to his school friends, studied for the bar and chucked it to write literary essays, married for love and read Wordsworth on his honeymoon, divided his time between business, politics, and literature, with a few hours for a canter on his horse across beloved English fields; his family circle was cultured and simple, his conversation brilliant, his heart in the right place, his sympathies liberal, his journalistic style lively; and in his articles he quoted long passages from the poets. All these qualities have become the staple for the current biographies of the English gentleman-scholar.

The psychological gulf between Bagehot and the patriarchs whom he so perilously resembled was that while the English patriarch, adolescent-like in at least one respect, takes himself seriously to his dying day, Bagehot at some point broke himself of that habit. It is difficult to know when or how it took place. But this much may be ventured: it was at the point when the deadening influence of his formal education was removed; and it was connected with one or two other fundamental changes in his character. That break was the point in Bagehot's life, crucial in the life of any man, when he ceases to be merely clay for events to shape.

It was no easy thing in those days, no more perhaps than it is in these, to break through the crust of an education. It was all the

harder with the particular kind Bagehot had received. His father
was a banker, general manager of Stuckey's bank at Langport. He
was an intelligent Unitarian gentleman who remained a banker
because he conceived it a duty to his family, but whose taste really
lay in the literature of political unction. His spells of illness were
his only opportunities to indulge himself in this taste, and he welcomed a cold because he could then in all conscience read the *Life*
of Mackintosh or Cobden's speeches. When Walter was twelve what
could such a father do but set him to writing essays on Alfred the
Great, and the Battle of Mantinea, and the life of St. Augustine, and
such matter? When Walter was at Bristol College, an eager boy who
had outstripped all the others, what letters could such a father write
him but long discussions of the Corn Laws, and a letter which read:
"Work as hard as you can, but be modest, for to be so is a great
charm in boys, and the more so the cleverer they are"?

Walter was in great danger of growing up as much a prig as the
other boys, friends of his, who had equally exemplary fathers. At
sixteen, while attending University College at London and living
with several young gentlemen at the house of a Dr. Hoppus, he
had reason to be convinced that two of his fellow-students were
guilty of acts "involving wrong conduct and deception." With great
moral courage he undertook the office of tale-bearer to Dr. Hoppus.
"My resolution," he wrote to his father, "has not been taken without
the most careful deliberation, and, I may add, earnest prayer." Dr.
Hoppus was indignant, the boys' fathers were sent for, the mis-
creants were duly ejected. Walter found some friends who admired
his conduct. Together they founded a debating society, where they
orated on vast abstract questions. And from their rooms long and
earnest theological discussions floated out to add to the London
night and fog.

Then—when he was in his early twenties—something happened;
or perhaps it was a series of things. An adequate biographer will
one day be clearer about the matter. Bagehot owed at least one
important debt to his father. Largely because the latter, as a Unitarian, objected to the doctrinal tests at Oxford, Bagehot had escaped its conventional literary-religious atmosphere. At Bristol
College he had come under the influence of the ethnologist Prich-
ard, and at University College he was deeply attracted by the skeptical and introspective mind of Arthur Hugh Clough. He now read

for an M.A. in economics—it was at the end of the eighteen forties, in the heyday of John Stuart Mill—and he read mainly by himself, with little guidance and less of the deadly earnest discussion. He studied law and was called to the bar. He also tried his first public writing—some essays for the *Prospective Review* on currency and on Mill's recently published *Principles of Economics*. He probably learned for the first time that he could put words together prettily. And also about that time his mother's mind had become unhinged with grief at the death of two of her sons—Walter's half-brothers.

This last event pulled him up by the roots and threw him back on himself for growth. For a while it made him morbid. He himself suffered something of a breakdown, and at odd moments then and in later days he would write and speak of the "darker realities." But the phrase itself is an indication of what so convulsive an event may have done for him in dispelling the narrowing and imitative influences that had been effective in his education. Finally there was the trip to Paris. What with anxiety about his mother and too much study, his health had broken down. He was twenty-five and he enjoyed the scene. There were "small French girls" to waltz with, and there was a genuine revolution that he bumped into—the *coup d'état* of Napoleon III in December 1851. His letters home about it are filled with fun and a shrewd political sense. He wrote some Paris letters on the revolution for the *Prospective Review* that show a germinating cynicism and a realistic sense of the political scene. He must have enjoyed shocking the Unitarian readers of the journal with the statement that the coup of Napoleon was the best thing that could have happened to France, and that no quality is more desirable in a people than political stupidity.

And so one that should have been attuned by his milieu to the proper pitch went off key. They had tried to give him convictions and a sense of mission, seriousness, and high purpose; and here he was dancing with girls in Paris and writing sportively of the sanctities of representative government. In the next few years he made himself master of the literary essay, with sprightly articles on the Oxford academic mind, on poor Hartley Coleridge, and on the first Edinburgh reviewers. These essays on English literary figures he was to write for several decades, and they were finally collected after his death as *Literary Studies* (2 vols., 1879). They have given Bagehot a place in the history of English literary criticism not much below that of Matthew Arnold. In them the approach was throughout psychological, with Bagehot's eye always on the relation of the writer's mind and personality to his work.

The shock of his mother's insanity, the dramatic events at Paris, the sense of mastery over a literary form—perhaps they will in some degree account for the change in Bagehot. Less than that is necessary for a young fellow, who has life in him to begin with, to throw aside the slumbrous veils of his education.

A desire to be near his mother made him enter his father's banking house on his return from France, and abandon any intention of making the life of thought his chief occupation. His father, with his orderly, conscientious habits of mind, was seriously disturbed by the flippant way in which Walter treated the principles of banking, and the short-cuts which he took to dispense with its routine. A curious mind grew impatient with what seemed an arid business technique, restless at merely doing things; there was so much material—right under a banker's nose—for theorizing about. But his father was to find a valuable ally—a marriage which eventually brought Walter closer to banking and public affairs.

The six Misses Wilson, daughters of James Wilson, M.P., and high official of Her Majesty's Treasury, heard that a Mr. Bage-hot, a young banker from the west of England—or was it a young barrister?—was coming to Claverton Manor to see their father about writing for his journal, the *Economist*. They were not interested in young bankers from the west of England. Another one of those bores, probably, who would talk interminably about Peel's Banking Acts and about "the laws of economics, sir." So they continued imperturbably with their German governess in the schoolroom at Claverton Manor. The next morning a tall slender man of a little past thirty, with long delicate hands and a mass of black hair and playful black eyes, appeared at the breakfast table. Breakfast over, the German governess walked out of the room. The young man turned quickly on the Misses Wilson with: "Your governess is like an egg." "At once," writes one of them in a memoir, "we saw that she *was* like an egg."

What a beginning for a Victorian courtship! Miss Elizabeth Wilson, if we may trust a sketch of her, had the dignity of a Greek goddess with the grace of a pre-Raphaelite head. She held out for a year and a half, and then the engagement took place. Walter writes to her:

I go about murmuring: "I have made that dignified person commit herself. I have, I have," and then I vault over the sofa with exultation. Those are the feelings of the person you have connected yourself with. Please do not be offended at my rubbish. Sauciness is my particular line. I am always rude to everyone I respect. I could write to you of the deep and serious feelings which I hope you will believe are really in my heart, but my pen jests of itself and always will.

There is not much more in the life of such a man to record. There were no great victories; rather, three successive defeats when he stood unwillingly for Parliament. Even the solid ground of a victory would have crumbled before his questioning spirit. That is why it is just as well that he was denied also the triumphs of a life of scholarship—most vulnerable of all triumphs. The burst of applause from an admiring press as each new exhaustive volume appears—the salvos that greeted Mill's *Principles* and Bryce's *American Commonwealth*—were spared him. He never wrote an exhaustive volume. At the most it was a quick theoretical sortie of some kind, or a series of essays as in *Physics and Politics;* more often it was a single essay, and then away nimbly to fresh fields. He did not approach a subject, as is the scholar's wont, with his forces marshaled in serried ranks, and all the impedimenta trailing after; rather, a forced march, a deft attack—and he had come away with his spoils.

Thus in jesting earnest he wrote for a quarter-century, making no great noise in England or anywhere else. As he approached and passed the prime of life, his interests shifted more and more from banking, from literature even, to economics and the logic of statecraft. He became before all else a commentator on the shifting financial and political scene. His weekly editorials in the *Economist* —he had succeeded his father-in-law in its management—were regarded with great respect by politicians and Treasury officials; Gladstone consulted with their author on matters of financial policy. But the real gusto of his thought found expression, I suspect, rather in the more theoretical writings: the longish sketch of *Lombard Street,* the papers on *The English Constitution,* and that amazing *jeu d'esprit, Physics and Politics.* Death found him, in 1877 at fifty-one, writing that sort of stuff; and from the bigwigs came graceful appropriate tributes.

Bagehot's economic writing ranks with the best in the English tradition. The most enduring result of his increasing interest in banking, *Lombard Street* (1873), has become classic for its realistic description of the English banking system and its analysis of the logic of its functioning. It shifted the emphasis in the literature of the subject from the discussion of banking legislation and mechanics to an examination of the body of working rules and their effect. It resulted in a new understanding of the function of the Bank of England in keeping the banking reserves of the community.

But Bagehot's mind was not content with pragmatic work of this sort. In his *Economic Studies* (collected in 1880, after his death) several essays deal with an analysis of the two basic postulates of English economic theory—the transferability of labor and of capital —and an examination of their validity in the changed economic world that Bagehot knew. In these and in a series of essays on Smith, Ricardo, and Malthus he effectively refuted any notion of the eternal validity of the theory of the founders and showed its necessary context in the England of their own time. Coming at a time when criticism of classical economics was maturing in England, these essays were influential for the cogency with which they called for revision of the classical body of theory within the limits of its own logical premises.

Much the same approach had even more far-reaching results in political science. Bagehot's *English Constitution* (1867) is probably his most widely read book. In it he abandoned the contemporary preoccupation with political forms, as he abandoned also most of the preconceptions derived from physics. He sought to substitute a discussion of the actual functioning of the political institutions of his day in their cultural and traditional setting. There is something of an anthropological note here, as there is also in *Lombard Street:* it is the actual working rules that interest him, and he strips away everything unimportant to get at them. His exposition of the theory of Cabinet government, of the survival value of such institutions as an English monarchy and the House of Lords, and of the function of the House of Commons as an organ of administrative control, has been formative for all subsequent discussions. When anyone sets out today to write a realistic analysis of the English Constitution, like as not he has Bagehot in mind as his archetype. In fact, the book has achieved so complete an acceptance as representing the reality of English government that it has doubtless influenced the shape that political institutions tended to take. Looking back at it now, it seems difficult to decide which was the reality and which the representation. Resting its ultimate explanations of British political institutions on the nature of the British mind it takes its place as a pioneer essay in national political psychology.

The most original and ambitious writing that Bagehot did in social science was his *Physics and Politics* (1869), in which "physics" is metonymy for natural science and "politics" for social science. It is the first important attempt to bring out whatever implications Victorian science, especially Darwinism and the new ethnographic writings of Tylor and Lubbock, possessed for the study of the political community. Although its principal premises are thus the premises of biology—evolution and natural selection—and its material largely anthropological, it is in essence a brilliant essay in social psychology, mapping the significance for human history of such forces as custom and revolt, innovation and imitation, conflict and discussion, law and force. Modern social psychology has to a great extent followed in the wake of these leads.

In the heyday of the democratic dogma, Bagehot was an aristocrat at heart—almost an aristagogue. He would have considered himself too hard-headed to feel except at high-wrought moments any real sympathy for the democratic mass. Brilliant in his domestication of Carlyle's *O altitudo* concept of leadership, he showed the myopic spots in his outlook mainly in underestimating the masses as a creative political force. The common man was to him, as to Carlyle, merely so much human material to be governed well.

On the whole he found little fault with the government that existed. The English Constitution was a creditable achievement; Commons and Cabinet were pleasingly responsive to the electorate; Lords and King served to check a possible mobocracy and heighten the tone of politics. Nor was he less satisfied with the economic fabric. Lombard Street in his book manages to get its work done somehow. Did the scratchings of Karl Marx's pen in the British Museum, and the noise of the discussions in his stuffy parlor, reach Bagehot in the offices of the *Economist*? It is doubtful. He was a banker, one of those who possess the earth. His table was full, he had a horse to ride, cultured men as friends, and a magazine to accept everything he wrote.

I have set down these shortcomings that I might seem to extenuate nothing. It would be folly to claim for Bagehot more than he can lay claim to. He was little concerned with exploring the realm of social possibility. He was a realistic conservative—in some ways a reactionary. But whatever he was, he was a first-rater. What recommends him is his infernal wisdom, and it is that which will make him for a long time modern. If he never attained to the height of inspiration, if he never had any genuine social vision, he was also very rarely fooled. He has opened up for us few areas for social construction, and there is little in him that is gleaming for the eager eye. But there is little in him also for time to corrode.

What a way this Bagehot had of avoiding the flurries and pitfalls of his generation! When everyone else was swallowing Ricardo whole, he saw that the "laws of economics" applied in Ricardian form only to industrialized communities like England, and even to them only approximately. When they were prating about checks and balances and all the pulleys and weights of a mechanistic concept of politics, he wrote his essays on the English Constitution to reveal a living organism. When they were talking about the principles of banking, he wrote a book about Lombard Street—about English bankers as people and the English banking system as a tradition and a going concern. While English dons were still discussing Aristotle's classification of constitutions, or arguing the ethical theory of the state, he mixed a strange concoction of physics and politics and talked about the survival-power of states. In each case his contemporaries have been outlived.

Many of his readers in this decade have been struck with wonder at his insistent psychological approach. He is always reducing his inquiries to terms of how men act and why. Yet this is only a facet of the characteristic that gives all his work some unity—a clear-eyed unfooled realism. He was a psychologist because it helped him to visualize the better what concepts were involved in the situation. A succession of unlike characters marches across his pages. He gave much thought to each of them—Gibbon, Macaulay, Hartley Coleridge, Shelley, Sydney Smith, Adam Smith, Disraeli, Gladstone, Peel, Clough, Napoleon III, Lord Brougham. He studied the man of letters, the banker on Lombard Street, the politician in Parliament. Like Emerson, he saw them as the realities; institutions were their shadows.

He had, in short, a quantity of that merciless sense that survives half-centuries and fails to evoke the most modern smile of derision. He represents what the modern spirit, whittling away the pompous and the sentimental from Victorian thought, can still retain as a credible core.

1930

4

Graham Wallas: the Fabian or the Tiger?

GRAHAM WALLAS's mind was the most fertile and flexible of his whole generation of English political thinkers. His most incisive work falls in the period (1908–1920) that saw the appearance of his three great books—*Human Nature in Politics, The Great Society,* and *Our Social Heritage.* As we look back now at that decade and its political thinking we can see it as a struggle between a growing revolt against rationalism on the one hand, and on the other a desperate attempt to save the bases of society by gradual and rational change. Most thinkers of the period can be safely contained within one or another of these strains. It was Wallas's fate to be caught in both, and no small part of his talent that he managed to poise himself perilously between the two.

His intellectual career began with the Fabian enthusiasm of the late eighties in England, and he was one of the contributors to the original volume of *Fabian Essays.* The curious reader will find in Pease's history of the Fabian Society a delightful drawing of Bernard Shaw, Wallas, and Sidney and Beatrice Webb seated in an English meadow, planning in all probability some Fabian manifesto. Shaw looks half jocose, half admonitory; *das Ehepaar Webb* have with them their unfailing notebooks and their enraptured statistical air; while Wallas has the fine, serious, and withal tentative look of the classical schoolmaster not yet turned thirty who is becoming engrossed in the social problem.

But his mind, thoroughly empirical, refused to be contained within anyone's intellectual system, and his mental appetite was too lusty to be satisfied with the stuff that passed for food in his day. Even the diluted Marx-Mill-Henry George concoction of the

Fabians proved unpalatable. He stayed away from the easy generalizations of the dogmatists, from the paradoxes of the *littérateurs*,
from the messianisms of the economists. He turned to English
history for the roots of contemporary problems, and wrote one of
the best studies we have of the history of ideas, the *Life of Francis
Place*. In it he studied and traced the relations between early nineteenth-century economic theory, the Combination Laws, and the
trade-union movement. His thought matured slowly and it was not
until he was fifty (in 1908) that he found at last the field for his best
thinking—the relation of the proper ordering of the state to the
nature of the human mind.

Wallas's name is chiefly connected with the rise of the rather
treacherous "science" of social psychology. With him this was no
grandiose affair, as it was, for example, in Pareto's *The Mind and Society*, but an honest attempt to establish political thinking on the
firm basis of the actual facts of the human mind. His *Human Nature
in Politics* (1908) and *The Great Society* (1914) represent a revolt
against a false rationalism and intellectualism in the study of the political animal. Bergson and Sorel in France, Pareto in Italy, Nietzsche (a good deal earlier) in Germany belonged to the same strain. So
also did the books on crowd psychology and the mob mind and the
instincts of the herd by Le Bon, Tarde, McDougall, Trotter, and
Martin. Throughout Europe and America political thinkers were
beginning to discover the tiger in man, those primal drives below
the level of consciousness that led Spengler somewhat later to refer
to man as "a beast of prey." The greatest discoverer in this realm
was, of course, Sigmund Freud, who saw the province he was stak-
ing out as "the psychology of the depths."

Wallas was no Freud and no Spengler. He was neither a technical
psychologist nor a philosopher who swept all human history. He
was too hard-headed, moreover, to fall for the "instinct" school that
played such havoc with social thought in the pre-war and post-war
years. He was in the tough-minded empirical tradition of British
social theory. It was he, more than anyone else, who carried over
into British—and perhaps American—social theory the viewpoints
of the new revolt against rationalism. He saw on the one hand the
force of instinctive dispositions and social habits in men's lives. He
saw on the other hand the complexity of what he called the Great
Society, and the wholly new conditioning it gave to the business

of living in the twentieth century. And he saw the growing discrepancy between the two.

To him more than to anyone else in the English tradition we owe our present knowledge that political behavior is irrational, that politics is the business of manipulating and exploiting the basic yet complex drives of men, and that all political progress must reckon with those drives. After the arid Victorian decades he brought a fresh realism back into English political thought, as Bagehot and Burke and Hobbes had done before him for their own generations. But while their writing spans the period when the democratic structure was being built up to its full strength, Wallas wrote at a time when it was cracking. Although he saw clearly the discrepancy between men's original dispositions and the demands made upon them by the complex life of the Great Society, he failed of an adequate analysis of the causes of the democratic collapse, and even more of an adequate program.

The ground of his failure must be sought not so much in the limitation of his own vision as in the intellectual resources upon which the Anglo-American thought of his day characteristically drew. His generation witnessed the idiocy of the international and industrial muddle and the mounting desperation of the capitalist state. It saw the world going to smash—and all that the political thinkers of the period could finally contrive was a series of new quirks and refinements in the practice of representative government. The waters were rising, and like a legion of good boys they stuck their intellectual thumbs into the dikes and talked of realism and objectivity.

Wallas himself was caught between seeing man as Fabian and seeing him as tiger. His earlier, pre-war work was a protest against the false assumption of rationality; his later, post-war work was equally a protest against the false conclusion that it was necessary to surrender to the cruel drift of events. On the one hand he talked of men as creatures of habit, instinct, and fear; on the other hand he talked of the collective organization of the will and the intellect. Someone has said of George Santayana that his views on religion can be summed up thus: "There is no God, and Mary is His mother." So too it would be possible to make a similar witticism about Wallas: that his views on political psychology were that there is no rationality and that the way to organize it is on a collective basis.

But this would be unfair to him, as it would be to the whole present intellectual movement that seeks to combine the recognition of political irrationalism with a program for organizing collectively the best rationality that men can muster. Wallas emphasized enormously the role of what he called "political invention." One of his heroes was Jeremy Bentham, whom he recognized as primarily concerned with the use of thought for refashioning social institutions. Like some others of his generation, such as the pluralists and the guild socialists, Wallas sought the undiscovered cadres on which society could build new collectivities in place of the unwieldy and collapsing capitalist state. Toward the end of his life, he went so far as to write a sort of handbook for political inventors: the *Art of Thought* (1926). In the detailed, meticulous fashion that was characteristic of him, he described his own thinking procedures, the rules that he had laid down for himself, the ways of surprising "fringe thoughts" and jotting them down in little notebooks. The last mental picture I have of him goes back to the time when he was lecturing at the Robert Brookings Graduate School at Washington. It was a lecture on property, and as Wallas spoke he would from time to time take out a little leather notebook and jot down something that had evidently occurred to him for the first time in the course of his lecture, and that seemed to him worth preserving.

But his desire for social change was an intellectual desire rather than one springing from a driving power of class conviction. And for that reason Wallas was never in any sense a revolutionist. He could never bring himself to face the problems of sheer political power involved in the transfer of dominance from one ruling group or class to another. One of his most significant books is *The Social Heritage* (1921), in which he pointed out the delicacy of the threads upon which modern civilization hangs, how if our knowledge of the industrial and the economic and political arts were snuffed out we should speedily find ourselves wandering about in Wellsian fashion, a few savages grubbing for food in the ashes of our world. It was a vivid image, but the uses to which others put it were to defend the *status quo* against any sort of radical change. The whole theory of the preciousness of the social heritage is, of course, one of the most conservative forces in our thinking. It was what made

Wallas at heart a Fabian, even after he had dissociated himself from the movement; and it was what made him avert his gaze more and more from the tiger in us.

1932, 1939

5

Engels and Marx—a Partnership[1]

THINK of a philosopher who was also one of the great military scientists of his day. Think of a profound theorist of history who surrounded himself always by the din of action. Think of a textile manufacturer and millowner who was the chief of staff of the world proletarian revolution. And if these paradoxes have not left you incredulous, add the final paradox of a brilliant writer who was content to dim the light of his own fame in order to enhance that of his friend, another writer. Friedrich Engels has been thus far, for English readers at least, an unclear and shadowy figure— known chiefly as the "—— and Engels" part of a literary collaboration that produced the *Communist Manifesto*. It is the merit of Gustav Mayer's biography [2] that we can now see Engels for what he was—one of the most full-blooded and complete personalities in European history, a figure almost Homeric in its proportions and Homeric too in the simplicity and strength and grace of its contours.

To those who think of revolutionists as puny and crabbed, I recommend the life of Engels. No life lived in nineteenth-century Europe approximated more closely to the Goethean norm of completeness and maturity. It achieved its balance, however, as the Greeks did—not by any inner check or by the starving of one faculty or another, but by the uninhibited exercise of every faculty. Here was a man who could ride to hounds with the English gentry for the sheer joy of it and despite his conviction that they were a decaying and oppressive class; a man who knew how to run a successful business and spent his hours studying the causes of capitalist col-

---

[1] This was published in somewhat abbreviated form in the *Herald Tribune Books*. I give here the original essay.

[2] *Friedrich Engels: a Biography*. With an introduction by G. D. H. Cole. New York, Knopf, 1936.

lapse; a man who could one month be fighting in the German Revolution of 1848, with the bullets whistling about his head, and the next month be off on a walking tour through Burgundy, "charmed by the Burgundian girls, with whom he lay in the grass, laughing and talking, and eating grapes and drinking wine." Not only from Engels's thought but from his life as well, communism emerges with a distinctly humanistic emphasis.

Professor Mayer's book is the distillation of years of research. The present translation is from a condensed version of the author's classic two-volume study of Engels, the first volume of which appeared sixteen years ago in Germany and the second last year in Holland. He has written a rich book which has clarity, compactness, above all penetration. The author writes from a fullness of knowledge which makes every phrase count, yet he is unpedantic. His long study has somehow failed to produce in him either the obliquity of vision or the obsessive grubbing for details that usually form the occupational diseases of lifelong devotion to a single subject. He makes short shrift of the usual stock of crises, epochs, and turning-points in the history of Engels. But in his studied underemphasis he has tended to err somewhat on the other side, and has thus sacrificed some sharpness of outline. Nevertheless, this book, along with Franz Mehring's recently translated *Life of Marx*, will furnish an admirable introduction to the history of international socialism.

How Engels ever managed to tear himself away from his class roots and the deeply Pietistic religious roots of his family, and grow into a revolutionist, is one of those questions that is ultimately insoluble. We can trace the process, just as we can trace a somewhat similar process in the life of our own Jack Reed, but we cannot lay our hands on the particular configuration of chance, cultural impact, and heredity that produced it. Professor Mayer is unusually skillful in tracing the perilous voyage of the mind of a young man coming to intellectual maturity, fighting out in his own mind the political and literary battles being waged around him.

Born in 1820, Engels grew up at the time of the Young German movement; his first heroes were Heine and Ludwig Börne; from them he moved on to Hegel, and then to the Young Hegelians such as Moses Hess and Bruno Bauer, who almost destroyed their master's thought in deriving from it; he ended with communism. Little did his worthy and well-to-do Pietist father, smug with that unrivaled smugness of a successful and respected middle-class German, know what his son was thinking in those days when he was attending school, serving as apprentice in a counting-house, and enlisted in the King's Guard. Little did he know, and still less could he understand. Engels's wanderings from the trim hedges of his family's life led to the usual tragic break—a break symbolized on that awful day during the 1848 revolution when the elder Engels, on his way to church, encountered his son wearing a revolutionary sash and directing the gunners in preparing the defenses of a strategic bridge.

Engels's *Lehrjahre* in England were crucial. He had already come to revolutionary conclusions by his study and thinking in Germany, and these were to be confirmed by his friendship with Marx and later put to a fiery test in the crucible of action. But England was the link. He went there to manage one of the family textile mills, and he was to remain there (with the exception of certain revolutionary intervals on the Continent) until his death. On his first visit of two years he got the feel of the Manchester cobblestones and the sense of the leaden Manchester sky, got to know the workers, lived in their quarters, fell in love with an Irish working-girl— Mary Burns—who was to be his companion until her death. He read Carlyle, Disraeli, Tom Hood, Mrs. Browning—all the literature of social protest; he threw himself into the Chartist movement. He was full of impulsive enthusiasms, and yet he was not all impulse. He studied, observed, pondered. England was his laboratory —England, which had freedoms only dreamed of in Germany; England, where the industrial bourgeoisie had already replaced the feudal landlords (as they had not yet done in Germany) and come to power, thus (as Engels hoped) paving the way for social revolution. There was something very dramatic and just a little absurd about this strapping, impulsive Rhinelander, who came looking like a young Teutonic god but speaking almost flawless English, with his head full of a medley of Young Hegelian and communist ideas, telling the tenacious, placid, empirical English that their country was fated to play a great historical role in the coming proletarian struggle for power.

In Paris, on his way back from Manchester, Engels ran into Karl Marx. Thus began a friendship which was to blossom into one of the most amazing and productive partnerships in history. Engels, when they met on this occasion in 1844, was twenty-four; Marx was twenty-six. From that time until the death of Marx forty years later, the life of each of the friends was the life of both. Everything they thought and wrote, whosoever might be the signature, was in the deepest sense a common product. Together they fashioned a conception of history and philosophy, an analysis of their contemporary world, a logic and a strategy of revolution and workers' organization. Together they dedicated themselves to their audacious world mission.

Never did a task as gigantic as this depend so closely on a friendship; never was a friendship so interlaced with a common task. They were young, they were sanguine. They had high revolutionary hopes. They had not yet tried themselves against the crude and final power of the State. Together they wrote *The Holy Family,* attacking their former comrades, the Young Hegelians, and showing that a dialectical scheme had to be put on a materialist base. Together they also wrote the *Communist Manifesto,* their clarion call for world revolution, delivered to a sprinkling of London and Paris revolutionists. They even had a hand in the fighting when it came, and Engels after four battles remarked that the courage required for hand-fighting was the most ordinary thing in the world. They had their fill of police, passports, spies. But they were not aiming at revolution by conspiracy. They saw it as their task to organize uprisings of workers when the movement of economic events had made such uprisings possible.

As they saw their hopes extinguished by the failure of one revolutionary movement after another, they dug in more deeply for "the permanent revolution." Marx turned his attention to economics and spent his days in the British Museum working on his great treatise, *Capital.* Engels turned to military studies and became an expert on tactics, fortifications, generalship. Both of them watched international affairs with the greatest interest: a war, an economic crisis, might any day bring the revolutionary conditions they were awaiting. When a crisis finally came in 1857, they were beside themselves with joy. They felt it was ushering in the *dies irae* they had been prophesying.

Engels, despite his business losses, rejoiced at every sign of panic on the exchange. Marx increased the pace of his economic studies:

he wanted them ready when the deluge came. Engels, with perhaps a slight tinge of rationalization, threw himself even more deeply into his military studies—and hunting. "For hunting," he wrote to Marx, "is the real cavalry school." Marx buried himself in figures about overproduction, credit expansion, speculation. When finally the crisis failed to lead to world disaster, the two friends could only console themselves by matching explanations as to why it had not come off. Their efforts after that were directed to perfecting their theory, and to the workers' movements in each country. The amazing thing is not that they failed to realize their youthful hopes, but that they succeeded as well as they did. When Marx died in 1883 there was already a working-class movement all over the world.

Marx's economic relation to Engels has often been commented on disparagingly. But that is unwarranted. Engels held it his duty to help support Marx and his family; around that duty he organized his whole life, scrimping on his own expenses, staying at his hated commercial occupation until he could retire from it with a competence for both of them. But with all that Marx often lived in the most horrible poverty, and his letters to Engels are full of anguished cries of despair that he should have to dun his friend so persistently. He tried to get employment. He even tried for a job as a railway clerk, only to be refused because of his handwriting. The two friends did hackwork together for an American encyclopedia. Marx became a correspondent for the New York *Tribune* in the days of Dana, but to spare him for his economic studies, Engels cheerfully wrote the articles for him. They had common friends, common (often unreasoning and ungenerous) hatreds. Living in the tense, unhealthy, neurotic atmosphere of the German émigrés in England, it was a wonder they kept themselves as whole as they did. There was only one occasion on which their relation was dangerously strained. Engels had written to Marx of the death of Mary Burns, with whom Engels had been living. Marx, after a few cool and casual words of regret, went on to speak of his own financial difficulties. Engels was deeply distressed, but it is a measure of the greatness of the two men that there was finally no break. Both understood that Marx's work was not only his own. The relation meant a sacrifice for both of the friends, but it was a sacrifice not so much to each other as to the common struggle in which each was engaged.

Professor Mayer does well to develop many of Engels's traits of personality by comparing them with Marx's. Indeed the relation of the two men was almost dialectical. Each brought (the "thesis") his own peculiar qualities: Engels a facile and fertile mind, immense energy, an understanding of business activity, a genius for exposition, a passion for tactics; Marx, a deeply searching mind, a tortured but unforgettable pen, a genius for system-building, an unparalleled daring. Each developed and stressed in relation to the other (the "antithesis") qualities he might never otherwise have realized. Out of their confrontation grew their common product (the "synthesis"), much more than the sum of the qualities of each. In a friendship that lasted as long as theirs, with its many hardships and tensions, there was need for one of the two to be unusually flexible. This role was undoubtedly Engels's. "Genius," Engels wrote to Bernstein, "is such an exceptional thing that we who have it not always know that we cannot attain it." He insisted on doing "what I was meant for, to play second fiddle." Of course he underrated himself, as he always did with his "brazen modesty." Marx was generous in his estimate. "You know I am always slow to grasp things," he wrote to Engels, "and that I always follow in your footsteps."

The truth is that while it is possible to analyze the differences of their qualities, it is hopeless to disentangle the strands of their achievement. Without the other each would still have been a genius and made a splash in world history. But without Engels, Marx might have remained a profound philosopher, and never written his economics nor held together an international movement; and without Marx, Engels might have remained a brilliant revolutionary journalist, without the capacity for systematizing his insights and without a movement in which to display his brilliant tactical sense.

After Marx's death Engels lived for ten years as the recognized leader of the world workingmen's movements. His house was the Mecca toward which all socialists turned; in the words of an unfriendly estimate, he was "the Teutonic Grand Lama of Regent's Park." With a burning desire to pursue his own studies, he nevertheless spent most of his leisure editing and completing the second and third volumes of *Capital* from Marx's notes. There were no longer any new beginnings for him in life: there were only the sequels, continuations, completions of earlier days. But he followed with interest every event that might have a bearing on his life-task. He saw, with a great acuteness, the special national characteristics that retarded the American labor movement. Applying his historical analysis to events, and projecting it into the future, he foresaw the World War and its harvest of excessive nationalism.

As a personality Engels was one of the most magnificent figures in the whole revolutionary tradition—a tradition which, despite its emphasis on principles, impersonal economic forces, and mass movements, has none the less turned very considerably on leadership. He did not have the bitter, searching intensity of Marx, nor the steel strength of Lenin. He was better rounded than either, more human—and his influence has been more humanizing. The episode of Lizzy Burns furnishes a symbol. Lizzy was Mary's sister, like Mary an unlettered Irish girl with wit and passion. Engels loved her and, after Mary's death, lived with her. His views on bourgeois marriage had kept him from going through the wedding ceremony with either. Nevertheless, at Lizzy's deathbed he married her.

It is this combination of an iron framework of theory and conviction which nevertheless is not allowed to go unrelaxed or defeat its own purpose that measured Engels's stature. The materialist interpretation of history, which is the basis of all Marxian thought, was as much his creation as Marx's. Its best statement is in the *Anti-Dühring* published under Engels's signature. But the mind that could help fashion the framework of historic law for the unfolding of human society was not a mind to be caught in that framework as in an iron trap. Engels's influence was always in the direction of a humanistic, undogmatic, unmechanical theory, whether of economics or literature or revolution. That, along with the greatness of his life, is his chief heritage.

1936

6

Lenin's *The State and Revolution*

THERE is probably nothing in the history of political thought that equals in dramatic power Lenin's achievement in linking in his own life the analysis and enactment of revolution. He was one of those rare persons in whom life drives no paralyzing wedges and in whom therefore there is no gap between the idea and the act. Our psychologists call this the "integrated personality" and our educators pant for it; and in the next breath they would both dismiss whomever they found possessing it as a "fanatic." This single-mindedness of purpose is an essential condition of revolutionary success; and the interplay between action and analysis has been generalized by the Marxian tradition as "the unbroken web of theory and practice." But it was Lenin's summit achievement, topping that of every other revolutionary leader we have known, to make out of his life the enduring symbol not only of tenacity of striving but of the clear unity of thought and deed. Nor are we dealing here with a reckless extremism. The extremisms belong rather with the world's Hamlets and Genghis Khans, with the paralyzed intellectual as a symbol at one pole and the extroverted world conqueror at the other. Lenin's greatness lies exactly in his resolution of these polar extremes.

Yet it is not a resolution aiming merely to untie the knots in one individual's life. If Lenin sought to resolve the tensions and dilemmas in his own life, it was in order to make of himself a sharper instrument in the social struggle. The goal was always effective action; in the interlocking of thought and deed, the end-product was the deed and not the thought. One may detect in him a mild anti-intellectualism which never fails to thrust the idea back in its place whenever it seeks to become an end. In the postscript to *The State and Revolution* he explains why the book is truncated and why the final chapter was never written as planned. It was to have been on "The

326

Experience of the Russian Revolutions of 1905 and 1917." What interfered was the second (October) Russian revolution. "Such interference," writes Lenin with a gentle irony, "can only be welcomed. . . . It is more pleasant and useful to go through the 'experience of revolution' than to write about it." More pleasant and useful: a whole way of life is summed up in that phrase; and in it the entire tradition of the *littérateurs* who have dallied with the revolutionary dream stands rebuked.

How *The State and Revolution* came to be written contains no inconsiderable part of its meaning. In 1917 Lenin and his wife Krupskaya were living in Switzerland as one of a little band of revolutionary exiles from all countries. Ten years before they had left Russia because the Bolshevik Central Committee agreed that they must not become the victims of the tsarist repression that followed the unsuccessful revolution of 1905. They just managed to escape the death-clutch of the terror that was grimly called at the time "Stolypin's necktie." In a weird Uncle Tom's Cabin night they fled across the breaking ice from the Finnish mainland to an island where they could board an unwatched mail steamer for Sweden. For a decade they had wandered over the face of Europe, from Stockholm to Geneva to Paris to Cracow and back to Geneva. It was a decade of shattering loneliness. The strength of the Russian workers and peasants seemed utterly broken after the 1905 revolution and the terror that followed it. Factional struggles splintered whatever strength remained. One had to face espionage and repression from without, and treachery and inconstant purpose from within; one lived on the edge of starvation, a jangled life of frayed nerves and obscure strivings, most tragic because it was severed from the proletarian Russian soil. When the war broke out in 1914, the Social-Democrats in every country voted war credits, and workers confronted workers across the trenches. Lenin's answer was given at the Zimmerwald and Kienthal conferences, where he rallied the remaining anti-war socialist leaders; it was given in his book *Imperialism* (1915), a pitiless analysis of the internal capitalist breakdown from which the external capitalist rivalries sprang.

But there was a deeper answer still. The betrayal of the Marxist tradition by its accredited spokesmen (even Plekhanov, whom Lenin had always admired, turned patriotic; no wound could have gone deeper) shook Lenin to the roots of his being. An individualist thinker might have turned to an autobiography, a religious thinker to solitude. Lenin turned to first principles. Since he had organized his life not around a single event but around a conception of history, it was to a re-examination of the movement of history that he had to return in these years of crisis.

The writing of *Imperialism* had enabled him to see the implications of the World War for the revolutionary path that was to follow it. But *Imperialism* was a work of economic analysis. The real questions Lenin was now concerned with—revolutionary tactics, the seizure of power, political construction and reconstruction, state forms and their succession—were political questions. Now there was strictly speaking no body of political theory in the Marxian tradition—in the sense, for example, that *Das Kapital* embodied an economic theory and *The Communist Manifesto* a theory of history and the class struggle. There was only Engels's *The Origins of the Family, Private Property, and the State,* full of brilliant leads lost in a quagmire of the anthropology of the day; and there were hints in the historical and polemical writings of Marx himself. Lenin was to bring these suggestions together, melt them in the passionate urgency of his own mind, pour the metal into a mold of doctrine, hammer it into a reasoned logic of revolution.

The first stage was a set of notebooks that Lenin called *Marxism and the State.* He had evidently begun these in a random way not long after 1907; and he had pursued them in the libraries of various European cities. After the outbreak of the war his pace increased. Cut off from action, he sat day after day in the libraries at Zürich and Berne, sharpening the outlines of a revolutionary theory of the state.

That the revolution was coming he had no doubt. He listened eagerly for every rumbling from the Russian masses, who were growing ever more discontented under the collapse of the feudal-capitalist economy and the bureaucratic war machine. He knew that when the revolution came it would be different from the 1905 revolution and different from the Paris Commune: the outward thrusts of the objective economic development that underlay revolution were unyielding. Yet even he did not know how close revolution was. News did not come easily to Switzerland through the war barricades around it. There were anti-war demonstrations in Russia in January, serious strikes in February. Yet as late as the end of January, in a lecture he gave on the 1905 revolution to a group of young socialists, he said, "We of the older generation may not live to see the decisive battles of this coming revolution."

Krupskaya has left us in her memoirs an account of how Lenin first got the news that the Tsar was overthrown:

Once after dinner, when Ilyich was getting ready to leave for the library, and I had finished with the dishes, Bronsky ran in with the announcement, "Haven't you heard the news? There is a revolution in Russia!" . . . We went to the lake, where on the shore all the newspapers were hung up. . . . There really was a revolution in Russia. Ilyich's mind worked intensely. I do not remember how the rest of the day and evening passed.

Lenin's reaction was immediate. The "old European pattern" of revolutions, where mass revolt has always ended with some "constitutional" middle-class regime, had for once to be broken. There came the frantic efforts to get to Russia, wild schemes of landing in an airplane, ingenious schemes for getting through on a Swedish passport and, since he did not know the language, pretending to be a deaf mute. Finally came Martov's plan of going through Germany in exchange for interned German prisoners—a plan which was finally followed and which led to the famous "sealed train" episode and the charges of being in the pay of the German government. Ralph Fox, in his vivid biography of Lenin, has described Lenin's arrival at the Finland Station, the enthusiastic ovation of the sailors and workers, his quick perception that they were now not only more revolutionary in temper than the Provisional Government but more so even than the Bolsheviks themselves reckoned.

There followed months of agitating, organizing, pamphleteering. After the July Days a period of extreme repression set in; Lenin was hunted and had to go into hiding. Just before he left Petrograd he wrote a note to Kamenev:

Entre nous. If they get me I ask you to publish my little notebook *Marxism on the State* (stranded in Stockholm). Bound in a blue cover. All the quotations are collected from Marx and Engels, likewise from Kautsky against Pannekoek. There is a whole series of notes and comments. Formulate it. I think you could publish it with a week's work. I think it important, for it is not only Plekhanov and Kautsky who got off the track. My conditions: all this is to be absolutely *entre nous*.

The notebook was somehow procured. Lenin worked over it during August and September while hiding first in a hayloft and then in a twig hut on a worker's farm and finally at Helsingfors.

It is clear from Lenin's letter that he set enormous store by his book. If he were killed, it would be his legacy to the revolutionary movement. "It is not only Plekhanov and Kautsky who got off the track"—in that restrained line Lenin packed the whole bitter experience of his discussions in the Central Committee of the past months. And so, between sending memoranda to his comrades on the Committee, Lenin wrote *The State and Revolution*. Before he could get at its final chapter, he was once more swept up in the October Revolution itself. The press had such a mass of more urgent work that the book was not published until the next year. By that time Lenin was at the head of the new Soviet government. And the book which had been begun and written as a guidebook for the revolutionary movement now took on fresh meaning as the blueprint of political construction in the Soviet state.

To the superficial eye *The State and Revolution* seems only a hundred-page pamphlet, stripped of adornment, filled with the clichés of the Marxist terminology. Its method is the glossator method so common in the literature—the appeal to the basic texts of the Marxian fathers, the elucidation of the texts, and the use of them to refute one's opponents. It is sometimes heavy-footed and unfailingly rasping in its polemics. Where then lies its greatness?

Only the dullard will fail to see through the outward skin the ribbed intellectual strength of the book. Lenin's greatest pamphlets have with his speeches the same quality of strict economy, the same intellectual flame burning the more strongly because nothing else is permitted to obscure it. Neither did he make any pretense to originality, and he follows the method of gathering and commenting on the *loci classici* of Marx and Engels all the more severely because he wishes to play down his own role. He felt that his job was not to create but to restore the Marxian theory of the state. His attacks on Kautsky and Plekhanov were directed against the whole Social-Democratic literature of the Germans, which had "transplanted . . . with an accelerated tempo the immense experience of a neighboring, more advanced country to the almost virgin soil of our proletarian movement." He felt he had to destroy the influence of these writings. Hence the savage polemical method. It is as if Lenin were seeking to light up the doctrinal darkness with the dazzling flash of knives.

Actually, however, Lenin's book is amply creative in its elements of synthesis and reinterpretation. The bricks for a Marxian theory of the state were available to anyone, but no one had ever put them together. And in the process he had to view old political forms in the light of new economic realities, with the genius for the modern instance that Lenin above anyone possessed.

Lenin begins with a masterly restatement of the class-domination or class-instrument theory of the state. The state is simply the special apparatus of force used by the dominant class to keep the underlying classes in subjection. By its very nature it arises out of the irreconcilability of class conflicts. This is true of capitalist democracy as it is of every other state, except that subtler means to maintain class power are used instead of force: "A democratic republic is the best possible political shell for capitalism." The whole form of the state is determined by the class uses to which it is put. As class succeeds class, the state machinery does not adjust itself to the demands of the new class power. The whole state apparatus—police, armies, bureaucracy, judiciary—must be violently shattered by the class rising to power, which replaces it by its own state apparatus. The bourgeois classes, when they came to power, created a state apparatus, basically parliamentary and bureaucratic, for their own purposes. The proletariat will have to do the same, changing the character of the state machinery in turn in accordance with *their* objectives.

Thus far Lenin's exposition has run along the traditional Marxian lines, but his emphases are interesting. One emphasis—or rather, lack of it—is the striking neglect of the theory of the class struggle proper. Lenin states it, demonstrates it, and gets over with it. It is simply "not true" that "the main point in the teaching of Marx is the class struggle." It "was *not* created by Marx, but by the bourgeois *before* Marx, and is, generally speaking, *acceptable* to the bourgeoisie" (how much light this throws on Charles Beard's insistence, for example, that he got his class theory not from Marx but from Madison). "A Marxist is one who *extends* the acceptance of the class struggle to the acceptance of the *dictatorship of the proletariat*." Which leads, accordingly, to another of Lenin's emphases:

on the inevitability of the capture and destruction of the bourgeois
state power by the proletariat. Engels's theory of "the withering
away of the state," he insists, has been distorted. It is not the bourgeois state that withers away, but eventually the proletarian dictatorship. The bourgeois state power must be captured and dis-
solved.

When he comes to the question of what is to replace it, Lenin
reaches the heart of his argument. The experience of the Paris
Commune of 1871 becomes central. The commune as a political
form replaced parliamentary bureaucracy. It remained a representative institution, but ceased to be a parliamentary "talking shop."
It became "a working body, executive and legislative at the same
time." It leveled the distance between the working class and its
ruling committees; it reduced the pay of all state officials to workers'
pay. And while destroying the parasitic network of centralized
French bureaucracy, the Communards aimed at building up and
extending the genuine national unity through a new centralism—
a commune of communes. Lenin would, of course, have developed
this theme further in his discussion of the soviets as the political
units of the Russian Revolution, had he ever written his last chapter. But he wrote enough to make it clear that the new proletarian
state forms already existed in revolutionary history, and that they
did not have to be spun out of the minds of theorists.

These living historical forms Lenin calls the dictatorship of the
proletariat, and the whole book must be seen at once as an argument for its inevitability and a paean to its nature. It has, according to Lenin, two principal features. On the one hand it is a *dictatorship*, in which the proletariat shares power with no other class,
and in which the hypocrisies of the sharing of power are stripped
away. On the other hand it is an *expansion of democracy:* "democracy for the people and not democracy for the rich folk." What
seems to us a paradox—the combination of dictatorship with democracy—is to Lenin no paradox at all. Democracy for the vast
majority, he argues, is possible only when accompanied by suppression of the exploiting minority through force. When the latter task
has been achieved, the state machinery itself becomes useless, and
increasingly withers away. The first phase of communist society—
socialist production—gives way to the "higher" phase of a completely classless and therefore a completely stateless society. Social-

ism will make possible a huge technological development, which will in turn give labor a new dignity and change the whole character of consumption habits. How long a time will be necessary for this transition, Lenin insists, or what forms it will assume, it is impossible to say in advance: like all other questions of political forms, that of the withering away of the state depends on an economic base of changing institutions and habits.

It would take a volume at least as long as Lenin's to discuss with any thoroughness the meaning and validity of his argument. Actually an entire literature has already developed around the book. Lenin has been used by every group in the struggles of the Marxists since his death. What is more pressing is for those who seek to stand outside the factions to examine what his thought means for the socialist tradition in the crisis democracies.

It is almost a quarter-century since Lenin's book was written. That quarter-century has witnessed the enactment of part of his vision and the dissolution of another part. The dictatorship of the proletariat in the Soviet Union has proved its strength and its capacity to fashion its own economic and political forms. But the world proletarian revolution has not been realized, and in its place fascism has become the aggressive force. In this context the bourgeois democratic states present a facet which Lenin recognized but did not emphasize—that of temporary barricades against the threat of universal barbarism. The crisis of the socialist tradition revolves today around two basic and interrelated questions. First, how can fascism best be fought and a democratic socialism achieved? Second, what attitude does this imply for left-wing democratic groups toward such crisis democracies as the America of the New Deal?

There is one line of political reasoning current today that runs directly counter to Lenin's whole position: the contention that the state is not the political instrument of any class, but a sort of broker or mediator between classes. The vivid illustration advanced in behalf of this view is the New Deal itself, which can scarcely be spoken of as an instrument of the capitalists without arousing more ironic laughter than any theory can bear. But Lenin has anticipated it by quotation from Engels: "By way of exception . . . there are periods when the warring classes so nearly attain equilibrium that the state power, ostensibly appearing as a mediator, assumes for the moment a certain independence in relation to both." And one may add from the experience of today's crisis democracies that such a state arises only in periods of dire capitalist emergency, that it always minimizes the necessary concessions to the working class, that its hands are tied by reactionary elements within its own ranks, and that when threatened by genuine proletarian militancy it never fails to make common cause with the capitalists who hate it. I have found nowhere in the literature of political theory insights so acute as Lenin's into the ways by which democratic political forms are used to mask the fact of actual economic inequality. Maury Maverick, for example, is miles away from being a Marxian, as also is Thurman Arnold. Yet *Blood and Ink,* like *The Folklore of Capitalism,* spells out in terms of the American experience the ways in which the forms and the rhetoric of our culture conceal the actual logic of oligarchy within it.

But if the class-domination theory remains valid as against the mediation theory, what shall we say of Lenin's insistence that the machinery of the capitalist democratic state must inevitably be captured and shattered, and that there is no path of continuity without violence between it and a democratic socialism? I do not propose to enter here into the interminable discussion whether the new Comintern line has betrayed Lenin's reasoning or is merely fulfilling it under conditions he did not foresee. What interests me much more is that Lenin's own book contains two divergent lines of direction, from each of which the clashing schools of Marxian thought today derive their strength.

One of these strains is the inevitability of a violent revolution. The other is the uniqueness of each national experience, and of the economic development, the political forms, and the revolutionary temper of each. The first leads to an austere anti-reformism and a bitter rejection of the Fabian assumptions. The second leads to an emphasis on the "national question," on national traditions and temper, and, in Engels's works, on the theme that "the working class can only come to power under the form of the democratic republic." Can these strains be reconciled? If ever a generation will have the impulsion to reconcile them, it will be one like ours, conscious through fascism of the tenacity with which the ruling class can cling to power, but conscious also of the reckless costs of violence as a method. What is healthy in Lenin's tough-mindedness is the insistence that Fabianism is never in itself a solution, since the ruling class will never in the end surrender power without a desperate attempt to smash democracy itself. But we may argue, nevertheless, that Fabianism and violence do not exhaust the alternatives; that, by Lenin's own reasoning, the fulfillment of the promise of a democratic republic leads in the deepest sense to a democratic socialism; and that revolutions of the majority, such as the Jeffersonian, Jacksonian, and the New Deal revolutions, must in the end, if conducted with courage and skill, make an anti-democratic capitalist coup merely suicidal adventurism.

Less immediate but no less important are the implications of Lenin's analysis of the nature and pace of socialist development itself. Our American generation will not accept his thesis that in a socialist state the workers' government will share power with no other class. What this has come to mean historically is the one-party system and the suppression of all opposition groups. But does this necessarily follow even from a class-domination theory of the state? There can be no doubt that in a minority-dominated capitalist state, the capitalists find it possible to share their power with the other classes. Why should this not be even more possible in an eventual majority-dominated workers' state?

This is not to deny Lenin's thesis that each new social system must fashion its own political instruments in terms of its own social purposes. But it is to deny that this means a clean sweep of the political machinery of the past. In fact, the essence of the Marxian theory of history is that the most valid elements of one stage survive in the next. Lenin himself insists, in his chapter on the Paris Commune, on the distinction between its discarding of parliamentary forms and its retention of representative forms. In the same way, the basic elements of the democratic tradition—the competition of ideas and of political opinions, and the democratic control of bureaucratic action—must not only be retained but expanded in a socialized culture.

In his analysis of the administrative machinery under socialism, Lenin mixes a good deal of hard sense with some curious Utopianisms. He saw the need for administrative centralism if the economic machine were to run. He anticipated the *expertise* of the Soviet state when he remarked, in answer to Kautsky's "superstitious reverence" for the "ministers" of the Prussian state: "Why can they not be replaced, say, by commissions of specialists working under sovereign all-powerful Soviets of Workers' and Soldiers' Deputies?" He relied, for democratic checks on the bureaucracy, on the recall of officials, the leveling down of their pay to that of the workers, and the imposition of executive responsibility on them which would force them to test their plans in practice. What seems Utopian is his belief that eventually all distinctions between the officials and the population as a whole would disappear. "Under socialism, *all* will take a turn in management, and will soon become accustomed to the idea of no managers at all." Certainly that has not happened in the Soviet state after two decades, nor is it likely to happen anywhere. We are more and more coming to recognize that the modern state, whether socialist or capitalist, cannot do without a bureaucracy but must learn to control it. In the beginning of socialized planning the state technicians are bound to have a power that strains the limits of democratic safety. But in the end the problem of democratic controls must be confronted squarely.

I prefer to omit, as beyond my interest or powers, all discussion of Lenin's theory of the transition from socialism to the "higher stage" of a classless, stateless society. Some day this may have some relevance for us. Today it remains in the realm of the luxuries of speculation. What is not in that realm is the democratic temper which pervades Lenin's whole life, and in the light of which his militant plea for dictatorship must be judged. There is no one in the history of political thought who guided himself more surely by contact with the masses, and by an amazing genius for discovering what the ordinary man thought and felt and an invincible belief in his essential dignity.

This book by the stocky bald little revolutionist, with its bristling militancy and its crabbed style, does it seem strange that it should have shaken our world? It has become a truism to say that the success of the Russian Revolution was unthinkable without the genius of Lenin's leadership. By the same token it was unthinkable without the confident analysis that enabled him to bludgeon the Central Committee into heeding his plans for a seizure of state power. But the converse is also true: the successful establishment of the Soviet state gave the book an authenticity and a prestige that has made it one of the great twentieth-century classics.

LENIN'S *THE STATE AND REVOLUTION*

No book that has been discussed thus far in this series [1] has been so widely read as Lenin's. In America it sells in editions of a hundred thousand, in the Soviet Union in editions of millions. Tens of millions have read it all over the world, and their minds have beaten to the rhythm of its logic. Lenin has become the supreme symbol of the revolutionary tradition, and through that symbolism even his mannerisms and his excesses have been ratified. After Lenin the dwarfing revolutionists without his talent nevertheless aped his withering phrases and, without his saving flexibility, they pursued his rigor.

Yet this is of trifling moment when weighed in the balance of Lenin's legacy as a whole. He wrote his book on the eve of a successful revolution; we read it today on the threshold of what may be a black period of reaction. Yet if we recall that Lenin began his researches for it in a similar period, during the years of exile after the 1905 failure, it should do much to dispel our sense of defeatism. For the long view that Lenin took is as valid in our day as in his. If we reject some of his formulations, it is because we have learned something from that history from which he himself was always learning and which he helped to shape. To the Marxist tradition he has given its most effective figure, and in the movement of Western political theory he is in his realism one of the two or three towering figures since Machiavelli.

1939

---

[1] The *New Republic* series of articles, "Books That Changed Our Minds."

7

Harold J. Laski

Laski and the Class-Domination Theory

HAROLD LASKI has written a book of iron mood to usher in an iron age. It is a book on the state,[1] but it does not serve up again the old honeyed platitudes that the philosophers love so, or wake the echoes of dead men's words. It is restrained in tone, yet it deals unflinchingly with the realities of the political struggle today—with death and terrorism and the seizure of power, with revolution and counter-revolution, with the repression of civil liberties and the selfish guarding of class interests. It is in form a sober treatise on political theory, in direction and temper a tract for the times, in substance the most powerful and realistic analysis of the capitalistic-democratic state that has thus far been written by a contemporary. The prospect with which it confronts our generation is so desperate that it must be set down finally as a book without hope.

The growing social tension today has been paralleled by the author's own intellectual pilgrimage to the left, and the fusion of the two finds expression in these pages. Mr. Laski has traveled a long way since the days of 1917, when, a youth just out of Oxford, he made a meteoric descent upon America and left the professors of political science aghast at his attack on the theory of the omnipotent sovereign state. For close to a decade, he championed the doctrine of pluralism. He asserted the right of other associations in communal life, such as the churches and the trade unions, to share with the state the privileges of sovereignty, and gave a good deal of ingenuity to evolving subtle and complicated techniques for reforming the structure of the democratic state. That period of Mr.

---

1 *The State in Theory and Practice*, New York, Viking, 1935.

Laski's writing was rounded out and summed up in his *Grammar of Politics,* published in 1925.

In the past decade, he has been concerning himself less with the theory of sovereignty and more with the struggle for power. Back in 1919, when Mr. Laski was still a young lecturer at Harvard, he spoke out in favor of the Boston police strikers and got a taste of what the state is like in practice—and incidentally found half the academic world come tumbling around his ears. Since then he has passed, like other members of the British Labour Party, through the experience of seeing his party come into office, attempt a piecemeal reform of the social system, and fail dismally. Events have pushed him continually farther left until now, although he is still a member of the Labour Party, he is a left-winger who feels that if there is to be a change at all in social arrangements it must be complete and cannot avoid being drastic. The real hero of the intellectual drama that lies beneath the over-prosaic title of the book is Nikolai Lenin, who knew how to make the most of the favorable moment for the seizure of state power.

In one sense, then, this book may be regarded as a farewell to pluralism. Mr. Laski makes short shrift of his former preoccupations with the rights and the wrongs of state power. The essence of the state, he says, is coercion; at any given time it is the existing government that exercises the entire coercive power of the state, and it has behind it the force of the army; when it comes to a showdown in a crisis the state is in fact supreme. But more important than Mr. Laski's farewell to pluralism is his final acceptance, in its fundamentals, of the Marxian theory of the state. This was foreshadowed a couple of years ago by his brilliant book *Democracy in Crisis.* It is fulfilled here. What was only implicit in the earlier work is in this book given the explicitness and finality of a considered theory of the state. If Mr. Laski was ever hesitant about taking the final step and aligning his thinking with the political theory of Marx, Engels, and Lenin, he has now definitely burned his bridges.

What does such a theory amount to? It says, first of all, that the state is always in the last analysis the instrument of the dominant economic class in a society. We call the modern state in England and America democratic, but it is in reality, says Mr. Laski, a capitalist democracy, protecting the property interests and expressing the way of life of those who own the instruments of production.

All great theory is an adventure in exploring what F. H. Bradley called the problem of appearance and reality. Behind the confused jangle of action, thought, and desire that make up our political life and find expression in our morning newspapers, there must be a set of determining forces that give shape to what happens. Mr. Laski finds these forces in the class relations of our society. He gives an impressive historical analysis of how the democratic forms of the capitalist state were evolved, how the peculiar economic set-up of the nineteenth century provided a plenty of commodities for distribution which eased the class tensions and allowed the growth of tolerance, how capitalism has been willing to make concessions to the underlying classes (thus creating a social-service state) so long as those do not threaten the basic fabric of capitalist power. He argues that under conditions of economic collapse, the causes of which he finds inherent in the development of capitalist economy, the demands of the masses as expressed through the mediums that a democracy affords them may reach the point where the capitalist governments bring in the entire coercive power of the state to stifle the protests, even when it means the suppression of civil liberties. He cites Italy and Germany as examples of how, when faced by the alternatives of surrendering their power as a class or scrapping the democratic character of the state, the capitalists have chosen the latter. He finds no instance in history where any class has ever abdicated its position of privilege and power without "heavy fighting," and he concludes that we are again faced with the same fate.

This is, of course, only the skeleton of the argument, and as such it does no justice at all to an analysis that even its opponents must recognize as tight, bold, and stark. It is evident that, although there is nowhere in the book an extended analysis of fascism as such, it is the recent triumph of Hitler that has acted throughout as the focus and dynamic of Mr. Laski's thought. He sees two principal revolutionary possibilities in the state today—the suppression of capitalism and the suppression of democracy. The proletarian movements aim at the first, the fascist at the second; the one is an economic revolution, the other a political one which leaves the seat of economic power unchanged. Mr. Laski's conclusion is that those who own the instruments of production will, when their dominance is seriously threatened by the first, accept the second and throw their force behind it.

The main outlines of such reasoning are traditionally Marxian. Mr. Laski comes to his Marxian convictions, however, from an intellectual starting-point quite different from that of the German, Russian, or American revolutionary theorists. He had steeped himself formerly in John Stuart Mill and T. H. Green, in Maitland and Figgis, in the British labor movement and the English university tradition, and he adds to that an intimate acquaintance with American legal theory and political practice. The result is not only a tone far less strident than that of most Marxian writings; he departs from them also in the range and flexibility of his reasoning. He recognizes (what the most subtle exponents of the materialist dialectic have always admitted) that the economic forces shaping government practice do not get translated into specific events except through the mediation of intricate psychological factors. He grants a far-reaching importance to the weight of national tradition. He deplores, but none the less takes account of, the fatal cleavages within the ranks of the workers' movements. He sees the middle classes as holding today the balance of power in the struggle for the state, and he even recognizes that there has been a growing *embourgeoisement* of the proletariat. But the heresy which, of all, will be considered the most unpardonable by the thoroughgoing Marxist is Mr. Laski's denial that the dictatorship of the proletariat is inevitable. Even where the fascist state, after crushing the working-class organizations, will have been swept into war (and for Mr. Laski war is an inescapable part of the international community of capitalist nation-states) it is "at least as possible that the outcome of war will be a reversion to barbarism as the victory of the working class."

It will be apparent that the final note of the book is that of a hopeless doom for our generation. Writing as one who is on the side of the proletariat, he has little expectation that the workers' parties can capture the imagination of the people sufficiently to gain a parliamentary victory, since all the organs of mass persuasion are on the other side. Even if they do, he says, the threat of such a victory would lead in England to its sabotaging by the House of Lords and eventually to a fascist coup. Even if the workers were successful in capturing power constitutionally, the two alternatives that would confront them would both point toward disaster: piecemeal reform is never possible without the co-operation of the property owners, and leads eventually, as in Germany, to counter-revolution; and drastic social reconstruction would be possible only if it could count on a united support from the workers and the middle classes which would be difficult to obtain while the nation was facing always the threat of war or of economic collapse. If all these hurdles could conceivably be cleared, the cost of revolution and civil war would still be a frightfully heavy one. The final chapter of the book, in which Mr. Laski outlines these prospects, is a piece of writing as eloquent and sustained as any I have yet met in the contemporary literature of political theory.

This book will inevitably be compared with John Strachey's *Coming Struggle for Power*. Both are proletarian in their premises and predilections. Both are a product of Marxism and the British university tradition. Each has a literary finish and a persuasive power which will make it dangerous reading for anyone whose convictions are still capable of being uprooted. But Mr. Laski's manner is less brash than Mr. Strachey's. It is thoughtful, temperate, almost ingratiating. One of the best measures of their difference lies in the way they use the refutation of an opponent's position to advance their own. Mr. Laski subjects the views of Professor Robbins and Professor Gregory, his colleagues at the London School of Economics, to as severe a drubbing as Mr. Strachey administers to J. M. Keynes and H. G. Wells. But while Strachey writes of them with a disdainful and savage *élan,* as of one who stands on the heights of communism and sees below him the antlike movements of the bourgeois economists and historians, Laski addresses his victims with something of a reproachful sadness that they should be so wrong on issues of such moment.

Ultimately this difference between the two books is tied to something much deeper. Strachey joyfully feels himself part of a class, destined to rise to victory on the crest of a historical wave. Mr. Laski is Marxist enough to say "farewell" to the existing social order; yet the immediate future is so dark that it holds not promise but doom. And he cannot find it in his heart to say "hail" to it. He finds refuge at the end of his book in vague verbalizations about "adding creative dignity to the human adventure" which, after his realistic analysis, come as an anti-climax.

1935

Liberalism's Family Tree

I CAN recall few books that left me in a more saturnine frame of mind than Harold Laski's *The State in Theory and Practice.* It swept with a clean logic to a prophecy of doom for my generation and then called on me and my fellows to embrace a fighting faith which by Mr. Laski's own logic had something less than a fighting chance of success. Mr. Laski's new book [2] is written in the same mood. It takes our most cherished ideals of liberty and individualism, links them with an unanswerable cogency to the achievement of power by the capitalist class, and leaves us to console ourselves with what moral we can muster. He seems himself to be of a divided mind in the matter. Liberalism as the garment of the capitalist ideal he handles with a mercilessly ironic detachment. But liberalism is today also one of the principal hurdles in the path of fascist barbarism. And this liberalism Mr. Laski cannot despise or abandon. The result is a strangely moving *odi et amo* mood that lends an eloquence and intensity to the writing at the same time that it withholds the note of finality which a book written in less troubled times would possess.

Being a political theorist, Mr. Laski is concerned primarily with the shape of power. Being also one of the most civilized human beings alive, he is sensitive to the fragile career of the human spirit, which power may serve but which crude and naked power can so easily crush. His writings contain, therefore, a masterly analysis of the capitalist state as an instrument of class power. But he is too canny a thinker to rest in the belief that naked force, whether it be political or economic, represents the mainstay of the existing class structure. In his latest book he has accordingly sought to get at the real fabric of capitalist power—its panoply of ideas. These ideas, it is his thesis, sum up in the main to the doctrine of liberalism. Mr. Laski has set out to dig into the past, to write a historical survey of the rise of the liberal doctrine and its full flowering, to give us, in short, liberalism's family tree.

As a study in the history of ideas the book is superb. It is a historical epistle addressed to the academies but written from the

---

[2] *The Rise of Liberalism: the Philosophy of a Business Civilization.* New York, Harper, 1936.

battlefields of Europe. Mr. Laski has for years been reading the tracts of seventeenth-century religious worthies and eighteenth-century mercantilists; he knows the bullionists as he knows the monarchomarchs; he has been through the literature of the Physiocrats as he has been through the literature of the levelers and the fifth-monarchy men and the French imaginary voyages. What he has given us is nothing less than a rewriting of the history of European social thought in the seventeenth and eighteenth centuries, with a prelude for the century before and a postscript for the century after. And because he is passionately interested in the conflicts of power today and because he has followed Maitland's injunction to write history backward, the scholarship in the book takes on life and meaning. The rise of liberal doctrine is narrated as part of the moving current of social history as affected ultimately by European economic development.

This is therefore one of the important attempts in English not to expound or defend Marxism but to use it as a technique in the history of ideas. Mr. Laski's problem was immensely difficult. Liberalism is the body of doctrine that claims for the individual freedom from interference of any kind—in his religious life, in the expression of his opinion, in his economic activity. Its philosophical core is the doctrine of individualism; the canons of its ethics are those of the individual conscience; in the realm of science it moves to the conviction that man may by rational inquiry become master of the universe; its religious corollary is the idea of tolerance and freedom of belief from the power of the state; its political faith is the rule of law and the doctrine of *laissez-faire;* its economic program is the Manchester ideal of free trade, free enterprise, and the competitive system; its legal vestments are freedom of contract and the sanctity of property; it is saturated with an optimism about human possibilities; its dream is the dream of progress. Liberalism is thus not a simple and satisfying universal formula but a complex tissue of belief ramifying into every area of life.

Liberalism found a Europe caught in the icy grip of feudalism and ecclesiastical authority. Today, after three centuries, the scene of its action is a Western world dominated by the struggle between the big property interests and the forces of labor. In the span between the two the role of liberalism has been to express in the realm of ideas the deep social struggles and economic changes. It aided these changes, adjusted itself to them, realized itself through them. It is Mr. Laski's strength that he understands, like Pareto, that formal doctrine and popular opinion are rationalizations of deeper drives in men. But unlike Pareto he does not regard any body of social thought as mere word magic and self-deception. He sees it as the orientation of each era to its new set of living conditions. Liberalism was hammered out by the same forces that hammered out the reign of business enterprise. Once in being it was used to justify the operation of the new economic system and its set of values.

Mr. Laski gives a sense of the inevitability of its progress—an inevitability that came from powerful impulsions within the system of production and the alignment of economic power. It is these impulsions, and not its own beauty or consistency, that make a doctrine succeed, spread, conquer. But Mr. Laski is wise enough to see that not only is there an outer logic of the relation of ideas to events, but within ideas themselves an inner logic that shapes a doctrine and contributes to its victory.

In liberalism this inner logic manifested itself most clearly in its drive toward the universal. Men's imaginations could not help being caught—even our own imaginations today are still caught —by the claims which liberalism staked out for the freedom and tolerance and expansion of the human mind. But as happens with all doctrine, the men who stood to profit from the triumph of liberalism identified these lofty claims with their own class interests. They equated their own power in society with the universal and permanent truths they had discovered about human beings everywhere. Liberalism as a revolutionary instrument had helped bring the new revolutionary capitalist class into power; they made out of it, in the sweep of their zest and recklessness, a universal; but when a new class took this universal, and extracted its implications and learned its lessons all too well, the bourgeois thinkers called a halt. They tried to prune liberalism, limit it, hedge it in. They saw that the liberties they had with its aid wrested from the feudal nobility and the Church potentates and the despotic monarchs could by the same token be wrested from them by the underlying population. Cromwell and the English merchants in the seventeenth century saw that the liberal doctrine, pushed far enough, might lead to genuine social revolution. Voltaire and the French men of substance in the eighteenth century saw the same. And when in the nineteenth century an increasing chorus of voices invoked the promise of liberalism for the new proletariat that industrialism had created, liberalism was converted from a credo for freeing the oppressed into a code for keeping them in their places.[3]

This is what the capitalist class is still seeking to do with liberalism. But liberalism is too fluid to stay confined thus. What has happened to liberalism, so far as America is concerned, is that it has split into four fairly distinct tendencies. The first represents the atrophied liberalism of the past, coming out more or less unashamed as the defender of the existing class alignment, and using in defense of the modern Bourbons all the old catchwords that had once served to beat a Stuart despot with: this is the liberalism of Alfred Landon, Walter Lippmann, Nicholas Murray Butler. The second, represented by figures as diverse as Justice Brandeis, Senator Borah, Dorothy Thompson, cares passionately for human rights but shares the distrust which the old liberals had for governmental activity: it is in essence Jeffersonian. The third, represented by Mr. Roosevelt and his group of advisers, cares passionately for human rights but turns increasingly to governmental activity and the social-service state in order to protect them. The fourth, the liberalism of the progressive labor movements, seeks to reaffirm for our own age the original direction of liberalism, calling for a new class base for it, claiming for the rising ranks of workers and professionals the protection of the civil liberties which once helped the rising ranks of merchants and factory-owners to come to power. Liberalism no longer exists as a unity. What does exist is the gigantic struggle over democracy in which liberalism plays a varying role.

Whether liberalism can ever be converted into genuine democracy, without convulsing the whole world, remains to be seen. Can the basic doctrine of the able and enlightened élite be converted into the doctrine of the informed and creative mass? Above all, can liberalism ever be stripped from the body it has thus far clothed—the body of capitalist power—and used to qualify and eventually

---

[3] Some of the sentences in this paragraph have been embodied in chapter I of my book, *It Is Later Than You Think*.

transmute that power? Mr. Laski, who is concerned only with the history of liberal doctrine, does not attempt an answer. The answer will be written in another generation by another historian.

1936

8

Pareto's Republic

Take a Machiavelli, with his amazing sense of the springs of human conduct and his cynicism about ethics; soak him in the modern worship of scientific method; hard-boil him in a hatred for democracy in all its manifestations; fill him with an intense animus against proletarian movements and Marxian theory; add a few dashes of economic fundamentalism; stir it all with a poetic feeling about the ruling élite; sprinkle thoroughly with out-of-the-way erudition; season with a good deal of acuteness and homely wisdom; and serve at interminable length. If you follow this recipe you should have something that resembles Pareto's treatise on *The Mind and Society*.[1]

I do not want to underestimate the personal achievement that these four volumes represent. Here is prodigality—of ideas, of learning, of spleen. Here is a far-flung exploration of history and human foibles, in two thousand pages with an enormous footnotage. Here are a million words, and many of them not at all foolish, poured into the huge mold of an argument. Pareto was an old man, well on toward seventy, when he wrote this work. He could look back on a career in which he had been successively mathematician, engineer, political journalist, professor of economics at Lausanne. Now, almost alone on his large Swiss estate, suffering from heart disease and insomnia, surrounded by his cats whom he adored and relatively unmolested by the pallid democratic beings whom he despised, he gathered his strength for his greatest effort. It would chart human history and social behavior, as cold and unswerving in its course as the calculations of the movements of the heavenly bodies.

---

[1] *The Mind and Society*. Edited by Arthur Livingston. Translated by Andrew Bongiorno and Arthur Livingston, with the advice and co-operation of James Harvey Rogers. New York, Harcourt, Brace, 1935.

348

Although he failed (as anyone would fail in such an effort) his failure has a ring of greatness in it. But over this greatness there hangs the pall of death. Written on the eve of the World War, in the midst of class tensions such as the great strikes in France and the Red Week in Italy, this book bears on it marks of the death agony of a culture.

Pareto seeks to apply the logico-experimental method of celestial mechanics to the very uncelestial events of this planet. Nothing will be held valid except what can, if necessary, be reduced to graphs and algebraic symbols. As though by a compulsion neurosis he plasters almost every page with manifestoes of this intent. His search for purity of method takes on the aspect of a religious quest. The reader stands uncomfortably in the presence of someone who is being washed of all bias in the blood of the scientific lamb.

Let it be said unmistakably that such a logico-experimental man as Pareto sets himself up for, squeezed dry of all emotion and values, never existed except possibly on Swift's island of Laputa, where the inhabitants cut their clothes by trigonometry. Everything valid in Pareto's method can be summed up in the injunction that applies in every field to think as rigorously, honestly, realistically as possible. The rest is mumbo-jumbo. When a social scientist seeks to wrap himself in a divine objectivity you can make a shrewd guess that he is either naïve and is looking for a false sense of security, or that he has his tongue in his cheek and is trying to hide something, or else that he is more or less willfully obscuring the basic issues of social policy involved.

Pareto's central theory, that of residues and derivations, is in reality a brilliant intuition. Stated baldly it holds that human behavior is irrational (non-logical); that it is based on certain deep-lying drives (residues) in human nature; and that theories, theologies, programs, faiths are so many variable expressions (derivations) of these underlying drives. But before he is through with his theory Pareto has analyzed, classified, and subclassified these residues and derivations until he has made the whole thing cumbersome, arbitrary, and just a bit absurd. He groups the residues into six general classes; of these I take it that the "instinct of combinations" covers the drive toward inventiveness and intelligence, and that "group persistences" are what American social thought has termed, with a varying emphasis, traditions, folkways, institutions. The derivations are grouped into four classes. Each of the classes is minutely subdivided. The entire structure is a triumph of ingenuity and shows a taxonomic talent of the first order. But when you try to use it bewilderment turns into chagrin and finally into despair.

I do not mean that the game lacks its attractiveness. Take any item of behavior on the part of your pet aversion in politics, and place its various elements in Pareto's tables of residues and derivations. It can become a fine art of annihilation. It is the Benthamite calculus of today. A Pareto scholar should not lack for mental stimulus the rest of his life, and there will be so many amateur Paretians among American intellectuals that I make bold to prophesy a seven-year plague of residues and derivations. But as a working instrument of analysis Pareto's scheme has some essential defects. He has not decided in what sense his residues are basic and in what sense his derivations are derivative. At times he seems to regard the residues as instincts, at other times as deep-lying "hungers" or human tendencies of an ever-vaguer character; often (as in the case of many of the group persistences) they are only socially conditioned folkways or traditions. The derivations are sometimes the logical coating that we apply to our own non-logical actions in order to save face, and sometimes the tricks and stereotypes by which we manipulate the actions of others. The whole scheme suffers from being a classification on a single plane rather than an analysis on various planes, and leaves in darkness the basic problem of sociology—the relation of invariant traits to the variable conditionings of cultures and institutions.

Pareto's emphasis on the irrational mind will, however, have an abiding influence. He is, in a sense, the Bentham of the irrational. In fact, he is strikingly like Bentham in many of his mental traits —his narrowness, his formalism of reasoning, his crotchets and obsessions, his Linnaean bent of mind, his barbarous terminology. Somewhere during his life he picked up a corrosive realism which eats through surfaces to reveal non-logical traits in man that are unlovely to those who believe in *Homo rationalis*. But the theory of residues is one of the few glimpses of this sort into the depths of life that the reader gets from Pareto. He is otherwise dismally bare of the sudden insights that one finds in Swift or Nietzsche. What

Pareto gives best is not a rigorously valid analysis of the irrational, or an artistic probing of it, but a fascinating travelogue through its darkest Africas. He roams through history and ethnology, a rather ponderous Frazer, finding instances of how men have used magic and it has passed for reason.

Clearly Pareto must be seen as part of the revolt against reason, swelling the anti-intellectualist currents of the past half-century. He must therefore be related to Nietzsche, Bergson, Sorel, Freud, Lawrence, and Spengler. What partly obscures this connection with them is that while they celebrate man's irrationality, he is content to lay it bare; and while they throw scientism overboard, he holds onto it, and in fact celebrates it. In this respect Pareto, despite his merciless attacks on Comte, Buckle, and Mill, represents a carry-over from the positivist thought of what John Strachey has called "the century of the great hope."

But this attempt to reconcile a current of intellectualism with a current of anti-intellectualism pervades the whole school of social psychology. Pareto's book was contemporary with Graham Wallas's *Great Society*, Trotter's once-famous herd books, Le Bon's crowd books, and McDougall's instinct books, as well as a host of lesser siblings. It shares their loose and ramshackle instinct psychology, and it shares also their sense of how blind or stupid or animal-like the masses of men are when they vote or fight or unite to revolt. The Pareto vogue, on account of the peculiar translation lag, comes fifteen years after the social-psychology vogue. But the generation that feels itself on the brink of revolutions should accept the emphasis on the irrational as eagerly as the generation that felt itself on the brink of a catastrophic war.

Unlike his theory of how we think, Pareto's social theory is like an iceberg: much the greater and more sinister portion of it lies beneath the surface. It is most clearly intelligible if it is referred back to the outlines of Marxian thought, for its underlying intention is to build a counter-system to Marxism. Marxian social economics and its theory of surplus (exploited) value are matched (as developed in Pareto's earlier books) by a "pure" economics with its famous Paretian law of the distribution of income, in which income distribution is shown to follow the same curve as the distribution of ability traits. The Marxian doctrine of the class struggle is matched by the Paretian theory (borrowed from Mosca) of the circulation of the élite. Marxian economic determinism as a theory of social causation is confronted by a theory of society as a web of interdependent and mutual relations. The Paretian theory of revolution ignores the Marxian emphasis on the movement of economic forces which prepare the ground, and concentrates on the resistance that the élite can offer through their morale, and on the weakening of proletarian leadership by class circulation. Finally the Marxian dialectic of history is matched by a semi-Spenglerian theory of rhythmical undulations in history, in which the moving forces are not the changes in the materialist basis of society but the waxing and waning of group persistences.

The central thread that runs through this network of theory is the notion of a militant élite. In the theory of class circulation the men of strength and intelligence come to the top; but there is a continuing process of decadence among them, a sloughing off of the old rot and a drawing upon new vigor. Their susceptibility to the residue of combinations weakens the élite, while the masses are retaining their stamina because of their susceptibility to the group-persistence residue. Thus the matter of relative stamina in the ruling and the underlying class at any time furnishes the rationale of revolutionary success or failure. It is the militant and cohesive élite that can become the decisive force in history. Pareto seems to have been influenced, through his friend Sorel, not only by the Bergsonian *élan vital* (in the form of class stamina) but also by Sorel's theory of violence. To Sorel violence had a transcendent and cleansing virtue, and helped to keep the body politic sturdy. Pareto's ultimate exhortation to the élite is to keep its spinal column straight and its fighting instincts in trim—and the ruling classes in Italy and Germany have illustrated his thesis.

This confronts us with the much debated question of Pareto's relation to fascism. In any sense of direct participation or influence, Pareto's fascism has been negligible. Mussolini's insistence that his mind was shaped as a student under Pareto at Lausanne, and his offer (unrejected) of senatorial honors to Pareto after his march on Rome, are inconclusive. They prove less about Pareto than they do about Mussolini's desperate efforts to rig up a respectable intellectual lineage for his own fascism.

What is much more to the point is that Pareto's theory and his preconceptions follow the approved pattern of fascist thought as we have come to recognize it. At the core of Pareto's attitude is a hatred of socialism and a contempt for democracy. He uses the epithet "socialist" vaguely, as many Americans do today with "communist," to describe anything from unemployment insurance to feminism and the new criminology; but he never utters it without a hiss. In his earlier book, *Les Systèmes Socialistes,* he was chiefly concerned to show socialist doctrine to be fallacious, crotchety, millennial; but in this book, more than a decade later, it is hard to find even a vestigial scholarly urbanity in discussing it. He seems to regard socialism as the final term in democratic degradation, since it has not only given a new messianism to labor movements but has even corrupted the élite.

But it is democracy that is the principal target. Pareto regards it, with humanitarianism, as the central deity of the new Pantheon that includes all the "modern Gods"—Progress, Tolerance, Democracy, Humanitarianism, Universal Suffrage, Solidarism, Pacifism, Tolstoyism. Against these reigning divinities he hurls his Promethean defiance. He reveals the plutocratic character of modern democracy, in which cowardice skulks behind money to buy votes and bribe legislators. His rather unalgebraic symbolism to convey the temper of plutocratic democracy rests on the distinction between the Lions and the Foxes. The Foxes are the men of craft who replace the Lions, the men of force, in governmental posts in an attempt to buy off mass unrest instead of suppressing it. Being himself (to use William James's phrase) tough-minded, Pareto has an admiration not only for tough-minded thinkers such as Aristophanes, Machiavelli, Nietzsche, and Sorel, but also for ruthless leonine men such as Bismarck. The Foxes are eating away at the morale of the élite. They form an unholy alliance with plutocrats and trade-union leaders in order to keep peace and divide the spoils, and their method of keeping peace is direct bribery and social reform.

This raises the question of the exact nature of Pareto's class attitudes. An obituary notice called him "the bourgeois Karl Marx," and several American critics have taken up the expression and dubbed him the Marx of the middle class. In our American sense of middle class this would of course be wide of the mark. Pareto

despised the indecisiveness of the middle class, its humanitarianism, its vulnerability to all the new modern cults and mass religions,
its swarming democracy. If to be a fascist theorist is to be a theorist
of middle-class revolt against the capitalists, as is sometimes asserted, Pareto does not fit the formula. Nor can he be called the
theorist of the capitalist bourgeoisie, using the term in its stricter
Marxian sense. Pareto draws a distinction in his thinking between
the Speculators (whom he calls the S's) and the investors or *Rentiers*
(the R's). In its European context this is a distinction between the
predatory restlessness of the new plutocratic bourgeoisie, and the
sturdy group persistences of the more conservative industrialists
and the large landowners. I take it also that this is not very far
from Feder's distinction in the early Hitlerite ideology between
the interest slavery imposed by unproductive (Jewish) capital and
the social beneficence of productive (Junker and Thyssen) capital.

Thus, the essence of Pareto's position is that of a capitalist-
aristocrat who despises democratic equalitarianism and who seeks
within capitalist society the more exclusive and traditional forces
that will renew its vigor and steel its resistance to the proletarian
thrusts. Pareto was writing in a Europe that was already on the
brink of the precipice. These volumes give evidence that he was
quite realistically aware of the meaning of the deepening crisis,
with its heightened nationalist feeling, its conflicting imperialisms.
its huge scandals of political corruption, its class tensions. That
meaning lay not in the road to war but in the road to fascism. Quite
strikingly the pattern of Pareto's thought reveals that fascism was
not merely a post-war growth but was already integral in the European situation in 1914. If Pareto was not a fascist theorist, then
fascism may be said to have cast its shadow before in the shape of
Pareto's treatise.

All this leads quite obviously to the conclusion that Pareto has
not so much written a scientific work as a very able and vigorous
polemic in defense of the traditional forces within capitalist society.
And in doing so he has given us, as Plato did, a picture of his republic. Every social theorist gives his vision of the world, whether
he presents it as scientific reality or Utopian dream. Even when he
seeks to thrust his own values into the background, they operate
just as effectively as preconceptions. Pareto's values burst the mold

of his elaborate scientific categories with an emotional force all the greater for his attempt at suppression. Every scientist is at bottom a poet, and any analysis of a society implies, on the writer's part, an ideal society. Dig deep into any social theory and you will strike a poetic myth.

What was Pareto's republic like? It must be remembered that Pareto's own origins were those of a capitalist-aristocrat. He was descended from a family of Genoese merchant princes whom Bonaparte elevated to the nobility and who afterward fought in the cause of Italian nationalist liberties. He learned to hate, with an inverted Mazzinian intensity, the compromises of Italian and French democracy. His book seeks to evoke a polity in which the older aristocracy will come back to strengthen a decadent capitalist élite, and together the landed aristocracy, the *rentier* class, the army, and the most militant of the industrialists will carve out their world. They will sweep plutocratic democracy aside, suppress the proletarian rabble, and replace the false humanitarianism of the middle class by derivations from real group persistences.

It will be a republic ruled by fierce young conquering gods, continually renewed by fresh blood. And the ruling gods will not hesitate to use force, both as a way of holding the masses in their place and as a way of maintaining their fighting instincts. The trade unions will no longer be allowed to keep labor in feudal darkness. The masses will be so much material to be shaped in the image of the desires of the ruling gods: they will be valuable for harboring the group traditions and for their hatred of novelty, but the only art they need to know is the art of being ruled. As for the rest of the population, a Catonian severity will prevail toward anything humanitarian (even Christianity) that may weaken their primitive stamina. Criminals, pacifists, and socialists will be hunted down like disease-bearing rats. In war and in foreign affairs it will be the courage of the Lions that will be the glory of the republic.

But enough. It must be clear by now that if the real test of the validity of a republic is its capacity to get itself enacted, Pareto has the advantage. "That illustrious Greek dreamer," as he calls Plato, had to be content with his book. But Pareto's republic is now a reality: it is Hitler's totalitarian state.

1935

9

Hitler as Thinker

1

THERE is no autobiography in history that can match the fantastic quality of *Mein Kampf*. Reading it we are in a universe of grotesque proportions—a nightmare Wonderland in which we are all Alices watching the distorted perspectives. World movements like Christianity, socialism, democracy, are reduced to items in the ego-displacement of a little Austrian water-color dauber. Whole nations and continents become the stamping-ground of his restless personality. His tastes and traumata are expanded into universals to decide the destiny of millions. Here is, in Nietzsche's terms, a "transvaluation of values" with a vengeance. In fact Nietzsche often comes to mind in reading these pages. Not Nietzsche the thinker-craftsman, nor the believer in the "European man," nor the creator of the "gay science"—but he of the autobiography, *Ecce Homo,* written in the fitful gleams of sanity preceding his complete collapse. Dostoyevsky also comes to mind, stripped of his literary genius and the depth of his insights, but the Dostoyevsky of the masochistic rejection of reason and the epileptic trances of the spirit.

There are those who have compared *Mein Kampf* with *Das Kapital* on the ground that both are the bibles of world movements and rationalize the revolutionary impulses of millions. But to compare Hitler's book with Marx's is unfair to both. Marx, for all his vanity, was no megalomaniac; *Mein Kampf* may be described as the anatomy of megalomania. Since Marxism is nothing if not rationalistic, its key-book is a pitiless analysis, in the Ricardian tradition, of the dynamics of our economy. But the key-book of Nazism describes the tempestuous voyage of a tortured mind. It is a mind that has rejected our gods, broken through the taboos that we call civiliza-

356

tion, and fashioned a god in its own image and a demonology of its own.

For despite its tirades against individualism, *Mein Kampf* is in reality the individualist dream run amuck. The personality that emerges from its pages is a blending of all that is grandiose in the European Bonapartist tradition with the most fantastic elements of the American success-story. It is a cross between Napoleon and Horatio Alger. It is the Little Corporal dreaming of world empire; it is also the saga of Pluck and Luck, the Boy from Braunau Who Made Good. You have here the apotheosis of sheer individual will imposing itself on the flux of events. Here is a sick mind, a lonely and dwarfed personality, that was able to convert its sickness and frustration into hate, its hate into vengeful ambition, its ambition into cold steel, its steel into an empire and a religion.

The book is at once autobiography, credo, handbook for party leaders, blueprint for world domination. It is the product of an untrained mind—a mind that makes a fetish of external discipline because it could never brook internal discipline. Hitler is neither a systematic nor an original thinker. The unity his book possesses is a psychic unity. He has breathed into his random materials the daemonic force of a great will and a consuming hate. I am reminded of the cosmological theory that an intense sun shining on inert and decayed matter transformed it eventually into reptilian life.

But it will not do on that account to dismiss *Mein Kampf* as a farrago of nonsense, not worth our attention. Its premises are not our own, its reasoning is faulty, its conclusions are hideous to us. Nevertheless its very quality of not making sense is exactly what gives it effectiveness. We must rid ourselves of the view that only logical ideas can be political weapons. Ideas in politics are much like poetry: they need no inner logical structure to be effective. Edward Lear's nonsense verse merely extends a principle inherent in poetry as a whole. And Hitler is, in a sense, the Edward Lear of political thinking. He has taught us that, just as a limerick drives Shakespeare out of our minds, so by a similar Gresham's law illogical political ideas drive out the logical.

And whether or not he makes sense, his book has become the profoundly evocative philosophy of millions of people. The *New Republic* has been running a series on "Books That Changed Our Minds." Unless the "our" refers to a narrow circle of American intellectuals, *Mein Kampf* should have been included. It has already changed the minds of countless people in France, England, Spain, Denmark, and the Near East, as well as in Germany, Austria, Hungary, Italy.

One may well ask whether Americans will remain immune. Given conditions of decency and social peace, we could afford to laugh at the obsessive intensity with which Hitler rides his anti-liberal, anti-humanitarian, anti-Christian, anti-Semitic, anti-socialist, anti-democratic hobbies. But we do not have the conditions of social peace. Nor do we have the foundations of an enduring social decency. And for millions of people who are ready to cement their collapsing psychic world by hate and illogic, *Mein Kampf* will offer the cement.

2

Hitler's is a spoken rather than a written book. He dictated the first half of it to his secretary while he was a prisoner at the fortress at Landsberg on the Lech, after the 1923 Beerhall Putsch. And it has all the marks of a book that has been *talked*. It is a congeries of unconnected fragments held together only by the sustained psychic tension of the speaker, rather than something set down reflectively with logic and inter-connection of its parts.

Such surely must have been the talk at the Munich *Stammtische* where *habitués* of all descriptions gathered over their beer and quarreled about the diverse roads to a commonly held Germanic mission. Such must have been the rhapsodic talk that Hanisch, Hitler's companion during the years when his fortune was at its lowest ebb, tells about: Hitler with his emaciated derelict face and his Jewish beard and his long tramp-cassock, declaiming against Marxism in the flophouse at Vienna-Brigittenau; Hitler sitting in the cheap Vienna restaurants while the customers discussed the daily headlines, and holding them spellbound with his attacks on the Jews and the Weimar government. Such must, finally, have been the speeches Hitler made at the huge Zirkuskrone mass-meetings, when the rising young party leader stood for hours on the platform and loosed a wild torrent of talk that swept his listeners along with him.

Among the passages in Hitler's book that ring truest are those in praise of the spoken word and in contempt of the goose-quill. "Every great movement on this globe," he says in his Preface, "owes its rise to the great speakers and not to the great writers." *Mein Kampf* as a spoken book holds the only thinker Hitler ever was—Hitler the talker, projected on the printed page. "Nevertheless the basic elements of a doctrine," he explains in his Preface, "must be set down in permanent form." What are these elements in the case of his own doctrine?

Hitler has urged foreigners to uncover the metaphysical roots of Nazism; and one might well start with his book. To many it will seem incongruous even to think of such a mélange as having serious metaphysical roots. And it is true that Hitler is pitiably amateurish in his handling of political and social concepts. Early in the history of the Nazi Party, Hitler struck an alliance with one of its poets and intellectuals, Dietrich Eckart. From him he may have picked up some of the going ideas of the young conservative intellectuals and some of the patter of their vocabulary. For Hitler, like many other men of action, does not explore ideas but absorbs them. They become part of him not through study and mastery but through a process of osmosis. Yet it is obvious that, if we take metaphysics to mean first principles with respect to thought and society and human beings in it, then even Hitler has a metaphysic. It lies not so much in the articulate doctrine he sets down as in his inarticulate major premises, the things he takes so completely for granted that he finds it unnecessary to do more than allude to them.

The metaphysical roots of Hitler's doctrine must be sought in the soil of the German intellectual tradition. There are two major attitudes current today toward that tradition. One is that we have no quarrel with the German people—that what the Nazis are doing is superimposed on them, and runs counter to every important element in the German past. The second attitude is that our quarrel is exactly with the German people, that they have a Nazi government today because they are Nazi at heart and have always been, and that the whole German intellectual tradition has been building up to Hitler. Neither of these is true. Actually, there are two German traditions, one humanist and the other anti-humanist, one stretching from Goethe and Lessing to Max Weber and Thomas Mann, the other from Fichte and Jean-Paul Richter to Spengler, Carl Schmitt, and Alfred Bäumler. The first stresses freedom, the life of reason, and the possibilities of human existence; the second

stresses authority, the brutal and tempestuous in man, and the
transcending of the human by the heroic and daemonic. One subordinates the state to culture, the other subordinates culture to the
state. One is European, the other fiercely nationalistic; one is democratic, the other feudal. In the great representative Germans the
two are intertwined; yet in every German thinker, however complex, an emphasis on the one or the other is unmistakable.

The basic assumptions in *Mein Kampf* are not far from those of
the body of Nazi social theory as set forth, for example, in Kolnai's
War against the West, which—although a very stiff dose for the
general reader—deserves much more study by American social
scientists than they have thus far given it. They are the assumptions
that the masses of men are irrational creatures, acting from deep-
lying drives of hunger, fear, imitation, herdism, sadism; that there
are natural *Stände,* or gradations of rank, among men, from the
slave-mass to the élite and finally to the *Führer* himself; that corresponding to these are varying *Stufen,* or levels of consciousness,
forming a mystical base for an eventual caste system; that the social
world, like the biological, is a jungle; that man is, in Spengler's
terms, "a beast of prey," and that only the strongest are worthy of
survival; that where there is no room for the weak, Christianity is
a luxury, humanitarianism runs against the grain of life, liberalism
is folly, and democracy a crime; that there are sound and healthy
tendencies in any community which have been poisoned by the
Jews, weakened by Christianity, and undermined by international
capitalism and international socialism; that the core of any community (*Gemeinschaft*) is a people around a leader, tied together
by idealistic bonds and by a sense of duty to the leader, and that the
highest stage of such a community is the *Volksgemeinschaft,* or
national community; that communities are not mechanisms but
organisms, and that the element of spontaneity and organic growth
is the essential element in them; that what is important about them,
as about anything, is the *Geist,* or spirit, that informs them; that
the *Geist* of a healthy community must run counter to the material-
istic spirit of the modern age, and must return to the sense of duty,
community honor, and fealty to the leader that characterized the
earlier Germanic community; that this *Geist* expresses itself most
strongly in a blood-community of race and in adherence to a native
and common soil; that in the perception of such values there can

be no logical categories but only an intuitionism that is its own principle and its own justification; that in the pursuance of them there will be a return to the basically masculine and military virtues, a substitution of force for the hypocrisy of legality, a substitution of dictatorship for the corruptions of democracy, and the creation of a new élite to replace the massism of the democracies; and that in the achievement of this objective one may count upon the destiny of a people, the divine mission of a leader, and upon the daemonic force within the élite that converts men into heroes.

To understand a body of thought one must always first see it as a systematic unity (even if more systematic than the way in which its proponents themselves see it). In the case of the Nazi doctrine our very aversion to it makes it necessary for us to recognize that it is not all nonsense. I have tried so to state Hitler's metaphysic as to bring out the elements in it that have some strength and some universal appeal.

Leonard Woolf once wrote an absorbing little book called *Quack, Quack,* in which he dealt with the quackeries of men like Keyserling, Spengler, and Bergson in the intellectual field and of Mussolini and Hitler in the political, linking them with the mumbo-jumbo of primitive kingship. But what did not emerge from the book was that Bergson and Spengler, while preparing the ground unconsciously for Hitler, were utterly honest craftsmen; and that Hitler's quackery is not limited to the political field but has deep roots in the intellectual. Nietzsche, for example, talked of the *Übermensch*, or superman; but he was referring to a height of spiritual mastery within the individual, and would have been horrified at the application of the idea in Hitler's book so as to compass the subjection of workers to an employer under the *Führerprinzip*. Spengler talked mystically of race, as Nietzsche did; but Nietzsche would have protested, as Spengler did, against the cry *Juda verrecke* (may the Jews die!) echoed by the Nazi youth, which represents Hitler's application of the race principle. One would look far in the whole anti-humanist intellectual tradition for the elaborate charlatanism of the concepts of *Geist* and *Volk* that one finds in Hitler's book.

In short, Hitler's relation to the German intellectual tradition is that of a quick and mobile intelligence who has picked up some leading ideas and conscripted their intellectual and emotional force skillfully to his own uses. There are long passages in his book in which he accuses the Jews of being parasites on the host of modern culture; but his own position toward the ideas on which he builds is in the very same sense parasitic.

3

I have spoken of the ideas that Hitler assumes. How about the ideas he selects for discussion? He has himself given us a clue to his principles of selection which is a thoroughly pragmatic one. "Every great revolutionary movement," he writes, "will untiringly try to make clear to the others the new train of thought, draw them over to its own ground, or at least make them doubtful of their own previous conviction. The propagation of a doctrine . . . has to have a backbone." That is to say, the concepts that Hitler emphasizes in his book are those that will give his propaganda persuasiveness. He looks for the ideas that will be effective in undermining the liberal and democratic beliefs on which the survival of the republic depended, and effective also in meeting the thrust of Marxist beliefs. He has three tasks: he must create a demonology that will unify his followers in a common hatred and a common sense of superiority; he must fight the liberal-democratic and Marxist systems of thought; he must build an intellectual structure of authority and obedience for the Nazi state to come.

The devices that Hitler uses in creating a demonology will appear more relevantly when we discuss Hitler as propagandist. But the theory underlying that demonology, as indeed it underlies the whole of Hitler's intellectual system, is that of blood and race—or better, racism. To an extent, in dealing with the racial interpretation of history, Hitler follows the traditional lines of Count Gobineau, who is the master of all the racial fanatics; Houston Stewart Chamberlain, whose *Foundations of the Nineteenth Century* was probably one of the books Hitler read with more than casualness; Bötticher (who wrote under the name of Paul de Lagarde) and Moeller van den Bruck, whose *Dritte Reich* was one of the Bibles of the pre-Hitler reactionaries; and Rosenberg, whose *Mythus des zwanzigsten Jahrhunderts* was published five years before Hitler wrote his book. Yet when you are dealing with the literature of racial genius, racial purity, racial superiority, you can scarcely trace a direct course. You are on an uncharted sea of mysticism and the subjective, where every mariner steers his own course.

Hitler proceeds by an elaborate division of races into three groups —the culture-creators (only the Aryans belong here), the culture-bearers (for example, the Japanese), the culture-destroyers (presumably only the Jews, yet Hitler includes the Negroes as well). This is a clever classification, for it enables Hitler to specify the perfect race and the parasite race while remaining vague about all the intermediate ones. Even in that paradise of the nebulous, the literature of race, Hitler is unparalleled in his vagueness. He brushes aside as irrelevant all questions of proof, of origins, of race history, of the relation between biological strains and psychological and cultural characteristics. He does not trouble to define race but appeals to the reader's consciousness of its reality. He makes no attempt to place the French, the Italians, the Americans, the English, the Slavs in his hierarchy: it would be both difficult and dangerous—hence the safe choice of the Japanese for the sterile but harmless "culture-bearers." Above all, despite the fact that he calls his principal chapter on racism "Nation and Race," he nowhere compares the two or distinguishes between them.

Is it because such a distinction might prove inconvenient to Hitler's aims? For the cultural nationalists of the nineteenth century, from Herder and Mazzini to Renan, had talked far more of nation than of race: and where they had talked of race it was as a vague abbreviation of the national character. To perform its function in the wars of liberation, nationalism had to be a unifying concept for the entire population. It could be exclusive in respect to other nationalities but it had to be inclusive in regard to its own. But Hitler's nationalism, since its function in the political revolution was to create both a heroic and a diabolic element, had to be at once unifying and divisive. Having to make use of every device he could lay his hands on, he had to use both the myth of race and the myth of nation and somehow blend them together. The focus of his concept of nationalism is not the German spirit as built up culturally in the history of German institutions, and therefore including all creeds and all biological strains: it is the German spirit as somehow discovered by contrast with its opposite, the Jewish spirit in international history.

So drastic a reversal of the whole European tradition of cultural nationalism would have been almost impossible were it not that Hitler was addressing a bitter and defeated nation. Moeller van den Bruck, whose *Dritte Reich* influenced Hitler deeply, has spoken of the historical function of catastrophe in evoking the great revolutionary energies of a people. Hitler's nationalism is in that sense a nationalism bred of catastrophe. His is a dual appeal to a defeated people: first, to assign the blame to the "November criminals," presumably Marxists and Jews, and thus make the Germans feel that they were betrayed from within rather than defeated from without; secondly, to evoke the energies of a defeated people for a great effort of renascence. His concept of the nation is thus a twisted and stunted one, narrowed down to fit the purposes of a group seeking to lead a humiliated people in a war of *revanche,* and seeking also to turn men's sense of insecurity into the politically profitable channels of counter-revolutionary hate. "From Tacitus to Gobineau," writes Jacques Barzun in his informative book on *Race,* "the great racial ideals have come from disappointed men." He might have added that they have grown up in cultures in despair.

But the contradictions between the race and nation concepts are not the only difficulties Hitler runs into. There is an essential contradiction within the race concept itself. To be unifying, a concept of racism must be idealistic—must stress the spirit of a race, its creativeness, its genius, its invincibility. But to be an effective demonology it must be specific and material, pointing a finger at the impure and the unelect, and devising ways of discovering them infallibly. As long as Hitler talks of the beauty and genius of the Aryan, he is on the spiritual plane; as soon as he talks of the Jews he is on the material plane. It is not sufficiently emphasized that Hitler's race theory was confronted by two traditions—that of the lofty glorification of race, as in Gobineau, Nietzsche, Spengler, Rosenberg; and that of anti-Semitism pure and simple. And confronted by these two traditions he preferred not to choose between them but to combine them. The first was necessary in appealing to ideal strivings; the second was necessary in fixing an object of hatred. Hence the experience the reader of *Mein Kampf* has in moving from misty vaporings about Aryanism to the macabre passages of vivid imagery, such as the famous one about the diabolic black-haired Jewish boy waiting in ambush for the unsuspecting Aryan girl and defiling her with his blood, or the one about the Jews' bringing the Negroes to the Rhine to bastardize the Aryans. But once Hitler is on this plane he has to break with Nietzsche and Spengler and the other race-theorists who were not anti-Semitic. And he is forced also to be specific about tests for Aryanism. Race theorists have always encountered difficulties in creating objective tests for racial purity and impurity. A French physician during the war, avid to give concreteness to the inferiority of the German strain, undertook to prove that you could tell a German through a urinalysis. Similarly in Hitler the genealogical precision of the Nürnberg laws and the movement for sterilization become logical consequences of his doctrine—but they bring it down from the lofty plane on which it started.

Hitler's race doctrine remains, with his anti-Marxism, the most exportable part of the theory of his book. They are the part that can be used best by the Mosleys, the Coughlins and Kuhns. They are the spearhead of the Nazi International. Now that Hitler's power-politics has forced him to drop his anti-Bolshevism, he must rely increasingly on his racism to rationalize his imperialist foreign policy as well as his internal tyranny. In fact, it has always been the blood concept that has linked his domestic with his foreign policy. In the case of anti-Semitism, it is blood-purity; in the case of imperialism, blood-unity. But since Munich and since his attack on Poland, even blood-unity and the need for uniting Germans everywhere under one banner has proved inadequate, for Hitler has been extending the trajectory of his power beyond the boundaries of the countries where there are problems of German minorities. More and more therefore he is likely to move away from the rhetoric of race and blood that fills the pages of *Mein Kampf,* back to the naked imperialist slogan that appears in the book as "the conquest of the world by the Germans." More and more, as Rauschning points out in his *Revolution of Nihilism,* his anti-Semitic theory is likely to become archaic. Its place has already been largely taken by the geopolitics of General Haushofer, and his conception of how geographic and economic strategy can be used to capture further *Lebensraum* and make strong states stronger.

Less archaic is the totalitarian theory in *Mein Kampf.* We use the word "totalitarian" today as loosely as we use the word "ideology"

—to refer to any theory we dislike. Actually a totalitarianism may be defined as a social organization in which the government occupies the totality of the field in every area of the individual's life: in politics, in economics, in education, in peace and war, in expression, in religion, in culture. In a long, rambling, and chaotic chapter on "The State," at the beginning of his second volume, Hitler seeks to construct a rationale for this belief that the state has an exclusive claim to every allegiance of the individual. The state, he says, is quite simply the instrument of the nationality—that is, of the bearers of the national culture. It follows that citizenship is not a matter of course but a privilege to be either denied or granted. There are citizens of the state and subjects of the state. Hitler argues that a mechanical democratic conception bestows citizenship even on the syphilitic: hence the need for rigorous exclusions from citizenship. By a trick of logic he thus manages to lump his political opponents and the vast mass of innocent Jews who were not even his political opponents, with the syphilitic.

And as citizenship may be denied, so too it is granted only on condition of the complete surrender of the individual to the state. Boiled down to its essence, Hitler's whole approach to the state is to see it as an instrument of power to be used by a governing group—a sort of inverted Marxism that substitutes the dominant élite for the dominant class. Hitler shrinks from a cultural approach to the state, as he shrinks from an economic approach. "The quality of a state," he writes, "cannot be evaluated according to the cultural height or the significance of power of this state in the frame of the rest of the world, but exclusively according to the degree of the quality of this institution with regard to the nationality involved in that particular case." Which, translated from its reckless Father Divine slinging-about of words, means probably that a culture (like the German culture under the republic) may rank high in world history yet fail to make full use of the heroic resources of the people. And to do that, says Hitler, it needs order, authority, discipline, leadership. Let it be noted here that those among our own thinkers who in the present crisis stress freedom merely as opposed to authority are playing into Hitler's hands. The intellectual problem of our day is not the opposition between freedom and authority: for the step between "freedom" and "anarchy" is for most people a short one, anarchy being merely the freedom that you don't like; and the

association between "authority" and "order" is a close one, order being merely the authority of your own crowd. The antithesis
is thus converted from one between freedom and authority to one
between anarchy and order. And when that has been done, half the
distance toward preparing a people for a totalitarianism has already
been traversed. Throughout his book Hitler is careful to associate
the images of order and energy with the Nazis and the images of anarchy and exhaustion with the Jews and the socialists and the Weimar regime.

When Hitler speaks of the innate qualities and the energy of the
German people, he draws most heavily on the "folk" concept and
comes dangerously close to the position of the numerous "folkish"
movements in post-war Germany. These movements wanted to
move away from the cosmopolitanism of the liberals and socialists
to a more severely national culture. Hitler did not want his movement to be associated with theirs in people's minds, yet he was loth
to lose the chance of capitalizing on the gains they had made. The
result is a weak and wobbly attitude toward them on his part, the
gist of which is that if a state is to be a "folkish" state it must not be
so as a dreamy concept, but it must be ruthless and disciplined and
allow no other allegiance than to itself. It must embody the *Führerprinzip* in every walk of life—which means in effect the complete
control by the party (and therefore by him) of economics, education,
propaganda, religion, bureaucracy, and the military. He speaks of
this as a process of "integration"—"to integrate through frantic energy the force of a people." Actually it is a process of excluding
everyone except his own group from any control over the springs of
energy in a culture.

4

It is when we come to the question of ways and means for capturing power, extending it, consolidating it, that we reach Hitler's only
real greatness in the history of thought—a greatness that cannot be
denied even by those who hate what he stands for. Hitler is probably
the greatest master of propaganda and organization in modern history. To find his equal one must go back to Loyola and the Jesuits.
His insights are not insights into theory but into strategy. In fact, it
would be possible to follow Kenneth Burke's lead in his brilliant essay, "The Rhetoric of Hitler's 'Battle,'" and regard the whole of

Hitler's theory as a set of strategic devices for influencing opinion. Burke's method is nowhere quite as pat and relevant as when applied to Hitler, whose charlatanism as a thinker puts most of his concepts on the plane of manipulation.

What makes him a master in manipulation? "The organizer," he says, and he is speaking of the propagandist as well, "has to be primarily a psychologist." But if we are to speak of Hitler as a psychologist, it is not in the ordinary sense. Professor Gordon Allport has recently told his fellow academic psychologists, in a presidential address, that from the standpoint of understanding how men's minds actually work they are inferior to statesmen and head waiters. Hitler knows nothing of academic lore, nothing of the neuro-physiological basis of the mind's behavior, nothing of the refinements of our sensory and motor apparatus. The organizer, Hitler continues, "has to take man as he is. He has to take account of the weakness and of the bestiality equally." He takes men as he has found them empirically and he builds his appeals on his experience with them.

That experience has, in Hitler's case, been a curiously specialized one. He has scarcely ever confronted people except to impress, persuade, browbeat, cajole, rouse them. Even before he became a public figure he had public attitudes. If ever a man since Machiavelli went to the school of power, it was Hitler. The result is that life has presented to him only one mask—the mask of power; and only one problem—how to gain and hold power. And because life has thus limited itself for him, denying him the luxury of experiencing private decency and loyalty and love, he has taken his revenge by forming a low opinion of human nature and using it to the hilt.

He divides men into "the heads and the masses," the leaders and the herd. "Only a fraction of mankind," he says, "is energetic and bold." The rest are cowards and gulls. But the leaders can command the herd only by battering down the walls of opinion and the institutions of state power by which a previous ruling group has surrounded the herd. Hitler understands that the fight for power, whether to capture or retain it, must be conducted on two fronts: in the nerve-centers of men's minds and in the actual nerve-centers of the state—economic, administrative, military, diplomatic. Hence his distinction, in his famous chapter on "Propaganda and Organization" between the members and the followers of a movement. "If a movement," he writes, "has the intention of pulling down a world and of building a new one in its place," it "will have to divide the human material it has won into two great groups: into followers and members." The followers are the mass whose ideas have been changed by the movement and who will in turn change the ideas of other followers. They are the hangers-on; without winning them over or neutralizing them, a movement cannot succeed. The members are the ruthless, disciplined group who will stop at nothing in the struggle for power. The followers should be as numerous as possible, and heterogeneous; the members must be kept few, and as thoroughly disciplined as soldiers. The problem with respect to the first is that of propaganda; with respect to the second, it is organization.

On both scores Hitler and the Nazis borrowed extensively from the Marxist parties, but especially with respect to organization. Hitler studies the Marxists, if not in their literature as he claims, then certainly in their utterances and tactics. It has been pointed out by several critics that Hitler's hatred of the Marxists may have arisen from his inability to answer their arguments in the days when he was trying out his mind against socialist intellectuals and trade-unionists. Time after time he was thrown into confusion among the dialectical windings of a complex intellectual system. Time after time he returned, schooling himself painfully in the art of answering these arguments. "We had a chance," he writes, "to become acquainted with the incredible discipline of our opponents' propaganda, and still today it is my pride to have found the means . . . for beating finally its very makers. Two years later I was master in this craft." It is interesting to note the pride of craftmanship Hitler shows here, for he is more in his *métier* as a propagandist than as anything else. When he joined the little group of six or seven men that called themselves the German Workers Party and established his place in it, the first job he took for himself was that of propaganda leader. It is here that his combination of imaginative daring, ruthlessness, and startling insight into men's weaknesses was most valuable. When he had to fight the Marxists in order to build his movement he saw that the problem was to play off national feeling against class feeling. When, having been admitted into the government by the von Papen group he had the problem of capturing the government so that he could be the master rather than the prisoner of that group, he did it by the daring coup of the Reichstag fire. When he had the problem of capturing Austria and Czechoslovakia, he did it by playing off the class feeling of the ruling classes in England, France, and even in the victim countries themselves, against their national feeling.

He addressed himself with passion to the task of mastering propaganda. He went to school not only to the Marxists; there are indications in his book that he knew how much was to be learned from other sources as well. He has a great admiration for the organization and methods of the Catholic Church. He speaks again and again of how much he learned by studying the propaganda the British used during the war. And he expresses admiration for American advertising techniques. Put all these together, add the fact that some of the insights of the Freudian school into the "psychology of the depths" must have penetrated to the Nazi circles in their early years, and add finally a mind eager to learn from every experience with men in the mass during the years of war and revolution and reconstruction— and you have the materials out of which Hitler the propagandist and organizer was fashioned.

But these materials would have been nothing had it not been for the fanatical life-and-death earnestness of Hitler himself. This is not the place to explore the psychic springs of this driving will: that must be left to the students of abnormal psychology. But it is clear that very early Hitler mastered the first principle of the success of any movement: that, given a favorable soil and climate for development, a movement is the shadow of a man. Hitler's basic assumption is that in a world of inertia, everything must give way to a driving will; amidst hesitation, assurance will triumph; amidst complexity men will cling to something that is simple; amidst disbelief they are eager for belief, even if externally imposed; in a world of passivity men want the experience of participation; in a world of humanitarian scruples the ruthless use of force will ultimately not be resisted. Finally, that we live by symbols, that the easiest and surest symbol is the person, and that the personification of the leader is at the basis of politics as it is at the basis of religion.

These are the principles on which Hitler's work as propagandist and organizer was based. The specific and rule-of-thumb injunctions with which his book is sprinkled may be traced back to them.

They explain the advice he gives that you must always exaggerate your claims, even if fantastically; that you must never concede the slightest justice to your opponent's cause, else men will begin to doubt yours; that your platform, once formulated, must remain fixed; that you must hammer away always at a single idea; that the continued iteration of it will finally induce belief; that there is nothing so likely to be believed in the end as the daring and the unimaginable; that the masses "want the victory of the stronger and the annihilation or the unconditional surrender of the weaker." The principles I have mentioned explain also the tactics that Hitler used in the internal organization of his party: the hierarchy in which the only allegiance is to the leader at the top; the theatrical handling of public meetings; the ritual and insignia of membership; the complete contempt for democratic procedure; the use of drilling and marching; the policing of meetings by storm-troops.

I have spoken of some of the sources of these methods and insights. But in every case Hitler surpassed his masters in boldness, in shrewdness, in scope. He borrowed much from the Marxians, but what he did not borrow was their doctrinairism and their essential belief in men's rationality because they projected their own rationality on others. He copied from the Catholic Church, as well as from the Bolsheviks, the principle of a party ruled by iron discipline, yet neither Loyola nor Lenin made of their followers the completely amoral and inhuman automatons that Hitler has made of his. He also took two other principles over from the Catholic Church: from the priesthood the idea of an élite continually renewed by fresh blood; from the Jesuits (perhaps also from the Greeks: see Werner Jaeger's *Paideia*) the strategic political importance of the control of education: yet the uses to which he has put both principles would be unrecognizable by their originators.

In the long run Hitler's reliance is on two things: maintaining an able and disciplined ruling group, and keeping the mass of the population in subjection not only through force but especially through control over every agency of expression and education. Hitler's book is obviously addressed to the young, to their ruthlessness and their sense of frustrated possibilities. The men with whom he surrounded himself were young men: it is perhaps a sign of the slowing up of his movement that more and more there has been a hardening of the

Nazi bureaucracy, the growth of vested leadership-interests, a concentration of power in ever fewer hands, a dearth of new faces. The Napoleonic "career open to talent," which furnished no small part of the dynamic of the Nazi movement has given way to a caste system relieved only by the uncertainties of national policy and the turbulence of world political change. The appeal to the young today lies no longer in the depiction of a world ruled by new young gods. It is an appeal based on the imperialist destiny of Germany, on freedom from the old religious ties, but especially on a new sexual freedom.

Hitler's emphasis on the state control of education is so great that much of his chapter on the state is devoted to a minutely detailed agenda of instruction. There is a good deal of talk in it about physical health and physical education: part of this is the "folkish" accent, part a literary carry-over from the Spartan scheme. But in the main Hitler's conception of the educational function of the state is Treitschkean. We are too prone to forget, being Americans and constitutionalists, the strength of the army in the German tradition and the extent to which Hitler is an army man. The young are to be taught military virtues, history bowdlerized by the drill-sergeant, duties and sacrifices. Education is to "find its culmination in branding, through instinct and reason, the race sense and race feeling into the hearts and brains of the youth." Education, in short, is to be narrowed to the purposes of the ruling group, instead of the ruling group being increasingly broadened by education. But even more: hatred is to be raised to the height of the primary educational principle, and thus the primary cohesive force in a community that has no inner principle of cohesion.

5

Virginia Woolf, in one of her acute critical essays, has a sentence on James Joyce that even more relevantly applies to Hitler. "A desperate man," she calls Joyce, "who feels that in order to breathe he must break the windows." It is not a question here of *Lebensraum* for a nation, but *Lebensraum* for one man: and not all the geographical expanse of the earth and the planetary system would ever medicine him again to a sense of sufficiency. Some men have had this fanatic desire for personal imperialism and ended either as millionaires or lunatics. Hitler's genius was political, and he had the fortune to live at a time when he could use and be used by the forces of reaction. The intellectual and psychic expression of that role may be found in *Mein Kampf*.

Göring has spoken somewhere of how Hitler proceeds "with the assurance of a somnambulist." If so it is a sleep-walker who has now plunged the world into another war. What the outcome will be, for Germany as well as for the whole of humanist culture, it is too early to know. It would be a good guess however that Hitler's assurance has finally played him false, and fatefully so. He succeeded in Germany so long as he could manipulate his strategy so that he never encountered a superior force. That too has been the secret of his diplomatic successes. Had he been willing to wait after Munich, consolidate his gains, allow the opposition to be split by divisions, he and Nazism might have been able to postpone the reckoning a long time. But the hypnotist came finally to hypnotize himself. The symbols about German destiny and his own which he sold so successfully to the German people he finally sold to himself. He went too far to extricate himself. And the result is a war in which, whatever the outcome from a military standpoint, Nazism as an intellectual system and as a system of values cannot emerge the victor.

The reason is that Hitler's values are life-denying values. Rauschning has called them "nihilism," by which he means the absence of fixed principle. But it is better to call them anti-humanist. For the Rauschnings of this world, in their desire for the static and their fear of change, pick exactly the strong parts of Hitler's doctrine to oppose. What has given Hitler strength is that there is a good deal of the revolutionist in him. He has promised men to open the windows for them, and they have flocked around him for breath: only to find that when they had smashed the windows he led them into a poisoned room. It is the poison—the anti-humanism, the barbarism—which is the real indictment of Hitler: not the restless desire for change and even for personal aggrandizement. If Hitler is ever defeated it will not be the military strength of the western Allies that will defeat him but the intellectual strength of a humanism which embraces the revolutionary values as well as the permanent. It will not be the war but the peace afterward, provided (what a big proviso!) it is a humane peace and one that does not repeat the follies of Versailles. It will not be the Chamberlains that will ever defeat Hitler but the Thomas Manns.

1939

10

Thomas Mann: Hero of Our Time

THOMAS MANN's little book [1] is the sharpest and noblest political utterance that has come out of exiled Germany. In form an expansion of a lecture delivered to American audiences from coast to coast, it is actually a manifesto composed on the battlefields of the human spirit, and addressed to the young in all countries who will decide the outcome.

Put briefly, the book calls for a democratic renaissance that will end the fascist adventure. Thomas Mann is a traditionalist—he calls himself a conservative—who has in the past thought of his own artistic task as distinct from that of the "political man," introducing in his thought a distinction where life itself admits of none. It took the obscene clangor of fascism to awaken him from his dream of the past, and to close the breach between the political and the artistic man. The awakening has evoked in Mann a wholeness, a moral clarity, a power that he never showed before. He has become a political thinker without ceasing to be an artist; he has become a democrat without ceasing to be a traditionalist.

Because of his biography, he does not fall into the cruder Marxian habit of regarding fascism wholly as a weapon that the capitalists wield and control. Nor does he fall into the cruder liberal habit of regarding it wholly as a perverse lapse from the divine grace of civil liberties. He sees fascism for what it is—a desperate revolt against the implications of the democratic principle, using the rhetoric of anti-bolshevism to attract and then enslave the capitalists, the rhetoric of socialism to attract and then enslave the masses, the rhetoric of nationalism to gloss over its own disunities and its cultural barbarism. He sees this as a realist. But he see farther. He sees the cowardice of fascism, its sadism, its tinsel glories,

---

[1] *The Coming Victory of Democracy.* New York, Knopf, 1938.

its gaudy external symbols, its negation of culture and of the human spirit itself.

But how meet this barbaric force? Not, says Mann, by denying its relevance to our own destiny, not by creeping into our shells, not by isolationism. Nor yet by admitting the paralysis of democracy, by defeatism. The answer lies in understanding the nature and strength of democracy, in acting in accordance with that nature and to the full measure of that strength. It is a youthful and militant democracy that Mann calls for—not the insipid textbook concept, but the living creed of grown men and women conscious of the stakes of the conflict, determined to save the world of their values, and willing to risk what is already doomed unless they risk it.

And here we must distinguish Mann's attitude from some of the attitudes toward democracy current in America today. There are, first, the liberals, who see in democracy only capitalist survival, the doctrine of free markets bolstered by a passive adherence to the shibboleths of civil liberties. There are, secondly, the fragments of revolutionary groups, who will have nothing to do with democracy unless they can conscript it to the uses of an impossible leftism. And there are, finally, the progressives of the past, who, having lost their belief in the forces of labor, think to vanquish fascism by borrowing some of the irrationalisms, the symbols and economic procedures, of fascism in the cause of national survival. It is part of Mann's deepest wisdom to understand that the democracies must call on their own inner strength, by the socialization of industry and the socialism of the human spirit which the rule of an informed majority implies. Above all, there must be an interplay of rationalism and realism. Mann quotes a sentence from Bergson which may well become the fighting slogan of our era: "Act as men of thought, think as men of action."

Because it is a statement of faith and not an analysis of trend, Mann's book is not without its weaknesses. He is too prone to see both democracy and fascism in terms of universals, which is the disease of the philosopher and artist, rather than in terms of change and movement, which is the disease of the historian. Of the two, I find the second today preferable. Seeing democracy as a universal, Mann tends to blur it with liberalism, and nothing today is more important than to understand that while the democrat must include liberalism in the scope of his thought, the liberal does not include democracy. And nowhere does Mann do more than hint at some of the central problems of political power that are involved in the survival and triumph of democracy—the problem of majorities and minorities in a transitional state, the obstructions against socialization that come from the vested interests of capitalist property and thought, the tyranny over opinion exercised by our oligarchies, the relentless struggle the ruling class will wage before it will yield its power.

But even without this, Mann has given us enough. He is a hero of our time; for in a democratic era heroism consists not in the individual exploit, but in bringing to consciousness and fruition the collective possibilities of human life. In my own mind I shall place this book next to a similar manifesto of an American humanist, Walt Whitman's "Democratic Vistas."

1938

PART FOUR

Ideas and Society

1

Do Free Markets Make Free Men?

E were discussing liberalism the other night—and discussion of liberalism is today, as much as it was five years ago, the occupational disease of liberals. We were having a hard time defining a liberal. We had in mind as a symbol, of course, not your new-fangled type, on whom the name is only grudgingly bestowed and who is in reality only a sort of realistic believer in democracy, but the lofty and unexceptionable ones, such as Walter Lippmann or Dorothy Thompson, who wear the mantle of liberalism with the easy assurance of ancient prerogative and vested habit. We found it easy to define a liberal in the economic realm, because generally he believes in the free market and the absence of government restraints on individual economic activity—or, at least, he believes only in those restraints that are applied in a gentlemanly way and can be carried through without sweat and discomfort. We found it easy to define him also in the intellectual and spiritual realm, because he believes passionately in the free man, and will fight the powers and principalities of darkness to protect man's freedom. And we saw that to be a lofty liberal, you have to believe in both. Among my scattering of friends in the Wall Street section, there are some who believe in the first and not the second; so they don't belong. And I know other people, including myself, who believe deeply in the second but don't put much stock in the first; so we don't belong.

And as we talked we saw that your classic liberal must not only believe in both, but he must see a necessary causal connection between the two. Without free markets there can be no free men. And conversely, when men lose their hold on freedom, don't be surprised to find them slipping from the ideal of free markets to government restraints on business and a controlled economy. Your liberal, then, in so far as his thought is an organic whole, sees two causal connections: free markets make free men, and man's fate hangs ultimately on his keeping himself uncontaminated by the taint of collectivisms.

At this point, one of our group, who had been listening to us silently as we unfolded the dialectic of true liberalism, interrupted with a question. If what we said was true, he asked, what was to distinguish the liberal of today from the eighteenth-century liberal? The answer, much as we racked our brains, was that there was no distinction. In the liberal of today the thought of the late eighteenth and early nineteenth centuries is most completely realized. The basic difference is that whereas the liberalism of that time had meaning for an emerging class in a rapidly shifting world, the liberalism of today is important only as rationalizing a nostalgia for the past. The earlier liberalism was dynamic; today's is static. The earlier liberalism represented the new currents in the advancing stream of Western thought; today's represents its minor eddies and backwaters. The liberal of today believes, like his brother of yesterday, in Nature's Simple Plan for governing the world through the sum of individual selfishnesses. Of course, we have learned some sophistication and we talk in a modernized vocabulary. But what the classical liberal of today wants most to do is to rebuild the world on a streamlined eighteenth-century model.

The position of classical liberalism today and its dilemmas are set forth with admirable clarity in two recent books—one by an American, Walter Lippmann, and the other by an Englishman, Lionel Robbins.

Walter Lippmann is easily the ablest rhetorician among American political thinkers. His early books, from the era of Teddy Roosevelt's "new nationalism" to America's entrance into the World War, were written with a nervous, glancing vitality that borrowed some of its staccato character from the staccato pace of events in a real world. He admits in his present book that he believed in those years in "a spaciously planned and intelligently directed social order." But the war knocked the underpinning from this belief. It taught him how easily men are swayed by propaganda. It taught him some of the unlovely realities of action by pressure groups, so that he was compelled to relax his belief in popular sovereignty. It strengthened in him a certain anti-massism, much like that of Ortega y Gasset, to which liberalism has always been prone. He became a frightened and bewildered man in a changing universe, clinging to outworn platitudes about individual liberty and freshening them with his enormous talent. He came to identify the forces of social change with the excesses of the mass and the dangers of collectivism. And he has now for so long set his face against these currents of change that his career, by the very fact that it has stood still, may be used to measure the degree of movement in American life in the past twenty years.

What Mr. Lippmann's new book [1] amounts to is a preface to his influential column in the daily papers. It is the whole of which the columns are fragments; without it they can scarcely be understood, for he has here set down the premises about men and society to which his columns are footnotes. Mr. Lippmann's is an austerely logical mind: he is really writing part of a serial each day. And since the *Herald Tribune* cannot supply with each issue a synopsis of the premises—historical, economic, psychological—on the basis of which Mr. Lippmann condemns and praises every morning, each column becomes as fragmentary and meaningless as an episode in those endless serial stories when we are not let in on who the characters are and what they have done. But the synopsis may be found here. It is orderly, lucid, impassioned. It is, in all probability, the best statement this generation is likely to have in America of the case for the free market as conditioning human freedom.

To say this is far from saying that the case itself is a good one. What Mr. Lippmann's argument sums up to is this: liberalism, given its origins in Adam Smith, started well as a revolutionary doctrine seeking to sweep away the feudal and mercantilist restraints upon economic activity. Smith's *Wealth of Nations* flowed from his insight into the newly emerging system of industrialism and the new division of labor that went with it. But after this brave start, liberalism hardened into the negative dogma of *laissez-faire* and never became a positive principle of social order. Since 1870, especially, the "latter-day liberals"—and Lippmann uses Herbert Spencer and the justices of the United States Supreme Court as

---

[1] *The Good Society*. Boston, Little, Brown, 1938.

typical—have "gone up a blind alley and come to a dead end."
They use liberalism to defend the *status quo,* and posit a natural
economic order and a social vacuum within which social control
is unnecessary. They have thereby left the entire field of control to
the Marxian collectivists. Actually, says Lippmann, liberalism must
be "not the rationalization of the *status quo,* but the logic of the
social readjustment required by industrial revolution." He then
proceeds to sketch out the positive "agenda of liberalism." What
they amount to is an attempt, through legislation and litigation, to
create a framework within which the competitive market can be
made to work. Lippmann believes that all collectivisms are reactionary—a throwback to the medieval controlled economy, and
that partial or gradual collectivisms clog up the functioning of the
free market and are, governmentally, "the polity of pressure
groups." He expends an enormous amount of rhetoric, now reada-
ble and now merely turgid, upon "the will to be free" and on "man
the inviolable." He even concludes with a section called (*sic!*)
"Watchman, What of the Night?" But what rhetoric and analysis
finally sum up to is that by social controls exercised through the
tradition of the common law and the machinery of litigation, the
free market must again be made to function.

I have tried above to get at the heart of Mr. Lippmann's argument and to state his case as fairly as I know how. Mr. Lippmann
characterizes his own position as "the radical conservatism of liberalism." Which may be a good way of telescoping for the advantage of his own doctrine the prestige of all three attitudes, but
which succeeds only in making a hash of all of them. Mr. Lippmann's basic psychological premise is that men cannot grasp the
totality of their social system. That is what underlies his fear of
economic planning and his objection to it. He gets this premise
from Graham Wallas, who in his *Great Society* first made clear to
social thinkers that since the Industrial Revolution our social system has become immensely complex, fragile, interdependent.
Wallas wrote *The Great Society* on the eve of the World War. What
Lippmann fails to point out is that Wallas's conclusions from his
premises are very different from his own. In his later books he made
it clear that the "great society" merely increases the need for an
"organization of will" whereby men can cope with the new problems. Wallas, in short, used the great society as proof of the bank-

ruptcy of *laissez-faire* and the need for moving on to partial and gradual collectivisms. Lippmann uses it, on the other hand, to attack every form of planning and collectivism. Without perhaps being aware of it, he is fashioning a new sort of religious fundamentalism. He pushes the processes by which men fashion their destinies in society into the realm of the unknowable. And thus, despite his brave assertions of the possibilities of order-through-litigation, he is contriving a form of economic surrender to the cruel drift of forces that the free market is incapable of mastering, very much like the religious surrender to the *status quo* because of the fears about the unknowable that lies beyond.

It is this basic irrationality that pervades Mr. Lippmann's liberalism, despite the elaborate ritual of bowing before the rational that he goes through. I know that he is anti-fascist. I know that he is filled with horror, as the rest of us are, at the ravages of the Nazi totalitarian state. But the nature of his anti-fascism is in the end self-defeating. For he not only lumps together the fascist and Soviet dictatorships—which has a measure of truth with respect to political method, but not with respect to their impact upon economic institutions and upon the lives of the plain people; but, more importantly, he puts the Roosevelt administration, which he calls "the providential state," in the same category of tendency. The result is to brand as dictatorship every step that is taken through government action toward control over our economic structure. The principles on the basis of which he attacks rational economic planning are principles which, when projected, can be used against social action of any sort—except perhaps the maintenance of a free market through the litigation of the courts. And this is, of course, exactly what the enemies of all reform and social control want to have said.

It is in this sense that the classic liberals of today end up by being illiberal and anti-rational. Whatever Mr. Lippmann may say about the need for shaping human affairs through reason, he recoils at the thought of applying those rational processes to the economic system itself. His argument is that economic planning leads of necessity to political tyranny and economic breakdown. For the planning group must be entrusted with enormous power if they are to make their plans work. And even if they have that power, they are incapable of making the adjustments among capital accumulation, production, and consumption which the free market presumably makes when enabled to function freely. The economic argument I should like to examine more closely in the next section, for Mr. Lippmann is not particularly strong as an economist, and takes his views second-hand from the Mises-Hayek school which has become the Riga of economic theory today. He never once grapples as an economist with the causes of capitalist breakdown; he never essays an appraisal of the extent to which Mr. Roosevelt's partial collectivism has helped or hindered the processes of recovery; he is not candid enough to give us the outlines of Soviet economic construction and the immensity of their achievement in the industrialization of the country. Instead he lays it down that a planned economy must conscript labor and ration consumption. And there he ends.

It is the tragic failure of the liberals not to see that the poverty, unemployment, and breakdown which have become the concomitants of corporate capitalism are not accidents and not mere excrescences of the capitalist process, to be lopped off by control through the courts. They are integral to an economic system where the power to make all the crucial decisions about prices, production, and investment is in the hands of a scattered group of powerful individuals and corporations, and where those decisions are made in non-social terms. Partial collectivisms, like that of Mr. Roosevelt or formerly of the Blum government in France or the Labor government in England, retain many of the defects of the old system while adding some defects of the new. That is inevitable with all pioneering attempts to forge new economies, and it is chiefly a consequence of having to attempt experiments in the social control of the market in the face of the antagonism of the powerful corporate groups who still maintain their crucial place in the market. This has been true at every step in the building of the New Deal policy, but it is especially true of the process of capital accumulation and investment. In England, in France, and in America the powerful corporate groups, whether through unconscious fear or conscious sabotage, have withdrawn their funds from investment and thereby paralyzed a partial collectivism. But to recognize this is a far different matter from saying that all attempts at planning lead inherently to collapse.

Mr. Lippmann's political objections to planning and partial

planning are based on the assumption that democracy and the free market are inseparable, that democratic responsibility would interfere with the planners, and that the planners would through their key positions control the people. The basic failure here is the failure to distinguish between democratic responsibility and the administrative process. Economic planning is a matter of administration: it can be carried on by an *expertise* of a body of technicians equipped to do their job in much the way that the British civil service or the staff of some of the more recent American administrative commissions are equipped to do theirs. The electoral machinery is used only to set the goal and direction. And it is as fantastic to say that elections would scrap the whole planning process as it would be to say that a change in ministries scraps the continuous functioning of the British civil service.

One cannot escape the suspicion that Mr. Lippmann's bias against the social and property implications of economic planning has led him to launch his elaborate attack upon all forms of it, as also his own intricate plan for avoiding planning. I call it an intricate plan, for nothing less than a complete network of social controls and legal rules would be necessary in order to create a framework within which competition could be coerced into functioning. We use the procedures of litigation in our anti-trust laws, along with the procedures of governmental investigation and complaint. Disregarding for a moment the ineffectiveness of that litigation, think of what it would mean to set up litigation machinery for the entire economic process which would be capable of countering the enormous weight of corporate power. It would mean that the total weight of social control would be thrown on the courts—on the branch of our government which is fullest of delays, most ritualistic in its procedures, most advanced in the degree of its ossification. I cannot believe that Mr. Lippmann or his fellow-liberals have actually studied the functioning of common-law procedures in the history of Anglo-American economic life. If they had they could not deify these procedures as they do. For they would know that for centuries both in England and in America we have sought to rely on them, and that we have found them finally inadequate.

Mr. Lippmann's book is chiefly valuable for the extent to which a sensitive and intelligent student, in his reaction against contemporary trends that he finds unpalatable, will go in seeking remedies for our situation within the very defects that have produced it. The book is the symbol of the attempt of an era to rescue itself by its own desperate inner logic.[2]

The toughness of economic fiber that Mr. Lippmann's book lacks will be found in the book [3] by Lionel Robbins. A professor at the London School of Economics, Mr. Robbins is the sharpest of the younger scholars who are today harnessing the neo-classical economics to the uses of Tory social theory. He has a cold and brittle intelligence—most savage in his effect as a polemicist when he is calmest in his manner. His writing has a clarity in the best tradition of the English economic school, and reminds me most strongly of people such as John Neville Keynes, father of the current Keynes, who loved to write on scope and method in economics, and succeeded both in purifying and in narrowing what they touched. Minds like that of Robbins are stronger at extracting the implications of a line of thought than they are at originating it. It is not surprising, therefore, that Robbins should have achieved his importance in expounding for English readers the doctrines of the Mises-Hayek school of economic theory, which has found new and subtle arguments for bolstering the very unsubtle dominance of the owning classes. He has infinitely more grace and clarity in his writing than the heavy Teutonic theorists from whom he draws the outlines of his thinking, but the outlines are largely theirs. Yet he makes up in authority what he lacks in originality: his writings tend to take on the tone of critical manifestoes, much as the essays of T. S. Eliot once did in another field.

He is not so well known to Americans as he might be, considering the zeal with which he defends values dear to most of our newspaper editors. He has consistently upheld the position that concessions to governmental interference with the free market are infractions of the order of nature. His little book on *The Nature and Significance of Economic Science,* published several years ago, views economics as a severely logical system of deduction from given assumptions. It leaves out of account as irrelevant the processes of

---

[2] For a discussion of Mr. Lippmann's book from a somewhat different angle, see the essay above, "Lippmann Agonistes."

[3] *Economic Planning and International Order.* New York, Macmillan, 1937.

economic change and movement, the framework of property institutions, and all consideration of social purposes. His later book, *The Great Depression,* may be read as a philosophical *apologia* for Hoover economic policy, in whatever country it crops up. It argues that the depression, so far from being the result of a breakdown of *laissez-faire* economy, was rather the result of government interventionism in the fields of money, trade, and industry; and that recovery has been impeded, not hastened, by further doses of the same.

It is the great merit of Mr. Robbins's new book that it broadens the area of discussion. The struggle between the pros and cons of economic planning has thus far proceeded within the national boundaries of the individual state. Almost the entire American controversy over the New Deal and its merits, in so far as it has not been merely the mouthing of vague epithets about socialism and the Constitution, has revolved around national prosperity or depression, the health and disease of industries, the grappling with the unemployment problem, the use and fate of capital investment. But the framework has been invariably a national one, and ever since Mr. Roosevelt's precipitate abandonment in 1933 of the international economic conference, neither side has sought to extend the horizons of the controversy to the farthest limits of international life. Rather has there been a tendency to shrink and contract the discussion by common consent, as if in the scramble to salvage something out of the wrack of humanity, it was now indubitably a matter of every nation for itself. Democrats, Republicans, and the labor forces in this country all tend to agree that an ocean-bounded country had better stay ocean-bounded; and Mr. Roosevelt, Mr. Landon, and Mr. Lewis differ chiefly on the scope and character of the groups to be benefited or burdened by a restrictive nationalist economic policy. Our premise is to further the strength and prosperity of the nation, rather than to release the restrictions that impede the wealth of nations.

Mr. Robbins is an internationalist, and as such he does not go along with these premises. He has written a brilliant book which is a merciless attack upon every form of deviation from the ideal of a completely free international market. He attacks tariff walls of all kinds, trade agreements, tariff unions, international cartels, international labor regulation. He bases himself squarely on the classical theory of international trade—the theory that each political unit must be allowed to put its energies into the production of those things in which because of resources or skill it has a comparative advantage over other countries, and that in this way there will be the best allocation of the productive resources of the world and the maximum possible economic gain to the consumer. This is the calculus that Mr. Robbins uses for measuring not only all trade and tariff arrangements between nations, but every proposal for economic control within a nation as well. Like the "felicific calculus" of Bentham, whom he so greatly admires, he uses the calculus of comparative advantage for sifting and appraising the entire set of economic value problems which is proving so puzzling to men today.

I have said the book is an attack on all deviations from the ideal of the free international market. But it is much more than that. If it were only that, one could admire Mr. Robbins for having the courage of the convictions of Adam Smith and Richard Cobden, and let it go at that. The book is chiefly interesting because it uses the theory of international trade as the medium for an attack on all forms of economic planning. Again, as in the case of Mr. Lippmann's book, a body of rhetoric is used—here, international economic freedom, there, political freedom; again, the rhetoric is one thing, the target aimed at quite another; and again the target is economic planning of any sort.

But I will not be unfair to Mr. Robbins. He does not reject *all* planning. He so defines planning—"an attempt to shape means to ends"—that the free international market is included within the category of plan ("international liberalism as planning"). What he objects to is planning from a center, with the coercive element entering. Like Mr. Lippmann, Mr. Robbins is determined to strip liberalism of the negativism that has thus far dogged it, and give it an element of affirmative strength. He is of the orthodox church in economics, but he wants to transform it into the church militant. He too feels that the early liberals were the true liberals—Hume, Adam Smith, Bentham, Ricardo. Both Mr. Robbins and Mr. Lippmann go back for their orthodoxy to the primitive church. And both believe that somewhere in the middle or third quarter of the nineteenth century a decadence set in upon liberalism. Here they differ: while Mr. Lippmann attributes the decadence to the *laissez-*

faire theorists of the *status quo* such as Herbert Spencer and the Supreme Court judges, Mr. Robbins attributes it to the rise of nationalism and of nationalist economic thought; his devils are Bismarck, Friedrich List, Gustav Schmoller. Both our authors consider socialism, like fascism, a reactionary throwback to medieval restrictions. Both of them wish to re-establish liberalism. Both seek to cure the evils of the present order by doing away with all forms of state interventionism except those that are necessary to maintain a free market. They share with the socialists the common dream of a Golden Age, save that their Golden Age is situated in the past instead of the future. Both represent an attempt to find the principle of salvation within the *status quo*—within the system of capitalist property institutions with a minimum of state regulation.

I shall confess that Mr. Robbins's chain of syllogisms leaves me almost as unconvinced as Mr. Lippmann's jeremiads on the new tyranny. I cannot get enormously interested in their lamentations over lost glory, or in the problem that dogs them so—who killed Adam Smith? I do not believe that Adam Smith was done to death either by the inactivity of his friends (as Mr. Lippmann thinks) or by the activity of his enemies (as Mr. Robbins believes). The truth is that he died of old age in a changing and turbulent world.

Mr. Robbins treats the theory of international trade as if it embodied the eternal verities, and as if the movement in the nineteenth century toward a system of international trade were a case of the world's learning to conform to those verities. Actually the theory of international trade was the rationalization, by English economists, of England's position at that time in the world economy. England got the jump in the Industrial Revolution, and it needed free world markets. It became the manufacturing center of the world and the distributing point to countries with inferior industrialisms. Then what happened was that the other countries learned all too well from England, borrowed England's industrial techniques, and built on them their own economic nationalisms; and then the world market broke down. The struggle for markets led to the World War, and the aftermath of the War was an intensification of nationalisms. And a theory that rationalized nineteenth-century conditions is no longer, however sadly we may feel about it, an adequate rationalization for our own time.

What Mr. Robbins is doing, therefore, is taking a paper construct that had some application in the century of the Great Peace, and seeking with it to undermine the various forms of economic control with which each country is attacking the problem of the Great Depression of capitalism. He has one advantage, in that the body of principles he is appealing to was established a century and a half ago and has assumed a classic form, while the economic controls he is attacking have not yet achieved a systematic rationalization. He is thus able to set his clear stream of theory over against the muddy and turbulent waters of the collectivisms and partial collectivisms of today, and say: "See how much better my stream is." But if it is better it is only because, having no traffic with reality and having long since ceased to carry the freightage of actual economic policy, it can remain uncontaminated. Liberal economic theory has the perfection of art, the unruffled perfection of "a painted ship upon a painted ocean."

It is a sign of vitality, however, that the institutional growths looking toward collective control of economic life have not yet perfected their theory. Mr. Robbins, like Mr. Lippmann, wins easy victories by attacking them through attacking communist and socialist theory, which is in itself a kind of painted ship, and which posits an international community of socialist nations that does not exist. Actually, neither perfect socialist theory nor the perfect theory of comparative advantage in international trade can be applied with any fruitfulness to the TVA or the SEC or the Labor Relations Board or the farm-subsidy program. They are working institutions in process of being hammered out; if they survive, it will not be for their perfection of theory but because they accomplish their objectives of increasing and distributing the national income. And when they have done that, the rationalizations of how they did it will follow.

Mr. Robbins uses as the prime criterion in his evaluation of economic programs the concept of the best allocation of the productive resources of the world. Given a state of peace, social order, equitable property institutions, and a satisfactory distribution of the world's wealth among nations, this is undoubtedly a good economic criterion. To be a system of organization—a system of *planning*—it would even then, Mr. Robbins recognizes, involve the displacement of our present nation-states by a world political federation. I find that an inspiring ideal for a distant future: my only qualification would be that a world federation can never be achieved nor could it run smoothly unless the individual polities in it were first able to socialize their property institutions. Meanwhile, however, it is a strange kind of doctrinairism to subject the efforts being made everywhere to stave off collapse and build internal stability and prosperity to the standard of the theory of comparative advantage. It is, in a sense, a new form of Taylorism—like preaching to an unemployed and starving man about that extra gram of efficiency he could extract if he made time-per-operation-unit the basis of his work.

I cannot conclude without referring to a book [4] that has just been published by another Englishman, Professor Pigou of Cambridge. I bring it in partly because it contains interesting answers to many of the problems that the free-market liberals are trying to solve by chasing phantoms and hunting witches, and partly because—while part of the same intellectual tradition as Mr. Robbins and Mr. Lippmann—Professor Pigou is so different in his intellectual temper.

Let me say first that Professor Pigou is no radical. He is the successor to Alfred Marshall's chair at Cambridge, and one of the great line of orthodox British economists including Adam Smith, Ricardo, Mill, and Marshall. Like Marshall and Mill, he is very much concerned about human welfare, but he has always discussed it in rigidly economic terms, without going into class theory or into political and humanitarian considerations that the classical economists have always regarded as outside their realm. I may cite as symbols of his preoccupations the titles of two of his books: *The Economics of Welfare,* and *The Economics of Stationary States.* He belongs to what Thorstein Veblen called the "taxonomic" approach to economics, as do the other members of the neo-classical tradition.

That is what gives special importance to his new book. The task he sets himself is to determine whether, viewed simply as functioning economic systems and aside from any sentimental or social considerations, capitalism or socialism presents the better case. And his conclusion, in terms of their capacity to allocate the productive

---

[4] A. C. Pigou, *Socialism versus Capitalism.* New York, Macmillan, 1937.

resources, to keep men employed, to promote and consolidate technical efficiency, to provide an incentive for economic effort, to exploit to the full the potentialities for national income, is on the side of socialism.

This represents a sharp confrontation of the entire tradition of liberal economic theory. John Stuart Mill alone, among the members of the school, showed leanings toward socialism. But as a whole the school has been as passionately opposed to socialism as it has been sturdily the apologist of free-market capitalism. Latterly the opposition to socialist theory and to Fabianism and other forms of gradual collectivism has enrolled under the leadership of the Austrian branch of the neo-classical school, following Ludwig von Mises and Friedrich Hayek. It is under the Mises-Hayek banners, as I have said, that Mr. Robbins and Mr. Lippmann fight New Dealism and every other form of economic control.

The crushing argument that this school has believed itself to be directing against economic planning is the argument on the lack of a pecuniary calculus in a planned society once the free market has been abolished. They apply both to international and internal economics the doctrine of comparative advantage. They argue, on psychological premises, that human wants are limitless but that the capacity to satisfy those wants is limited. Hence it follows that there must be a mechanism for guiding production into those channels where there will be the most economical use of resources with the maximum satisfaction of wants. That mechanism is presumably furnished under a free capitalist market by competition over costs and prices in the labor, capital, and consumers' markets, and in that way there is an automatic rational allocation of productive resources. The argument was that planning does away with the whole cost-price-profit relationship and hence breaks down the system of consumers' choices on which rational allocation of resources depends. This has been thoroughly answered by the theorists of planning, who point out that planning will retain the entire system of price, cost, and accounting, and will only displace the profit drive as the dynamic of the process, and substitute for it the administrative process. It is the great merit of Professor Pigou that he shows in detail how such a calculus would function under a planned economy.

Deprived of the argument of the collapse of planning from this direction, the free-market liberals such as Mr. Lippmann fall back on their second defense line—that planning would collapse because it would involve political tyranny over the entire social system by the planners, in which all the freedoms that the Western world has built up would be lost. Their great argument for this lies in the example of Soviet Russia and Nazi Germany. And those examples illustrate the danger of the indiscriminate lumping of collectivist economies. For what both of them illustrate is merely that given political traditions and methods which are undemocratic to begin with (as was true of both the Russian and Nazi revolutions) economic planning cannot remedy the defects of the political methods. What it can do—and that Russia, and Germany only to a considerably lesser extent, illustrate—is to build effective economic structures even within those political traditions.

Let us keep in mind the fact that the task of the future, despite Mr. Lippmann and Mr. Robbins, is not to rebuild the shining city of the eighteenth century; it is to explore the entire range of methods of social change and political administration which will enable us to get the economic benefits of planning without paying the price of democratic breakdown. The path of the future is along the line of gradual socialization, experimenting with methods of economic control until a planned society is achieved. When that happens, men will not have to narrow the range of their freedom to the costly and empty freedoms of the market.

1938

2

Materialism and History [1]

MARXISM as a system of thought has made the greatest impression in the academic world in the form of a theory of history. There are several facts that help to account for this. History, as the oldest of our social sciences, has raised the most enduring problems of method and philosophy. The question of how to explain the movement of life through time in the direction in which it does move opens up the problem of social causation in its barest and most acute form. It is presented, moreover, in a form in which it has captured the imagination not only of scholars but of the general reading public as well. "As I grow older," Charles Beard once wrote, "I feel with Buckle that there is something in history. Just what it is, is very difficult to determine." And many others have felt the same lure to find out what there is in history, if not the same sense of the difficulty of discovering the answer.

Actually, of course, the materialist interpretation of history, as part of the entire Marxian configuration, implies the whole of it. The Marxian theory of history implies the whole of the Marxian sociology, including basically its economic theory, its theory of social classes, and its theory of the state. Let me put it in a more generalized form. Any theory of history implies a complete social theory. It implies, secondly, a basic philosophy of human life and nature. It implies, thirdly, a social order in which it has grown up and toward the problems and puzzles of which it is directed. It implies, finally, a program of action with respect to that social order, whether in accepting or upholding it, or in rejecting and seeking to change or displace it. Thus you have five entities held

---

[1] A paper read at the meeting of the Eastern Sociological Association at New Haven, March 1936.

in suspension in relation to one another and each implying the others; a theory of history, a social theory, a basic philosophy, a social order, and a program of action. While I choose the theory of history as a starting point I do not forget that it is part of a configuration.

One other preliminary remark. We know that human life is complex, and all of social theory may be seen as an attempt to reduce that complexity to some sort of pattern. All thought simplifies the bewildering and unyielding stuff of life itself. But to simplify in that sense is the price that we pay for the order that thought seeks to achieve. One form of order is the concept of causation. Recently some of our theorists, especially those in the field of natural science, have been telling us that causation does not exist. I am ready to believe it. More and more I find myself ready to believe in the non-existence of things in whose existence I had formerly believed. But that sort of nihilism is for the working thinker a luxury that he can ill afford, because it reduces him to non-existence as well, and his whole craft to futility. Recently I have had occasion to read statements by two distinguished historians, Carl Becker and Charles Beard, gently railing at the materialist interpretation of history because it does not and cannot explain life. I agree with them that economics and the material forces in society do not explain history, and that history does not explain life. I am ready, although I cannot prove it, to agree that nothing completely causes or explains anything else.

But having said this, we must get on. We do not want final explanations. What we want is an approach to the movement of history, a way of analyzing it and interpreting it, a way of relating the different phases of the whole of social life to one another—ideas and institutions and *mores* and technologies and religions and political systems. What we want above all else is to discover—whether in a simple or a complex form—the dynamic of the processes of history and social life. If any theory or combination of theories will give me that, and will function as a good working hypothesis; if the serious attempts made to apply it to the task of historical interpretation and to project it into the future to the task of social prediction, meet with a greater degree of success than some other theory or lack of theory, then I am willing to use it until some better one offers itself.

Let me give briefly my own notion of the materialist theory of history. In doing this I am aware that, pretty much as Justice Holmes once remarked that Supreme Court judges have a way of reading Herbert Spencer's *Social Statics* into the Constitution, so I run the danger of reading my own hopes and fears and difficulties into the Marxian thesis. But I am not too terrified at the prospect. In the house of Marxian theory, as in any other theory, there can be many mansions. There is or need be no more of the sacerdotal or the authoritative within the framework of Marxian thought than there is or need be within the framework of Platonism or Aristotelianism. In the history of any intellectual movement, especially those that are closely related to social struggles, zeal and dogmatism often tend to crowd out intelligence and flexibility. You will remember that rationalism, during the days of the French Revolution, had its Garbo-like goddess, and that positivism, in the days of Comte and Frederic Harrison, could not decide for a while whether it was a doctrine or a church. But there is no inherent hieratic character in Marxian thought. It has now reached the stage where it should be able to slough off whatever rigidities or sanctities it has had.

The materialist interpretation of history is premised on the assumption that history has a rationale and a sequence, and is not merely whimsical. The key to the historical sequence is to be found in the interplay between the material conditions of life and the economic institutions on the one hand, and on the other the cultural and ideological superstructures built on this base and in turn helping to transform it. In this interplay, while there is mutuality of relation and influence, the conditioning forces and the determining forces are the economic. They set the boundaries within which men's efforts toward forming and transforming their social lives can be effective. They furnish the starting-point and the tools for this task. On the principle that whatever men do influences what they are, the material conditions of any age set the entire psychological tone of that age, and condition its folkways and thoughtways.

But most important of all, more important than the function it performs of psychological conditioning, the material structure of a culture—its technology, its modes of production, its state of the

industrial arts, its resources—influences enormously the stratification of that culture. In Marxian terminology, the conditions of
production determine the relations of production. They determine
the class structure of a society—in short, its social order—not in the
sense of a rigorous and mechanical determinism, but in the sense
that they represent a tough and unyielding compulsive in a society,
with which the social order has to reckon and on which it must be
based. Given a similar technological development, as for example
in Germany and the Soviet Union today, very different systems of
class relations may be based upon it, at least temporarily. But a
change in the productive forces and the conditions of production
will sooner or later bring about a redistribution of social power and
a change in the relations of production.

Technological change in relation to the natural and productive
resources of the culture is therefore the *primum mobile* of the materialist theory. But it must not be taken as the central element in
the theory. It is the relations of production—the class relations of a
society—that are central. That is what keeps the Marxian theory
from being too crudely a technological interpretation of history.
The relations of production give shape to the entire institutional
structure of a culture—the distribution of power, the use of the
state machinery, the contours of the family, the educational system,
morals, religion, literature, and art.

But these changes again do not flow mechanically. They must
first be channeled through men's minds and men's actions. They
produce tension and strife, a conflict of interests, and a series of
misunderstandings and all too clear understandings between groups
—what the Marxians call the class struggle. This tension and strife
forms the focus of thought and effort, and the framework within
which activity is carried on. When they grow great enough and
when the cleavage between the forces of production and the relations of production grow so great as to produce a collapse in the
productive system, a period of revolutionary change has arrived.
In the unequal pace of social transformation, whether in periods of
preparation, revolution, or consolidation, the framework for social
activity is set by the conditions and relations of production, the
dynamic of change is the struggle between social classes for a share
in the distribution of the total social income and for control of the

modes of production, but the effective agencies for all these changes and transformations are the activities of human beings.

Now it will be asked: What are the elements that enter into this approach to history, and how do they combine into a usable instrument of historical interpretation?

There is, first of all, *determinism*. This introduces the vexed question of historical "laws." I take it that what historians and social theorists are seeking is a pattern of historical change and therefore of social change. I take it that we are not concerned now with finding or celebrating a view of history that leaves everything to blind chance and the accident of the individual genius. I take it also that we are not concerned with the metaphysics of any immanent principle in historical development, or with any mystical or supernatural aids or hindrances to historical change. Determinism to me means that there is a pattern in history, and materialist determinism means that the pattern is traced by man's increasing control over the forces of nature and the development of his economic institutions.

But to say that there is a pattern and a sequence does not mean to say that there is *inevitability* in history. Certainly there is no inevitability as applied to the nuances or minutiae of history, to its backchamber conspiracies or its anteroom gossip. Also there is room and to spare within the framework of economic forces for individual caprice and talent, for the entire play of the accidental and contingent, for the several millimeters between the length that Cleopatra's nose had and the length it might have had. Nor is there any inevitability even in the large. For example, it was not inevitable that fascism should have triumphed in Germany. What was inevitable was that somewhere within the framework of struggle over a collapsing capitalism, following upon an era of imperialist war and as part of that era, there should be an attempt by the capitalist interests to secure a death-hold upon their slipping power. That it could have been avoided in Italy seems unlikely. That it could have been avoided in Germany seems, however, more likely, if the cards had been played right. Moreover, it is not at all inevitable that the cause of the proletariat will triumph throughout the world, just as it was not inevitable that it should have triumphed in Russia. It is quite conceivable that in a collapsing culture such as the West

European or the American, war accompanied by the death-grip of reaction should produce not proletarian triumph but sheer barbarism, a barbarism worse than that which followed the fall of the Roman culture.

There is therefore no inevitability in history, no stern unyielding law such as that of the stars in their courses. That might have been the dream of a Pareto, who thought he could apply the procedures of celestial mechanics to the behavior of men living in a society. You will not find, in the Marxian system of thought, the fond illusion that the course of human actions can be reduced to graphs and algebraic symbols. You will not find a sense of divine objectivity which assumes that the thinker can strip himself of all biases and apply to the study of society the methods of precision instruments. You will find neither inevitability nor scientism, because both of them dispense with the primary fact that we are human beings whose actions are human and therefore not entirely predictable.

But you will find a sense of *historical laws.* I do not mean here exactly the same thing as the laws of the physical world. And yet I do not mean anything that is wholly different, either. I mean ascertainable sequences in history, repeated correspondences between changes in the economic and material elements in a culture and the other elements, objective sequences in men's behavior in society. Obviously the laws of the physical world are not inflexible and depend for their functioning upon given conditions which, while they may be isolable in the laboratory, are to be found only imperfectly known; although we have every reason to believe from the fact that the universe does not smash up and go whirling off into chaos that the laws exist even when we have not yet ascertained them. The same is true, though to a greatly qualified degree, of the laws of human life and society and historical change.

Men and conditions under which they live are part of the objective world. Like the phenomena of nature they exist apart from our consciousness of them. This, as philosophy, is objective *materialism* or naturalism, as opposed to idealism of any sort, which sees only ideas as real entities and the material world as a reflection of some static or developing idea. Since the entire fabric of our social life and our cultures is part of the material world, it is organic; there is, in short, an organic base upon which our super-organic cultural and ideological structures rest. And this organic base develops according to the laws of all cultural growth.

To Marx and to Engels, as to their teacher Hegel and a host of other thinkers, the deepest law of organic growth was the *dialectical*. Marx and Engels held that the causes of organic and social growth are to be found within and not outside the social system, that in the unfolding of society no force outside society need be called upon for explanation, but that each period, economic system, culture holds in suspension the period or system or culture that is to follow and contains within itself, phoenix-like, the seeds of its own destruction and its own reconstruction farther on in the organic scale of development. They held that the shifting technologies create shifting class relations and class conflicts in such a way that each era and each social system, out of its own energies and tensions, fulfills itself and gives way to the next.

To put it, as they put it, in the form of the constituent elements of the dialectic process—thesis, antithesis, and synthesis—is useful but not indispensable. It is the language of the time of Marx and Engels, the sociological terminology of their day. We have our own terminology. But what is essential is not the sociological or philosophical patter but the social and historical pattern. What is essential is to understand that human effort is limited by and contained within a developing framework of economic, technological, and material elements, that as they change the social order built upon them changes as well, that it is forced on to change by the contradictions that develop between the demands of production and the framework of class power under which production is carried on.

This brings us to what is perhaps the most vexed problem in the whole range of problems connected with a theory of history: the role of human effort and of contingency within the framework of economic determinism. Men have to work within the limits imposed by the economic forces, but within those limits they do make their own history. One of the charges that has been most persistently made against the materialist theory of history is the charge that it somehow degrades the human spirit because it irons free will out of the scheme of things and lets necessity reign alone. Scrupulously examined, the charge is absurd. The great value of the materialist theory is that it sets the framework within which human effort *can* be effective.

Its whole emphasis is that men do make their history. But with three necessary qualifications. It is not the great men who make it, as part of the accident of their genius, but whole classes of men under the leadership of great men, and as a consequence of their class position and the historic function of the class. Here the role of human effort is to be sharply distinguished from the Carlylean and Nietzschean "great man" theory and from the Spenglerian or Paretian theory of the role of the élite. Second, men's efforts are exercised not arbitrarily or whimsically but within the limits set by the changes in the material conditions of life and in the ensuing class relations. Third, and this is related to the preceding, the materialist interpretation is therefore no philosophy of voluntarism. It is not enough that men should decide to do something, and succeed in doing it by the sheer force of their will or wish. Graham Wallas has somewhere spoken of human society as "the organization of will." It may be so, yet the will can be socially effective only when it flows with rather than against the stream of history.

But when men's efforts stay within the realm of what is humanly and historically possible, they become the center of gravity of the materialist theory. It is human activity, human effort, human intelligence that have acted as the agents of social transformation in every period of history; it is upon these that we must depend for the necessary social transformation that will make sense out of our own society and save it from barbarism. The materialist theory of history is thus in the best sense a humanistic theory.

But while it deals with living men and their efforts, it concerns itself less with them as individuals than as social groupings, and less with their motives than with the consequences of their acts. The materialist interpretation thus avoids the mere pursuit of psychological subtleties and literary effects in history—although it must be said that there are few histories that display as much of both qualities as Trotsky's *History of the Russian Revolution* or Harold Laski's *The Rise of European Liberalism*. But then the psychology is not an arid psychologism; it is brought in mainly where it illuminates and flows from the play of economic and social forces.

I have spoken of *chance* and *contingency*. There is room for them as well within the framework of historical materialism. To hold that they play no part in history would be to hold to a fatalistic mechanism by which everything that happened was predetermined from the very beginning. Obviously this is not so. If we define chance as that which has no cause within the social system, we must obviously exclude it. But if we define it rather as contingency, as something whose cause does not come within the scope of the relevant active forces, then we must make room for it.

But more important than chance is *mutuality,* or what Engels calls *Wechselwirkung.* While it is true that the relations of production are the final determinants of social change, they do not operate in a vacuum. They determine the form and pattern of the social structure as a whole, but they are themselves in turn influenced and transformed by the institutional and ideological elements in the rest of the social structure. The best illustration of course is offered by the relations between technology and science. The economic structure of a society determines the extent to which science can develop; yet science in the very process of development adds to the state of the industrial arts and thereby transforms the economic structure.

Finally there is the question of *tradition* and the social *lag.* It is clear that the various elements of a social order or of a social system change at various rates. Historical materialism is a temporal and dynamic rather than a static philosophy; it explains idea-systems and institutions in terms of a changing social complex. Yet it recognizes also persistences and continuities as well as changes and transformations. These persistences are partly due to the laws of organic growth, partly also to the dead weight of tradition. There are thus all sorts of lags within a social system—lags that are most noticeable when we compare men's social attitudes and opinions with their objective class position and their actual economic interests. But while tradition and the social lags distort and delay the historical process, they do not change its essential character or direction.

In fact, their very operation depends upon the operation of the class factors in history. The social-lag concept which has become so current in the American sociological school is meaningless unless the origin of the lag is itself explained. Unless the explanation is to be theological—a sort of primal curse of indolence or backwardness in the human mind—it must be traced to the operation of social factors. Thorstein Veblen has given us in *The Theory of the Leisure*

Class one of the best clues to the mechanism of the social lag. It arises from the control over the neutral stereotypes of the underlying population that is exercised by the dominant class through the force of imitation, prestige, and economic compulsion; and it is maintained by the power which the dominant class has over the instruments of education and opinion.[2]

How valid is such a theory of history? That is, of course, almost impossible to answer. A theory of history is valid not in any absolute sense but if it serves as a useful instrument for clarifying and illuminating the processes and events of history. It is valid, in short, to the extent that it is a *usable* theory of history.

I think it can safely be said that, at least for the history of the Western world since the Greek city-states, the materialist theory has been the most usable theory we have discovered thus far. Despite the fact that it has been a pariah among the academic castes, they have not been able to ignore or neglect it. It has become the storm-center of their work and their methodological discussions; always when they would have been most disposed to forget it they have been drawn toward it with an almost magnetic force. Some of them have even adopted elements of it more or less unconsciously, as is true of most of the historians of imperialism, the World War, and fascism.

What social-theoretical systems of history has the materialist interpretation had to contend with? (1) Scientism, which by aiming at a godlike objectivity stripped historical facts of everything except the bare garment of their factness, and thus actually abandoned the "facts" to the blind mercies of the prevailing preconceptions that happen to be established as to social cause. (2) Multiple-causationism, deeply rooted especially in American social-process theory, with its belief that history is a sort of common carrier that has to admit all factors as equally and mutually causative, and cannot regard any one element as determining.[3] (3) Subjectivism or psychologism of some sort, usually taking the form of emphasis on

---

[2] For an elaboration of the theory of the social lag given here, see my essay above, "The Shadow World of Thurman Arnold," section 5, "Institutions and Lag." For an elaboration of the theory of opinion control, see "Freedom in the Opinion Industries" above.

[3] For a further discussion of the multiple-causation theory, see the chapter on "The Theory of the Social Process" below.

spiritual or idealistic factors or else of emphasis on the psychological elements of the minds and personalities of great men or else the habits of the masses. Much of our intellectual history, synthetic history (the so-called "new history" in America), "cultural" history, and "social" history belongs in this category. Through the emphasis on psychological factors, and in the name of subtlety and complexity, the role of personality and of great men in history is re-established, and the motives of acts are examined to the exclusion of their consequences. (4) The cyclical and undulatory theories of the thinkers in the countries which have now turned to fascism, stressing racial factors in history and the voluntaristic ("will to power") factors in an élite.

These are, I think, the principal schools of historical theory that have developed either independently of or in opposition to the theory of historical materialism. But none of them has shown itself to be as usable in its approach to the problems that agitate us today (whatever may be its utility in solving the so-called "ultimate" problems of history or philosophy), none explains as well the forces that have led us into the present state of our culture and social organization, and none indicates as well the lines of future development.

It is in some such terms that I should put the utility of the materialist interpretation today. It traces most clearly the main lines of forces that lead from the past to the dilemmas and tensions of today. It lays bare the essential elements of contemporary institutions—separating what is contingent in them from what is of real moment in dominating the present and shaping the future. By projecting the lines of force from the past into the future, it gives a basis for prediction which, while never infallible or exact, nevertheless furnishes a starting-point for action.

1936

3

Literature and Society [1]

V IEWED as a whole a body of literature like a body of magic or a system of law is part of the entire culture of a people. The characteristic qualities that distinguish it from other literatures derive from the characteristic qualities of the life of the group. Its themes and problems emerge from group activities and group situations. Its significance lies in the extent to which it expresses and enriches the totality of the culture.

Although the groups with which anthropology ordinarily concerns itself are preliterate, the functionalist viewpoint as developed in anthropology is illuminating when applied to the setting of literature in a culture. Seen thus, literature is neither an esoteric activity, as the formalists would contend, nor a purely instrumental activity, directed to external ends in the group life, as the extremist element in the Marxian school would have it. It is an integral part of the entire culture, tied by a tissue of connections with every other element in the culture; yet possessing a function of its own and ministering best to the life of the group where it performs that function with the greatest artistry and the deepest congruity with the basic assumptions and the accredited purposes of the group. And it should be added, to point the complexity of relationship, that these basic values are not something given but are the end-products of a past in which literature has itself played a substantial part in the process of cultural construction.

Literature is thus both culture-forming and culture-ridden. Its

1 This is a section of the article, "Literature," originally published in the *Encyclopaedia of the Social Sciences* and written by Edwin Mims, Jr., and myself. We planned out the article as a whole together, then each of us wrote a section, which was in turn subjected to editing by the other. The section for which I was primarily responsible seems in itself enough of a unity to be published separately; but I want to emphasize that it is in a real sense the product of collaboration. And I want to thank Mr. Mims for generously making it available for this book. Many of the illustrations from literary history which fill out the bare skeleton of the theory are his and not mine.

connections with society are so integral and pervasive that there is a temptation within every sociological school of criticism to press to the conclusion that society is the play itself and not merely the backdrop against which the play is enacted. Certainly the range of social influences on literature is as broad as the entire range of operative social forces: the prevailing system of social organization —including the class structure, the economic system, the political organization, and the deeply rooted institutions; the dominant ideas; the characteristic emotional tone; the sense of the past and the pattern of the future; the driving aspirations and "myths," and their relation to the contemporary realities. There is nothing in the compass of social life that does not play its part—small or large, directly or by deflection, immediately or by varying removes—in giving literature the impress of its surrounding world.

The sort of determinism which this involves is not, however, the rigid and mechanical determinism that has played havoc with the charting of relationships in the entire realm of social life. It cannot afford to isolate a single element in society—whether economic or ideological—and assign to it a causal role in the final determination of literature; nor can it premise an immediacy of relation between literature and the social factors or a quantitatively equal response to the impact of social forces. The whole of the social process—including material, conceptual, emotional, and institutional elements—may be regarded as containing the potential determinants of the direction and character of the literature of a period. At any time the pace and character of social and intellectual change sharpen issues, pose problems, precipitate conflicts, and establish harmonies that are distinctive for that time; a "social situation" is brought into the area of operative influence which, in its selection of elements and in its orientation, is unlike any other social situation. And while this selective process is projecting certain dynamic and significant issues into the consciousness of the time and obscuring others, another selective process is at work, from the side of the writer, singling out those elements which have managed to produce an impact on him and weaving them into a pattern which is compatible with his standards of art and his view of human life. Where these two mechanisms of selection interlock in the work of a particular writer a point of contact is established between literature and society.

In terms of such a dynamic and selective process some justice can be done to the subtle and complex connections that link literature to the operative social whole. Critics who attempt to test the hypothesis of a socially determined literature by measuring the degree to which certain great writers were absorbed in the public issues of their day set up a mechanical unilinear determinism which they find no difficulty in destroying. Thus it might be shown that Chaucer's poetry is a poor mirror of the more obvious political issues of the England of his day, and that even Shakespeare was alive to the glory of the victory over the Armada but not to the realities of the enclosure movement. But such a line of inquiry assumes a simplicity that does not exist in the functioning of the social process. Any appreciable change in the social process communicates itself to the body of literature not directly but through a ramifying network of social relations, with every chance that its force may be multiplied or deflected in the devious process of transmission, or that its influence will be complicated, distorted, or nullified by some other change arising elsewhere in the social process.

For society is neither neat structure nor unobstructed process: it is a complex of end-products from the past, of functioning institutions in various stages of development, of tangled idea and emotion, of hesitant purpose and frequent cross-purpose. In such a milieu the surprising fact is not that there is so little clear evidence of the transmission of social change to the literary process, but that there is so much. In the case of particular writers the relation seems of course even more erratic than in the case of a body of literature. For to what extent the social process will push its significant changes across the threshold of the writer's consciousness, and to what extent he will embody even that proportion in the emotional pattern that constitutes his artistic vision, can be explained only by the conjunction of his own biography with the history of the society.

The essential task of literature is to lay bare the foundations of human emotion: to this revelatory process the social forces can give only direction, impetus, and an ideological impress. It is a commonplace of criticism that literature transcends the boundaries of the particular culture, that it speaks "the universal language of the human heart." Whatever the culture, its basic literary themes are the same—birth and death and love and jealousy, individual conflict, communal experience, triumph and defeat. They are linked to the biological bases of life, to its psychological invariances, to the necessities of the collective experience. It is significant that the literatures of the most varied cultures have meaning and beauty for an outsider even when their social organizations seem to him bewildering and their basic values absurd.

For the artistic imperative to which literature is the response is universally operative. Everywhere the writer takes the stuff of experience in the life of the group and washes it in the powerful emotional stream of his personality. The drab incident is made vital, the abstraction human and dramatic, the idea imaginative. Homer's gods survive across the centuries because they are humanized; Dante's theme of divine love is made immediate and dramatic; and the group activity that is the theme of modern proletarian writing is translated into terms of its impact on individuals. For the literary process society is only the river bed; the stream itself is the flow of human life.

In fact the two elements are scarcely as distinct as that. The emotional pattern of the individual writer, which could claim, if anything could, to be a primary datum, is as a matter of actuality socialized in the very process of construction, and the individual artistic vision is a selection from potential elements; the emotional response of the reader is the product, as Tolstoy points out, of a sort of social contagion and certainly proceeds in an emotional milieu already socially conditioned; the valuation of the writer and the guidance of the reader—the dual task of a highly subjective body of criticism—proceed by canons which, to avoid being chaotic, must be socially rooted. Literature is whatever reaches through words to the human; but in the process the entire social realm must be traversed.

Literature is seen in clearest social perspective as an institution —a cluster of structure, usage, habit, idea, technique—the whole containing a principle of growth of its own but responding always to the change and stir in the varied life of the institutions with which it is interwoven. And as such it consists of a scheme of controls, through which it performs its social function by organizing the verbal expression of experience and thus integrating on an emotional level the activities of the group with its underlying view of life.

The basic material of literature is thus experience. But the experience that has found expression in literature has never been as broad as that of the entire culture. It is always a limited experience that is thus embodied—the life and the vision of life of particular groups within the culture. In the literature of Periclean Athens it is the experience of the male citizenry that is expressed, but not of the metics or the slaves or the women; in the literature of imperial Rome it is the experience largely of a leisure aristocracy and not of the industrial population or the serfs or, with some exceptions, of the provincials; in the literature of medieval Europe it is the experience only of a fighting, jousting, and love-making nobility; in the literature of China it is the experience of a high officialdom or of a petty bureaucracy, but not of the masses of peasantry. Sometimes the confines of expression have been determined by the class groupings, sometimes by the distribution of literacy and leisure, sometimes by arbitrary and traditional taboos.

In fact literary history could be approached illuminatingly from the point of view of the forces that have drawn various groups and strata of the culture into or kept them out of the body of literary expression. In the Western world there has been since the breakdown of feudalism a steady extension and widening of the limits, so that new groups have been continually drawn into the literary process—first, generally, as readers and then as writers. The entire period since the commercial revolution has been dominated by the rise of the middle class to the literary hegemony in the new capitalist nation states that succeeded the feudal regime. And the anti-capitalist revolutionary movements of the past hundred years have carried with them, both as result and as an integral part of their purpose, the opening of channels of expression for the experience of the underlying population—from the workmen's literature of Chartist England and of the France of George Sand to Gorky's delineation of the life of outcasts in tsarist Russia on the eve of the revolution and the direct and unvarnished writing of worker correspondents in the Soviet Union.

The large tidal changes in making new and untapped resources of experience available for literary expression have resulted from changes in class stratification. Another accession of experience, that of women, was made possible by the breaking down of the taboo which women's inferior economic position had placed about the

masculine monopoly of writing; the timidity with which Jane Aus-
ten and Emily Dickinson wrote indicates the gap between their
period and that of the present, when it is often possible for a woman
to have, in Virginia Woolf's phrase, "a room of her own."

But tied up with these changes affecting class and sex groupings
there have been shifts of intellectual horizon, contacts with hitherto
unfamiliar cultures, reorientations in the effective moral codes,
which have broadened and deepened the experience of the entire
culture and which have uncovered new levels within the individual
consciousness. The effects of the Crusades and of the Renaissance
on West European literature, of the geographical and scientific discoveries on Elizabethan literature, of the rise of urban life on the
eighteenth-century novel, of European expansion into the exotic
regions of the Far East on late nineteenth-century French literature, of the disintegration of rigid bourgeois morality upon the
entire range of Western literature at the turn of the twentieth century, as exemplified especially in Hardy, Ibsen, and Dreiser, and of
psychoanalytical research and speculation on the modern novel,
are instances of how the large and pervasive social forces uncover
new strata of experience. The forces mentioned are of course in
no sense primary or crucial; they are themselves merely links in
the endless interlocking chain of causation and concomitance that
constitutes the process of history; but from whatever source they
proceed, the part they play in broadening, enriching, or impoverish-
ing the field of human experience constitutes their primary significance for literature.

While organizing this experience in language patterns literature
in turn heightens it as well; it selects and points out evocative
values not appearing on the surface. But to do this consistently requires more than a philosophic or deeply human sense of values,
although that is indispensable. It requires also a preoccupation,
much like that of the philosopher or the scientist in his own realm,
with the dramatic and significant in human behavior; a disciplin-
ing of sensitivity and perception; a familiarity with a far-flung body
of traditions; a mastery of a technique. In this sense literature takes
on the apparatus and the conscious scrupulousness of the other arts.
Vergil's desire, after years of constant polishing of the lines of the
Aeneid, to destroy the whole poem at his death because some passages still remained inferior and Flaubert's balancing of *le mot*

juste are merely the more familiar instances of an inherent pressure toward refinement in the literary process.

The result is the differentiation of a specialized literary group from the main stream of the activities of a culture. Such a group tends to become intellectually ingrown and to narrow the field of its exposures. Euphuism and Gongorism, the schools of Donne and of Rimbaud, the barriers within which Joyce or the Sitwells or Gertrude Stein enclose their incommunicable symbols, are end-products of the introversion that is implicit in every stage of the building of a literature. Here as elsewhere in the culture process the inner impulsions of a specialized discipline must be reconciled with the larger demands for growth and freshness.

Literature faces thus continually the need for rebarbarization. In terms of the response to that need many of the excursions into new regions of experience take on meaning. The most persistent of these has been the recurring cult of the folk and the folk mind. The folk itself is rarely drawn into the ambit of literary expression, except indirectly through the frequently sentimentalized mediation of "literary" treatment. But it does find its expression orally in ballads, tales, heroic songs, fables, proverbs, gnomic sayings, and legends. Whatever its origin, this folklore or folk literature grows by repetition and accretion and constitutes at any time the larger proportion of the verbal expression of a culture. In periods before the formation of a literary language, as in Russia's dark centuries before Lomonosov, and among groups cut off by economic subjection, isolation and illiteracy from individualized literary expression, as with the peasant populations of Europe and the American Negroes and hill folk, the folk literature is the only literature.

Because such folk expression appears to rise straight from a deeply rooted experience and because it appears to be the product not of a single great individual talent but of successive generations living highly patterned and custom-incrusted lives, writers and critics have found in it a vigor, an immediacy, and a refreshing sincerity that they have commonly found wanting in the "literary" literature. Since the medievalist movement of the eighteenth century this admiration of the folk mind has played a large part in critical thought and in literary expression. That Goethe and Grimm expressed great admiration for the Yugoslav folk ballads was as characteristic of their day as the contemporary American interest in Negro spirituals. In fact many have found in the folk mind the source not only of the folk literature but ultimately of all literature. In the wake of the romantics nineteenth-century literary theory held that the literature of medieval Europe was not the result of individual creation but was forged in the rich life processes of the medieval folk. This is now radically questioned, and the acceptance of Bédier's researches on the origins of the *chansons de geste* would indicate a tendency, at least in the case of the more sustained literary works attributed to the folk mind, to emphasize the creative role of particular individuals in gathering and fusing into an individualized expression what must undoubtedly have been traditional folk material.

It is not difficult to find in the intellectual stream since the early eighteenth century the currents which have produced the emphasis on the folk mind. The cult of nature which found expression in the Lake poets as well as in Rousseau and the *philosophes;* the differentiation between the simple sincerity of the rural mind as contrasted with the civilization-contaminated life of the cities; the construction of a "noble savage" whose idyllic happiness flows from his obedience to "Nature's Simple Plan"; the discovery by nineteenth-century anthropologists of primitive civilizations, whose tightly knit cultural integrity lay in the dominance of custom and the supposed subordination of the individual to the group, and the idealization of the European peasant by intellectual and literary groups as far removed as Tolstoy and the Russian *narodniki,* Hamsun and the earlier Ibañez—these were not so much the forces behind the folk cult in literature as themselves a related expression of deepest-lying social forces.

A function of rebarbarization similar to that which contact with the folk spirit has performed for the literary mind has been performed also by cults of the heroic, from the Eddas and the Homeric heroes and the Prometheus legend to the Napoleon pattern in European literature and the superman philosophies of Carlyle, Emerson, and Nietzsche. More recently a new primitivism has arisen, largely under the stimulus of anthropological researches into primitive art and sex life and imperialistic contacts with primitive groups, and constituting something of a literary Gauguinism. In another realm of experience many writers, following in the wake of the Freudian researches, have plunged into the jungle of the submerged and repressed sexual impulses; or have, like D. H. Lawrence in *Lady Chatterley's Lover* and James Joyce in *Ulysses,* broken down the taboos that, through moral codes and through the more directly institutionalized forms of censorship, have in the Western Christian civilizations hedged about the exploration by literature of the physical sexual experience.

All these literary allegiances—to the folk mind, to the hero cult, to the primitive mode of life, to preoccupation with sex activity— spring in common from the continually felt need for the rebarbarization of a literature in which the experience represented is continually threatening to grow thin. But they differ from the large movements which brought the experience of the middle class, the proletariat, and women within the range of literary expression; they do not represent on the part of the writers a direct exposure to new areas of experience. They are derivative and vicarious. They have been as much escapes from experience as accessions of it.

Before a developed technique emerges in any literature even the best of individual achievement is but random expression, and whatver progress it has made in charting experience may at any time slip away again. In this sense the accumulated technology of literature—what may be called, in paraphrase of Veblen, the state of the literary arts—becomes part of the social heritage. All literary technique is concerned in some way with the manipulation of words and word patterns. The word, with its sound values and its emotional connotations, is the basic constituent of the technical apparatus, just as experience is the material to which it is applied. Language may thus be regarded as implementing literature, and, as Boileau emphasized, the richness and flexibility of a language will often condition the potentialities for greatness in the literature which is linked to it. The crude stage of the Roman language, as reflecting the undeveloped culture of Rome, at the period when Ennius first attempted to force it into the complicated literary molds of Greece, accounts in no small part for that lack of *ars* with which the more flexible Augustans taxed him. The emergence of literary expression in the vulgar tongues of the Romanic nations had to wait upon the slow process of linguistic evolution in which the competing languages attained at least a rudimentary balance. The advance represented by the Pléiade in France and the Elizabethans in England is incomprehensible without an understanding of the immediately preceding or accompanying climax in linguistic development.

Much of comparative literary criticism has concerned itself with such contrasts of the basic linguistic materials and their effect upon literary expression. But on the whole it is probable that most of what seems thus in the nature of linguistic differences may be referred back to differences in the texture of the culture. For while it is conceivable that words should serve only as quasi-mathematical symbols of communication and that whatever emotional values they ultimately contain should derive from their technical handling and their literary patterning, it is actually true that the words themselves come already laden with pleasure values and with connotations out of the culture. It is upon this substructure of connotation that the literary artist builds his superstructure of emotional values; and he often finds that because the words that he uses are already emotionally tinged they are not bare obedient instruments of his will but living things whose accretions from the culture are hostile to his purposes. Language may thus be as much an obstacle as an aid to literary expression.

The literary technician arranges his language in word patterns, aiming thereby to achieve patterns of sound and thought which are emotionally evocative. Rhyme, rhythm, and assonance belong in the first category; imagery and idea in the second. These technical elements may be combined into further patterns, as in the sonnet, the ballad, the classical oration, or the epic poem. These larger patterns may vary from a more or less rigidly determined mold such as the sonnet, to the larger literary types or genres, such as the drama or the novel.

As technological forms these elements are products of a process of invention and development which must have involved a succession of individual experiments and adaptations, each building on the level previously reached. Brunetière placed a good deal of hope in a natural history of literary forms and styles, but the suggestiveness of his prologomena was never fulfilled by the results of his research. With few exceptions the origins are lost in the mist of history, and the developments upon them proceed by almost imperceptible gradations or, obscured in the creative process, elude all attempts at isolating them. The origins of the early clusters of nature legends, which may be found in very similar forms in Egypt, Babylonia, India, Judea, Greece, and the Celtic and Teutonic tribes, their relation to each other and the method by which they reached their historical distribution are still extremely controversial. With the epic there emerged a highly developed literary form, which winnowed and re-sorted the ballad clusters that had grown up about the myth-legend content. But the processes by which these ballad clusters were forged into the formal epics are only dimly charted, as is also the transition from the dithyramb to the tragedy and from the village satyric choruses to the comedy. With advancing research the origins of the novel and the short story are being continually pushed back to a remoter antiquity.

All literature which is of any value is of course invention; but the fashioning of new literary forms and genres involves a special sort of invention which bears somewhat the same relation to the creative process that invention in the industrial arts bears to the economic arts. But there is a greater inertia in the literary process: there is not the same pressure which capital accumulation and economic competition exert upon technological invention; nor is there the same rate of obsolescence which technical advance forces upon industrialists. But the sharpest difference lies in the fact that every literary form becomes a vested interest. The prestige of the tried pattern tends to deflect the craftsmanship of each writer from the search for new forms to the extraction of all the implications that the existing ones hold. The operative considerations are aesthetic rather than utilitarian, and the continuous need for effecting functional readjustments to a developing, larger situation is not so apparent in literature as in economics. In fact aesthetic and sentimental considerations often induce a reversion to archaic forms.

But while such a functional adjustment is not apparent in the immediate sequence of experimental changes in literature, it would be dangerous to conclude that it was not operative in the larger areas of change. Actually the great importance of the study of the genre in literary history lies in the relation which it bears to the cultural compulsions of the period. These compulsions do not operate unswervingly and equally on individual writers; there is the obvious fact that every period shows so great a divergence of literary expression that there is often a greater affinity between two writers of different periods than between two of the same period. To that extent there is an element of significance in Lytton Strachey's remark that Pindar could have written under the Georges and Keats on the eve of Marathon. And in any period the process of literary experiment consists obviously of numberless innovations varying from tentatives toward a slightly changed form to heroic attempts at transforming an entire genre—each of these experiments responding to complex personal and often erratic motivations.

The effect of the social forces of the period in determining the literary form is not a direct and unilinear one: it is selective. From the array of potential variations certain ones are over a period of time selected for survival. And the criteria of selection lie in the changing experience of the time. Changes in social structure and in ideological currents bring new experience, and this experience refuses to be crowded into the old forms. They are no longer adequate to express it. And the new literary forms that emerge out of the survival and persistence of certain experimental changes and the lapsing of others may be said to be functionally related to the new experience.

For example, the intensification of cleavages between social classes which tends to accompany a period of urbanization may result in the emergence of new forms or the re-emergence of forms long neglected. The social realignments and tensions of seventh- and sixth-century Greece, which shattered the older tribal homogeneity, ushered in on the one hand a new and flexible type of personalized lyrical poetry, represented by Alcaeus, Sappho, and Anacreon, and on the other the naturalistic satiric poems of Archilochus and Simonides of Amorgos. The further growth of the city-states stimulated the development of two new literary forms, the choral odes and the drama, both more adapted to the amusement and edification of the urban collectivities. The growing importance of urban life in the modern period, typified most strikingly in the activities of the Spanish towns, found its reflection in the picaresque novels portraying the urban sharpers who awaited their guileless victims from the country. The popularity of this genre in its French and English forms created a demand among the growing urban middle classes of these countries for a more wholesome use of the prose narrative technique. Thus the rise of the homely novel of sentiment and chastity, which became the hallmark of subsequent bourgeois culture, is best considered against the accompanying economic transformation rather than as a revival of the abstract novel form, which may be traced to the Hellenistic romances, or by the more archaeological-minded to Egyptian prototypes.

So closely is the literary form tied to the culture out of which it has grown that when another culture attempts to take it over there is a tendency toward a transfer of the ideological patterns of the older culture. Vergil, in an age which stood heir to the concepts generated in the long period of intellectual quest and spiritual restlessness that had intervened since Homer, attempted nevertheless to think of his hero and his problems after the patterns and in the atmosphere of the Homeric heroes. The medieval fame of Vergil in its turn deflected Dante's portrayal of the Middle Ages; although drawing upon the ethos of its own age the *Divina Commedia* strikingly reflected, often unconsciously, the pre-Christian world. Tasso was led by his love for older models to stray from the narrow path of sixteenth-century Catholicism, and the Puritan hatred of Satan was curiously transformed in Milton. The unsuccessful attempts of Chapelain, Mesnardière, and the literary intimates of Richelieu to forge an epic worthy of the new dignity of France illustrates how futile may be the transplanting to an uncongenial soil of a form which flourished in the soil of its own culture. The epic machinery, which had been fashioned in anthropomorphic polytheism, collapsed when placed in a Protestant setting, as is indicated by the offense caused to Dr. Johnson's religious sensibilities by Milton's familiarity with God.

If the forms and genres of literature respond to the social compulsions of a period, the responsiveness of theme is even more striking. There are of course permanent human themes that run through the literatures of all cultures, but in each cultural situation the basic theme is clothed in a new form. This may be illustrated by the varied treatment accorded the theme of love. As Marx recognized, the sexual instinct is universal, but the forms of marriage and courtship vary with the underlying economic relationships. While not a few of the variations in the conception of love—at least as they are reflected in literature—seem adventitious, the relationship is generally clear. Infidelity, the recurring tragic theme of the ballad stage of society, becomes the spice of Restoration comedy. The love of the flesh, sublimated by the scholastic poets of the Middle Ages into love of God, remained to haunt the less unified generation of Petrarch and to delight the lusty burghers immortalized by Boccaccio. The mistress worshiped at a distance by the platonic troubadour in the last stages of feudal society was displaced by the insatiable Wife of Bath.

But the outburst in the fourteenth and fifteenth centuries of anti-feudal satires and *fabliaux* which attempted to reveal the true character of woman in all its designing ramifications could not permanently supplant the tendency to sentimentalize the weaker sex. When the descendants of the insurgent burghers of those centuries became in their turn the entrenched middle class of the eighteenth and nineteenth, the genteel tradition of chivalry and sentimental love received a new impetus. It is significant, however, as a reflection of changing class ideals that the sentimental literature of the later period was intensely preoccupied with the institution of marriage and with the economic advantages of a successful marriage. Among certain of the romantic poets there is revealed a tendency to regard the woman as an intellectual equal, and with the growing social and economic emancipation of woman the modern novel is stressing the desirability of sexual as well as intellectual equality.

One of the crucial facts about a writer is his kit of values. This is recognized in criticism, where writers are characterized and classified in terms of their affiliation with one or another of a group of schools or literary philosophies, such as classicist, romanticist, realist, humanist, naturalist. These philosophies determine what they shall select for treatment and from what viewpoint they shall treat it. They represent the handle by which the writer grasps reality. But they are not only instruments in the creative process; they are also embodied in the critical method of an age, serving to canalize the creative stream. They arise in response to social change. A comprehensive change in the social structures may call for a reformulation or reorientation of the prevalent conception of life. This is accomplished in a systematic fashion by the philosophers and through an imaginative and emotional projection by the artists and writers. The connections between the two groups may often be distinctly traced, as in the cases of Euripides and Socrates, Lucretius and Epicurus, Boileau and Descartes, the Schlegels and

Schelling, Zola and Comte. The direction of influence is generally from the philosopher to the writer, but the influence is not necessarily one-sided; in reality both formulations may be followed back to the same source.

Conceivably any *ism* can constitute such a philosophy for an author. Any issue that has been long wrangled over may attain the dignity of a school and then of a movement, and after being fought for tenaciously may end by organizing literary expression. Actually there have tended to be certain relatively stable points of view that have served this purpose. Whether these points of view are permanent aspects of human thought, as has been claimed for classicism and romanticism, is very doubtful. Such a division of the field normally involves a straining and extension of each term, so that it becomes practically meaningless.

But it must be admitted that there are discernible throughout literary history certain poles between which literary expression has oscillated. The power attributed to the gods and the invisible forces guiding human life measures man's estimate of the limitations of his own power. The sense of human power and self-sufficiency shown in the *Iliad* or the Eddas, where the gods are symbols of the superhuman courage of the warrior, has never proved lasting. Homer is followed by Hesiod and the Eleusinian mysteries, *Beowulf* and the *Battle of Maldon* by *Sir Gawayne and the Green Knight*. The anthropomorphic is engulfed by the animistic, by a folklore of magic and witches and monsters. Instances could be multiplied from the ancient and medieval literatures of recurring cycles of humanism and supernaturalism. But even in those literatures the antithesis is oversimplified. And by the time of the Renaissance, in which so many historical traditions and fresh social forces converged and cultural boundaries were broken down, the idea of polarity is no longer useful. In the heightened confusion each writer had to find or fashion for himself an artistic credo to serve as a center of stability. And if this credo narrowed his imaginative scope or distorted his vision of reality, it was only a hazard that has to be run in every imposition of a more or less formal philosophy upon an artistic process.

But every writer has not one but two philosophies—his more or less conscious artistic credo and, lying deeper than that, his often unconscious vision of life and scheme of values. The first is the rhetoric of his writing; the second its logic. Through the first he is assimilated to some "school" within the craft; the second fixes him in the setting of his larger world—his place in the social structure, his economic position, his orientation toward the vital issues of the day, his responsiveness to the contemporary aspirations and realities. In a writer such a social *Weltanschauung* is likely to lie not on or near the surface but out of sight, where it is the more deeply embedded and the more difficult to quarry.

This more basic philosophy involves the relation of literature to the totality of society. But society is in this case too inclusive a term to be useful in analysis. It must be split up into elements which fall, to start with, into two main groups—those relating to social organization and those relating to ideology. In the first group may be placed technology, economic activity, the organization of the state, the structure of classes, social relations of dependence and domination, the important institutions, and the distribution of power; in the second, intellectual temper, emotional tone, ethical and religious conceptions, aesthetic achievements. The Marxist approach subordinates the second group to the first, making of it a superstructure (*Überbau*) which rests on the first as foundation. It is truer to say, if the inquiry is into the forces exerting an active influence on literature, that it is responsive to the whole of society, including not only the social organization but also the ideological structure, of which literature is itself a part. And it is responsive to the whole of society seen not structurally but dynamically, so that at any time it is only the elements that have been projected by change and conflict into the arena of operative forces that need to be considered.

Literature will be thus most responsive to the dynamic of a society in transition. Social change is going on at all times in all social orders: there is no stationary state. But the sense of it and the compulsions it sets in motion vary in intensity just as change itself varies in pace. When the pace becomes sufficiently great so that it no longer represents merely variation within a social system but a sequence looking to its breakdown, the result is a transition society. By its very nature the period of transition has in it elements at once of disintegration and construction. It does not start until something that was a unity begins to break down; it does not end until something new that is a unity has been achieved. Between those termini the sense of wrack or the vision of construction, the stress of conflict, the emergence of order, leave a deep impress on experience.

But it is a fevered impress, lacking the strength and firm dignity that arise out of an integrated culture. Routh points out that the *Iliad* shows the marks of having been written in a society that was a unity, the *Odyssey* for a conquered race in a society that had crumbled before the Dorian invasion. Petrarch wrote in an Italy whose Dantean unity—an ideological unity, not political or economic—was breaking up. Shakespeare wrote when Elizabethan unity was in the forging, with the moving vision of the emergence of a new collectivity—English nationality—before him; the metaphysical poets, descending the arc, wrote in the break-up of the Elizabethan unity. There is in both the Elizabethans and the metaphysicals the feverish tone of a transition literature; in both a preoccupation with death; but while in the Elizabethans death was the great tragedy, it held for the metaphysicals a strange fascination. In the post-war disintegrative period of modern capitalist society, with the strong focusing of its contradictions, has come again an interest in death, represented strikingly by Thomas Mann and Robinson Jeffers; the one looking upon it as the soil out of which art and beauty spring, the other looking upon it as the final breaking through to reality—the only escape from the body of this life.

In the entire complex of forces making up a society the economic organization, and especially the class structure, have quite generally, under Marxian influence, been singled out as determining the form and the idea patterns of literature. Translating this into terms of a changing society it has been the dynamic of the class structure—the class struggle—that has been thus singled out. The assumption that this has always affected literature directly is used only by the less critical thinkers of the school; the more considered position is that it attains its effects as a selective process and generally through the mediation of the ideological elements in society. The impact of society on literature lies in the dynamic convergence of both sets of factors—social organization and ideology—each influencing and influenced by the other. The richest body of material that has yet been uncovered for the study of this complex relationship lies in the history of the periods of economic transition in various cultures from the tribal social organization to the feudal, from the feudal to that of petty trade and industry, and from that to capitalism. In the history of the capitalist social system the significant relationship is that between capitalistic enterprise, individualist thought, and the romantic strain in literature. The present period, which is considered by Marxians to be a transition period representing the disintegration of capitalism, is being widely analyzed from this general point of view.

The processes by which literature has responded to the operative social forces are the ordinary processes associated with the life of institutions. Innovations and tradition, insurgency and the vesting of interests, cultural borrowing and native growth, the carryover of intellectual patterns, the compulsive power of myth—these processes, found throughout the cultural fabric, have also left their mark on literature, adding their purposes and rationale to its own. But literature is also an active instrument: through its evocative power it molds behavior, carries over the propaganda, conscious or unconscious, of its intellectual setting, plays its part in building and breaking social movements, and creates beauty values to invest an old order or sanction a new.

1933

4

The Supreme Court and American Capitalism

1

THE American state has developed two of its institutions to a degree never before attained—the capitalist form of business enterprise and the judicial power. At first sight the combination seems paradoxical, joining in a single pattern an exploitative type of economic behavior with the objectivity of the judicial process. But those who have studied the building of the American state know that the paradox lies only on the surface. It is no historical accident but a matter of cultural logic that a Field should grow where a Morgan does; and a Brandeis is none the less organic a product of capitalist society than is a Debs. If the contrast between the first pair and the second is precipitous, it is none the less contrast and not contradiction. Between our business enterprise and our judicial power there is the unity of an aggressive and cohesive cultural pattern. They seem of the same fiber; have, both of them, the same toughness, richness, extravagant growth; hold out at once portent and promise.

Capitalist business enterprise, while it has reached its most consummate form in the United States, is generic to the whole Western world. But the judicial power—or more exactly, judicial supremacy—is a uniquely American institution: [1] it could arise only in a federal state which attempts, as we do, to drive a wedge of constitutional uniformity through heterogeneous sectional and economic groupings. The core of judicial supremacy is of course the

---

[1] There have perhaps been states in the past more completely under the judicial sway than America. But that the rule of judges through their veto power over legislation is the unique American contribution to the science of government has become a truism of political thought.

power of judicial review of legislative acts and administrative decisions.[2] And the exercise of that power by the United States Supreme Court has made it not only "the world's most powerful court"[3] but the focal point of our bitterest political and constitutional polemics.

At the heart of these polemics is the recognition that the real meaning of the Court is to be found in the political rather than the legal realm, and that its concern is more significantly with power politics than with judicial technology. The Court itself of course, in its official theory of its own function, disclaims any relation to the province of government or the formation of public policy; it pictures itself as going about quietly applying permanent canons of interpretation to the settlement of individual disputes. If there is any truth in this position the Court's quietness must be regarded as that of the quiet spot in the center of a tornado. However serene it may be or may pretend to be in itself, the Court is the focal point of a set of dynamic forces which play havoc with the landmarks of the American state and determine the power configuration of the day. Whatever may be true of the function of private law as restricting itself to the settlement of disputes and the channeling of conduct in society, public law in a constitutional state operates to shift or stabilize the balance of social power.

There has been a tendency in some quarters to regard the power function of the Court as the result of an imperialistic expansion by which the justices have pushed their way to a "place in the sun." We still think in the shadow of Montesquieu and view the political process as an equation in governmental powers. The growth of the Court's power has, by this conception, taken place at the expense of the legislative and executive departments, and the American state has become the slave of a judicial oligarchy.

[2] The literature on judicial review is extensive and polemical. E. S. Corwin, *The Doctrine of Judicial Review* (1914), is still unsurpassed for the history of the doctrine and his article on "Judicial Review" (1932), 8 *Encyclopaedia of the Social Sciences* 457, is at once sane and penetrating. Boudin, *Government by Judiciary* (1932), in the course of a vigorous attack on the institution, presents a valuable although overaccented examination of the sequence of Supreme Court decisions from the viewpoint of the development of the judicial power.

[3] The phrase is that of Felix Frankfurter, "Mr. Justice Brandeis and the Constitution," in Frankfurter, ed., *Mr. Justice Brandeis* (1932), at 125; but the appraisal represented is a general one.

The literature in which this enslavement is traced and expounded is voluminous, polemical, and, even when very able, somewhat dull. It is dull with the dullness of a thin and mechanical *leitmotiv*—the theory of usurpation, of the deliberate annexation by the Court of powers never intended for it. This theory is part of the general philosophy of political equilibrium which, originating with the eighteenth-century *philosophes,* was reinforced by nineteenth-century physics. It holds that the safety of the individual can be assured only by maintaining a balance between the departments of the state. Whatever may have been the validity of such a philosophy in a pre-industrial age, it has become archaic in a period when government is itself dwarfed by the new economic forces. It is as if generals in a besieged city should quarrel over precedence while the enemy was thundering at the gates.

There was, let it be admitted, a period in which the problem of judicial usurpation was a lively issue. Readers of Beveridge's volumes on Marshall [4] are struck by the bitter political tone of the early years of the Court, beginning even with its decision in *Chisholm v. Georgia.*[5] Charge and countercharge, invective and recrimination were staple, and in the din of party conflict it was no wonder that the still small voice of judicial objectivity was often completely drowned. In such an atmosphere usurpation had meaning and utility. The polity was in its formative stage, and there was little about the constitutional structure that was irrevocably settled. The Revolution had hewn out a new world but, as we who have been contemporaries of another Revolution can well understand, the task of giving that world content and precision of outline still remained. In the jockeying for political position and the general scramble for advantage, every argument counted, and much of the political theory of the day can be best understood in terms of this orientation toward the distribution of power. But what counted even more than theory was the *fait accompli.* Every new governmental step was decisive for later power configurations, and might

---

[4] *The Life of John Marshall* (1916–20). This was of course due to some extent to the general bitterness of party polemics in a period of political realities. See also Warren, *The Supreme Court in United States History* (1922), for a vivid depiction of a similar effect. Both Beveridge and Warren drew copiously upon newspaper material.

[5] 2 Dall. 419 (U. S. 1793).

some day be used as precedent. And the battles of the giants, Marshall's battles with Jefferson and Jackson, were the battles of men who knew how to use the *fait accompli.*

The Court has then from the very beginning been part of the power structure of the state, acting as an interested arbiter of disputes between the branches of the government and between the states and the federal government, and with an increasingly magistral air distributing the governmental powers. But to a great extent the significant social struggles of the first half-century of the new state were waged outside the Court. Each period has its characteristic clashes of interests and its characteristic battlegrounds where those clashes occur. In the pre-industrial period the party formations measured with a rough adequacy the vital sectional, economic, and class differences in the country. The party battles of the period had some meaning, and accumulated stresses could find release through changes of party power. The function of the Supreme Court in this scheme lay rather in settling the lines of the polity than in resolving disputes that could not be resolved outside. But when party formations grew increasingly blurred and issues such as slavery and industrialism arose to cut across party lines, an attempt was made, notably in the Dred Scott case, to draw the Supreme Court into the struggle over social policy. The attempt was of course disastrous, for the slavery issue reached too deep to the economic and emotional foundations of the life of the day to be resolved by a counting of heads of more or less partisan judges. It is significant that the most direct effect of the Dred Scott decision was the sudden growth to power of a new political party, which should settle the basic question of public policy in the approved manner at the polls. The subsequent resort to war revealed that there might be some issues so basic that they could not be settled at all within the constitutional framework.

The coming of industrialism cut clear across the orientation and function of the Court as it cut across every other phase of American life. The doctrine of judicial review, whatever may have been its precedents and whatever the legalisms of its growth, had become by the middle of the century an integral part of the American political system. But it was not the dominant political institution, nor had it acquired the compelling incidence upon public policy that it has today. Before that could happen there had to be such a shift in the nature of the state that the characteristic clashes of interest would be taken out of the sphere of democratic control. In short, only through the building of an extra-democratic structure of reality upon the framework of a democratic theory could the judicial power be given a real vitality or the Supreme Court attain its present towering command over the decision of public policy.

That transformation was effected by the maturing of capitalism with its strange combination of individualism as a pattern of belief and the corporation as a pattern of control. Business enterprise furnished the setting within which the Court was to operate, and in this setting the ramifications of the problems that came up for solution effected a complete change in the meaning and function of the judicial power. That power had always, when exercised, had far-reaching effects upon the process of our national life; even when in abeyance it had been a force to be reckoned with. The Court by expounding and applying the written Constitution had always itself been one of the elements that determined the shape and direction of the real constitution—the operative controls of our society. But the real constitution became under capitalism merely the *modus operandi* of business enterprise. Between it on the one hand, and on the other the ideals of the American experiment and the phrases in which the eighteenth century had clothed those ideals, there was an ever-lengthening gulf: it became the function of the Supreme Court to bridge that gulf. Capitalist enterprise in America generated, as capitalism has everywhere generated, forces in government and in the underlying classes hostile to capitalistic expansion and bent upon curbing it: it became the function of the Court to check those forces and to lay down the lines of economic orthodoxy. For the effective performance of its purposes capitalist enterprise requires legal certainty amidst the flux of modern life,[6] legal uniformity amidst the heterogeneous conditions and opinions of a vast sprawling country, the legal vesting of interests amidst the swift changes of a technological society: to furnish it with these

---

[6] It is generally accepted that one of the essential elements of law is certainty, and that it is especially essential for the development of capitalism. It encourages accumulation and investment by certifying the stability of the contractual relations. But it is to be conjectured that a speculative period in capitalist development thrives equally or better on uncertainty in the law. And in periods of economic collapse the crystallized certainty of capitalist law acts as an element of inflexibility in delaying adjustments to new conditions.

was the huge task which the Supreme Court had successfully to perform. The Court had of course other functions, and may be regarded from other angles. But if we seek a single and consistent body of principles which will furnish the rationale of the judicial power in the past half-century, we must find in it the dynamics of American business enterprise.

2

The steady growth in the judicial power and the increasing evidences of its economic affiliations have made the Court one of the great American ogres, part of the demonology of liberal and radical thought.[7] It has served, in fact, as something of a testing-ground for political attitudes of every complexion. The Marxist, making the whole of politics merely an addendum to capitalism, sees the Court as the tool and capitalism as the primary force. The contemporary Jeffersonian, fearful of all centralizing power and zealous for the liberties of the common man, fears Wall Street and the Supreme Court alternately, uncertain as to which is the shadow and which the substance. His cousin the liberal, if he is of a constructive turn, counts on using the machinery of the Court to control in a statesmanlike fashion a developing capitalism which it is futile to turn back; or, if he has lost faith in the efficacy of tinkering with governmental machinery and has become an ethical liberal, he refuses to regard either Big Business or the Supreme Court in itself important, but looks to the quality of the American experience that flows through them both. The technological liberal, who thinks in blueprints and plans for state planning, regards the Court as the great technical obstruction that his plans must meet, and racks his brain for ingenious ways of avoiding the encounter.

The contemporary indictment of the Court, which furnishes the point of departure for all these shades of opinion, is in the large well known. It holds that the Court's decisions can be better explained by economic bias than by judicial objectivity, and that its trend has been to bolster the *status quo*. This indictment is itself

---

[7] In America the liberals have been extremely critical of the power of judicial review. In republican Germany, however, on the question of introducing it, the liberals supported it while the conservative parties opposed it. See C. J. Friedrich, "The Issue of Judicial Review in Germany" (1928), 43 *Political Science Quarterly* 188.

of course far from objective. It is the expression of an attitude. And that attitude can be best studied in relation to its genesis in the Progressive movement, which ran its brief course between the turn of the twentieth century and the American entrance into the war. To that movement may be traced the current "economic interpretation" of the Court, which links its decisions with the growth of capitalism. The Marxists might of course claim this approach as deriving from their own "materialist" conception, diluted or vulgarized in the course of its transmission to our shores. But whatever the degree of logical identity with Marxist materialism, in its actual historical growth the economic interpretation of the Supreme Court is a native product. It was out of the characteristic social conflicts of the Progressive period that the economic approach to the Court emerged, and from the intellectual dilemmas of the period that it received its formulation. In fact, if one still detects in the attitude of liberal critics of the Court an equivocal and confused note, it may be found not wholly alien to the irresoluteness, the divided sense of hostility and acceptance that lay at the heart of the Progressive movement.

The Progressive period was one of great ferment in thought and gallantry in action.[8] A peculiar emotional intensity surrounded the public life. From the western plains the storm of agrarian Populism had already broken, in the form of state Granger legislation, an Interstate Commerce Act, and all manner of heterodox currency proposals. The trust-busting offensive, which had opened with the Sherman Act, and had startled Wall Street in Roosevelt's drive against the Northern Securities combine, was moving on to the scrutiny of the Money Trust in the Pujo investigation. In the cities the muckrakers were canvassing the tie-up between political corruption and the "Interests," and more solidly the labor movement was closing up its phalanxes and pressing for social legislation. Intellectually there was a prevailing *malaise*. The confidence in the national destiny was slipping, as was the faith in the adequacy of the democratic structure. Not since the days of Emerson and John Brown had Americans been forced thus to search their hearts and

---

[8] John Chamberlain, *Farewell to Reform* (1932), gives a brilliant survey of "the rise, life, and decay of the Progressive mind." 3 Parrington, *Main Currents in American Thought* (1930), left incomplete by the author's death, throws out a few suggestive leads, especially in the Introduction and the last chapter. Hacker and Kendrick, *The United States Since 1865* (1932), gives an excellent account of the period.

inquire into the direction of the national drift. The answer of the
activists was the liberal revolt in politics against the increasing
entrenchment of the illiberal forces. To that revolt the political
thinkers made a definite contribution.[9] Probing the principles underlying the American venture, they dug beneath the political
ideals to their economic basis. They emerged with the discovery
that the tie-up with the economic "Interests" applied not only to
current politics but to the very fabric of the state; that the august
Supreme Court and the still more august Constitution [10] which it
expounded and guarded were not, as had been supposed, detached
and self-contained; and that between them and the realities of the
marketplace there was an unlovely traffic.

This discovery was made not, as the muckrakers and the Populists
had discovered Corruption and the Interests, through a journalistic
foray into contemporary reality, but through a vast historical research. The revaluation of American democracy was pushed back
to the Founding Fathers themselves, and with explosive results.[11]
To be sure, the dynamite was already at hand, in the temper and
intellectual equipment of the period. The "vague terror" which
"went over the earth" when "the word socialism began to be
heard" [12] at about this time had to some extent been felt as far
away from German Marxism as were the American centers of academic thought, and the class struggle as well as the materialist
interpretation of history was not unheard of. Veblen in 1904 had
shown in a chapter [13] of his *Theory of Business Enterprise* that the
business influence extended to American law through a carry-over

---

9 For an interesting analysis of this contribution and the intellectual situation which
evoked it, see Parrington, *The Beginnings of Critical Realism in America* (1930),
introductory chapter, xxiii–xxix, and "A Chapter on American Liberalism," at 401–
413. Much of the same ground is covered in Parrington's introduction to J. Allen
Smith, *The Growth and Decadence of Constitutional Government* (1930). "Considered
historically," he says of the Progressive thinkers, "their main contribution was the
discovery of the undemocratic nature of the Federal Constitution."

10 For an account of the hold of Constitution-worship on the American mind,
see Hamilton, "Constitutionalism" (1931), 4 *Encyclopaedia of the Social Sciences* 255.

11 It should be noted that some of the Fathers themselves were attracted by the
idea of economic determination. This is especially true of Madison, whose realistic
awareness of the relation between economic interest and political action was striking.
See Beard, *Economic Basis of Politics* (1922). In fact it may be said that the contact
with Madison's thought became an element which has strengthened the hold of
economic determinism in American thought.

12 Holmes, *Collected Legal Papers* (1920), at 295.

13 Chapter VIII, "Business Principles in Law and Politics."

of the eighteenth-century natural-rights philosophy in the interests of Big Business. Even Turner's theory of a moving frontier, expounded as early as 1893,[14] had suggested how important might be the economic base of political attitudes. But these stray leads of scholarship counted for less than did the felt realities of the day. The air was filled with the clash of group and class economic interests: what easier than to project this clash back to the founding of the Republic?

This was exactly what J. Allen Smith did in 1907 in his *The Spirit of American Government*.[15] It was not a great book, as Veblen's books are great or Turner's essay. There was no titanic outpouring of social analysis in it, no brilliant and clean-cut theory. But it was a courageous book and a dogged one. It hung onto its thesis that the American state had been shaped in its growth by conflicts of interest that were at bottom economic. Smith was followed and buttressed by Charles Beard. In his *Economic Interpretation of the Constitution* (1913)—a title which in itself bore witness that a new Higher Criticism had been born—Beard's search of Treasury records, convention debates, and contemporary journals turned up formidable evidence to the effect that the Constitution was an "economic document" and had been railroaded through by the property interests of the time that stood to gain by it.[16] The reverberations of these books were considerable,[17] but whatever the anathema or discipleship that they stirred up, the venture in historical research had done its work. Through the attack on the Constitution a flank attack had been delivered on the Supreme Court.

But the analysis was now extended further, by a host of scholars

---

[14] "The Significance of the Frontier in American History," reprinted in Turner, *Frontier in American History* (1921). Chamberlain, *op. cit. supra*, note 8, has an interesting analysis of the relation of Turner's thesis to the Progressive movement.

[15] For estimates of the place of this book in the thought of its day, see Parrington's introduction to Smith, *op. cit. supra*, note 9; and Walton Hamilton's review of it (1930), 40 *Yale Law Journal* 152.

[16] Beard analyzed the "personalty interests" as "money, public securities, manufactures, and trade and shipping"—*Economic Interpretation of the Constitution* (1913), at 324. See also chapter V, "The Economic Interests of the Members of the Convention." His last chapter contains a clear and forceful statement of his theses, which have the uncompromising ring of Luther's and were doubtless intended to be nailed up on all the academic doors of the day. See for a similar analysis of the first decade of the new state, Beard, *Economic Origins of Jeffersonian Democracy* (1915), especially chapter VI, "Security-Holding and Politics."

[17] It is perhaps not without significance that this period represented the impressionable intellectual years of the present generation of American constitutional scholars.

and publicists.[18] It was not enough to show that the Constitution which the Court expounded had not the stainless objectivity which was claimed for it; the charge was now made that whatever the origins of the Constitution, the Court was not really expounding it but that the justices were reading their own class interests into it. Granted the validity of the historical thesis of Smith and Beard, this was indeed a logical consequence, for it was not to be supposed that a process operative in the creation of the Constitution should cease to be operative in its interpretation. Bentley's *Process of Government* (1908), which made an impression on the scholars of the day, had shown government not as a formal structure but as a dynamic process twisted and turned in various directions under the pressure of group interests. This theory of pressures Bentley had applied to the judicial process as well, and it fitted in with the prevailing pluralist attack on nineteenth-century Austinianism and the new emphasis given to the reality of economic groupings.[19] The result was a general assumption among the students of the Court that the decisions of the justices could be explained by their economic interests and sympathies—an assumption which rarely went as far as Gustavus Myers did in his uncompromising *History of the Supreme Court* (1912), but was often present as a preconception even where it was not avowed. Most of the discussion in the years immediately preceding the war was concentrated on judicial review. Its incidence and its historical validity were hotly debated, and the issue was even projected into the political campaigns in the form of proposals to strip the Court of its power, or at least determine the conditions under which the power could be exercised.

We can see now that this entire Progressive critique of the connection of the Court with capitalism was itself a phase of capitalist development. It came at the crucial turn in the history of American business when it began to be clear that the system of controls set up by a democratic pre-industrial society was futile under the

[18] Much of the literature about the judicial power appeared in the decade after publication of Smith's book, and the writers (Beard, Goodnow, Corwin, McLaughlin, Hadley, Farrand, Boudin, Davis, Haines, Weyl, Warren, and others) used as their point of departure, on one side or the other, the thesis of economic interest.

[19] The fusion of these two strains—pluralism and the emphasis on economic realities —in the political thought at the beginning of the war is illustrated in Charles Beard's survey of tendencies, "Political Science in the Crucible" (1917), 13 *New Republic*, Nov. 17, part II, 3.

new conditions of life, and it marked the awakening of the middle class to that fact. Little Business felt itself being crowded out by Big Business, and for a brief moment the farmers, the traders, the unions, and the small bourgeoisie huddled together to check its further career. But as Walton Hamilton has put it, "their best wisdom was the product of a social experience that was passing." [20] Their anti-trust legislation, armed to cope with a situation produced by an exhausted individualism, continued to use the technique of that same individualism. When even that technique was burked by the decisions of the Court, and when more positive attempts at social legislation and government control met with a similar fate,[21] the relation between the Court and Big Business took on an unmistakable clarity for the thinkers who expressed the world of Little Business.

Perhaps too great a clarity. The intellectual phase of the Progressive movement suffered from the Populist tendency of the period toward the personal identification of villainy. Myers, fresh from his investigations of the direct personal corruption of the Tammany braves, and of the unscrupulous careers of some of the builders of great American fortunes,[22] carried over the same mechanical approach to the very different sphere of the judicial process,[23] and tried to show how a reactionary majority opinion might rest on the stock-holdings of the justice who had written it, or on his previous associations as a corporation lawyer. Beard too, on his mettle perhaps against academic hostility, tried to prove more than he had to; and while his investigations into the direct "personalty interests" of the framers of the Constitution are a *tour de force* of historical research, the very concreteness of his approach did much to pave the way for a too mechanical economic interpretation of the Court. The search has been throughout for light on direct pressures and the personal motives of the judges.

---

[20] "The Control of Big Business" (1932), 134 *Nation* 591, 592.
[21] The stripping of the Sherman Act of much of its significance, the crippling of the Federal Trade Commission, and the attempts to qualify the powers of the Interstate Commerce Commission are important chapters in American administrative history. See Sharfman, *The Interstate Commerce Commission* (1931); Henderson, *The Federal Trade Commission* (1924); Myron Watkins, "The Federal Trade Commission" (1932), 32 *Columbia Law Review* 272; Keezer and May, *The Public Control of Business* (1930); *The Federal Anti-Trust Laws, a Symposium* (1932).
[22] *History of Tammany Hall* (1901); *History of the Great American Fortunes* (1910).
[23] *History of the Supreme Court of the United States* (1912).

Even those who are averse to the economic interpretation tend to resolve the whole problem of the judicial process into a matter of personal judicial whim. How unfruitful both these approaches are—the mechanical economic interpretation and the atomistic personal interpretation—I hope to show in the last section of this paper. But before that it will be necessary to inquire to what extent a developing American capitalism did represent an impinging force upon the Court, and how the Court—as a whole and through its various ideological groups—reacted to that impact.

3

In itself capitalism is merely the name we give to a system of free individualist enterprise which allows and fortifies the accumulation of wealth.[24] It is thus in essence a scheme of economic organization going back to the beginning of modern times and resting upon legal institutions, the most important of which are private property and contract. Within these limits capitalism has more recently developed on the one hand a set of technological methods and on the other a set of working rules [25] which we call respectively industrialism and business. Both these lines of growth have wrought vast changes in the character of capitalist society. Industrialism in production has brought the factory, the machine process, the large city, and the working class, and has given our world the characteristic outer stamp that it bears. Business enterprise has brought the corporation, the credit structure, the investment banker, and the marketing mechanism, and has given our world its inner living spirit.[26] In both realms the working rules have changed so rapidly and with such fateful

---

24 In addition to Marx's classic analysis of capitalism, see Hobson, *The Evolution of Modern Capitalism* (1926 ed.); and the writings of Thorstein Veblen, especially *The Theory of Business Enterprise* (1923), and *Absentee Ownership* (1923). The point of departure for Veblen's work is the form that capitalism has taken in America. The emphasis of the present article is therefore rather on the Veblenian analysis than on the Marxist.

25 I take the phrase "working rules" from the suggestive analysis in Commons, *Legal Foundations of Capitalism* (1924).

26 It is in this contrast between the matter-of-factness of industrialism and the sophisticated and devious business structure imposed upon it that Veblen finds the central contradiction of capitalism. See his *Theory of Business Enterprise* (1923), *The Instinct of Workmanship* (1914), *Absentee Ownership* (1923).

consequence as to merit the designation of "revolution." [27] But these revolutions, however drastic, have not shattered the outlines of the capitalist system. They have merely realized its inherent trends and possibilities.

It is obvious that the large movements of modern law can be understood best in relation to this development of a capitalist society. The ways of life and the property attitudes of this society while it was still rural and bourgeois have written themselves into the Anglo-American common law. They have written themselves also into American constitutional law, as embodied first in the written document drawn up by a group of "men of substance" acting as spokesmen for the more or less property-conscious American society of the late eighteenth century, and as interpreted by a property-conscious Supreme Court. In all societies the historical function of law has been to elaborate, rationalize, and protect the dominant institutions and the accredited ways of life, and the function of public law has been to apply ultimately the coercion of the state toward maintaining the outlines of those dominant institutions.[28] American constitutional law, whatever may be its unique modes of operation and principles of growth, is not exempt from this function.

But here as everywhere the large historical generalization conceals great dangers. To say that American constitutional law rationalizes and gives sanction to American capitalist society is of little value unless the relation between the two is traced historically and with an eye to the evolving character of each. As with all words that have grown to be symbols and are moved about as counters in argument, capitalism has taken on for us a singleness of meaning that beclouds more issues than it illumines. Actually of course it is not only an exceedingly complex institution, reaching out into many domains of

---

[27] The revolution in technology has been called the Industrial Revolution; the more recent technological developments have been called by Meakin the "Second Industrial Revolution"; Berle and Means, *The Modern Corporation and Private Property* (1932), speak aptly of the drastic changes in the scale and methods of business as the "corporate revolution."

[28] Maitland's remark, that "our whole constitutional law seems at times to be but an appendix to the law of real property" (*The Constitutional History of England* [1908], at 538), was probably intended mainly to express his sense of the erratic logic of development in history. But it is significant also in showing how the line of development in public law is the legal elaboration and protection of the dominant institutions—in this case property.

what men do and how they think, but it is also a rapidly shifting one. Its tremendous importance for the Supreme Court flows from this fact of its change. For to a static capitalism, however baleful or beneficent, the Court and the nation could eventually work out a harmonious adjustment, balancing somehow the demands of constitutional rules with the interests of constituent groups. But a changing capitalism is continually undoing what is done even before it has been entirely done. Being a growing thing it creates conflicts of interest, problems of control, disorders in the "economic order" while the ink is scarce dry on the statute or decision which attempted to heal the ravages of some previous change. Its superior mobility over previous systems of economic organization, such as the feudal or slave systems, derives from the fact that it rests on a rapidly moving technological base and appeals to the free and even reckless flow of individual energy. We have as a consequence the characteristic transitionalism of modern Western society and that instability of institutional arrangements which gives it its vitality. And in the United States the pace of capitalist development has been extraordinarily rapid, abbreviating the earlier stages upon which the European societies lingered for centuries, and setting the pace for the entire world in the latest stages.

The history of American capitalist development falls roughly into four periods. With due awareness of the danger of schematism, and with an eye especially to their impact upon the problem of legal control, the periods may be described as (1) pre-industrial capitalism, (2) industrial capitalism, (3) monopoly capitalism, and (4) finance capitalism.[29] Pre-industrial capitalism is a catch-all for the various

[29] Periodization in modern economic history has varied of course with the point of view adopted (see, for example, works by the Hammonds, Clapham, Weber, Gras, Cunningham). Since capitalism is a Marxist concept, periodization from the point of view of capitalist development has been attempted by the Marxist writers or those deriving from them, and has been tied up intimately with the general development of Marxist theory. Werner Sombart's division of capitalism into *Frühkapitalismus, Hochkapitalismus,* and *Spätkapitalismus* is well known. Marx's own division was between pre-industrial capitalism, industrial capitalism, and monopoly capitalism. John A. Hobson, *The Evolution of Modern Capitalism* (1894), follows similar lines. Largely as a result of Hobson's analysis of imperialism in his book of that name, and also as a result of Hilferding, *Finanzkapital* (1910), and the logic of events at the outbreak of the war, the Marxists, especially Lenin, *Imperialism,* added another stage which they called variously and by its respective aspects "imperialistic capitalism" and "finance capitalism." In American economic history there has been little attempt to lay out a broad analysis of stages, other than that involved in the concept of industrialism. See for representative classifications, Faulkner, *American Economic*

phases of development lying in European history between the commercial revolution and the early decades of the nineteenth century; in America, between colonization and the first railroad network in the eighteen forties. It was an economy still basically agricultural, with a growing superstructure of trade and small manufacture. In America as in Europe the juristic importance of this period lies in its having laid the foundations for the capitalist state, hewn out the institution of property, and fashioned the master ideas, such as individualism and natural rights, which were to exercise so tenacious a hold upon the modern mind.

What the pre-industrial period seems so neatly to have settled, industrial capitalism proceeded to unsettle. In America we may block out the four decades from the eighteen forties to the eighties as marking the rise of an industrial society. The machine process, large-scale industry, a far-flung system of transportation and communication, and an urban way of life represented the principal lines of development. The growth of monopoly and of a financial structure was not at all absent in this period, but it was accompaniment rather than main theme; its possibilities, scarcely dreamed of, awaited later phases of capitalism. The sectional distribution of industrial development was uneven: until the Civil War it was so completely identified with the northern states to the exclusion of the southern that an only mildly heterodox theory of the Civil War attributes it to this antinomy rather than to a struggle over human rights.[30] Large stretches of the West also have remained agrarian to this day. The main drift however toward the creation of an industrial state meant a vast displacement of pre-industrial institutions. The actual meaning and social incidence of property were radically shifted. The gap between the propertied and the propertiless was widened and given significance, and the general lines of economic distribution and social stratification were drawn with the emergence of a capitalist entrepreneur class, a middle-class trading and professional class, and a class of workers of varying degrees of skill.

History (1924), and Kirkland, *History of American Economic Life* (1932). Commons, *History of Labor* (1926), divides American developments into the custom-order period, the merchant-capitalist or job-capitalist period, the middleman period, and the corporation period; his point of view is that of the dependence of the laborer upon shifting entities with the extension of markets and of bargaining power over wider areas.

[30] 2 Charles and Mary Beard, *The Rise of American Civilization* (1927), chapter XVIII, "The Second American Revolution."

Where the pre-industrial period had laid the property foundations of capitalist society, the industrial period laid its class foundations. But perhaps the outstanding achievement of the period was
its fulfillment of the philosophy of individual initiative and competition as the organizing principles of economic society. The idea
of a triumphant capitalism—the strongest force in American history
—received here its decisive impetus. Despite the intensifying of class
lines, this capitalist myth—and "myth" is used here neutrally to
mean any evocative idea that patterns men's lives—stirred the energies of rich and poor and created a united front in the interests of
capitalism.[31] There was as yet relatively little hostility manifested
toward the propertied class by the propertiless: there could scarcely
be hostility toward what every man hoped some day to attain.[32] The
whole of American society was turned into an open state in which
capitalist enterprise was given free movement and bidden Godspeed.

The period of monopoly capitalism, from the eighties to the
decade before the World War, offers to the historian a striking dual
visage. It was marked by a rapid concentration of economic power,
but also by a disenchantment with capitalism.[33] The period witnessed not only the heightening of the movement for industrial consolidation, but also the building of a credit and banking structure,
a technique of salesmanship and a set of business *mores* that all attested to the continuing vitality of capitalism.[34] But the united front
was gone. In its place was the "independent" entrepreneur confronting the invincible aggression of the trusts. The competitive
ideal, however neat had been the conception of it as the dominant
control in the economic mechanism, had failed practically in organizing economic life. The open state was found to be a dangerous
program, and some of the legislatures now began to throw up bar-

[31] The concept of the "myth" as used here derives from Sorel, *Reflections on
Violence* (1912). Sorel applied it primarily to the myth of revolution, but he also
showed how it can be used of other master-ideas in the history of civilization.

[32] See Hadley, *Undercurrents in American Politics* (1915), lecture II, "The Constitutional Position of the Property Owner." The common man, says Hadley, "was
not ready to declare war against an industrial society that offered him so many in-
ducements to become one of its members."

[33] For an analysis of this disenchantment, written just before the war by one of the
Progressives, and couched in political rather than economic terms, see Walter Weyl,
The New Democracy (1912), chapter I.

[34] For the classic statement of the outlines of the American business structure at
the end of this period, see Veblen, *Absentee Ownership and Business Enterprise: the
Case of America* (1923).

ricades against its further extension. Agrarianism, Populism, trust-busting, muckraking, and progressivism grew to alarming strength. They represented, as we have seen, an inner cleavage in the forces that formerly had fought side by side in the advance of capitalism.

The final period—that of finance capitalism, covering the last quarter-century—was marked by a shift of axis in the economic world from industrial organization to financial control. The growth of the giant corporation found its significance not so much in the matter of magnitude as in the separation that it effected between the ownership and the management of industrial enterprise, and the opportunity it gave for the subtleties of corporation finance. Investment banking became the central activity of the higher reaches of economic behavior, and such investment houses as that of Morgan the symbol of economic power. The attempt to check the monopolistic trend came to seem increasingly hopeless, and attention was transferred to the dangers of financial concentration and banking control of industry.[35] The capitalist myth, so far from receding, received an accession of strength from two decades of mounting prosperity, but its type-figure was now cast not in the image of the entrepreneur but in that of the speculator or the financial promoter. The *bloc* that had been formed in the previous period to stem the growth of the large corporation and the money power found that their task had become archaic, and that the principal concern of the community lay in a fair distribution of profits and risks *within* the corporate and pecuniary structure. The failure of the old controls seemed established by the crisis of 1929, and the search for new controls began along the line of economic planning by the government or some form of autonomous rationalization within the business structure.

These successive shifts of focus in American economic reality have done much to determine the large sweep of American constitutional law. They have done so in a threefold way: by setting the characteristic problems that have appeared for decision before the Supreme Court, by creating the conflicts and the clashes of interests which have given those problems importance for the community, and by fashioning the ideologies which have to a large degree influenced the decisions. Put in another way the impact of American capitalistic

---

[35] Brandeis, *Other People's Money* (1914), especially chapter IX, "The Failure of Banker-Management."

development on the Court has been at once to pose the problems and to condition the answers.

The increasing push and thrust of economic problems upon the business of the Supreme Court has been noted by Professors Frankfurter and Landis.[36] Within this larger trend it is interesting to analyze by what dynamics of the economic process the varied range of problems is brought into the area of decision. The ordinary groupings around legal subject matter, or the groupings around clauses in the Constitution or around devices in the Court procedure, are not entirely revealing. To know that a case is an injunction case, or that it came under a writ of certiorari, or that it appealed to the due process clause of the Fourteenth Amendment, conveys little of the context of emotion and belief that might give it meaning. The groupings might more realistically be built around those clashes of interests within the economic system or clashes of attitude about it out of which the cases proceed.

These clashes of interest are as varied of course as the economic life that they mirror. They are at once evidences of maladjustment and challenges to control. Some are concerned with the organizational aspects of capitalism, others with the incidence of its functioning, still others with the distribution of its flow of income. Thus one may find clashes of interest between workers and employers over wages or hours or working conditions or plans for social insurance; between groups of businessmen over trade practices (in the sphere of business *mores*) or the maintenance of competition (in the sphere of economic ideology); between consumers and public-utility groups over rates and services; between consumers and other business groups over prices and standards; between ownership and control groups within the corporate structure over the division of profits; between agricultural and industrial groups, Big Business and Little Business groups, groups being taxed and the government as taxer; between all sorts of groups who would stand to gain from a particular government policy, such as a grant of direct relief or an issue of legal-tender paper, and those who would stand to lose; between the interests of autonomous business control and those of state-enforced competitive enterprise; between the interests of in-

---

[36] *The Business of the Supreme Court* (1927), chapter VIII.

dividual enterprise and those of collective control; between those who have a property interest in the *status quo* and those who have a humanistic interest in changing it.

In short, capitalism pushes ultimately before the Court the clashes of interest that are attendant on the growth of any economic system, with the displacement in each successive phase of elements that had been useful in previous phases, with the antagonisms it generates among those who are bearing its burdens and the rivalry among those who are dividing its spoils, and with the inherent contradictions that it may possess. If it be added to this that modern capitalism is perhaps the least organic system of economic organization the world has seen—"often, though not always, a mere congeries of possessors and pursuers," J. M. Keynes has called it [37]—and that the American social and political structure within which it operates is perhaps more sprawling and heterogeneous than that of any other major capitalist society, some notion may be had of the confusion of interests and purposes out of which it is the task of the Court to bring certainty and uniformity.

The dimensions of the task must, however, be qualified in several respects. Not every case that comes before the Court involves grave conflicts of interest or broad issues of public policy; it is only the exceptional cases that do. Moreover, the pressures and interests summarily analyzed above apply to the entire governmental process in a capitalist state, and not merely to the Court. In fact, the Court does not fight on the front lines but must be considered a reserve force. The brunt of the attack and the task of reconciling the conflicts is met by the legislatures and the administrative agencies, which are more amenable to democratic control than is a small tribunal holding office for life. It is only what survives the legislative barriers and also the jurisdictional exclusions of the Court, that comes finally to pose its issues. And even of this group not every case involving an important conflict of interests will exact from the Court that intense absorption with its social values and implications which creates the nexus binding the judicial process to the economic system. Many a case which, if it had come later or earlier in the country's development, might have been decided differently or constituted a leading

---

[37] Quoted in Tawney, *Religion and the Rise of Capitalism* (1926), at 286.

case fails at the time to call into play the entire concentration of the Court's social philosophy.[38] For at any period neither the Court nor the country can focus its energies on more than a few dominant issues. It is the area that includes these issues—let us call it the "area of vital conflict"—that determines the path of growth in the judicial process and fashions the outlines of constitutional law.

4

When we turn to the sequence of decision in the history of the Supreme Court, do we find in it any of the movement and stir that have marked the growth of American capitalism? To most the question would seem to call for a definite answer in the negative. There is a tendency, whenever economics and the judicial process are brought into relation, to regard the first as the active and the second as the passive element, the first as marking the line of growth and the second as adjusting itself—or rather, failing to adjust itself—to that growth.[39] There is so much in legal history which seems to confirm this view that our great danger lies in being tempted to regard it as true. The sociologists have built a theory of the "legal lag" on the assumption of its validity,[40] and much of the "liberal" criticism of the Court's decisions attributes to that tribunal a distressing medley of imperviousness and ferocity toward economic reality. The conception is often extended to include the backwardness and inertia of the whole of legal science.

In reality this view embodies only a half-truth, and at present the more dangerous half. We may guess that it had its origin and per-

---

[38] It has been noted that the Court in its present composition is likely to be liberal with regard to cases affecting personal liberties, but conservative with regard to the protection of property rights: see Shulman, "The Supreme Court's Attitude toward Liberty of Contract and Freedom of Speech" (1931), 41 *Yale Law Journal* 262. An explanation for this might be sought in the fact that issues of personal liberty are not at present as squarely in the area of vital conflict as are property issues. In time of war or of war hysteria we should expect that inconsistency to be ironed out.

[39] For a clear statement of this theme, see Henderson, *The Position of the Foreign Corporation in American Constitutional Law* (1918), at 3–9, where he speaks of economic change as the "dynamic element" in constitutional development, and formal doctrine as the "state element."

[40] The entire conception of the legal lag—which owes much to Dicey, *Lectures on the Relation between Law and Public Opinion in England during the Nineteenth Century* (1905), to Ogburn, *Social Change* (1923), and to American sociological jurisprudence—needs to be re-examined more thoroughly than the limits of this paper will allow.

haps found its validity in the attempt to bolster the fighting reformist faith of the Progressive movement by building a somewhat ramshackle sociology for legal thought. It dates from the period when a sociological jurisprudence had considerable intellectual appeal, and it seemed to receive confirmation whenever the Court definitely placed obstacles in the path of social legislation. But it tends to obscure the important fact that law is as much a growth as is economics. The principle of growth of a legal doctrine is undoubtedly not that of an economic technique. It is likely to be more tortuous and elusive, and to attain its results rather by indirection than by a steady processional sequence. But legal doctrines do have their life histories.[41] The very fictions they embody are, by the fact of being fictions, vehicles of change. Instead of positing an antithesis between a dynamic economic activity and a static law, it is truer to see the growth of each interwoven with the other and conditioning the other. Just as the meaning of American constitutional law emerges best from the dynamics of American capitalism, so the meaning of capitalism is most securely found in the developing legal institutions of property, liberty, and contract, and their aggrandizement through the doctrine of due process.

The course of Supreme Court decision when viewed thus falls, like the course of capitalist development itself, into fairly well-defined periods. It will be well in blocking them out to abstain from ethical designations, such as "liberal," "conservative," and "reactionary," which are confusing because of the continual shift of criteria as new forces and alignments come into play.

The line of judicial growth in the first half-century of the Court lay in a pronounced nationalism as expressed in the subordination of the state legislatures and the protection of vested property rights.[42] Of these the limitation of state power was probably more in the forefront of Federalist consciousness than the protection of property, although the two motives were often fused. But it was more than an article of Federalist faith; it was already a constitutional

---

[41] For a general theory of the life history of legal doctrines, see Walton Hamilton's article on the "Judicial Process" (1932), 8 *Encyclopaedia of the Social Sciences* 450. See also by the same author, "The Ancient Maxim Caveat Emptor" (1931), 40 *Yale Law Journal* 1133; and "Affectation with Public Interest" (1930), 39 *Yale Law Journal* 1089.

[42] C. G. Haines, *Revival of Natural Law Concepts* (1930), chapter IV, is especially full on the growth of judicial doctrine in this early period.

tradition holding over from the ideology and temper of the Constitutional Convention. There was a prevailing distrust of anything that the states might do in a new society, a distrust which was part of that fear of the people that pursued Federalist thought throughout. State legislatures were deemed dangerous because they had yielded basely to the pressures of the multitude, cutting debts, issuing paper money, canceling obligations. To prevent such irresponsibility a line of cases, of which *Fletcher v. Peck* [43] and *Dartmouth College Trustees v. Woodward* [44] were the most notable, interpreted the "obligations of contract" clause of the Constitution in a way that has made it of far-reaching economic importance. The Court evidenced thus at the very beginning a concern for property that was to grow in intensity, and incorporated it in a doctrine of vested rights which Professor Corwin has noted as one of its first doctrinal creations. [45]

Of course, it is quite easy to read our own property conflicts into the phrases of the day, and make an identification where there is room only for a comparison. Private property was not on the defensive in the America of Marshall as it was to be in the successive Americas of Field, Peckham, Pitney, and Sutherland. It was part of the rising society and connected with the future of the new state, and the judicial support of it was an expression of the prevailing ideology. It is noteworthy that on the issue of the desirability of social protection of property rights—as distinct from the issue of whether the task was a fit one for the judiciary to perform, and the issue of states' rights that was involved—there was little disagreement between the Federalist and Democratic administrations before Jackson. Even the early "populist" outbreaks, such as Shays's Rebellion, were not organic revolts against the ominous features of an economic system as was the Populist movement a century later, but were part of the revolutionary unsettlement and the post-war economic impoverishment. And the Jacksonian revolution, with its extension of the suffrage and its frontier democracy, did not materially change the constitutional position of property. On the frontier, as

---

43 6 Cranch 87 (U. S. 1810).

44 4 Wheat. 518 (U. S. 1819).

45 E. S. Corwin, "The Basic Doctrine of American Constitutional Law" (1914), 12 *Michigan Law Review* 247, 275. See for a good general treatment of this period, with an eye to its economic development as well, C. G. Haines, *op. cit. supra*, note 42, especially chapter IV.

President Hadley has pointed out, property rights had greater sanction and more immediate protection than human rights.[46] One of the striking mélanges of the period, incidentally, is to be found in the manner in which Federalist jurists conscripted the Jeffersonian ideology of natural law in the service of a doctrine of vested rights which restricted the powers of Jeffersonian state legislatures at the same time that it protected property dear to both parties. That Marshall's motivation throughout was national unity in the interests of the smooth functioning of the increasing commercial activity of the country [47] is shown further in his decision in *McCulloch v. Maryland*,[48] in which congressional control of monetary affairs was upheld, and the decisions interpreting the commerce clause,[49] especially *Gibbons v. Ogden* [50] and *Brown v. Maryland*.[51]

The period of judicial nationalism had coincided roughly with the pre-industrial period and expressed its ways of thought and life tolerably well. The second period of the Court's history, extending from the eighteen thirties to the Civil War, reflected to a degree the coming of industrial capitalism. It was in its juristic ideas a definitely transitional period, marked by no consistent drive except a disinclination to place obstacles in the way of the forging of an industrial society. The relatively tolerant attitude of the Court toward state legislation in the first two decades of Jacksonian democracy (1830–1850) was followed in the next decade by a reaction against the reck-

---

[46] "The small protection given to the rights of man, as compared with that which was accorded to the rights of property, is a salient feature in the history of the early American state—and continues in its later history as well"—Hadley, *op. cit. supra*, note 32. He speaks in the same place of the "democratic concern for the interests of the property owner and the democratic unconcern for the interests of humanity."

[47] Boudin, *op. cit. supra*, note 2, chapter XII, "John Marshall and the Rise of Nationalism," speaks of Marshall as being one of the real leaders of the "Young America" movement, and therefore more closely identified with Madison and Clay than with the elder statesmen of the Federalist Party. Mr. Boudin also contends that there is an ideological break in Marshall's career between his earlier and his later opinions, conditioned by this new development. Although Mr. Boudin intends it to show that Marshall was important despite *Marbury v. Madison,* and that he was not the founder of the modern doctrine of judicial review, the chief importance of this lead for the present discussion lies in its fortifying the view that Marshall, like Clay, Webster, and the rest of the nationalist group, was interested in clearing the field for the extension of commerce and industry.

[48] 4 Wheat. 316 (U. S. 1819).

[49] Frankfurter and Freund, "Interstate Commerce" (1932), 8 *Encyclopaedia of the Social Sciences* 220, trace incisively the course of interpretation of the commerce clause in American constitutional law in relation to our economic development.

[50] 22 U. S. 1 (1824).

[51] 25 U. S. 419 (1827).

less land and currency activities of the western legislatures. The idea of implied constitutional limitations on the state power was used as a convenient doctrine; but though it followed logically from the sanction that natural law gave to vested rights, and although there was vigorous agitation for it by Story and Kent and later by Cooley, the Court in this period gave only a hesitating allegiance to it.[52] Its attitude was on the whole pragmatic. Industrialism, with its introduction of a system of transportation and a marketing area that cut across state boundaries and shattered the validity of the state-nation concept as a dichotomy, was bringing problems that could not be solved by a single formula. In the interpretation of the commerce clause a series of decisions which, despite the prevalent confusion of purpose, had since *Gibbon v. Ogden* clung to a pragmatic insistence on defining state power in regulating interstate commerce by examining its consequences, was summed up in *Cooley v. Board of Wardens*,[53] which in effect opened the way for sustaining state regulation where that would facilitate the progress of industrialism. The slavery issue was the great jarring note of emotional absolutism. It was an unavowed participant in many of the opinions, and by polarizing the emotions of the country it introduced into the decisions of the Court a more marked political bias. But the Dred Scott decision may itself be interpreted in terms of the "sweep of economic forces." [54] It marked a crucial recognition by a landowning capitalism that the industrial capitalism that was rising in the northern states was more than a principle of economic organization but reached to the fabric of the state, and would have to be combated with the weapons of constitutional law.

The period of constitutional interpretation that extended from the end of the Civil War to the middle of the eighties presents as interesting and challenging a sequence of decision as any in the Court's history. Since it measures the transition from a competitive industrialism to a monopolistic capitalism, it contains the genesis of many of the problems of regulation that dominate the subsequent history of the Court. Coming also immediately after the Civil War, it marks

---

[52] Haines, *op. cit. supra*, note 42, at chapter IV.
[53] 53 U. S. 299 (1851).
[54] The phrase is from Charles and Mary Beard, *op. cit. supra*, note 30. Chapter XVII contains a good account of the economic and emotional setting of the Dred Scott decision.

the convergence of a set of attitudes relating to business enterprise
with a set of attitudes relating to Reconstruction—to the confusion
of both. Thus in the early part of the period, while the Reconstruction issue was still fresh, the economic influences which would
otherwise have helped shape the course of judicial decision are
qualified and confused; and in the latter part, when the economic
ideologies reassert themselves, a constitutional amendment intended
primarily as a guide for the problem of reconstruction is increasingly
pressed into service to bolster a theory of economic statesmanship.
Not only do the cases smell of powder but often of the powder of
two different battles.

The Fourteenth Amendment, which has laid its hand so heavily
upon American constitutional law, seems to have come into being
with less attendant innocence than had until recently been believed.
Professor Kendrick's edition of the journal of the committee [55]
which prepared the amendment indicates that the notion of using a
Negro rights amendment to restrict state-legislative raids upon business interests was not wholly absent from the minds of the members.
It did not receive definite expression before the Court, however,
until Roscoe Conkling's argument in the San Mateo case.[56] But even
clearer was the intent on the part of the radical Republicans to use
the amendment as an entering wedge to effect a complete constitutional subordination of the states to the nation, not so much in the
interests of property as in the interests of northern control.[57] The
first test of the amendment in the Slaughterhouse case [58] was therefore not a clear-cut decision on the economic issue of regulation that
was involved but was oriented toward the political issue, which was
more directly in the area of vital conflict of the day. But the most
important parts of the decision are the brief of ex-Justice Campbell
and Justice Field's dissenting opinion that was based on it. Campbell's line of reasoning, by which the due process clause could be
interpreted to support property rights against legislative restriction,
was subsequently hammered away at the Court in a series of power-

---

[55] B. B. Kendrick, *The Journal of the Joint Committee of Fifteen on Reconstruction,*
39th Congress, 1865–1867 (1914).
[56] *County of San Mateo v. Southern Pacific Ry. Co.,* 116 U. S. 138 (1885). For a discussion of this case, see Kendrick, *op. cit. supra,* note 55, at 28–36.
[57] Kendrick, *id.,* at chapters VII, VIII.
[58] Slaughterhouse cases, 16 Wall, 36 (U. S. 1872).

ful dissenting opinions by Field [59] and his supporters until their triumph in *Allgeyer v. Louisiana*.[60] Whatever the orientation of the majority in the case, the Field orientation was economic. It is as if he had a prevision of the future needs of capitalist enterprise and how those needs would be supplied. The second and more crucial test of the Fourteenth Amendment, in *Munn v. Illinois*,[61] was, because of its setting in the Granger revolt [62] rather than the Reconstruction issue, fought on new ground. The impact of the monopolistic trends upon the farmers, whose position in a capitalist society is at best anachronistic, had led to the passage of regulatory state legislation. The reaction of the business community to the Waite opinion, with its attitude of judicial toleration of the state acts, and Justice Field's dissent as the expression of that reaction, marked the beginning of a *grande peur* which seized the property interests and scarcely abated for several decades until they had arrived within the secure confines of *Allgeyer v. Louisiana* and *Lochner v. New York*.[63] It was scarcely a coincidence that this epidemic of fear coincided with the publication of Cooley's *Constitutional Limitations*.[64] But the most significant phase of the campaign for a new conception of due process lay in the steady insistence of the counsel for the corporations that the justices owed a duty to the society they lived in to conserve its most sacred institution even in the face of the strict constitutional logic of the situation.[65] This was

---

[59] Walter Nelles's review of Swisher, *Stephen J. Field* (1930), in (1931), 40 *Yale Law Journal* 998, is a remarkable analysis of the relation between Field's opinions and the forces active in the developing society in which he lived. An adequate treatment of the relation between the Supreme Court and American capitalism must wait upon the publication of other such analytic studies of the other Supreme Court justices.

[60] 165 U. S. 578 (1897).

[61] 94 U. S. 113 (1876); also the Granger cases, 94 U. S. 155 (1876).

[62] See Solon J. Buck, *The Granger Movement* (1913), and *The Agrarian Crusade* (1920); also Hacker and Kendrick, *op. cit. supra*, note 8, part I.

[63] 198 U. S. 45 (1905).

[64] Haines, *op. cit. supra*, note 42, at 122; see also William Seagle, "Thomas M. Cooley" (1931), 4 *Encyclopaedia of the Social Sciences* 356.

[65] A rather remarkable example is contained in Choate's argument in *Pollock v. Farmers' Loan and Trust Co.*, 157 U. S. 429, 532, 534, 553 (1895): "I believe that there are rights of property here to be protected; that we have a right to come to this Court and ask for this protection, and that this Court has a right, without asking leave of the Attorney General or of any counsel, to hear our plea. The act of Congress we are impugning before you is communistic in its purposes and tendencies, and is defended here upon principles as communistic, socialistic—what shall I call them?—populistic as ever have been addressed to any political assembly in the world. . . . I have thought that one of the fundamental objects of all civilized government was the preservation of the rights of private property. I have thought that it

the first important manifestation of the social animus of the new corporation lawyers and of the effects of their association with the ideology of business.

This period in the Court's history from the Civil War to the first victory of the Field cohorts in the mid-eighties was thus one of the fateful periods in our national life. It marked a parting of the ways between a policy of judicial tolerance and one of the further extension of judicial review. The Court stood poised between the agrarian revolt, which had been stirred by the growth of monopoly capitalism, and the business interests, whose new militancy concealed their uneasiness. We know of course which policy eventually prevailed and what a difference that has made in our national life. It is relatively easy from the vantage-ground of the present to say that a real choice never existed, and that the development of monopoly capitalism made the outcome for the Supreme Court an inevitable one. But inevitability is a summary word that solves too many difficulties. Capitalist development certainly weighted the scales. It set the wider limits outside of which no choice was possible. But within those limits the country had a chance at a choice—and took it.

The doctrine which came to the fore in the mid-eighties and dominated the Court for a quarter-century was on the economic side a militant expression of *laissez-faire* and on the legal side a no less militant extension of the economic scope of due process. It seems at first sight surprising that a period which was seeing the individualistic ideal of competition give way to monopoly should call for a *laissez-faire* policy in its Court decisions. But *laissez-faire* is to be distinguished from individualism; the latter is a philosophy, the former a mandate.[66] *Laissez-faire* may conceivably proceed from a cherishing of individualist values, but since it would in such an event have to qualify its imperative claims for freedom from legisla-

---

was the very keystone of the arch upon which all civilized government rests. . . . If it be true . . . that the passions of the people are aroused on this subject, if it be true that a mighty army of sixty million citizens is likely to be incensed by this decision, it is the more vital to the future welfare of this country that this Court again resolutely and courageously declare, as Marshall did, that it *has* the power to set aside an act of Congress violative of the Constitution, and that it will not hesitate in executing that power, no matter what the threatened consequences of popular or populistic wealth may be."

[66] For the connection between the program of *laissez-faire* in the American situation, and the theory of natural rights of which it makes use, see Veblen, *The Vested Interests and the Common Man* (1920).

tive interference by a recognition of the individualist values which
are injured by such freedom, its relations are likely to be solely empirical. The change from the individualism at the basis of the previous period of judicial toleration to the *laissez-faire* of the new
restrictive period measured the difference between the two intellectual climates. There was of course a new alignment in the Court;
the old minority had become a majority. But it was a new Court in
a new society. It was not a sport, but an organic part of a period
which has come down in the history of American life as thin in its
cultural fiber and crass in its political morality. One may hazard
that much of the responsibility is to be laid to the disillusioning
effect of the competitive breakdown under the pressure of new and
unscrupulous business *mores*.

The period of judicial toleration had, we have noted, been a
crucial period, hesitant and divided when confronted by bewildering problems of a new industrialism. The period of judicial restriction was, when confronted by a dangerous revolt against the incidence of the new forms of capitalist enterprise,[67] decisive and
militant. And it was in its own way remarkably creative. On every
important front of public policy it transformed the existing doctrine
with considerable ingenuity [68]—in the field of railroad regulation

---

[67] Not least among the causes for the militancy of the possessing classes, reflected
in the militancy of the Court, was the influx of immigration and the growth of a
labor movement which, while in the main a "business unionism" variety, was often
engaged in violent clashes with employers. The fear of the immigrant worker, and
the contempt for him, have been influential in American history not only in heightening the clash between capitalists and laborers, but in putting behind the former
a united body of opinion representing middle-class respectability. The Court in its
decisions in this period reflected the prevalent Catonian attitude toward the labor
movement, which called for its extirpation. I Commons, *op. cit. supra,* note 29, at 9,
points out, however, that the courts by blocking labor's way toward reform probably
made the trade-union movement even more aggressive.

[68] The sequence of steps by which the Fourteenth Amendment was pressed into
use for the protection of business interests against legislative regulation seems to
have been somewhat as follows: (1) The decision that corporations are "persons"
within the meaning of the amendment; (2) the decision that equal protection of
the laws applies to foreign corporations as well as to individuals from outside states;
(3) the decision that the due process clause applies to legislative and administrative
attempts to regulate rates and other matters connected with the conduct of business
enterprise; (4) the decision that liberty of contract is a right of liberty (or of property)
within the meaning of the amendment; (5) the decision that the police power and
the public interest doctrine must be narrowly and urgently construed in determining
exemption from the due process clause; (6) the decision that the reasonableness of
state legislation is not a matter of presumption by the fact that the legislation passed
the gantlet of the legislative process, but is open to examination by the Court.

(Santa Clara County v. Southern Pacific Ry.; [69] *Chicago, Milwaukee and St. Paul v. Minnesota;* [70] *Smythe v. Ames* [71]), business control *(Allgeyer v. Louisiana),* federal taxation *(Pollock v. Farmers Loan and Trust),*[72] regulation of hours *(Lochner v. New York),* social legislation *(Employers' Liability cases),*[73] and anti-trust cases *(United States v. E. C. Knight Company).*[74] It was in this period that the powerful conceptions of contemporary constitutional law—due process,[75] police powers,[76] liberty of contract,[77] and the rule of reasonableness [78]—received their real impetus and elaboration.

In the past quarter-century the trend of judicial decision has again become vacillating for lack of some decisive movement within capitalist enterprise itself to give it firmness and direction. The second decade of the century is generally considered to have been "liberal," and *Muller v. Oregon* [79] was hailed as a significant turning-point; the third decade is regarded as a "reactionary" return to normalcy; during the past several years liberals with their ears to the ground have again detected pulsations of hope. A closer analysis, however, of these three phases of the period fails to reveal any striking contrasts.[80] Nor do they show a unified line of growth. At the bottom of their failure to achieve direction lies the character of the finance-capitalist society in which they have been working. Its pace of change in the field of both corporate and human relations has been too rapid to leave the earlier legal rules untouched, but too insecure to furnish a means of transforming them. It has ceased to

---

69 118 U. S. 394 (1886).

70 134 U. S. 418 (1890).

71 169 U. S. 466 (1898).

72 157 U. S. 429 (1895).

73 207 U. S. 463 (1908).

74 156 U. S. 1 (1895).

75 See Haines, *op. cit. supra,* note 42, at chapter VI; Hough, "Due Process of Law —Today" (1919), 32 *Harvard Law Review* 218.

76 See Freund, *Police Power, Public Policy and Constitutional Rights* (1904).

77 See Walton Hamilton, "Freedom of Contract" (1931), 6 *Encyclopaedia of the Social Sciences* 450; Roscoe Pound, "Liberty of Contract" (1909), 18 *Yale Law Journal* 454; Shulman, *op. cit. supra,* note 38.

78 See Haines, *op. cit. supra,* note 42, at chapter VII.

79 208 U. S. 412 (1908).

80 For such an analysis, see Boudin, *op. cit. supra,* note 2, at chapters XXXVIII, XXXIX. The basis of Boudin's skepticism is partly the failure of the decisions to evidence any intention on the part of the Court to declare any self-denying ordinances with regard to the judicial power; partly that even in the "liberal" decisions the Court—as regards the larger trends of the rule of reasonableness, or any *rule* for future cases—was timid and even reactionary.

be merely a monopoly capitalism, but it has not yet articulated a technique to control its new creatures, the giant corporation and the expanding credit structure. It has outgrown its complete imperviousness to the plight of the underlying classes, but has not yet found a way of meeting either their demands or their requirements. The old individualistic controls are clearly a thing of the past; to cling to them would involve drastic results for the entire economic structure. But pending discovery of controls that will replace them the Court has waited for a crystallization of capitalist attitudes.[81] The tentativeness of this period has of course furnished the able and decisive minority group with a golden opportunity to influence the trend of decision. But a minority can work only interstitially, within the limits set by the dominant institutions, and never against the grain of current economic development. Whether capitalist enterprise can crystallize its new purposes and perfect its techniques sufficiently to give the Court again a clear faith and an articulated ideology remains to be seen.

5

The nexus between the course of Supreme Court decision and the realities of American capitalism [82] poses some crucial problems as to the nature of the judicial process. It is upon this broader question that all our current theoretical interests in American constitutional law converge, for it is here that one approaches the dynamics of growth in the law. Contemporary American thought on this question is in the transitional stage attendant upon having shattered the old absolutes without having yet arrived at new formulations. It

---

[81] The critics of the Court have in one respect uniformly done it an injustice. They have not recognized sufficiently the tremendous task that devolves upon the Court—once it is agreed that legislation is to be scrutinized at all—to make the legislation harmonize with the fundamental purposes of a capitalist economy. For these purposes are not always clear, even to industrialists and bankers. And in the confusion of counsel that characterizes present trends within business, the task of the Supreme Court is all the more difficult.

[82] This brings us back to the problem of the legal lag touched on above. As a matter of fact, it might be said—if it were not so paradoxical—that there is less lag in the conservative decisions than in the liberal criticism of them—lag, that is, with regard to economic reality, and not with regard to enlightened opinion. It is often difficult for liberal minds to understand that the reality does not necessarily conform to their view of it.

has rejected the rhetoric and the traditional mumbo-jumboism with which the reverent generations had invested the fundamental law. It finds it no longer possible to regard the judicial utterances as Delphic,[83] and takes an almost irreverent delight in uncovering the bonds that link Supreme Court justices to other human beings. The myths have fallen away. But the absence of myths does not constitute theory; it is at best merely preparation for it.

It will be well to distinguish two aspects of contemporary thought on the Supreme Court and its economic relations. One has to do with the function that the Court decisions perform, the other with the forces determining them. The prevailing view of the function of the Court is thoroughly realistic. It sees the Court as a definite participant in the formation of public policy, often on matters of far-reaching economic and social importance. Viewed thus, the Court through its power to veto legislation has also the power to channel economic activity. In that sense it has been often called a super-legislature, exercising powers tantamount to the legislative power, but more dangerously, since it is not subject to the same popular control. The main contention here is sound, although the particular formulation it is given is often overstressed. Whether we shall call the Court a super-legislature or a super-judiciary has in reality only a propagandist relevance. Except from the viewpoint of a separation-of-powers ideal or a shattering of intellectual myths it is of little import. But what is of great import is the fact that the Court has become, through its exercise of the judicial power in the intricate context of contemporary capitalist society, a crucial agency of social control. As such it is part of our fabric of statesmanship and should be judged in terms of its effect upon American life.

The second aspect of the problem relates to an adequate theory of judicial decision. The contemporary trend is to regard each judge as acting upon his own economic beliefs and his own preferences as to social policy, and as rationalizing or deliberately manipulating his legal views into conformity with his social views. This represents of course an extreme revulsion against the traditional view of the judge as objectively expounding a body of law that has some superior truth-sanction. It looks toward

---

[83] For the "discovery theory" of law, see Corwin, "The 'Higher Law' Background of American Constitutional Law" (1928), 42 *Harvard Law Review* 149, 153.

a complete and perhaps unfruitful atomism: *tel juge, tel jugement.* It would hold that the course of judicial decision is the sum of the personal choices of the judges, and that the policy of the Court is determined at any time by the chance concatenation of nine arbitrary wills. Side by side with this there is another trend toward a sort of environmentalism or economic determinism. While holding to the atomistic view of the judicial process, it emphasizes in each judge not the volitional and whimsical elements but the non-volitional and determined. It examines his early life, education, economic affiliations, and property interests, and by a selective process with which every biographer is acquainted it shows the inevitable flow of what he is from what he has been. Both these approaches stress the compelling reality of the judge's views of social policy as over against his adherence to legal rules in determining his decision; in this respect they mark a change from the tendency a decade or more ago to make the antithesis one between logic and experience, between a mechanical adherence to *stare decisis* and a realistic awareness of the changing needs of the day.

Such a theory of the judicial process obviously contains much that is sound and fruitful along with elements that tend to be merely impressionistic. Its atomism derives probably from influences similar to those which led Justice Cardozo to focus his analysis of the nature of the judicial process on the individual judge and the individual decision. Cardozo's discussion of the various intellectual procedures open to the judge comes dangerously close to a new Benthamism by which the isolated judge balances the compulsions of logic against the claims of philosophy and both against the persuasions of sociology. By a similar Benthamism in the current atomistic view the judge is made a lightning calculator not of competing intellectual methods but of his own desires and devices. Both views are helpful through their insistence that whatever influences the judicial decision must pass through the mind of the judge. But they do not take sufficient account of the fact that his mind is itself largely a social product, and that he is a judge within an economic system and an ideological milieu. Their influence is operative even when he is not applying the "method of sociology," or using law consciously as an instrument for social ends.

For the problem of the relation of capitalism to the Supreme Court the construction of a theory of judicial decision is of crucial

importance. If the historical analysis presented in the last two sections is valid, much in the development of American constitutional
law is explainable in terms of a developing capitalism. Such an influence, to be effective, would have had to be operative somehow on
the minds of the judges, through whom alone constitutional law
grows. But how? In what form and through what agencies have the
effects of economic development been transmitted to the minds of
the judges? The easiest answer of course would lie in a theory of
pressures. But while this might be valid for some of the lower reaches
of the American judiciary, it has no meaning at all for these men,
who are placed by their exalted and permanent positions beyond
the reach of corruption, as they are placed also beyond that of
democratic control. A theory of interests is likely to be more valid.
The judge is a member of an economic class, of a social grouping,
of a geographical section. He shares their interests and will, even if
unconsciously, direct his policy-forming function to their advantage.
But unless this theory is broadened to include general ideological
influences as well as direct interests, it will suffer from the oversimplified and mechanical interpretation that has been applied to
the framing of the Constitution.

An adequate theory of the judicial process in the Supreme Court
would have to take account of a number of factors. (1) The Court
works first of all with a set of traditional and technical legal elements. It must stay within the framework of a Constitution, confine
itself to the facts and issues of actual cases brought before it, observe and create for itself a body of procedure. It must maintain so
much continuity with its own past decisions as to achieve the necessary minimum of legal certainty, and so much consistency with its
own past reasoning as to make the body of constitutional law a somewhat orderly intellectual system. In the process it creates concepts
and develops doctrines, such as due process, liberty of contract, and
police power, giving them thereby a directive force over its future
decisions. There has been a tendency in recent thought to treat all
these legal factors in the judicial process less as rules than as techniques—fairly flexible and accordingly subservient to the more
deeply rooted purposes of the judges. (2) The Court works within
a cultural and institutional framework which the justices share with
their fellow-citizens. They live in and are sworn to preserve a society
which is the end-product of a historical growth but is also changing

under their very fingers. This society is dominated by its capitalist system of economic organization and is therefore best viewed as a capitalist society. Its institutions and modes of thought are partly incorporated in the Constitution, partly in the body of constitutional law, but are mainly resident in the life of the society itself. (3) The Court works in a world of ideas which the justices share with their fellow-men. These ideological elements—conceptions of human nature, human motive, social possibility, and ethical values —may be "preconceptions" and therefore submerged in consciousness, or they may be avowedly held and deliberately applied. Many of them, such as the competitive ideal and the right of property, proceed from the economic world; those that do not, such as human nature, individualism, and natural law, have nevertheless a definite bearing on economic problems; all of them are social products and are affected by changes in the social and economic structure. (4) There are personal and intellectual differences between the judges —differences of background, philosophy, social convictions, and sympathies.

Of these factors the second and third groups—the world of social fact and the world of social idea—include and are conditioned by the nature of our economic life. The selection that any particular judge makes of them will constitute what Thomas Reed Powell has called the "logic" of his decision; the selection that he makes of the first group of factors—the legal tradition and technology—will constitute the "rhetoric" by which he supports and rationalizes his decision.[84] For an explanation of the main trend of constitutional decision we may therefore look to the institutional and ideological elements that exercise their compulsive force on the minds of the judges, and to the changes wrought in these elements principally by economic development. For an explanation of the groupings within the Court, we may look to the variations in outlook and belief as between the individual members.

---

[84] See T. R. Powell, "The Logic and Rhetoric of Constitutional Law" (1918), 15 *Journal of Philosophy, Psychology and Scientific Method* 645. This essay was one of the most important in shifting American juristic thought. The accepted theory of the judicial process had been that the judge was like the priestess of Apollo at Delphi who, upon being presented with the problem that called for decision, stupefied herself with vapors and listened to the dim voices that came to her; or, in other words, that the judge brought to bear ancient lights to illumine modern instances. Professor Powell's emphasis was that the judge brought to bear his current outlook to manipulate the ancient rules.

This raises a question about the Court which is as important for social action as for juristic theory. What technique can be employed for shifting and controlling the trend of the Court's decisions? What are the chances, for example, that the Court will reverse the secular trend of its decisions during the past half-century and adopt an attitude toward private property that will tolerate experiments in the direction of a controlled and articulated economy? The contemporary emphasis on the judge's capacity to make his rhetoric march to the tune of his social beliefs has as corollary the view that the crucial concern, whether of liberals or conservatives, should be the selection of the right judges—a sort of eugenics program for the judicial process. It seems clear, however, that such a view is overoptimistic. It stops at the judge and does not push its analysis to what it is that determines his view of life. The judge's convictions and social preferences run in terms of the current ideologies of his day; through those ideologies the operative economic forces and master trends of the period find their way into the Court's decisions. In such a sense it has been said that a period deserves whatever Supreme Court it gets—because it has created the judges in its own ideological image. A period in which capitalist enterprise is on the aggressive and the individualistic ideal sweeps everything before it is not likely to read anything but an individualistic philosophy into its constitutional law. A period such as the present, in which the individualistic ideal has been undermined by worldwide economic collapse, is likely to be increasingly tolerant of departures from an absolute conception of liberty or property.

This does not involve, however, a rigorous determinism, either economic or ideological. The judicial process is not, as a too mechanical view might hold, powerless in the clutch of capitalist circumstance. The current institutions and ways of thought of a period determine only the larger outlines which the constitutional law of the period is likely to take. Within that framework there is room for a fairly wide selection and variation of emphasis. The Supreme Court effects a nexus between our fundamental law and our fundamental economic institutions. But by its very position as an agency of control it is powerful to change the contours of those institutions. The same constitutional fabric that contains the absolute individualism of Justice Sutherland gives scope also to the humanistic individualism of Justice Holmes and the social constructivism of Justice Brandeis. The judicial process in the Supreme Court is no exception to the order of things everywhere. Within the limits set by its nature and function it can be carried on with creativeness and purpose or it can become merely a form of submission to the current drift.

1933

5

Minority Rule and
the Constitutional Tradition[1]

1

"L AW," Aaron Burr once remarked, "is that which is boldly asserted and plausibly maintained."[2] I prefer this insight, crude as it may seem, to much of the wisdom of the whole array of schools of legal philosophy.[3] Burr must have had an uncanny prescience about the development of American constitutional law. Into the increasingly bold assertion of judicial supremacy—the history of the judicial power—I do not propose to enter here.[4] It has been explored a good deal recently and is a matter of record in the annals of the Supreme Court. That record is one of tortuous maneuverings and bold *faits accomplis* in the field of governmental practice. The men who have guided the destinies of the judicial power, from Alexander Hamilton and John Marshall to Chief Justice Hughes in our own day, have been masters of the art of political manipulation and anything but novices in the technique of presenting the enemy with the completed actuality of a decision.

I am not one of those who regard the bold assertion of judicial

---

[1] First read at the meeting of the American Historical Association at Philadelphia, December 30, 1937. First published in the *University of Pennsylvania Law Review* for March 1938, and reprinted in Conyers Read, ed., *The Constitution Reconsidered* (1938).

[2] Quoted in Nelles and King, "Contempt by Publication in the United States" (1928), 28 *Columbia Law Review* 401, 428.

[3] I say this, of course, while recognizing that Burr's remark represents in itself a school of legal philosophy—something that would correspond to a cross between the American realists and the glorification of the survivor contained in some of the German jurists. But while we may formalize Burr's remark thus, Burr himself did not.

[4] This is dealt with in the chapter above, "The Supreme Court and American Capitalism."

461

supremacy as an act of usurpation.⁵ It is a truism, of course, that the power of judicial supremacy over the whole governmental process is nowhere to be found expressly granted in the constitutional document. It is a body of inferences, a system of "givens" and "therefores," an intellectual construction. But it has by this time become accepted as a living institution, and I have too much respect for any part of an organic going concern to think that it can be exorcised out of existence by legalistic discussions of whether it was actually intended. The judicial power has by this time *written itself* into the Constitution by Court interpretation and prescriptive right, just as much as if it were clearly granted in the document. In short, it is a colossal gloss upon a text not given, a gloss with which we must deal as we would with any political actuality.

It is time that American thought on the Constitution moved away from the question of original intent, away from *whether* the men in the Constitutional Convention intended judicial review, to the question of *how* judicial supremacy has been built up and maintains itself in what is presumably a democracy. To move from the *whether* to the *how* is, perhaps, always a step forward—from what can be only subjectively guessed at to what can be objectively observed, from theology to science, from polemics to history. What can be said of intent with respect to judicial review, although it will undoubtedly prove eternally interesting, is actually rather little, and that little is uncertain. One may balance the warily expressed desires of the framers against the clear aversion of the people at the time and get nowhere.⁶ What can be said of the logic of the way in which the judicial power has been built up is clearer—that it is the natural outcome of the necessity for maintaining the rule of a capitalist minority under the forms of a democracy. Judicial review has not flowed merely from the will to power of individual justices, but has been the convenient channel through which the driving forces of a

⁵ The theme of usurpation, either in assertion or denial, is the grand underlying theme of most of the recent literature on the Supreme Court. Thus also the theme of exploitation has been used as the grand theme of much of the recent literature on capitalism. But the abstract question of legalism would seem to have as little to do with political power realities as the abstract question of social justice with economic power realities. In either case they are usable primarily as evocative myths.

⁶ Paraphrasing Lord Justice Buckley in *Hanau v. Ehrlich* (1911), 2 K. B. 1056, 1069, one may say that it is a century and a quarter too late to apply our own minds independently to the task of determining whether judicial review was intended by the Constitution.

developing business enterprise have found expression and achieved victory.

Let us, however, turn to the last half of Aaron Burr's definition. "Law is that which is boldly asserted *and plausibly maintained.*" Bold assertion is pursued in the realm of political action and economic pressure. Plausible maintenance proceeds in the realm of symbols, interest structures, and idea-systems. The aggressions of the judicial power cannot be understood unless we see them as part of the attempt to maintain the existing power structures in our peculiar form of capitalist democracy. But the defenses of the judicial power are also formidable. Every going institution seeks to build a triple line of defense. First, there is the area of *symbols,* or what Professor Elliott calls "social myths" and Thurman Arnold calls now "symbols" and now "folklore." [7] The realm of symbols is most often an unconscious realm; when they have become too articulate their spell is broken. I have sought to examine elsewhere in a paper the interrelated symbols that the Constitution and the Supreme Court have built up in the mind of the common man, and especially the symbolism of the divine right of judges.[8] Secondly, there are *interest structures,* the pulls and thrusts of class relations that make various groups defend the judicial power and that have made the Supreme Court defend those groups; these interest structures are generally unconscious and operate best on the level of unconsciousness, but in times of tension they tend increasingly to become articulate. In between these two there is the third area—that of *formal apologetics* —the ideology by which the judicial power has operated and has been defended. Thus we have, in a triple defense-ring around the judicial power, symbolic structures, interest structures, and idea structures. It is with the relation of the last two that I am here principally concerned.

2

The Court's own *apologia* for its power—what may be called the "official" theory of the judicial function—is well known, but I shall take the liberty of recapitulating it. It runs somewhat as follows. We

---

[7] Elliott, "The Constitution as a Social Myth," in Read, ed., *The Constitution Reconsidered;* Arnold, *Symbols of Government* (1935) and *Folklore of Capitalism* (1937).
[8] See Lerner, "Constitution and Court as Symbols" (1937), 46 *Yale Law Journal* 1290.

have a fundamental law, in the form of a written Constitution, over-riding legislative enactments that are not in harmony with it. We have a federal system, in which powers must be divided between the states and the central government; and a system of separated powers, in which the lines must be drawn between the departments of the government, and the encroachments of one upon the others avoided. We have thus in two respects a system that would result in chaos or tyranny unless there were a final arbiter. We have, moreover, the danger that men in power will aggrandize their power at the expense of other men, and invade their rights; we have a people safe from such invasion only under the protection of the Constitution. We have finally a judicial body, deliberately placed above politics and beyond partisan control, and empowered to assure for us a govern-ment of laws and not of men. The fund of knowledge and principles to which this body appeals is to be found in the Anglo-American common law, the precedents of constitutional law, and a "higher law" resident in the "genius of republican institutions."

In its way this official theory is something of a masterpiece. It is, to be sure, a mosaic pieced together from diverse materials: the *Federalist Papers*, Court decisions and dicta, commentaries by scholars such as Kent and Cooley, classic speeches such as those of Webster; but, while it is a mosaic, it is a thing of beauty nevertheless, neat, logical, close-fitting, comprehensive—so long as you grant its premises.

Let me set out some of those premises, generally unexpressed.[9] The official theory assumes that a fundamental law must be superior to all legislative enactments, despite the example of the English sys-tem, where the line of constitutional growth lies in parliamentary enactment rather than judicial construction. It assumes that other departments of the government may not be as capable as the judici-ary of the task of constitutional construction—assumes, that is, a fund of exclusive and inspired knowledge of the law on the part of the judges. It assumes that the binding obligation of a litigant at law to accept the Court's construction of a statute is binding as well upon Congress. It assumes on the part of the executive and the legis-lature an imperialistic thirst for power and expansion, and despite Justice Stone's agonizing cry *de profundis* in the Butler case ("the

---

[9] I am indebted here to some extent to Edward S. Corwin's acute article, "Judicial Review" (1937), 8 *Encyclopaedia of the Social Sciences* 457.

only check upon our own exercise of power is our own sense of self-restraint"),[10] despite this cry, the official theory makes no similar assumption about the stake the judges have in their own power. It assumes that all government is dangerous, and thus adopts a negativist attitude toward governmental powers. It assumes that the legal aspects of a governmental problem can be separated and abstracted from its real aspects. It assumes, in short, a closed Constitution in a malignant universe, instead of an open instrument of government in a changing and challenging world.

I have spoken thus far of the formal ideology of the judicial power. But an ideology is not merely a series of linked propositions drawn from related premises. It sometimes draws its greatest strength from allies—ideas in this case not directly within the official *apologia* of the Court's power, but embedded in the popular mind and strengthening the acceptance of that power. I want to pick four of them for brief discussion—the doctrine of limited governmental powers, the doctrine of the sanctity of property, the doctrine of federalism, and the doctrine of minority rights.

The Constitution was born in a century obsessed with the notion of limited powers, a century overhung by the shadows of Locke and Rousseau. Conservative thought clung to the rights of minorities against the tyranny of the majority; and radical theory, such as that of Jefferson and the great European rationalists, took the form of belief in the perfectibility of man and the malignancy of government. But the pattern of the century contained a curious inner contradiction in its thought. Its prevailing economic policy was mercantilistic, with all the close and comprehensive controls that the mercantilist state exercised over economic life, and with all its resulting concentration of authority.[11] Its prevailing political thought, however, was atomistic, with its emphasis on individual liberties and governmental dangers. The men who framed the Constitution and ran the government that it created were caught in this contradiction. Their conservative economic interests dictated a strong central mercantilist government; the prevailing political ideas of the time, fortifying their fear of democracy, made them place that government of expanded powers in an intellectual framework of

---

10 *United States v. Butler,* 297 U. S. 1, 79 (1936), (dissenting opinion).
11 For the mercantilist character of the economic thought of the era of the Constitution, see Hamilton and Adair, *The Power to Govern* (1937), 103–144.

limited powers. Hence, to a large extent, the confusion of the Constitutional debates. The interesting fact is that judicial ideology still clings to this doctrine even in a world where to act on it would be grotesquely tragic, and where the popular impulse is to abandon it.

When we pass to the doctrine of the sanctity of property, we find that the sense of property has assumed a variety of forms in our history, but always the protection and support it has accorded to the judicial power has been a continuing factor in the Court's life. American life has pushed forward along a variety of trails—farm, frontier, and factory; plantation and city; trade route, logging-camp, mining-town, and real-estate boom; corporation and co-operative. But through all these the common base-line has been a persistent and pervasive sense of property. It first took the form of the land-mysticism and land-hunger of Physiocratic thought, deeply resident in the whole movement of colonial land-settlement, and from which Jefferson eventually drew much of his support; then the sense of vested rights and the deep sense of contractual obligation, to which Marshall gave doctrinal expression in his "contract decisions," [12] and which, using and twisting somewhat Sir Henry Sumner Maine's terminology,[13] provided a new sort of status for an age of capitalism; then the sense of property individualism, born of the movements for European liberation, blessed with the approval of Protestant capitalism,[14] flourishing in the wilderness of the American frontier, turned into *laissez-faire* by the conditions of a reckless and exploitative capitalism; and finally, when individualism could no longer thrive as an idea because it had been extinguished as a fact in economic life, the clinging to the profit system and the cash-nexus as bulwarks against social anarchy and the destruction of the social fabric. This sense of property, even when its widespread social base has been so largely destroyed in the age of absentee ownership, is still a powerful ally for the judicial power.

When we turn to the theory of federalism and states' rights, we are

---

[12] See Isaacs, "John Marshall on Contracts—a Study in Early American Juristic Theory" (1921), 7 *Virginia Law Review* 413.

[13] I am referring, of course, to his famous distinction between status and contract. See Maine, *Ancient Law* (6th ed., 1876), 170.

[14] See Tawney, *Religion and the Rise of Capitalism* (1926) (following Weber); and apropos of the Weber-Tawney thesis, see Laski, *The Rise of European Liberalism* (Eng. ed., 1936), 29–34.

dealing with a powerful intellectual and sentimental force that the Supreme Court has at times had to fight and more latterly has been calling to its aid. We are all acquainted with the kinds of arguments which, like ghosts, are continually looming up in the world of ideas, which rule us from the past by their wraith-like being, although we are aware that they no longer represent actualities. The idea of free opportunity under capitalism is one, and it lingers on even in a world dominated by monopoly. In the political realm the most potent and assertive American ghost is still federalism.[15] Most of its former functions have been stripped from it; it haunts a nation in which every force drives toward centralization, both economic and political. But when I call it a ghost, I do not mean it is no longer a fact to be reckoned with. The strength of a ghost, it must be remembered, rests in its capacity to get itself believed; and that, in turn, depends more than anything on our own needs and fears. And the fear of overcentralization, of the wiping out of the traditional political and cultural landmarks of the states, is a very real fear, especially in the light of what the fascist dictatorships have done to federalism.[16] And it is a fear which the Supreme Court, as witness the AAA case,[17] has not been averse to exploring and exploiting.

It may be said of the doctrine of minority rights and individual liberties that recent events have given them or seem to have given them even greater meaning than they once possessed. This tradition of minority rights has always been an important source of strength for judicial supremacy. The doctrine of vested rights,[18] the sanctity

---

[15] Lest this be interpreted as an attempt to depreciate the value of the federal principle, I want to say that I value our regional cultures highly. But one must not confuse such personal valuations with the stream of tendency. And while I believe that an element of the federative principle will always remain in American political history, I must recognize that the strength of federalism lies in the past and not in the future. The corporation has not obliterated federalism in political theory, but it has done so in economic fact. I have found much of interest on federalism in Dicey, *Introduction to the Law of the Constitution* (8th ed., 1915), especially the introduction to this edition; Friedrich, *Constitutional Government and Politics* (1937), chapter XII; McMahon, "Federation" (1937), 6 *Encyclopaedia of the Social Sciences* 172.

[16] For a moving account of the German experience, written by a German liberal of the old school to whom the federative principle meant much, see Mendelssohn-Bartholdy, *The War and German Society* (1937).

[17] *United States v. Butler*, 297 U. S. 1 (1936).

[18] Edward S. Corwin's articles on vested rights are, of course, well known. I have sought to treat the subject further in the chapter on "Vested Rights and Vested Interests," below.

of contract and liberty of contract,[19] the doctrine of due process of law—all have drawn upon this tradition. In fact, most of the Court's decisions invalidating legislation hostile to property might be interpreted as proceeding from its zeal for minority rights, rather than from any untoward zeal for business interests. Nevertheless, as long as a strong rationalization for capitalist power existed in economic thought and opinion, the civil-liberties and minority-rights argument was secondary. Now, however, two things are happening to push it to the fore. One is the decline of *laissez-faire,* both in practice and in thought. The second is the spread of fascism in Europe and the fear of it in America. The first has made the businessmen and the judges turn increasingly to the rhetoric of civil liberties; the second has made the liberals and the middle classes more ready to accept the Court's guardianship of civil liberties, even if it means a measure of judicial control over economic policy.[20]

About civil liberties and minority rights and the liberals I shall have more to say later. But I want to pause here for a moment to survey the meaning of these four ideological allies of the judicial power. All four, viewed historically, have their roots in majority movements, and have played a great and even revolutionary role in the history of the Western world. And all four have been turned to the uses of minority rule as parts of the constitutional tradition. Take, first, the idea of a government of limited powers. The notion of a higher law; the idea of natural rights of individuals, which adhere to them independently of government and even in despite of government, and which must be protected against government; the necessity of disobedience to a government that violated these rights —these had once been living parts of a revolutionary movement that swept Western Europe from the parliamentary champions of the struggle against the Tudors and Stuarts to the philosophers of the French Revolution. They were majority movements, aimed at limiting the powers of minority governments of the dying classes. They rationalized the actual movement toward parliamentarism in

[19] See Hamilton, "Freedom of Contract" (1937), 6 *Encyclopaedia of the Social Sciences* 450. See also Laski, *op. cit. supra,* note 14, at 237–264, where he treats of the liberalism of the Supreme Court majorities and concludes that it serves only to clothe the business interests that they guard.

[20] During the public controversy in 1937 over President Roosevelt's Court reorganization plan, many liberals who had earlier been critical of the Court's decisions came to its defense, motivated largely by the fear that "packing" the Court or weakening its prestige would remove the principal guarantee of civil liberties.

England and toward middle-class democracy in France. But in taking them over, judicial review turned them to quite different uses
—to defeat parliamentary supremacy and hedge democracy around
with severe limitations—in short, to the uses of minority rule. And
the same may be said of that property sense which has been part of
the American democratic experience, of the democratic localism
that underlies federalism and states' rights, and of the democratic
movements that generated the doctrines of civil liberties and minority rights. All have been twisted out of their original context,
and turned to the uses of minority rule.

3

I want now to examine more closely what I mean by three concepts I have been using—democracy (or majority will), minority
rule, and minority rights. The relation between these three is central to an understanding of the ideology of the judicial power.

Scratch a fervent believer in judicial supremacy, and like as not
you will find someone with a bitterness about democracy. The two
are as close as skin and skeleton. When I speak of *democracy* here, I
want to distinguish it sharply from *liberalism*. There is no greater
confusion in the layman's mind today than the tendency to identify
the two. American history has been the scene of a protracted struggle
between democratic and anti-democratic forces.[21] Anti-democracy
began as aristocratic thought, with emphasis on a neo-Greek élite.
Alexander Hamilton, heart-broken because the new American state
could not be a monarchy with George Washington as king and himself as king-maker, sublimated his monarchical passion in a dream
of America as an aristocracy of property. And a whole school followed him. But it soon became clear that in a country where a
revolutionary war had been fought to achieve democracy, an aristocratic body of thought could not form the base of any party successful at the polls. The collapse of the Federalist Party proved it.

---

[21] The sharpest delineation that I know of this struggle in American history is
to be found in Parrington's three-volume work *Main Currents in American Thought*
(1927–1930). Parrington stood on the shoulders of J. Allen Smith, whose two books,
The Growth and Decadence of Constitutional Government (1900) and *The Spirit
of American Government* (1907), are not as well known as they deserve to be.
Latterly the work of the Marxist historians has begun to realize the implications
for American history of this struggle between democratic and anti-democratic forces.

A shift was made, therefore, to liberalism; and so powerful an aid did liberalism become to the anti-democratic forces that even conservatism grew shamefaced and, in order to survive, had to don the garments of liberalism. In the South alone, in the period of tension preceding the Civil War, slavery as an economic base caused aristocratic theory to linger on, and the spokesmen for the slavocracy defended it as an élite that had re-established a Greek republic among the roses and cotton bolls below the Mason-Dixon line.[22] But the Civil War proved by blood and iron that aristocratic theory was, like slavery, an unnecessary survival from archaic times. The northern financial oligarchy that rose to unchallenged political power out of the Civil War spoke thereafter in the name of an orthodox, if slightly cynical, liberalism. And it has continued to do so.

Let us be clear about it; minority-rights liberalism (which becomes in practice minority-rule liberalism) furnishes the only reasoned defense of the capitalist power that we have in America. This liberalism has three facets: a defense of individual civil liberties against society, a defense of minority rights (including both human and property rights) against the possible tyranny of the government, and a belief in rationalism and in the final triumph of the idea. In the course of the liberal revolutions in Europe, democratic forces were unleashed which sought to carry the implications of the libertarian movements to their logical conclusion not only for the middle class but for the underlying population as well, not only for political but for economic freedom and equality. These forces are what I shall call the "democratic impetus" or the "democratic thrust." They began to loom as the great threat to the privileged position of the middle classes. Fortunately for those classes, they could find in the armory of liberalism the intellectual weapons they needed for fighting the democratic threat. The basis of democracy is that the majority will shall prevail; its premise is that the common man can fashion his own political destiny, and that government must consist of representative institutions to carry the majority will into execution. To this, liberalism has opposed the proposition that

---

22 I do not mean to say here that the Athenian republic was a slavocracy in the sense in which the American South was. The recent researches of Zimmern and others have shown that the slave base of Athenian society was by no means as rigorous as had been previously believed (see Westermann, "Ancient Slavery" [1937], 14 *Encyclopaedia of the Social Sciences,* 74–77); but it did furnish a convenient *apologia* for the classical-minded defenders of the southern economic system.

the freedom and rights of the individual and the minority were more sacred than the will of the majority. In that lies the essential distinction between liberalism and democracy.

In their fear of majority will the propertied groups have depicted the democratic mass movements in the darkest colors of extremism. They have called the Jeffersonians "Jacobins," the Jacksonians "Locofocos," the Abolitionists "Niggerlovers," the agrarian radicals "Populists," the trade unionists "Reds" and "Bolsheviks." The democratic forces in turn have responded by calling the propertied groups "Monarchists," "plutocrats," "economic royalists." The two barrages of epithets have enlivened American politics, but failed to illuminate it. But behind the battle of the epithets there has been a very real struggle between the thrust of majority will, ever present in a nation whose collective life has been based on democratic premises, and the counter-thrust of minority rule.

This has been the basic paradox of American life—the necessity we have been under of squaring majority will with minority rule— that is, democratic forms with capitalist power. It has made us, in one sense, politically speaking, a nation of hypocrites. But it has also spurred our wits and sharpened the edge of our political inventiveness. Out of it have emerged our peculiar institution of judicial supremacy and that whole idea structure of the defense of judicial supremacy which I have outlined.

The mistake we are all too ready to make is to pose an antithesis between the Constitution as such and the democratic impulse, an antithesis that does not exist. We have been led into this error partly by the excellent work of Charles Beard and his school in proving that the Constitution represented the property interests of the minority.[23] That is true enough. But we must also remember that the Constitution, without the accretion of judicial review, could (whatever its origins) have become an instrument of the majority will. The whole animus behind it, despite the system of checks and balances, was a flexible one. It was meant, as has recently been pointed out with great effectiveness by Professor Hamilton [24] and Professor Cor-

---

[23] I refer, of course, to his *Economic Interpretation of the Constitution* (2d ed., 1935). I do not mean that Mr. Beard has himself fallen into the error of posing an antithesis between the Constitution and the democratic impulse, but that the emphasis in his early work lent credence to that error.

[24] Hamilton and Adair, *The Power to Govern* (1937).

win,[25] to adapt itself to the changes and chances of the national life. It is significant that the majority groups, who were first rather sullen about it, and then accepted it after affixing to it a bill of rights guaranteeing individual liberties, finally became enthusiastic about it. It is well known that Jeffersonians as well as Hamiltonians and Marshallians vied in their praise of the Constitution.[26] What they differed about was the judicial power. The real antithesis is between the democratic impulse and the judicial power.[27] And with Jefferson and the so-called Revolution of 1800, which saw the triumph of Jeffersonianism, began that series of democratic thrusts, upsurges of the majority will, that has enlivened and vitalized American history. In Jefferson and Jackson, notably in the Bank War and the Dorr Rebellion, in Lincoln, to an extent in Cleveland, in the Populist movement and Bryan, in Theodore Roosevelt and Woodrow Wilson, in Eugene Debs, in Franklin Roosevelt and the New Deal, and in John L. Lewis and the CIO, we have had repetitions of that democratic thrust at the seats of minority power. It became the task of the propertied minority to ward off those thrusts. And they have been thus far enabled to do it through the instrument of judicial supremacy, the ideology that surrounds and defends it, and especially the ideology of liberalism.

In two senses judicial supremacy has smoothed the way for minority rule. In one specific instance after another, measures of policy which the majority has desired have been invalidated by the courts. If the people of Georgia wanted to undo a corrupt grant of land,[28] or the people of New York wanted an eight-hour working day in bakery shops,[29] or the people of Oklahoma wanted to restrict the number of ice-plants,[30] their wishes were so much dry stubble to be trod under foot by the minority will of the Court.

---

[25] Corwin, "The Constitution as Instrument and Symbol" (1936), 30 *American Political Science Review* 1071.

[26] For the best statement of this development, see Schechter, "The Early History of the Tradition of the Constitution" (1915), 9 *American Political Science Review* 707.

[27] Louis B. Boudin has brought out with the greatest sharpness the distinction between the Constitution, as embodying the democratic experience of the past and democratic potentialities for the future, and judicial supremacy as an instrument of minority power. See Boudin, *Government by Judiciary* (1932), and especially Boudin, "The United States Constitution 150 Years Later," *New Masses*, September 21, 1937.

[28] *Fletcher v. Peck*, 6 Cranch 87 (U. S. 1810).

[29] *Lochner v. New York*, 198 U. S. 45 (1905).

[30] *New State Ice Co. v. Liebmann*, 285 U. S. 262 (1932).

But there is an even deeper sense in which the Supreme Court has acted as the final barricade against the assaults of democratic majorities. We must remember that the process of the triumph of the democratic majority is a long and tedious process, as majority leaders from Jefferson to Franklin Roosevelt have discovered. It is a process of seeking to displace the enemy from one position after another. There is the vast inertia of the party system, with an autonomous force of its own even after popular sentiment has changed; there is the political apathy of the masses, the tendency they have of forgetting to remember. There is the pressure of special interests, blocking up committees, arranging filibusters. There is the control that the vested interests exercise over our newspapers and our very patterns of thinking. And there is, finally, the effective weapon the propertied minority has in withdrawing capital from investment and thus paralyzing the economic process. And after all these positions have been captured, the anti-democratic forces retreat to their last barricade—judicial review. There, behind the safe earthworks of natural law, due process, minority rights, the judges can in the plenitude of their virtue and sincerity veto and outlaw the basic social program of the majority.

4

The democratic forces of the country have known, in intervals of lucidity, what they were up against and what they were fighting. But in addition to all the difficulties of mustering the necessary big electoral battalions, they have become increasingly confused recently. And their confusion has arisen from the fact that the rationalizations that are used to explain and defend the Supreme Court power are the rationalizations that flow from the premises of liberalism—that minority rule uses the theory of minority rights, and manages somehow to equate the two.

Minority rule has recently had to work very subtly to defeat majority will. There was a time, in Alexander Hamilton's day, when the anti-democratic theorists could say frankly, when confronted with the accusation that they had defeated the people's will: "Your people, Sir, is a great beast." [31] Or they could speak more gravely, as did Fisher Ames, of "a government of the wise, the rich, and the

[31] 1 Henry Adams, *History of the United States during the Administration of Jefferson* (1930), 85.

good," [32] as if all three were coterminous. Later they had to convert the Bill of Rights and the Fourteenth Amendment, the heart of the protection of minority rights, from a charter of liberties to a charter of property protection. The task, as is well known, was a difficult one, and involved two major intellectual somersaults—twisting due process of law from a procedural meaning to a substantive meaning, and endowing the corporation with all the attributes of human personality. But, while the task was well done, it was done with a certain cynicism that is particularly apparent in the political commentaries between the Civil War and the World War, as well as in the Court decisions of that period. Now, however, in the midst of world tensions in which democracy has taken on a new meaning and a new prestige for us, it is necessary to be more subtle in defense of minority rule. The new defense is, therefore, not only a plea of minority rights, powerfully evocative in itself in these days, but a new interpretation of majority will as well.

That interpretation is to be found in its most finished form not in the Supreme Court decisions, in all of which it is implicit, nor even in scholarly commentary, but in two popular commentators, Mr. Walter Lippmann and Miss Dorothy Thompson. It is significant that Mr. Lippmann embodies it in his book *The Good Society,* which is an attack on economic planning, the most dangerous threat to the economic power of the minority. It is even more significant that Miss Thompson's theory, which is the more sharply delineated, is to be found best in a series of three articles which form a critique [33] of Mr. Roosevelt's Roanoke Island speech.

The new theory (I use Miss Thompson's articles as a model) reinterprets the democratic principle so that it becomes something quite different from the naked principle of majority will. First, not only must minorities be protected from majorities, but majorities must even be protected from themselves. [34] Second, if true democracy

---

[32] Ames's writings are the classic repository of anti-democratic comment. "Our country," he wrote in 1803, "is too big for union, too sordid for patriotism, too democratic for liberty"—*Id.,* at 83. And George Cabot, another high Federalist, wrote in 1804: "We are democratic altogether; and I hold democracy in its natural operation to be the government of the worst"—2 *id.,* at 165.

[33] Thompson, "The President's Political Philosophy," New York *Herald Tribune,* Aug. 23, 1937, p. 15, col. 7; Aug. 25, 1937, p. 17, col. 7; Aug. 27, 1937, p. 15, col. 7.

[34] "But the converse of oligarchic rule is not rule by an unchecked majority, for there can be an oligarchy of the majority as well as of the minority. The converse of minority rule is the restoration in this country of genuine popular constitutional

does operate in terms of majority will, it is not the will of a numerical majority, but a very different conception.[35] Third, the notion of numerical majorities really smells of fascism.[36] And having arrived at that position, one falls back in fright on minority rights, even if it involves scrapping the TVA, the Wagner Act, the Securities and Exchange Commission, and the Labor Relations Board.

When we say that majorities must be protected from themselves, the premise is the anti-democratic one—that the common man may be good material for being ruled but that he has no capacity for governing.[37] When we go on to talk of "true" democracy, as distinguished from majority will, what are we saying? We are saying that democracy is nothing so vulgar and demagogic as a counting of heads, but that there is a "real" national will, as distinguished from the one that expresses itself at the polls. That real national will is somehow a trusteeship [38] of the minority. For the few know what is

---

government, of government by law, to which not only minorities but majorities and bureaucracies, Congresses and the government itself, must give obedience"—*id.*, Aug. 23, 1937, p. 15, col. 8.

[35] "For the American tradition conceives of democracy not as something which functions periodically, in the form of ratifying or rejecting plebiscites, but as something which functions continually; which derives authority, not from the majority, but from the whole people . . . and which avows that every individual is invested with certain natural rights, which not even a majority of 99 per cent can divest him of. . . .

"The parents of American democracy never advocated mass rule or the will of the majority as the final and sole authority"—*id.*, Aug. 25, 1937, p. 17, cols. 7, 8.

[36] "The important thing about the President's conception of government—of the unchecked reign of the majority expressed in the form of a blanket mandate—is that it is not incompatible with dictatorship but does, indeed, furnish the philosophical justification for modern dictatorships which have conquered the state by democratic means"—*id.*, Aug. 23, 1937, p. 15, col. 7.

"The conception that the majority's ratification of any executive program is the final expression of the democratic principle is, therefore, a revolutionary idea. Its adoption will inevitably lead to a change in the spirit and the form of American government. . . . The appeal to that principle is what Machiavelli recommended to his prince. The German socialists taught it to Hitler. And Aristotle was familiar with it, in the fourth century before Christ. It is revolutionary, but it is not liberal. It is, I believe, deeply reactionary"—*id.*, Aug. 25, 1937, p. 17, col. 8.

[37] This conception of the common man is embodied in the anti-democratic philosophy of Nietzsche and other German romantics; it deeply influenced the thought of Carlyle, Ruskin, and other English writers of the nineteenth century. See Brinton, *English Political Thought in the Nineteenth Century* (1933); Lippincott, *Victorian Critics of Democracy* (1938). It has also found expression in such contemporary writers as Wyndham Lewis, *The Art of Being Ruled* (1926); Mencken, *Notes on Democracy* (1926).

[38] There is an interesting parallel between this notion of political trusteeship by the minority for the majority, and the notion of economic trusteeship by the propertied minority for the propertyless majority. It is worth noting that the minorities

to the interest of the many better than the many know themselves. This whole conception of the national will as something transcending numbers and having no traffic with the felt desires of the day is an essentially mystical conception.

It has always been the role of reactionary thought to retreat to a mystical conception of the body politic, as witness Burke, de Maistre, Adam Müller, and the French Catholic school.[39] For mystical notions enable you to escape from the fact of the naked majority will. And conservative minority groups have always regarded the majority as unsavory, as meaningless by the very fact of numbers, strident and mechanical like the clashing of weapons through which the primitive Germanic tribes indicated their assent by the greatest noise.[40] What is novel is the fact that all this is now said—and believed—in the name of liberalism. And yet not so novel if we consider the extent to which the ingredients of liberal thinking—that is, minority-rule thinking—have entered into the traditional defense of the judicial power under the Constitution.

What has happened, of course, cannot be blamed on the Constitution. What has happened is that there has been built in America an extra-democratic structure of economic reality which dare not operate through the democratic machinery; for the democratic machinery is too easily turned into an instrument for leveling economic privilege. When this extra-democratic structure of economic reality (I use it as an academic phrase for the structure of corporate power) is challenged, and a successful attempt is made to take our democratic theory literally and nakedly, how far will the corporate groups allow this attempt to go? To my mind, this is the most important question that the Constitution faces in the calculable future,

---

and majorities are roughly the same in the two instances. Economic realism has made Americans increasingly skeptical of the notion of trusteeship in the economic realm, and cautious in accepting the claim, voiced most articulately once by George F. Baer of anthracite fame, that God had granted the captains of industry their wealth to hold in trust for the welfare of the masses. They have not yet applied a similar acidity to the parallel claims in the political realm. Ultimately, of course, the concept has been extended—notably by Henry Sumner Maine—to the fabric of society itself. Maine held that all civilization was a trust held by the few for the many. See Smellie, "Sir Henry Maine" (1928), 8 *Economica* 64.

[39] For an interesting study of liberal Catholicism that sought to mitigate the rigors of de Maistre and Chateaubriand through the writings of Lamennais, Ozanam, Donoso Cortés, and Bishop Ketteler, see Götz Briefs, "The Dispute between Catholicism and Liberalism in the Early Decades of Capitalism" (1937), 4 *Social Research* 91.

[40] See Konopczynski, "Minority Rights" (1937), 10 *Encyclopaedia of the Social Sciences* 525.

and it faces it more dangerously than it has confronted any problem since the Civil War. Does the economic interest of the corporate groups so far outweigh their sense of commonwealth as to make them ready either to keep their minority rule or scrap the whole democratic framework? My own conviction is that this is their attitude, and that they will insist on one or the other of these alternatives. When the corporation cannot win its fight against democracy by economic means, it may call in military and political means and become (if I may give the term a twist) the corporative state.

If this is so, the new attack on the majority principle, represented by Miss Thompson and Mr. Lippmann, takes on a disquieting importance. A counter-thrust against a successful labor government, for example, will look for a theory to attach itself to. Here is a theory ready-made. The naked majority principle, Miss Thompson tells us, is really fascist; it is part of a totalitarian state. I find a readiness in surprisingly intelligent quarters to accept this paradox. If that readiness spreads, corporate power will not lack those intellectual garments which it needs to stave off a socialized democracy —intellectual garments which the liberals are now spinning just as assiduously as the Parcae once spun other fateful garments.

1938

6

Vested Rights and Vested Interests

W HEN an activity has been pursued so long that the individuals concerned in it have a prescriptive claim to its exercise and its profits, they are considered to have a vested interest in it. When this interest is given legal sanction it becomes a vested right. The prescriptive claim may be enforced against other individuals or even against the state itself seeking to encroach upon it. In this broadest sense vested interests and vested rights are as old as human history and as broad as social life. Property may be traced back ultimately to the vesting of ownership or other proprietary rights in individuals and groups who have carved out their claim by conquest or effort or ingenuity, and made it secure by force or continued exercise of it. Roman law, however tenacious of the sanctity of property rights, recognized *usucapio,* the taking by continued use, in order that there might be no sustained uncertainty about ownership. The whole of legal history may be regarded as the sequence of vesting rights in individuals whose claims for one reason or another come to be regarded as sufficient.

The rise and fortunes of capitalism in the Western world have given the concept the most specific consequence for social thought. Feudalism was a system of frozen rights and relationships; and while it sanctioned the established, it did not, except through a certain residual continuity with Roman law, smile upon more newly acquired rights. With its disintegration scope was given to the exercise of arbitrary power over private property by the prince and the creation of a system of aristocratic privilege. The whole effort of a rising capitalism in the sixteenth and seventeenth centuries, as exercised through the natural-law jurists of that period, was to place bounds around the dynastic power and privilege and to open a path for the vesting of the claims which a new merchant class was pressing. On the Continent this struggle found intellectual expression in the writings of Grotius, Pufendorf, and other natural-rights philosophers. In England it conditioned the constitutional conflict of the seventeenth century, with its insistence upon subjecting an arbitrary monarch to the rule of law.

The culmination of both movements of thought was the eighteenth-century natural-rights philosophy of the French and English intellectuals, finding its most significant formulation in Locke's definition of property as whatever a man has mixed his labor with. This flung the gates open for a legitimation of the claims of the capitalist class as rapidly as they were acquired; and once the rights were vested, it placed barriers against the encroachment of the state upon them. The vested interests of a rising capitalist class were written into the English common law as they were written into natural-rights philosophy, and by the latter part of the eighteenth century Lord Mansfield declared it an established doctrine that vested rights must be protected. As capitalism matured in nineteenth-century England, the task of removing the disabilities which political inequality imposed upon the vesting of new interests was completed by the reform movements and Benthamite jurisprudence in the period between 1832 and 1870.

The *locus classicus* of the vested interests, however, is American business enterprise and its accompanying body of constitutional law. In fact the history of American constitutional law is most clearly intelligible as a record of the varying legal sanctity of the vested interests. The Constitutional Convention itself may be seen as a concerted attempt to entrench the vested interests against agrarian discontent and the lingering revolutionary *élan*. In the judicial interpretation of the Constitution a series of bulwarks was erected against the interference of state legislatures with this property-conscious intent of the framers. The mechanism was the establishment of judicial supremacy and the power of judicial review of legislative enactments. The doctrine principally relied upon before the Civil War was that of vested rights. While this doctrine sought to protect the constitutional guarantee of equal protection of the laws and the constitutional prohibition of the impairment of the obligation of contracts, it had no substantial underpinning within the Constitution for negating hostile state legislation and had to seek it outside the Constitution in the theory of implied limitations on state power. These limitations were found to be implied in natural law, in the social compact, in the character of republican government, and in the genius of American institutions. Ultimately of course they were nowhere more clearly implied than in the genius of an expanding American capitalism.

The first important statement of the doctrine of implied limitations as the basis for vested rights is given by Justice Chase as an *obiter dictum* in *Calder v. Bull* [3 U.S. 386 (1798)]. Chief Justice Marshall in his first great decision, *Marbury v. Madison* [5 U.S. 137 (1803)], showed the trend of his thought in this direction by saying: "The government of the United States has been emphatically termed a government of laws, and not of men. It will certainly cease to deserve this high appellation, if the laws furnish no remedy for the violation of a vested legal right." His statement of the doctrine reached its most significant form in *Fletcher v. Peck* [10 U.S. 87 (1810)], when he refused to inquire into the reputedly corrupt circumstances surrounding the Yazoo land grants on the ground that they had created a vested right, and *Dartmouth College v. Woodward* [17 U.S. 518 (1819)], when he declared rights vested by a state charter of incorporation irrevocable. Marshall's tenacity of purpose and the clarity with which he saw the stakes of the conflict were given substance and circumstance by the erudition of his friend Justice Story and of Chancellor Kent. The latter set down in his opinions in the New York court and in his *Commentaries* (4 vols., New York, 1826–30), delivered as the lectures of a law professor, the fullest and most reasoned exposition of the doctrine of vested rights before Cooley. From the end of Marshall's dominance over the Supreme Court until after the Civil War the vested-rights philosophy was thrust into the background by the Jacksonian supremacy, the slavery conflict, and the needs of federal expansion. It continued, however, almost uninterruptedly in state judicial review in another form—that of the due process clause, which, while unavailable in the federal Constitution against state legislation, was available in the state constitutions. The New York court, which invalidated a whole series of statutes between 1840 and 1860, set the pattern for other states.

After the Civil War the swift expansion of business energies and business power brought again the threat of control by hostile state legislatures. To meet this threat the due process clause of the Fourteenth Amendment was conscripted into service by the Supreme Court for the protection of vested rights, and it was used with greatest effect in those cases where the denial of due process was alleged to constitute a deprivation of liberty of contract. Actually the concept of vested rights, along with that of due process, is vague and malleable. Vested rights have had a varying sanctity in the functioning of the judicial process. In a significant sense the history of American constitutional law is the record of advances and retreats on the battleground of vested rights, the contending forces being those groups who have sought to extend the area of state control and those who have sought to limit it. At bottom these conflicts have been between economic interest groups. But the reality of the battle has been considerably obscured by the rhetoric of democracy thrown over it—in Marshall's day nationalism and after the Civil War individual liberty.

Heartened by its triumph, American business enterprise in the 1880's and after turned from the defensive and sought a free field for industrial mergers and the concentration of power. What had previously been mainly a desire to protect existing vested rights against state encroachment became, in a period of monopoly capitalism, an effort to wrest and hold power for new vested interests. This alternation of periods of defense and aggression, of the protection of existing vested rights and the creation of new vested interests, is integral to the history of capitalism. In America the new vested interests not only broke the competitive pattern of the older economic society but threatened the established political forms. Accordingly two successive generations—in the late 1880's and at the turn of the century—threw themselves into the task of curbing the vested interests. The culmination of the efforts of the first generation was the Interstate Commerce Act and the Sherman Anti-Trust Act; of the second, Roosevelt's trust-busting, Wilson's New Freedom, and the Pujo investigation into the money trust. The legislative efforts were largely frustrated by Supreme Court policy, especially as formulated in the rule of reason with respect to monopolies; and the official attacks and investigations served only to put the vested interests on the defensive again until after the World War.

The attack on the vested interests was a phase of the muckraking era. Denunciations of the "interests" were common in the 1880's and 1890's, especially in the western agrarian movements, the fiction of Frank Norris, and the writings of Henry Demarest Lloyd. But with the turn of the century they became epidemic in the influential magazines and produced a unique periodical literature. Ida M. Tarbell's "History of the Standard Oil Company" (*McClure's Magazine,* 1902–04) and Thomas W. Lawson's "Frenzied Finance" (*Everybody's Magazine,* 1904) were the opening guns of the campaign. C. E. Russell, Upton Sinclair, David Graham Phillips, Alfred Henry Lewis, Burton J. Hendrick, Ray Stannard Baker, and Lincoln Steffens all had a hand in exposing the power of the vested interests and the malignancy of the "system." Their attacks became the foundation of magazine fortunes and writing reputations. The tone of the articles was often as frenzied as the financial operations they described; there was generally more heat than analysis in them; and several of the writers later joined or returned to the fold that they had depicted as a pack of wolves in disguise. The entire movement was probably as episodic in the span of American life as it turned out to be in the lives of the principals. Yet it left some impress on politics, and it subsequently furnished the basis for more detached analysis of the new phases of business enterprise.

The high point of such an analysis was attained in the writings of Thorstein Veblen. He took the term vested interests out of the popular literature of the muckraking period and gave it a laborious and yet ironic precision. His definition of a vested interest as "a marketable right to get something for nothing" (*The Vested Interests,* p. 100) has, however, a greater sharpness in itself than is contained in his actual analysis. The latter suffers from being at once too broad and too narrow, the reference being now to the whole of business enterprise and now to the strategic position of being able to make use of the technique of "sabotaging," or "conscientious withdrawal of efficiency," in the pursuit of maximum profit. With Veblen as with the more popular writers of the muckraking era the term vested interests must be regarded not as a sharply analyzed concept but as a symbol with a shifting reference.

Yet Veblen's analysis has taken on an increased meaning in the period of corporate growth and banker control in the 1920's and in the wrack and reconstruction of the depression period in the 1930's. While the doctrine of vested rights arose originally to protect a socially valid claim against the encroachment of other individuals and was as such sanctioned by the state, it has become increasingly a matter of vesting the right against the state itself. In an era of corporate concentration vested rights have paralyzed the effective functioning of state control and overshadowed the very existence of the state. A communist state finds no place for them. A fascist state, however, after rooting out certain dissident or dangerous vested rights by its totalitarian power, entrenches those that remain more securely than in a democracy. So much have vested interests come to be part of the legal and constitutional fabric that even proletarian movements, such as that of the English Labour Party, include in their plans for a seizure of power the compensation of vested interests.

In the current schemes of economic planning for a controlled capitalism vested interests enter as an important factor; the Tugwell drug-control bill was opposed by some on the ground that if the consumer knew in advance all the conditions of marketing, valuable vested interests in advertising would be lost; on the other hand, the liquor control set up under President Franklin D. Roosevelt expressly provided that nothing contained therein could be later construed as having created vested interests which could be defended against governmental action. Latterly among democratic thinkers a tendency has shown itself not so much to fight the vested interests as to extend vested rights and thereby a stake in social stability to the lower middle class and the skilled worker. This may well become an important factor in the future in meeting the threat of revolution. But whatever the drift, the idea of vested interests, whether as reality or as symbol, will remain of value so long as a capitalist economic system continues to create legal sanctions for its own operations.

1935

7

The Jungle of Legal Thought

IT must have required considerable daring to hack a way into the jungle of modern legal thought and make as much of a clearing as the authors of this symposium [1] have achieved. The London School of Economics is to be congratulated for having seen the need for a presentation of the outstanding modern legal theories and for having arranged this series of ten lectures to fill it. For the varieties of legal experience are more than matched by the varieties of legal thinking. The institutional restraints and lags which hem in the development of actual legal systems do not operate so effectively to check the growth of intellectual systems seeking to explain them. The passion for justice or the dunderheadedness of the Supreme Court is each in some measure kept within bounds by the case system, the Constitution, the needs of statesmanship, and the compulsions of the economic process. But the intellectual passion or dunderheadedness of commentators on the Supreme Court can take a bewildering multiplicity of forms, and the only bounds each knows are the bounds of possibility. All the moot problems of the philosophic tradition combine with differences in social and political outlook, economic loyalties, aesthetic temper, and national psychology, to produce the chaos which is modern legal thought.

Such are the crooked paths which the ten lecturers who contributed to this symposium have not feared to tread. Instead of attempting, however, to write a history of recent legal thought, they have contented themselves with selecting certain representative or significant thinkers and schools. Certainly this was the more compassable task. The jurists selected are Petrazycki, Stammler, Duguit, Hauriou and Renard, Pound, Kelsen, Geny, Maine, Austin, and the American realists.

The selection itself raises, as any selection probably would, ques-

---

[1] *Modern Theories of Law.* New York, Oxford, 1933.

tions both grave and carping. An essay on Pound and one on the realists that concentrates on Jerome Frank are scarcely adequate to express American legal thought; one wonders at the inclusion of Petrazycki, unless it be on the principle that the small nations should have at least one representative; Stammler and Kelsen give some of the flavor of German thought, but both are neo-Kantians, and one misses the Hegelian tradition of either the right or the left; among the French someone like Demogue, outside of the pluralist-sociologist currents of thought, might have found room; although such schools as the American realists and the French institutionalists are given, one misses an essay on the present-day Marxian conception of law such as Professor Laski would have been so qualified to write; finally one wonders whether our English editors are being overly modest or overly frank when they include no English theorist later than Austin and Maine, one of whom wrote in the shadow of Victoria, the other of her empire.

The criticism intended here is not in the direction merely of national representativeness or even modernity of thinking. I am rather raising the question whether the realities of modern legal thought emerge at all from an analysis of the systems of selected individual theorists. Like the biographical approach to history, such a method simplifies the reality, although it may achieve a compensating illusion of concreteness or certainty. The points at which the import of modern juristic thinking is most clearly discernible do not lie somewhere in the completed systems of Stammler, Geny, Kelsen, or Austin, with their patterns of syllogisms like so much frozen architecture. They lie rather in the thick of the polemical struggle, in the making of jurisprudence through the contact and conflict of conceptions. They are often most clearly revealed by reference to the work of writers outside the proper sphere of legal theory. Thus there is more to be learned about contemporary English legal thinking from the work of Maitland in legal history, of Malinowski in anthropology, and of Laski in political theory than is to be discovered through a re-examination of Maine and Austin. According to this conception legal theory is most alive in the clash of schools and at its points of contact with other disciplines. It is as if there were a process of Platonic dialectic at work, clarity about legal thought being evolved through the confronting and resolution of opposites.

But what is not revealed directly in the systems of the subjects of the essays is more likely to be revealed indirectly through the pre-conceptions of the essayists. Each individual essay, as well as the en-tire selection of subjects, is loaded with a hypothesis on the part of the writer as to what are the significant issues and positions today. Unless it is so random and casual an affair as to constitute merely a *causerie,* it must proceed from a genuine analysis of trends and schools. The sum of the ten analyses, or ten sets of preconceptions, contained in the book gives a not inadequate picture of the stuff of contemporary legal thinking. To be sure, it is not the picture or the impression the authors intended: they do not so much give it as give it away.

The common issues that run through all these essays are not the issues that agitated the eminent jurists discussed. They are rather those that are now agitating the writers. It is a commonplace of criticism that we write ourselves and our pet notions into our dis-cussions of other people's ideas. In fact, other people's ideas are generally the safest currency with which to speculate. Mr. T. S. Eliot once wrote, in an unsparing essay, that when Medea in the play of Euripides is made to say in the Gilbert Murray translation: "This thing undreamed of . . . hath sapped my soul: I dazzle where I stand, the cup of all life shattered in my hand," some of the phrases were a gift from Mr. Murray. "It is he who has sapped our soul and shattered the cup of all life for Euripides." What is so true of all criticism and inherent in the task of translation is even more ob-vious in the analysis by one legal philosopher of the system of legal ideas of another. We cannot help translating into the intellectual currency of our day and circle. The Medea that appears in Mr. Mur-ray's pages is not the Medea of Euripides, but is Medea as seen by Mr. Murray through the eyes of the pre-Raphaelites, especially Swinburne. The Hauriou, the Maine, the Geny that appear in the pages of this book are seen through whatever haze or clarity the con-temporary climate of opinion, especially in English academic circles, offers.

One thing emerges clearly from these essays: the issues that agitate the writers are not such as to fall easily into the traditional classifica-tions into schools—as, for example, analytical, historical, philosophi-cal, sociological. Such divisions no longer express the significant rifts between theorists. They have been broken up into other divisions or, what is more likely, are criss-crossed by them. The issue of realism and empiricism crops up in a variety of forms; the claim for a normative or formal science of law is pitted against an institutional emphasis of one sort or another; pluralism and state power receive, as may be expected, greater emphasis in a book coming from the London School than in one that might come, say, from the Yale Law School; a concept-jurisprudence is still under attack variously by those interested in social change and those interested in an open-eyed inductive approach; the struggle of intellectual absolutisms against pragmatic or instrumental approaches has taken on fresh and sharp meanings; radical and conservative approaches to economic institutions cast their shadow, although they do not appear in the foreground. On the whole the quarrels turn out to be ultimately not quarrels of method or even of doctrine, but of the directions in which the body of legal institutions and doctrine is to be shaped. The body of legal thought as it comes down to us in any one intellectual generation is a curious blend of elements from the past that are archaic, some which possess continuing vitality, preoccupations of the present, foreshadowings of the future. Each school, in its attempt to shape this material to its own purposes, will lay a varying emphasis on the entities with which legal thought deals: on legal rules, legal doctrines, legal institutions and agencies, logical and philosophical truth, social institution, social fact and policy, class interest, state power.

Within this common circle of interests many of the essays have a richness of implication and a freshness of their own. Professor C. A. W. Manning writes with intelligence, discrimination, and considerable wit of Austin and Austinianism. He revisits Austin as Wordsworth once revisited Yarrow, and he finds, as Wordsworth did, that the reality rivals even the fond memory of earlier days. Since Austin first sought, in his *Province of Jurisprudence Examined,* to keep jurisprudence within well-marked limits, the stars in their courses have fought against him. The historical and sociological movements in jurisprudence have both crept aboard; new and strange growths have arisen in anthropology, psychology, political theory, radical economic policy—growths that have made the province of jurisprudence even more cluttered and untidy than Austin found them in his day; he has become a fair mark for every young theorist impatient of the restrictions of an imperative theory of law or feeling himself too hemmed in by the precision of Austin's method. We have grown accustomed to, and like Professor Manning a bit tired of, hearing Austinianism called narrow and mechanical. The very volatile and amorphous character of legal thinking today makes it all the more necessary not to minimize the achievement of a man for whom law was granite and whose mind was a deftly handled chisel.

Mr. Robson's just and ordered essay on Sir Henry Maine presents that amazingly fertile mind as a sharp contrast to the rigid analysis, the unsentimental and persistent way that Austin had of keeping his eye always on the object. Mr. Robson emphasizes Maine's "brilliant, comprehensive, illuminating generalizations," the "eminent peak from which he surveyed the world," the fact that "he blazed a great trail and opened up the heavens"; but he points out also that later knowledge has shown many of Maine's conceptions to be quite fantastic, and he adds some strictures especially upon his conservative political theory. There is much in the ferment of Maine's mind that makes him "modern" although he wrote seventy-five years ago, and the explorations which we are making today into related fields in the interests of jurisprudence are in the tradition of the forays that Maine made. Despite these wide views Maine's mind was not flabby and liberal; it was tough and Tory; and he wrote some of the toughness of his Tory outlook into his glorification of private property which he put ostensibly into the form of a discourse on *Ancient Law*. Mr. Robson notes (and this view may be found stated with greater particularity in Mr. Smellie's very suggestive article on Maine in *Economica*) that for Maine private property and civilization "are inextricably entangled." Maine should have sat on our own Supreme Court. He would have been a worthy successor to Marshall, and he could have fought lustily in the days after the Fourteenth Amendment for due process and liberty of contract and the fabric of civilization—so lustily that it would have taken half a dozen Brandeises to undo his work.

The frontal attack on Austinianism comes, however, not from Maine's historical and comparative school but from some of the French and English jurists outside of it, and it has been directed not only against the imperative theory of law but especially against the monistic view of sovereignty. This attack is quite adequately represented here. Mr. Ivor Jennings, the editor, writes of the French institutionalists Hauriou and Renard, who break a lance for the Catholic Church and natural law and attempt a fusion of neo-Thomism and recent institutional theory in their attack on the state. Mr. B. A. Wortley writes of Geny, who is attacking the too rigorous method of interpreting the French Code and who makes a plea for greater judicial discretion and for law as a social science. Professor Laski, himself a leader of the pluralist forces, contributes in his unfailingly lucid and trenchant manner an essay on Duguit's conception of the state, in which he points out that while Duguit is effective in his criticism of the exclusive claim of the state to sovereignty his own constructive formulation of his legal theory is indecisive.

"It never does harm," says Mr. Jennings at the conclusion of his essay on the French institutionalists, "to be told repeatedly that the state is only one among institutions." I should grant such a statement my mild assent, but I should point out the possibility that too continued repetition might in the end prove merely boring. And I should subscribe wholeheartedly to Professor Laski's warning that it will not do merely to deny the exclusive sovereignty of the state; such a denial must, in addition to rejecting the metaphysic it is attacking, construct for itself a new and more satisfactory metaphysic. And that is the one thing that both pluralism and institutionalism, whether in economics, political theory, or law, have thus far failed to accomplish. The analysis of social institutions given by Hauriou and Renard seems pitifully inadequate when compared with the analyses of Veblen, MacIver, or Hamilton; yet even they have some of the indicia of transitional gropings for a reality not found in the narrower formulations.

For the German theorists this metaphysical realm is the realm of certitude. The unfailing logic of Stammler and Kelsen has a terrible, insistent sequence even when it is crossing the widest of abysses. Professor Ginsberg's sympathetic and discriminating analysis of Stammler is all the greater achievement when it is remembered that nothing short of expository genius would be adequate to make transparently lucid the thought of a man who defines law as *das unverletzbar selbstherrlich verbindende Wollen*. Mr. Lauterpacht's essay on Kelsen is so conscientious in its fidelity to the original body of thought that it cannot help being arduous in the reading; but it is ultimately rewarding. It requires a continuous intellectual athleticism to follow the far-roving and exacting mind of Kelsen, and at least one reader can testify to being muscle-bound in the end. But no legal thinker today is so rich and challenging in all the resources and implications of his thought as Kelsen is.

Both Stammler and Kelsen are rationalists; both are neo-Kantian in persuasion and critical in method; both are impatient of the current fashions in the direction of empiricism and sociologism. But Stammler ends by basing himself vaguely on a theory of the objective ends of law, to be ascertained by reason; Professor Ginsberg points out acutely that it is too abstract a view of reason, "which, while doing lip-service to a remote idea of reason, leaves actual law and actual morals at the mercy of empiricism and the blind force of tradition." Kelsen on the other hand not only manages to make metaphysical ends meet in his system, but also gives an overwhelming impression of the richness of philosophical resources and the breadth of social vision which he possesses but which he is deliberately excluding from his legal theory. His thinking represents the most heart-breaking form of intellectual asceticism that one is likely to encounter. I cannot help deploring that sort of hara-kiri, because I feel that what is required today is not an austere dissociation between moral *Weltanschauung* and legal science but an equally austere and heroic attempt to effect a thorough integration of the two. Nevertheless, Kelsen will continue for a long time to have real validity for American legal thinkers. That validity lies in his unsparing treatment of the "needs of life" schools which are forever making the adaptation to social change an excuse for slovenly or emotional thinking.

This is a charge to which sociological schools of law are always laying themselves open. Recent American thought, which is largely sociological, offers thus a delicate problem for analysis: in the march of legal thought it has been definitely in the vanguard, yet it may be questioned whether it has not pushed ahead so unheedingly as to cut itself off from its base of supplies. Sir Maurice Amos's essay on Dean Pound does not raise any such disquieting suggestion. It is on the whole an urbane commentary in which one could hope that some of the urbanity had been replaced by the sort of thoroughgoing critical analysis which Pound's importance warrants. Such an analysis would reveal that Dean Pound's thought is neither so summary in its outlines nor so static as Sir Maurice's essay gives it the impression of being. Not so summary, because Pound has qualified and subtilized his sense of law as primarily an ideological entity, moving on an ideological plane, as also his animus against the "in-human strictness" and the "coldly syllogistic method" of the Aus-tinian school; not so static, because Pound's thought has always oriented itself toward some specific intellectual and institutional situation in the law, seeking to change or reform; and it can accord-ingly be best understood in terms of such a development. But a rigorous analysis of Dean Pound might reveal also that, large as he will loom in the final history of American legal thought, he has been attempting an essentially impossible task. His thought has sought to move in two worlds. On the one hand, it has emphasized the lag of the law behind the realities of economic change, and has sought to close the gap; on the other hand it has consistently denied that economic realities have anything to do with the movement of legal ideas or institutions. This bifurcation has become increas-ingly obvious as Pound's labors have borne fruit in the field of legal-institutional reform and attention has been shifted from his "social engineering" conception of law to his emphasis on the autonomous development of legal ideas.

The American realists, while they have much in common with Dean Pound, find themselves on the whole leading the opposition at present. It is unfortunate that Professor Goodhart's essay on them is the only one in the book which is so unsympathetic to the intellectual system of the subjects discussed as to put the reader definitely on his guard. Professor Goodhart gives the impression of being on a heresy hunt, and of having a decided flair for it. He writes with wit and abandon, and some of his sentences pack a lot of dynamite. The useful thing he has done has been to isolate five rather popular tendencies in present-day American thought and subject them to thoroughgoing analysis: the stress on the uncer-tainty and atomism of the law, the attack on logic, the stress on psychology, the attack on legal terminology, and the tendency to measure the law in terms of its effects.

Some of these I should wish to deplore almost as much as Profes-sor Goodhart does. But I should hesitate to regard them as consti-tuting a school. One would be hard put to it to discover among these five traits any common or unifying element. Much of the confusion in the discussion of American "realism" lies in the fact that it does not constitute a philosophical category or position. It is more likely to be based on an economic attitude or a social *Weltanschauung*. It derives from the general revolt against formalism, which it shares however with Pound, Holmes, Cardozo, and even, to some extent, a rationalist such as Cohen. It derives more specifically, however, from a pragmatist-behaviorist-institutional set in social thought, and from a common economic liberalism. The real meaning, for example, of the intellectual passage of arms that Professor Goodhart describes between Jerome Frank and John Dickinson is revealed less clearly in the pages of any book than it is in the work that these two men did within the Roosevelt administration. Pascal's remark that "three degrees of elevation of the pole reverse the whole of jurisprudence" might be equally applicable if the reference were not to the physical climate but to the climate of economic opinion.

1934

8

The Theory of the Social Process

THE history of the social-process concept is closely tied up with the history of the emergence of sociology as an autonomous study. Albion Small wrote that "all sociologists since Comte have more or less consciously assumed this concept as their major premise." [1] And it was Charles Horton Cooley's opinion that "the first requisite in the making of a sociologist is that he learn to see things habitually in this way." [2]

The influence of the concept on the American sociological tradition has been enormous. Small, in seeking to clarify the concepts by which an adequate foundation could be built for sociology as an architectonic science, selected social process as the basis for his construction and embodied an analysis of it in his book *General Sociology* (1905), which he afterward described as "a treatise on the category 'social process.'" Earlier in the same year E. A. Ross had analyzed the concept at some length in his *Foundations of Sociology*, which Small described as "the first [book] in English to put much stress on the term 'process' as a scientific social category." He added, however, that "Ratzenhofer had anticipated both books, and the term 'social process' has been used in a semi-unconscious and amateurish way by a great many people." Small's influence was important, since he was principally a student of the history of ideas and brought to the attention of the American group an account of the sociological tradition from the time of Montesquieu and Savigny which ran principally in terms of the making of social-process theory. The theory had a marked effect upon the thinking of Ward, Giddings, Bentley, Ellwood, Dewey, Mead, and Thomas in

---

1 Small, *Origins of Sociology* (1924).
2 Cooley, *Social Process* (1918).

493

America, and of Simmel, Oppenheimer, and von Wiese in Germany. But after Small the most important name in its development was that of C. H. Cooley, whose *Social Process* (1918) summed up the state of thought on the concept which American sociology had reached in its maturity. Since then there has been a tendency to carry it to an extreme, notably in the "Chicago school," where it became the central conception of sociology and the principal instrument of analysis. Society came to be viewed not only and primarily as process but as a network of innumerable processes.

Negatively the concept of social process represents an important reaction against static theory. It is characteristically opposed to the conception of society as structure, or society as a formal or static arrangement of blocks of material. As such it is closely tied up in the history of ideas with evolutionary thought, which did for the whole of social thinking what the philosophers of history had succeeded in doing for themselves only by a gigantic intellectual effort: it shaped social thought in a temporal perspective. It thrust into the foreground of the philosophic consciousness the notion of society as a developing organism achieving its continuity through some sort of selective process related to the performance of function. The study of the formal and the logical gave way to the study of development and activity.

Where evolutionary thought was not completely triumphant a literature of reconciliation arose, well illustrated in English thought by the writings of Bagehot, Ritchie, and Caird. It is on the whole quite easily explainable that the idea of process should have flourished in the intellectual climate of an age of rapid movement in inventions, of swift social change, an age with its codes and standards in flux. To this historical reason must be added a more strictly psychological one, indicated by Henri Bergson's remark: "The consciousness we have of our own self in continual flux introduces us to the interior of a reality, on the model of which we must represent other realities." Similarly G. H. Mead, in a shrewd essay on Cooley, says that he discovered his society "from the inside. . . . Finding it in living, it was a process." [3]

At the core of social-process theory is thus the notion of movement, change, flux—of society as a continual becoming. "Society,"

---

[3] "Cooley's Contribution to American Social Thought," *American Journal of Sociology*, 35 (1929-30), 693-706.

writes R. M. MacIver, "exists only as a time-sequence. It is a becoming, not a being; a process, not a product. . . . Society . . .
lives on only as a changing equilibrium of present relationships." [4]
Georg Simmel in fact took the position that, since society is never
a product but only a process, one should not speak of society at all
but only of socialization. And Ross called the social process primordial, since it not only constituted society but logically preceded
it. But apart from the negative value of furnishing an antidote
against an undue structural emphasis in social thought, there is
little in process theory itself that makes it a valuable instrument of
analysis. The mere flux, continuity, becoming, finally emerge as
ends in themselves, and they tend to inhibit questions of the purposes or direction of the process or of differences of value in it.
Social-process theory thus becomes a species of raw vitalism, in
which the stuff of social experience is set up as the supreme and
unquestioned value and as the final term in explaining itself.

But this does not exhaust the importance of the idea. It must be
seen as the center of a whole configuration of concepts ranged
around it which are both historically related to it and logically
implicit in it. These are: first, the concept of process itself; second,
the concept of social interaction, or of society as a flow of relations
between individuals; third the concept of historical and social continuity; fourth, the concept of the organic connection between the
individual and society; fifth, the concept of the social heritage; sixth,
the concept of society as an organic unity; seventh, the concept of
multiple factors and the rejection, in the problem of social causation, of any particularist or determinist elements.

The conception of society as an organic whole of interrelated
parts goes back to Montesquieu, whose *esprit des lois* arose from the
relation that the laws themselves bore to the whole of the social
order, that whole constituting the *esprit général*. But it received its
classic expression in Hegel, with his sense of society as an organic
whole. In Hegel's thought this theory of organic unity was combined with a theory of historical dialectic which emphasized the
continuity of history. A similar emphasis is to be found among
the traditionalists, notably Burke and de Maistre, who counted

---

[4] *Society: Its Structure and Changes* (1931), chapter XX.

upon the ordered continuity of religion and tradition to knit together the social fabric and who insisted upon the organic connection of the individual and society. Comte, whose formative thinking was not very far removed from the shadow of the European revolutions, followed the traditionalists in their appreciation of the unity of society and the continuity of history. He saw history as development, although after a hierarchical fashion that was his own contribution; and he saw society and the realm of thought itself as organic wholes.

To the influence of Hegel, Comte, and, later, Darwin in forming social-process theory there were added in the nineteenth century Marxian thought and the repercussions it aroused. This gave rise to a polemical struggle which revolved about two axes: the validity of what was primarily a conflict theory in the interpretation of social change, and the validity of the materialist interpretation of history with its selection of a single set of factors as constituting the dynamic of historic change. In sociology the conflict theory was represented by Gumplowicz and Ratzenhofer. While not in the main line of the Marxian tradition, they were largely inspired by the doctrine of the class struggle and extended a similar analysis to the sociology of racial and national conflict. They had considerable influence upon American sociology, principally through Small and Ward.

The problem of the materialist interpretation, however, even more than the theory of conflict, became the storm center of European sociology in the last quarter of the nineteenth century. The counter-statement to the Marxian position found much support by reverting to Eichhorn's theory of the complexity of society and the multiplicity of factors that must be invoked to explain the movement of events. Multiple causation became the rallying cry of those who opposed or feared Marxian thought. This counter-statement took extreme form among the Russian liberal sociologists, such as Lavrov, Mikhailovsky, and Kareyev, and among the French solidarists; both set out to defend the theory of multiple causation in the interest of libertarian democracy. Representing the middle ground between Marxism and traditionalism, they sought in historical continuity for the laws of progress which would justify and fortify their libertarian efforts. They debated incontinently the questions of the relation between the personal and the impersonal factors in the historical process and of the relation between the individual and society in the social process. The prevailing point of view was that of the organic unity between the two. This is represented in German thought also in the work of Stammler, Simmel, and Dilthey, and the basic preoccupation is perhaps best expressed in Dilthey's phrase, the *Strukturzusammenhang,* or inner unity, between the individual and society.

It is significant that Cooley's *Social Process,* which stands at the end of this whole historical sequence in the sociological tradition, includes the entire configuration of elements in social-process theory. Indeed the logical connection between them is clear. If society is a process and not a product or an agglomeration, it follows that it can be only a flow of relations or interactions between individuals. Von Wiese's definition is helpful: "We are all 'relatives' in the old, now obsolete, meaning of the word—that is, we are all persons relative to, connected with, or dependent on others. . . . Social process . . . is the dynamic aspect of any given social relation." [5] And if society is a flow of relationships, it follows that history is an unbroken continuity of such relationships—an evolutionary process in which, as in the organic world, nature makes no leaps and in which the most catastrophic act is the attempt to break with the past. For the individual by himself is helpless; he lives only through his relations with other individuals around him and even more through his relations with the individuals who have preceded him; it is the social heritage that they pass on to him, in the form of accumulated knowledge and crystallized institutions and vested interests, which enables him to muster the requisite skill and order through which he may survive. Thus in such a train of reasoning the question of the individual versus society becomes pointless, as social-process theorists are careful to point out: the individual lives only through society.

This organic connection obtains, however, not only for any individual and the society of which he is a part but for the society as a whole; the primary note here is the Hegelian "altogetherness of everything." Not merely history but society itself is a seamless web which the thinker can break only at his own peril. The Marxian theory, borrowing as it does from Hegel, is also an organic theory;

[5] L.M.W. von Wiese, *System der allgemeinen Soziologie,* adapted and amplified by Howard Becker as *Systematic Sociology* (1932).

but in it the dialectic of history is moved by a set of particular causes: the organization of production is so bound up with the other social manifestations that changes in it produce corresponding changes in them. But the main line of social-process theory is organic in a quite different sense. It does not admit of any particularist emphases, and it sees a qualitative homogeneity in the entire social process. The problem of social causation becomes thus infinitely complex, permitting no simplification. A change in any part of the social process is to be accounted for only in terms of changes (which are both cause and effect) in a multiplicity of factors in the rest of the social process and, by ultimate logic, in the whole of it.

The implications of this entire complex of theory for social change and its consequences for social action are far-reaching. By stressing the unbroken continuity of history and society it tends to bolster the *status quo* and to inhibit revolutionary action which might break with the past and endanger the fragile social heritage. The change that the theory envisages is in reality only that of continuity and not radical or revolutionary change. By positing the organic relation of society and the individual it places the locus of the social process and the locus of change in the mind of the individual, denying society as an objective reality and denying also the sweep of impersonal forces in history.

On the whole, social-process theory represents the liberalism of the realm of sociology. It has furnished the foundation for progressivism in political and educational movements and for an entire program of social work and social reform. Sociologists have for the most part followed Cooley's injunction and adopted it as their fundamental intellectual attitude. But its very indecisiveness has done much toward preventing the achievement of an adequate theory of social change or social causation. And through its function of rationalizing the adherence to the *status quo* and the fear of revolutionary action it has in the movement of events carried implications of a definitely anti-liberal character.

1934

9

The Pattern of Dictatorship[1]

THE contemporary concern over the advance of dictatorships
is not merely the expression of our democratic bias but
proceeds from deeper intuitions. There are moods in history
when the world map is in essence a military chart, and every governmental change in even the least important country comes like a
bulletin from the battlefield, laden with fateful significance for the
entire world outlook. Our present mood is one of these. There are
still some minds, of course, that persist in regarding the new dictatorships as momentary departures from the democratic norm,
just as there are some at the other extreme to which they seem completely catastrophic, spelling the end of the world, the jumping-off
place for civilization. We must reject both these perspectives. But
one thing may be said for certain: we are dealing here not with a
few sporadic and abnormal seizures of power but with the political
fiber of an entire period. The question may well be posed whether
we are not entering upon a new age of despots.

If so, it means that the liberal-democratic state—whose foundations were laid in the English constitutional struggles of the seventeenth century, which achieved its great victories in the American
and French Revolutions, and which reached its classic form in the
nineteenth century—is in that classic form no longer possible. So
completely has it dominated the whole span of the past few generations that it has been accepted in rhetoric even where it was not followed in actuality, and under its influence Marxist theory itself
tended to interpret the dictatorship of the proletariat in constitutional terms. That era of unquestioned acceptance is at an end; the

---

[1] This was a paper read at the meetings of the American Historical Association,
December 1933, first published in the *Yale Review* in 1934 as "The New Age of
Despots" and later reprinted in Guy Stanton Ford, ed., *Dictatorship in the Modern
World* (1935; 2nd ed., 1939). Although events have moved rapidly in the past five
years I have thought it better not to make any changes since the original publication.

present struggle for power marks its passing. Even if the democratic state survives in some form and is not completely swept away, it will re-emerge in a new shape, bearing the impress of the struggles it is now waging with dictatorship.

But the very sharpness of the clash between democracy and dictatorship exposes us to the danger of simplifying both and of thinking of them as two absolutes, locked since the beginning of the centuries in mortal struggle and now again confronting each other. Dictatorship is undoubtedly old, as democracy is old or kingship. It has a tradition of its own. But in such matters tradition is unimportant, except in so far as it enters as an element into the intellectual climate of the new regime, causing Mussolini to talk about Caesar and strut like Bonaparte, and Hitler to revive the glories of the Cromwellian revolution. My meaning will be clearer if I put it into extreme paradoxical form: that the dictatorial power itself is far from being the important fact about the modern dictatorship. We have grown accustomed to thinking of any sort of concentration of power in the hands of a man or of a group as despotism, and are prone to guard too jealously a democratic dispersion of power. But the reality today is not dictatorship as an abstract idea, opposed in a timeless dualism to the idea of democracy, but dictatorship as it is set in the struggles and dilemmas of our own age. What really counts is the scheme of society and view of life represented by the dictatorial regime, the process of building it, and the consequences that flow from it. The power of the dictator is, of course, the central fact of this scheme. But it derives its meaning, whether sinister or salutary, from its relationship to the rest of the pattern. It is this pattern of dictatorship that must be subjected to analysis.

It is now almost two decades that dictatorship and the threat of dictatorship have dominated the political scene in the Western world. The collapse of the great Central and Eastern European empires even before the end of the World War left the ground completely open for that struggle for power which is always latent, even at the height of order and security; and constitutional democracy was not strong or militant enough to seize and hold the power. In almost every country of Europe that has been hard hit by the war three groups fought it out for supremacy—the liberal-socialist *bloc*, the communists, and the conservative *bloc* of large landholders, heavy industrialists, and bankers. Three principal types of dictatorship were evolved. First, the constitutional dictatorship by the liberal-socialist *bloc,* represented typically by the Kerensky, Karolyi, and Brüning regimes. These were generally the first to profit by the revolutionary overthrow of the monarchist and reactionary governments that had fought in and in most cases bungled the war. Between the anxious passions at the extreme left and right their *via media,* however, proved unstable. Second, the communist dictatorships of Lenin and Bela Kun, which moved like a specter across Europe in the days just before and after the Armistice, like a specter dominated the wranglings at Versailles, but except in Russia left only spectral and impermanent results. Third, the counter-revolutionary or White dictatorships, successful where the socialist and communist revolutionary movements proved premature or unstable—in Poland, Finland, Hungary—and leaving in their wake a White Terror that will rank among the most ghastly episodes in all history.

To these must be added a fourth type—the fascist dictatorship—which has thus far proved more durable and effective than any of the others. As it evolved, principally in Italy and Germany, it has been closely related in spirit and objectives to the counter-revolutionary movements but has included more affirmative elements. It has sought not merely to fight Marxism defensively but has developed an affirmative ideology that would make it more effective in the struggle. It has wakened responsive movements in countries as diverse as Austria, the Balkan states, France, England, Ireland, America, and Japan. It is today the focal type of dictatorship, growing continually in definiteness and universal applicability, engaging the energies and loyalties of ever-wider groups, constituting itself the opponent at once of the constitutional-democratic state and of Marxist movements. There was for a time a disposition to say that fascism was a polity unique to Italy, to be explained only in terms of Italian national psychology and traditions. But the movement of events finally took this question out of the realm of academic dispute. After Hitler's great parliamentary gains Mussolini remarked: "Whoever says that fascism is not an exportable commodity is mistaken." It is on this "exportable commodity" that our analysis of the pattern of dictatorship will center, drawing also, of course, upon the communist and earlier counter-revolutionary dictatorships wherever that can be done without doing violence to their own contexts. On the whole, however, it must be made quite clear that in terms of purpose, ideology, and tradition there is between the fascist dictatorships and the dictatorship of the proletariat a deep and unbridgeable chasm.

But it is not only the contemporary persuasiveness of fascism and its position as the focal point for anti-democratic action that make it the important pattern of dictatorship today. Even more crucial is its continuity with the whole line of development of the Western state. There has been a marked tendency to attribute the growth of fascism to post-war conditions—to the Carthaginian peace with its stigma of national humiliation, its unsatisfactory territorial adjustments, its problems of demobilization and unemployment, its widespread monetary inflation, its legacy of national hatreds. This is sound enough as far as it goes, but stopping there it is truncated and provincial. These influences are themselves merely the crystallization of forces inherent in modern economic and political development. The war, the peace that followed it, the depression that followed both, were the logical consequences of our capitalist-individualist economic organization and our system of nation-states. Wherever the dominant economic groups found that neither the liberal-democratic state nor the constitutional dictatorship could preserve national unity and fight the threat of communism, they were willing to scrap both types of government and accept in their place the anti-liberal, anti-proletarian fascist dictatorship. By what was more than a happy coincidence, their own interests and those of the fascist movements were rooted in a militaristic nationalism. The fascist dictatorship has thus become the mailed fist thrust out in defense of the capitalist nation-state. In the future wherever proletarian movements or economic collapse threatens the two basic institutions of capitalism and nationalism, and wherever the democratic state is unable or unwilling to defend them, we may expect that the struggle for power will center in the fascist dictatorship. If, in short, we are really to have a new age of despots, then here is the design for the despotism.

This design should not be conceived as too clearly and sharply etched. Actually fascism smells of the blood and dust of battle, in which fixed principles are so many impedimenta. It has had to make its way amidst treacherously unstable national and international conditions. It has had to be above all else mobile, and light-ning-quick in its adaptations. "The *fascisti*," Mussolini himself has said, "are the gypsies of Italian politics; not being tied down to any fixed principles, they proceed unceasingly toward one goal, the future well-being of the Italian people." And Hitler, despite the "unalterable" character of the twenty-five propositions early laid down in the party platform, has proved himself a consummate op-portunist. But pattern there is none the less in the fascist dictator-ship—not in the ordered consistency of doctrine and action but in the significant relation between the objectives, techniques, and doctrines of the dictatorship and the interests it represents.

In the making of any dictatorship three principal stages are dis-cernible—the preparation for power, the thrust at power, and the entrenchment in power. The first is occupied with the laborious building of a movement, and must find ways of reaching and enlist-ing mind and heart and will. It creates therefore an ideology, a leader, a technique of persuasion, and an organization for action.

Of these the ideology, or system of ideas, is the most conspicu-ously paraded—and is perhaps the least important. It constitutes at best the rhetoric rather than the logic of dictatorship, and is to a large extent a rationalization after the fact. The fascist ideology falls rather naturally into several groups of elements. There is first what we may call the *anti* group, in which fascism declares itself anti-liberalism, anti-tolerance, anti-parliamentarism, anti-election-ism, anti-equality—in short, against the whole machinery and all ideals of the liberal-democratic state. The indictment, which has by this time thoroughly entered the modern consciousness, is that the democratic state consists mostly of talk, that in crucial emergencies it has produced paralysis rather than action, and that through its weakness it has permitted the victory of alien and bolshevist ele-ments. Against these—communists, socialists, Jews, foreigners—it directs its primary hatred, holding them responsible for the de-cadence or the anarchic violence of the preceding regimes.

The second group of elements in the ideology consists of the cult of the nation-state and of the related patriotic and militaristic vir-tues that are to heal its wounds and restore it to its former glory. The nation is the cohesive force that must override every class, sec-tional, economic, or religious loyalty.

The third, and in a sense the crucial element is the concept of

order. Unlike the loose-knit law-and-order concept of the constitutional state, this is a militant, driving concept. It seeks to stamp out
all dissident elements, create the structure of the corporate or totalitarian state, bring firmness and authority where libertarianism
and tolerance had existed, establish a set of known relationships in
a system of status, and a hierarchy at the apex of which stands the
leader of the party and the guardian of the state.

Finally, add to these three groups of elements the myth of a
cultural renaissance, and you have a complete and rounded ideology. The renaissance as embodied in Italian fascism has its varied
roots in the Roman imperialist tradition, the old *Risorgimento*,
Marinetti's Futurist movement, and Mussolini's own contempt for
the old men and his zest for *giovinezza*. In Germany there are none
of the futuristic elements, more stress upon the return to the primitive Teutonic virtues, and the intention of eliminating all racial
strains except the "Aryan," which has been traditionally the carrier
of those virtues.

Such an ideology, given the purposes it is to serve, is an immensely skillful construction. It shows that its framers have learned
the primary principle of the whole business—that an ideology must
create and manipulate hatreds as well as loyalties, that it must make
use of the most deeply ingrained habits and prejudices, that it must
lull inferiorities and direct cruelty and despair into politically useful channels. The spirit or *Geist* of fascist and Nazi culture is more
than a literary expression. It has served like a huge tide to float an
entire political revolutionary movement.

The most important symbol and emotionally the most evocative
figure in the entire movement is the leader himself. But to say this
is to say nothing more than could be said of any outstanding Hollywood star, whose appeal lies partly in her beauty, partly in the kindness of lighting and the make-up artists, and partly in the expertness
of direction and the ministrations of a huge sales and publicity staff.
The dictator, like the movie star, has been excessively romanticized.
A glamour-starved populace, both in his own country and abroad,
creates the myth of a superman who focuses all the energies of his
time and dares put an end to inaction. By enlarging his stature they
succeed in compensating for their own dwarfed and stunted stature
in an industrial age. He is *il Duce, unser Führer*. He sways tens of
thousands by his daemonic oratory; he moves about in a continuous

hysterical parade; wherever he goes heels are clicked, hands rise to salute, hoarse and eager throats do him homage. In due course this begins to tell on him, for he is generally a person capable of persuading and hypnotizing not only others but even himself. If, to begin with, he was only a man who wanted to be dictator, he ends by becoming a combination of Caesar and Messiah. And naturally so, for he comes at the end of a long romantic sequence. All the centuries of romanticism, by emphasizing genius and leadership and a Promethean defiance of fate, have contributed to his construction. He stands there, mystic, adventurer, orator, fanatic; the man of action who moves by his words, the man of words who incites to action; the hero of our time, which had begun to fear that it had lost its capacity for hero-worship.

But this is only half the story. The other and more important half is that the building of a dictatorship is, under the modern conditions of the machine age, a large-scale industry, and the leader himself, therefore, a part of the machine process. A successful movement toward a dictatorship must enlist a membership, arrange meetings and speeches, gain the help of the press or establish a party press, distribute propaganda, win over the aid or connivance of the police and the army, penetrate the churches, clubs, and trade unions, build a party organization with local units and leaders, equip, arm, and pay a private army. It must, in short, add to all the business requirements of running a successful party the further burden of running a military establishment, staging a revolution, and preparing for a new social order. All this requires organization, advertising, salesmanship, and financing. The dictator is, then, really the product of romanticism who finds himself part of a huge administrative organization. He is a Byronic figure caught in the machine age. He stands thus at the confluence of two worlds, an enduring witness that history is not a matter of clear sequences but shuttles back continually from present to past in weaving its unbroken web.

Thus the leader not only rides the movement but is ridden by it. He becomes part of a whole train of needs and purposes and techniques and consequences. He may become not a symbol but merely an instrument, used by the interests that can afford to dig down in their pockets to furnish the sinews of war, incapable of retreat, unable to go on without them. Once they have accepted him it becomes immaterial whether he really possesses the Nietzschean qualities attributed to him; if he does not, they can be created for him.

The earlier analysts of the fascist dictatorship, impressed by the fact that it had found fertile soil in the despair and desolation of the middle class, held that it was a middle-class movement to secure the interests of that class against both the proletariat and the capitalists. But this is to mistake a favorable soil for an effective force. Like the Russian peasantry in regard to communism, the middle classes in Italy and Germany were willing to tolerate and even aid the fascist movements. Theirs was the nationalism that was whipped up to a fury; theirs, the most credulous, was the intolerance; theirs, the least class-conscious, was the hatred of class groupings; theirs, the most stereotyped and culturally starved, was the reveling in the symbolism, the insignia, and all the trappings of an *opéra bouffe*.

But the real stakes were those of the industrialists and landowners. It was a large banking house that first gave Mussolini financial backing, and the Thyssen steel *bloc* that gave Hitler his. In both movements there was a definite progression away from the mild socialism with which they had begun to an out-and-out conservatism. The invectives against bankers in the Nazi propaganda grew increasingly milder until they ended lamely in the distinction drawn by Feder, the party ideologist, between productive and unproductive capital, the latter presumably belonging to the Jews. Long before the party purge of June 30, 1934, Hitler dissociated himself from the left wing of the party, represented by Strasser and the Nazi-bolshevists, after which he was able to be more persuasive in the speeches he made before private gatherings of the great industrial magnates. They, on their part, when they had got over their initial distrust of demagogic methods and irresponsible personalities and had seen through some of the phrase-making, were not unwilling to join their fortunes to a movement that could vitalize the flagging opposition to radicalism. They shrewdly saw that the two could march to power together. There was one clear common ground on which the industrialists could meet the Nazi and fascist leaders—common hatreds and common nationalist zeal. Not only were they tied together by economic interest; they were both tied impalpably to the nation-state by all the symbols in which they had come to believe.

With an ideology, a leadership, an organization, financial support, the enthusiasm of the middle class, and the backing of the vested interests, the remaining task in the preparation for power is systematic terrorism. In the terrorism that follows the successful establishment of a dictatorship there is little to choose between the Reds, the Whites, and the fascists, except, of course, as one may sympathize more or less with the particular aims that terrorism serves. But terrorism as a systematic preparation for power, as a way of keeping one's own military impulses in trim while crippling and demoralizing the enemy, is a specific characteristic of the fascist movements. The basis of operations is the party army—in Italy the black-shirt fascist squads, in Germany the brown-shirt storm troops. Similar private armies are found, in a more or less developed state, wherever a fascist movement has taken hold.

Such an *imperium in imperio* would have seemed inconceivable in a strong nation before the war, but the disintegration of the state power in both countries after the war reduced the state to a police force attempting to keep the peace between armed camps. The typical activity was squadrism—terrorization by bands roving over the countryside or squads descending suddenly upon a trade-union headquarters or a newspaper establishment and destroying it, or kidnaping some too troublesome member of the opposition and beating him into unconsciousness. Such strong-arm work often got beyond the control of the leaders themselves, who strove to discipline some too zealous squadrists or storm troopers, or attempted to dissociate themselves from specific acts of violence, as Mussolini did in the instance of the murder of the socialist deputy Matteotti. But this must generally be taken as an official dissociation, which does not necessarily exclude the usefulness of the act to the movement or even a personal desire that it be carried out. When an entire movement is deliberately founded upon a philosophy of violence, it is somewhat casuistical to repudiate particular acts. To an American with a law-and-order tradition inherited from Anglo-Saxon constitutionalism, it would seem unthinkable that private armies or strong-arm squads should be allowed within the state if it were not that we had our own racketeering and gangsterism as instances. In either case the state's capacity to enforce order has broken down, and private organizations for protection and attack operate interstitially in the particular area of activity where the state is powerless.

To be effective, such a preparatory reign of terror must have the sympathy, or at least the toleration, of the police, the army, and the magistrates. Here a fascist movement, appealing to nationalist and militarist attitudes, has in a capitalist-minded people a definite advantage over whatever private armies the socialists or communists may possess. In Germany the republican regime made its crucial error by carrying over the police, the judiciary, and the army officers from the monarchy. They stood by inactive while the strength of the republic was being whittled away by civil dissension, allowed assassination and terrorist acts to go unpunished, and, when the crucial time came for the *coup d'état*, aided the transfer of power. In Italy there was open camaraderie between the squadrists and the police, and in the March on Rome, Mussolini was able to make a grand gesture by placing at the head of each of the five divisions of his Black Shirts a regular army general.

Given such a situation, the actual thrust at power is less dramatic, less dangerous, and—if we may put it so—less crucial than is generally conceived. If the preparatory work has been done thoroughly, it is a relatively formal affair, those in power being less concerned with a militant defense against the movement for dictatorship than that they be offered a sufficient show of force to save their faces. The March on Rome served this purpose quite adequately, and neither the prime minister nor the king cared to engage Mussolini in an actual trial of strength. In Germany Hindenburg and Papen counted on being able to control Hitler more effectively when he was given the responsibilities of ministerial office. In both countries the nature of the cabinet system gave the transfer of power a parliamentary form, ironic enough considering the anti-parliamentary character of the movements. The genuine danger to the realization of the dictatorship comes not from the existing regime but from the possibility of a general strike. But this possibility is considerably decreased by the memory of past terrorism, the speedy destruction of the workers' press, and cleavages in their own ranks.

With the dictatorial party in power, the road to the establishment of the dictatorship itself is, even under a parliamentary system, swift and certain. The party can accomplish under the guise of legality what it could not have accomplished as a revolutionary movement. This was especially true in Germany, where the reverence for the state and its functionaries is deeply ingrained in the individual burgher. The first task before the new government in dissolving the parliamentary state is to stamp out all opposition. All the opposition armies are disbanded, their parties outlawed, their press destroyed, their funds confiscated. The reign of terror is intensified: it becomes incredibly brutal, merciless, calculated; it is now directed against those who are defenseless and pleading. Those who are spared death and do not succeed in fleeing the country are, as in Germany, placed in concentration camps or, as in Italy, exiled to penal colonies. The tactical principle governing all these operations is that everyone in any way connected with one's enemies is, if not already a political offender, at least potentially one, and should therefore be put out of the way.

With equal thoroughness all the government services are purged and refilled with party men. This not only assures the entrenchment of power but takes care of the supporters who have been clamoring for jobs and helps the movement to get on the bandwagon. The government's licensing function is used to rid the professions of undesirable elements, and even the large business corporations have party agents placed on their boards of directors. The technique of effecting so complete an entrenchment in power has measurably improved with experience, so that Hitler was able to accomplish within a few months what it took Mussolini as many years to do. But in Hitler's case the added speed and ruthlessness overshot their mark: hence the jerry-built structure of coercion and the need for terroristic purges within the party.

The dictatorship is now ready to lay down the lines of its completed polity. This includes the single-party system, the thoroughgoing local party organization, both in local communities and in the factories, the transformation of the party army into a party militia, the control of all the agencies of communication and education, the focusing upon youth of a propaganda that associates with the discipline of the movement their holidays and social pleasures, the all-powerful "blood and iron" state, and the hierarchical concentration of party leadership and state power in the hands of the dictator. Some of the main lines of such a polity—given, of course, the fundamental differences that may exist in aims and consequences—are common to both the developed communist and the developed fascist dictatorship. Sidney Webb's phrase describing the

Communist Party as the "steel frame of Soviet society" would apply equally to the Nazi and Fascist Parties. Relieved of the usual need of competing with other groups for power, the single-party system represents a new conception of the function of the party. It becomes, along with governmental services, an arm of the administration, and the more effective arm—watchful, zealous, setting the pace, and taking the leadership in every area of social activity. This requires discipline and periodic purgings of the party membership. It requires also a far-flung local party organization. In the Italian polity this led to the system of *rasses* or small party bosses exercising continuous and often irresponsible local coercion—a system whereby, as one Italian deputy put it, Italy had not only a central dictator but "9362 miniature dictators, one in each town." Germany, too, is covered with little Hitlers and Russia with little Stalins. The fiber of the central regime cannot help penetrating to every crevice of the entire polity.

The other important cadre of fascist political organization is the corporate or totalitarian state. This involves characteristically the organization of the economic groups that compete for the distribution of the national income into government-supervised associations, or "corporations," with the government holding the balance of power. All open conflict in the form of strikes and lockouts is banned and the labor movement is nationalized. But this does not mean that the dictatorial regime involves a genuine system of economic control or even of state capitalism. The essential outlines of private property as an institution and individual profits as an incentive are retained. What the dictatorship aims to do is to prune capitalism of its irresponsible individualism, assure it a steady return, and insure it against labor difficulties. The corporate state is then far from being the *stato forte* in the economic sphere. If it is a despotism, it is here a benevolent despotism. But everywhere else its sway is undisputed, with the important exception of the Church. Both in Italy and Germany only the churches continue to compete with the state for the allegiance of the individual citizens. The state has not been able to make much headway in absorbing them, largely, perhaps, because the belief in religion is an act of faith more richly and deeply rooted even than belief in the nation or in a great leader.

The part of the dictatorship which is put to the greatest strain by the accession to power is the dictator himself. Overnight he is compelled to assume a double role—to combine the glamour of the revolutionary extremist waging *mein Kampf* with the sobering responsibilities of power, which call continually for compromise and qualification. He must continue to preach militarism and huge armaments, yet somehow keep from getting embroiled in an inconvenient war; must continue his anti-labor policy, yet keep the productive forces of the nation going; must continue to be a myth, yet function as a reality. Yet his prestige grows, even with every fresh factional split in his party; for the essence of party divisions in a single-party system is the vying over loyalty to the leader. His best security is the knowledge that on him and him alone depend the little islets of power he has created for every man in the organization.

But though their immediate aim may be spoils and power, the ultimate vision of the adherents to a dictatorship is far different. The democratic bias ends too easily in attributing to any dictatorship only a vision of earth and no vision of heaven. The dictator's heaven is contained in the society he is aiming to establish. This society contains three essentials: it is aristocracy, it is built upon a definite system of status, and its thought and culture have been purified of all imperfect elements.

The notion of the "élite," which has taken the imagination of the fascists, represents the revival of old impulses toward aristocracy which democratic industrialism had completely repressed. The aristocracy of the upper bourgeoisie under capitalism had never really been a satisfactory one; it had been too mobile, too new and callow, too accessible to Jews and upstarts. The fascist dictatorship aims to create a new élite, or else to entrench the old landowning aristocracy and give it an official stamp. Below this there will be a system of status, forming an ordered and stable society in which each individual shall have his definite place. The women are to be taken out of industry and brought back to their old position in the home and encouraged to rear children. All the elements of the population that cannot fit into such a scheme must be stamped out or allowed to wither away, and there has even been some discussion in the German dictatorship of sterilization for the non-"Aryan" elements. Thought and culture too must be brought under political control, lest the heavenly city of the dictator and the élite be tainted by earthly dross.

It will not do to dismiss all this as a madman's dream of power. It is a complete scheme of life. It seems at first sight to represent a reversal of our whole cultural and political drift during the past three centuries. Actually, however, it is a direct and natural outgrowth of our present society. The dilemmas that fascism seeks to resolve are our dilemmas, the institutions it wishes to conserve are the basic economic institutions of our society, the loyalties it appeals to are the loyalties that attach to the nation-state which we have created, the militarism it exploits is the same militarism that leads to our own wars, the passions it channels to its purposes are the race and class passions that grow out of the competitive struggle inherent in our society.

Most significant of all, the techniques upon which the dictatorship chiefly relies, both in building and maintaining its power, are in reality those used, though less arrogantly and with a less explicit political intent, in a democratic society. I am not referring to the Black Shirts and the Brown Shirts, to the March on Rome or terrorism, but to that entire mastery of mass persuasion without which all the shirts would have been only so many yards of cloth and the March on Rome merely a paranoid fantasia. The democratic state has had to dispose of an increasing amount of unneeded products that its machines were turning out, it has had to drum up the war fever, and it has had to give its masses the illusion of power while withholding the actuality. To do all this it evolved a technique of advertising and of high-pressure salesmanship, a flamboyant journalism, a radio and a cinema that stamped the same stereotypes on millions of brains. We have been naïve enough to believe that our nationalism and militarism, our race and class conflicts, our advertising and salesmanship, our techniques for influencing opinion and manipulating the effective symbol in swaying mass emotion would always remain in the same pattern. But under fascism an economic and political convulsion has disarranged the pattern and is forming its elements into a new one. "We think with our blood," says Hitler, and there seems to be something a bit alien and shocking about the irrationalism that underlies such a statement. But actually that is the basic premise of all the techniques of mass persuasion which we have ourselves been using. The most damning blow the dictatorships have struck at democracy has been the compliment they have paid us in taking over (and perfecting) our most prized techniques of persuasion and our underlying contempt for the credulity of the masses.

The recurring question about the fascist dictatorships that have established themselves is how long they will survive. It is evident that they have effectively stamped out opposition, and that they are using with consummate skill the entire apparatus of school and press and radio in inculcating civic loyalties and "teaching the young idea to shoot," to their own purposes. Short of economic collapse or a catastrophic war there is no reason to believe that these dictatorships will not endure on into the calculable future. What strains and stresses may be developing meanwhile that may cause their eventual disruption we have no means of telling. There is a copybook maxim that "nature, expelled with a pitchfork, ever returns." This would be a consolation to the believers in democracy—if only they could be certain that nature is on their side and not on the other. It is possible that responsible constitutional government under the conditions of industrialism demands too much both of the human brain and the human will. It is possible that democratic government has been able to survive as long as it has only because it has operated under the surplus economy of the period of an expanding capitalism. In either case the real aberration will prove to have been the democratic effort of the past few centuries; and the pattern of dictatorship with its submission to authority, its entrenchment of the powerful economic interests, its gaudy adornments, its system of status, its intolerance, will invest with a deep security a new age of despots.

1933

10

The School and the Common Man

I N A capitalist democracy the position of the school system is
something of a puzzle. It is the arm of the state and the faithful
servant of the economic interests that the state gives political
expression to; yet it is also one of the main reliances of the underlying population which by accessions of knowledge seeks to prepare itself for power. The school system is the channel through
which all the impalpable but powerful social conventions that support the *status quo* can be directed to the point of greatest effectiveness—the minds of young people; yet at the same time there
is instilled in those minds that most powerful corrosive of social
institutions—the capacity to read. Seen as a polarity within the
state this may go some way toward explaining the dual strain in
our educational history—*étatisme* and academic freedom. Seen as
an inner contradiction in education itself, it gives point to the
desperate confusion in the social thought of outstanding American
educators.

It is with a considerable awareness of this fundamental duality
that Professor Curti has written his analysis of the social ideas of
our educational thinkers.[1] It is not a book that dissects educational
thought in a vacuum. It silhouettes it against a developing system
of business enterprise. It is a rich, detailed, well-documented study
—but, more important than that, it is one that could have been
written only for a generation whose principal interest in education
is the way in which it affects the survival and transformation of
state power.

The theme itself has a dramatic force that American intellectual

[1] *The Social Ideas of American Educators,* by Merle Curti (*Report of the Commission on the Social Studies: Part X*). New York, Scribner, 1935.

514

historians have never done justice to. The real protagonist through-out is the common man and the making of his mind. Each succes-sive movement in American life left a deposit on his consciousness, and it left also its imprint on the school system which helped form his consciousness. The American Revolution was never to a great extent a social revolution because it was never consolidated within the mind of the common man. The Revolution swept by education and left it relatively unchanged. The schools were allowed to keep their class foundations. A new constitutional structure strength-ened the old oligarchic lines of the polity which the schools were now conscripted into strengthening further.

When the radicals finally came back into power—under Jefferson and again under Jackson—they were either unwilling or too weak to use the schools deliberately as a democratic weapon with which to challenge the holders of economic power. For they were pri-mari'ʃ western farmers and city mechanics, and the reach of their demands was the extension of state-subsidized education to the children of the common man. So long, however, as the schools were under the old controls and taught the old religious and political dogmas, this was the sort of advance that left the armies of democ-racy more vulnerable than ever, deep in the enemy's own territory.

The triumph of business after the Civil War was also decisive in the history of the school system. The sweep of enterprise carried along with it the schools and the educators. It swept immigrant groups, frontier groups, urban groups into a more intensive indi-vidualism and into a way of life that stressed personal success rather than collective action, social distinctions rather than mass democ-racy. It made all the new human material that was going into the forming of our culture a plastic surface on which to stamp the im-print of business values. And in this process it was the schools and the educators that made the common man accessible to the propa-ganda of the rulers.

Professor Curti's treatment of the educational implications of the democratic and anti-democratic movements before the Civil War is the best I have ever met in the literature. His discussion of the social ideas of the American educators who have influenced the common schools deserves to be read as a supplement to Thor-stein Veblen's *Higher Learning in America*. The chapters on Wil-liam James and Stanley Hall subject to a new scrutiny the social consequences of their thought, with drastic results. The chapter on Edward Lee Thorndike is a masterpiece of cold analysis. One could wish that the chapters on the author's own masters—John Dewey and George S. Counts—had been equally rigorous.

There is one basic cleavage within the book itself. Like Parrington and Beard before him, Professor Curti tries to resolve the points of view of Jeffersonianism and Marxism—and ends by veering from one to the other. From Marxism he takes the conception of the school as an arm of the state, imprinting the stereotypes on which, even more than on the military and the police, the power and viability of the state rest. From this angle a choice between different methods of educational organization and different types of educational thought is nothing more than a choice between varying malevolences. From Jefferson he takes the conception of the possible development of influence and importance for the common man within the prevailing institutional framework. Mr. Curti's plight is the plight of our whole generation of realistic thinkers, outside of education as well as within it. It is the plight of those who are concerned about the fate of the common man and his culture in a social system that is weighted against both.

What brightens somewhat the prospect for our generation is that the school system, as Professor Curti shows, has behind it a great democratic tradition which can be evoked to confront the compulsives of business enterprise. The energies for building our common schools came originally from the common man, even though their control passed into the hands of the possessing groups. If education is ever to be swung from capitalism to democracy, it must be moved by a process that will at the same time make it a releasing rather than a standardizing force. The schools as standardizers create robots for the existing power groups. Schools that will take the mass energies that are pent up in them and give those energies release and direction will be freeing themselves—and the social system as well.

1935

11

Democracy with a Union Card

1

IT IS a sign of labor's coming of age that the newspapers have turned sedulously to examining the nature and extent of trade-union democracy. A weak labor movement does not deserve or get that much attention, either from its enemies or from its friends. As long as the American Federation of Labor stayed within its narrow preserves of craft unionism and refrained from hitting at the great nerve centers of the capitalist structure—the mass-production industries—it could be as undemocratic as it chose. As soon, however, as the Committee for Industrial Organization split off to do the actual job of organizing the unorganized, and succeeded amazingly in getting the job done, its internal mechanisms of power became a matter of enormous moment to everyone.

Which is as it should be. Democracy is not a classroom concept, worth pursuing because of the beauty of its contours or for some absolute validity it possesses. Democracy is only a pragmatic assurance that power will, on the whole, be used for and not against the community interests. That is why democracy never becomes vital until the question of power has entered. No one concerns himself about how an empty hulk is captained and manned. And the question of power has now entered the labor movement with a vengeance. I have talked with businessmen, toughened to their own corporate despotisms, who could think only of the danger of despotism in trade-union leaders. I have heard state and national politicians speak of the new power of labor with a disquieting incertitude as to what it might do to their political futures. I have heard even the liberals, perhaps I should say especially the liberals, discuss the new forces of labor as educated Romans must once have discussed the barbarian hordes beyond the Danube and the Rhine. To listen to them, one would feel certain that the Goths were veritably here.

The comparison may actually be not without a certain force. Our historians tell us that some of the strongest elements in the democratic practice of the Western nations go back, not to the imperial institutions of Rome, but to the tribal practices of the barbarian Germanic peoples. It needed the synthesis of Greek thought, Roman political organization, and Teutonic folk custom to produce what we call Western democracy. In this mixture the vitalizing force came probably from the last of the three, where the democratic impulse was strongest because it arose from day-to-day communal experience and the necessities of communal organization. In the same way, it is possible that the eventual American democracy will be again the result of a fusion. To the idea of majority will that we got from the French revolutionary thinkers, and the idea of minority rights that we got from the English parliamentary struggles, we may be able to add the actual functioning democracy of the everyday work-life of the trade unions.

For our American democracy may, so to speak, stand in need of some sort of rebarbarization. The original democratic impulse, as it emerged from our revolutionary struggle against Great Britain, has been overlaid by a powerful plutocracy and all but stifled in the climate of business success. But it is not beyond hope of revival. For political life is only a glove: the hand underneath, which gives social reality to it, is the daily work-life of each person and the habits of thought that it engenders. There is a chance that we shall be able to put more and more social substance into our formal political democracy. But that chance lies only in our being able to democratize the basic units of our economic life, which determine the conditions of our living and the patterns of our thinking. Those units are the corporation and the trade union. Democratize the corporation and the trade union, and you have laid the basis for genuinely democratizing the state. Of these two, it is less likely that the corporation will insure democracy in the trade union than that the trade union will bring democracy to the corporation. Only, to do that, it must first clean its own house and make itself democratic as it grows in power.

Unfortunately, the unions have not consistently seen this. They, and those in sympathy with unionization, have lately tended to think mainly in terms of power, of a labor organization strong enough to protect the interests of its membership. This single-mindedness is intelligible, since any organization in process of growth must think first of winning and consolidating its power. But that is not enough. On the other hand, those employers who have not set their faces stonily against every form of unionism have been thinking exclusively in terms of union responsibility to the state and under the law. This single-mindedness is also intelligible, since a labor war creates a panic mood in the minds of employers. But this is not enough, either. We must all face the problem of creating a framework within which labor can be powerful enough to secure its rights and achieve its valid social purposes; responsible enough to gain the respect of open-minded employers and the alliance of the middle class; democratic enough to insure its future against the racketeer, the bureaucrat, and the dictator. If we fail in solving that problem, we confront a bitter social conflict which may result in no social gain but only in chaos.

These are some fears and hopes about trade-union democracy. Without a democratic structure, the labor movement may relapse to the feckless swivel-chair bureaucracy of the 1920's. Or it may become an irresponsible giant, using its strength for purposes determined not by its rank and file but by some inside clique. With a genuine democracy, on the other hand, it may not only gain its demands in wages and working conditions, but it may became the spearhead of a drive for recasting our institutions until they assume, under the economic conditions of today, the shape that the democratic elements in our past have intended them to have. Not all who call loudly for democracy in the labor movement envisage this end, and many of them would be frightened by it. But I am not writing this analysis to please those who talk about labor violence and call for labor responsibility merely because that is the best stick they can find to beat the labor dog with. Liberals and conservatives alike who invoke democracy in the labor movement must face the consequences of democracy. They must face the fact that just as it is the growing power of labor that has produced all the concern over labor democracy, so an increasing democracy and responsibility in the labor movement cannot fail to swell its strength further and make it one of the great shaping forces in our national destiny. For democracy means nothing less than the health of the labor movement.

2

The thing to remember about the new labor movement is that it is really new, and not merely a continuation of the old. Something has happened in American labor in the past few years that is comparable to what happened fifty years ago, when the Knights of Labor felt their power slipping, struggled for a time against the inevitable, and finally gave place to the American Federation of Labor. I think it can scarcely be doubted that the CIO, like the A.F. of L. in the late eighties, carries with it the whole brunt and burden of historical development. We have come again to what Henry Adams would have called a "change of phase" in labor history.

Why do I speak of it as a change of phase? When the Knights yielded to the A.F. of L., a vague movement of social insurgency gave way to a definite and conscious trade-union movement. That was a change of phase. The Knights were in many ways superior to the new Federation: they were broader in their social views, less jealously an organization of the skilled alone. But they did not form as good a fighting unit. They spread amorphously over the field of labor, including in their ranks middle-class groups, farmers, and intellectuals—drawing the line only at the exploiting classes. Samuel Gompers, the little Jewish cigarmaker who served as the Napoleon of the new forces, was shrewd enough to see what Terence Powderly, the leader of the Knights, could not see—that labor stood a better chance of gaining its aims if it restricted them and made them concrete. Like Napoleon, Gompers reduced a social program to a military campaign.

The strength of Gompers and the Federation was that they knew what they wanted. Instead of gazing starry-eyed toward a vague social ideal, they wanted better wages, shorter hours, better working conditions. They held themselves realistically within the economic limits of their task and achieved an almost Marxian emphasis on the material basis of the worker's life. When asked at a congressional investigation what it was that labor wanted, Gompers said, in effect: "Labor wants more and more and still more." A little Marxism may in the end prove a dangerous thing, and the smattering that Gompers got from some of the German immigrants was only a smattering; but Gompers did succeed in analyzing what it was that had

produced the weakness of the Knights of Labor. He saw that it was
on the one hand their broad and too inclusive middle-class radicalism, and on the other their milk-and-water welfare, Friendly Society sort of unionism. Both defects could be remedied by a militant
trade unionism that directed itself to the job of the worker and
pressed always for the immediate concessions that the union's
strength warranted.

The new labor movement of today has similarly analyzed the
weakness of the A.F. of L.: it is the weakness of a trade-union organization which has failed to use its full powers in organizing the unorganized and unskilled, and which refuses to adopt an industrial-
unionism base for fear of challenging the vested interests in the
craft unions. As of Gompers, it may be said of John L. Lewis and
his associates on the CIO that they knew what they wanted, with a
decisiveness that brought success in its wake. They wanted renewed
militancy in labor, based on industrial unionism, and capable of
confronting the new strength of the banker-controlled giant corporation. Of course, the fact that action based on this analysis led
to enhanced power, not only for labor but for the CIO leaders as
well, was to them a by no means negligible fact. Nor must we forget
that if they had been allowed to remain within the A.F. of L., their
purpose of using an industrial-union base might not have been
pushed with so relentless a disregard of craft-union vested interests.
But the important thing about men in public life is not how snow-
pure their motives are, but how they act, given the position in
which history has placed them. And the CIO leaders have been
placed in the position Gompers occupied fifty years ago—where
their own power interests are identical with the vigorous forward
movement of labor.

The change in the American labor movement cannot be reduced
to a single term. There is a new base for organization—the industrial-union base. There is a new leadership. There is a new temper
and militancy, both in leadership and in the rank-and-file membership. There is a new readiness for political action and a consciousness of its importance. Together these sum up to what I have called
a change of phase in American labor. If any single element were to
be selected out of this sum to express the meaning of the change as
a whole, I should say it was the new perspective in both leaders and
men. There was a saw current some years ago in labor circles that

American workers could be grouped as follows: soup-conscious, job-conscious, class-conscious, and unconscious. The perspective today is none of these things, but *labor-consciousness*. Coal workers organize steel workers; garment and auto workers organize textile workers. The thinking is no longer in craft terms; nor is it yet, if indeed it will ever be, thinking in clear-cut class terms. It sees the labor movement for the first time as something of a totality, and is willing to use what means are necessary to make it an organized totality. That is what gives it strength; that is what elicits the Dionysian energy that courses through the labor movement today. Beyond the mustering of that energy and the achievement of that totality, this thinking does not go.

This raises, of course, the persistent question of how long this impetus will last. The A.F. of L. also started out bravely. But in labor, as elsewhere throughout the social organization, the original impetus gives out, leaders become bureaucrats, vested interests grow up, and the impulse toward expansion is replaced by a fatal tendency toward constriction. Above all else, labor forgets to view its role in terms of the whole fabric of economic development.

The wisdom of the A.F. of L. originally lay in seeing that if labor wanted to share in the fruits of business prosperity, it must be prepared to bargain for them on the economic plane. Hence the concentration on trade unionism, pure and simple. Hence also the restriction of organization efforts to the skilled aristocracy of labor. For given the skills on which the industrial structure depended, and given the still undeveloped integration of industry, a strike among skilled workers was an adequate bargaining weapon. A labor movement, moreover, had to have continuity through the successive phases of the business cycle, in hard times as well as good: that meant it had to accumulate dues from the workers best able to pay them—the steadily employed skilled workers. But what started as a measure of sound policy became perpetuated through fear of the vested interests in labor. The very principle of restriction to the skilled groups was to prove fatal to the A.F. of L. The type of labor organization that was suitable to cope with the capitalism of the turn of the century became unsuitable to cope with the capitalism of the 1930's. For the latter represented giant corporations, many of them enjoying a monopoly position or easily capable of uniting on a common line of action, pyramided so that their control lay in the hands of a small banking group.

It is significant that the central object of Gompers's attention was the need for meeting business enterprise on a strictly economic plane. It is equally significant that the central fact that Lewis has grasped is the present integration of industry and the pyramiding of financial power in our society. From the social insight of each man has flowed the corresponding change of phase in labor history.

3

I have dwelt on the historical perspective because without it a good deal of the current controversy over labor democracy will seem so much sound and fury, unmotivated and undirected. If you understand the historical forces that have shaped the labor movement, you will not be seduced into the cloud-cuckooland of wishful thinking on either side. You will not believe that you can exorcise the strength of labor by calling Mr. Lewis names, or by lashing the unions to the mast of governmental restrictions. You will not believe, on the other hand, that no one need worry about where labor is going, that the energies of labor will necessarily find their own sound direction. The broad movements of history give the framework for action. What happens within that framework is a matter of human personality and leadership, of techniques and strategies and policies.

The principal problem within labor organization, as everywhere in the state, is the problem of leadership and the lack of it, of power and its abuse. The failures of labor leadership and the abuses of labor power fall under four heads: grafting and racketeering, chair-warming inactivity, dictatorship, violence and legal irresponsibility. The first two are generally charged against the earlier phase of labor history; the second two against the present phase.

Racketeering and grafting are diseases not of the labor movement but of commercialism itself, of the ethos of our entire economic world. Those diseases have extended themselves to labor, as they have extended themselves to every other part of the social organism. Considering how easy a prey labor is to the racketeer, the surprising thing is not that so much of labor, but that so little of it, has been affected. Taking racketeering in its strict sense—the shakedown of employers in the name of "protection," the cut-in on workers' salaries in the name of "job insurance," the appropriation of union funds as a private treasure-trove, the annexation of whole unions by mobsters as a supplementary source of income—such charges can be brought against only a fraction of the labor movement: among the building trades, the motion-picture operators, the musicians, some of the painters' locals, the restaurant workers, and the retail clerks. The clarity and forthrightness with which the American Labor Party in New York supported the racket-buster Thomas E. Dewey for the District Attorneyship is an index of how marginal racketeering is to labor. And it is notable that where the new labor spirit has produced rank-and-file revolts against corrupt leaders, racketeering has been most courageously and effectively fought.

Far more serious is the problem of the labor skate—the walking delegate who has worn his feet flat and the swivel-chair executive who has worn his pants shiny. There is nothing quite like the labor bureaucrat. He is a combination of Rotarian, southern Congressman, and Grand Army veteran, with almost equal portions of petty money-mindedness, spread-eagle oratory, and reminiscences of past battle scars. These bureaucrats have for decades controlled the old-line unions, like a praetorian guard in control of the state—except that they are wooden and not real soldiers. What makes the problem of bureaucratic leadership worse in the labor movement than it is in government or in business is the loneliness and isolation of the union leader. Once chosen, he has no retreat. For the gulf between an ordinary worker and a union leader is so broad that the span across it is traversed in only one direction. If union leaders are to have the dignity that their bargaining status requires and if they are to be immune to the wooing of industry, they must get salaries considerably above the union wages and live on a new level of comfort. And they do not want to return to their old jobs. Their loneliness, their love of power, their desire for a sinecure make the problem of rotation in office extremely difficult. This means the building up of political machines, the creation of a hierarchy of henchmen, the slow death of union militancy from the top down. Above all else, it means the tragic waste of the potential resources of leadership in the rank and file.

The CIO has changed this situation in several respects. Partly because it is still new, partly because its success depends on ever-wider organizing gains, partly because its entire base is close to the realities of the labor struggle, it has cleared out its dead wood with great effectiveness. Its top leaders are, to be sure, men of experience who have held their jobs as labor officials for years—men such as Lewis, Hillman, Murray, Dubinsky, Brophy, Howard. But they have retained their vitality throughout, as indeed the entire CIO venture witnesses. More important, no organizing campaign in the mass-production industries could have been carried through so swiftly except by the devoted efforts of the progressives and radicals —and some of the best leadership reflects this leftward emphasis. Finally, and most important, below the top leaders there is what we may call a rank-and-file leadership—in the locals, joint boards, shop councils, state centrals, and organizing staffs—a group of young, confident, and realistic men who reveal what resources of leadership had been lying around unquarried within the ranks all this time. These factors are an assurance that at least for the calculable future the problem of the new labor movement will not be one of inertia in leadership.

There are fewer assurances against its being one of overactivity in the struggle for power. The new danger is generally considered to be that of a labor dictatorship. There is a new specter to haunt our minds—the massive figure of John L. Lewis, with a head whose prognathous outlines suggest the barbaric and ruthless *Machtmensch*. Since fear is a response to the unknown rather than the known, one may find, underlying the fear, an uncertainty as to the potential strength of the vast labor masses undergoing organization. What power Lewis may in the future be able to amass and hold is anyone's guess. I incline not to be too fearful of the prospect, for several reasons.

One is that Lewis is being watched with a cold and skeptical scrutiny as no leader has ever been watched, with the exception of Mr. Roosevelt. For the spread of fascism, with its *Führerprinzip*, has put us all on our guard against the dictator growing up within a democracy. Lewis, moreover, is only *primus inter pares*. As events have already shown, the other CIO leaders are not merely lieutenants, but co-leaders with minds and purposes of their own. Finally, it is clear that Lewis understands the forces that have raised him to his present position—the desire of the workers for effective organization—and he knows that his own power hinges upon his being able to deliver the goods. Powderly tried to hold the rank and file of his Knights of Labor too tightly bound, and in breaking loose they swept him aside. The IWW leaders were much too far ahead of the American workers, who never caught up with them. The A.F. of L. leaders have lately gone dead on their following. Lewis and the other CIO leaders are too realistic to make the same mistake. Lewis's whole career shows that, with all his stubbornness, he still has the quality of flexibility, of "give." He talks resolutely and defiantly, and the workers like him for it, as a contrast to the sense of inferiority that previous leaders have had when confronted by the grandees of business and government. But this big talk is largely for the purpose of maintaining morale. In this respect, Lewis reminds me of no one so much as the Russian general Kutuzov, as he is depicted by Tolstoy in *War and Peace*. For Kutuzov knew that the leader was there only to give assent and form to the upsurging energies of his followers, and that without that energy he was helpless.

But all this is my own set of guesses. Political communities should minimize their guesses, however, and leave as little as possible to chance. The best insurance against the abuse of power by Lewis or anyone else is a strong and responsible democratic labor movement, which understands its objectives, knows its relation to the law, and has developed inner techniques for checking whatever personal imperialisms may develop. Since strong leadership is always necessary and, even with safeguards, always dangerous, the wise course to adopt toward any leader is to see to it that the path which leads to the attainment of his own power is a path that leads through the achievement of the objectives of the whole organization.

4

The recent growth of the labor forces has been attended, as was inevitable, by violence on both sides. The lions who roar daily in our newspaper columns and editorial pages have assumed an attitude of outraged indignation which does scant justice to their knowledge of history. For violence has always been a part of labor struggles in America. Anyone who doubts it has only to read the record in Louis Adamic's *Dynamite* or Samuel Yellen's more recent

American Labor Struggles. More than that; violence is deeply rooted not only in our labor struggles but in the whole American tradition. It has been part of the American experience from the time we liquidated the Indians and took the continent away from them, up to the present time when the record of our contemporary violence is written in the pages of every daily newspaper. But I do not mean to imply that violence is in any mystical sense part of the American national character. It proceeds rather from the historical fact that a mixture of vigorous peoples has sought to exploit the resources of a continent in the ruthless spirit of a competitive capitalism. Labor violence, in its clash with the violence of the impersonal corporation, has been part of that picture; and the blood spilled at Haymarket, at Homestead, at Ludlow, at Herrin, has flowed from the main arteries of American experience.

The anxieties today are not only over direct violence but also over such "secondary violence" as contract-breaking, wildcat strikes, and sympathetic strikes. Two bodies of opinion have arisen among businessmen in viewing this whole question of labor militancy. One is determined to fight it to the death, believing that any concession to a powerful labor movement will only make it more powerful. Its vision is conditioned by the payrolls of today and the ballot-boxes of tomorrow; it believes labor gains to be an economic loss for business, and labor organization to be a prelude to a labor government, and it sees in labor militancy a determination to achieve both at all costs. This view is typically represented by the Little Steel executives, who fought and to an extent broke the Little Steel strike. The second view sees labor violence as a direct outgrowth of the repression of labor in the past through espionage, company unions, the stretch-out, and vigilantism. This view is represented typically by the Big Steel executives, who signed with the CIO and have recently renewed their agreement. There is a touch of the Promethean even about a businessman, and both these groups see themselves driving a salient into the future by means of which the battle over industrial relations will be decided.

It can scarcely be anything but clear to observers that the labor violence of the past few years flowed from the suppressions of the past. I do not believe that violence in itself justifies retaliatory violence. I do believe that violence begets violence, and that the violence of labor is puny and trivial compared with the mammoth violence that has been practiced on labor by employers, police, and courts. One has only to compare the labor order in Big Steel with the unrest in Little Steel and the sporadic outbreaks in the automobile industry. In Big Steel there was a systematic organizing campaign and a voluntary settlement; in Little Steel there was an unsuccessful strike; in automobiles, there was a successful but bitterly fought strike, at the end of a hasty organizing campaign. The moral is dual. If employers sow the wind, they must be prepared to reap the whirlwind. And where the CIO has had a chance to do the painstaking work of organization, it has combined responsibility with strength.

What this means is that labor responsibility and labor discipline are better achieved from within than from without. The present movement to impose labor discipline from without is based on a tragically false premise. The premise is that you can produce either responsibility or democracy by fiat. Trade unions can be successfully regulated only when they have already achieved their basic objectives. Compare, for example, the situation of railroad labor and maritime labor. The Railroad Labor Board employs a system of conciliation whose machinery for delay and arbitration has effectively prevented strikes and settled disputes. Railroad labor accepts it and is tolerably happy under it. But when Mr. Kennedy proposed the same plan for maritime labor, he was bitterly fought by the CIO maritime unions. And they had reason. For the Railroad Labor Board came into being only after a long history of railroad labor struggles which had resulted in complete organization. Being on a plane of equality in bargaining position, the unions can now afford to work within the framework of governmental arbitration. But the maritime unions, despite their amazing growth in the past few years, are not yet fully organized; and there are serious internal dissensions between old-line and CIO unions. The machinery for delay and arbitration could easily be used to prevent organizing efforts and break strikes; it could also be used to stifle the rank-and-file revolt which is displacing the old-line leaders.

This example will illustrate the suspicion with which the unions regard the whole group of proposals for making them more responsible under the law—the proposals for incorporation, for publicity of accounts, for the outlawing of sympathetic strikes, jurisdictional strikes, sit-down strikes, for revisions in the Wagner Act, and for compulsory arbitration. Individual items in this program may be relatively harmless; the program as a whole, however, when applied to a trade-union movement that has not yet reached maturity, must result either in stifling trade-union growth or in further outbreaks of resistance and violence. Those who point to England as an indication of the success of such a program have both their facts and their premises wrong. For England, despite its reactionary Trades Disputes Act of 1927, which bans sympathetic strikes and which was put through after the collapse of the general strike of 1926, does not compel either incorporation of trade unions or arbitration of disputes. And even the Trades Disputes Act was not passed until British labor had already gone through its CIO phase and reached a measure of mature strength and political expression.

Labor order cannot be legislated into existence at this stage of our industrial history, if ever. To pursue such a policy leads, by the easy stages of descent that Vergil once described, down to the hell of the corporate state. Labor order is the organic outgrowth of two conditions: a healthy state of industrial relations, for which equality of bargaining position and an advanced degree of organization are necessary conditions; and internal democracy, within both the corporation and the trade union. The only regulatory function over labor that government can safely perform today is to provide a framework within which labor and industry can achieve these conditions of organic health. The government can seek to guarantee the maintenance of civil liberties in labor struggles, as it is doing through the splendid work of the La Follette investigating committee; it can provide machinery for collective bargaining and for easing the settlement of jurisdictional disputes, as it is doing through the Wagner Act and the work of the National Labor Relations Board; and it can set minimum standards of wages and working conditions in industry, which are still being fought for in the form of the wage-hour bill and the Child Labor Amendment. Beyond that government action is fraught with grave danger.

5

The energies that have produced a militant labor movement have been turned not only outward, against employer domination, but inward, against boss-manned and racket-riddled machines as well.

This energy has generally taken the form of rank-and-file tactics organized by minorities—tactics employed, incidentally, in the American Revolution as well. Such rank-and-file movements have become democratic as they have got under way, even when the original steps were taken by only a few. It is for this reason that the communists have a place in the CIO beyond their numbers or importance: they have the energy and zeal and discipline for these tactics of inaugurating democratic revolts against a bureaucracy, as they have also for starting new unions. Once in office, they have in several of the unions retained an influential place by the extent of their responsiveness to the needs and desires of the union members.

There has been a tendency in the press to show alarm over this fact. I see no real reason for it. What should be alarming, on the contrary, is the Red-baiting movement that has appeared in several CIO unions. The present influence of communists in some of the unions, along with the influence of every other shade of opinion, is an indication that the new labor movement has not become congealed. It is still fluid. And something of the same conclusion may be drawn from the inner dissension in high CIO circles. The Dubinsky-Lewis row, for example, is an index of the wide variety of personal temperament and trade-union philosophy that the CIO leadership has had scope for. There is reason to believe that the basic cause for the collapse of peace negotiations between the A.F. of L. and the CIO was the fear the A.F. of L. had of being overwhelmed if the CIO unions were readmitted unconditionally, and the fear the CIO had of being dismembered otherwise. The public row among the leaders over this question is pretty good evidence that the CIO is still more an assemblage of allies than an organic army. American labor has been notoriously afraid of ideas, of social philosophies, and of social programs; and the CIO exhibits this trait. It shows every sign of being a young, unjelled labor movement which, for all its exciting seven-league strides toward growth, is still in its early stages and still overflowing with energy. From the viewpoint of the maintenance of a responsive leadership and the perfection of a democratic structure, this is enormously important.

Nevertheless, the diversion of energy to labor dissension endangers the efforts toward democratic control. An army surrounded by enemies must turn its energies to fighting, and its own needs become secondary. That is why workers' education has made so little headway, even among the newer unions. Education is the indispensable base for trade-union democracy; it is a prime condition for trade-union health. The A.F. of L. unions have never cared much about it, and still do not. This is largely due to the anti-ideological bent that "pure and simple" unionism gave to American labor at the start. Just as education is said to spoil a good field hand, so it has been suspected of having the power to spoil a good craft unionist. And as for the CIO unions, while there have been leaders such as John Brophy who have seen the importance of educational efforts, the movement as a whole has been too preoccupied with other matters. First there was the gigantic task of recruiting and organization. Then, when the recession came, there was the equally difficult task of consolidating and retaining the membership gains in the face of lay-offs and wage-cuts. And always there has been the labor-split to divert energy from constructive work. The result has been that even for the CIO education has remained a luxury. It is no secret that the two dominant CIO leaders, John L. Lewis and Sidney Hillman, have little patience with schemes for extending education; they have a feeling for realistic tactics of organization, struggle, bargaining, but education tends to seem goody-goody to them. There are seven million American workers organized: less than 2 per cent of those—roughly 100,000—are meeting regularly in study classes and recreational groups. This is a pitiable proportion for a movement that hopes to build an economic democracy in America.

The level at which educational effort must start is, judged in ordinary terms, disheartening. Organizers who have been in the field for an extended period come back with a kind of shell-shock. There is widespread illiteracy, not in the ordinary sense, but in the sense of social illiteracy. This is less true of the immigrant groups than it is of the areas in the South and Middle West, where an organization drive must not only achieve its immediate objectives but also, in the span of a year or two, create a new social consciousness. Most of the people being brought into the textile unions have previously lived in the social context out of which the Ku Klux Klan emerged. The men now enrolled in the automobile unions were, many of them, members or potential members of the Black Legion. There are areas in New England where the shoe unions, for example, are hurling themselves against the political stolidity of the workers as against a wall of granite. And where all this is true, educational efforts are likely to be pretty rudimentary. In a survey of workers' education, for example, I find listed among the signs of an awakening educational interest the fact that a union carnival in Tennessee featured a spitting contest in which the ammunition was union-label tobacco.

While this indicates the difficulties of educational work, it also underlines the need for them. Given such social material, trade-union organization that concentrates on numbers and militancy without thinking of social objectives and without educating the workers for them may as easily lead to some sort of fascist adventure as to economic democracy. Education is not a solvent for trade-union problems, but it builds a wall against reactionary possibilities. It is a dynamic force for democracy within the union. It gives the rank and file the techniques and the confidence for union participation, and in such an atmosphere bureaucratic leaders do not thrive. It gives trade-union tactics and social programs a broad base. It is proof against dictatorial power and also against the catchwords under which ambitious careerists camouflage their thrusts for dominance. I will not say that education in this sense has not made beginnings. There are evidences of such beginnings, especially throughout the CIO, that are distinctly encouraging. There are study groups, recreational activity, labor theaters, labor newspapers and magazines, beginnings even in movie and radio work. But when it is remembered that all these efforts must be made within a hostile framework of American society as a whole, when it is remembered that our powerful newspapers, radio chains, and motion-picture companies are controlled by groups unsympathetic to labor organization, then the task of labor education becomes all the more pressing.

Beyond education, there are political procedures and safeguards for trade-union democracy. I name some at random: periodic union meetings and conventions (important when you consider that the Carpenters' Union did not have a convention for eight years), rotation in office, the calling of special meetings by petition, centralized accounting systems, a degree of autonomy for the locals within a union and for the unions within a federation. But these are formal procedures, and some have not been lacking in the past. What is more essential is to go beyond formal safeguards to the everyday experience out of which democracy is built. Americans have shown they can solve the problem of evolving political techniques; the real task is the organization of will and thought for democracy. There must be genuine democracy in the factory or mill or mine itself; the rank and file must be trained on shop committees, griev-ance committees; they must participate actively in the day-to-day work of the union; and where the base is sound the structure will be sound. The shop steward of today is the creative trade-union leader of tomorrow.

Such democratic forces, coming from within rather than imposed from without, represent the only chance for combining trade-union responsibility with continued vigor. The dynamite for blasting out the swivel-chair bureaucrat and the dictator is rank-and-file revolt; but the only specific for keeping other bureaucrats and dictators from developing is day-to-day democracy and a sustained educa-tional drive. Labor has an arduous road ahead. Its path is not smooth in these days of planetary crash and turmoil. It must face ignorance and hostility from without, dissension and the drive toward conformity from within. The odds are heavily against it in a social system whose values are pecuniary rather than technological or social. We can expect no overnight miracles. Yet leg over leg the dog got to Dover. Out of the democratic union of today may come the socialized democratic state of the future. Unless the process is interrupted by war or some other social disaster, America is likely to find that a union card is a good passport to democracy.

1938

12

The Voyage of the American Mind [1]

M AY I give some brief reflections on the papers read here this afternoon? I want to deal with the voyage of the American mind and the foreign ports at which it has touched.

We started with a pretty complete provincialism, as colonials subject not only to the English political system but to the British intellectual hegemony as well. We emerged from our subjection to both on the crest of the eighteenth-century revolutionary current that swept like a tidal wave over Europe and America, leaving its effects principally through the American and French Revolutions upon the political thought and practice of the Western world. It is worth noting, however, that while our revolutionary fervor, as symbolized in the Declaration of Independence, derived from French egalitarian thought, the constitutional order that followed it drew principally from the English theory of the protection of propertied minorities against the propertyless masses. Taken as a totality, our revolutionary and constitutional experience was thus a peculiar American amalgam of foreign intellectual materials. The democratic revolution and the consolidation of it in a post-revolutionary democracy were adaptations of those materials to the native elements in our culture.

It is not surprising, therefore, that the early nineteenth century in America witnessed the growth of a new cultural nationalism. While Calhoun was dreaming in South Carolina of a Greek republic transplanted to the slave soil of the South, the New England thinkers were reaching toward a universalism cast in a national

---

1 This was read at the New School for Social Research, in New York, at a symposium of the Graduate School ("The University in Exile"). The papers presented at the symposium dealt with migrations and their consequences.

mold. Emerson, as the type-thinker, ransacked the universe for his materials: borrowed through Carlyle the transcendental elements of German romantic idealism, borrowed the mysticism of Swedenborg, the gnomic wisdom of the Eastern sages; but the final product was the Self-Reliant American Scholar.

After Emerson, however, this fusion of the national and the universal, the contingent and the invariant, was transformed into a national egoism that hardened itself against all foreign importations. It took the form, economically, of a tariff protectionism that sought to shut out the products of the rest of the world; it took the form, diplomatically, of an isolationist system; it took the form, psychologically, of the narrow individualism of the American frontier mind; it took the form, intellectually, of a uniquely American clannishness and imperviousness to foreign ideas.

More recently the extent to which we are all caught in the common destiny and doom of Western capitalism has tended to break down this intellectual autarchy. Our intellectuals have moved toward Marxian thought; in our institutional life we have within our own framework borrowed some of the cultural elements of the Russian Revolution; we have all watched with a morbid fascination the tragic enactments in a Europe half lost to fascism. Once more the Western world finds itself in a period comparable to that of the late eighteenth century.

And once more we can detect, I think, a tendency to fit materials gathered internationally into a characteristically national structure. We are, as a century and a half ago, on the threshold of a constitutional re-formation. But since we live in an age of fierce economic conditionings, the larger process through which we are going is the re-formation of our economic constitution. And in a "time of troubles" in which the first task of capitalist democracies has been to ward off fascism—to contrive a way of avoiding the break in the fabric of legality, the collapse of political and intellectual freedom, the hardening of economic inequality, which go with fascism—in such a time the experience of other countries has once more become of immense moment in the voyage of the American mind.

It is in this framework that, as an American, I regard the transplanting to America of the best of German and Italian scholarship in the social sciences. I shall confess that I have learned more from my contact with the members of the University in Exile than I could have learned from a whole five-foot shelf of learned treatises on democracy and fascism. These are the men whose cultures, so similar in many respects to ours, have been stamped out. We can learn from them how high are the stakes in the conflict; we can learn how inextinguishable, and yet how defenseless, thought is when it does not wear the garments of power. We can learn what methods not to use in confronting our own situation. Whether we can also learn what methods to use is, however, quite another matter, and one still in the realm of trial and error.

Because of this immigration of crucial and comparable social experience American thought should be considerably enriched. Provided always that the experience *is* comparable. And here we must sound several warnings. One is that we must, each time we attempt to draw conclusions from a comparative treatment, take account of the relative economic development: thus Italy and America differ in their degree of capitalist maturity; in Germany and America the strength and quality of the labor movement are quite different. A second is that we must take account of the place that the institution in question occupies in its culture: thus I have felt that some of the lessons drawn from Germany and Italy of the fascist danger latent in President Roosevelt's recent Supreme Court reorganization plan have suffered from a failure to see judicial review in its American context of economic power. It is easy to become the tragic victims of analogy.

On the whole this intellectual immigration has put American social thought in the fortunate role described by Thorstein Veblen in his passage "On the Merits of Borrowing" (*Imperial Germany and the Industrial Revolution*). Veblen pointed out that when one culture borrows technological or other traits from another, it borrows them in completed form and does not have to incur the penalty which the first country incurred for taking the lead; it does not have to take over, along with them, the institutional encumbrances that had grown up around them.

I hope we will show perspicacity of this sort in the process of borrowing from the newcomers to our country. I should, in this connection, like to make one sharp criticism about several of the papers that have been read this afternoon. They have been eloquent; they have been learned; they have been subtle—but they might just as

well have been set in Swift's island of Laputa. There has been a
tendency to see the intellectuals as forming a unique group, entirely dissociated from the rest of the community, dissociated especially from those economic classes which alone can furnish them
the sinews of continuing strength and the sources of periodic renaissance. Professor Tillich has opened for us universal vistas of intellectual migration; Professor Lasswell has impressed us with the
iron rigor of his detachment, and made us shrink from the prospect
of any possible "skill deteriorations" in the intellectual migrant
groups; Professor Speier has won our admiration by the persuasiveness and charm with which he has balanced the dualities in the
life of the mind. But meanwhile we have been allowed to forget
that intellectuals are intellectual workers; that what they think is
given meaning and value by the culture in the context of which
they do their thinking; that the value of thought lies in the valu-
ing audience, and its viability in the capacity of that audience to
enact the thought into living institutions; and that the significant
audience in a capitalist society is made up of the workers and other
functional economic groups within it.

If I read recent history correctly, it is just this sort of dissociation
of the intellectual groups from their social context that has caused
democratic cultures to be snuffed out. In our borrowings from the
experience of those cultures I hope this will be one of the encumbrances we will not take along.

1937

ACKNOWLEDGMENTS
AND
INDEX

Acknowledgments

In the few instances where I have changed the title of an article or review, the original title appears in brackets.

1. Ideas Are Weapons   Unpublished
2. Freedom in the Opinion Industries   Unpublished

PART TWO

1. John Marshall's Long Shadow — *New Republic,* 84:148–52, Sept. 18, 1935

2. Taney Redivivus — *American Historical Review,* vol. 43, no. 2, pp. 415–8, Jan. 1938

3. The Heritage of Emerson — *Encyclopaedia of the Social Sciences,* 5:487–8, 1931

4. Thoreau: No Hermit — *Encyclopaedia of the Social Sciences,* 14:621–2, 1934

5. The Lincoln Image — *New Republic,* 98:134–6, Mar. 8, 1939

6. Mr. Justice Holmes
   Justice Holmes: Flowering and Defeat — *Nation,* 142:746–7, June 10, 1936
   The Scar Holmes Leaves — *Yale Law Journal,* 46:904–8, Mar. 1937
   Holmes, Frankfurter, and the Austerity Theory [Holmes and Frankfurter] — *Nation,* 147:537–9, Nov. 19, 1938

7. Mr. Justice Brandeis
   The Social Thought of Mr. Justice Brandeis — *Yale Law Journal,* 41:1–32, Nov. 1931; also in Felix Frankfurter, ed.: *Mr. Justice Brandeis* (Yale University Press, New Haven, 1932), pp. 7–45

   Brandeis and the Curse of Bigness — *New Republic,* 83:53, May 22, 1935, and New York *Herald Tribune Books,* Mar. 17, 1935, p. 6

   Homage to Louis D. Brandeis [Homage to Louis D. Brandeis; Brandeis at Eighty] — *Nation,* 148:222, Feb. 25, 1939; *Nation,* 143:565–6, Nov. 14, 1936

8. Woodrow Wilson: the New Freedom and the New Deal [The — *New Republic,* 76:251–2, Oct. 11, 1933

New Freedom and the New
Deal]
9. Thorstein Veblen
    Recipe for an American Genius   *Dictionary of American Biography,*
    19:241–4, 1936

    Veblen and the Wasteland   *New Freeman,* vol. 2, no. 24, pp.
    565–7, Feb. 25, 1931

    What is Usable in Veblen?   *New Republic,* 83:7–10, May 15, 1935;
    also in Groff Conklin, ed.: *New
    Republic Anthology, 1915–1935,*
    (Dodge Publishing Company, New
    York, 1936)

    Veblen's World [Gateway to   *Nation,* 142:321–2, Mar. 11, 1936
    Veblen's World]
10. The Social Thought of Hadley of   *Encyclopaedia of the Social Sciences,*
    Yale   7:239–40, 1932
11. The Legal Economics of John R.   *Harvard Law Review,* 49:360–5, Dec.
    Commons   1935
12. Charles A. Beard
    Beard's Economic Interpreta-   *New Republic,* 100:7–11, May 10, 1939
    tion
    Charles Beard Confronts Him-   *Nation,* 142:452–4, Apr. 8, 1936
    self
    Midpassage—toward What?   *New Republic,* 100:164–5, June 14,
    1939
13. John Reed: No Legend   *Nation,* 142:552–3, Apr. 29, 1936
14. The Liberalism of O. G. Villard   *New Republic,* 98:342–4, Apr. 26, 1939
15. Walter Lippmann
    Lippmann Agonistes   *Nation,* 145:589–90, Nov. 27, 1937
    Lippmann and the Supreme   *Nation,* 144:230, Feb. 27, 1937
    Court [Lippmann and the
    Court]
16. Thurman Arnold
    Capitalism as Magic   *Nation,* 146:46–7, Jan. 8, 1938
    The Shadow World of Thur-   *Yale Law Journal,* 47:677–703, Mar.
    man Arnold   1938
17. Morris R. Cohen: Law and the   *Harvard Law Review,* 47:380–6, Dec.
    Life of Reason   1933
18. Corwin and the Judicial Power   *Harvard Law Review,* 52:1033–5, Apr.
    1939
19. Carl Becker: Historian of the   *Yale Law Journal,* 42:1143–8, May
    Heavenly City   1933
20. Roosevelt and History   *Nation,* 146:533–4, May 7, 1938
21. Jim Farley: Soldier and Artist   *New Republic,* 97:69–71, Nov. 23,
    1938
22. Mr. Justice Black
    Hugo Black—a Personal His-   *Nation,* 145:367–9, Oct. 9, 1937; *Na-*
    tory [Hugo Black—a Per-   *tion,* 145:337–8, Oct. 2, 1937
    sonal History; The Educa-
    tion of Hugo Black]

Mr. Justice Black, Dissenting [Justice Black, Dissenting]   *Nation*, 146:264–6, Mar. 5, 1938

23. William O. Douglas: Diogenes on Wall Street [Wall Street's New Mentor]   *Nation*, 145:429–32, Oct. 23, 1937

24. Robert S. Lynd: the Revolt against Quietism   *New Republic*, 100:257–8, July 5, 1939

25. Sinclair Lewis, Caliban, and the Federal Power [Caliban on Main Street]   *Stage*, 14:78, Dec. 1936

26. The America of John Dos Passos   *Nation*, 143:187–8, Aug. 15, 1936

PART THREE

1. Jonathan Swift: Literary Anthropologist   *Encyclopaedia of the Social Sciences*, 14:489–90, 1934

2. The Paradox of Adam Smith   Introduction, pp. v–x, to Adam Smith: *The Wealth of Nations* (Modern Library, New York, 1937)

3. Walter Bagehot: a Credible Victorian   Unpublished

4. Graham Wallas: the Fabian or the Tiger?   Unpublished in present form; incorporates material from an editorial by the author in the *New Republic*, 72:33, Aug. 24, 1932

5. Engels and Marx—a Partnership   New York *Herald Tribune Books*, May 17, 1936, p. 3

6. Lenin's *The State and Revolution*   *New Republic*, 100:92–6, Aug. 30, 1939

7. Harold J. Laski
   Laski and the Class-Domination Theory   New York *Herald Tribune Books*, Mar. 10, 1935, p. 3
   Liberalism's Family Tree   *Nation*, 143:396–7, Oct. 3, 1936

8. Pareto's Republic   *New Republic*, 83:135–7, June 12, 1935

9. Hitler as Thinker   Unpublished

10. Thomas Mann: Hero of Our Time [Thomas Mann's Democratic Manifesto]   *Nation*, 146:726–8, June 25, 1935

PART FOUR

1. Do Free Markets Make Free Men?   *Southern Review*, vol. 3, no. 4, spring, 1938

2. Materialism and History   Unpublished

3. Literature and Society   *Encyclopaedia of the Social Sciences*, 19:523–41, 1933

4. The Supreme Court and American Capitalism — *Yale Law Journal*, 42:668–701, Mar. 1933; also in Douglas Maggs, ed.: *Selected Essays on Constitutional Law* (Foundation Press, Chicago, 1938)

5. Minority Rule and the Constitutional Tradition — *University of Pennsylvania Law Review*, 86:457–70, Mar. 1938; also in Conyers Read, ed.: *The Constitution Reconsidered* (Columbia University Press, New York, 1938), pp. 191–207

6. Vested Rights and Vested Interests — *Encyclopaedia of the Social Sciences*, 15:240–2, 1935

7. The Jungle of Legal Thought — *Yale Law Journal*, 43:854–8, Mar. 1934

8. The Theory of the Social Process — *Encyclopaedia of the Social Sciences*, 14:148–51, 1934

9. The Pattern of Dictatorship [The New Age of Despots] — *Yale Review*, 24:293–310, Dec. 1934; also in G. S. Ford, ed.: *Dictatorship in the Modern World* (University of Minnesota Press, Minneapolis, 1935), pp. 1–23

10. The School and the Common Man — *New England Quarterly*, 9:168–71, Mar. 1936

11. Democracy with a Union Card — *Virginia Quarterly Review*, vol. 14, no. 2, pp. 209–28, Apr. 1938

12. The Voyage of the American Mind — *Social Research*, vol. 4, no. 3, pp. 334–337, Sept. 1937

Index

Thompson, Dorothy, 195, 346, 381, 474, 477
Thompson, Ralph, 196
Thoreau, Henry David, 45–7, 84, 132
Thorndike, E. L., 516
Thorstein Veblen and His America (Dorfman), 117, 129–38
Thucydides, 258
Tillich, Paul, 537
Times, New York, 157
Tolstoy, L., 414, 526
totalitarianism, 187–8, 510
trade unions, 79–80, 96, 182–3, 517–33
tradition, 404–5
transaction, 148–9
transcendentalism, 42
transition, 172
Treitschke, H. von, 372
Trevelyan, G. M., 72–3
Trotsky, L., 403
Trotter, William, 351
trusteeship, 475–6
trusts, 212–6
Tufts, James H., 119
Turner, Frederick J., 152–3, 159, 433
TVA, 21, 173, 282–3, 392
Tylor, E. B., 311

United Gas Public Service Company v. Texas, 363–4
University in Exile, 534, 535–6
U.S.A. (Dos Passos), 285–9
U.S.S.R., 333, 337, 385–6, 395, 399

valuation (rate), 93–4
values, 206–7, 213–6
Van Devanter, Justice W., 251
Veblen, Thorstein, 95, 114, 117–41, 146, 147, 148, 149, 153, 165, 181, 183, 196, 199, 203, 209, 211, 215, 270, 273, 287, 288–9, 393, 404, 415, 432–3, 436, 440, 451, 481, 483, 489, 515, 536
Vergil, 412, 419
vested interests, 122, 135, 213, 478–83
vested rights, 32, 478–83
vigilantism, 14

Villard, Henry, 181
Villard, O. G., 178–85
violence, 352, 526–8
Voltaire, 199, 236, 239, 346
voluntarism, 167

Wagner, Adolf, 142
Waite, Justice M. R., 450
Wallace, Henry, 248–53
Wallas, Graham, 11, 76, 314–8, 351, 384–5, 403
Wall Street, 267–74
Walras, A. A., 147
Ward, Lester F., 119, 137, 493, 496
Warren, Charles, 233, 427, 434
Watkins, Myron, 435
Wealth of Nations, The (Smith), 297–304
Webb, Beatrice and Sidney, 76, 314, 509–510
Weber, Max, 40, 277, 359, 466
Webster, Daniel, 33, 50, 161, 464
Wells, H. G., 239, 287, 342
Wertheimer, M., 147
Westermann, A. L., 470
Weyl, Walter, 434, 440
White, William Allen, 18, 23
Whitehead, A. N., 5, 209
Whitman, Walt, 60, 289, 377
Wicksell, K., 147
Wiese, Leopold von, 494, 497
Wilson, Woodrow, 76, 77, 106, 112, 113–116, 153, 179, 180, 183, 184, 252, 472, 481
withering away of the state, 332
Wood, Leonard, 179
Woolf, Leonard, 361
Woolf, Virginia, 372, 412
Wortley, B. A., 489
Wu, John C. H., 58, 60

Yale University, 118, 129, 142–4
Yellen, Samuel, 526–7
Young Hegelians, 320, 322

Zimmern, Alfred, 470
Zola, Emile, 420